Street by Street

HERTFORDSHIRE

PLUS CHALFONT ST PETER, HARLOW, LUTON, STANSTED AIRPORT, WALTHAM ABBEY

Enlarged Areas Hemel Hempstead, St Albans, Stevenage, Watford

1st edition May 2001

© Automobile Association Developments Limited 2001

This product includes map data licensed from Ordnance Survey® with the permission of the Controller of Her Majesty's Stationery Office. © Crown copyright 2000. All rights reserved. Licence No: 399221.

All rights reserved. No part of this publication may be reproduced, stored in a retrieval system, or transmitted in any form or by any means– electronic, mechanical, photocopying, recording or otherwise – unless the permission of the publisher has been given beforehand.

Published by AA Publishing (a trading name of Automobile Association Developments Limited, whose registered office is Norfolk House, Priestley Road, Basingstoke, Hampshire, RG24 9NY. Registered number 1878835).

Mapping produced by the Cartographic Department of The Automobile Association.

A CIP Catalogue record for this book is available from the British Library.

Printed in Italy by Printer Trento srl

The contents of this atlas are believed to be correct at the time of the latest revision. However, the publishers cannot be held responsible for loss occasioned to any person acting or refraining from action as a result of any material in this atlas, nor for any errors, omissions or changes in such material. The publishers would welcome information to correct any errors or omissions and to keep this atlas up to date. Please write to Publishing, The Automobile Association, Fanum House, Basing View, Basingstoke, Hampshire, RG21 4EA.

Ref: MD117

Key to map pages — ii-iii

Key to map symbols — iv-1

Enlarged scale pages — 2-13

Street by Street — 14-231

Index – towns & villages — 232-235

Index – streets — 236-283

Index – featured places — 283-293

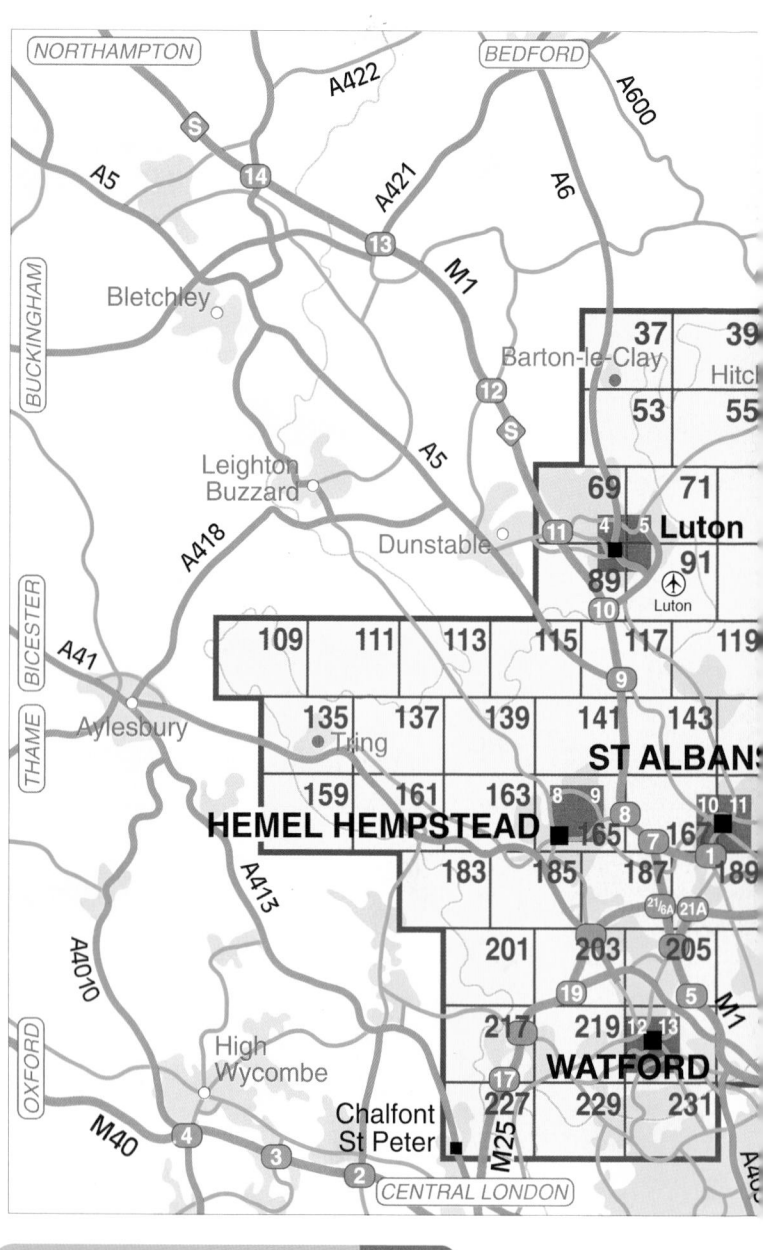

ii

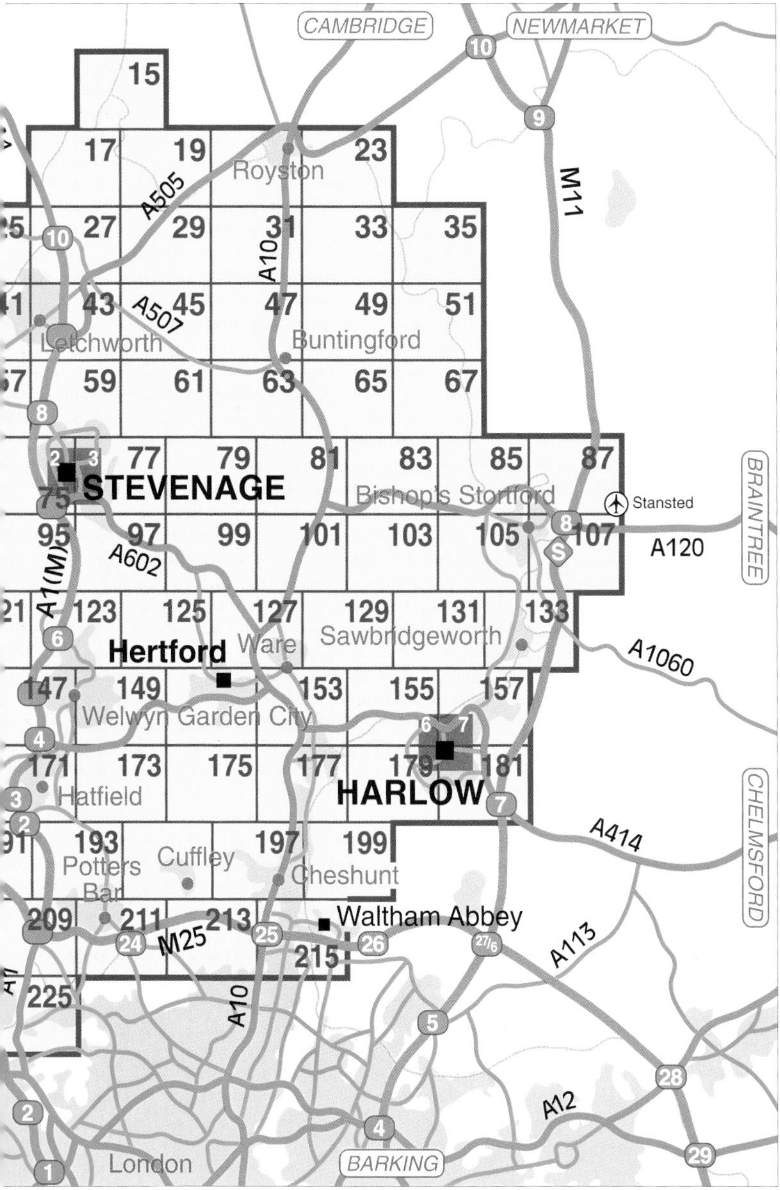

CAMBRIDGE   NEWMARKET

15

17   19   *Royston*   23

A505

25   10   27   29   A10   31   33   35

M11

41   43   A507 45   47   49   51

Letchworth   *Buntingford*

57   59   61   63   65   67

8

2 3   77   79   81   83   85   87

75   **STEVENAGE**   *Bishop's Stortford*   ✈ Stansted

95   97   99   101   103   105   8 107   A120

A602   S

21   A1(M) 123   125   127   129   131   133

6   A1060

Hertford   *Ware*   *Sawbridgeworth*

147   149   153   155   157

4   *Welwyn Garden City*   6 7

171   173   175   177   179   181

3   **HARLOW**   A414

2   *Hatfield*   7

91   193   *Cuffley*   197   199   A113

Potters   *Cheshunt*

Bar

209   211   213   25   ■ *Waltham Abbey*

24   M25   26   27/6   A113

225   215

A10   5

A12

2

London   BARKING

28

1   4   29

BRAINTREE

CHELMSFORD

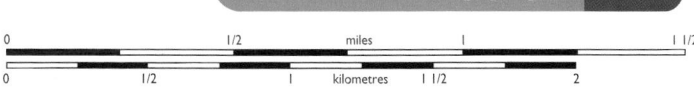

2.5 inches to 1 mile   **Scale of main map pages**   **1:25,000**

0   1/2   miles   1   1 1/2

0   1/2   1   kilometres   1 1/2   2

Junction 9	Motorway & junction	P+🚌	Park & Ride
Services	Motorway service area	🚌	Bus/coach station
	Primary road single/dual carriageway		Railway & main railway station
Services	Primary road service area		Railway & minor railway station
	A road single/dual carriageway	⊖	Underground station
	B road single/dual carriageway	⊖	Light railway & station
	Other road single/dual carriageway	++++++++	Preserved private railway
	Restricted road	_LC_	Level crossing
	Private road	•—•—•—	Tramway
← ←	One way street	- - - - - -	Ferry route
	Pedestrian street	....	Airport runway
- - - - - -	Track/ footpath	— · — · — ·	Boundaries- borough/ district
▯▯▯▯▯▯	Road under construction	▼▼▼▼▼▼	Mounds
⌐ - - - ⌐	Road tunnel	**93**	Page continuation 1:25,000
P	Parking	**7**	Page continuation to enlarged scale 1:17,500

	River/canal lake, pier		&#9855;	Toilet with disabled facilities
	Aqueduct lock, weir			Petrol station
465 ▲ Winter Hill	Peak (with height in metres)		PH	Public house
	Beach		PO	Post Office
	Coniferous woodland			Public library
	Broadleaved woodland		i	Tourist Information Centre
	Mixed woodland		♟	Castle
	Park			Historic house/building
	Cemetery		Wakehurst Place NT	National Trust property
	Built-up area		M	Museum/art gallery
	Featured building		†	Church/chapel
⊓⊔⊓⊔⊓	City wall		Y	Country park
A&E	Accident & Emergency hospital			Theatre/performing arts
	Toilet			Cinema

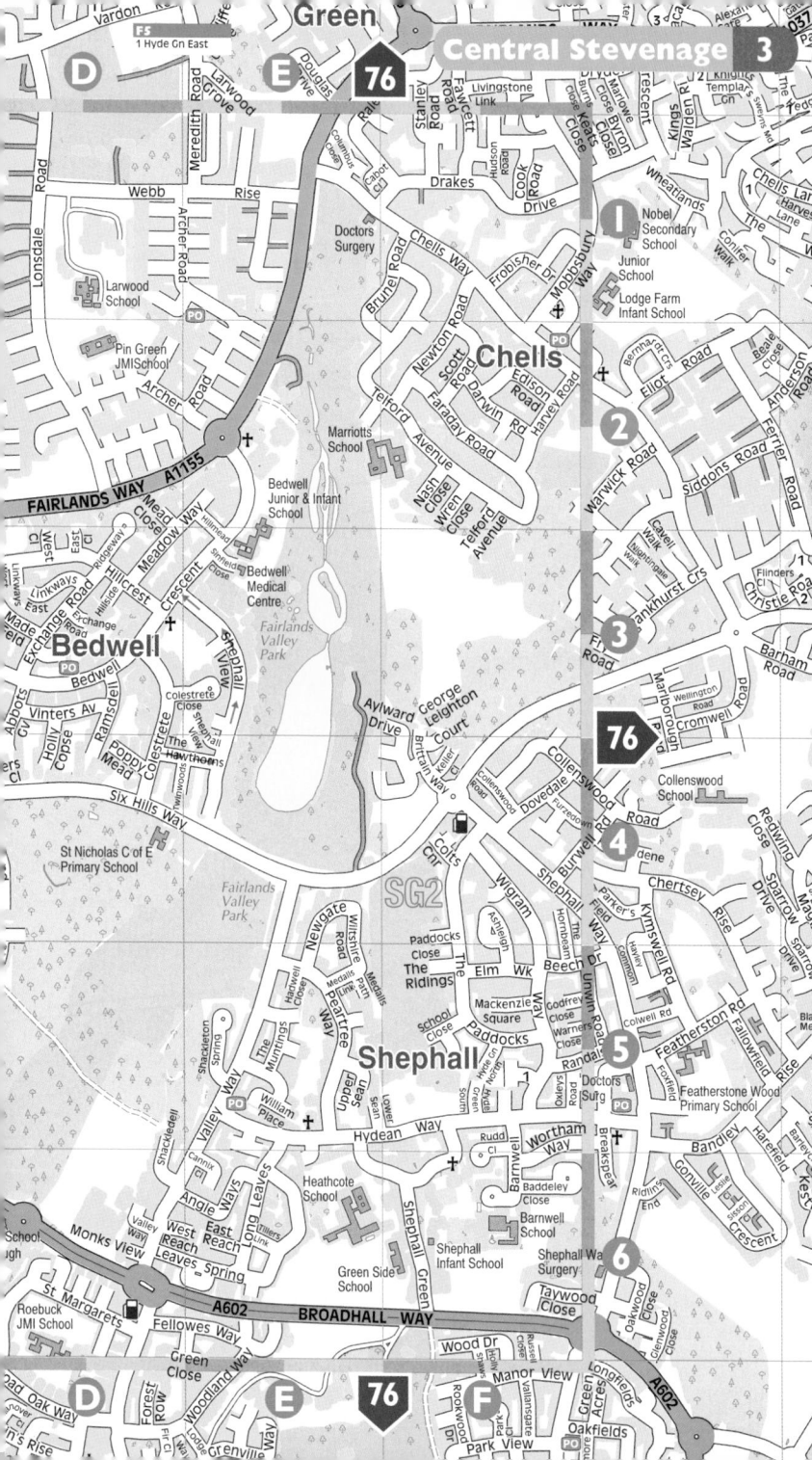

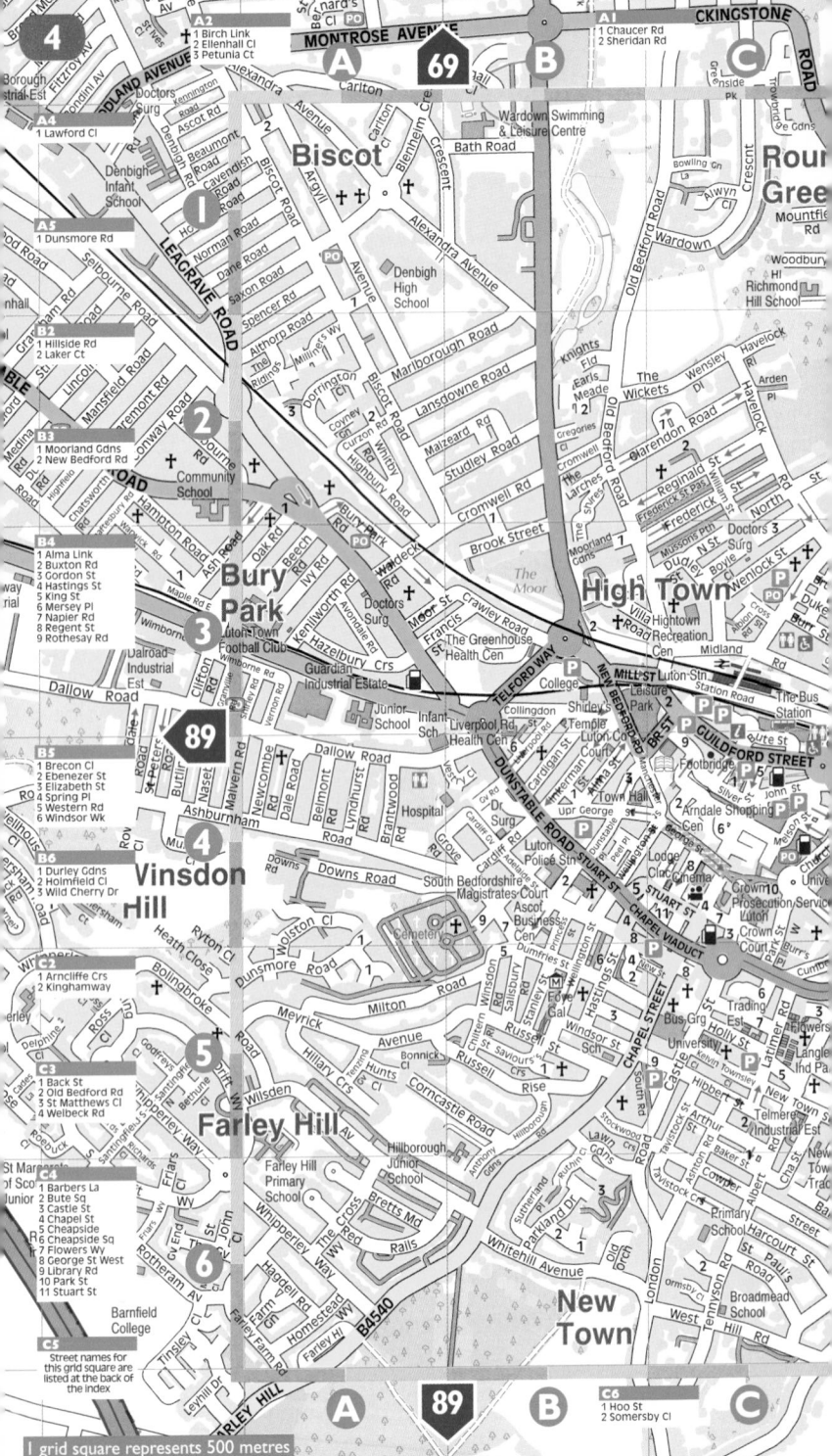

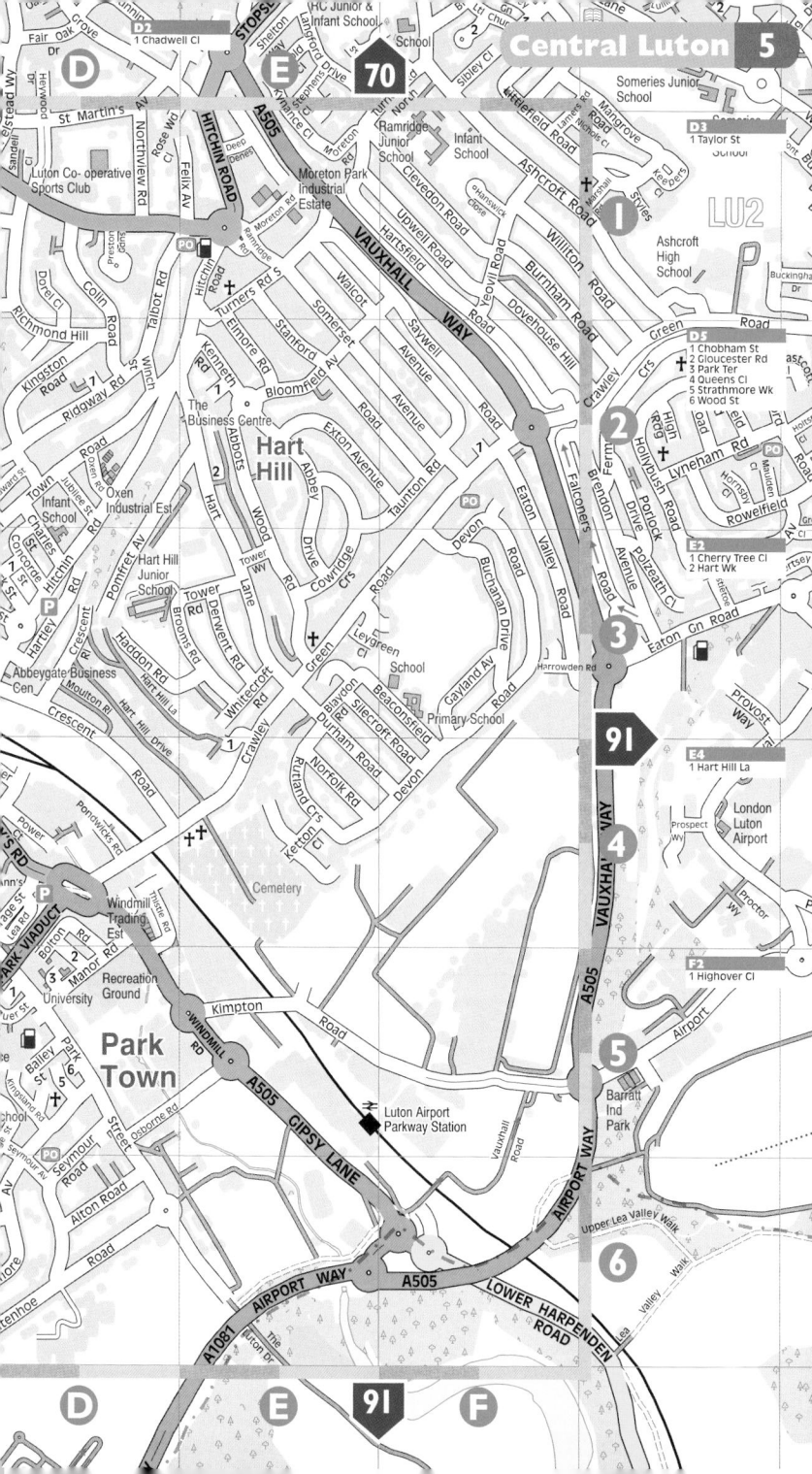

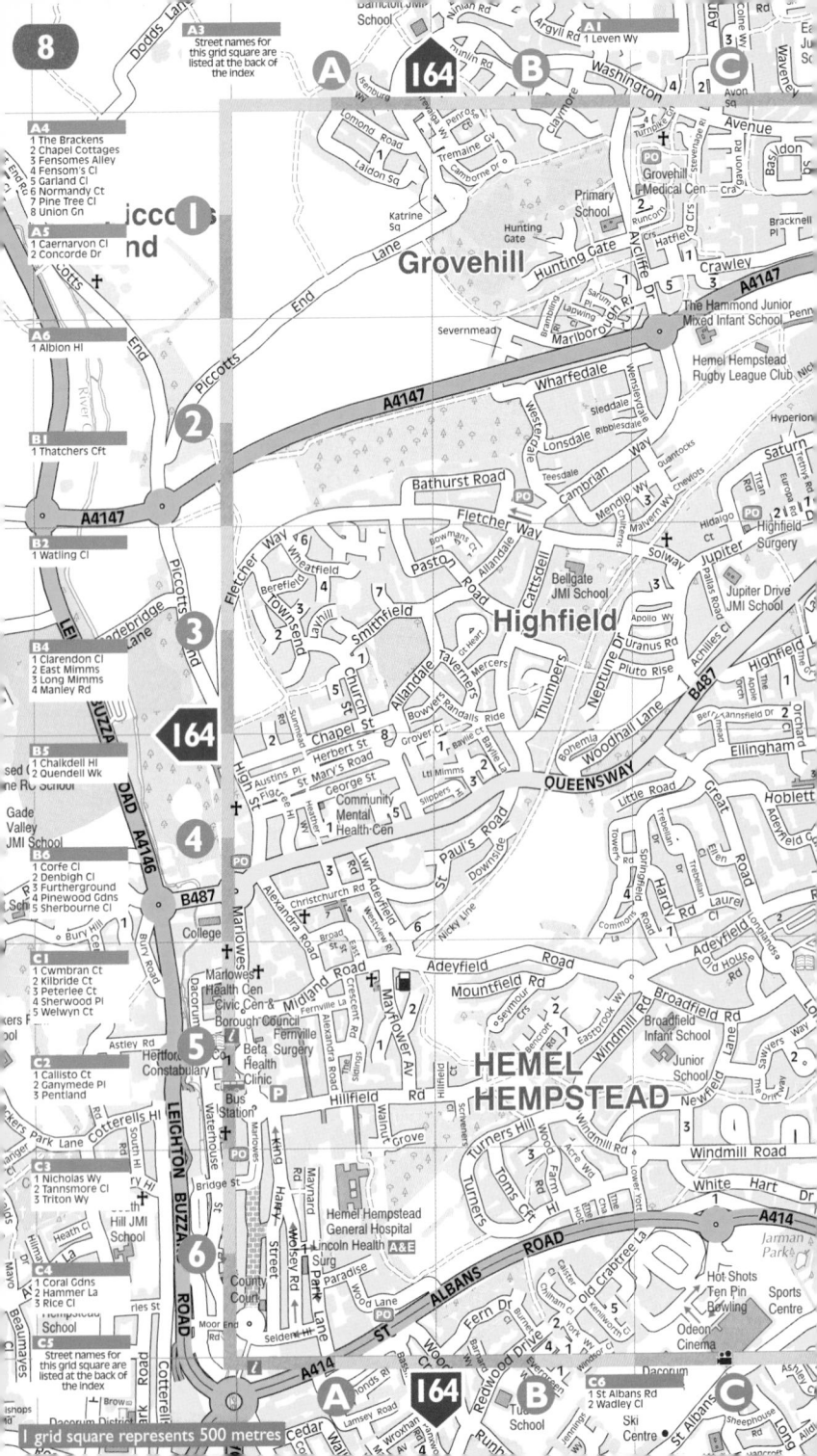

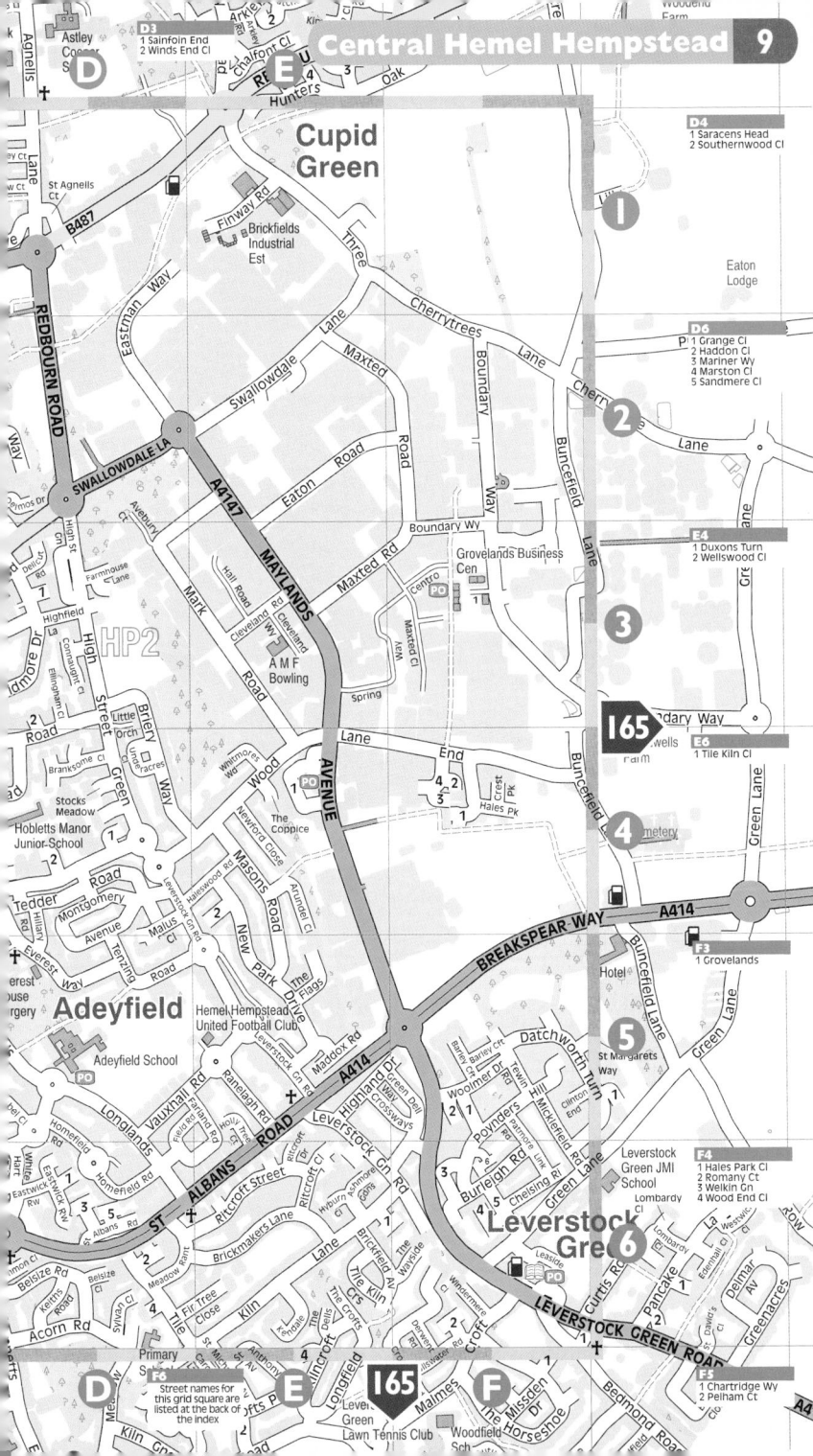

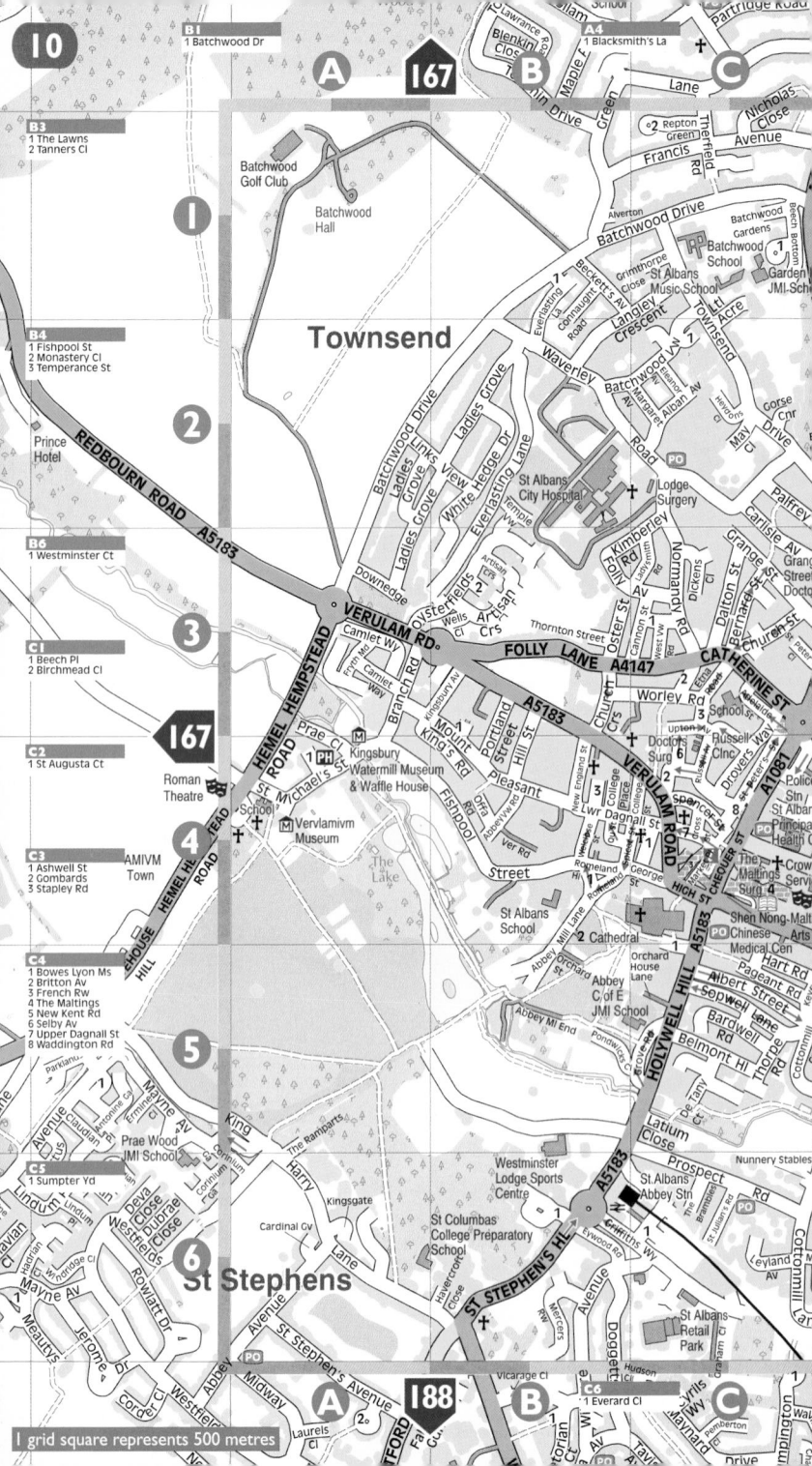

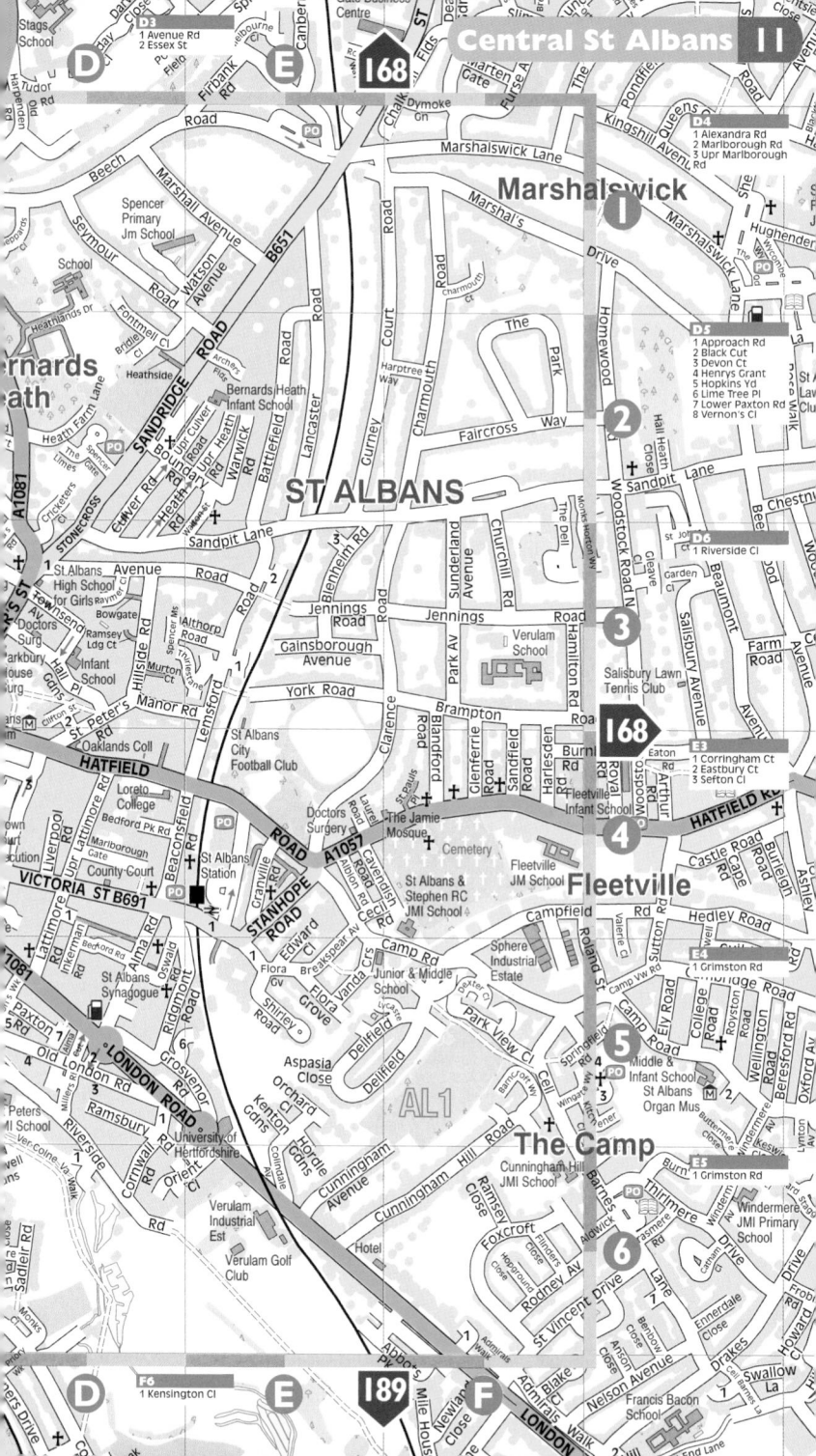

220

221

220

1

2

3

4

5

6

Oxhey

Watford Heath

F G H J K

1
2
3
4
5
6
7
8

Flecks Lane

River Cam or Rhee

Potton Road

Little Green

New Road

Cemetery

Great Green

North Brook End

North Brook End

Guilden Morden

Drove Knoll Road

Fox Hill Road

Fox Hill

Guilden Morden School

Worboys Court

Pound Green

Church Street

Church Lane

Swan Lane

High Street

Thompsons Meadow

Morden House

Silver Street

Buxtons Lane

Trap Road

Bogs Gap Lane

Hillside Farm

Brook End

Steeple Morden

Hay Street

Craft Way

Steeple Morden School

Jubilee End

Cheyney Street

Cheyney Close

Highfield Farm

Ashwell Road

Church Street

Church Farm Lane

The Green

Litlington Road

Morden Green

F G H **18** J K

Wyndmere Farm

Westbrook Close

Potton Road

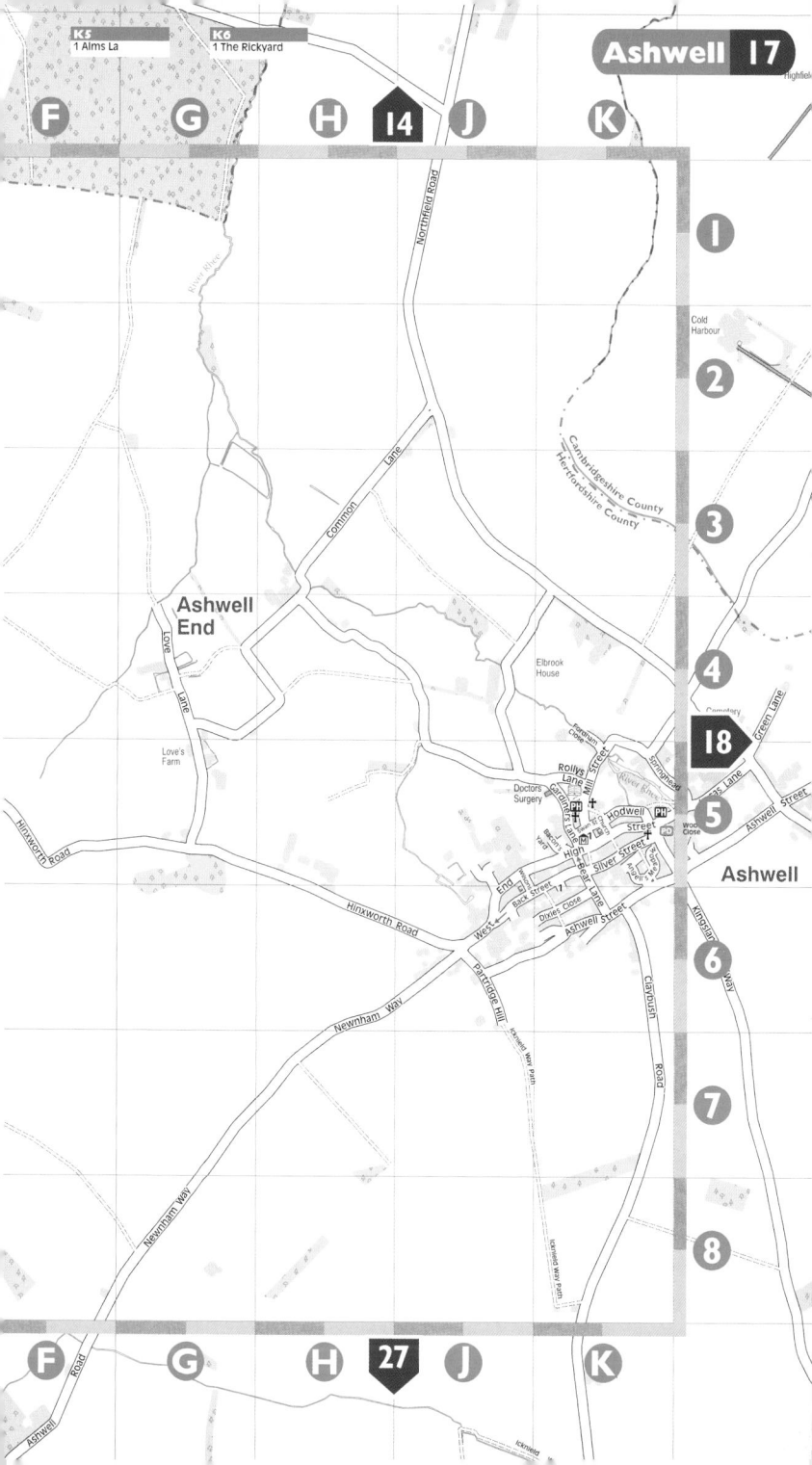

18

A **B** **15** **C** **D** **E**

Highfield Farm

Ashwell Road

Church Farm Lane

The Green

M
G

I

Ashwell Road

Wyndmere Farm

Westbrook Close

Station Road

Gatl
End

Cold Harbour

2

Cambridgeshire County
Hertfordshire Co

3

High Farm

Icknield Way Path

4

brook
ouse

Cemetery

Green Lane

Lucas Lane

Station Road

17

Rollys
Lane

Mill Street

PH

Woodforde Close

5

PH

PO

High

Silver Street

Ashwell Street

Ashwell

Station Road

Cambridgeshire County
Hertfordshire County

Ashwell Street

Kingsland Way

6

Claybush Road

Redlands Farm

Station Road

7

8

Icknield Way Path

O

The Knoll

A **B** **28** **C** **D** **E**

Pembroke Farm

I grid square represents 500 metres

Road

Utlington

Anvil Aven

Cottbill C

Combe Ln

Foxton Road

F **G** **H** **J** **K**

Ickfield Way Farm

1

Highfield
Cottages

2

3

Highfield
Farm

Morden
Grange
Farm

4

20

*Morden
Grange
Plantation*

A505

5

Kings
Ride

BALDOCK   ROAD

6

Cambridgeshire County

Herfordshire County

**The
Thrift**

Cheyneys
Lodge

Chain Walk

Chain walk

Lower
Coombe Farm

7

Chain   Walk

A505

Ashwell & Morden Station

Station Road

8

Coombe Road

Coombe Farm

F **G** **H** **29** **J** **K**

Chain Walk

Heath Farm

20

A B C D E

1

2

Cambridgeshire County
Hertfordshire County

3

Highfield
Farm

Ivy
Farm

Baldock Road

4

LC

A505 BALDOCK ROAD

Golf Course

◀ **19**

Therfield Heath
Nature Reserve

5

A505

Kings
Ride

Greys

BALDOCK ROAD

6

**The
Thrift**

Chain Walk

Duckpuddle
Bush

7

8

Coombe Road

Chain Walk

Coombe Farm

A B **30** C D E

Park Farm

Mill Lane

Royston 21

ROYSTON

F8
1 Greenbury Cl

F G H J K

North Hall Farm

Icknield Way Path

New Road

Icknield Way Path

I

Icknield Way Path

2

New Buildings Farm

3

BARLEY ROAD

B1368

4

5

B1368

New Road

6

CAMBRIDGE ROAD

ROYSTON RD

Baker's Lane

B1368

HIGH STREET

PICKNAGE ROAD B1050

The Surgery

CHISHILL ROAD

BARLEY   ROAD

B1039

Chishill Windmill

The Pudgell

Herdon

B1039

7

Hertfordshire County
Cambridgeshire County

Barley

Hanager Dr

Barley Vp School

Church
Church Lane
Churchfield

Smith's End Lane

LONDON ROAD

Stackenhoe End

May Street

Maltings Lane

8

F G H **33** J K

Smith's
End

Booms

Stackenhoe
End

Little   Road

J3
1 Hallworth Dr
2 Hunters Cl
3 Wycklond Cl

J4
1 Howard Cl

F G H J K

Waterloo Farm

A507

Stotfold Road

Church ...nd

...e Farm

Ariesey Road

Lakeside Surgery

The Gardens

Stotfold Health Centre

Brook Street

Melbourn Close

Coppic...

Roe Close

Pix Road

Hitchin Road

High Street

Church Street

The Avenue

Baldock Road

The Coppens

I

K2
1 Netherstones
2 Old Brewery Cl

2
Stotfold

K3
1 Upperstone Cl
2 Walnut Cl

St Marys Voluntary Lower School

3

K7
1 Crossleys

4

26

5

K8
1 Pelican Wy

6

Bedfordshire County
Hertfordshire County

7

West Drive

Fairfield Hospital

Stotfold Road

Stonehill JMI School

Lower Wilbury Farm

Gaunts Way

Gaunts Way

Grange Junior Mixed School

Northfields Infant School

Northfields

Danescroft

Southfields

Southfields

8

41

Standalone Farm Centre

Midhurst

Orchard Way

Lammas Way

Stonnells Close

Wilbury Road

Norton School

F G H J K

16

E8
1 Aldridge Ct
2 Brewery La
3 Farriers Cl
4 Jackson St
5 Lavender Ct
6 Meeting Ho La

A8
1 Paynes Cl

A3
1 Rook Tree Cl

Caldecote

A   B   C   D   E

Taylor's Rd

Caldecote Road

Stotfold Road

Wrayfields

A1(T)

Radwell Grange

Malthouse Lane

Stotfold

Mill Lane

St Marys Voluntary
Lower School

Cemetery

Roecroft
School

Braves
Manor

Church Street

Newnham Road

Junction 10

Baldock Road

A507

The Coppens

25

Radwell

Radwell Lane

A1(M)

A507

Norton Road

River Ivel

Norton Bury Lane

Norton

Mill Lane

Blackhorse
Farm

NORTH ROAD

Gaunts Way

Grange
Junior
Mixed
School

Northfields
Infant School

Norton Bury

St Nicholas
Junior & Infant School
Church

Croft Lane

Danescroft

Southfields

Lammas Way

Wilbury Road

Norton Road

42

Blackmore

A1(T)

HITCHIN

A   B   C   D   E

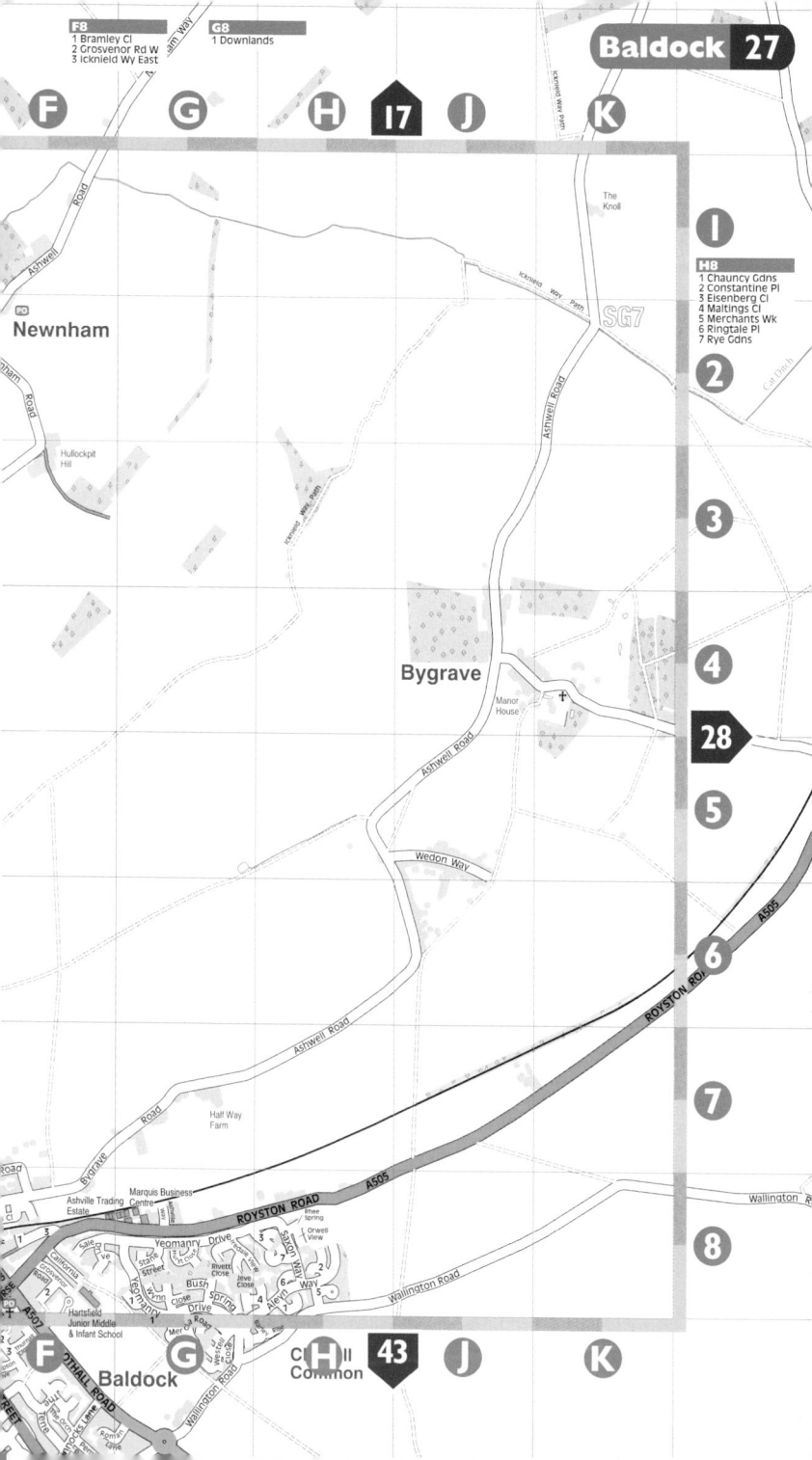

F8
1 Bramley Cl
2 Grosvenor Rd W
3 Icknield Wy East

G8
1 Downlands

F **G** **H** **17** **J** **K**

The Knoll

I

Ashwell Road

Newnham

H8
1 Chauncy Gdns
2 Constantine Pl
3 Eisenberg Cl
4 Maltings Cl
5 Merchants Wk
6 Ringtale Pl
7 Rye Gdns

Icknield Wy Path

SG7

2

Hullockpit Hill

Icknield Way Path

Ashwell Road

3

4

Bygrave

Manor House

28

Ashwell Road

5

Wedon Way

6

Royston Road

A505

Ashwell Road

7

Half Way Farm

Wallington R

Marquis Business Centre

Ashville Trading Estate

Bygrave Road

A505

8

ROYSTON ROAD

Three Spring

Orwell View

Wallington Road

Yeomanry Drive

Saxon Way

State Street

Bush Close

Rivett Close

Jeve Close

Spring Way

California

Spring Drive

Hartsfield Junior Middle & Infant School

F **G** **H** **43** **J** **K**

Baldock

Church Hill Common

Wallington Road

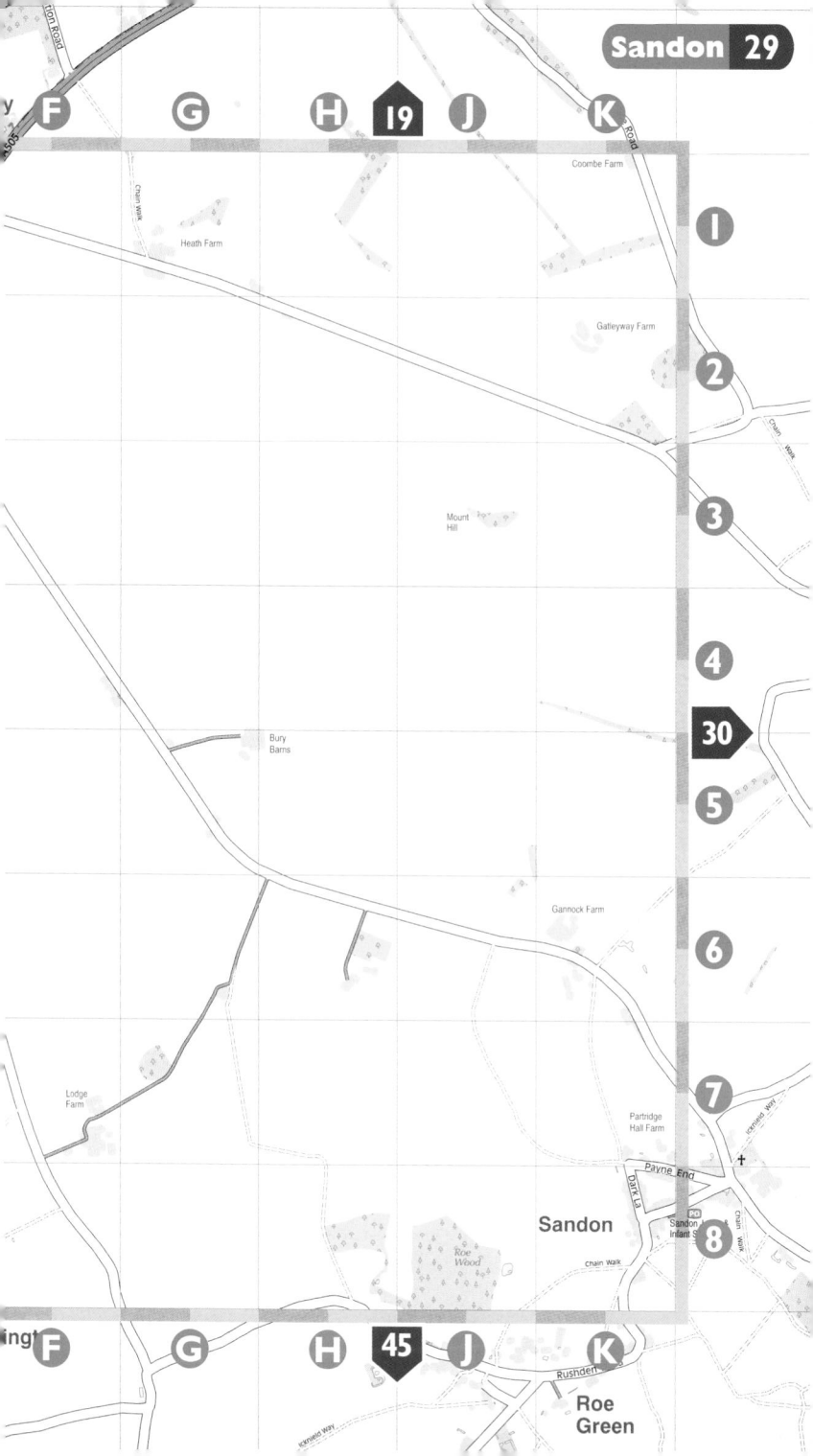

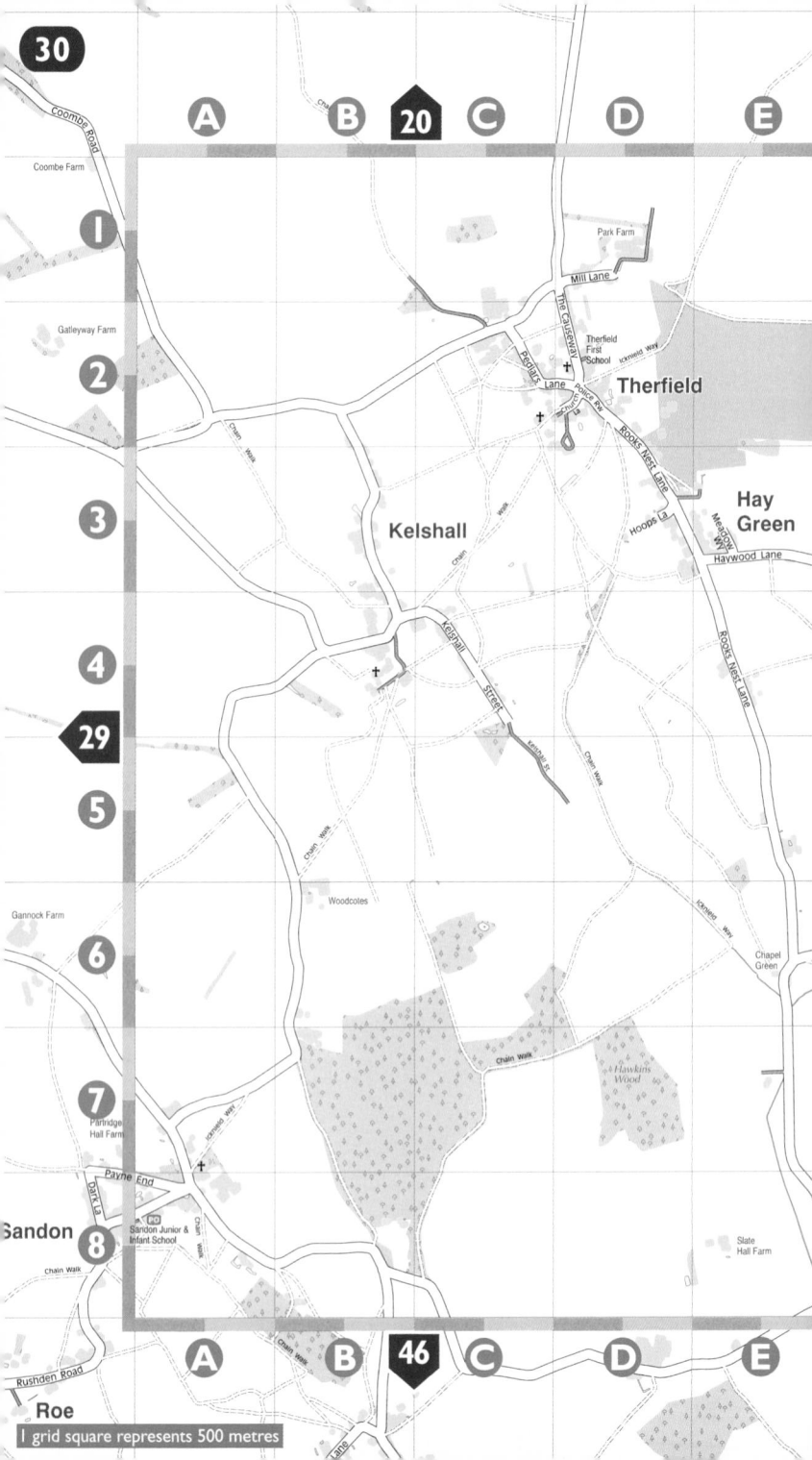

30

A B **20** C D E

Coombe Road

Coombe Farm

1

Galleyway Farm

2

Park Farm

Mill Lane

The Causeway

Therfield
First
School

Vicarage Way

Therfield

Peoples Lane

Rooks Nest Lane

Hoods La

Hay
Green

Haywood Lane

Kelshall

Chain Walk

3

Chain Walk

4

29

Kelshall Street

Chain Walk

Chain Walk

5

Gannock Farm

Woodcotes

6

Ickfield Way

Chapel
Green

Hawkins
Wood

7

Partridge
Hall Farm

Payne End

Chain Walk

Sandon

8

Sandon Junior &
Infant School

Chain Walk

Slate
Hall Farm

Chain Walk

Rushden Road

Roe

A B **46** C D E

1 grid square represents 500 metres

London Road

Barley Vp School

Hanager Cr

PH

Smith's End Lane

Churchfield

Smith's End

Bogmoor Road

Shaftenhoe End

Little Chishill Road

Bogmoor Road

Abbotsbury House

Li Chishill

Walk Wood

Cross Leys

34

Morrice Green Farm

Hertfordshire Way

Nuthampstead Bury

Hertfordshire Way

Bell Farm

Bell Lane

Park Farm Lane

Nuthampstead

Hertfordshire Way

Rooting Lane

Farm

49

Scales Park

34

A B C D E

1

Building
End

2 Little
Chishill

3

*Cross
Leys*

4

◀ **33**

5

6

7

8

A B **50** C D E

Building End Road

B1039

The
Hall

*Chrishall
Common*

Cambridgeshire County

Essex County

River Stort

Park Lane

Park Lane

Bull Lane

Langle

The Hall

Lower
Green

New Farm

Scales Park

River Stort

Essex County
Hertfordshire County

1 grid square represents 500 metres

Lower

Church Vale
Hillfoot
Cl

F G H J K

Little
Ion

Ion Bridge
Farm

Brookside

Church C

I

John Bunyan Trail

High Road

Church

**Hanscombe
End**

Hanscombe End Road

2 **Apsle
End**

Dean

Manor
Farm

3

**Higham
Gobion**

Apsley Bury
Farm

Apsley Bury Rd

4

Shillington

38 ▶

Hexton
Common

Bedfordshire County
Hertfordshire County

5

Bunyan Lane

6

John Bunyan Trail

Mill Lane

7

Manor
Farm

Bury Farm

PH

Hexton

PO

Hexton
Manor

Pegsdon

Pegsdon W

BARTON RD. **B655**

Hexton Junior
Middle & Infant
School

HITCHIN R B655

8

Ravensburgh
Castle ✖

F G H **53** ▼ J K

F5
1 Docklands
2 St Mary's Cl

F

Mayfield
Farm

G

H

J

K

Holwellbury Farm

A600

I

Gurney's Lane

Holwell

Holwell Road

2

Meadow
Farm

Ashcroft
Farm

Range Meadow

Pirton Road

Lordship
Farm

Bedfordshire County
Hertfordshire County

Waterloo
Lane

3

Holwell Road

New Wrights
Farm

**Burge
End**

West Lane

Little

Burney Close

Royal Oak Lane

Hambridge Way

Bury End

Crunnells Green

High Street

Maltings Orchard

Walnut

Walnut Tree
Farm

Ickhield Way Path

4

Pound
Farm

40

5

Ickhield Way Path

6

Westmill Lane

7

Highdown
Farm

Oughtonhead
Common
(Nature Reserve)

Swinburne Av.

Hine Way

Westmill

8

Birchen Road

Moss Way

Infant
School

F

G

H

55

J

K

HEXTON

Hitchin Road

Oughton Head
Farm

Oughtonhead Lane

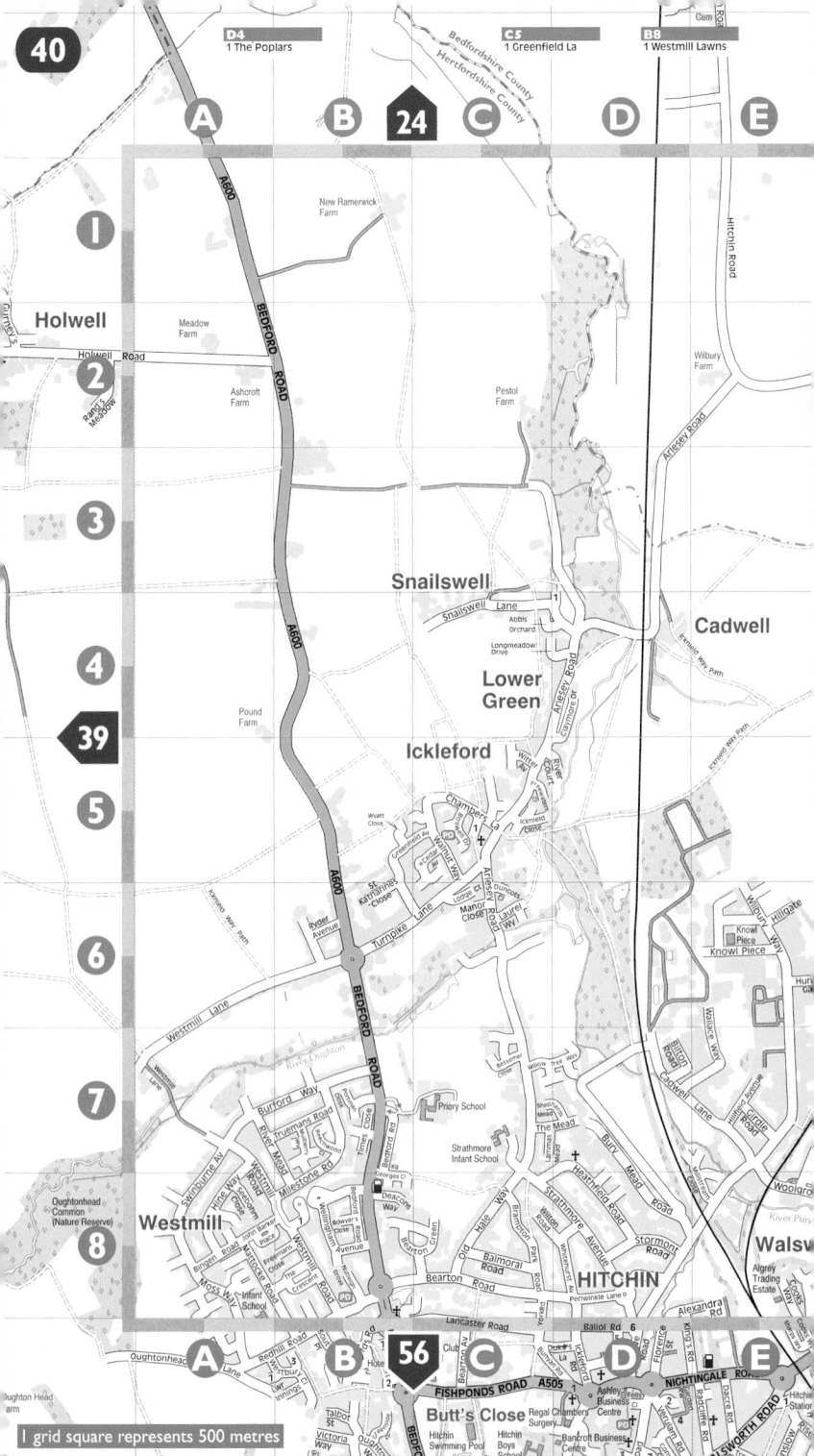

I grid square represents 500 metres

Baldock **43**

F1
1 Elm Pk
2 Riddell Gdns
3 The Twitchell

F2
1 Elmwood Av
2 Providence Wy
3 South Cl

A505

27

J

K

I

F3
1 Clare Crs
2 Templar Av

2

G1
1 Weavers Wy

3

H8
1 Post Office Rw

4

44

Clothall

5

Hickman's Hill

6

7

Green End

8

Weston

Weston Bury

Church End

F **G** **H** **59** **J** **K**

Damask Green

Baldock

Clothall Common

Hartsfield Junior Middle & Infant School

Baldock Health Cen

Baldock Industrial Estate

Warren Lane

CLOTHALL ROAD

A507

Warren Lane

CLOTHALL ROAD

A507

CLOTHALL ROAD

Warren

Laxton Gardens

Beechwood Close

Chalk Hills

Hatch Lane

Extend Way Path

Extend Way Path

Hertfordshire Way

Hertfordshire Way

Ashgrove Lane

Lannock Manor Farm

Hatch Lane

Fore Street

Mill Lane

Maiden Street

Hitchin Road

Friars Road

The Snipe

Manor Ho

Marlborough Cl

Woodhall Mead

Damask Green Road

Hertfordshire Way

Church Lane

LONDON ROAD

Chiltern Road

Pixmore Road

Clothall Road

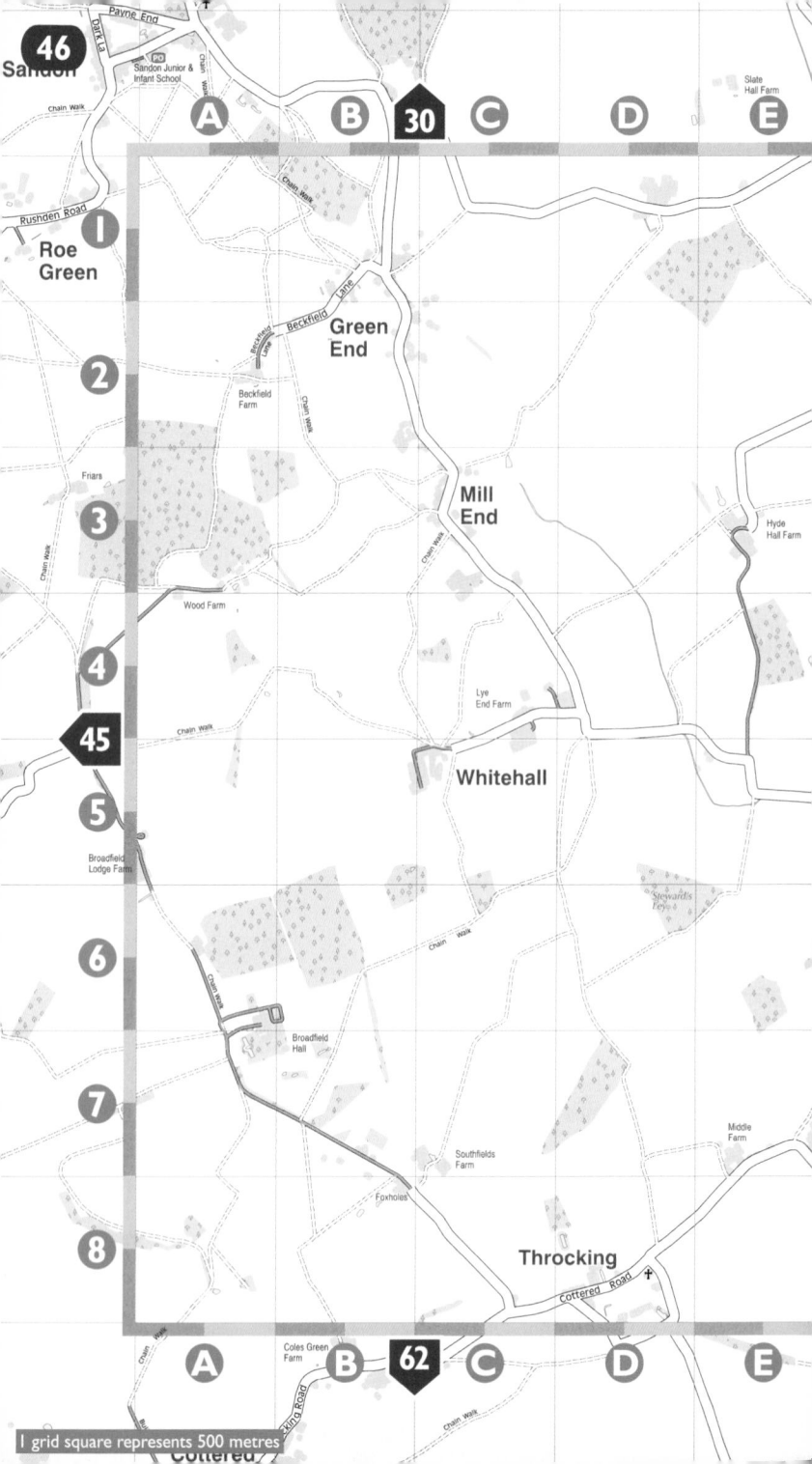

46
Sandon

Payne End
Dark La

Sandon Junior &
Infant School

Chain Walk

A   **B**   **30**   **C**   **D**   **E**

Rushden Road

1

**Roe
Green**

Chain Walk

Beckfield Lane

**Green
End**

2

Beckfield
Farm

Slate
Hall Farm

Friars

3

**Mill
End**

Hyde
Hall Farm

Wood Farm

4

Lye
End Farm

45

Chain Walk

Whitehall

5

Broadfield
Lodge Farm

6

Stewards
Leys

Chain Walk

Broadfield
Hall

Chain Walk

7

Middle
Farm

Southfields
Farm

Foxholes

8

Throcking

Cottered Road

A   **B**   **62**   **C**   **D**   **E**

Coles Green
Farm

King Road

Chain Walk

Cottered

1 grid square represents 500 metres

F G H **31** J K

①

Buckland

Bull Lane

HILL VIEW

Back Lane

Whiteley Lane

2

Hodenhoe Manor

A10(T)

3

4

Canons Wood

Chipping

The Sq

Royal Oak Ct

48 ▶ Wyddial

5

Ermine St

Moles Lane

6

Moles Farm

Parkside

7

Throcking Lane

8

SG9

A10(T)

Park Farm Industrial Estate

School

F G H **63** J K

Edwinstree Middle School

Bowling Green

Norfolk Road

Ind

Vicarage Road

Wyddial Road

Causeway

The

Layston First School

The Medical Ctr

Church St

The Pyghtle

48

A   B   **32**   C   LONDON ROAD   D   Barkway Equestrian Centre   E

1

B1368

2   Biggin Manor

3   B1368   BIGGIN HILL   Cave Gate Cottages

Capons Wood

4

47   B1368   River Quin

Wyddial

5

6   Moles Lane   Beauchamps   Silkmead Farm

Moles Farm

7   Bradbury Farm   B1368

8   SG9

Layston First School   Causeway

A   B   **64**   C   B10   D   HARE STREET ROAD   Cemetery   E   B10

Hare Street

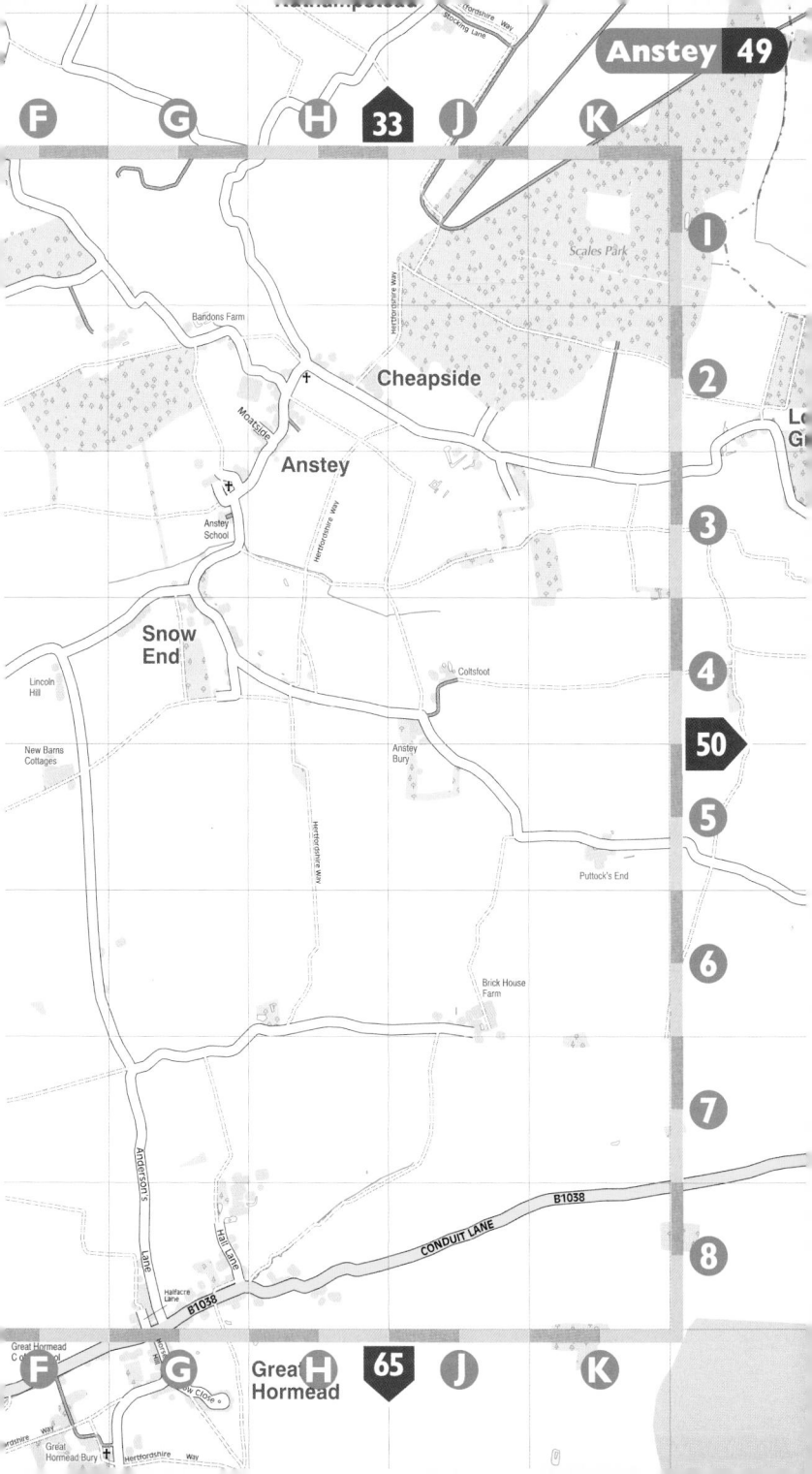

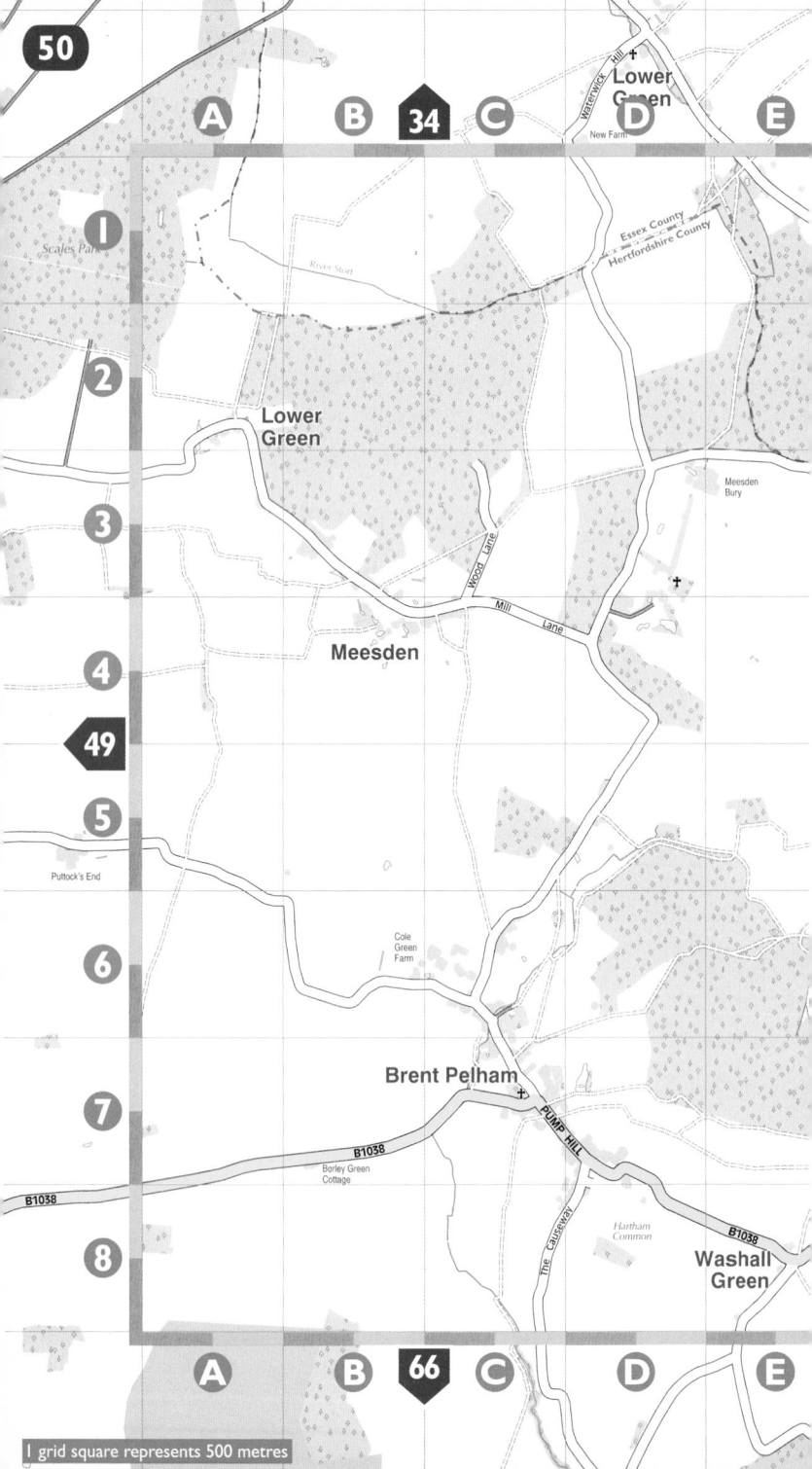

34

A   B   C   D   E

1

Scales Park

2

Lower
Green

Essex County
Hertfordshire County

River Stort

Meesden
Bury

3

Wood Lane

Mill
Lane

4

Meesden

49

5

Puttock's End

6

Cole
Green
Farm

7

Brent Pelham

PUMP HILL

B1038

Borley Green
Cottage

B1038

8

The Causeway

Hartham
Common

B1038

Washall
Green

A   B   C   D   E

66

Lower
Green

Waterwick Hill

New Farm

I grid square represents 500 metres

Pegsdon Way

HITCHIN ROAD · B655

A · **B** · **38** · **C** · **D** · **E** · B655

1

Old Wellbury

Icknield Way Path

2

Bedfordshire County
Hertfordshire County

New Wellbury

Wellbury House

3

Icknield Way Path

Little Offley

4

Lilley Hoo

5

Cloudshill

Westend Farm

School Lane

6

Offley

Lilley Hoo Farm

Hexton Road

A505

High St

PO

West Lane

John Bunyan Trail

West St

Mimram
Luton Road

Salisbury Lane

County Court Cl

7

Rectory La

Gn

Acres

Limbrook Lane

Luton Road

Luton White Hill

Luton Road

Lilley

+

Lilley
Wood

Holdnough Hill

8

Lilley Bottom

A505

HILL

Dog Kennel
Farm

Luton Hill

Westbury
Wood

A · **B** · **71** · **C** · **D** · **E**

F G H 39 J K

I

Oughtonhead Lane

Hitchin Cricket Club

HEXTON ROAD B655

Hitchin Road

Oughton Head Farm

2

Pirton Cross

Foxholes

PIRTON ROAD

Be

3

Offley Bottom

Wibley Lane

Carters Lane

Wellbury Way

Wibley Lane

Offley Cross

4

56

Offley Grange

A505

5

Temple Close

Temple End

6

Great Offley

ey ace

Harris Lane

7

Walden Road

Offleyholes Farm

8

Offley Hoo

West Wood

F G H 72 J K

Willian Road

F **G** **H** 4I **J** **K**

F1
1 Arnold Cl
2 Burns Cl
3 Campbell Cl

F2
1 Mermaid Cl
2 Peppercorn Wk
3 Pullman Dr
4 Spurrs Cl
5 Worsdell Wy

North
Hertfordshire
College

Purwell

I

F3
1 Bramfield
2 Hensley Cl

2

G2
1 Holden Cl
2 Nimbus Wy
3 Stirling Cl

William Ransom
School

Oakfield

Uplands Avenue

Linten

Wymondley
Road

Hitchin Road

Great
Wymondley

3

Graveley Road

Graveley Lane

4

58

5

Kingshott
School

Ashbrook

Arch Road

Wymondley
Junior & Infant
School

Grimstone Road

Little
Wymondley

Priory View

Priory Lane

Stevenage Road

Ashbrook Lane

Blakemore End Road

St Ippollitts
School

Cemetery

Ippollitts

Redcoats

Wymondley
Bury

A602

Titmore
Green

Todd's
Green

7

8

Fishers
Green

F **G** **H** 74 **J** **K**

Weston
Bury

Church
End

Church Lane

A   **B**   **44**   **C**   **D**   **E**

I

Harveyshill
Farm

2

Fairclough Hall
Farm

Weston
Lodge

Luffenhall

3

PH

**Warren's
Green**

**Hall's
Green**

Dane End
Lane

4

Warren Lane

Howells
Farm

59

5

Dane
End

B1037

6

Richmond
Hy

*Churchend
Common*

WHITE HILL

7

Beecroft
Lane

Manor
Farm

Church
End

Kitcheners Lane

Boxbury
Farm

B1037

PH

Boxbury

8

Box
Wood

Gresley Way

Roman Gate

Walkern

HIGH ST

Winters
Lane

Totts
Lane

Froghall Lane

Brockwell
Shott

PO

Rushes
End

Autumn Glory

Cherry
Tree Mede

Moors Ley

The
Maltings

A   **B**   **77**   **C**   **D**   **E**

STEVENAGE

HIGH ST

1 grid square represents 500 metres

F G H 45 J K

I

Cottered

A507

The Cre

2

Brook
End

3

Chain Walk

4

Spring Lane

Cottered
Warren

62

5

A507

A507

Warren Lane

B1057

Hare
Street

Cromer

B1057

Bling Lane

Bury
Grange

Warren Lane

Gardners
End

6

Ardeley
Bury

Ardeley
School

School Lane

PH Ardeley

The Crescent

7

Chain Walk

Walkern
Bury Farm

8

F G H 78 J K

Bassus
Green

St John's
Wood

Chain Walk

H1
1 Aylotts Cl
2 Chequers Cl
3 Freman Dr

H2
1 Tylers Cl

F G H **47** J K

I

I1
1 Dell Springs
2 Ermine Ct

BUNTINGFOR 2

I2
1 Bridgefoot
2 Market Hi

3

I3
1 Barleycroft
2 Nut Slip
3 Peasmead

4

64

5

6

7

8

School
Ind Est
Vicarage Road
Wyddial Road
Causeway
Edwinstree Middle School
Norfolk Road
The Medical Cen
The Causeway
Layston First School
The Prydhie
HARE STREET ROAD
DOCK ROAD
BALDOCK ROAD
Longmead
Monks Walk
Monks
Riverside
Snells Mead
Owles Lane
Mill Close
Millfield First School
Luynes
Knights Close
Station Road
London Road
Owles Lane
Windmill Hill
A10(T)
Aspenden
A10(T)
Tudor Stud
Aspenden
Pinehill Farm
PO
Ph
Whatbarns Farm
Gaylors Farm
Westmill
Cherry Green
Peasefield
Tillers End Farm
Coles Park
Knights Hill Farm

F G H **80** J K

66

50

A B C D E

1

2 Great Horm Park

3

The Street

4

65

Furneux Pelham

Barleycroft End

5

Furneux Pelham C of E School

The Street

6

Hertfordshire Way

Patient End

7

The Causeway

8

Hole Farm

A B C D E

83

Grave End

Washall Green

Whitebarns Lane

Whitebarns

Hartham Common

The Causeway

B1038

River Ash

The Causeway

Hertfordshire Way

1 grid square represents 500 metres

Dewes Green

Berden Priory Farm

Dewes Green

F **G** **H** **51** **J** **K**

Dewes Green Road

Bonneting Lane

Vicarage Lane

The Street

Church Drive

Berden

I

2

The Crump

Stocking Pelham

Crabb's Lane

Ginns Road

Crabbs Green

Park Green

3

Brick House End

4

5

East End

6

Hixham Hall

Mallows Green

7

Mallows Green Road

Uppend

8

Watery Lane

Patmore Heath

F **G** **H** **84** **J** **K**

Patmore Hall

County Hertfordshire County

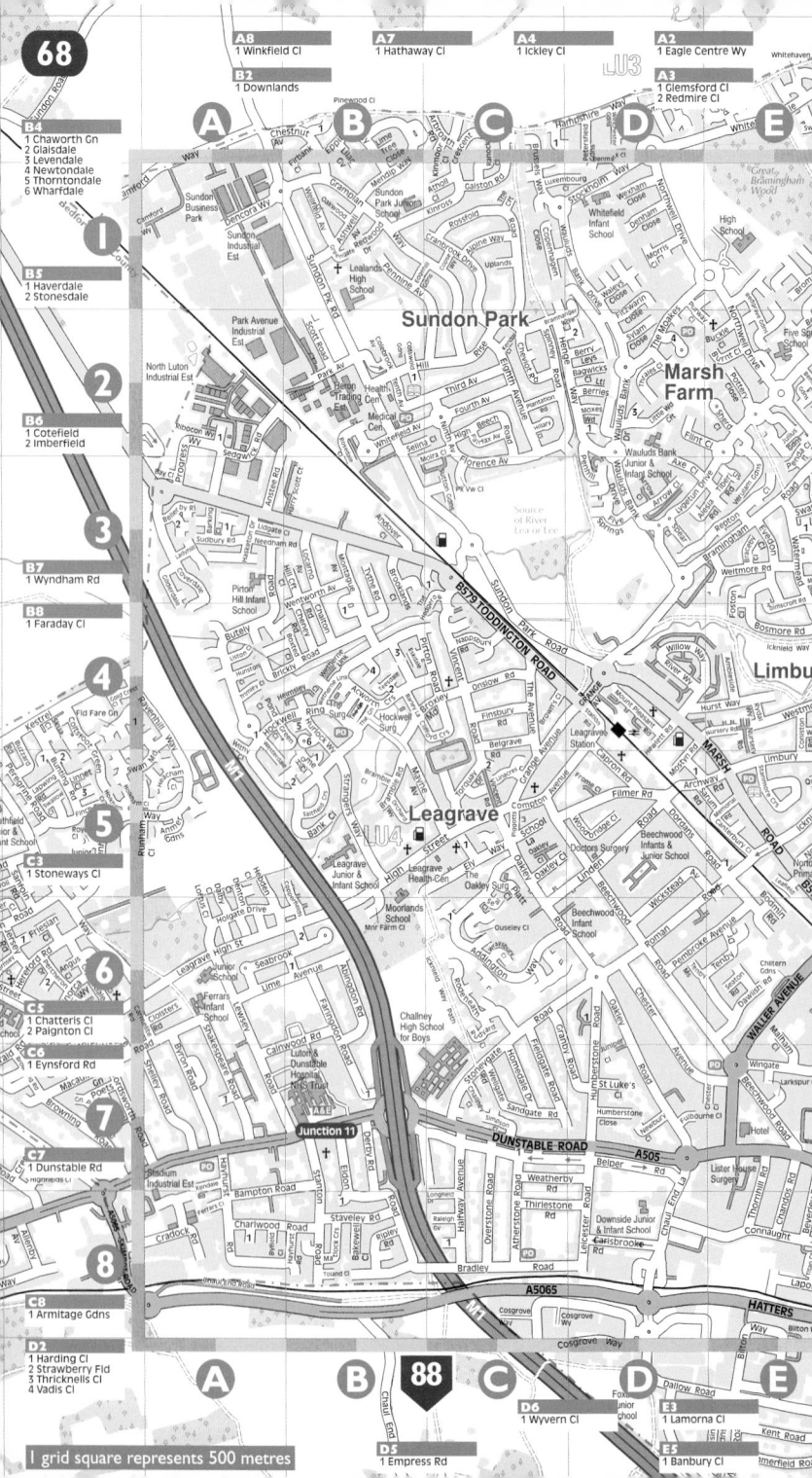

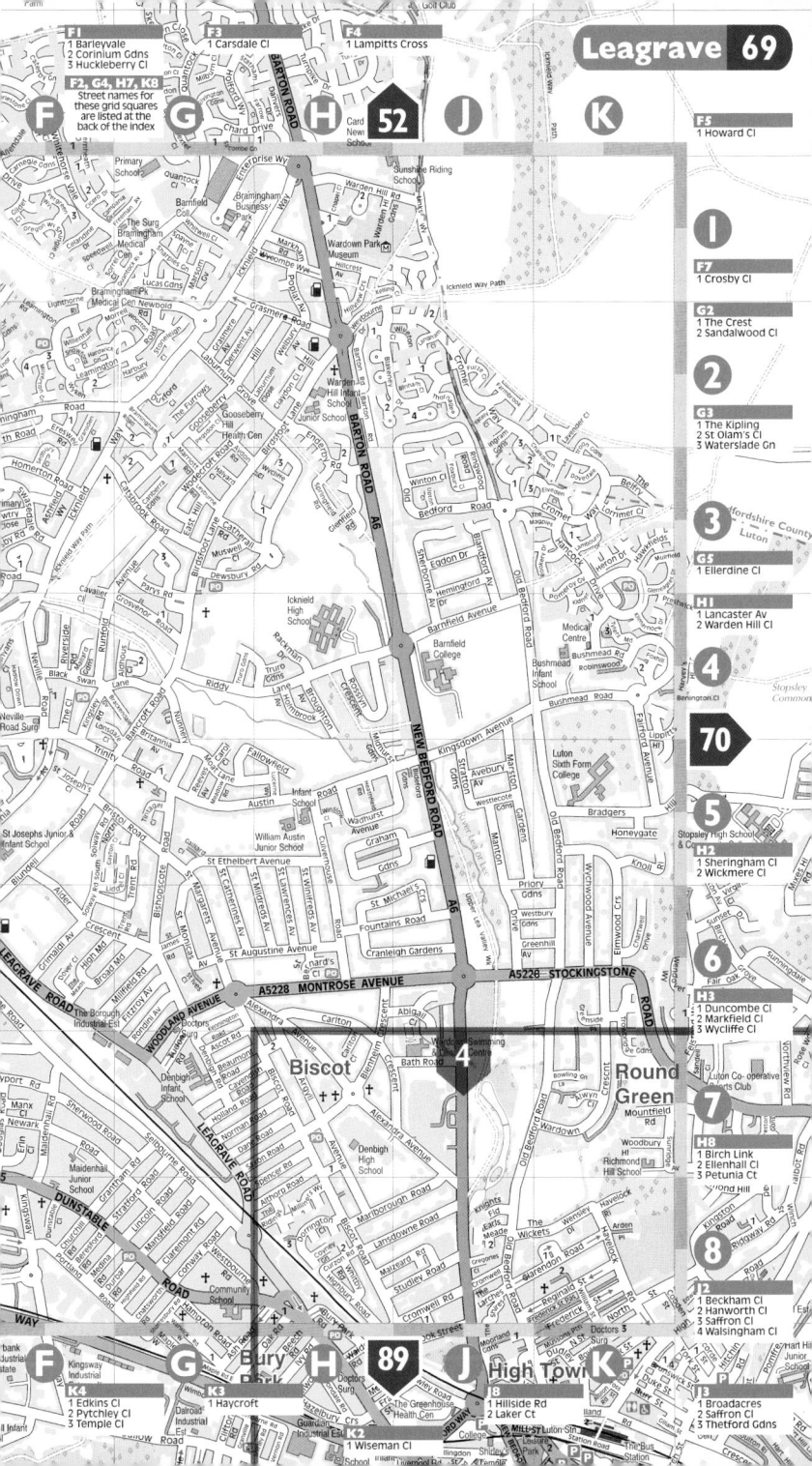

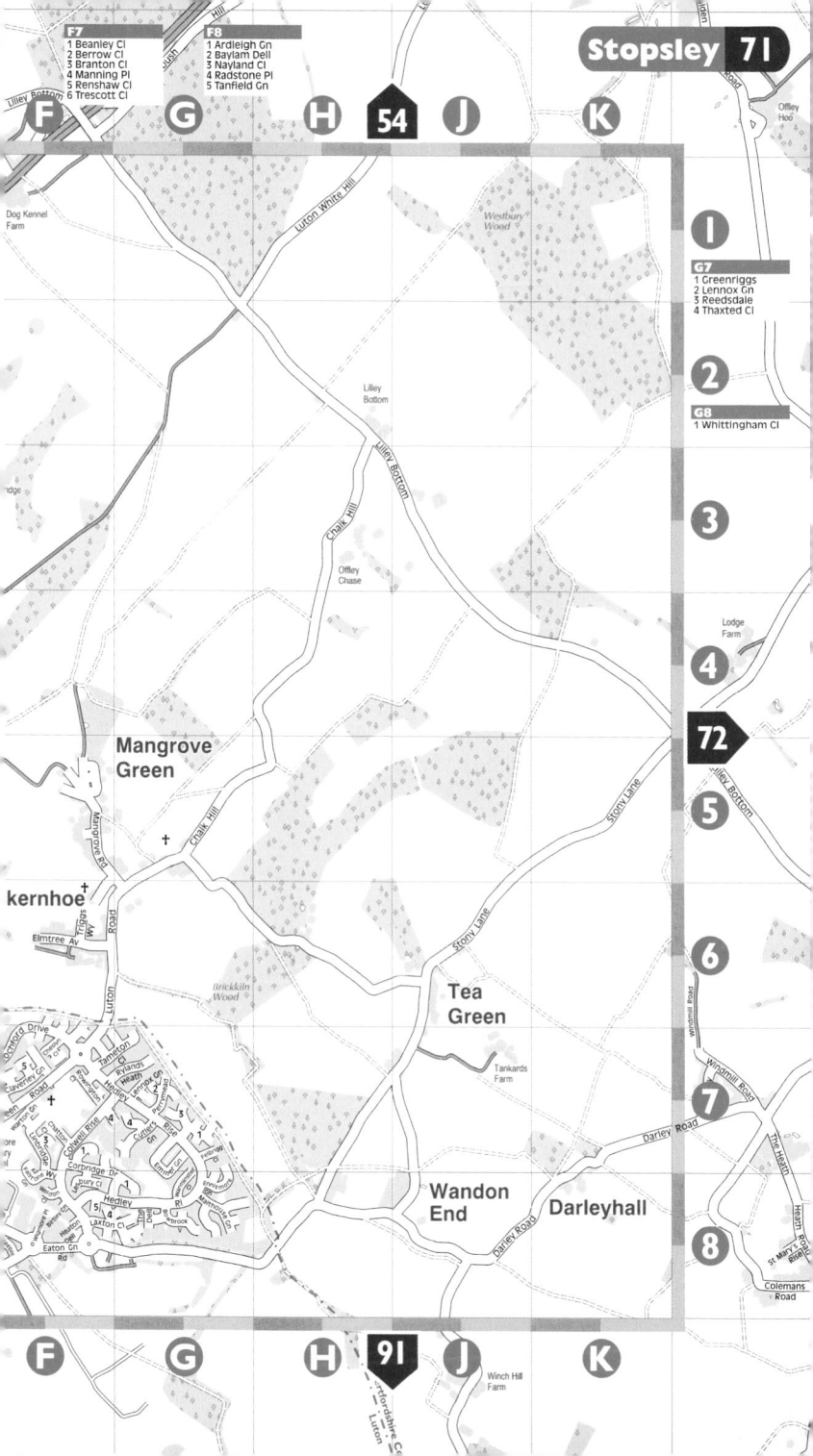

F7
1 Beanley Cl
2 Berrow Cl
3 Branton Cl
4 Manning Pl
5 Renshaw Cl
6 Trescott Cl

F8
1 Ardleigh Gn
2 Baylam Dell
3 Nayland Cl
4 Radstone Pl
5 Tanfield Gn

G7
1 Greenriggs
2 Lennox Gn
3 Reedsdale
4 Thaxted Cl

G8
1 Whittingham Cl

Offley
Hoo

Dog Kennel
Farm

Westbury
Wood

Luton White Hill

Lilley
Bottom

Lilley Bottom

Chalk Hill

Offley
Chase

Lodge
Farm

72

Lilley Bottom

Mangrove
Green

Stony Lane

kernhoe

Elmtree Av

Brickkiln
Wood

Windmill Road

Tankards
Farm

Tea
Green

Stony Lane

Darley Road

The Heath

Wandon
End

Darleyhall

St Marys Road

Eaton Gn
Rd

Darley Road

Colemans
Road

91

Winch Hill
Farm

Hertfordshire
Luton

F G H J K

F G H 54 J K

I 2 3 4 5 6 7 8

I grid square represents 500 metres

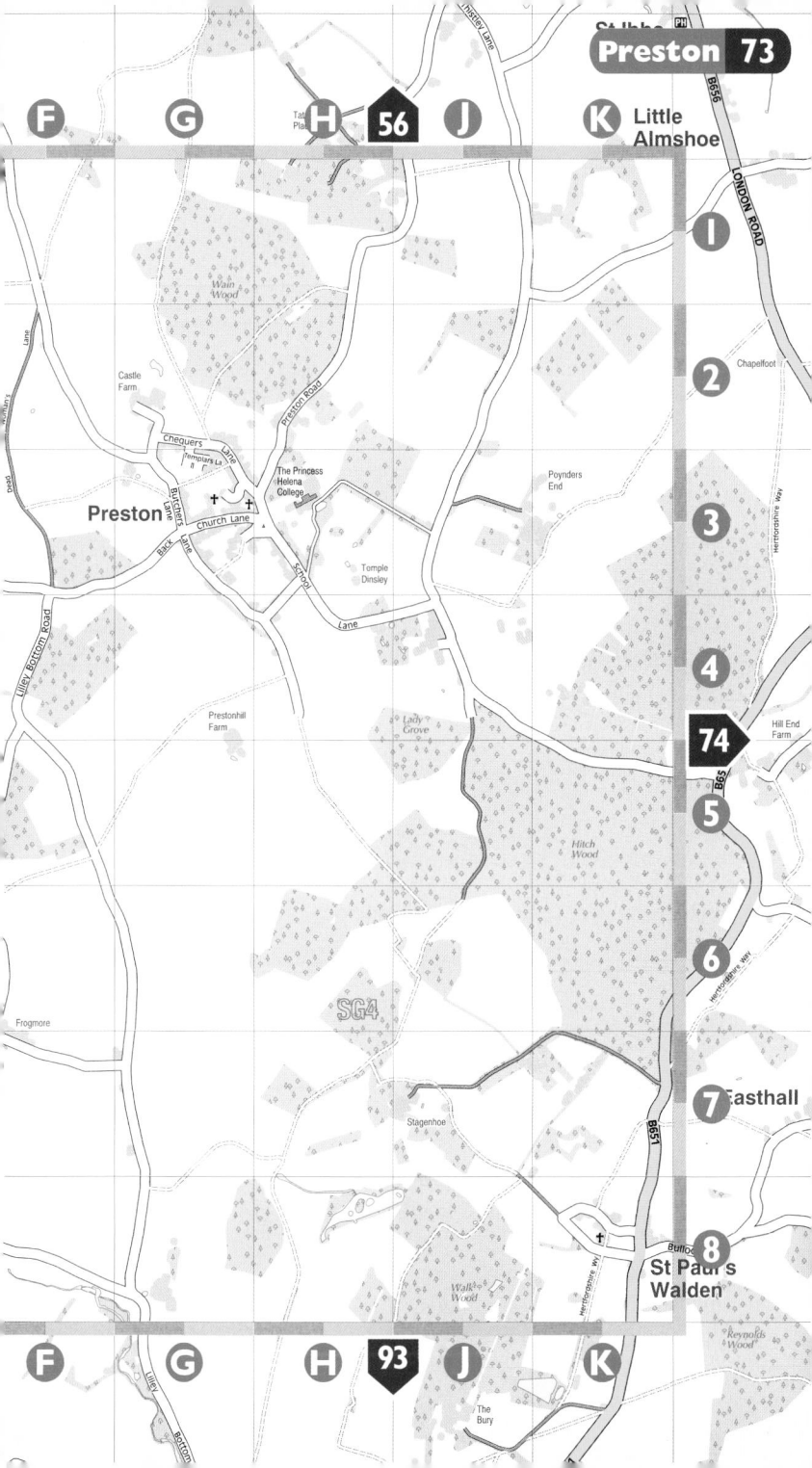

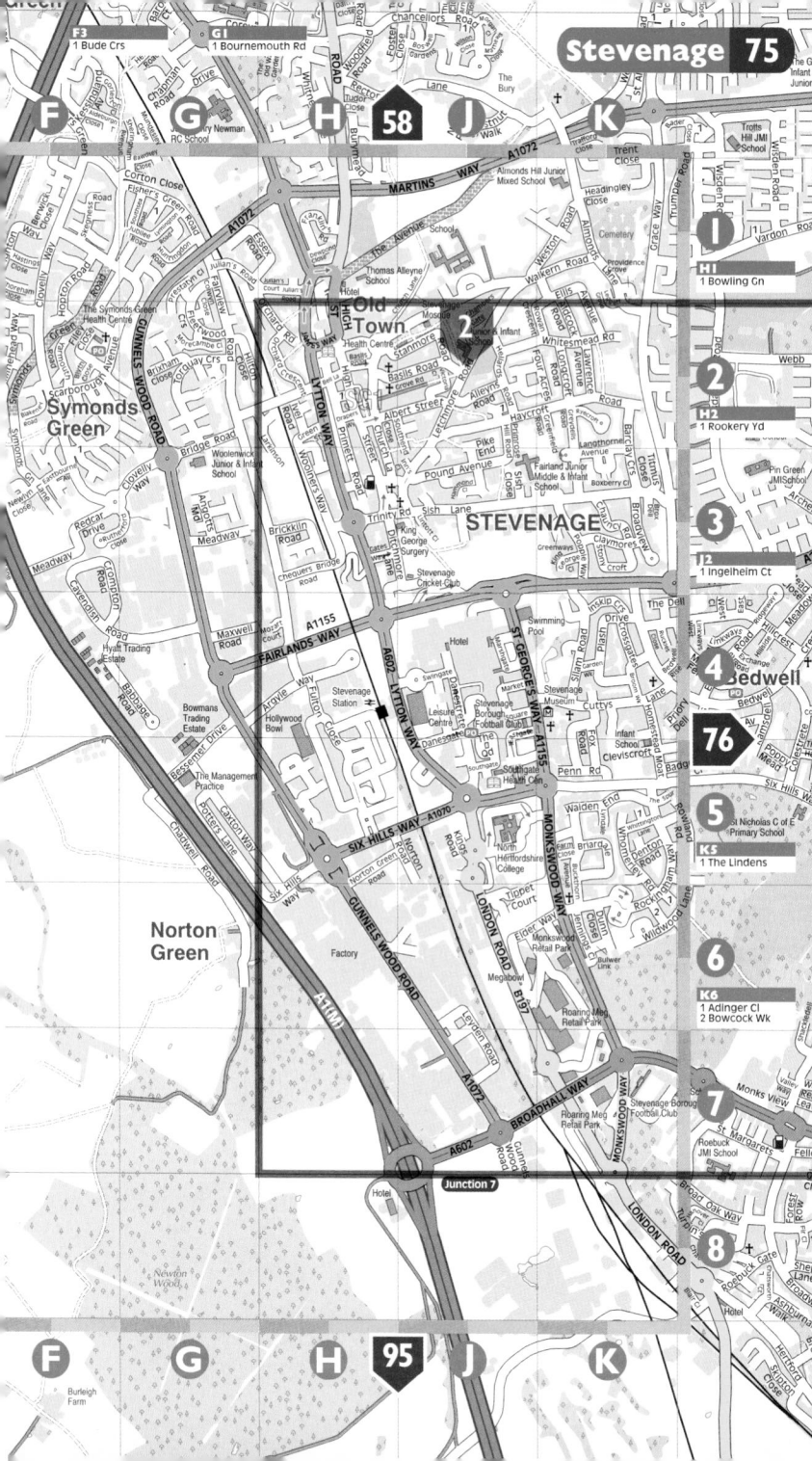

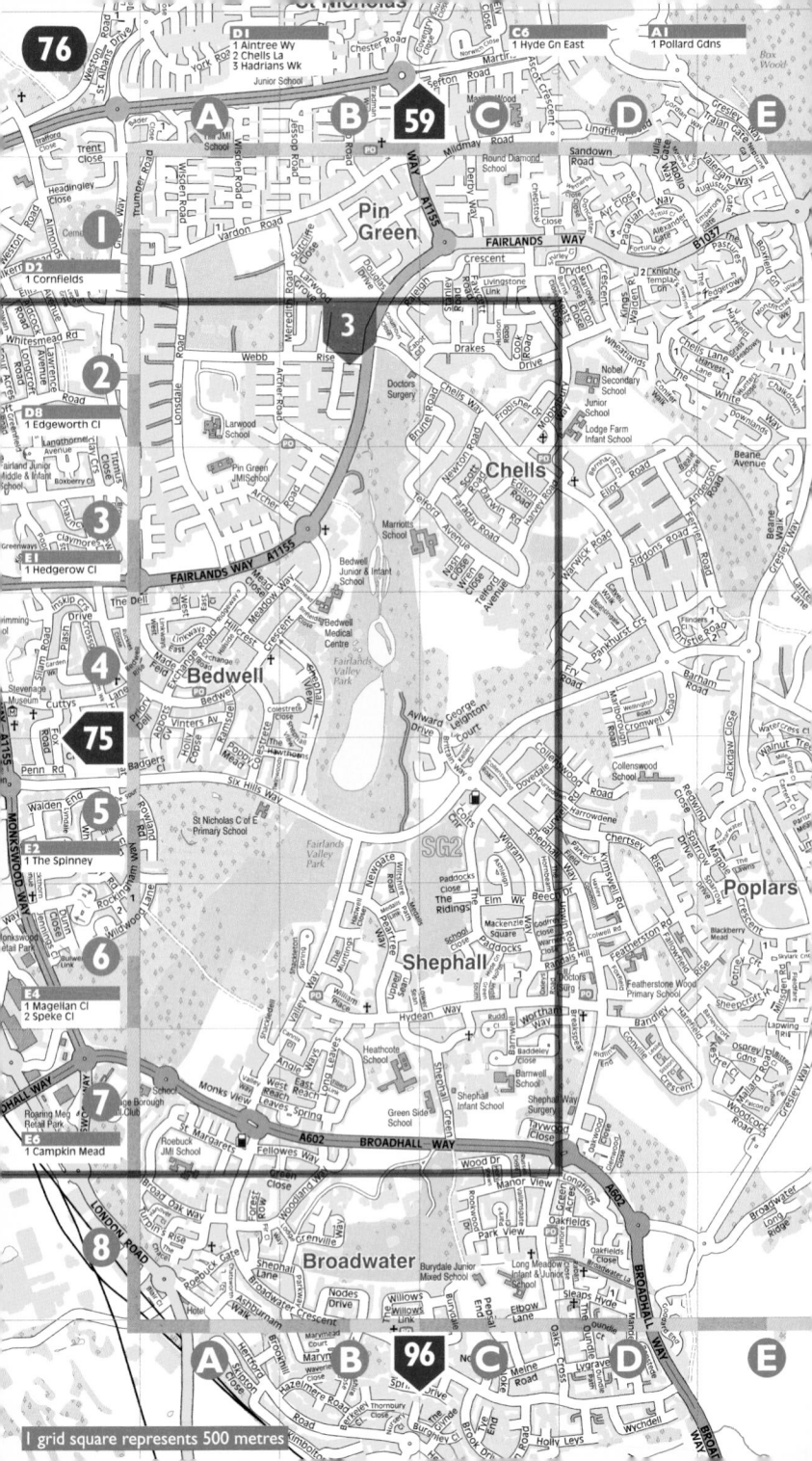

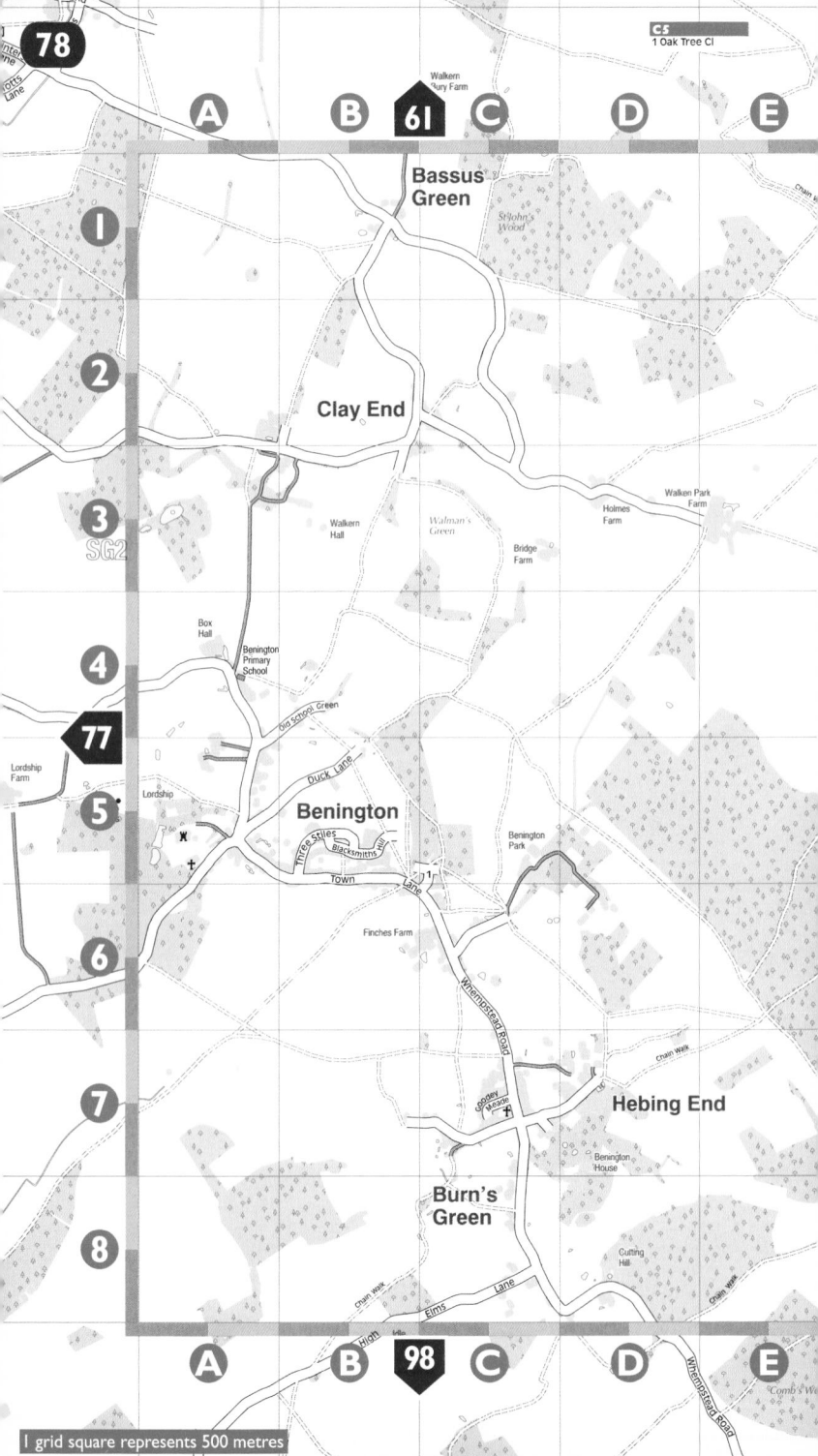

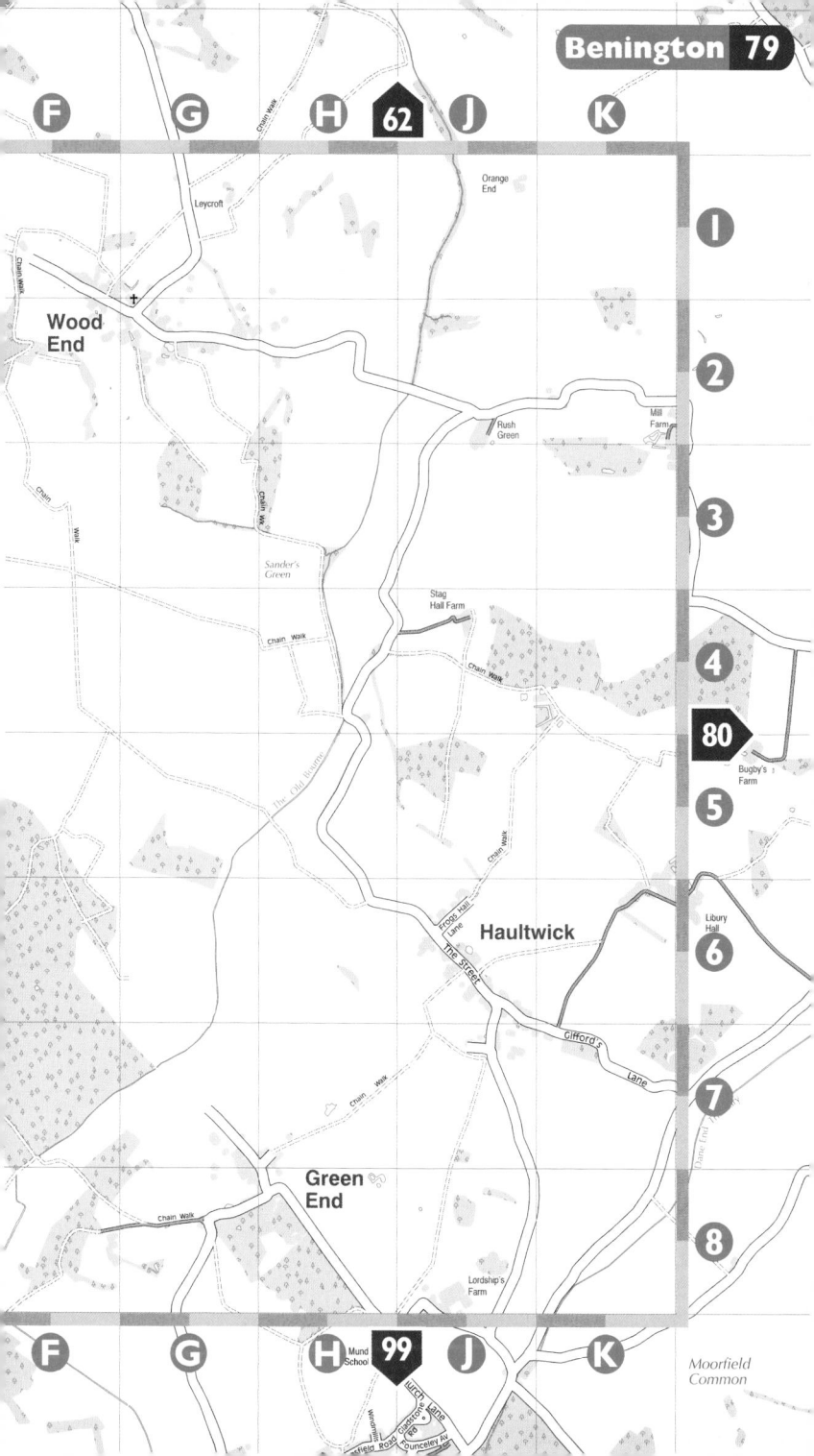

F G H **62** J K

I

Orange
End

Leycroft

Chain Walk

2

Rush
Green

Mill
Farm

**Wood
End**

Chain Walk

3

Sander's
Green

Stag
Hall Farm

Chain Walk

4

Chain Walk

80

Bugby's
Farm

The Old Bourne

5

Chain Walk

Chain Walk

Libury
Hall

Stag Hall
Lane

Haultwick

6

The Street

Gifford's
Lane

Lane End

7

Chain Walk

**Green
End**

Chain Walk

8

Lordship's
Farm

F G H **99** J K

Mund
School

Church Lane

Gladstone Lane

Pouncelcy Av

Mansfield Road

*Moorfield
Common*

F **G** **H** **64** **J** **K**

Quinbury
Farm

Coles
Park

Knights Hill
Farm

I

Gravelly

Green End

2

Hull Lane

Hamels Lane

Malting
Lane

Uplands
Green

B1368

Ford
Street

Broughing

3

Hamels Lane

Hamels
Park

East Herts
Golf Club

Station Road

4

Gatesbury

82

B1368

5

Mentley Lane

Mentley Lane West

Mentley Farm

Burntmill Road

Puckeridge

King's
Wood

6 SG11

The Moat

Clapham End

River Rib

1
Carisbrook
The Drive

St Johns

High Street

Park Lane

Roundmoor

Station Road

Roger De Clare
School

Standon
Health Centre

St Thomas of Canterbury
Catholic School

Fishers Cl

South Road

Station Road

Aston Road

7

Town Farm
Crescent

Cambridge Road

Standon Road

A10(T)

Stortford Road

Saffron

Gauldie Way

Southfields

Vicarage

Rib Close

STANDON HILL A120 **KENT'S LANE**

Standon

High Street

8

St Edmunds
College

Paper Mill Lane

Hadham Road

F **G** **H** **101** **J** **K**

A10(T)

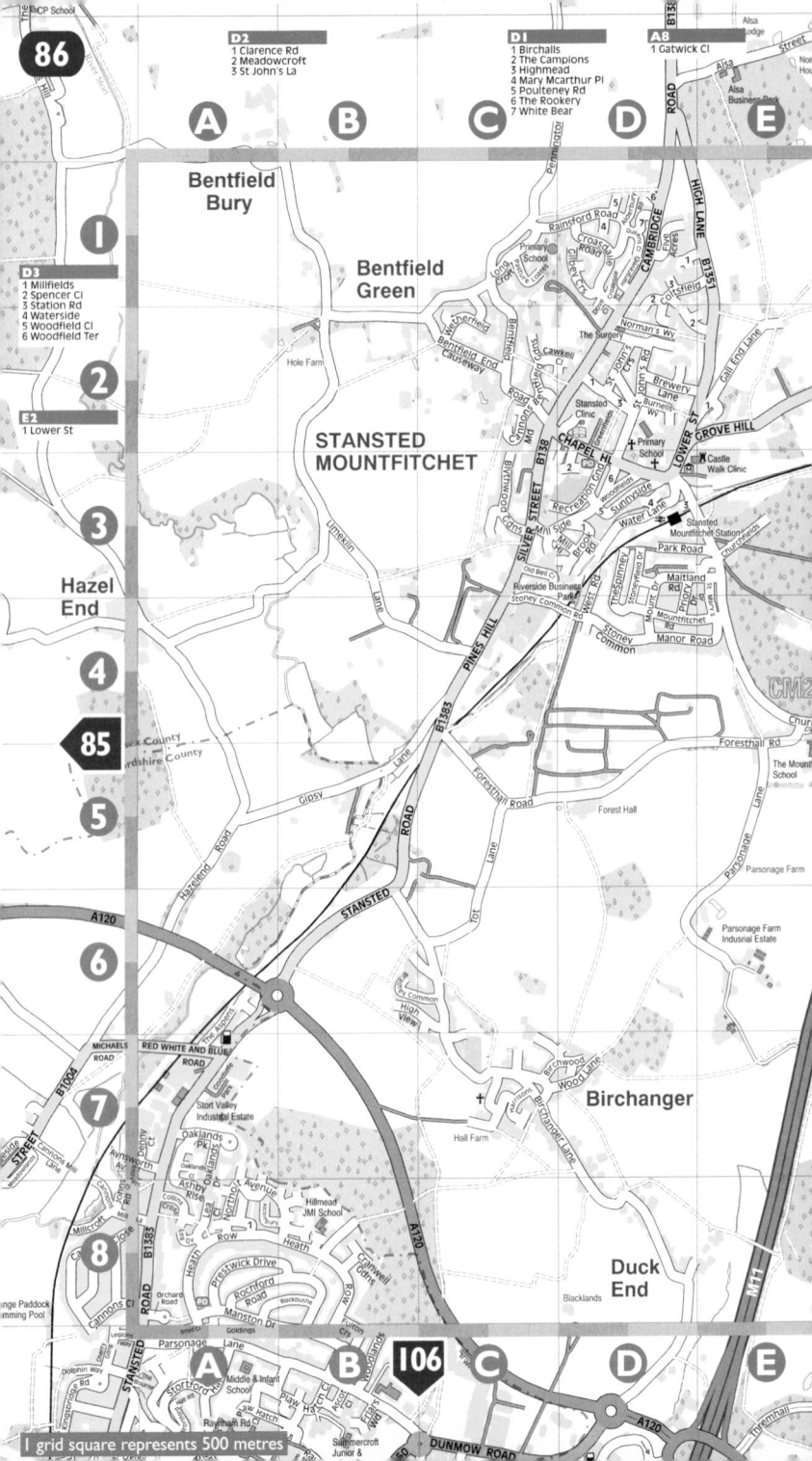

F G H J K

The Surgery

HENHAM

PH

STANSTED RD

Velan Drive

Robin Hood Rd

Mill Cl

Rush Lane

LC

Hall

Road

Church Lane

I

Fuller's End

2

Tye Green Road

Tye Green

3

Claypit Hill

The Arthur Findlay College

M11

Burton Bower

4

Burton End

Belmer Road

5

Sixth Avenue

Monks Farm

6

Thirtieth St

Bury Lodge

Bury Lodge Lane

Ninth Avenue

Eleventh

Fifth

Tenth Avenue

Third Avenue

Bassinbourn

7

Long Border Rd

Long Border Road

BASSINGB ROUNDAB

Thremh

8

Round Coppice Road

P

F G H **107** J K

PRIORY WOOD ROUNDABOUT

B1051

Stansted House

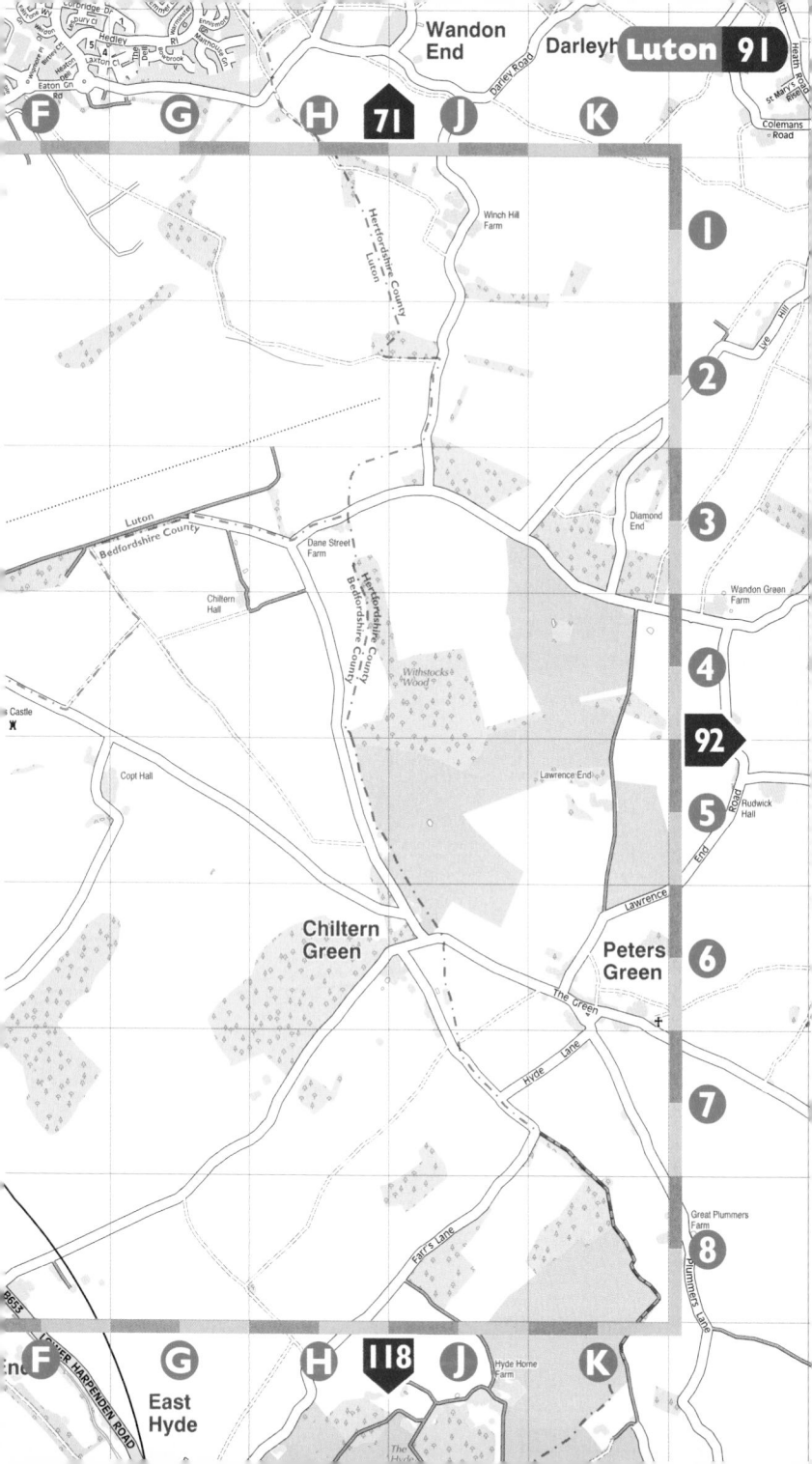

92

A Colemans Road

St Mary's C of E
Heath Rd

Orcha...
The ...
Oxford Rd **B**

72

C

D Law Hall
Farm

E

Chapel Road

Breachwood
Green

Holybush
Lane

I

Bailey's
Farm

Grove
Farm

Pasture

Bendish

2

Ive Hill

Lane

Whiteway
Bottom

Long Lane

3

Wandon Green
Farm

Whitewaybottom

Lane

4

91

Lawrence End

Road

Rudwick
Hall

End

Barleybeans

Whitewaybottom

5

Lane

Lawrence

6 P...rs
Green

The Green

Luton Road

Claggy Cott

Claggy

7

Hyde

Lane

Kimpton Road

**Ansells
End**

Luton Road

8

Great Plummers
Farm

Ramridge
Farm

Kimpton
Grange

B652

Plummers Lane

Saregbury

Lane

A

B

119

C

D

E

Tallents
Farm

BOTTOM

Coop...

1 grid square represents 500 metres

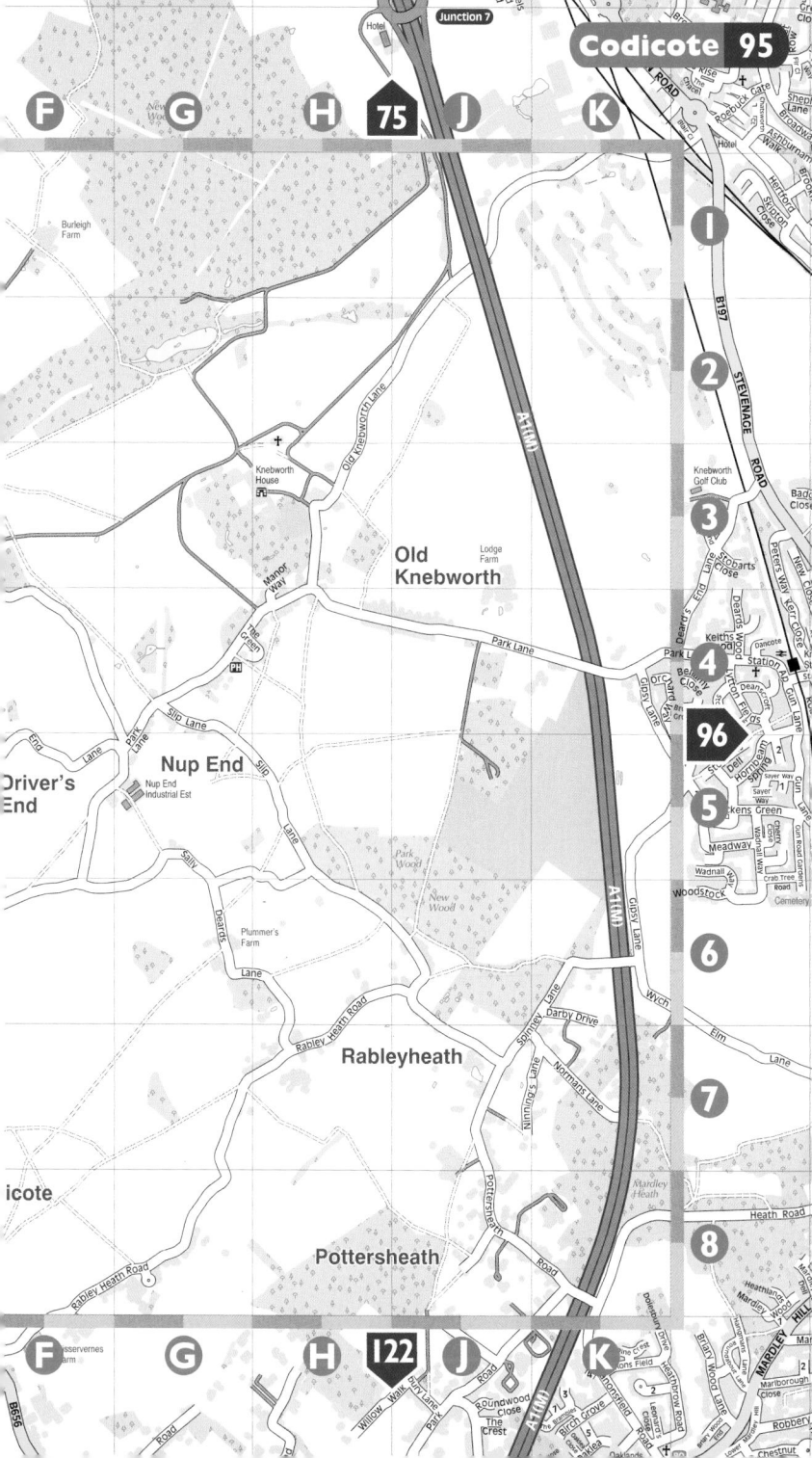

Green End

H2
1 Whiteley Cl

J2
1 Windy Ri

Chain Walk

F G H 79 J K

I Moorfield Common

Little Munden JMI School

Church Lane

Kingsfield Road
Gladstone Rd
Rounceley Av

Willowmead

Esmond Road
Kennedy Cl
Road
PO

Dane End

2

Whitehill Farm

Munden Drive
Chapman Drive

hempstead

Cock's Wood

3

Brookfield Common

Lodge Farm

ney Lane

4 Rowney Priory

100

Lowgate Lane

Sacombe Hill Farm

5 combe reen

Marshall's Lane

Sacombe Green Road

Sacombe

6

Sacombe
Pound

Sacombebury Farm

Sacombe House

7

The Clumps

8

Chain Walk

Burrs Green Farm

A602
WARE ROAD

Chelsing Farm

Hertfordshire Way

F G H 126 J Temple K

Temple Lane

Hertfordshire Way

Ⓐ　Ⓑ　**80**　Ⓒ　Ⓓ　Ⓔ

Levens Green

Old Hall Green

Ⓘ

Moorfield Common

High Trees Farm

Beggarman's Lane

Hill F

Whitehill Farm

⓶

Cock's Wood

Rigery Farm

Rigery

⓷

Potter's Hall Farm

Labdens Farm

Rowney Lane

Rowney Priory

Lowgate Lane

⓸

99

Lowgate Lane

Low Lane

⓹

Sacombe Green

Standon Green End

Marshall's Lane

Dane End Road

A10/T1

⓺

⓻

High Cross Puller Memorial Junior & Infant School

✝

Marshall's Lane

High Cro

Marshall's

Poplar Close

North Drive

⓼

Chen Wood

Chelsing Farm

Herts

Ⓐ　Ⓑ　**127**　Ⓒ　Ⓓ　Ⓔ ou

Wadesmill

A10/T1

F3
1 Parkins Cl

F G H **81** J K

Hadham Road

1

2

Harcamlow Way

Stort R...

3

Latchford

Arches Hall

4

102

5

6

Biggin's Farm

7

8

Rush Green

Dowsett's Farm

Colliers End

Plashes Wood

Plashes Farm

Barwick

Barwick Lane

Core Lane

Harcamlow Way

Sutes Woods

Great Barwick Manor

Harcamlow Way

Sawtrees Wood

F G H **128** J K

101

82

129

Standon

High Street

Harcamlow Way

Mill Lane

Paper Mill Lane

m Road

Standon
Friars

W...ond
Green

Balsams

Bromley

Bromley Hall

River Ash

Standon
Lodge

Latchford

Arches Hall

New Barns

Biggin's
Farm

Brand's
Farm

**Kettle
Green**

Nomans Bourne

Nobland
Green

Rush
Green

Camwe
Hall

A B C D E

A B C D E

1 2 3 4 5 6 7 8

I grid square represents 500 metres

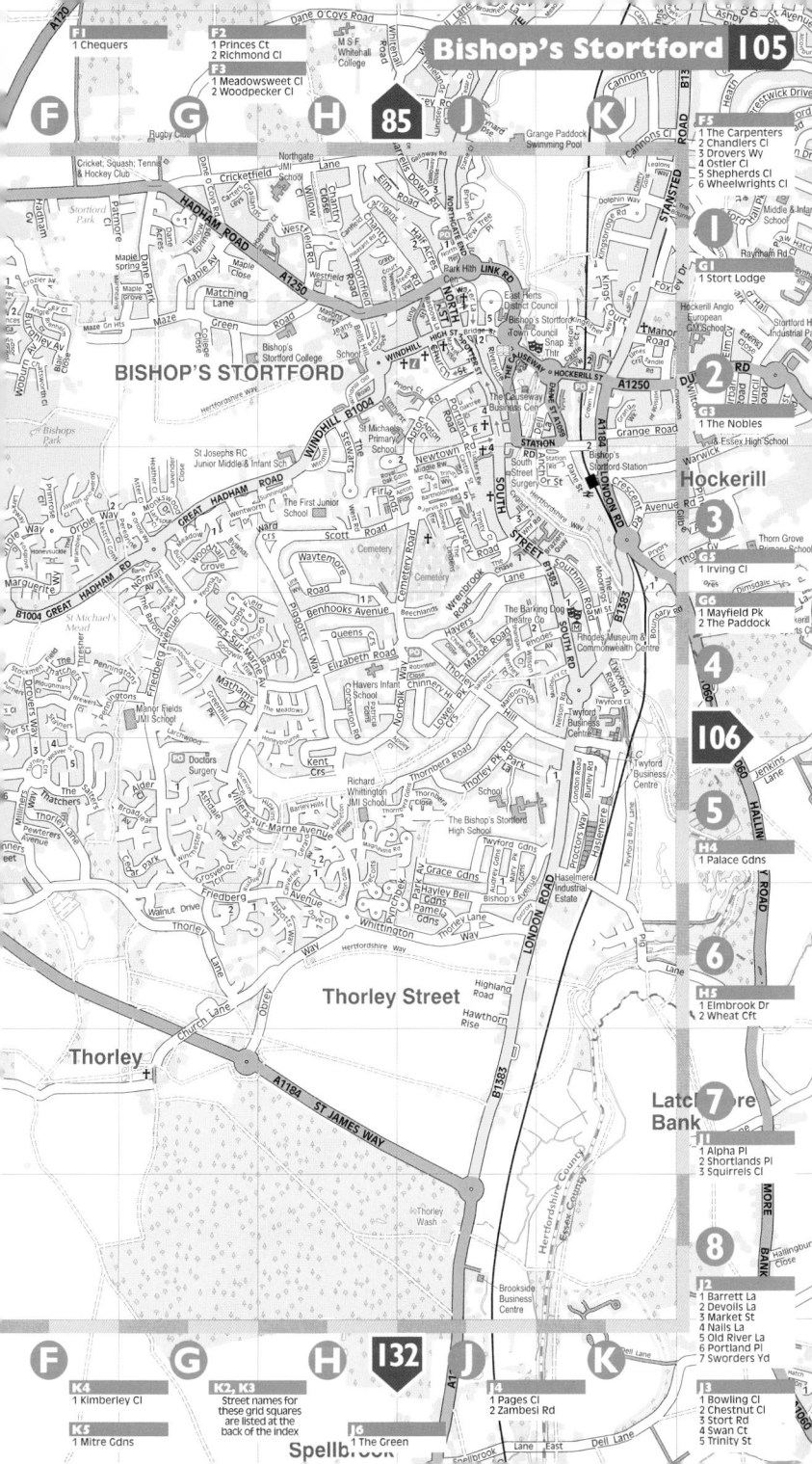

F G H 87 J K

I

Round Coppice Road

P

PRIORY WOOD ROUNDABOUT
Priory Wood Roundabout

20

art l

kiln
en

os Farm

Bury Lodge Lane

Thremhall Priory Farm

A120 DUNMOW ROAD

Flitch Way

CM22

2 20

Takeley Street

3

Hatfield Forest

Forest Way

edlar's
een

n Road

The Street

Beggar's Hall

Three Forest Way

Hallingbury Way

Hatfield Forest NT

4

Three Forests Way

Three Forests Way

5

Hatfield Way

Three Forests Way

Three Forests Way

Hallingbury Street

Hallingbury Way

Forest Lodge

Collin's Coppice

Little Barrington Hall Farm

6

Forest Way

Three Forests Way

Lodge Farm

7
Farm

Wall Wood

The Woods

8

Three Forests Way

Forest Hall

Forest Farm

F G H J K

Monk's Wood

Three Forests Way

Barrington Hall

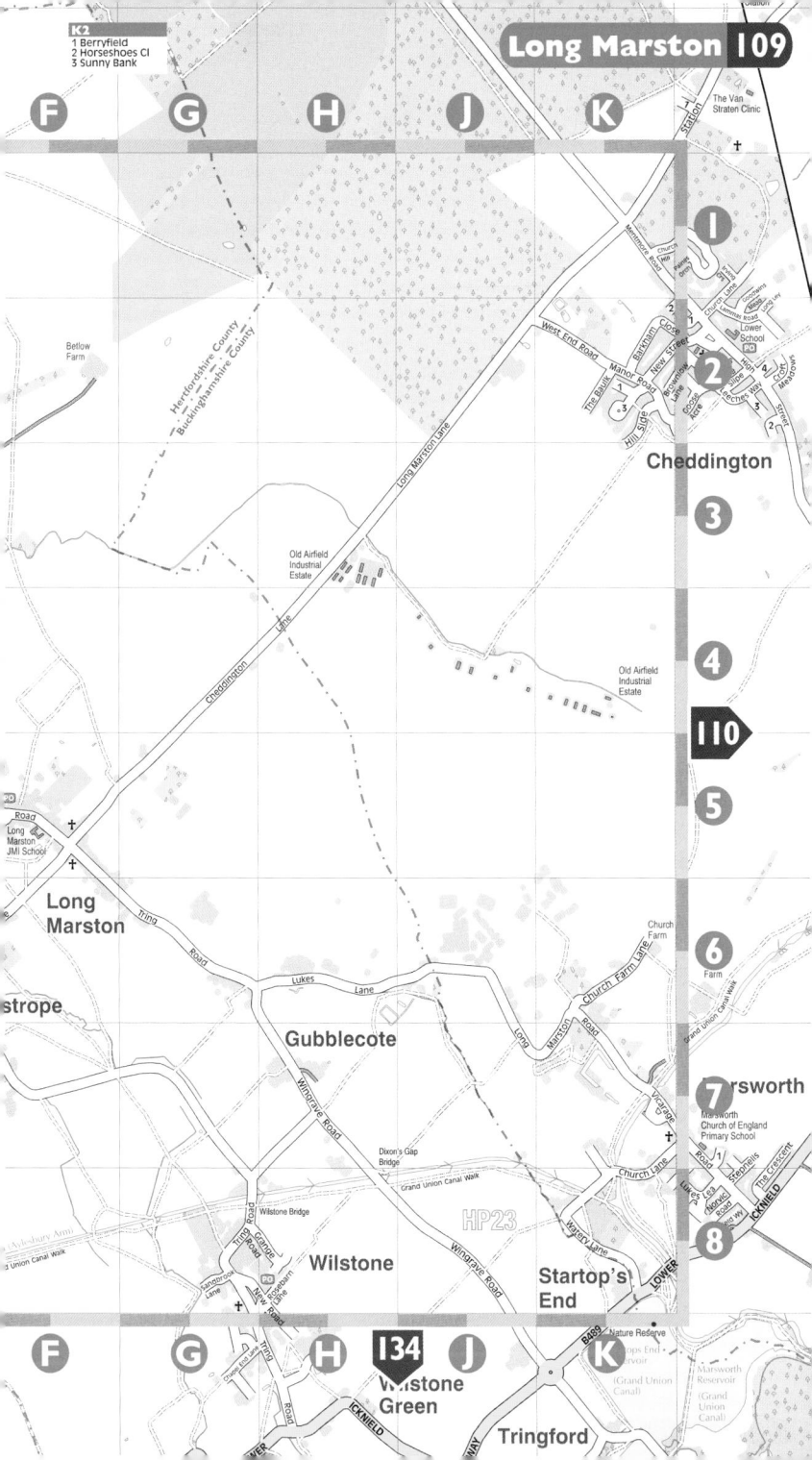

Ivinghoe
Aston

F
G
H
J
K

I

S

TRING ROAD

Coombe
Bottom

Crabtree
Cottage

Coombe
Hole

B489

2

Two Ridges Link

• Hill Fort

Ridgeway

3

vinghoe
Golf Club

Town
Farm

Icknield Way

4

112

Ivinghoe

B489

ROAD

B489

Icknield Way

5

Icknield Way

mill

Icknield Way

6

urst Farm

Icknield Way

Ridgeway

Down Farm

'Clipper
Down

7

Ivinghoe
Common

Pitstone Hill

Icknield Way

8

Duncombe
Farm

County

F
G
H
136
J arley
End
K

Icknield Way

E4
1 Chestnut Cl
2 Huntsmans Cl

A B C D E

1

Willow
Farm

Stet

Bedfordshire County
Buckinghamshire County

2
Coombe
Hole
B489

TRING ROAD

R A F
Edlesborough

Chiltern
Farm

3
Collyers

Fairview
Farm

Dagnall

4
Dagnall
Farm

Ward's
Coombe

III

5
Kensworth Way

Kensworth Way

RINGSHALL ROAD

6
Ward's Hurst Farm

Ringshall
Coppice

Well Farm

7
Clipper
Down

Beacon Road

RINGSHALL ROAD

B4506

Buckinghamshire County
Hertfordshire County

Ivinghoe
Common

Hall Farm

Ringshall

8
Duncombe
Farm

Deer Leap
Swimming
Pool

A B **137** C D E

Farm

F **G** **H** **J** **K**

B4540

Saddlebrook Rd

Tree
Cathedral

Icknield

I

Whipsnade
Health

B4540

Whipsnade

Eleanor Avenue

Dukes Avenue

The
Green

Centre

Studham Lane

Glenpool

Rise

Buckwood Lane

Oakway

2

Holywell

Mary Joans Ride

Cut
Throat
Avenue

Cut

Throat

Avenue

Valley

Close

Whipsnade
Park Zoo

Holywell Road

Holywell Rd

Holywell Cl

3

Sir Peter's Wy

Humphrey
Talbot
Avenue

Dunstable Road

Icknield Way

4

hite
on

Way

Icknield Way

Studham

Icknield Way

114

Whipsnade
Park Golf Club

Manor
Farm

Swanells Wy

Southern
Wy

Kens

5

Studham
Lane

Church

Church
Road

Church
Road

Valley
Close

Studham
VC Lower
School

Mansgrove
Farm

Valley Road

6

Common Road

Bury
Farm

SOUTH
A4146

7

Ravensdell
Wood

Young
Wood

Lamsey
Farm

Milebarn
Farm

A4146

8

HEMEL HEMPSTEAD

Pedley Hill

Church
Farm

F **G** **H** **138** **J** **K**

Road

HEMPSTEAD ROAD

K5
1 Carpenders Cl
2 Kinsbourne Crs
3 Penshurst Cl
4 Shepherds Wy

K6
1 Yeomans Av

F G H **90** J K

New Mill End
1

2

3

4

118

5

6

7

8

Home Farm

West Hyde

Lady Bute's Lodge

LONDON ROAD

Kennel Lane

Lady Bray Farm

White Walls

Kinsbourne Green

The Common

Denture Clinic

Thrales End

Annables Lane

Annables Farm

Turner's Hall Farm

Spring Road

Kinsbourne Green Lane

Roundwood Lane

Deigarth

Faulkners End Farm

Wood End JMI School

Ashley Gdns

Brackendale Grove

Roundwood Lane

Falconer's Lane

Roundwood Lane Primary School

Roundwood Park School

Townsend Lane

Claydate Avenue

Barns De

Hartwell Gardens

DUNSTABLE ROAD

Luton Lane

Redbourn Golf Club

Golf Course

Rothamsted Experimental Station

F G H **142** J K

118

B7
1 Moreton End Cl
2 Timbers Ct

B6
1 Bramble Cl
2 Lambourn Gdns
3 Moreton Pl
4 Otterton Cl

A8
1 Badingham Dr

A6
1 The Spinney

A5
1 Ridgeway
2 Ridgewood Gdns

A   B   **91**   C   D   E

New
Mill End

1

East
Hyde

B8
1 St Andrew's Av

2

C5
1 Highmoor

3

C6
1 Ambrose La
2 Stonemason Cl

C7
1 Hales Meadow
2 Old Rectory Cl

4
End

117

5

C8
1 Thompsons Cl

Wood End JM
School

6

Brackendale

D5
1 Masefield Ct
2 Rye Cl

7

D7
1 Connaught Rd
2 Devonshire Rd
3 Maldon Ct

8

D8
1 Poets Ct
2 Victoria Rd

E5
1 St Martins Cl
2 Someries Rd
3 Willow Wy

A   B   **143**   C   D   E

HARPENDEN

Rothamsted Experimental
Station

E6
1 The Bungalows
2 Lower Luton Rd

E7
1 Lyndhurst Cl

E8
1 Overstone Rd

1 grid square represents 500 metres

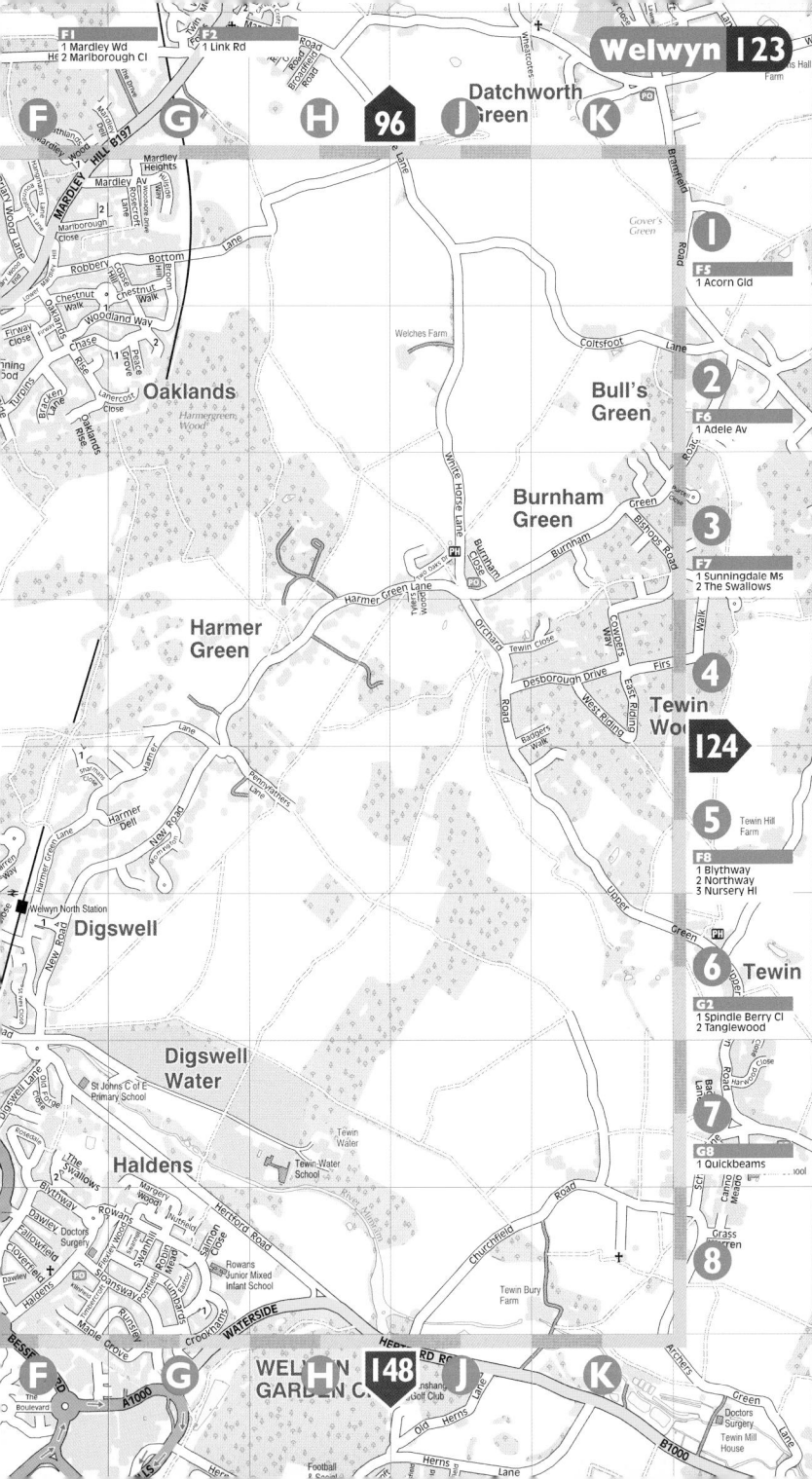

F1
1 Mardley Wd
2 Marlborough Cl

F2
1 Link Rd

F **G** **H** 96 **J** **K**

Datchworth Green

Gover's Green

I

F5
1 Acorn Gld

Welches Farm

Coltsfoot Lane

2

Bull's Green

F6
1 Adele Av

Oaklands

Harmergreen Wood

White Horse Lane

Burnham Green

Green

Bishops Road

3

F7
1 Sunningdale Ms
2 The Swallows

Harmer Green Lane

Burnham

Orchard Road

Tewin Close

Cowpers Way

Walk

Harmer Green

Desborough Drive

West Riding

Firs

East Riding

4

Tewin Wood

124

New Road

Renovations Lane

Harmer Dell

5 Tewin Hill Farm

F8
1 Blythway
2 Northway
3 Nursery Hl

Welwyn North Station

Digswell

New Road

Upper Green

PH

6 Tewin

G2
1 Spindle Berry Cl
2 Tanglewood

St Johns C of E Primary School

Digswell Water

Bad Lane

7

G8
1 Quickbeams

Tewin Water

Haldens

Tewin Water School

River Mimram

Hertford Road

Waterside

Rowans Junior Mixed Infant School

Crookhams

Churchfield Road

Tewin Bury Farm

Carlo Mead

Grass Warren

8

Archers Green

Doctors Surgery

Tewin Mill House

F **G** **H** 148 **J** **K**

WELWYN GARDEN C.

HERTFORD RD

Old Herns Lane

Herns Lane

124

A **B** **97** **C** **D** **E**

Watton Road
A7
1 The Hazels
Watkins Farm
Perry Farm
Hawkins Hall Farm
Bramfield Road
1
Perrywood Lane
Coltsfoot Lane
2
Bu... Green
Perrywood Lane
Bramfield Woods
urnham reen
3
Green
Burnham
Chain Walk
Queen Hoo Lane
Cowper Way
West R
4
Firs
Tewin Wood
123
Tewin Hill
Winding Shott
5
Tewin Hill Farm
Chain Walk
Bury Lane
B
Under Green
6
Tewin
Park Woods
Chain Walk
7
Back Lane
Hertford Road
Chain Walk
Westend
Bacon's Farm
School Lane
Cannons Meadow
Tewin School
8
Grass Warren
Mardley Hill
Chain Walk

A **B** **149** **C** **D** **E**
Green
Doctors Surgery
Tewin Mill
Hertford Road
Yarrengate Farm
B100...

I grid square represents 500 metres

F6
1 Church Fld

F7
1 Valley Cl

Youngsbury

1

G5
1 Amberley Gn

2

G6
1 Aldwyke Ri
2 The Blanes
3 The Brambles
4 Maplewood
5 Rolleston Cl

3 12

Col
Chr

H6
1 Cranbrook Cl

4

128

5

H7
1 Bourne Cl
2 Century Rd
3 Goldstone Cl
4 Orchard Cl

Fanhams

6

H8
1 Bluecoat Yd
2 Bridge Foot
3 George Wk

7

J6
1 Grasmere Rd

8

J7
1 Beazley Cl

Chelsing
Farm

Hertfordshire Way

Wadesmill

Thundridge
JMI School

Thundridge

Cold Christmas Lane

Cowards

Ashridge
Common

Moles
Farm

Woodson Park
Leisure Centre

Round
House

Great Cozens

WARE

The Chauncy
School

WESTMILL ROAD

WATTON ROAD

WADESMILL ROAD

Priory

Sacred Heart
RC School

HERTFORD ROAD

Ware Station

Mill Studio
Business Centre

STAR ST

B1004

152

F

G

H

J

K

K8
1 Barley Ponds Cl
2 Belle Vue Rd
3 Musleigh Manor
4 Widbury Gdns

K7
1 Spring Rd

1 Hampden Hill Cl
2 Jubilee Av

1 Herts
Clubhouse

K6
1 Rushfield Rd

J8
1 Common Whf
2 Wickhams Whf

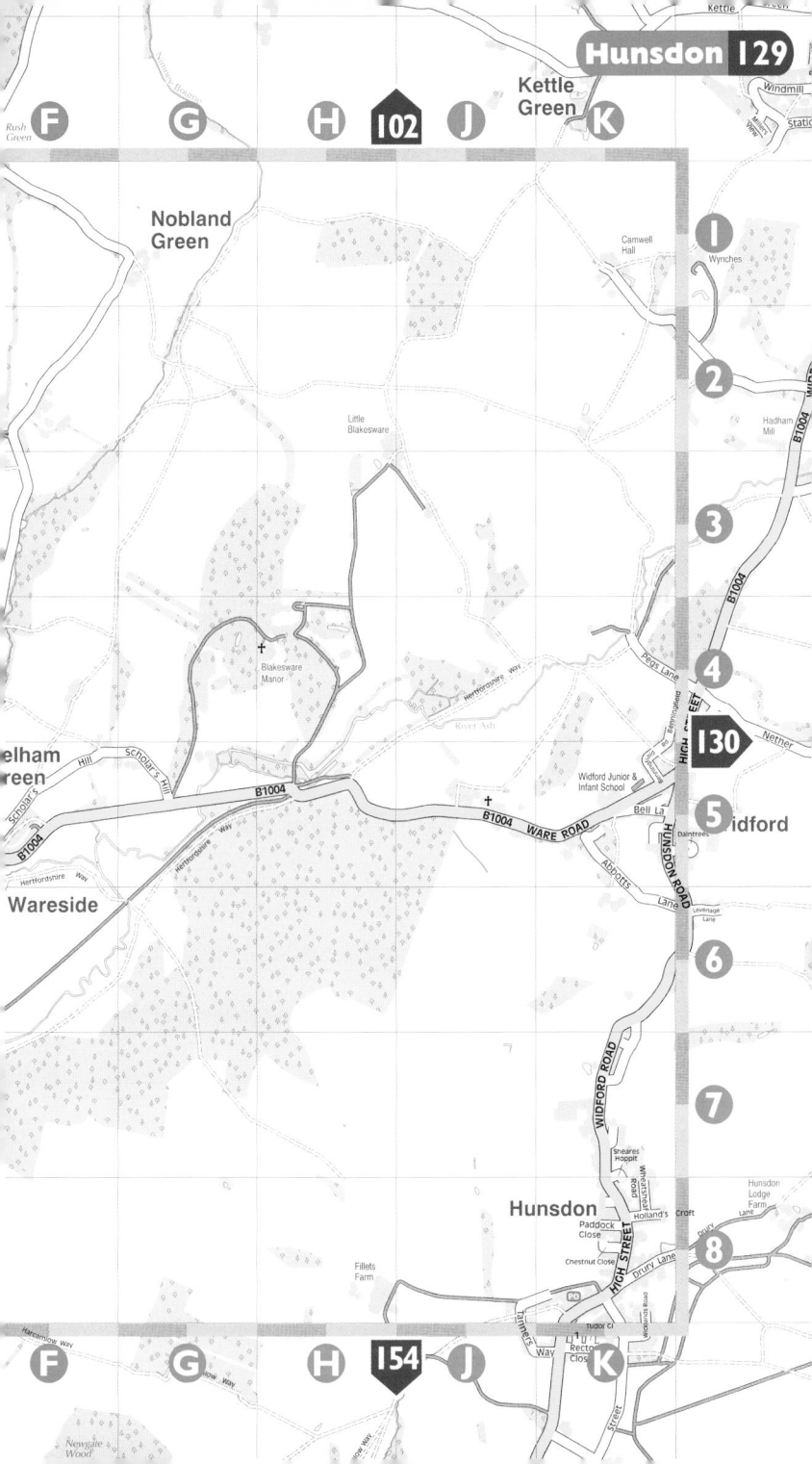

ettle
een

Kettle

Broadfield
Way

Broadfield

Windmill Way

Station Rd

SG10

Green
Tye

Stansted Hill

Ulfords

Hertfordshire Way

Cemetery

Bucklers
Hall Farm

1

Wynches

PH

**Perry
Green**

2

Hadham
Mill

Hertfordshire Way

3

South-end

Minges

St Elizabeths
School & Home

4

Lane

**Nether
Street**

HIGH STREET

Nether   Street

Widford Junior &
Infant School

5

HUNSDON ROAD

La

Daintrees

Widford

ARE ROAD

Abbotts

Lane

Leventage
Lane

6

Marshland Wood

WIDFORD ROAD

7

Sheares
Hoppit

Actons
Farm

nsdon

Holland's Croft

Hunsdon
Lodge
Farm
Lane

Paddock
Close

Chestnut Close

8

Drury

HIGH

Drury Lane

Tudor Cl

Rectory
Close

Way

Overhall
Farm

I grid square represents 500 metres

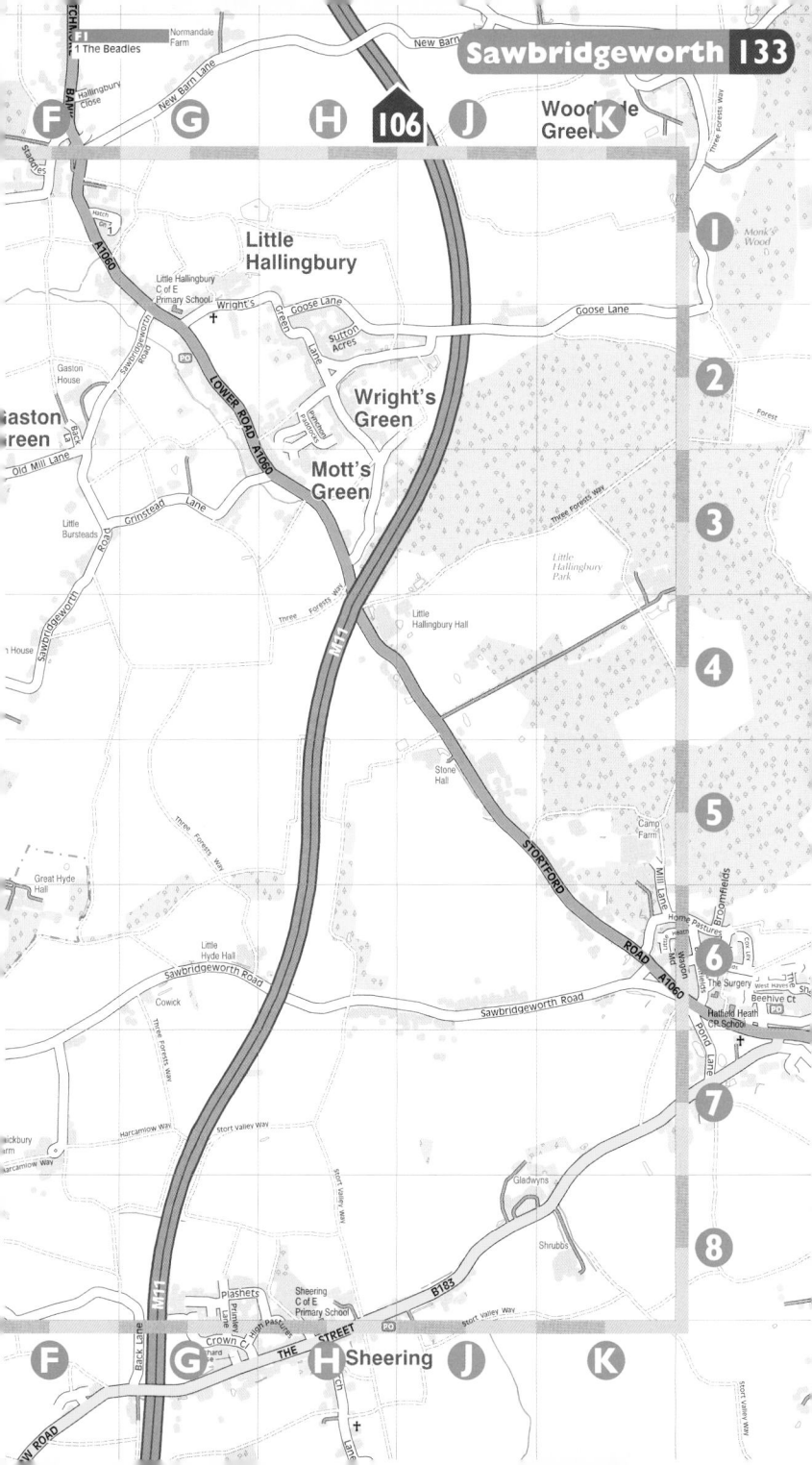

F
G
H
106
J
K

Wood'de Green

I

Monk's Wood

1 The Beadles

Normandale Farm

New Barn

New Barn Lane

Hallingbury Close

Little Hallingbury

Little Hallingbury C of E Primary School

Wright's Green Lane

Goose Lane

Goose Lane

2

Forest

Gaston House

aston een

Old Mill Lane

Wright's Green

Sutton Acres

Mott's Green

Three Forests Way

3

Little Hallingbury Park

Little Bursteads

Grinstead Lane

n House

Little Hallingbury Hall

4

Three Forests Way

Stone Hall

Camp Farm

5

Great Hyde Hall

Mill Lane

Home Pastures

Bloomfields

Little Hyde Hall

Sawbridgeworth Road

STORTFORD ROAD A1060

Watson Mt

The Surgery

West Haven

6

Cowick

Sawbridgeworth Road

Hatfield Heath C of E School

Beehive Ct

Pond Lane

7

ickbury

Harcamlow Way

Harcamlow Way

Stort Valley Way

Gladwyns

Shrubbs

8

Plashets

Priory

Crown

Upon Pastures

Sheering C of E Primary School

Stort Valley Way

B183

Stort Valley Way

F
G
THE STREET
H
Sheering
J
K

Back Lane

W ROAD

Stort Valley Way

F **G** **H** **110** **J** **K**

Bulbourne

Tring Wharf

Tring & New Mill Pre-school

New Mill

Grand Union Canal

Grand Union Canal

Mansworth Reservoir

Grand Union Canal

Manor House Farm

Folly Farm

Parkhill Farm

Marshcroft Lane

Grand Union Canal Walk

Station Road

Football Club

Hotel

Grove Road Primary School

Netherby Close

Dundale Infants School

Tring School

Tring Sports Centre

Tring Health Centre

Doctors Surgery

TRING

Upper Dunsley

The Arts Educational School

Tring Town Council

Akeman Business Park

British Museum (Natural History) Zoological Museum

Park Street

HIGH STREET

LONDON ROAD

A4635

A41(T)

A4251

A41(T)

Woodlands Farm

Tring Park

Oddy Hill

Wigginton

The Twist

Park Farm

The Bit

Vicarage Road

Hemp Lane

Hill Green Farm

Wigginton Bottom

I

2

3

4

136

5

6

7

8

F **G** **H** **159** **J** **K**

J8
1 Belmers Rd
2 Grimsdyke Rd
3 Pollywick Rd

H5
1 The Beeches
2 Hawkwell Dr

Wick Farm

H4
1 Danvers Cft
2 Hollyfield
3 Sulgrave Crs

138

A · B · **113** · C · D · E

I

Hog Wood

Lamsey Farm

Milebarn Farm

Church Farm

Church Road

Little Gaddesden JMI School

2 Little Gaddesden

Jossen Road

Hudnall

3

Hudnall Lane

Hudnall Corner

HEMEL HEMPSTEAD ROAD

A4146

Lower Gad. Farm

4 • Ashridge Estate (NT)

Home Farm

Hill Wood

137

Cromer

5

Nettleden Road

St Margaret's Farm

6

7

Nettleden Lodge

Nettled

Frithsden Beeches

Brickkiln Cott

8

Frithsden Gardens

A · B · **162** · C · D · E

Frithsden

Frithsden

I grid square represents 500 metres

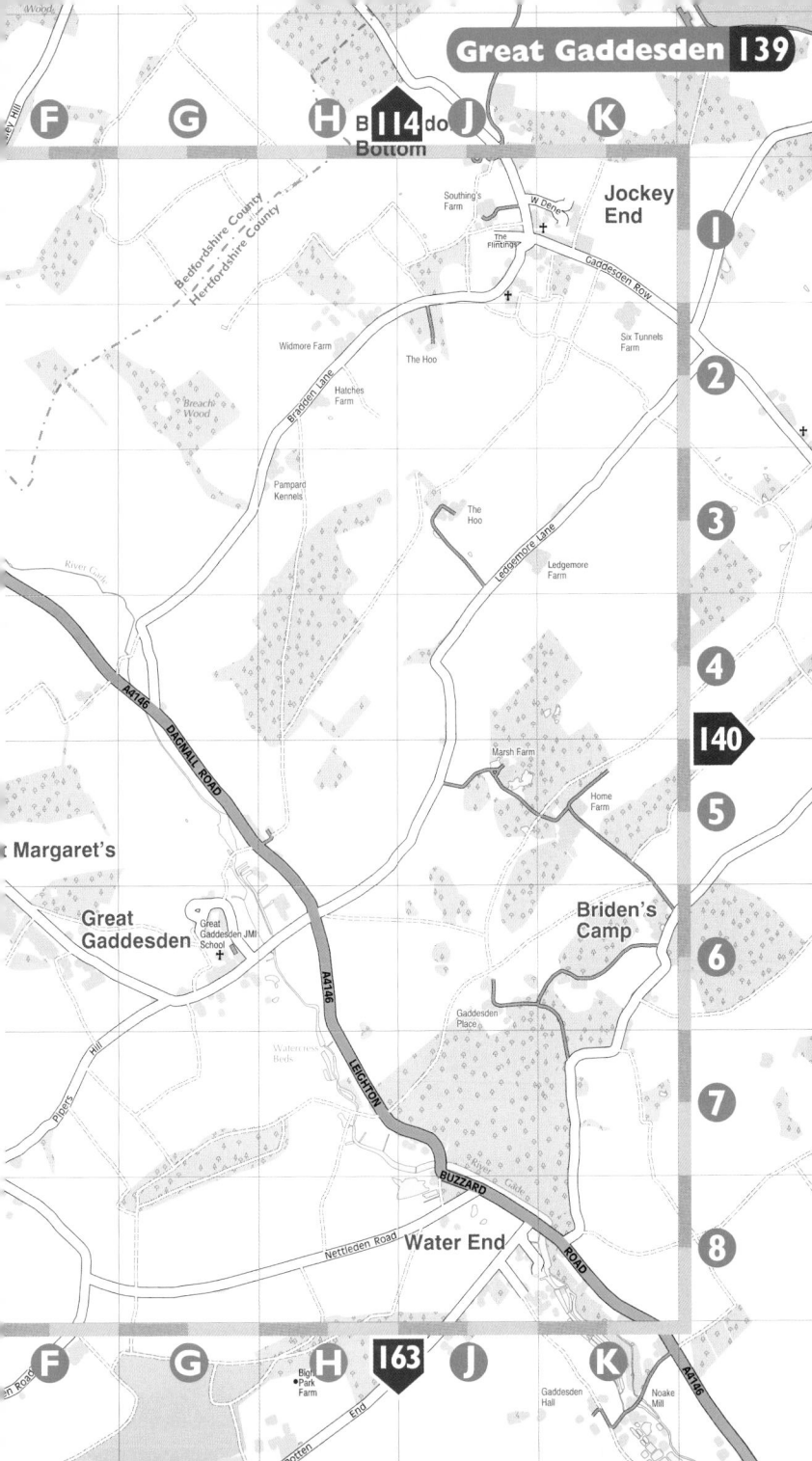

F G H J K

114

Bdo
Bottom

Jockey
End

Southing's
Farm

W Dene

The
Flinthall

Gaddesden Row

I

2

Six Tunnels
Farm

Bedfordshire County
Hertfordshire County

Widmore Farm

The Hoo

Broadon Lane

Hatches
Farm

3

The Hoo

Ledgemore Lane

Ledgemore
Farm

Pampard
Kennels

Breach's
Wood

River Gade

4

140

Marsh Farm

Home
Farm

5

A4146

DAGNALL ROAD

Margaret's

Great
Gaddesden

Great
Gaddesden JMI
School

Briden's
Camp

6

A4146

LEIGHTON

Gaddesden
Place

Watercress
Beds

Pipers Hill

7

Woods

BUZZARD

River Gade

Nettleden Road

Water End

ROAD

8

A4146

F G H J K

163

Bigh
Park
Farm

End

Gaddesden
Hall

Noake
Mill

Road

A4146

140

115 Farm

139

164

Valley Lane

Beechwood Park Preparatory School

A **B** **C** **D** **E**

Wood End Lane

Jockey End **I**

Gaddesden Row

Puddephat's Lane

Six Tunnels Farm **2**

Wood End Farm

Puddephats Farm

Gaddesden Row CP School

Upper Wood Farm

3

Ledgemore Farm

Gaddesden Row

4

Elmtree Farm

5

Home Farm

Corner Farm

Hawbush Farm

Cupid Green Lane

Briden's Camp **6**

7

Eastbrook Hay Farm

8

Lovetts End Farm

Wood Farm

HP2

Dodds Lane

ROAD

A4146

A **B** **164 C** **D** **E**

Gaddesden Hall

Noake Mill

Dodds Lane

Barntoft JMI School

Wootton Drive

Thames

I grid square represents 500 metres

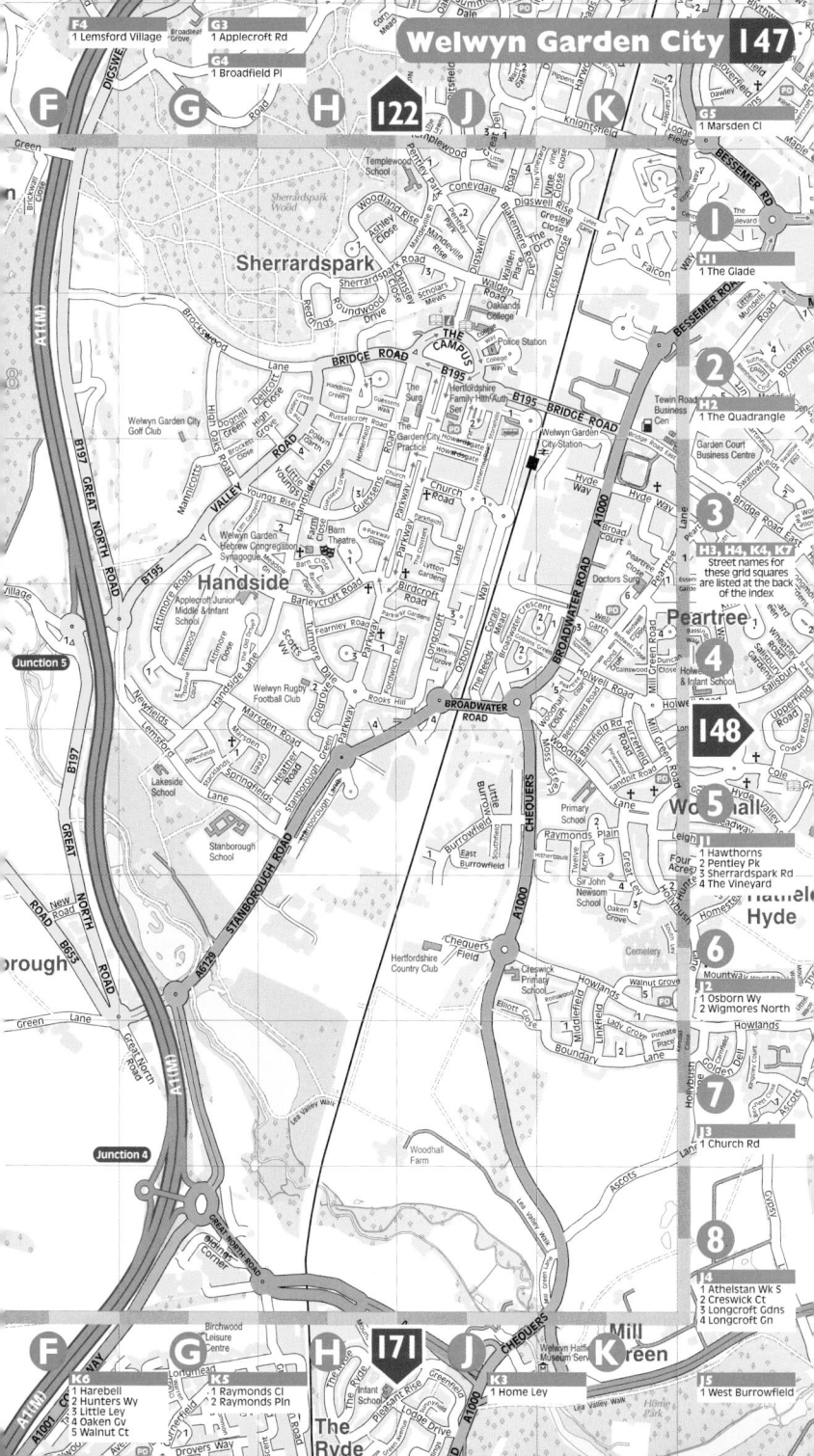

122

148

171

F1
1 Cumberland Cl
2 Mansfield Gdns
3 Woodhall Cl

F2
1 Archers Cl
2 Redwoods

F3
Street names for
this grid square are
listed at the back of
the index

F5
1 Glovers Cl
2 Pearsons Cl
3 Waterdale
4 Wilton Wy

F6
1 Mandeville Cl

G1
1 Glebe Cl

152

G3, J3
Street names for
these grid squares
are listed at the
back of the index

Hertford

G4
1 Peg's La
2 Queen's Rd

G5
1 The Arbour
2 Morgans Cl

H4
1 Greencoates

Hartham

HERTFORD

K3
1 Foxholes Av
2 Honeysuckle Cl
3 Spinney St

K2
1 King's Rd

J2
1 Meadow Cl

F2
1 Black Smiths Cl

F7
1 Galley Gn

F G VIDBURY HILL
B1004
G H 128 J K

Harcamlow Way

Mardocks Farm

Watersplace Farm

All Nations Christian College

Easneye

1
F8
1 Beyers Prospect
2 Bridle Wy
3 The Coppings

2
G4
1 Meridian Wy

3
G5
1 Hillside Crs
2 The Nook

Little Briggens

Newlands

B180

Home Farm Industrial Estate

4

154

Holycross Road

Cahill Lane

Chambers

Stanstead Abbots

5
G7
1 Chelsea Flds

Margarets

St Johns La
Amwell Lane

St John Baptist School

Hillside

B181

French's Close

Folly View

Scott Av
New River

Priory Gdns

Delhaun St

St Margarets Station

STATION RD HIGH ST

Millers Lane

ROYDON

HUNSDON ROAD

Cat's Hill

Netherfield House

Netherfield Lane

6
G8
1 Chittenden Cl
2 Estfield Cl
3 Parkland Cl
4 Theleway Cl

Amwell View School

A414

Hoddesdon Rd

Robin Close

The Granary

Ryegate Farm

7
H5
1 Lee Cl
2 Woodham Wy

Saint Margaret's Road

Caxton

Beechfield

Field

A414

Rye Meads

8

Bridle Way

Cranbourne School

Nursery Road

Wallers Way

The John Warner School

Rye Road

Ditchfield Road

The Drive

F G H 177 J K

J5
1 Abbotts Rl

H6
1 Kingfisher Cl

Rye House Station

Rye House Stadium

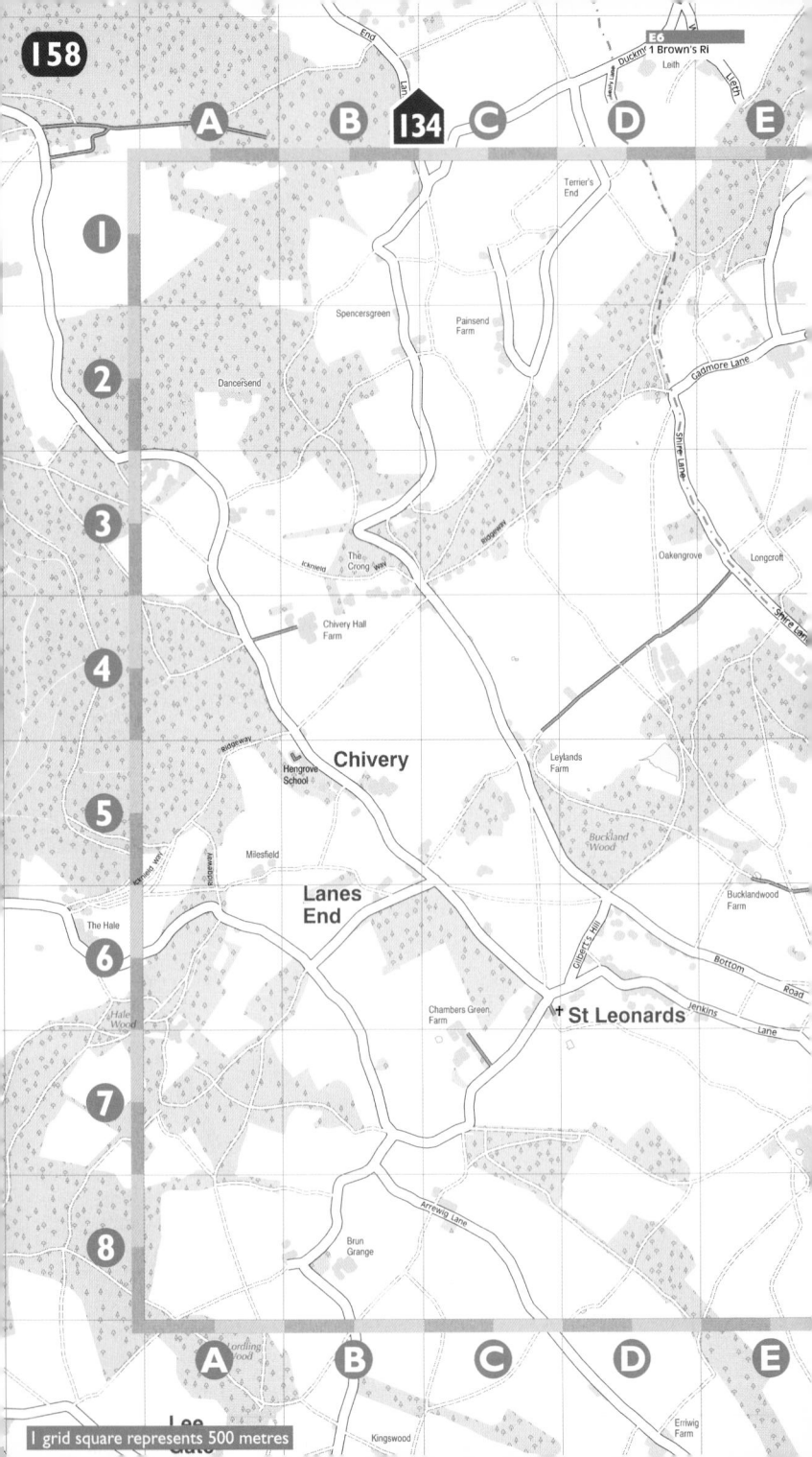

Wigginton Bottom

Hastoe

Hill Green Farm

Champneys

The Flats

Hertfordshire County
Buckinghamshire County

Tring Grange Farm

Hawridge Common

Buckland Common

Cholesbury

Hawridge & Cholesbury C of E Primary School

Braziers End House

Wood Row

Crawley's Lane

Champneys

Parrott's Farm

Shirelane Farm

Cherry Tree

Gyles Croft

Wood Farm

Bank Farm

Bellingdon Farm

Wick Farm

Kiln Farm

High Scrubs

I 1

2

3

4

160

5

6

7

8

F G H **135** J K

F G H J K

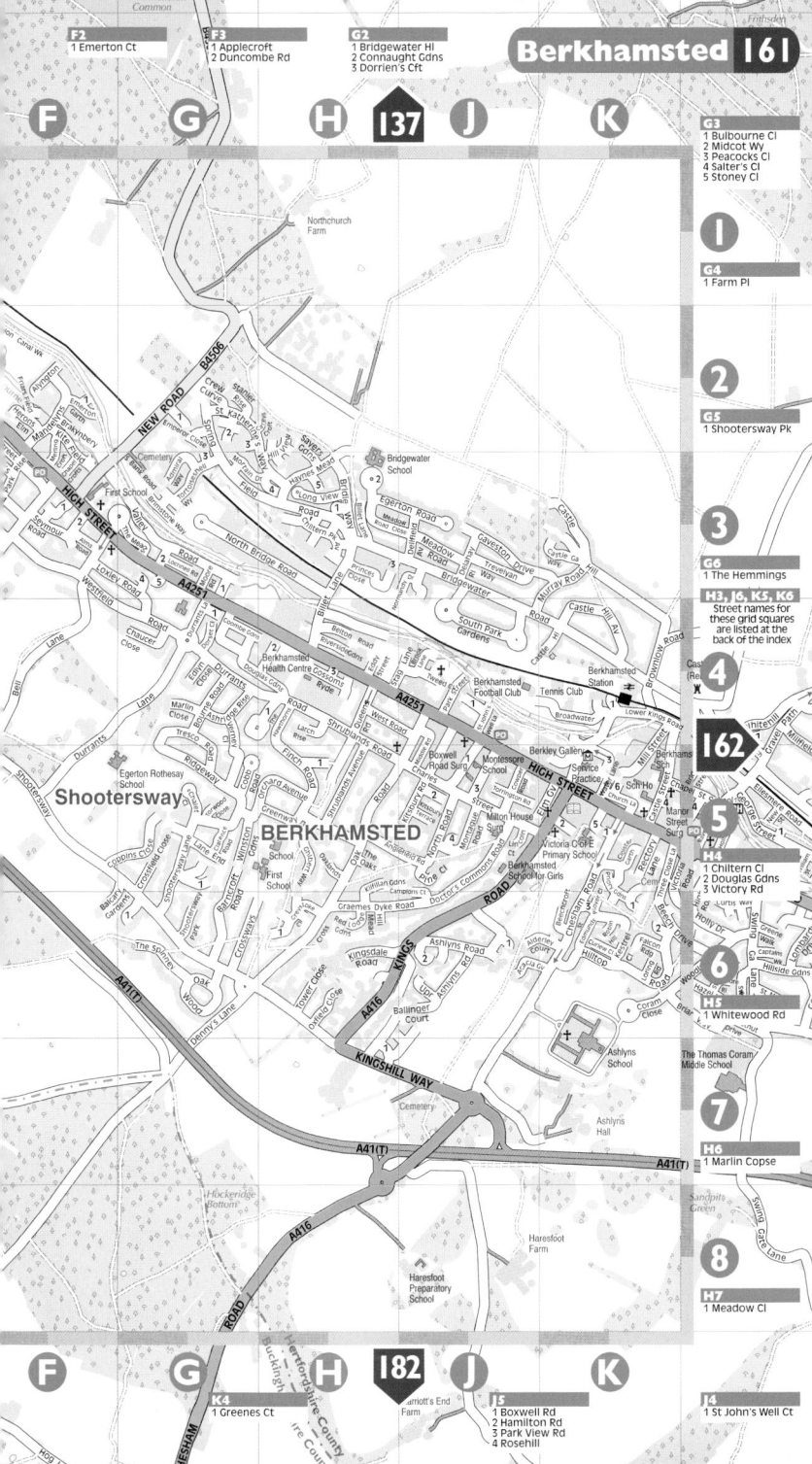

Berkhamsted

Shootersway

162

137

182

162

A

B

138

C

D

E

A6
1 Cedar Wy

Frithsden Gardens

A6
1 Cambridge Ter
2 Ivy House La
3 Little Bridge Rd
4 Manor St

A4
1 Hill Ct

Frithsden Beeches

Bricklin Cott

PH
Vineyard

Frithsden

1
B5
1 Paxton Rd

Frithsden Copse

Nettleden Road

2
E3
1 Water End Rd

Vicarage

Vicarage Gdns

Homefield

The Bank

PO

School

Berkhamsted Golf Club

Potten End

The Front

The Common

3

Castle

Murray Road

Castle Hill Av

Castle Hill

New Road

Haresfoot Senior School

Gutteridge Farm

Little Heath

Bacon Path

Shrublands

Bracken Hl

Littlle Heath Lane

4
Berkhamsted Station
161

Castle (Remains)

Lower Rd

Whitehill

Gravel Path

Gravel Path

Millfield

Clover Field

Meadway

House Lane

Ivy

Bluegessip Lane

HIGH STREET

Tennis Club

Broadwater

Buckley Gallery

Service Practice

Berkhamsted

Chapel St

Sch Ho

Lower Kings

St John's School

5
Victoria CofE Primary School

Manor Street Surg

PH

Bridgewater Road

George Street

6

Rectory Lane

Cheshen Road

Highfield Rd

Shrublands Road

Casthopp

Gun

Curtis Way

Greene Way

Holly Dr

Captains

Hillside Gdns

Longbury Drive

Cedar Road

Bank Mill Gdns

Bank

Mill Lane

Bankmill Bridge

River Bulbourne

LONDON ROAD

Old Mill Gdns

Woodfield

HIlltop

Falcon

Camelot

Hazel Way

St Margaret's Close

Chestnut

Hall Park

Hall Park Hill

Hall Park Gate

Fieldway

Upper Hall Park

7

Ashlyns Hall

Ashlyns School

Coram Close

The Thomas Coram Middle School

Broad Way

Long Green

Broadway Farm

Little Heath Lane

8
A41(T)

Sandpits Green

Swing Gate Lane

A41(T)

Sugar Lane

Bottom Farm

Bottour Cutters

Vale Farm

Stone

A

B

183

C

D

E

1 grid square represents 500 metres

Water End

139

F G H J K

H4
1 Warmark Rd
2 Whitebroom Rd

H5
1 Briarcliff
2 Jasmin Wy
3 Rosewood Ct

Bigham's
Park
Farm

Gaddesden
Hall

Noake
Mill

I

H6
1 Juniper Gn

Rumblers
Farm

2

H7
1 Bluebell Cl
2 Damask Gn
3 Hazeldell Link
4 Huntsmill Rd
5 Shepherds Gn
6 Sundew Rd

Housewood
End

Boxted Farm

3

1 Little Catherells
2 Parklands

Fennycroft
Road

Gadebridge

4

164

Fields
End

5

Cavendish

J5
1 Chardins Cl
2 Goosecroft
3 Harepark Cl

Warners End

Hammer

Counters
End

6

J6
1 Gt Sturgess Rd
2 Leggfield Ter
3 Small Acre
4 Westridge Cl

Pouchen
End

7

K3
1 Plantation Wk
2 Spencer Wy
3 Whitestone Wk

Chaulden

Green
End

Boxmoo

8

Bourne
End

LONDON ROAD

F G H **184** J K

K6
1 Gullbrook
2 The Rowans

K5
1 Bodwell Cl
2 Bullace Cl
3 Peartree Cl
4 Quartermass Cl

K4
1 Calley Hl
2 Marnham Ri
3 The Nokes
4 Plantation Wk
5 Robbs Cl

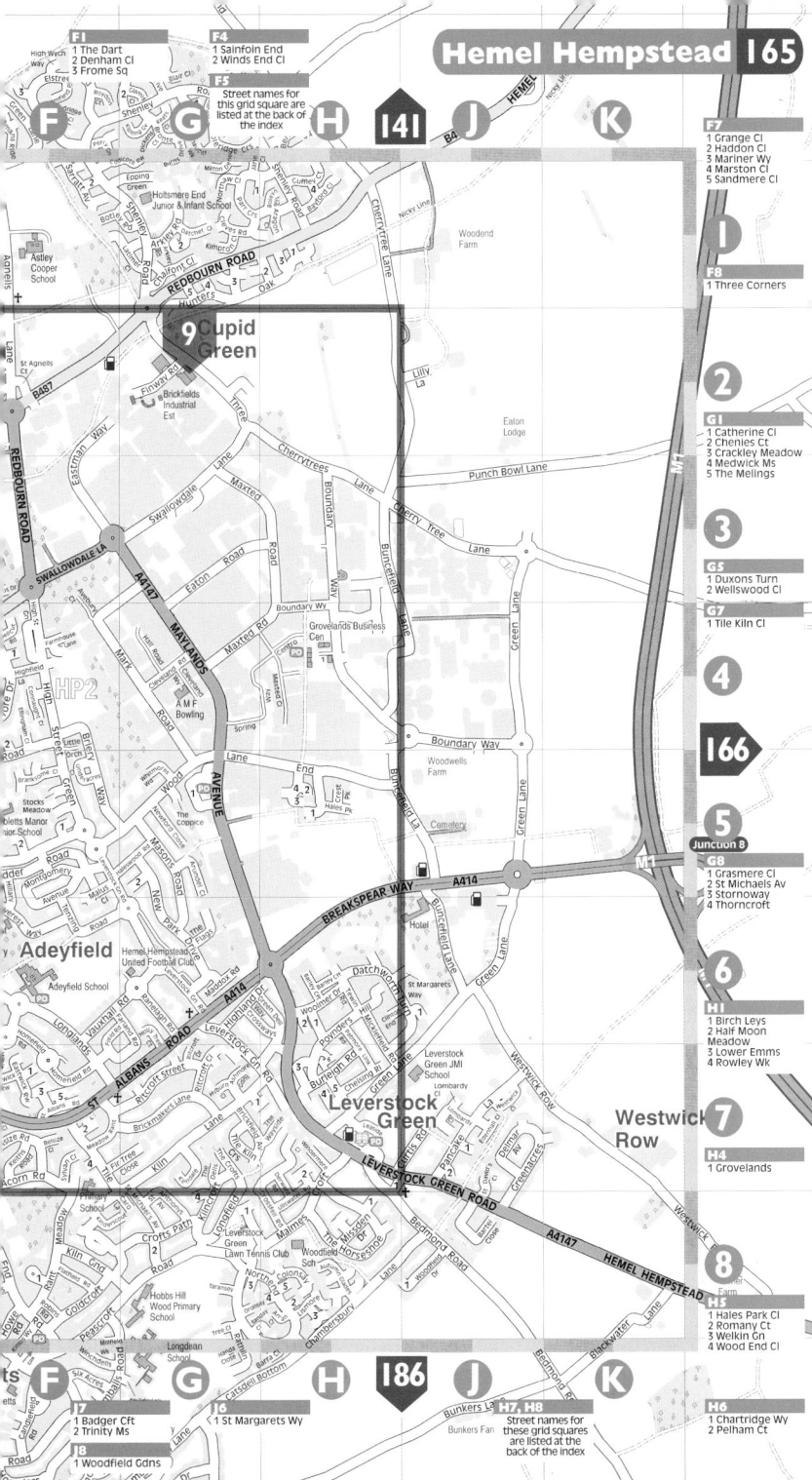

Cupid Green

HP2

Adeyfield

Leverstock Green

Westwick Row

141

166

186

I grid square represents 500 metres

F1
1 Aldbury Cl
2 Cotswold Cl
3 Ivinghoe Cl
4 Mendip Cl
5 Pistone Cl
6 Tilsworth Wk

F2
1 Belgrave Cl
2 Quantock Cl
3 Summersland Rd

I
F4
1 Wheatleys

2
F7
1 Edison Cl
2 Greensleeves Cl
3 Grenadier Cl
4 Sturmer Cl

3
F8
1 Ashbourne Ct

4

5
G2
1 Harley Ct

6
G3
1 Eastfield Ct
2 Hunt Cl
3 Thorpefield Cl
4 Westfield Ct

7
G6
1 Wynches Farm Dr

8

G8
1 Newfield Wy

G7
1 St Edmunds Wk

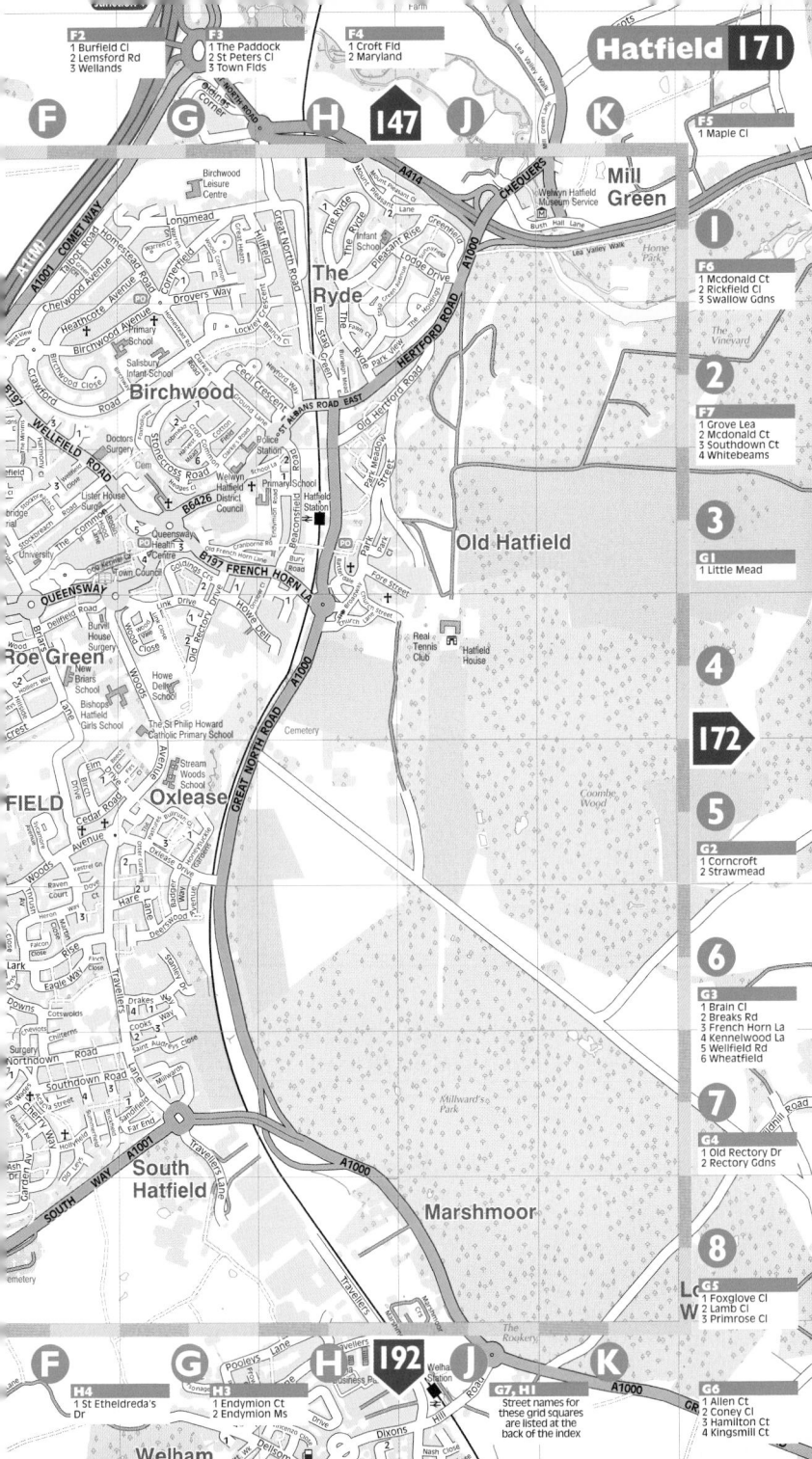

A **B** **148** **C** FORD ROAD **D** **E**

Burnside

Welwyn Hatfield
Museum Service

Mill
Green

1

Lea Valley Walk

Hall Lane

River Lea or Lee

Lea Valley Walk

Home
Park

The
Vineyard

2

Hillend
Farm

3

West End

4

West End Lane

171

Coombe
Wood

5

Park
Dairy

Pope's
Farm

6

Woodside
Place

Camfield
Place

Woodside

7

Wildhill
Road

Wildhill

8

AL9

Woodhill
House

Lower
Woodside

Westfield
Lane

Woodside

Grubbs Lane

A **B** **193** **C** **D** **E**

A1000 GREAT NORTH

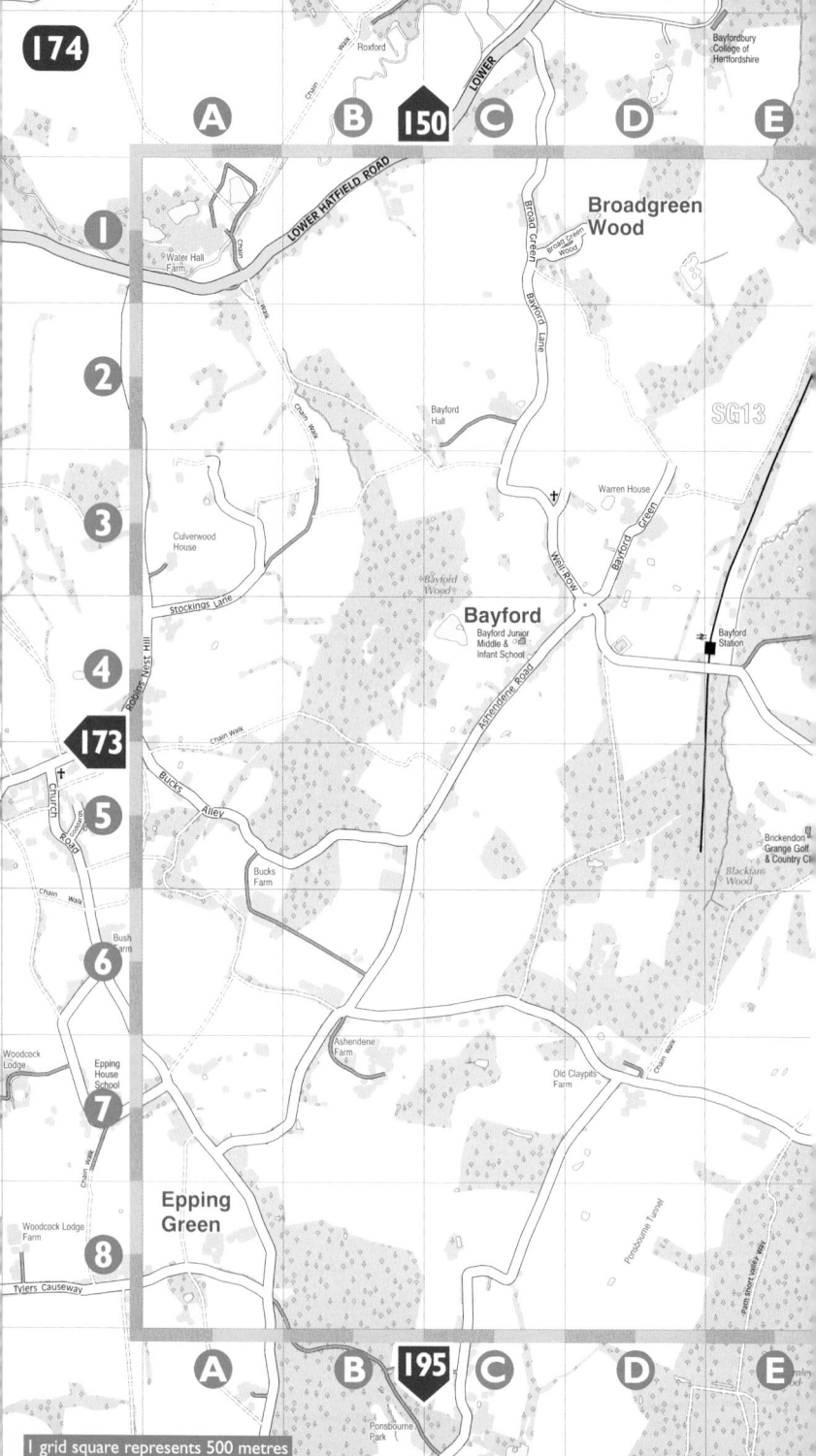

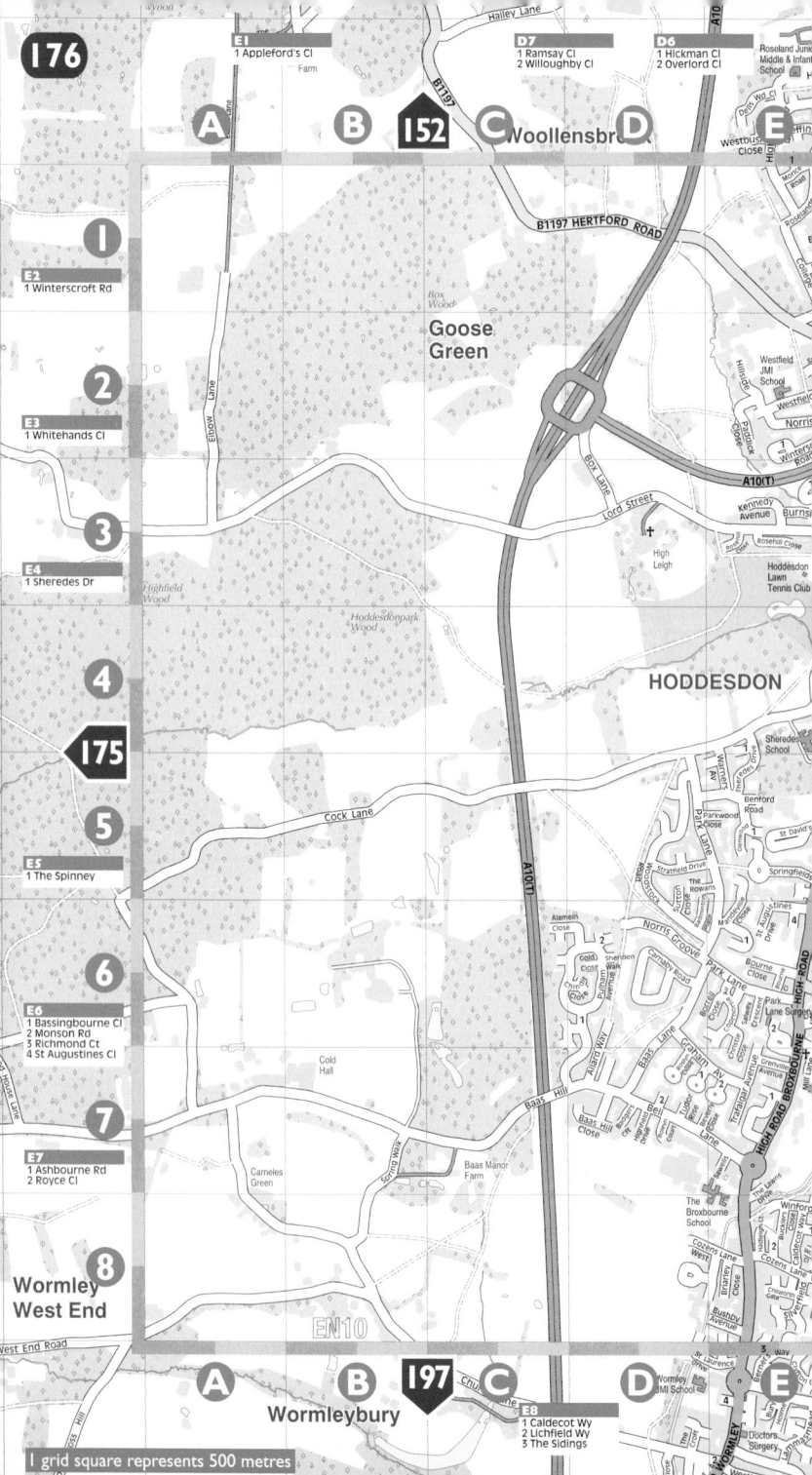

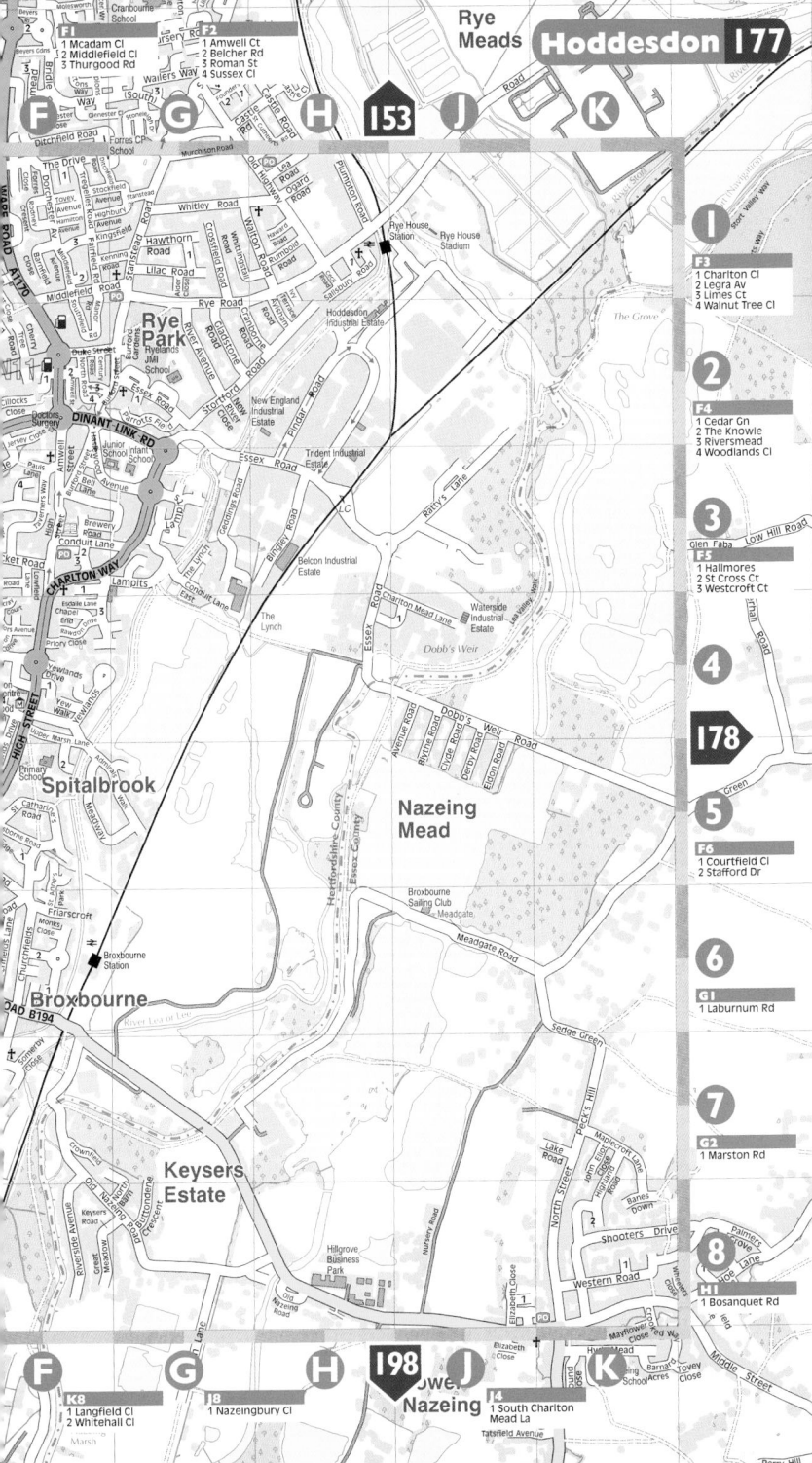

F3
1 Florence Cl
2 Jack Stevens Cl
3 Larkswood

F G H 157 J K

CM17

Roffey Hall

I

Church Langley

Florence Nightingale Health Centre

Threshers Bush

New Way La

2

Foster Street

Foster Street

3

4

Wynter's Farm

Potter Street

Hastingwood Road

Harlow Common

5

Mill Street

Wynter's Grange

Stort Valley Way

Harlow Park

Hastingwood

6

Latton Park

Junction 7

Hastingwood Road

PH

Paris Hall

Stort Valley Way

7

Glovers Farm

Canes Farm

8

Rundells

A414

CANES LANE

Little Weald Hall

ROAD

F G H J K

North Weald Golf Club

A414

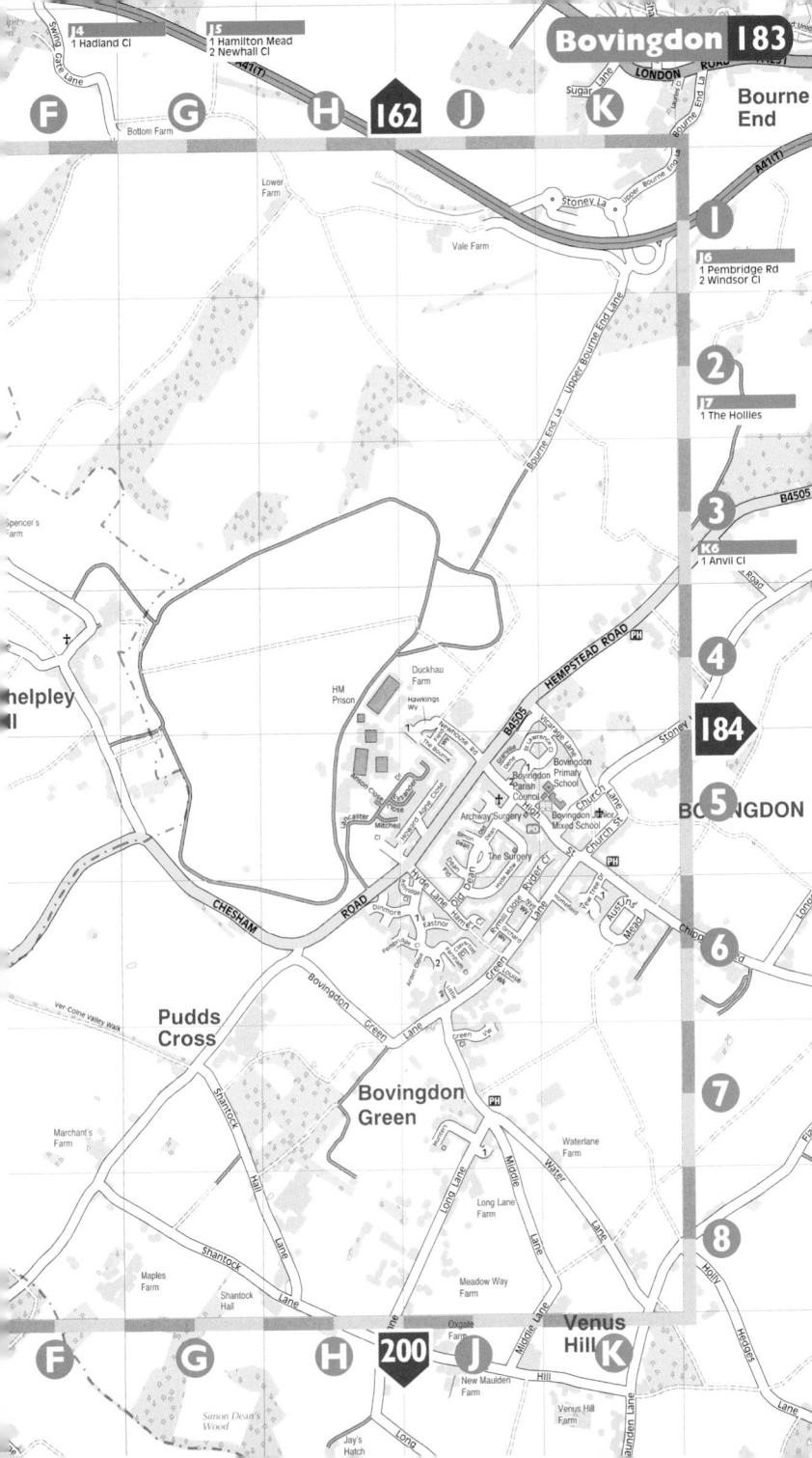

Bourne End

F G H **162** J K

J4
1 Hadland Cl

J5
1 Hamilton Mead
2 Newhall Cl

Swing Gate Lane

Bottom Farm

Lower Farm

Bourne End La

Bourne Gutter

Stoney La

Sugar Lane

LONDON

A41(T)

Upper Bourne End La

Vale Farm

1

2

3

4

184

5

6

7

8

J6
1 Pembridge Rd
2 Windsor Cl

J7
1 The Hollies

K6
1 Anvil Cl

B4505

Spencer's Farm

helpley II

HM Prison

Duckhau Farm

HM Prison

Hawkings Wy

HEMPSTEAD ROAD

PH

Stoney Lane

B4505

Bovingdon Primary School

Bovingdon Parish Council

Archway Surgery

Bovingdon Junior Mixed School

Church St

BOVINGDON

The Surgery

PO

PH

Chipp

Mead

CHESHAM   ROAD

Hyde Lane

Ryder Ct

Green

Sycamore Cl

Green

Eastnor

Dunmore

Pudds Cross

Bovingdon Green Lane

Bovingdon Green

PH

Waterlane Farm

Ver-Colne Valley Walk

Marchant's Farm

Shantock Hall Lane

Long Lane

Middle Lane

Water Lane

Maples Farm

Shantock Hall

Shantock Lane

Long Lane Farm

Meadow Way Farm

Oxgate Farm

Venus Hill

New Maulden Farm

Middle Lane

Venus Hill Farm

Holly

Hedges Lane

Flau

Leyhill Lane

F G H **200** J K

Simon Dean's Wood

Jay's Hatch

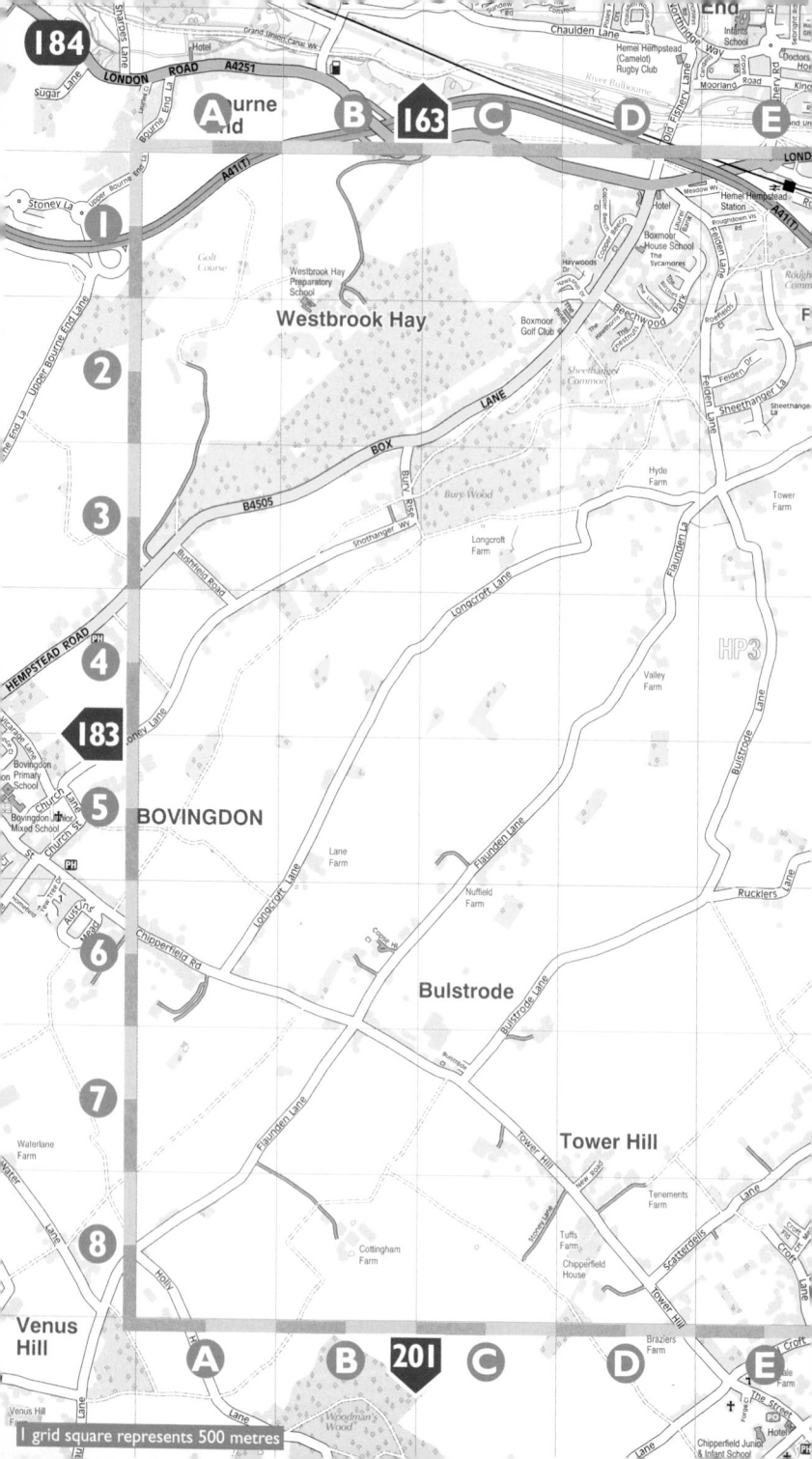

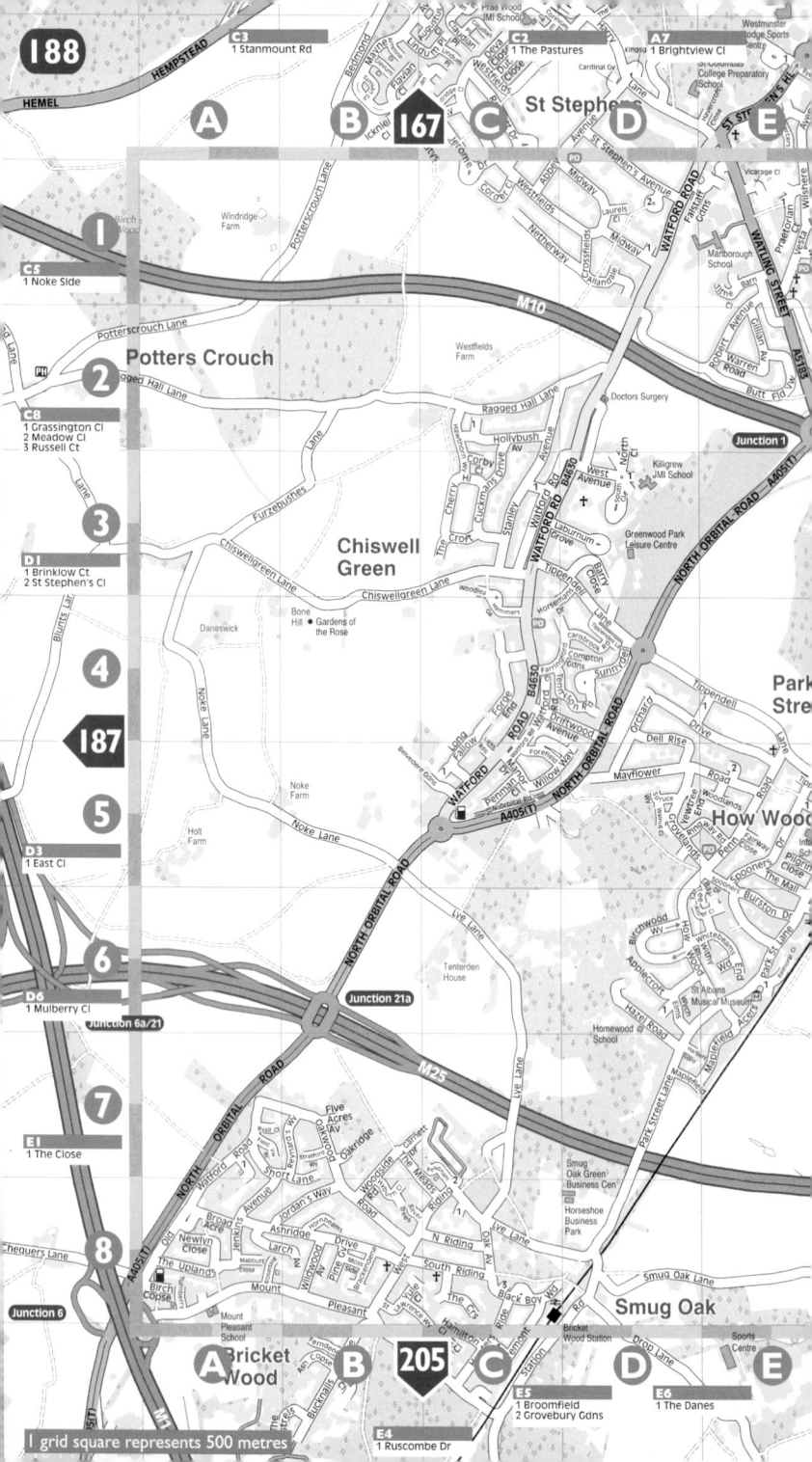

168

206

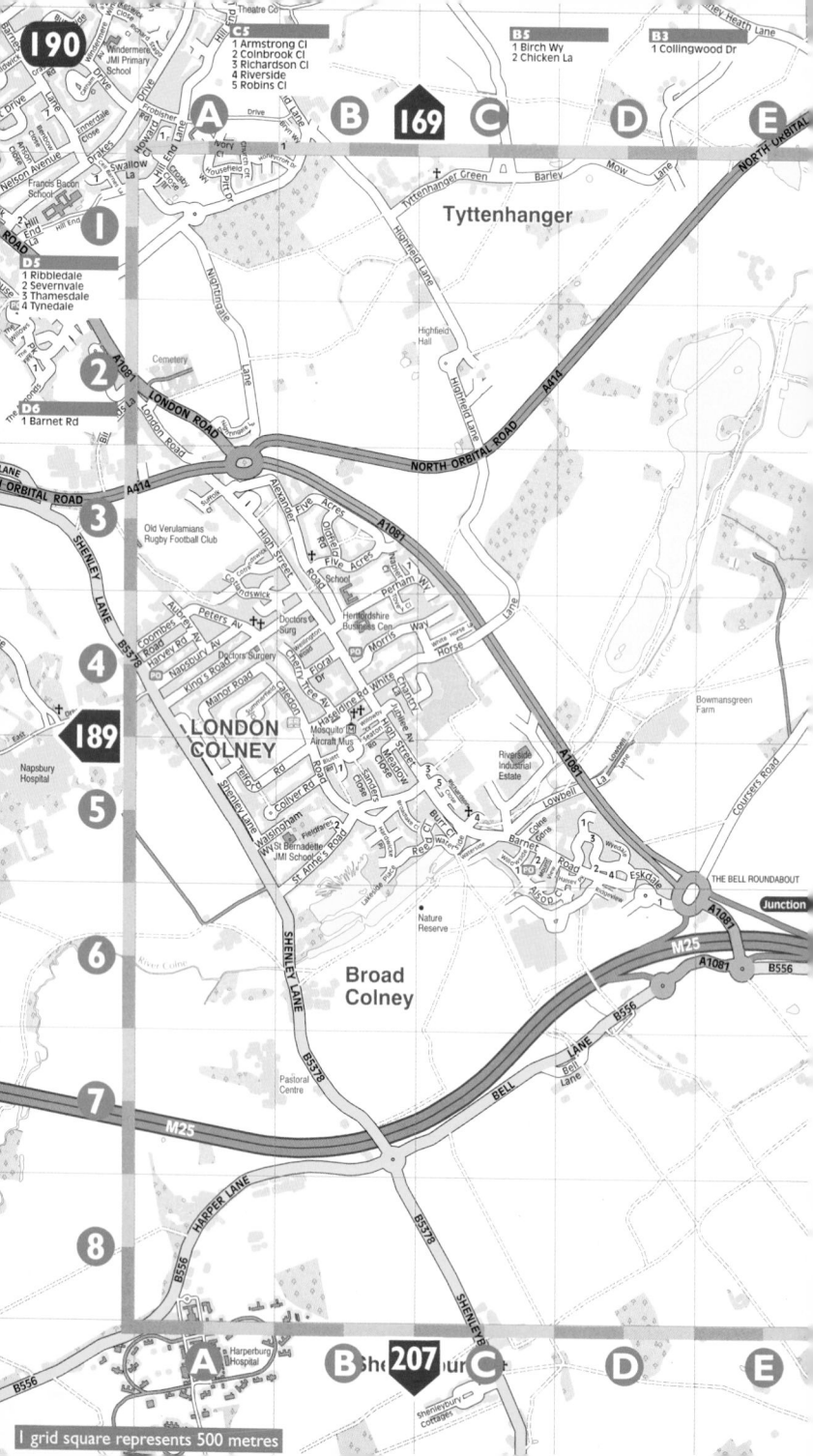

H1 1 Bennetts Cl
J1 1 Dellsome La

A414

St Mark's High

Colney Heath JMI School

F
G Colney Heath

Park Corner

H

170

J

Junction 2

K

Cemetery

Colney Heath Cfts

PO

I

High Street

ROESTOCK

Meadway

Address Close

Fellowes Lane

Roestock

Bullen's Green

Tollgate Farm

Dellsome

2

Warren Farm

River Colne

Tollgate Road

A1(M)

Tyttenhanger Farm

3

Tollgate

Coursers Road

Coursers Farm

✝

4

North Mymms Cricket Club

192

Walsingham Wood

5

6

Cobbs Ash

Salisbury Hall

quito raft

Potwells

Mymmshall Wood

7

Redwell Wood Farm

Redwell Wood

Hawkshead Wood

B556

Manor Lodge School

M25

Shenley Lodge

Ridgehill

Recton Lane

BLACKHORSE

LANE B556

Blackhorse Lane

The Grange

8

Blackhorse

F

G

H

208

J

SAINT ALBANS ROAD

K

194

173

Tylers Causeway

Warrenwood Park

Woodhill House

Tylers Cau

Woodcock Lodge Farm

A　　B　　C　　D　　E

Woodfield Lane

Barbers Lodge Farm

Coldharbour Farm

New Park Farm

1

2

3

Justice Hill

4

Great Wood

Copsey Brook

193

The Ridgeway

5

THE RIDGEWAY

The Ridgeway

B157

WAY

Ramsey Cl

Woodlands

6

Queenswood School

Well Wood

7

Leggatts Park

Nyn Park

Vineyards Road

Northaw Place

B156 JUDGE'S HILL

Northaw C of E School

Northaw

8

Church Lane

PO

NORTHAW

A　　B　　**211**　　C　　D　　E

COOPERS LANE

B156

Park Farm

WEST

Hook Wood

CAUSEWAY

1 grid square represents 500 metres

196

175

A B C D E

Wormley West End

West End Road

1

Beaumont Road

Beaumont Manor

Thunderfield Grove

2

Tanfield Stud Farm

3

Hammondstreet Road

Richardson Crescent

Appleby Street

4

Hammond Street

Hammondstreet Road

Upr Snot

195

Crouch Lane

5

Lucas End

Saint James's Road

The Parochial Church Council of Goffs Oak St James

Rosedale

Tanfields Junior Middle & Infant School

Stockwell Lodge Medical Centre

6

GOFF'S OAK

The Maples

The Gateways

Andrew Lane

Valence Driv

Conifer Close

B156

HILL Curley Hill

Moorhurst Avenue

Pembroke Drive

7

Little Piper's Close

Woodside JMI School

GOFF'S LANE

Burton Lane

B156

Hunters Reach

Thompsons Faints Close

Cattlins Close

Colesgrove Manor

Goffs School

Bonneygrove Junior & Infant School

8

EN7

Silver Street

Halstead Hill

Barrow Lane

Beverley Gardens

A B **213** C D E

Woodgreen Farm

Farm

LIEUTENANT

Burnt Farm

Wormleybury

Wormley

Turnford

Flamstead
End

CHESHUNT

Palmers Grove

F **G** **H** 178 **J** **K**

Nazeing Park School

Back Lane

Middle Street

Nazeing Common

Nazeingwood

I

Curtis Farm

Perry Hill

Middle

Perry Hill

Street

Nazeing Golf Club

Belchers

Belchers Lane

Stort Valley Way

2

Bumble's Green

Waltham

Road

Almsing

The Hts

Bumbles Gn Lane

Nazeing Parish Council

Nazeing Gate

The Avenue

3

Nazeing Long Green

Lane

Felsteads

Harold's Park Farm

4

Road

Galleyhill Green

Parville Farm

5

Claverhambury

6

Aimes Green

Claverhambury Road

Claverhambury Road

Maynards Farm

7

EN9

Deepark Wood

Copthall Road

Dallance House

Breach Barns

Fernhall Farm

8

Fernhall Lane

Long

Street

Three Forests Way

F **G** **H** **J** **K**

Warlies Park

Home Farm

Fernhall

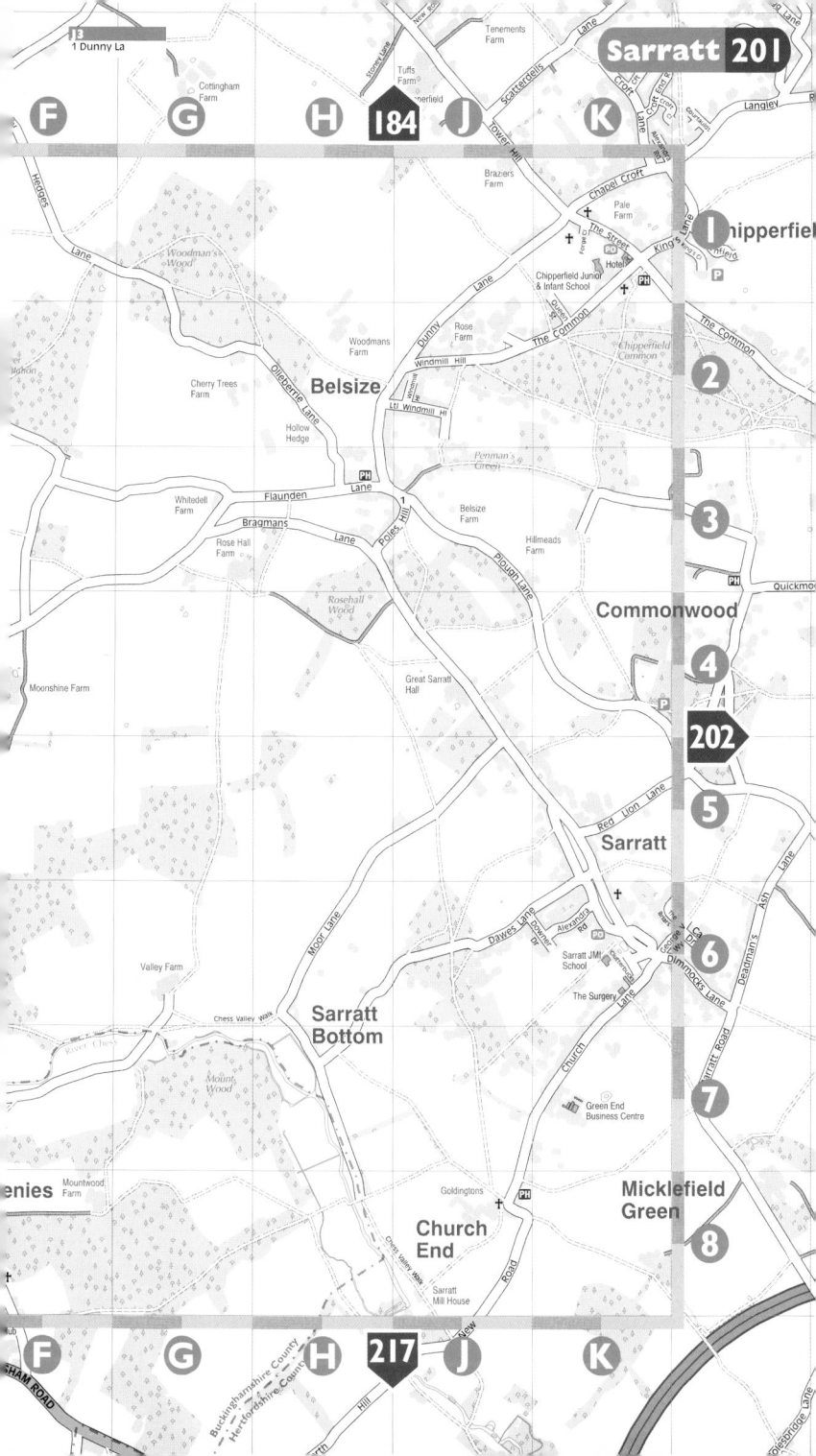

206

Colney Street

189

A   B   C   D   E

Sports Centre

1

C6
1 Lambourn Cha

Drop Lane

2

D4
1 Hawthorne Rd
2 Woodlands

River Colne

Netherwyde Farm

Houndswood

Hill Farm

3

D5
1 Scrubbits Sq
2 Thelusson Ct
3 Upper Station Rd

The Heath

The Warren

Business Centre

4

Blackbirds

205

Blackbirds Farm

5

D6
1 Christchurch Crs

Radlett Station

Radlett & Bushey Reform Synagogue

Red House Surg

Canons Cl

Newcerries

6

E4
1 Waterside

High Cross

Edge Grove

Fairfield Primary School

Doctors Surgery

Aldenham Parish Council

Radlett Parochial Church Council

Church

Cemetery

Cobden Hi
Infant Sch

Tabard Rugby

7

E6
1 Athlone Cl

RADLETT

8

Round Bush

Batlers Green

Little Kendals Farm

Delrow School

Crandge

A   **B**

222

C   **D**   **E**

Letchmore Heath

I grid square represents 500 metres

Pardents

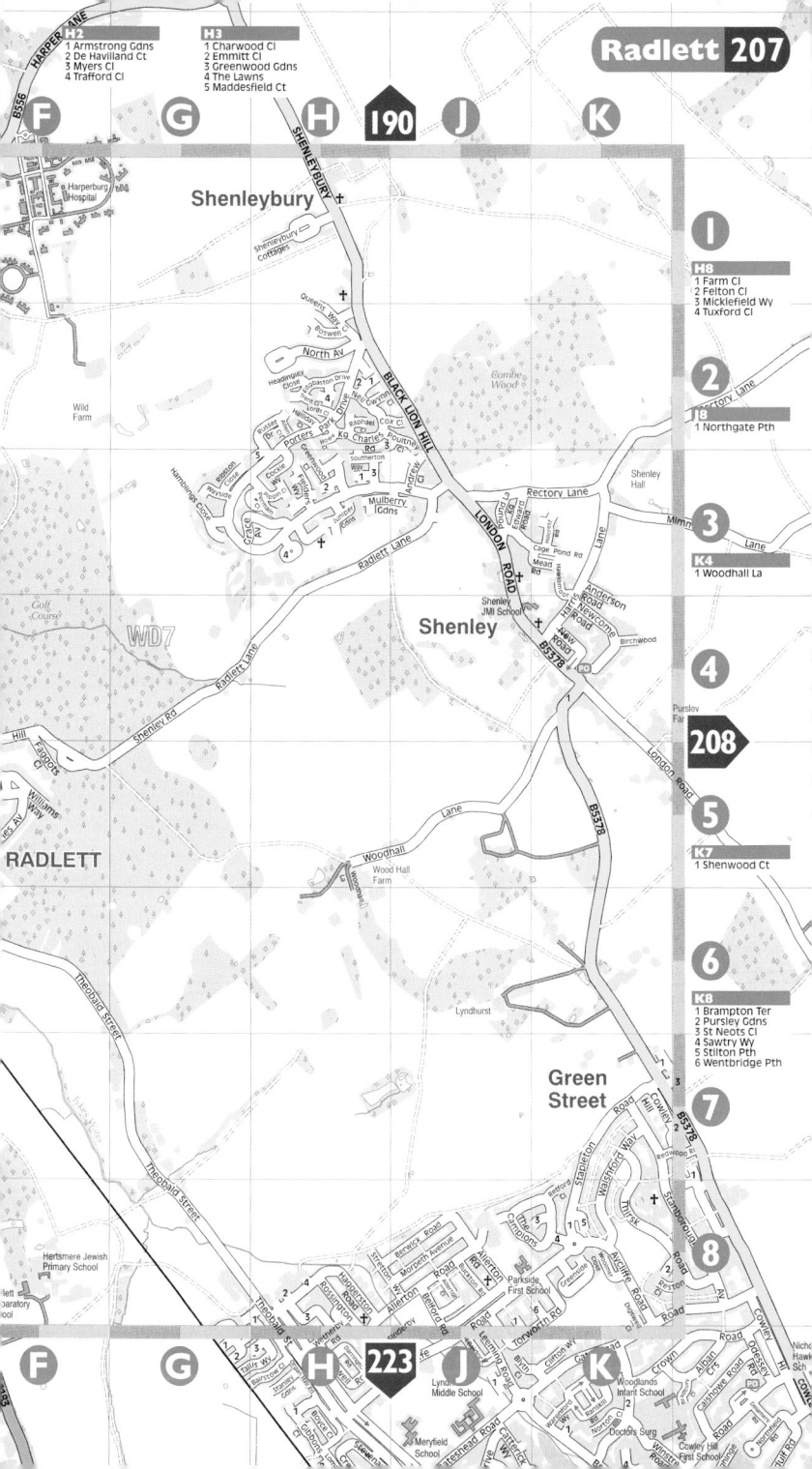

C8
1 Aragon Cl
2 Roundhedge Wy
3 William Covell Cl

A

B

195

C

D

E

Kingswell Ride

Wells Farm

Colesdale Farm

WEST

B156

Cattlegate Road

Cattlegate Farm

M25

Chalk Walk

Burnt Farm

BurntFarm Ride

The Paddocks

Glasgow Stud

Cattlegate Road

Crews Hill Station

Crews Hill

Holly Hill Farm

211

Crews Hill Golf Club

Crews Hill

Cr

The W of Tra

Beech Avenue

Cypress Avenue

Rosewood Drive

Wroxham Gardens

Theobalds Park Road

A1005

THE RIDGEWAY

Botany Bay

East Lodge Lane

Botany Bay Cricket Club

Crews West

St Johns C of E Junior & Infant School

Strayfield Road

A1005

EN2

London Loop

THE RIDGEWAY

The Kings Oak Private Hospital

Chase Farm Hospitals N H S Trust

Cemete

Hotel

Oak Avenue

Spring Court

Hadley Road

Ridge Crest

Conna Close

A

B

C

D

E

Farorna Walk

Fairview

Hardy Way

Hansart Way

Holtwh

Go

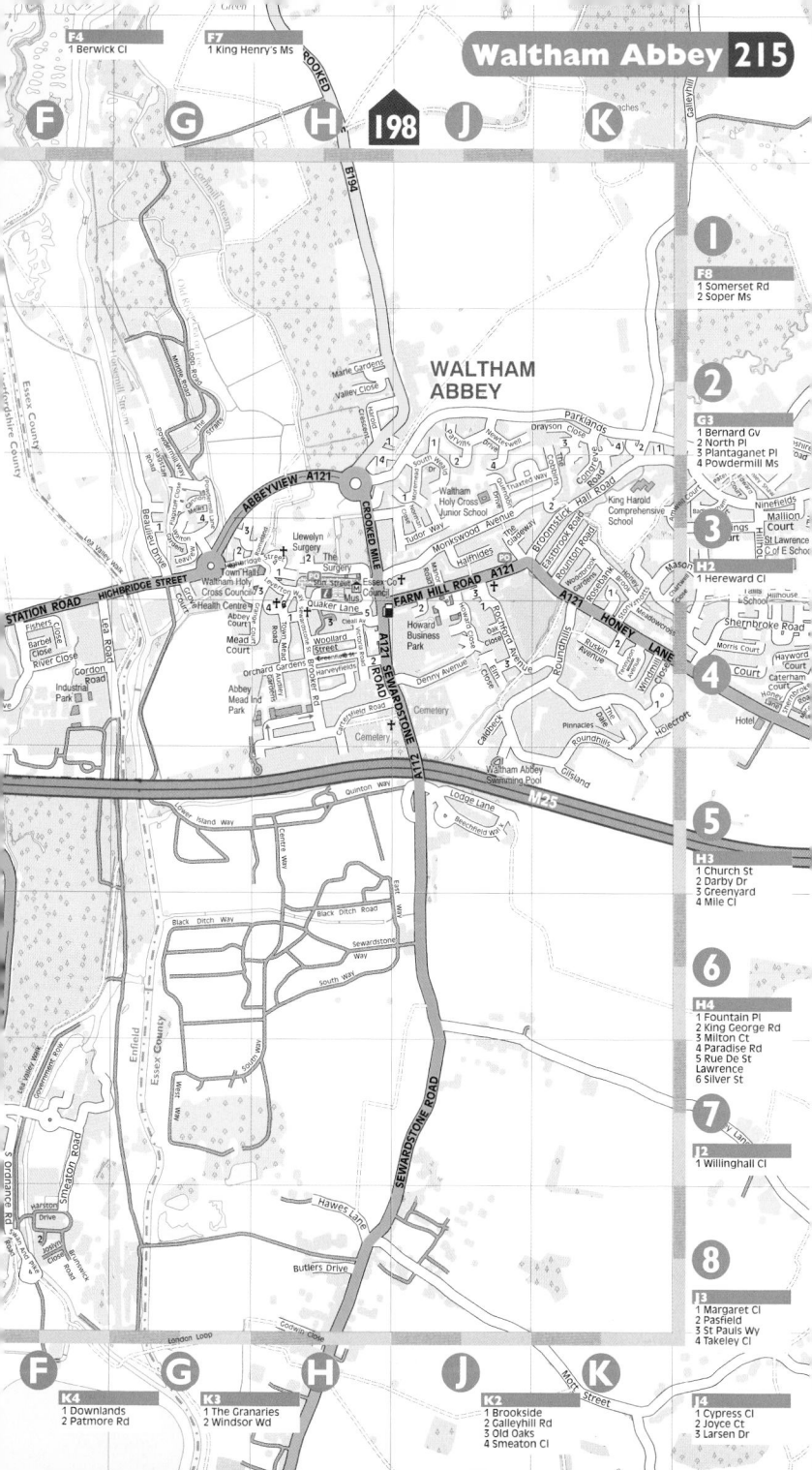

WALTHAM ABBEY

F4
1 Berwick Cl

F7
1 King Henry's Ms

198

1

F8
1 Somerset Rd
2 Soper Ms

2

G3
1 Bernard Gv
2 North Pl
3 Plantaganet Pl
4 Powdermill Ms

3

H2
1 Hereward Cl

4

5

H3
1 Church St
2 Darby Dr
3 Greenyard
4 Mile Cl

6

H4
1 Fountain Pl
2 King George Rd
3 Milton Ct
4 Paradise Rd
5 Rue De St
Lawrence
6 Silver St

7

J2
1 Willinghall Cl

8

J3
1 Margaret Cl
2 Pasfield
3 St Pauls Wy
4 Takeley Cl

K4
1 Downlands
2 Patmore Rd

K3
1 The Granaries
2 Windsor Wd

K2
1 Brookside
2 Galleyhill Rd
3 Old Oaks
4 Smeaton Cl

J4
1 Cypress Cl
2 Joyce Ct
3 Larsen Dr

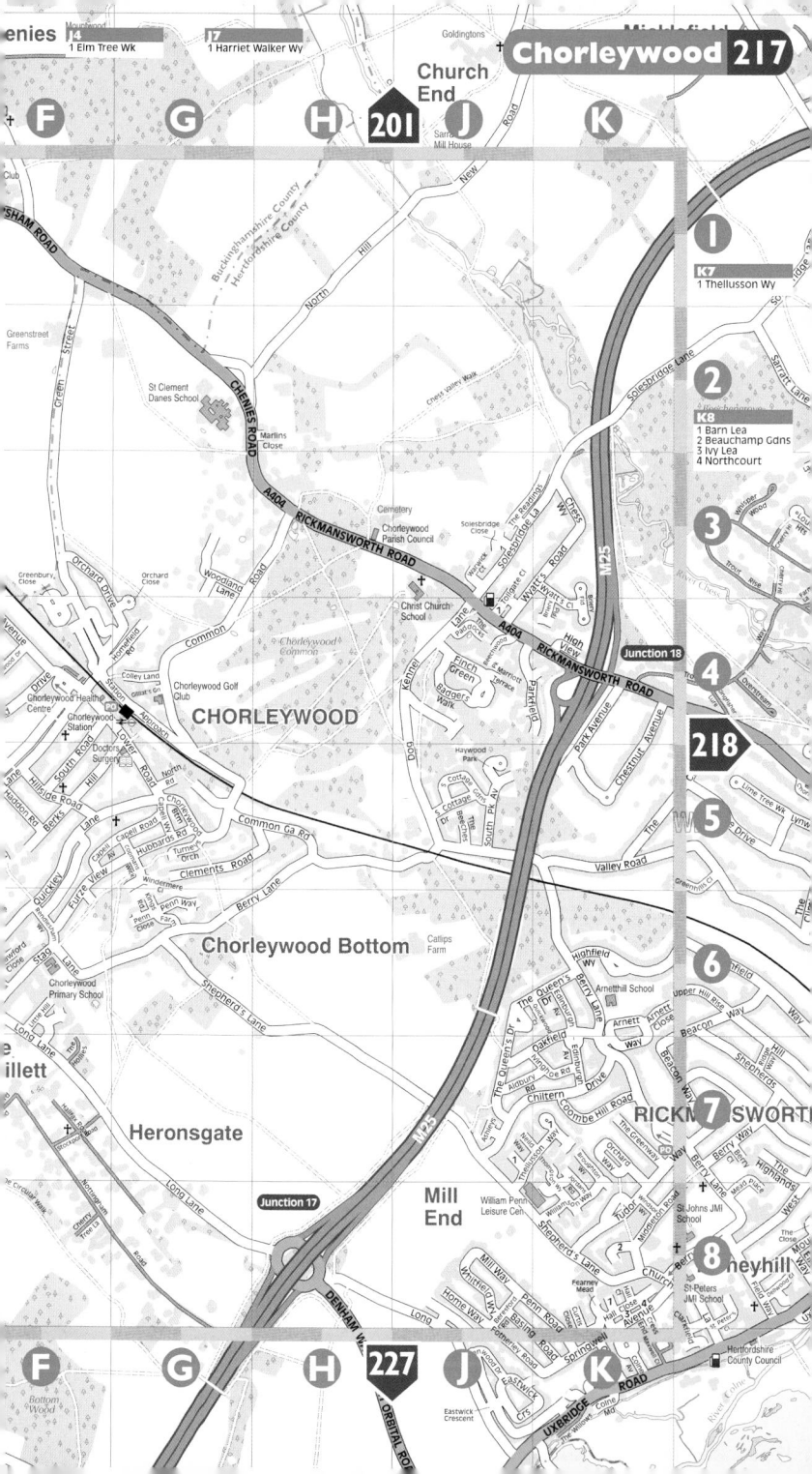

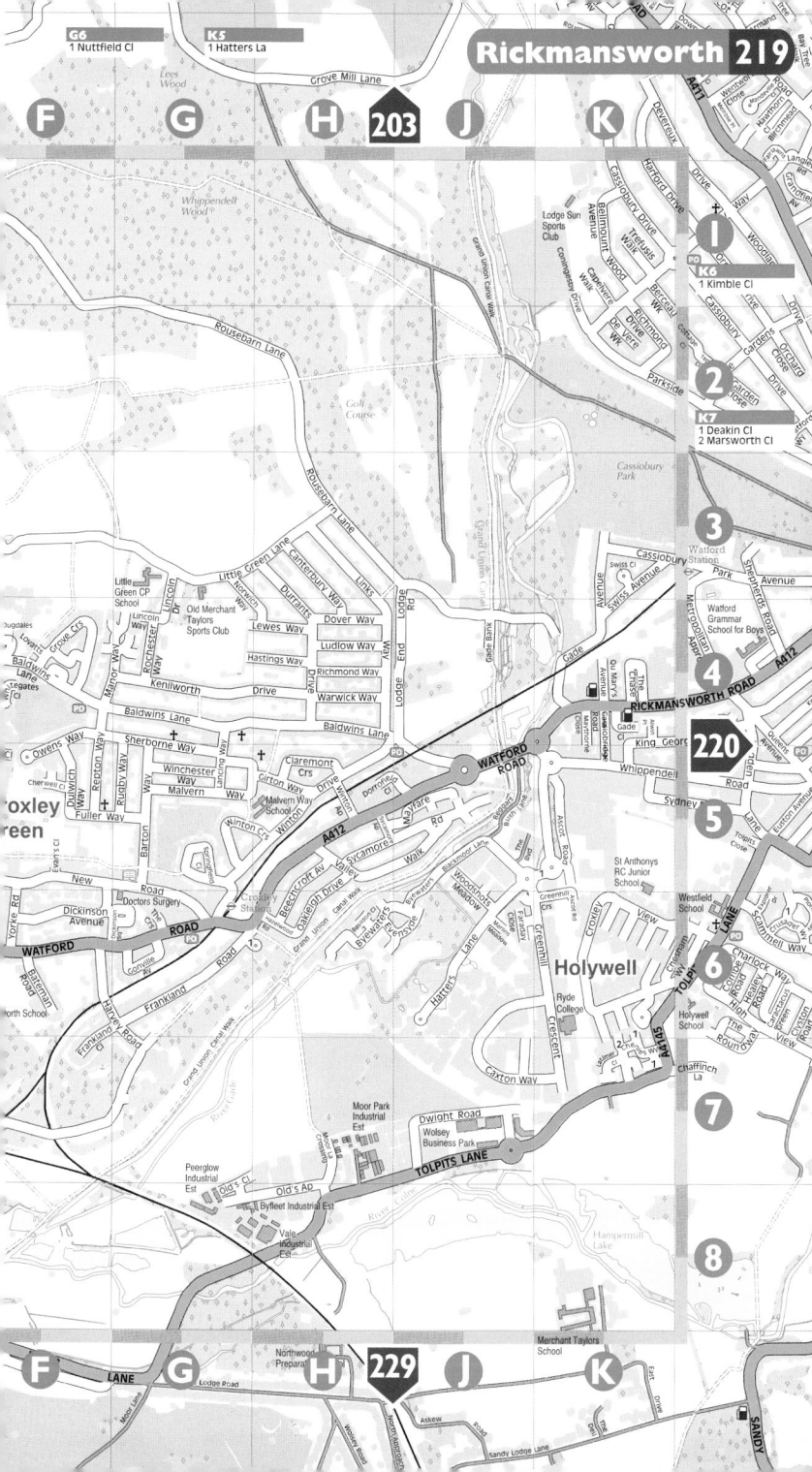

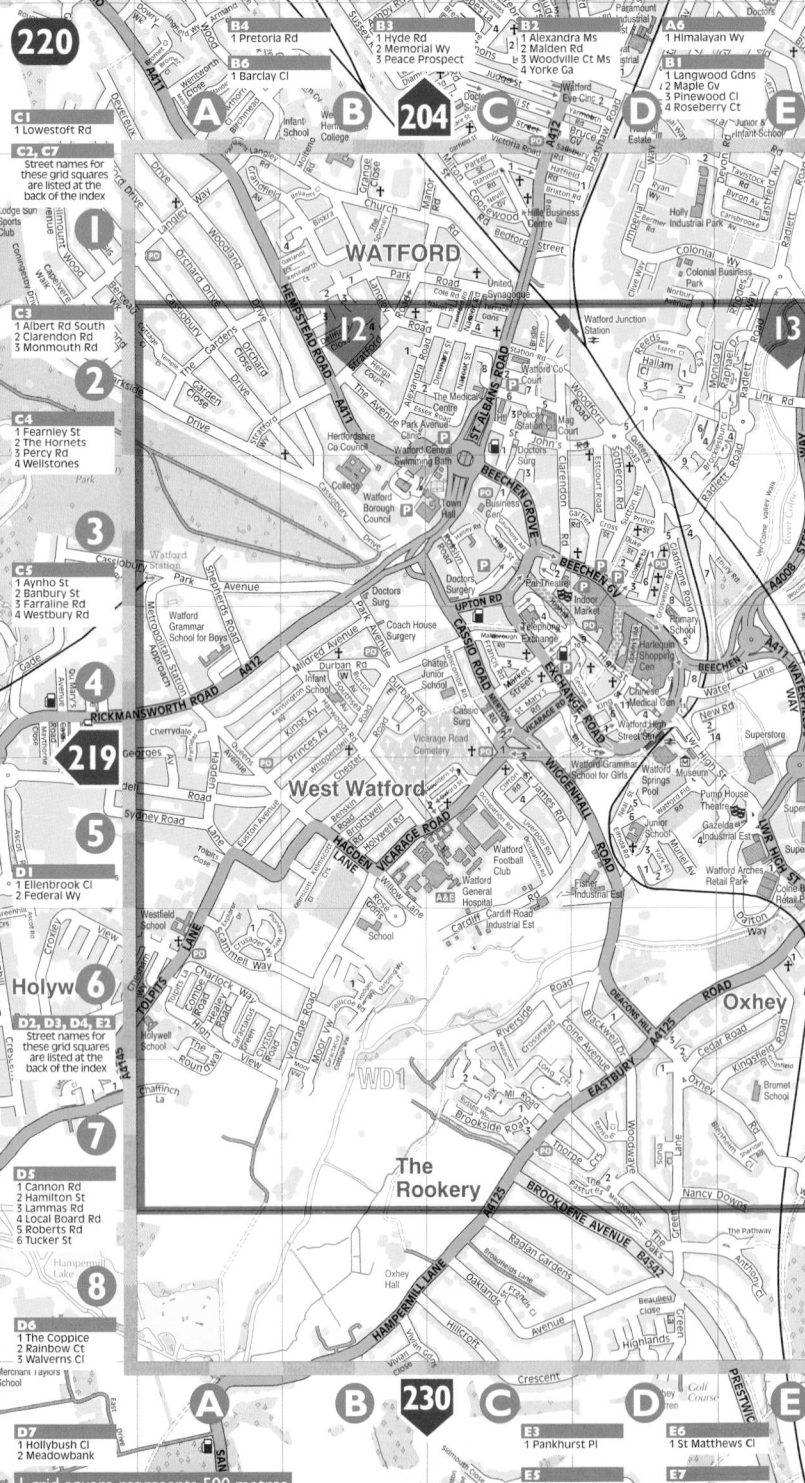

220

WATFORD

I2

I3

219

Holyw

West Watford

WD1

The Rookery

Oxhey

230

1 grid square represents 500 metres

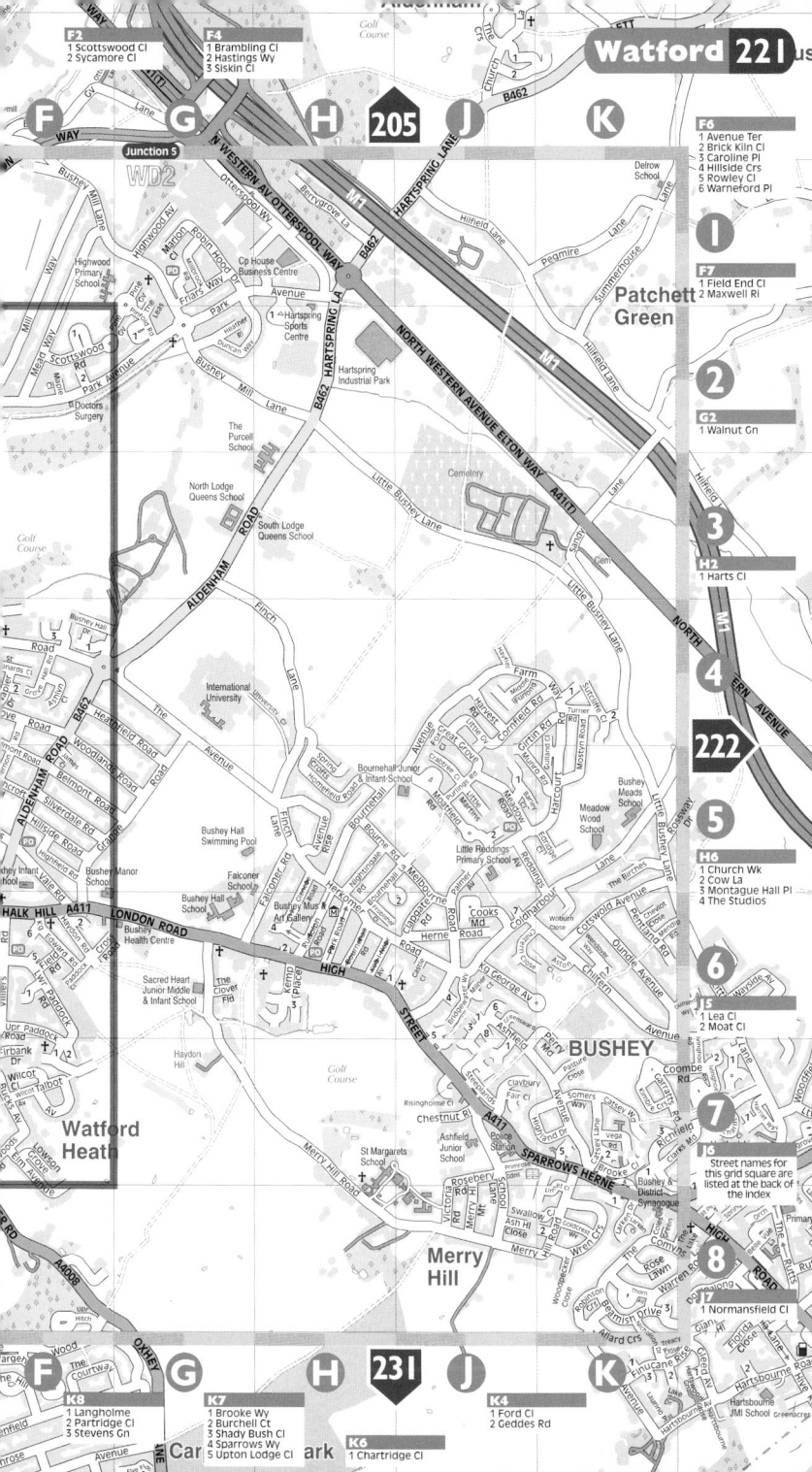

Watford 221

F2
1 Scottswood Cl
2 Sycamore Cl

F4
1 Brambling Cl
2 Hastings Wy
3 Siskin Cl

F6
1 Avenue Ter
2 Brick Kiln Cl
3 Caroline Pl
4 Hillside Crs
5 Rowley Cl
6 Warneford Pl

F7
1 Field End Cl
2 Maxwell Ri

G2
1 Walnut Gn

H2
1 Harts Cl

H6
1 Church Wk
2 Cow La
3 Montague Hall Pl
4 The Studios

J5
1 Lea Cl
2 Moat Cl

J6
Street names for this grid square are listed at the back of the index

J7
1 Normansfield Cl

K8
1 Langholme
2 Partridge Cl
3 Stevens Gn

K7
1 Brooke Wy
2 Burchell Ct
3 Shady Bush Cl
4 Sparrows Wy
5 Upton Lodge Cl

K6
1 Chartridge Cl

K4
1 Ford Cl
2 Geddes Rd

G1
1 Purcell Cl
2 Stainer Rd

G6
1 The Bartons
2 Fox Cl
3 Georges Mead
4 Oak Tree Ct
5 Romeland
6 Stuart Ct
7 Webber Cl
8 Westview Ct
9 Yew Tree Ct

G7
1 Dylan Cl

H1
1 Farrant Wy
2 Saxon Ct
3 Tomkins Cl

H2
1 Tudor Ct

I1
1 Barnsdale Cl

J2
1 Badgers Cl
2 Chiltern Cl
3 Holmdale Cl
4 Holme Pk
5 The Pines

J3
1 Orchard Cl
2 The Reddings
3 Tilehouse Cl

J4
1 Links Dr
2 Woodside

J5
1 Lowther Cl

K4
1 Brownlow Rd
2 Dunnock Cl
3 Goldfinch Wy

K3
1 Chatsworth Cl
2 Clarendon Ms
3 Lexington Cl
4 Welbeck Cl

K2
1 Badminton Cl

K1
1 Fairburn Cl
2 Grove Rd
3 Horbeam Cl
4 Spring Cl

BOREHAMWOOD

Elstree

Deacons Hill

220

229

South Oxhey

Eastbury

Pinnerwood Park

Pinner Green

Northwood

I grid square represents 500 metres

F2
1 Attenborough Cl

F3
1 Ganton Wk

Merry Hill

F G H 221 J K
1 Broadmead Cl

I

F8
1 Barrowdene Cl
2 Burhill Gv
3 Little Orchard Cl

2

G2
1 Highfield

3

G6
1 Cherry Croft Gdn
2 Helston Cl
3 St Cuthberts Gdn
4 Thorndyke Ct
5 Uxbridge Rd
(Hatch End)

4

5

G7
1 Littlecote Pl
2 Wellington Av

6

H6
1 Beeton Cl
2 Braeside Cl

7

J5
1 Meadway Cl
2 Wealdwood Gdns

8

J7
1 West Chantry

Carpenders Park

**Hertfordshire County
Harrow**

Old Redding

**Hatch
End**

UXBRIDGE ROAD (HARROW WEALD)

UXBRIDGE RD
(HATCH END)

F G H J K

K8
1 Almond Wy
2 Temsford Cl

K7
1 Bancroft Gdns

K6
1 Carrington Sq

K1
1 Gillan Gn
2 Mc Kellar Cl
3 Mungo-park Cl

Abbots Langley	203 K2
Adeyfield	9 D5
Aimes Green	199 F6
Albury	83 H3
Albury End	83 G5
Aldbury	136 D3
Aldenham	205 H7
Aley Green	88 D8
Allen's Green	131 H3
Amwell	145 F2
Ansells End	92 C7
Anstey	49 H3
Apsley	185 H2
Apsley End	38 A2
Ardeley	61 J6
Arkley	225 G5
Arlesey	24 E4
Ashley Green	182 B2
Ashwell	18 A5
Ashwell End	17 G4
Aspenden	63 H4
Aston	77 G7
Aston End	77 F4
Astrope	109 F6
Ayot Green	146 E1
Ayot St Lawrence	121 F3
Ayot St Peter	121 K6
Ayres End	144 C4
Babbs Green	128 D5
Bakers End	128 E2
Baldock	43 F1
Ballingdon Bottom	114 C8
Barkway	32 D5
Barley	23 G7
Barleycroft End	66 D5
Barley End	136 D1
Barnet Gate	224 D6
Barton-le-Clay	36 D6
Barwick	101 H5
Bassus Green	78 B1
Batchworth	228 E1
Batchworth Heath	229 F3
Batford	119 G6
Batlers Green	206 C8
Bayford	174 C4
Bedlar's Green	107 F4
Bedmond	186 E5
Bedwell	3 D3
Bell Bar	193 G2
Belsize	201 H2
Bendish	92 D2
Bengeo	150 E1
Benington	78 B5
Bennetts End	185 K1
Bentfield Bury	86 A1
Bentfield Green	86 B1
Bentley Heath	210 A5
Berden	67 K1
Berkhamsted	161 H5
Bernards Heath	10 C2
Birchanger	86 D7
Birch Green	149 K5
Birchwood	171 G2
Bird Green	51 G1
Biscot	4 A1
Bishop's Stortford	105 F2
Blackmore End	119 J3
Blue Hill	98 A4
Borehamwood	223 H3
Botany Bay	212 A6
Botley	182 C8
Bourne End	163 F8
Bovingdon	183 K5
Bovingdon Green	183 H7
Bower Heath	119 F3
Boxmoor	164 A8
Bozen Green	65 G6
Bragbury End	96 E2
Bramfield	124 E5
Braughing	82 A3
Braughing Friars	82 E4
Brays Grove	7 F5
Breachwood Green	92 B1
Brent Pelham	50 B7
Brickendon	175 F5
Bricket Wood	205 F1
Brick House End	67 K4
Briden's Camp	139 K6
Bridge Green	35 K3
Broad Colney	190 B6
Broadgreen Wood	174 D1
Bradley Common	178 E6
Broadoak End	150 C1
Broadwater	76 B8

Broken Green	82 D7
Bromley	102 D1
Brook End	62 A3
Brookmans Park	192 E4
Broxbourne	177 F6
Buckland	47 H1
Buckland Common	159 F6
Bucks Hill	202 B4
Building End	34 C2
Bulbourne	135 G1
Bullen's Green	170 D8
Bulls Cross	213 K6
Bull's Green	123 K2
Bulstrode	184 C6
Bumble's Green	199 G2
Buntingford	63 K2
Burge End	39 F4
Burnham Green	123 J3
Burn's Green	78 C8
Burton End	87 H5
Bury Green	104 B2
Bury Green	214 A1
Bury Park	89 G1
Bushey	221 K7
Bushey Heath	222 B7
Butt's Close	56 C1
Bygrave	27 J4
Caddington	88 E5
Cadwell	40 E4
Caldecote	16 D8
Caldecote Hill	222 C7
Campions	157 J4
The Camp	11 F6
Carpenders Park	231 G1
Chalfont Common	226 C3
Chalfont St Peter	226 D6
Chandler's Cross	218 E1
Chapmore End	126 A4
Charlton	56 B4
Chatter End	84 E2
Chaulden	163 G7
Chaul End	88 C2
Cheapside	49 H2
Cheddington	109 K3
Chells	3 F2
Chenies	201 F8
Cherry Green	63 H8
Cheshunt	197 H5
Cheverell's Green	115 H5
Childwick Bury	143 K8
Childwick Green	143 J7
Chiltern Green	91 H6
Chipperfield	202 A1
Chipping	47 H4
Chipping Barnet	225 K4
Chiswell Green	188 B3
Chivery	158 B5
Cholesbury	159 H7
Chorleywood	217 G4
Chorleywood Bottom	217 G6
Chorleywood West	216 D5
Church End	25 F2
Church End	84 A7
Church End	110 E7
Church End	142 B5
Church End	201 J8
Churchgate	197 F7
Churchgate Street	157 J5
Church Langley	181 G1
Clapgate	83 K3
Claverhambury	199 H5
Clay End	78 B2
Clay Hill	213 F7
Clement's End	114 B6
Clothall	43 K5
Clothall Common	43 H1
Cockernhoe	70 E6
Codicote	94 E8
Codicote Bottom	121 H1
Codmore	182 A8
Cokenach	32 E4
Cold Christmas	128 A3
Cold Harbour	118 E4
Cole Green	149 H5
Coleman Green	145 K4
Colliers End	101 F3
Colney Heath	170 B8
Colney Street	189 G8
Commonwood	201 K4
Cooper's End	35 J4
Cooper's Green	170 A1
Cottered	62 A1
Counters End	163 K6
Cow Roast	136 B8

Crabbs Green	67 F3
Cradle End	104 C1
Crews Hill	212 E5
Cromer	61 F4
Cromer-Hyde	146 B4
Croxley Green	219 F5
Cuffley	195 K6
Cumberlow Green	45 G2
Cupid Green	9 E1
Dagnall	112 E3
Damask Green	59 H4
Dancers Hill	209 H5
Dane End	99 J2
Danesbury	122 C3
Darleyhall	71 K4
Dassels	64 D4
Datchworth	97 F4
Datchworth Green	96 D5
Deacons Hill	223 K6
Deer's Green	51 J2
Dewes Green	51 H4
Digswell	123 F6
Digswell Park	122 D5
Digswell Water	123 G2
Drayton Beauchamp	134 B2
Driver's End	95 F3
Duck End	86 D7
Ducks Island	225 J2
Duddenhoe End	35 J1
Dudswell	160 E6
Eastbury	230 A4
East End	67 G2
Eastend	155 F7
East End Green	149 K2
Easthall	74 A1
East Hyde	118 B3
Eastwick	155 J1
Edworth	16 B2
Ellenbrook	170 C1
Elstree	223 H4
Enfield Lock	214 E2
Enfield Wash	214 D1
Epping Green	174 A8
Essendon	173 G2
Eyeworth	14 A3
Farley Hill	89 G3
Farnham	85 F3
Farnham Green	84 E2
Felden	184 E2
Fields End	163 G6
Fishers Green	74 E5
Flamstead	116 C3
Flamstead End	197 F4
Flaunden	200 D7
Fleetville	11 F4
The Folly	119 K3
Ford End	51 G7
Foster Street	181 J2
Freezy Water	214 D4
Friar's Wash	116 C6
Frithsden	162 D2
Frithsden Gardens	138 B8
Frogmore	189 G4
The Frythe	122 A3
Fuller's End	87 H4
Furneux Pelham	66 C2
Further Ford End	51 F5
Gadebridge	163 J3
Ganwick Corner	210 C5
Garston	204 D8
Gaston Green	133 F2
Gatley End	18 E5
Gilston	156 A4
Gilston Park	155 K3
Goff's Oak	196 A4
Goose Green	176 C2
Gorhambury	166 D5
Gosmore	56 D4
Graveley	58 C3
Gravel Hill	226 C2
Gravesend	83 H4
Great Amwell	152 D1
Great Gaddesden	139 F3
Greatgap	110 D3
Great Green	15 H4
Great Hallingbury	106 C2
Great Hormead	65 H4
Great Munden	80 C2
Great Offley	55 F7
Great Parndon	179 H5
Great Wymondley	57 J2
Green End	43 J4
Green End	46 B8
Green End	79 H2

Green End	81	J2
Green End	163	J7
Green Street	84	B8
Green Street	207	K7
The Green	113	H1
Green Tye	103	K8
Grovehill	8	A1
The Grove	203	H7
Gubblecote	109	H7
Guilden Morden	15	F4
Gustard Wood	120	A5
Hadham Cross	103	F7
Hadham Ford	103	J1
Hadley Wood	210	E8
Hailey	152	E7
Haldens	123	G7
Hall Grove	148	C5
Hallingbury Street	107	C5
Halls Green	178	D3
Hall's Green	60	A3
Hammerfield	164	A6
Hammond Street	196	A4
Handside	147	G4
Hanscombe End	37	J1
Harefield	228	D8
Harefield Grove	228	C6
Hare Street	6	A5
Hare Street	61	H3
Hare Street	64	D1
Harlow	6	C4
Harmer Green	123	G4
Harpenden	143	G1
Harpenden Common	143	J2
Hartham	151	G2
Hart Hill	5	E2
Hastingwood	181	J5
Hastoe	159	F2
Hatch End	231	F6
Hatching Green	143	G3
Hatfield	170	E5
Hatfield Garden Village	170	D1
Hatfield Hyde	148	A6
Haultwick	79	J6
Hay Green	30	E3
Hay Street	64	E8
Hazel End	85	K3
Heath End	160	B7
Hebing End	78	D7
Helham Green	129	F5
Hemel Hempstead	8	B5
Heronsgate	217	G7
Hertford	151	H4
Hertford Heath	152	A6
Hertingfordbury	150	D4
Hexton	37	H7
Higham Gobion	37	G3
High Barnet	225	H3
High Cross	100	E7
High Cross	206	A6
Highfield	8	B3
The High	6	B3
High Town	4	B3
High Wych	131	K8
Hill End	228	A5
Hinxworth	16	C3
Hitchin	40	D8
Hitchin Hill	56	C4
Hobbs Cross	157	K8
Hockerill	106	A3
Hoddesdon	176	D4
Hogpits Bottom	200	E2
Holwell	39	K2
Holyfield	198	C6
Holywell	114	A2
Holywell	219	K6
Hoo End	93	G5
Hook's Cross	97	H3
Howe Green	106	D7
How Wood	188	E5
Hudnall	138	B2
Hudnall Corner	138	D2
Hunsdon	129	J8
Hunsdonbury	154	D3
Hunton Bridge	203	G3
Ickleford	40	B5
Ivinghoe	111	F4
Jack's Hatch	179	J7
Jockey End	139	K1
Katherines	179	F4
Kelshall	30	B3
Kettle Green	102	D8
Keysers Estate	177	G7
Kimpton	93	G7
Kings Langley	185	J6

Kingsmoor	179	K6
King's Walden	72	C6
Kingswood	204	C4
Kinsbourne Green	117	H4
Kitt's End	209	K8
Knebworth	96	B3
Lanes End	158	B6
Langley	34	E7
Langley	74	E8
Langleybury	203	G4
Latchford	102	A4
Latchmore Bank	105	K7
Latimer	200	B7
Latton Bush	180	D5
Leagrave	68	B5
Leasey Bridge	119	H8
Lea Valley	119	H6
Leavesden Green	204	A4
Lemsford	146	E4
Letchmore Heath	222	B1
Letchworth	41	H3
Letty Green	149	H7
Level's Green	85	F4
Levens Green	80	C8
Leverstock Green	9	F6
Ley Green	72	C4
Ley Hill	182	D8
Lilley	53	K7
Limbury	68	E4
Little Almshoe	56	E8
Little Berkamstead	173	H5
Little Chishill	34	A2
Little Gaddesden	138	A2
Little Green	15	H3
Little Hadham	83	K7
Little Hallingbury	133	G1
Little Heath	162	D4
Little Heath	193	H7
Little Hormead	65	G2
Little Offley	54	C3
Little Parndon	6	A3
Little Tring	134	D3
Little Wymondley	57	H5
London Colney	190	A4
Long Marston	109	F6
Loudwater	218	C3
Lower Green	34	D8
Lower Green	40	C4
Lower Green	50	A2
Lower Nazeing	198	D1
Lower Sheering	132	E8
Lower Woodside	172	A8
Lucas End	196	A5
Luffenhall	60	E3
Luton	89	F2
Lye Green	182	B6
Mackerye End	119	G5
Mangrove Green	71	G5
Maple Cross	227	G3
Mardleybury	96	C7
Mark Hall North	7	F1
Mark Hall South	7	F2
Markyate	115	K4
Marshalls Heath	119	J6
Marshalswick	11	F1
Marsh Farm	68	D2
Marshmoor	171	J8
Marsworth	110	A7
Meesden	50	B4
Meriden	205	F6
Merry Hill	221	J8
Micklefield Green	201	K8
Mill End	46	C3
Mill End	217	J8
Mill End	171	K1
Moneyhill	218	A8
Monken Hadley	225	K2
Moor Green	62	B7
Moor Park	229	H3
Morden Green	15	K8
Mott's Green	133	H3
Mount Pleasant	228	A7
Much Hadham	103	F6
Nash Mills	186	A3
Nast Hyde	170	C5
Nasty	80	C3
Nazeing	178	C8
Nazeing Gate	199	J3
Nazeing Long Green	199	J3
Nazeing Mead	177	J5
Nether Street	130	B4
Nettleswell	7	D3
Nettleden	138	E7
Newgate Street	195	G2

New Greens	167	K1
New Ground	136	B7
New Mill	135	G3
New Mill End	117	K1
Newnham	27	F2
Newsells	32	D2
New Town	4	B6
Nobland Green	129	G1
The Node	94	E4
Nomansland	145	F3
Northaw	194	C8
North Brook End	15	K4
Northchurch	160	E3
North Watford	204	C7
Northwood	229	H7
Northwood Hills	229	J8
Norton	26	B8
Norton Green	75	G6
Nup End	95	G5
Nuthampstead	33	H7
Oakfield	57	F3
Oaklands	123	G2
Odsey	18	E8
Old Hall Green	80	E8
Old Harlow	157	F5
Old Hatfield	171	J3
Old Knebworth	95	J3
Old Town	2	A1
Orchard Leigh	182	D5
Otterspool	205	G2
Oxhey	13	E5
Oxlease	171	G5
Painter's Green	96	E7
Panshanger	148	B2
Park Green	67	K3
Park Street	188	E4
Park Town	5	D5
Passmores	180	A4
Patchetts Green	221	K1
Patient End	66	B6
Patmore Heath	84	A1
Peartree	147	K4
Pegsdon	37	J8
Pepperstock	89	H8
Perry Green	130	D1
Peters Green	91	K6
Piccotts End	164	B2
Pimlico	186	E2
Pin Green	76	B1
Pinnacles	179	H1
Pinner Green	230	D8
Pinnerwood Park	230	D6
Pirton	38	E5
Pitstone	110	D6
Pitstone Green	110	E5
Pitstone Hill	111	G8
Pond Street	35	H2
Poplars	76	E6
Porter's End	119	J2
Potten End	162	D3
Potter's Bar	210	E3
Potters Crouch	187	K2
Pottersheath	95	H8
Potter Street	181	G3
Pouchen End	163	G7
Presdales	152	D2
Preston	73	F3
Puckeridge	81	K6
Pudds Cross	185	G6
Purwell	57	H1
Puttenham	108	D7
Rableyheath	95	H7
Radlett	206	B4
Radlett	207	F5
Radwell	26	C5
Redbourn	142	C3
Redbournbury	143	F7
Redhill	45	G3
Reed	31	K5
Reed End	31	G3
Rickmansworth	217	K7
Ridge	208	E4
The Ridgeway	194	D5
Ringshall	112	D8
Roast Green	51	H3
Roe End	115	F5
Roe Green	45	K1
Roe Green	171	F4
Roestock	191	H1
The Rookery	12	B6
Rosedale	196	D6
Round Bush	206	A8
Round Green	4	C1
Rowley Green	224	E3

Roydon 154 C8
Roydon Hamlet 178 D5
Royston 21 F2
Rucklers Lane 185 J4
Rushden 45 G5
Rush Green 74 C5
Rush Green 152 B3
Rusling End 94 C2
The Ryde 171 H1
Rye Meads 153 J8
Rye Park 177 G2
Sacombe 99 H6
Sacombe Green 100 A5
St Albans 11 E2
St Ibbs 56 E8
St Ippollitts 56 E7
St Julians 188 E2
St Leonards 158 D6
St Margarets 153 F5
St Margaret's 139 F5
St Nicholas 59 G7
St Paul's Walden 73 K8
St Stephens 167 H8
Sandon 29 K8
Sandridge 145 F8
Sarratt 201 K5
Sarratt Bottom 201 H6
Sawbridgeworth 131 K7
Shaftenhoe End 33 H1
Shaw Green 45 F4
Shenley 207 J4
Shenleybury 207 G1
Shephall 3 E5
Sherrardspark 147 G1
Shootersway 161 F5
Sleapshyde 170 B7
Slip End 28 D3
Slip End 89 H7
Smallford 170 A5
Smith's End 33 G1
Smug Oak 188 D8
Snailswell 40 B3
Snow End 49 G4
Sopwell 189 G1
South-end 130 D3
Southern Green 45 J5
South Hatfield 171 G7
South Mimms 209 G2
South Oxhey 230 C2
Spellbrook 132 C1
Spitalbrook 177 F5
Staines Green 149 K5
Stanborough 146 E6
Standon 81 K8
Standon Green End 100 D5
Stanstead Abbots 153 K5
Stansted Mountfitchet 86 B2
Stapleford 125 G2
Starling's Green 51 H6
Start Hill 107 F2

Startop's End 109 K8
Steeple Morden 15 H7
Stet 112 A1
Stevenage 2 B2
Stewards 180 B6
Stocking Pelham 67 F2
Stopsley 70 B5
Stotfold 26 A2
Studham 113 K4
Sumners 179 H5
Sundon Park 68 B2
Swanley Bar 193 H6
The Swillett 217 F7
Symonds Green 75 F2
Tea Green 71 J6
Temple Fields 156 D5
Tewin 124 A6
Tewin Wood 123 K4
Therfield 30 D2
Thorley 105 F7
Thorley Houses 104 D4
Thorley Street 105 H6
Threshers Bush 181 K2
The Thrift 19 K6
Throcking 46 C8
Thundridge 127 J2
Tilekiln Green 106 E3
Titmore Green 57 J7
Todd's Green 58 A7
Tolmers 195 G4
Tonwell 126 D2
Totteridge 225 K7
Tower Hill 184 D7
Townsend 10 A2
Trims Green 132 A2
Tring 135 G6
Tringford 134 D1
Tring Wharf 135 G2
Trowley Bottom 141 G1
Turnford 197 H3
Two Waters 185 G1
Tye Green 6 C6
Tye Green 87 K3
Tylers Causeway 173 J8
Tyttenhanger 190 C1
Uppend 67 K8
Upper Dunsley 135 H6
Upper Green 35 F7
Upwick Green 84 B4
Venus Hill 200 E1
Wadesmill 127 H1
Wakeley 62 D7
Walkern 60 D8
Wallington 44 E1
Walsworth 40 E8
Waltham Abbey 215 J2
Waltham Cross 214 B3
Wandon End 71 J8
Ware 127 K7
Wareside 129 F6

Warners End 163 H5
Warren's Green 59 K3
Washall Green 50 D8
Waterdale 187 J8
Water End 139 J8
Water End 192 C4
Waterend 146 C1
Waterford 125 H7
Watford 220 B1
Watford Heath 13 F6
Watton at Stone 97 K5
Welham Green 192 B1
Well End 208 B8
Wellpond Green 82 D8
Welwyn 122 A4
Welwyn Garden City 148 C1
Westbrook Hay 184 A2
West End 172 E4
West Hyde 117 J2
West Hyde 227 H6
Westland Green 103 F1
Westmill 40 A8
Westmill 63 K7
Weston 43 J8
West Watford 12 B4
Westwick Row 165 K7
Wheathampstead 119 K8
Whelpley Hill 183 F4
Whempstead 99 F3
Whippendell Botton 185 G8
Whipsnade 113 J1
Whitehall 46 C5
White Hall 97 J1
Whitwell 93 H3
Widford 130 E5
Wigginton 135 J7
Wigginton Bottom 159 K1
Wildhill 172 D7
Willian 42 B7
Wilstone 109 H8
Wilstone Green 134 C1
Winsdon Hill 89 G2
Woodcock Hill 228 D3
Wood End 79 F2
Woodhall 147 K5
Woodside 89 F7
Woodside 172 B7
Woodside 204 C2
Woodside Green 106 E8
Woollensbrook 152 C8
Woolmer Green 96 C7
Wormley 197 J2
Wormleybury 197 F1
Wormley West End 175 K8
Wright's Green 133 H2
Wyddial 48 A5
Wymondley Bury 57 K6
Youngsbury 127 K1

USING THE STREET INDEX

Street names are listed alphabetically. Each street name is followed by its postal town or area locality, the Postcode District, the page number, and the reference to the square in which the name is found.

Example: **Abbey Rd** *CHES/WCR* EN8.............................. **214** D4 🔟

Some entries are followed by a number in a blue box. This number indicates the location of the street within the referenced grid square. The full street name is listed at the side of the map page.

GENERAL ABBREVIATIONS

ACC	ACCESS	
ALY	ALLEY	
AP	APPROACH	
AR	ARCADE	
ASS	ASSOCIATION	
AV	AVENUE	
BCH	BEACH	
BLDS	BUILDINGS	
BND	BEND	
BNK	BANK	
BR	BRIDGE	
BRK	BROOK	
BTM	BOTTOM	
BUS	BUSINESS	
BVD	BOULEVARD	
BY	BYPASS	
CATH	CATHEDRAL	
CEM	CEMETERY	
CEN	CENTRE	
CFT	CROFT	
CH	CHURCH	
CHA	CHASE	
CHYD	CHURCHYARD	
CIR	CIRCLE	
CIRC	CIRCUS	
CL	CLOSE	
CLFS	CLIFFS	
CMP	CAMP	
CNR	CORNER	
CO	COUNTY	
COLL	COLLEGE	
COM	COMMON	
COMM	COMMISSION	
CON	CONVENT	
COT	COTTAGE	
COTS	COTTAGES	
CP	CAPE	
CPS	COPSE	
CR	CREEK	
CREM	CREMATORIUM	
CRS	CRESCENT	
CSWY	CAUSEWAY	
CT	COURT	
CTRL	CENTRAL	
CTS	COURTS	
CTYD	COURTYARD	
CUTT	CUTTINGS	
CV	COVE	
CYN	CANYON	
DEPT	DEPARTMENT	
DL	DALE	
DM	DAM	
DR	DRIVE	
DRO	DROVE	
DRY	DRIVEWAY	
DWGS	DWELLINGS	
E	EAST	
EMB	EMBANKMENT	
EMBY	EMBASSY	
ESP	ESPLANADE	
EST	ESTATE	
EX	EXCHANGE	
EXPY	EXPRESSWAY	
EXT	EXTENSION	
F/O	FLYOVER	
FC	FOOTBALL CLUB	
FK	FORK	
FLD	FIELD	
FLDS	FIELDS	
FLS	FALLS	
FLS	FLATS	
FM	FARM	
FT	FORT	
FWY	FREEWAY	
FY	FERRY	
GA	GATE	
GAL	GALLERY	
GDN	GARDEN	
GDNS	GARDENS	
GLD	GLADE	
GLN	GLEN	
GN	GREEN	
GND	GROUND	
GRA	GRANGE	
GRG	GARAGE	
GT	GREAT	
GTWY	GATEWAY	
GV	GROVE	
HGR	HIGHER	
HL	HILL	
HLS	HILLS	
HO	HOUSE	
HOL	HOLLOW	
HOSP	HOSPITAL	
HRB	HARBOUR	
HTH	HEATH	
HTS	HEIGHTS	
HVN	HAVEN	
HWY	HIGHWAY	
IMP	IMPERIAL	
IN	INLET	
IND EST	INDUSTRIAL ESTATE	
INF	INFIRMARY	
INFO	INFORMATION	
INT	INTERCHANGE	
IS	ISLAND	
JCT	JUNCTION	
JTY	JETTY	
KG	KING	
KNL	KNOLL	
L	LAKE	
LA	LANE	
LDG	LODGE	
LGT	LIGHT	
LK	LOCK	
LKS	LAKES	
LNDG	LANDING	
LTL	LITTLE	
LWR	LOWER	
MAG	MAGISTRATE	
MAN	MANSIONS	
MD	MEAD	
MDW	MEADOWS	
MEM	MEMORIAL	
MKT	MARKET	
MKTS	MARKETS	
ML	MALL	
ML	MILL	
MNR	MANOR	
MS	MEWS	
MSN	MISSION	
MT	MOUNT	
MTN	MOUNTAIN	
MTS	MOUNTAINS	
MUS	MUSEUM	
MWY	MOTORWAY	
N	NORTH	
NE	NORTH EAST	
NW	NORTH WEST	
O/P	OVERPASS	
OFF	OFFICE	
ORCH	ORCHARD	
OV	OVAL	
PAL	PALACE	
PAS	PASSAGE	
PAV	PAVILION	
PDE	PARADE	
PH	PUBLIC HOUSE	
PK	PARK	
PKWY	PARKWAY	
PL	PLACE	
PLN	PLAIN	
PLNS	PLAINS	
PLZ	PLAZA	
POL	POLICE STATION	
PR	PRINCE	
PREC	PRECINCT	
PREP	PREPARATORY	
PRIM	PRIMARY	
PROM	PROMENADE	
PRS	PRINCESS	
PRT	PORT	
PT	POINT	
PTH	PATH	
PZ	PIAZZA	
QD	QUADRANT	
QU	QUEEN	
QY	QUAY	
R	RIVER	
RBT	ROUNDABOUT	
RD	ROAD	
RDG	RIDGE	
REP	REPUBLIC	
RES	RESERVOIR	
RFC	RUGBY FOOTBALL CLUB	
RI	RISE	
RP	RAMP	
RW	ROW	
S	SOUTH	
SCH	SCHOOL	
SE	SOUTH EAST	
SER	SERVICE AREA	
SH	SHORE	
SHOP	SHOPPING	
SKWY	SKYWAY	
SMT	SUMMIT	
SOC	SOCIETY	
SP	SPUR	
SPR	SPRING	
SQ	SQUARE	
ST	STREET	
STN	STATION	
STR	STREAM	
STRD	STRAND	
SW	SOUTH WEST	
TDG	TRADING	
TER	TERRACE	
THWY	THROUGHWAY	
TNL	TUNNEL	
TOLL	TOLLWAY	
TPK	TURNPIKE	
TR	TRACK	
TRL	TRAIL	
TWR	TOWER	
U/P	UNDERPASS	
UNI	UNIVERSITY	
UPR	UPPER	
V	VALE	
VA	VALLEY	
VIAD	VIADUCT	
VIL	VILLA	
VIS	VISTA	
VLG	VILLAGE	
VLS	VILLAS	
VW	VIEW	
W	WEST	
WD	WOOD	
WHF	WHARF	
WK	WALK	
WKS	WALKS	
WLS	WELLS	
WY	WAY	
YD	YARD	
YHA	YOUTH HOSTEL	

POSTCODE TOWNS AND AREA ABBREVIATIONS

BLGY	Abbots Langley
MP/FLIT/BLC	Ampthill/Flitwick/Barton-le-Clay
AMS	Amersham
AMSS	Amersham south
ARL/CHE	Arlesey/Church End
BAR	Barnet
BERK	Berkhamsted
BGSW	Biggleswade
BLDK	Baldock
BORE	Borehamwood
BRKMPK	Brookmans Park
BROX	Broxbourne
BSF	Bishop's Stortford
BUNT	Buntingford
BUSH	Bushey
CFSP/GDCR	Chalfont St Peter/Gerrards Cross
CHES/WCR	Cheshunt/Waltham Cross
CHESW	Cheshunt west
CHING	Chingford
CSHM	Chesham
CSTG	Chalfont St Giles
DEN/HRF	Denham/Harefield
DUN/HR/TOD	Dunstable/Houghton Regis/Toddington
DUN/WHIP	Dunstable/Whipsnade
EBAR	East Barnet
EDGW	Edgware
EN	Enfield
ENC/FH	Enfield Chase/Forty Hill
EPP	Epping
GSTN	Garston
GTMIS/PWD	Great Missenden/Prestwood
HARP	Harpenden
HAT	Hatfield

HERT/BAY..............Hertford/Bayford
HERT/WAS ....Hertford/Watton at Stone
HHNE..............Hemel Hempstead northeast
HHS/BOV..............Hemel Hempstead
south/Bovingdon
HHW..............Hemel Hempstead west
HLW..............Harlow
HLWE..............Harlow west
HLWS..............Harlow south
HLWW/ROY..............Harlow west/Roydon
HNLW..............Henlow
HOD..............Hoddesdon
HTCH/STOT..............Hitchin/Stotfold
HTCHE/RSTV...Hitchin east/Rural Stevenage
KGLGY..............Kings Langley
KNEB..............Knebworth
KTN/HRWW/WS..............Kenton/Harrow
Weald/Wealdstone
LBUZ..............Leighton Buzzard
LCOL/BKTW .....London Colney/Bricket Wood
LOU..............Loughton
LTN..............Luton
LTNE..............Luton east
LTNN/LIM..............Luton north/Limbury
LTNW/LEA..............Luton west/Leagrave
LWTH..............Letchworth
MHAD..............Much Hadham

MLHL..............Mill Hill
NTHWD..............Northwood
OXHEY..............Oxhey
PEND..............Ponders End
PIN..............Pinner
POTB/CUF..............Potters Bar/Cuffley
RAD..............Radlett
RAYLNE/WEN ....Rural Aylesbury north &
east/Wendover
RBSF..............Rural Bishop's Stortford
RKW/CH/CXG..............Rickmansworth/
Chorleywood/Croxley Green
ROY..............Royston
RYLN/HDSTN..........Rayners Lane/Headstone
SAFWS..............Saffron Walden south
SBW..............Sawbridgeworth
SDY/GAM/POT......Sandy/Gamlingay/Potton
STAL..............St Albans
STALE/WH..St Albans east/Wheathampstead
STALW/RED ....St Albans west/Redbourn
STAN..............Stanmore
STDN..............Standon
STSD..............Stansted
STVG..............Stevenage
STVGE..............Stevenage east
TRDG/WHET..........Totteridge/Whetstone
TRING..............Tring

WAB..............Waltham Abbey
WARE..............Ware
WAT..............Watford
WATN..............Watford north
WATW..............Watford west
WGCE..............Welwyn Garden City east
WGCW..............Welwyn Garden City west

Abb - All

Index - streets

A

Abbey Av STALW/RED AL3 .... 188 C1
Abbey Ct WAB EN9 .... 215 G4
Abbey Dale Cl HLWE CM17 .... 181 F2
Abbey Dr ABGLY WD5 .... 204 B2
LTNE LU2 .... 5 E2
Abbey Mill End STALW/RED AL3 .... 10 B5
Abbey Mill La STALW/RED AL3...... 10 B5
Abbey Rd ABGLY WD5 .... 204 B2
Abbey Vw RAD WD7 .... 206 C5
Abbeyview WAB EN9 .... 215 G3
Abbey View Rd STALW/RED AL3 .... 10 B4
Abbis Orch HTCH/STOT SG5 .... 40 C4
Abbots Av STAL AL1 .... 189 G1 🗓
Abbots Av West STAL AL1 .... 189 F1
Abbots Cl KNEB SG3 .... 96 E8
Abbots Gv STVG SG1 .... 3 D4
Abbots Pk STAL AL1 .... 11 E6
Abbots Ri KGLGY WD4 .... 185 G3
Abbots Rd ABGLY WD5 .... 186 E8
Abbots Vw KGLGY WD4 .... 185 K5
Abbotsweld HLWS CM18 .... 180 A4
Abbots Wood Rd LTNE LU2 .... 5 E2
Abbotts La WARE SG12 .... 129 K5
Abbotts Ri WARE SG12 .... 153 J5 🗓
Abbotts Rd LWTH SG6 .... 41 H3
Abbotts Vw BSF CM23 .... 105 H6
WARE SG12 .... 153 J5
Abdale La BRKMPK AL9 .... 192 B5
Abel Cl HHNE HP2 .... 9 D5
Abercrombie Wy HLWW/ROY CM19... 6 B6
Aberdale Gdns POTB/CUF EN6 ...... 210 A3
Aberford Rd BORE WD6 .... 223 K2
Abigail Cl LTNN/LIM LU3 .... 69 J6
Abingdon Rd LTNW/LEA LU4 ...... 68 B6
Abridge Cl CHES/WCR EN8 .... 214 C5 🗓
Abstacle Hl TRING HP23 .... 134 E6
Acacia La CHESW EN7 .... 196 E6
Acacia Ct BERK HP4 .... 161 L4
Acacia St HAT AL10 .... 171 F7
Acacia Wk HARP AL5 .... 144 A3
Acers LCOL/BKTW AL2 .... 188 E6
Achilles Cl HHNE HP2 .... 8 C3
Ackroyd Rd ROY SG8 .... 21 J1
Acme Rd WATN WD24 .... 204 B8
Acorn Gld WLYN AL6 .... 123 F5 🗓
Acorn La POTB/CUF EN6 .... 195 G7
Acorn Pl WATN WD24 .... 204 B7 🗓
Acorn Rd HHS/BOV HP3 .... 9 D6
Acorn St WARE SG12 .... 154 D2
Acremore St STDN SG11 .... 104 A2
Acre Wy NTHWD HA6 .... 230 A7
Acre Wd HHNE HP2 .... 8 B6
Acrewood Wy STALE/WH AL4 ...... 169 J6
Acton Cl CHES/WCR EN8 .... 214 D1 🗓
Acworth Crs LTNN/LEA LU4 .... 68 B4
Adamsfield CHESW EN7 .... 196 D4
Adams House HLW CM20 .... 6 C3 🗓
Adams Wy NTHWD WD24 .... 135 G4
Addington Wy LTNW/LEA LU4 ...... 68 C6
Addiscombe Rd WATW WD18 ...... 12 C3

Addison Cl NTHWD HA6 .... 230 B7
Addison Wy NTHWD HA6 .... 230 A7
Adelaide Cl EN EN1 .... 213 H8 🗓
Adelaide St LTN LU1 .... 4 B4
STALW/RED AL3 .... 10 C3
Adele Av WLYN AL6 .... 123 F6 🗓
Adeyfield Gdns HHNE HP2 .... 8 C4
Adeyfield Rd HHNE HP2 .... 8 C5
Adhara Rd NTHWD HA6 .... 230 A4
Adinger Ct STVG SC1 .... 2 C5 🗓
Admirals Cl STALE/WH AL4 .... 191 J1
Admiral St HERT/BAY SG13 .... 151 K3
Admirals Wk HOD EN11 .... 177 K3
STAL AL1 .... 11 F6
Admiral Wy HARP HP4 .... 161 G5
Adrian Cl DEN/HRF UB9 .... 228 C7
Adrian Rd ABLGY WD5 .... 203 K1
Adstone Rd LTN LU1 .... 88 E6
Ailsworth Rd LTNN/LIM LU3 ...... 69 F3
Ainsdale Dr OXHEY WD19 .... 230 D2
Aintree Rd ROY SG8 .... 21 K3
Aintree Wy STVGE SG2 .... 76 D1 🗓
Airport Approach Rd LTNE LU2 .... 90 E1
Airport Wy LTN LU1 .... 89 K6
LTNE LU2 .... 90 D3
Aitken Rd BAR EN5 .... 225 H5
Akeman Cl STALW/RED AL3 ...... 167 G8 🗓
Akeman St TRING HP23 .... 135 F6 🗓
Alamein Cl BROX EN10 .... 176 C6
Alandale Dr PIN HA5 .... 230 C7
Alan Dr BAR EN5 .... 225 K6
Alban Av STALW/RED AL3 .... 10 C2
Alban Crs BORE WD6 .... 224 A1
Alban Rd LWTH SG6 .... 42 C6
Albans Vw GSTN WD25 .... 204 C3
Albany Cl BUSH WD23 .... 222 A6
Albany Rd PEND EN3 .... 214 C7
Albemarle Av CHES/WCR EN8 .... 197 G6
POTB/CUF EN6 .... 210 C3
Albert Gdns HLWE CM17 .... 181 G2
Albert Rd ARL/CHE SG15 .... 24 E5
LTN LU1 .... 4 C6
Albert Rd North WAT WD17 ...... 12 C1 🗓
Albert Rd South WAT WD17 ...... 12 C2 🗓
Albert St STAL AL1 .... 10 C5
STALW/RED AL3 .... 115 J4
STVG SG1 .... 2 A1
TRING HP23 .... 135 F6
Albion Hl HHNE HP2 .... 8 A6 🗓
Albion Rd LBUZ LU7 .... 110 D4
LTNE LU2 .... 4 C3
STAL AL1 .... 11 E4
Albury Cl LTNN/LIM LU3 .... 52 A8
Albury Dr PIN HA5 .... 230 D7
Albury Grove Rd CHES/WCR EN8 ... 197 H8
Albury Ride CHES/WCR EN8 ...... 214 C1
Albury Rd BUSH WD23 .... 83 K7
Albury Wk CHES/WCR EN8 .... 197 C8
Alconbury BSF CM23 .... 86 A8
WCCE AL7 .... 149 F3
Aldbury Cl GSTN WD25 .... 204 E6
STALE/WH AL4 .... 169 F1 🗓
Aldbury Gv WGCE AL7 .... 148 C3
Aldbury Rd RKW/CH/CXG WD3 .... 217 J7
Aldcock Rd STVG SG1 .... 75 K1
Aldeburgh St STVG SG1 .... 58 A8
Aldenham Av RAD WD7 .... 206 D7

Aldenham Gv RAD WD7 .... 206 E
Aldenham Rd BUSH WD23 .... 13 F
GSTN WD25 .... 222 F
OXHEY WD19 .... 13 E
RAD WD7 .... 206 D
Alderbury Rd STSD CM24 .... 86 D
Alder Cl BLDK SG7 .... 42 E
BSF CM23 .... 105 C
HOD EN11 .... 177 C
LCOL/BKTW AL2 .... 188 C
Alder Crs LTNN/LIM LU3 .... 69 F
Alderley Ct BERK HP4 .... 161 L
Alderman Cl BRKMPK AL9 ...... 192 C2
Alders End La HARP AL5.......... 118 B
Alders Wk SBW CM21 .... 132 C
Alderton Cl LTNE LU2 .... 70 E8
Alderton Dr BERK HP4 .... 137 H
Alder Wk GSTN WD25 .... 204 C
Aldhous Cl LTNN/LIM LU3.......... 69 C
Aldock Rd WCCE AL7 .... 148 E
Aldridge Av PEND EN3 .... 215 H
Aldridge Ct BLDK SG7 .... 26 E8
Aldwick STAL AL1 .... 11 F
Aldwickbury Crs HARP AL5 .... 119 F
Aldwick Rd HARP AL5 .... 144 E
Aldwyke Ri WARE SG12 .... 127 G6
Aldykes HAT AL10 .... 170 E
Alesia Rd LTNN/LIM LU3 .... 68 E
Alexander Ga STVGE SG2 .... 76 E
Alexander Rd HERT/WAS SG14 .... 150 E
HTCH/STOT SG5 .... 25 H
LCOL/BKTW AL2 .... 190 A
Alexandra Av LTNN/LIM LU3 ...... 69 C
Alexandra Ms WAT WD17 .... 12 B1
Alexandra Rd BORE WD6 .... 208 C
HHNE HP2 .... 8 A
HTCH/STOT SG5 .... 40 E
KGLGY WD4 .... 184 E
KGLGY WD4 .... 186 E
RKW/CH/CXG WD3 201
STAL AL1 .... 11 D4
WAT WD17 .... 12 E
Alexandra Wy CHES/WCR EN8 214
Aleyn Wy BLDK SG7 .... 27 E
Alfriston Cl LTNE LU2 .... 70 E
Alington La LWTH SG6 .... 41 E
Allandale HHNE HP2 .... 8 E
STALW/RED AL3 .... 188 E
Allandale Crs POTB/CUF EN6 ...... 209 E
Allandale Rd PEND EN3 .... 214 E
Allard Cl CHESW EN7 .... 196 E
Allard Crs BUSH WD23 .... 231 E
Allard Wy BROX EN10 .... 176 E
Aldicks Rd HHS/BOV HP3 .... 164 E
Allen Cl RAD WD7 .... 207 E
STALE/WH AL4 .... 145 E
Allen Ct HAT AL10 .... 171 G6
Allendale LTNN/LIM LU3 .... 69 E
Allerton Cl BORE WD6 .... 207 E
Allerton Rd BORE WD6 .... 207 E
Alleyns Rd STVG SG1 .... 2 E
Allmains Cl WAB EN9 .... 199 E
All Saints Cl BSF CM23 .... 105 E
Allsaints Crs GSTN WD25 .... 204 E
All Saints La RKW/CH/CXG WD3 .... 219 E
Allum La BORE WD6 .... 223 E
Allwood Rd CHESW EN7 .... 196 E

Alma Cut STAL AL1 .... 11 D5
Alma Link LTN LU1 .... 4 B4
Alma Rd BERK HP4 .... 161 F3
   STAL AL1 .... 11 D5
Alma St LTN LU1 .... 4 B4
Almonds La STVG SG1 .... 75 K1
The Almonds STAL AL1 .... 189 H6
Almond Wy BORE WD6 .... 224 A4
   RYLN/HDSTN HA2 .... 231 K8
Almshouse La EN EN1 .... 214 A7
Alms La BLDK SG7 .... 17 K5
Alnwick Dr TRING HP23 .... 108 D2
Alpha Pl BSF CM23 .... 105 J1
Alpine Cl HTCHE/RSTV SG4 .... 56 E4
Alpine Wy LTNN/LIM LU3 .... 68 C1
Alsop Cl LCOL/BKTW AL2 .... 190 C6
Alston Rd BAR EN5 .... 225 K3
   HHW HP1 .... 163 K7
Altair Wy NTHWD HA6 .... 230 A4
Altham Gv HLW CM20 .... 7 D2
Altham Rd PIN HA5 .... 231 F6
Althorp Cl TRDG/WHET N20 .... 225 F7
Althorp Rd LTNN/LIM LU3 .... 4 A2
   STAL AL1 .... 11 D3
Alton Rd LTN LU1 .... 5 D6
Altwood HARP AL5 .... 119 F8
Alva Wy OXHEY WD19 .... 230 E1
Alverton STALW/RED AL3 .... 10 B1
Alwin Pl WATW WD18 .... 219 K4
Alwyn Cl BORE WD6 .... 223 J8
   LTNE LU2 .... 4 C1
Alyngton BERK HP4 .... 161 G1
Alzey Gdns HARP AL5 .... 144 A1
Amberley Cl HARP AL5 .... 118 D7
   LTNE LU2 .... 70 E5
Amberley Gn WARE SG12 .... 127 G5
Ambleside LTNN/LIM LU3 .... 68 C4
Ambrose La HARP AL5 .... 118 C6
Amenbury La HARP AL5 .... 118 C8
Amersham Rd AMS HP6 .... 216 A1
   CSTG HP8 .... 226 A3
   RKW/CH/CXG WD3 .... 216 E1
Amersham Wy AMS HP6 .... 216 B1
Amor Wy LWTH SG6 .... 42 B3
Amwell Cl GSTN WD25 .... 205 F5
Amwell Common WGCE AL7 .... 148 C4
Amwell Ct HOD EN11 .... 177 F2
   WAB EN9 .... 215 K3
Amwell End WARE SG12 .... 127 H8
Amwell Hl WARE SG12 .... 152 E3
Amwell La STALE/WH AL4 .... 144 C2
   WARE SG12 .... 153 F3
Amwell St HOD EN11 .... 177 F2
Anchor Cl CHES/WCR EN8 .... 197 H6
Anchor La HHW HP1 .... 164 A1
Anchor Rd BLDK SG7 .... 43 F2
Anchor St BSF CM23 .... 105 K5
Anderson Cl DEN/HRF UB9 .... 227 K7
Anderson Rd RAD WD7 .... 207 K3
   STVGE SG2 .... 76 D3
Anderson's La BUNT SG9 .... 49 G7
Andover Cl LTNW/LEA LU4 .... 68 B3
Andrew Rd RAD WD7 .... 207 J3
Andrews Cl HHNE HP2 .... 8 A3
Andrewsfield WGCE AL7 .... 148 D3
Andrew's La CHESW EN7 .... 196 C6
Anelle Ri HHS/BOV HP3 .... 185 K2
Angell's Meadow BLDK SG7 .... 17 K5
Anglefield Rd BERK HP4 .... 161 H5
Anglesey Cl BSF CM23 .... 105 F2
Anglesey Rd OXHEY WD19 .... 230 D4
Angle Wys STVGE SG2 .... 3 D6
Anglian Cl WATN WD24 .... 13 D1
Angotts Md STVG SG1 .... 75 G3
Anmer Gdns LTNW/LEA LU4 .... 68 B3
Annables La HARP AL5 .... 117 F5
Anns Cl TRING HP23 .... 134 D6
Anselm Rd PIN HA5 .... 231 G6
Anson Cl HHW HP1 .... 183 H5
   STAL AL1 .... 168 E3
   STALE/WH AL4 .... 145 F8
Anson Wk NTHWD HA6 .... 229 H3
Anstee Rd LTNW/LEA LU4 .... 68 A3
Anthony Cl OXHEY WD19 .... 220 E8
Anthony Gdns LTNN/LIM LU1 .... 4 B6
Anthony Rd BORE WD6 .... 223 H2
Anthorne Cl POTB/CUF EN6 .... 210 C1
Anthus Ms NTHWD HA6 .... 229 H3
Antoneys Cl PIN HA5 .... 230 E8
Antonine Ga STALW/RED AL3 .... 167 H7
Anvil Cl HHS/BOV HP3 .... 183 K6
Aplins Cl HARP AL5 .... 118 B7
Apollo Wy NTHWD HA6 .... 230 B4
Apollo Wy HHNE HP2 .... 8 B5
   STVG SG1 .... 76 D1
Appleby St CHESW EN7 .... 196 C4
Applecroft BERK HP4 .... 161 F3
   LCOL/BKTW AL2 .... 188 D6
Applecroft Rd LTNE LU2 .... 70 D5
   WGCW AL8 .... 147 G3
Appleford's Cl HOD EN11 .... 176 E1
Apple Glebe AMP/FLIT/B MK45 .... 36 C7
The Apple Orch HHNE HP2 .... 8 C3
Appleton Av WARE SG12 .... 128 E4

Appleton Cl HLWW/ROY CM19 .... 6 B5
Appleton Flds BSF CM23 .... 105 H5
Appletree Wk GSTN WD25 .... 204 C5
Applewood Cl HARP AL5 .... 118 A6
Approach Rd STAL AL1 .... 11 D5
The Approach POTB/CUF EN6 .... 210 A2
Appspond La LCOL/BKTW AL2 .... 187 J2
Apsley Cl BSF CM23 .... 105 H5
Apsley End Rd HTCH/STOT SG5 .... 38 A4
Apton Ct BSF CM23 .... 105 J2
Apton Flds BSF CM23 .... 105 J3
Apton Rd BSF CM23 .... 105 J2
Aquarius Wy NTHWD HA6 .... 230 B4
Aragon Cl ENC/FH EN2 .... 212 C8
   HHNE HP2 .... 165 H1
Aran Cl HARP AL5 .... 144 A3
Arbour Cl LTNN/LIM LU3 .... 52 A8
The Arbour HERT/BAY SG13 .... 151 G5
Arbroath Gn OXHEY WD19 .... 230 E2
Archer Cl KGLY WD4 .... 185 K7
Archer Rd STVG SG1 .... 3 D1
Archers BUNT SG9 .... 63 K1
   EPP CM16 .... 179 J6
Archers Flds STAL AL1 .... 11 E2
Archers Green La WLYN AL6 .... 148 E1
Archers Ride WGCE AL7 .... 148 C5
Archers Wy LWTH SG6 .... 41 H3
The Arches LWTH SG6 .... 42 A2
Archfield WGCE AL7 .... 122 E8
Arch Rd HTCHE/RSTV SG4 .... 57 H5
Archway Rd LTNW/LEA LU4 .... 68 C3
Arden Cl BUSH WD23 .... 222 C7
   HHS/BOV HP3 .... 183 J6
Arden Gv HARP AL5 .... 118 D8
Arden Press Wy LWTH SG6 .... 42 B3
Ardens Wy STALE/WH AL4 .... 169 G4
Ardleigh Gn LTNE LU2 .... 71 F8
Ardross Av NTHWD HA6 .... 229 H4
Argent Wy CHESW EN7 .... 196 B5
Argyle Rd BAR EN5 .... 225 H4
Argyle Wy STVG SG1 .... 2 A3
Argyll Av LTNN/LIM LU3 .... 4 A1
Argyll Gdns HHNE HP2 .... 164 D1
Arkley Dr BAR EN5 .... 225 F4
Arkley La BAR EN5 .... 225 F3
Arkley Rd HHNE HP2 .... 165 G1
Arkley Vw BAR EN5 .... 225 G4
Arkwrights HLW CM20 .... 7 E3
Arlesey New Rd LWTH SG6 .... 41 G2
Arlesey Rd HNLW SG16 .... 24 B1
   HTCH/STOT SG5 .... 25 H3
   HTCH/STOT SG5 .... 40 C5
Arlington Crs CHES/WCR EN8 .... 214 C8
Armand Cl WAT WD17 .... 204 A8
Armitage Rd RKW/CH/CXG WD3 .... 218 C4
Armitage Gdns LTNW/LEA LU4 .... 68 C3
Armourers Cl BSF CM23 .... 104 E5
Armour Ri HTCHE/RSTV SG4 .... 41 F7
Armstrong Cl LCOL/BKTW AL2 ...... 190 C5
Armstrong Gdns RAD WD7 .... 207 H2
Arncliffe Crs LTNE LU2 .... 4 C2
Arnett Cl RKW/CH/CXG WD3 .... 217 J6
Arnett Wy RKW/CH/CXG WD3 .... 217 K6
Arnold Av East PEND EN3 .... 214 E8
Arnold Cl AMP/FLIT/B MK45 .... 36 E7
   HTCHE/RSTV SG4 .... 57 F1
   LTNE LU2 .... 70 B2
   STVG SG1 .... 58 B8
Arnolds La BLDK SG7 .... 16 D3
Arran Cl HHS/BOV HP3 .... 165 H3
Arretine Cl STALW/RED AL3 .... 167 G4
Arrewig La TRING HP23 .... 158 B3
Arrow Cl LTNN/LIM LU3 .... 68 D3
Arthur Rd STAL AL1 .... 168 E6
Arthur St BUSH WD23 .... 13 E2
   LTN LU1 .... 4 C5
Artisan Crs STALW/RED AL3 .... 167 H3
Arundel Cl CHES/WCR EN8 .... 197 F6
   HHNE HP2 .... 9 E4
   STVGE SG2 .... 77 F6
Arundel Dr BORE WD6 .... 224 B4
Arundel Gv STALW/RED AL3 .... 168 A2
Arundell Rd ABLGY WD5 .... 204 B2
Arundel Rd LTNW/LEA LU4 .... 69 F7
Ascot Cl BORE WD6 .... 223 K5
   BSF CM23 .... 106 B1
Ascot Crs STVG SG1 .... 59 H8
Ascot Gdns PEND EN3 .... 214 B7
Ascot Rd LTNN/LIM LU3 .... 69 G7
   ROY SG8 .... 21 K3
   WATW WD18 .... 219 K5
Ascots La BRKMPK AL9 .... 147 K8
Ashanger La BLDK SG7 .... 43 K5
Ashbourne Sq NTHWD HA6 .... 229 K5
Ashbourne Cl LWTH SG6 .... 42 B5
Ashbourne Ct STALE/WH AL4 .... 169 F8
Ashbourne Rd BROX EN10 .... 176 E7
Ashbrook La HTCHE/RSTV SG4 .... 57 K8
Ashburnam Wk STVGE SG2 .... 76 A8
Ashburnham Cl OXHEY WD19 .... 230 E2
Ashburnham Dr OXHEY WD19 .... 230 B2
Ashburnham Rd LTN LU1 .... 89 G2
Ashbury Cl HAT AL10 .... 170 D4

Ashby Dr AMP/FLIT/B MK45 .... 36 C6
Ashby Gdns STAL AL1 .... 189 F2
Ashby Ri BSF CM23 .... 86 A8
Ashby Rd BERK HP4 .... 160 E2
   WATN WD24 .... 204 B8
Ash Cl ABLGY WD5 .... 203 J2
   BRKMPK AL9 .... 193 G3
   DEN/HRF UB9 .... 228 C7
   GSTN WD25 .... 204 C5
Ashcombe WGCW AL8 .... 122 E7
Ash Copse LCOL/BKTW AL2 .... 205 G1
Ashcroft PIN HA5 .... 231 H5
Ashcroft Cl HARP AL5 .... 144 B1
Ashcroft Rd LTNE LU2 .... 70 C5
Ashdale BSF CM23 .... 105 G5
Ashdale Gdns LTNN/LIM LU3 .... 52 A8
Ashdales STAL AL1 .... 189 F2
Ashdown LWTH SG6 .... 25 J8
Ashdown Crs CHES/WCR EN8 .... 197 J6
Ashdown Dr BORE WD6 .... 223 J2
Ashdown Rd BUSH WD23 .... 13 E2
   STVGE SG2 .... 96 C2
Ash Dr HAT AL10 .... 171 F7
   HTCHE/RSTV SG4 .... 56 E5
Ashendene Rd CHESW EN7 .... 195 K3
   HERT/BAY SG13 .... 174 C4
Ashfield Av BUSH WD23 .... 221 J6
Ashfields GSTN WD25 .... 204 A5
Ashfield Wy LTNN/LIM LU3 .... 69 F3
Ashford Gn OXHEY WD19 .... 230 E4
Ash Gv DEN/HRF UB9 .... 228 C7
   HHS/BOV HP3 .... 185 K2
   STALE/WH AL4 .... 120 A8
Ash Groves SBW CM21 .... 132 E7
Ash Hill Cl BUSH WD23 .... 221 J8
Ashlea Rd CFSP/GDCR SL9 .... 226 B8
Ashleigh STVGE SG2 .... 3 F4
Ashley Cl HHS/BOV HP3 .... 164 E8
   PIN HA5 .... 230 C8
   WGCW AL8 .... 147 H1
Ashley Dr BORE WD6 .... 224 B5
Ashley Gdns HARP AL5 .... 117 K6
Ashley Rd HERT/WAS SG14 .... 150 D4
   STAL AL1 .... 169 F6
Ashleys RKW/CH/CXG WD3 .... 217 J7
Ashlyn Cl BUSH WD23 .... 13 F3
Ashlyns Ct BERK HP4 .... 161 J6
Ashlyns Rd BERK HP4 .... 161 J6
Ash Meadow MHAD SG10 .... 103 J7
Ash Ml ROY SG8 .... 32 C6
Ashmore Gdns HHS/BOV HP3 .... 9 E6
Ash Ride ENC/FH EN2 .... 212 D5
Ashridge Dr LCOL/BKTW AL2 .... 188 A8
   OXHEY WD19 .... 230 D4
Ashridge La CSHM HP5 .... 200 A1
Ashridge Ri BERK HP4 .... 161 G4
Ash Rd LTNW/LEA LU4 .... 89 C1
   TRING HP23 .... 134 E5
   WARE SG12 .... 128 A6
Ashton Rd LTN LU1 .... 4 C6
   PEND EN3 .... 214 D6
Ashton's La BLDK SG7 .... 42 E5
Ash Tree Fld HLW CM20 .... 155 H7
Ash Tree Rd WATN WD24 .... 204 C6
Ashtree Wy HHW HP1 .... 163 K7
Ashurst Cl NTHWD HA6 .... 229 K6
Ash V RKW/CH/CXG WD3 .... 227 G4
Ashville Wy BLDK SG7 .... 27 G8
Ashwell Av LTNN/LIM LU3 .... 68 B1
Ashwell Cl HTCHE/RSTV SG4 .... 58 B5
Ashwell Common HTCHE/RSTV SG4 .. 58 B5
Ashwell Pk HARP AL5 .... 119 F8
Ashwell Rd BLDK SG7 .... 16 D4
   BLDK SG7 .... 27 F1
   BLDK SG7 .... 27 H7
   ROY SG8 .... 15 G8
Ashwell St BLDK SG7 .... 17 K6
   STALW/RED AL3 .... 10 C3
Ashwood Rd POTB/CUF EN6 .... 210 C3
Ashworth Pl HLWE CM17 .... 181 G1
Askew Rd NTHWD HA6 .... 229 H1
Aspasia Cl STAL AL1 .... 11 E5
Aspen Cl STVGE SG2 .... 96 C2
Aspenden Rd BUNT SG9 .... 63 J4
Aspen Park Dr GSTN WD25 .... 204 C5
The Aspens BSF CM23 .... 86 A8
   HTCHE/RSTV SG4 .... 56 E3
Aspen Wy PEND EN3 .... 214 C5
   WGCE AL7 .... 148 D4
Aspfield Rw HHW HP1 .... 164 A1
Ass House La KTN/HRWW/W HA3 ... 231 J3
Aster Cl BSF CM23 .... 105 C3
The Asters CHESW EN7 .... 196 B6
Astley Gn LTNE LU2 .... 70 E7
Astley Rd HHW HP1 .... 164 B6
Aston Cl BUSH WD23 .... 221 K6
   WATN WD24 .... 13 D1
Aston End Rd STVGE SG2 .... 77 F4
Aston La STVGE SG2 .... 97 F2
Aston Ri HTCHE/RSTV SG4 .... 57 F3
Aston Rd STDN SG11 .... 81 J7
Astons Rd NTHWD HA6 .... 229 H2
Aston Vw HHNE HP2 .... 141 F8
Aston Wy POTB/CUF EN6 .... 210 E2

Astrope La *TRING* HP23 .... 108 E6
Astwick Av *HAT* AL10 .... 170 E1
Athelstan Rd *HHS/BOV* HP3 ...... 185 J1
Athelstan Wk North *WCCE* AL7 ... 147 K4 🔲
Athelstan Wk South *WCCE* AL7 ... 147 J4 🔲
Athena Pl *NTHWD* HA6 .... 230 A7
Atherstone Rd *LTNW/LEA* LU4 ..... 68 C8
Atherton End *SBW* CM21 .... 132 C6
Athlone Cl *RAD* WD7 .... 206 E6 🔲
Athol Cl *PIN* HA5 .... 230 C7
Athol Gdns *PIN* HA5 .... 230 C7
Atholl Cl *LTNN/LIM* LU3 .... 68 C1
Atria Rd *NTHWD* HA6 .... 230 B4
Attenborough Cl *OXHEY* WD19 ... 231 F2 🔲
Attimore Cl *WGCW* AL8 .... 147 G4
Attimore Rd *WGCW* AL8 .... 147 G4
Aubrey Av *LCOL/BKTW* AL2 .... 190 A4
Aubrey La *STALW/RED* AL3 .... 141 K7
Aubreys *LWTH* SG6 .... 41 K7
Aubreys Rd *HHW* HP1 .... 163 H7
Aubries *STVGE* SG2 .... 77 J1
Auckland Cl *EN* EN1 .... 214 A7
Auckland Rd *POTB/CUF* EN6 ...... 209 J2
Audley Cl *BORE* WD6 .... 223 K3
Audley Ct *PIN* HA5 .... 230 D8
Audley Gdns *WAB* EN9 .... 215 H4
Audrey Gdns *BSF* CM23 .... 105 J6
Audwick Cl *CHES/WCR* EN8 .... 197 H6
Augustine Rd *KTN/HRWW/W* HA3 .. 231 J7
Augustus Cl *STALW/RED* AL3 ...... 167 H8
Augustus Ga *STVGE* SG2 .... 76 D1
Austenwood La *CFSP/GDCR* SL9 .. 226 A8
Austin Rd *LTNN/LIM* LU3 .... 69 G5
Austins Md *HHS/BOV* HP3 .... 183 K6
Austins Pl *HHNE* HP2 .... 8 A4
Autumn Glades *HHS/BOV* HP3 .... 165 H8
Autumn Gv *WGCE* AL7 .... 148 C5 🔲
Avalon Cl *GSTN* WD25 .... 205 F2
Avebury Av *LTNE* LU2 .... 69 J3
Avenue Ap *KGLGY* WD4 .... 186 A8
Avenue Ct *WLYN* AL6 .... 122 E2 🔲
Avenue One *LWTH* SG6 .... 42 E4
Avenue Ri *BUSH* WD23 .... 221 H5
Avenue Rd *BSF* CM23 .... 105 K3
HOD EN11 .... 177 J3
STAL AL1 .... 11 J5
Avenue Ter *OXHEY* WD19 .... 13 F5 🔲
The Avenue *BAR* EN5 .... 225 K3
BUSH WD23 .... 221 H5
HERT/WAS SG14 .... 150 E1
HHW HP1 .... 163 H5
HOD EN11 .... 177 J3
HTCH/STOT SG5 .... 25 K3
HTCHE/RSTV SG4 .... 56 E2
LTNW/LEA LU4 .... 68 C2
NTHWD HA6 .... 229 H5
PIN HA5 .... 231 J5
POTB/CUF EN6 .... 193 F8
RAD WD7 .... 206 D4
STVG SG1 .... 75 H1
WAB EN9 .... 199 J3
WAT WD17 .... 12 B1
WLYN AL6 .... 122 D2
Avia Cl *HHS/BOV* HP3 .... 185 J1
Avior Dr *NTHWD* HA6 .... 230 A3
Avocet *LWTH* SG6 .... 25 J8
Avon Cl *GSTN* WD25 .... 204 D4
Avondale Rd *LTN* LU1 .... 4 A3
Avon St *HHNE* HP2 .... 164 E1
Axe Cl *LTNN/LIM* LU3 .... 68 D3
Aycliffe Dr *HHNE* HP2 .... 8 B1
Aycliffe Rd *BORE* WD6 .... 207 J3
Aydon Rd *LTNN/LIM* LU3 .... 69 G3
Aylands Rd *PEND* EN3 .... 214 C6
Aylesbury Rd *TRING* HP23 .... 134 D6
Aylets Fld *HLWS* CM18 .... 180 B4
Aylotts Cl *BUNT* SG9 .... 63 H1 🔲
Aylsham Rd *HOD* EN11 .... 177 H1
Aylward Dr *STVGE* SG2 .... 3 E3
Aynho St *WATW* WD18 .... 12 C4 🔲
Aynsley Gdns *HLWE* CM17 .... 181 F1
Aynsworth Av *BSF* CM23 .... 85 K7
Ayot Gn *WGCW* AL8 .... 121 K8
Ayot Little Green La *WLYN* AL6 ... 121 K8
Ayot St Peter Rd *WLYN* AL6 .... 121 H5
Ayr Cl *STVGE* SG2 .... 76 D1
Ayres End La *HARP* AL5 .... 144 B3
Aysgarth Cl *HARP* AL5 .... 143 J1
Aysgarth Rd *STALW/RED* AL3 ..... 142 B3

B

Baas Hl *BROX* EN10 .... 176 C7
Baas Hill Cl *BROX* EN10 .... 176 D7
Baas La *BROX* EN10 .... 176 D7
Babbage Rd *STVG* SG1 .... 75 G4
Back La *BSF* CM23 .... 47 H1
GSTN WD25 .... 222 B1
HTCHE/RSTV SG4 .... 73 G3
RBSF CM22 .... 133 F2
WAB EN9 .... 199 J1
WLYN AL6 .... 124 A7

Back St *BLDK* SG7 .... 17 J6
LTNE LU2 .... 4 C3 🔲
The Back *BERK* HP4 .... 162 E2
Bacons Dr *POTB/CUF* EN6 .... 195 C6
Bacon's Yd *BLDK* SG7 .... 17 K5
Badeley Ct *STVGE* SG2 .... 3 F6
Bader Cl *STVG* SG1 .... 58 E8
WGCE AL7 .... 148 D3
Badger Cl *KNEB* SG3 .... 96 A3
Badger Cft *HHNE* HP2 .... 165 J7 🔲
Badgers *BSF* CM23 .... 105 J4
Badgers Cl *BORE* WD6 .... 223 J2 🔲
HERT/BAY SG13 .... 152 A3
STVG SG1 .... 2 C4
Badgers Cft *BROX* EN10 .... 176 D7
TRDG/WHET N20 .... 225 K7
Badgers Wk *RKW/CH/CXG* WD3 .. 217 J4
WLYN AL6 .... 123 J4
Badger Wy *HAT* AL10 .... 171 G6
Badingham Dr *HARP* AL5 .... 118 A8 🔲
Badminton Pl *BORE* WD6 .... 223 K2 🔲
STVGE SG2 .... 96 C2
Badminton Pl *BROX* EN10 .... 176 D6
Bagwicks Cl *LTNN/LIM* LU3 .... 68 D2
Bailey St *LTN* LU1 .... 5 D5
Baines La *KNEB* SG3 .... 96 A3
Baird Cl *BUSH* WD23 .... 221 J6 🔲
Bairstow Cl *BORE* WD6 .... 223 H1
Bakers Gv *WGCE* AL7 .... 148 D2
Bakers La *DUN/WHIP* LU6 .... 114 C1
ROY SG8 .... 23 F6
WLYN AL6 .... 94 E8 🔲
Bakers Rd *CHESW* EN7 .... 197 F8
Baker St *HERT/BAY* SG13 .... 151 K3
LTN LU1 .... 4 C5
POTB/CUF EN6 .... 209 K5
Bakery Cl *HLWW/ROY* CM19 ..... 178 D1
Bakewell Cl *LTNW/LEA* LU4 .... 68 B8
Balcary Gdns *BERK* HP4 .... 161 F6
Balcombe Cl *LTNE* LU2 .... 70 D5 🔲
Balcon Wy *BORE* WD6 .... 224 B1
Baldock La *LWTH* SG6 .... 42 B7
Baldock Rd *BUNT* SG9 .... 63 F2
HTCH/STOT SG5 .... 42 A4
LWTH SG6 .... 19 K6
ROY SG8 .... 21 G3
Baldock St *ROY* SG8 .... 21 G3
WARE SG12 .... 127 H7
Baldock Wy *BORE* WD6 .... 223 J1
Baldwins *WGCE* AL7 .... 148 C3
Baldwins La *RKW/CH/CXG* WD3 .. 219 F4
Balfour St *HERT/WAS* SG14 .... 151 F2
Baliol Rd *HTCH/STOT* SG5 .... 56 D1
Ballater Cl *OXHEY* WD19 .... 230 C3
Ballinger Ct *BERK* HP4 .... 161 H6
Ballslough Hl *HTCHE/RSTV* SG4 .. 93 C8
Balmoral Cl *CHES/WCR* EN8 ...... 214 C4
LCOL/BKTW AL2 .... 188 E6
STVGE SG2 .... 96 C2
Balmoral Dr *BORE* WD6 .... 224 C4
Balmoral Rd *GSTN* WD25 .... 204 B2
HTCH/STOT SG5 .... 40 C8
PEND EN3 .... 214 C6
WATN WD24 .... 204 D8
Balmore Wd *LTNN/LIM* LU3 .... 52 E8 🔲
Balsams Cl *HERT/BAY* SG13 .... 151 G5
Bampton Rd *LTNW/LEA* LU4 ...... 68 A8
Banbury Cl *LTNN/LEA* LU4 .... 68 E5 🔲
Banbury St *WATW* WD18 .... 12 C4 🔲
Bancroft *HTCH/STOT* SG5 .... 56 D2
Bancroft Gdns
KTN/HRWW/W HA3 .... 231 K7 🔲
Bancroft Rd *KTN/HRWW/W* HA3 .. 231 J8
LTNN/LIM LU3 .... 69 G5
Bandley Ri *STVGE* SG2 .... 76 D6
Banes Down *WAB* EN9 .... 177 K8
Bank Cl *LTNW/LEA* LU4 .... 68 B5
Bankmill Br *BERK* HP4 .... 162 C6
Bank Mill La *BERK* HP4 .... 162 B6
Banks Rd *BORE* WD6 .... 224 B2
Barbel Cl *CHES/WCR* EN8 .... 215 F4
Barberry Rd *HHW* HP1 .... 163 K6
Barbers La *LTN* LU1 .... 4 C6
Barbers Wk *TRING* HP23 .... 134 E6
Barclay Cl *HERT/BAY* SG13 .... 152 A5
WATW WD18 .... 12 B5 🔲
Barclay Ct *HOD* EN11 .... 177 F4
Barclay Crs *STVG* SG1 .... 2 C1
Barclay Rd *LTNW/LEA* LU4 .... 68 E5 🔲
Barden Cl *DEN/HRF* UB9 .... 228 B7
Bards Cnr *HHW* HP1 .... 164 A5 🔲
Bardwell Rd *STAL* AL1 .... 10 C5
Barford Ri *LTNE* LU2 .... 70 D3
Bargrove Av *HHW* HP1 .... 163 K7
Barham Av *BORE* WD6 .... 223 J3
Barham Rd *STVGE* SG2 .... 76 D4
Barkham Cl *LBUZ* LU7 .... 109 K2
Barking Cl *LTNW/LEA* LU4 .... 68 A3
Barkway Hl *ROY* SG8 .... 32 E3
Barkway Rd *ROY* SG8 .... 21 J4
Barkway St *ROY* SG8 .... 21 H4
Barley Cl *BUSH* WD23 .... 221 J5
Barleycroft *BUNT* SG9 .... 63 J5 🔲
Barley Cft *HERT/WAS* SG14 ...... 125 J6
HERT/WAS SG14 .... 151 G1

Barleycroft *STVGE* SG2 .... 76 B1
WARE SG12 .... 126 D5
Barleycroft Gn *WGCW* AL8 .... 147 H3
Barleycroft Rd *WGCW* AL8 .... 147 H1
Barley La *LTNW/LEA* LU4 .... 68 E8 🔲
Barley Mow La *STALE/WH* AL4 ... 190 C6
Barley Ponds Cl *WARE* SG12 ..... 127 K8
Barley Ponds Rd *WARE* SG12 .... 127 K8
Barley Ri *BLDK* SG7 .... 43 H7
Barley Rd *ROY* SG8 .... 23 H7
Barleyvale *LTNN/LIM* LU3 .... 69 F1
Barlings Rd *HARP* AL5 .... 143 H7
Barmor Cl *RYLN/HDSTN* HA2 ..... 231 H8
Barnacres Rd *HHS/BOV* HP3 ..... 185 J5
Barnard Acres *WAB* EN9 .... 198 E6
Barnard Gn *WGCE* AL7 .... 148 C4
Barnard Rd *LTN* LU1 .... 4 A6
SBW CM21 .... 132 C7
Barnard Wy *HHS/BOV* HP3 .... 8 B2 🔲
Barn Cl *HHS/BOV* HP3 .... 185 H7
RAD WD7 .... 206 D3
WGCW AL8 .... 147 H3
Barncroft *STDN* SG11 .... 83 J6
Barncroft Rd *BERK* HP4 .... 161 G6
Barncroft Wy *STAL* AL1 .... 11 H6
Barndell Cl *HTCH/STOT* SG5 ..... 25 H7
Barndicott *WGCE* AL7 .... 148 D4
Barnes La *KGLGY* WD4 .... 185 H8
Barnes Ri *KGLGY* WD4 .... 185 J8
Barnet By-pass *BORE* WD6 ...... 224 B2
Barnet Gate La *BAR* EN5 .... 224 A6
Barnet La *BORE* WD6 .... 223 J8
Barnet Rd *EBAR* EN4 .... 210 E4
LCOL/BKTW AL2 .... 190 D6 🔲
MLHL NW7 .... 224 D1
POTB/CUF EN6 .... 210 D3
POTB/CUF EN6 .... 210 D3
Barnet Way (Barnet By-pass)
MLHL NW7 .... 224 D1
Barnfield *HHS/BOV* HP3 .... 185 J8
Barnfield Av *LTNE* LU2 .... 69 K4
Barnfield Cl *HOD* EN11 .... 177 H1
WAB EN9 .... 178 D8
Barnfield Ct *HARP* AL5 .... 143 K1 🔲
Barnfield Rd *HARP* AL5 .... 143 J2
STALE/WH AL4 .... 169 J7
WCCE AL7 .... 147 K4 🔲
Barn Hl *HLWW/ROY* CM19 .... 178 C1
Barnhurst Pth *OXHEY* WD19 ..... 230 C3
Barn Lea *RKW/CH/CXG* WD3 ..... 217 K8
Barn Md *HLWS* CM18 .... 6 C6
Barns Ct *EPP* CM16 .... 179 K8
Barnsdale Cl *BORE* WD6 .... 223 J1 🔲
Barns Dene *HARP* AL5 .... 118 A8
Barnside Ct *WGCW* AL8 .... 147 H2 🔲
Barnston Cl *LTNE* LU2 .... 70 E4 🔲
Barnsway *KGLGY* WD4 .... 185 J8
Barnwell *STVGE* SG2 .... 3 F6
Baron Ct *STVG* SG1 .... 58 C5
Barons Rw *HARP* AL5 .... 144 A1
The Barons *BSF* CM23 .... 105 J3
Barra Cl *HHS/BOV* HP3 .... 186 A1
Barrells Down Rd *BSF* CM23 ..... 85 K8
Barrett La *BSF* CM23 .... 105 J2
Barrington Dr *DEN/HRF* UB9 ..... 227 K7
Barrington Rd *LWTH* SG6 .... 41 K6
Barrowby Cl *LTNE* LU2 .... 70 E4 🔲
Barrowdene Cl *PIN* HA5 .... 231 F8 🔲
Barrow La *CHESW* EN7 .... 213 K6
Barrow Point Av *PIN* HA5 .... 231 G6
Barrow Point La *PIN* HA5 .... 231 G6
Barrows Rd *HLWW/ROY* CM19 ... 179 F6
Barr Rd *POTB/CUF* EN6 .... 210 D4
Barry Cl *LCOL/BKTW* AL2 .... 188 D4
Bartel Cl *HHS/BOV* HP3 .... 165 K8
Bartholomew Rd *BSF* CM23 ...... 105 H4
Bartletts Md *HERT/WAS* SG14 ... 126 B4
Barton Cl *HARP* AL5 .... 118 C8
Barton Rd *AMP/FLIT/B* MK45 .... 36 A1
HTCH/STOT SG5 .... 37 G6
LTNE LU2 .... 69 K2
LTNN/LIM LU3 .... 52 D2
STALE/WH AL4 .... 145 J2
The Bartons *BORE* WD6 .... 223 G6 🔲
Barton Wy *BORE* WD6 .... 223 H6
RKW/CH/CXG WD3 .... 219 F6
Bartrams La *EBAR* EN4 .... 210 E4
Barwick La *STDN* SG11 .... 101 G8
Basbow La *BSF* CM23 .... 105 J3
Basildon Av *WATW* WD18 .... 219 K8
Basildon Sq *HHNE* HP2 .... 8 C2 🔲
Basils Rd *STVG* SG1 .... 2 C3
Basing Rd *RKW/CH/CXG* WD3 .... 217 J4
Bassett Cl *STALW/RED* AL3 .... 142 A4
Bassil Rd *HHS/BOV* HP3 .... 8 A4
Bassingbourne Cl *BROX* EN10 ... 176 E5
Bassingburn Wk *WGCE* AL7 ...... 148 C3
Batchelors *STDN* SG11 .... 81 K4
Batchwood Dr *STALW/RED* AL3 .. 10 B8
Batchwood Gdns *STALW/RED* AL3 .. 10 C7
Batchwood Vw *STALW/RED* AL3 .. 10 C8

Batchworth Hill London Rd
 RKW/CH/CXG WD3 .... 228 D1
Batchworth La *NTHWD* HA6 .... 229 H4
Bateman Rd *RKW/CH/CXG* WD3 .... 219 F6
Batford Cl *WGCE* AL7 .... 148 C2 🔲
Batford Rd *HARP* AL5 .... 119 F6
Bath Rd *LTNN/LIM* LU3 .... 4 B1
Bathurst Rd *HHNE* HP2 .... 8 A2
Batterdale *BRKMPK* AL9 .... 171 H3
Battlefield Rd *STAL* AL1 .... 11 E2
Battlers Green Dr *RAD* WD7 .... 206 B7
Battleview *STALE/WH* AL4 .... 145 H1
The Baulk *LBUZ* LU7 .... 109 K2
 LBUZ LU7 .... 111 F4
 LTNE LU2 .... 53 K7
Bawdsey Cl *STVG* SG1 .... 75 C1
Bay Cl *LTNW/LEA* LU4 .... 68 A3
Bayford Cl *HERT/BAY* SG13 .... 151 F5
 HHNE HP2 .... 165 H1
Bayford Gn *HERT/BAY* SG13 .... 174 D3
Bayford La *HERT/BAY* SG13 .... 174 C1
Bayhurst Dr *NTHWD* HA6 .... 230 A5
Baylam Dell *LTNE* LU2 .... 71 F8 🔲
Baylie Cl *HHNE* HP2 .... 8 B4
Baylie La *HHNE* HP2 .... 8 B4
Bay Tree Cl *CHESW* EN7 .... 196 D5 🔲
 LCOL/BKTW AL2 .... 188 E5
Bay Tree Wk *WAT* WD17 .... 204 A8
Bayworth *STVGE* SG2 .... 42 B4
Beacon Cl *CFSP/GDCR* SL9 .... 226 B6
Beacon Rd *BERK* HP4 .... 112 B7
 WARE SG12 .... 128 C1
Beaconsfield *LTNE* LU2 .... 5 E3
Beaconsfield Rd *HAT* AL10 .... 171 H3
 PEND EN3 .... 214 C7
 STAL AL1 .... 11 D4
 TRING HP23 .... 134 D6
Beacon Wy *RKW/CH/CXG* WD3 .... 218 A7
 TRING HP23 .... 135 H4
The Beadles *RBSF* CM22 .... 133 F1 🔲
Beagle Cl *STVGE* SG2 .... 76 C3
Beale Cl *STVGE* SG2 .... 76 E3
Beamish Dr *BUSH* WD23... .... 221 K8
Beane Av *STVGE* SG2... .... 76 E3
Beane River Vw *HERT/WAS* SG14 .... 151 F3
Beane Rd *HERT/WAS* SG14... .... 98 A5
 HERT/WAS SG14 .... 150 E3
The Beaneside *HERT/WAS* SG14 .... 98 A5 🔲
Beane Wk *STVGE* SG2 .... 76 E3
Beanfield Rd *SBW* CM21 .... 131 J5
Beanley Cl *LTNE* LU2 .... 71 F7 🔲
Beard's La *SAFWS* CB11 .... 35 J5
Bear La *BLDK* SG7 .... 17 K5
Bearton Av *HTCH/STOT* SG5 .... 56 C1
Bearton Gn *HTCH/STOT* SG5 .... 40 B8
Bearton Rd *HTCH/STOT* SG5 .... 40 C8
Bearwood Cl *POTB/CUF* EN6... .... 210 E1
Beasant House Gdns
 RKW/CH/CXG WD3 .... 217 K3 🔲
Beauchamp Pl *BORE* WD6 .... 208 A7 🔲
Beaulieu Cl *OXHEY* WD19 .... 220 D8
Beaulieu Dr *WAB* EN9 .... 215 G3
Beaumayes Cl *HHW* HP1 .... 164 A7
Beaumont Av *STAL* AL1... .... 168 C5
Beaumont Ga *RAD* WD7... .... 206 D5
Beaumont Hall La *STALW/RED* AL3. 142 C4
Beaumont Park Dr
 HLWW/ROY CM19... .... 178 C3
Beaumont Rd *BROX* EN10 .... 196 D2
 LTNN/LIM LU3 .... 69 G7
Beaumont Vw *CHESW* EN7 .... 196 B4 🔲
Beazley Cl *WARE* SG12 .... 127 J7 🔲
Becket Gdns *WLYN* AL6 .... 122 C5
Beckets Sq *BERK* HP4 .... 161 H3 🔲
Becketts *HERT/WAS* SG14 .... 150 D4
Beckett's Av *STALW/RED* AL3 .... 10 B1
Beckfield La *BUNT* SG9... .... 46 A2
Beckham Cl *LTNE* LU2 .... 69 J2 🔲
Becks Cl *STALW/RED* AL3 .... 115 H4
Bedale Rd *PIN* HA5 .... 215 F8 🔲
Bede Cl *PIN* HA5 .... 230 E7 🔲
Bedford Cl *RKW/CH/CXG* WD3... .... 200 E8
Bedford Crs *PEND* EN3... .... 214 D5
Bedford Park Rd *STAL* AL1... .... 11 D4
Bedford Rd *AMP/FLIT/B* MK45 .... 36 C4
 HTCH/STOT SG5 .... 40 A2
 LWTH SG6 .... 41 H2
 NTHWD HA6 .... 229 H3
 STAL AL1 .... 11 D5
Bedford St *BERK* HP4 .... 162 A5
 WATN WD24 .... 220 C1
Bedmond La *ABLGY* WD5 .... 187 G4
 STALW/RED AL3 .... 167 G8
Bedmond Rd *ABLGY* WD5 .... 187 F7
 HHS/BOV HP3 .... 165 J8
Bedwell Av *BRKMPK* AL9 .... 173 H4
 HERT/BAY SG13 .... 173 H2
Bedwell Cl *WGCE* AL7 .... 147 K4
Bedwell Crs *STVG* SG1 .... 3 D3
Bedwell Ri *STVG* SG1 .... 2 C3
Beech Av *ENC/FH* EN2 .... 212 D5
 RAD WD7 .... 206 D3
Beech Bottom *STALW/RED* AL3 .... 10 C1

Beech Cl *HARP* AL5 .... 143 K4
 HAT AL10 .... 171 F5
Beech Ct *BERK* HP4. .... 162 A4
Beech Crs *STALW/WH* AL4 .... 145 G2
Beechcroft *BERK* HP4 .... 161 K6
Beechcroft Av *RKW/CH/CXG* WD3 .... 219 H6
Beechcroft Rd *BUSH* WD23 .... 13 F4
Beech Dr *BERK* HP4 .... 161 K6
 BORE WD6... .... 223 J2
 SBW CM21 .... 157 F1
 STVGE SG2 .... 3 F5
Beechen Gv *WAT* WD17 .... 12 C2
The Beeches *HTCHE/RSTV* SG4 .... 56 E3
 LCOL/BKTW AL2 .... 189 F5 🔲
 RKW/CH/CXG WD3 .... 217 J5
 TRING HP23 .... 135 H5 🔲
Beech Farm Dr *STALE/WH* AL4 .... 169 J4
Beechfield *HOD* EN11... .... 153 F7
 SBW CM21 .... 132 C7
Beechfield Cl *STALW/RED* AL3 .... 142 C4 🔲
Beechfield Rd *HHW* HP1 .... 164 A7
 WARE SG12 .... 127 K7
 WGCE AL7 .... 147 K5
Beechfield Wk *WAB* EN9 .... 215 J5
Beech Gv HI *EBAR* EN4... .... 210 E8
 LTNE LU2 .... 70 D2
 LWTH SG6 .... 41 H2
Beech Hyde La *STALE/WH* AL4 .... 145 J2
Beeching Cl *HARP* AL5 .... 118 C5
Beechlands *BSF* CM23 .... 105 J4
Beech Ms *WARE* SG12 .... 152 C2
Beechpark Wy *WAT* WD17 .... 203 K7
Beech Pl *STALW/RED* AL3 .... 10 C1 🔲
 WATN WD24 .... 204 B3
Beechtree La *STALW/RED* AL3. .... 166 C8
Beech Wy *STALE/WH* AL4. .... 119 K3
Beechwood Av *POTB/CUF* EN6... .... 210 C3
 RKW/CH/CXG WD3 .... 216 E4
 STAL AL1 .... 168 E4
Beechwood Cl *BLDK* SG7 .... 43 F4
 CHESW EN7 .... 196 C4 🔲
 HERT/BAY SG13 .... 151 J3 🔲
 HTCH/STOT SG5 .... 40 B7
Beechwood Dr *TRING* HP23 .... 136 E4 🔲
Beechwood Pk *HHS/BOV* HP3 .... 184 D2
 RKW/CH/CXG WD3 .... 217 J4
Beechwood Ri *WATN* WD24 .... 204 C6
Beechwood Rd *LTNW/LEA* LU4 .... 68 D3
Beecroft La *STVGE* SG2 .... 60 D7
Beehive Cl *BORE* WD6... .... 223 G6
Beehive Gn *WGCE* AL7 .... 148 B5
Beehive La *WGCE* AL7 .... 148 B6 🔲
Beehive Rd *CHESW* EN7 .... 195 K6
Beesonend La *HARP* AL5 .... 143 G6
 STALW/RED AL3 .... 142 E7
Beeston Cl *OXHEY* WD19 .... 230 E3
Beeston Dr *CHES/WCR* EN8... .... 197 H5
Beethoven Rd *BORE* WD6 .... 223 F7
Beeton Cl *PIN* HA5 .... 231 H6 🔲
Beggarman's La *STDN* SG11 .... 100 C1
Beggars Bush La *WATW* WD18 .... 219 J5
Beggars La *TRING* HP23 .... 136 A5
Belcher Rd *HOD* EN11 .... 177 F2 🔲
Belchers La *WAB* EN9 .... 199 J2
Beldam Av *ROY* SG8 .... 21 H4
Beldams La *BSF* CM23 .... 106 A4
Belfairs *OXHEY* WD19 .... 230 E4
Belford Rd *BORE* WD6 .... 207 J8
Belfry Av *DEN/HRF* UB9 .... 227 K7
The Belfry *LTNE* LU2 .... 69 K3
Belgrave Cl *STALE/WH* AL4 .... 169 F2 🔲
Belgrave Rd *LTNW/LEA* LU4 .... 68 C4
Belham Rd *KGLCY* WD4 .... 185 K6
Bell Acre *LWTH* SG6 .... 42 B5
Bell Acre Gdns *LWTH* SG6 .... 42 B5
Bellamy Cl *KNEB* SG3 .... 96 A4
 WAT WD17 .... 220 B1
Bellamy Rd *CHES/WCR* EN8... .... 197 J7
Bell Cl *ABLGY* WD5 .... 187 F5
 HTCHE/RSTV SG4 .... 57 F5
 KNEB SG3... .... 96 B4
Bellerby Ri *LTNW/LEA* LU4 .... 68 A3
Belle Vue La *BUSH* WD23 .... 222 A8
Belle Vue Rd *WARE* SG12 .... 127 K8 🔲
Bellfields Gdns *HLWE* CM17 .... 181 F7
Bell La *ABLGY* WD5 .... 187 G5
 BERK HP4 .... 161 F4
 BRKMPK AL9 .... 193 G2
 BROX EN10 .... 176 D7
 HERT/WAS SG14 .... 151 G3 🔲
 HOD EN11 .... 177 F3
 LCOL/BKTW AL2 .... 190 C7
 PEND EN3 .... 214 C8
 ROY SG8 .... 33 H7
 STVG SG1 .... 2 A1
 WARE SG12 .... 129 K5
Bell Md *SBW* CM21 .... 132 C7
Bellmount Wood Av *WAT* WD17 .... 219 K1
The Bell Rbt *LCOL/BKTW* AL2... .... 190 E5
Bell Rw *BLDK* SG7 .... 42 E1 🔲
Bells Hl *BAR* EN5 .... 225 J5

 BSF CM23 .... 105 H2
Bells Meadow *ROY* SG8 .... 15 H4
Bell St *SBW* CM21 .... 132 C7
Bell Vw *STALE/WH* AL4 .... 169 G6
Belmer Rd *STSD* CM24 .... 87 J5
Belmers Rd *TRING* HP23 .... 135 J8 🔲
Belmont Hl *STAL* AL1... .... 10 C5
Belmont Rd *BUSH* WD23 .... 13 F3
 HHS/BOV HP3 .... 185 J1
 LTN LU1 .... 4 A4
Belmor *BORE* WD6 .... 223 K5
Belper Rd *LTNW/LEA* LU4 .... 68 D7
Belsize Cl *HHS/BOV* HP3 .... 9 D6
 STALE/WH AL4 .... 169 F1
Belsize Rd *HHS/BOV* HP3 .... 9 D6
Belswains La *HHS/BOV* HP3 .... 185 J2
Beltona Gdns *CHES/WCR* EN8... .... 197 H5
Belton Rd *BERK* HP4 .... 161 H4
Belvedere Gdns *LCOL/BKTW* AL2 .... 188 B5
Belvedere Rd *LTNN/LIM* LU3 .... 69 G4 🔲
Bembridge Gdns *LTNN/LIM* LU3 .... 68 E2
Ben Austins *STALW/RED* AL3 .... 142 D5
Benbow Cl *STAL* AL1 .... 168 E8
Benchley Hl *HTCHE/RSTV* SG4 .... 57 C1
Benchleys Rd *HHW* HP1 .... 163 J7
Bencroft *CHESW* EN7 .... 196 E4
Bencroft Rd *HHNE* HP2 .... 8 B5
Bendish La *HTCHE/RSTV* SG4 .... 93 C2
Bendysh Rd *BUSH* WD23 .... 13 F2
Benford Rd *HOD* EN11 .... 176 E5
Bengeo St *HERT/WAS* SG14 .... 151 F2
Benhooks Av *BSF* CM23 .... 105 H4
Benington Cl *LTNE* LU2 .... 70 A4
Benington Rd *STVGE* SG2 .... 77 C7
Bennett Cl *BRKMPK* AL9 .... 148 A7
 NTHWD HA6 .... 230 A6
Bennett Ct *LWTH* SG6 .... 42 A4
Bennetts Cl *STALE/WH* AL4 .... 191 H1 🔲
Bennetts End Cl *HHS/BOV* HP3 .... 164 E3 🔲
Bennetts End Rd *HHS/BOV* HP3 .... 8 C6
Benningfield *WARE* SG12 .... 129 K4
Benningfield Rd *WARE* SG12 .... 19 K5
Benskin Rd *WATW* WD18 .... 12 B4
Benskins Cl *BSF* CM23... .... 67 J1
Benslow La *HTCHE/RSTV* SG4 .... 56 E2
Benslow Ri *HTCHE/RSTV* SG4 .... 56 E2
Benson Cl *LTNN/LIM* LU3 .... 68 E2
Benstede *STVGE* SG2. .... 96 D1
Bentfield End Cswy *STSD* CM24 .... 86 C2
Bentfield Gdns *STSD* CM24 .... 86 C2
Bentfield Rd *STSD* CM24 .... 86 C2
Bentick Wy *HTCHE/RSTV* SG4 .... 94 E7
Bentley Cl *BSF* CM23. .... 105 J4
Bentley Dr *HLWE* CM17 .... 181 F2
Bentley Heath La *BAR* EN5 .... 209 K5
Bentley Rd *HERT/WAS* SG14 .... 150 B2
Benton Rd *OXHEY* WD19 .... 230 E4
Bentsley Cl *STALW/RED* AL3 .... 168 E2
Berceau Wk *WAT* WD17 .... 219 K1
Berecroft *HLWS* CM18 .... 180 A6 🔲
Berefield *HHNE* HP2. .... 8 A3
Beresford Rd *LTNW/LEA* LU4 .... 69 F8
 RKW/CH/CXG WD3 .... 217 J8
 STAL AL1 .... 169 F7
Bericot Wy *WGCE* AL7 .... 148 D3 🔲
Berkeley *LWTH* SG6 .... 42 A5
Berkeley Cl *ABGLY* WD5 .... 204 A2
 BORE WD6. .... 223 K5
 POTB/CUF EN6 .... 209 K2
 STVGE SG2 .... 96 B1
 WARE SG12 .... 127 G7
Berkeley Sq *HHNE* HP2. .... 141 H8
Berkhamsted La *HERT/BAY* SG13 .... 173 J6
Berkhamsted Rd *HHW* HP1 .... 163 J4
Berkley Av *CHES/WCR* EN8 .... 214 C4
Berkley Cl *STALE/WH* AL4 .... 169 F2
Berks Hl *RKW/CH/CXG* WD3 .... 217 F5
Bermer Rd *WATN* WD24 .... 220 D1
Bernard Gv *WAB* EN9 .... 215 G3 🔲
Bernard St *STALW/RED* AL3 .... 10 C3
Berners Dr *STAL* AL1 .... 189 F1
Berners Wy *BROX* EN10 .... 197 K1
Bernhardt Crs *STVGE* SG2 .... 76 D3
The Berries *STALE/WH* AL4 .... 168 D2 🔲
Berrow Cl *LTNE* LU2 .... 71 F7 🔲
Berry Av *WATN* WD24 .... 204 C6
Berry Cl *RKW/CH/CXG* WD3 .... 218 A7
Berryfield *LBUZ* LU7 .... 109 K2 🔲
Berry Grove La *BUSH* WD23 .... 205 F8
Berrygrove La *GSTN* WD25 .... 221 H1
Berry La *RKW/CH/CXG* WD3 .... 217 G6
 RKW/CH/CXG WD3 .... 218 A3
Berry Leys *LTNN/LIM* LU3. .... 68 D2
Berrymead *HHNE* HP2 .... 8 C3
Berry Wy *RKW/CH/CXG* WD3 .... 218 A7
Berwick Cl *CHES/WCR* EN8 .... 215 F4 🔲
 STVG SG1 .... 75 F1
Berwick Rd *BORE* WD6. .... 207 J8
Besford Cl *LTNE* LU2 .... 70 E7
Bessemer Cl *HTCH/STOT* SG5. .... 40 C7
Bessemer Dr *STVG* SG1 .... 75 C5
Bessemer Rd *WGCE* AL7 .... 148 A1
 WGCW AL8 .... 122 E7
Bethune Cl *LTN* LU1 .... 89 G3
Betjeman Cl *CHESW* EN7 .... 196 E6 🔲

Betjeman Wy *HHW* HP1 .... 164 A4
Betony V *ROY* SG8 .... 21 J4
Bettespol Mdw *STALW/RED* AL3 ...... 142 B3
Betts La *WAB* EN9 .... 178 D7
Betty's La *TRING* HP23 .... 135 F5
Bevan Cl *HHS/BOV* HP3 .... 164 C8
Bevan House *WATN* WD24 .... 13 E1
Beverley Cl *ROY* SG8 .... 21 F1
Beverley Gdns *CHESW* EN7 .... 213 J1
STALW/RED AL4 .... 169 G2
WGCE AL7 .... 148 D3
Beverley Rd *LTNW/LEA* LU4 .... 68 E3
STVG SG1 .... 59 H7
Beverly Cl *BROX* EN10 .... 176 D7
Bewdley Cl *HARP* AL5 .... 144 A3
Bewley Chr *POTB/CUF* EN6 .... 214 C1
Bexhill Rd *LTNE* LU2 .... 70 E7
Beyers Gdns *HOD* EN11 .... 153 F8
Beyers Prospect *HOD* EN11 .... 153 F8
Beyers Ride *HOD* EN11 .... 153 F8
Bibbs Hall La *HTCHE/RSTV* SG4 .... 120 C3
Biddenham Turn *CSTN* WD25 ...... 204 D5
Bideford Gdns *LTNN/LIM* LU3 ...... 69 J5
Bideford Rd *PEND* EN3 .... 214 E8
Bidwell Cl *LWTH* SG6 .... 42 B4
Biggin Hl *BUNT* SG9 .... 48 D2
Biggin La *HTCH/STOT* SG5 .... 56 C2
Bignells Cnr *POTB/CUF* EN6 .... 209 G4
Billet La *BERK* HP4 .... 161 H3
Billy Lows La *POTB/CUF* EN6 ...... 210 C1
Bilton Rd *HTCHE/RSTV* SG4 .... 40 D7
Bilton Wy *LTN* LU1 .... 68 E8
LTN LU1 .... 88 E1
Bingen Rd *HTCH/STOT* SG5 .... 40 A8
Bingley Rd *HOD* EN11 .... 177 H3
Binham Cl *LTNE* LU2 .... 69 J2
Birchall La *HERT/WAS* SG14 .... 149 F5
Birchalls *STSD* CM24 .... 86 D1
Birchall Wd *WGCE* AL7 .... 148 D2
Birchanger La *BSF* CM23 .... 86 A1
Birch Copse *LCOL/BKTW* AL2 ...... 188 A3
Birch Dr *HAT* AL10 .... 171 F5
RKW/CH/CXG WD3 .... 227 G4
Birchen Gv *LTNE* LU2 .... 70 A6
Bircherley Ct *HERT/WAS* SG14 .... 151 G3
Bircherley St *HERT/WAS* SG14 ... 151 G3
The Birches *BUSH* WD23 .... 221 K5
HHS/BOV HP3 .... 184 D1
LWTH SG6 .... 41 J1
WLYN AL6 .... 121 K1
Birchfield Rd *CHES/WCR* EN8 ...... 197 F7
Birch Gn *HHW* HP1 .... 163 J5
Birch Gv *POTB/CUF* EN6 .... 210 B3
WLYN AL6 .... 122 E1
Birch La *HHS/BOV* HP3 .... 200 E3
Birch Leys *HHNE* HP2 .... 165 H1
Birch Link *LTNW/LEA* LU4 .... 4 A2
Birchmead *WAT* WD17 .... 204 A8
Birchmead Cl *STALW/RED* AL3 ..... 10 C1
Birch Pk *KTN/HRWW/W* HA3 .... 231 K6
KNEB SG3 .... 96 C8
Birch Tree Gv *CSHM* HP5 .... 182 D8
Birch Tree Wk *WAT* WD17 .... 204 A7
Birch Wy *HARP* AL5 .... 143 K1
Birchway *HAT* AL10 .... 171 F2
Birch Wy *LCOL/BKTW* AL2 .... 190 B5
Birchwood *BSF* CM23 .... 86 C7
RAD WD7 .... 207 K4
Birchwood Av *HAT* AL10 .... 171 F2
Birchwood Cl *HAT* AL10 .... 171 F2
Birchwood Wy *LCOL/BKTW* AL2 .... 188 D6
Birdcroft Rd *WGCW* AL8 .... 147 J4
Birdie Wy *HERT/BAY* SG13 .... 152 A2
Birds Cl *WGCE* AL7 .... 148 C5
Birdsfoot La *LTNN/LIM* LU3 .... 69 J5
Birds Hl *LWTH* SG6 .... 42 A3
Birkbeck Rd *ENC/FH* EN2 .... 213 G8
Birkdale Gdns *OXHEY* WD19 .... 230 E2
Birkett Wy *CSTG* HP8 .... 216 A3
Birklands La *STAL* AL1 .... 189 K2
Birling Dr *LTNE* LU2 .... 70 C7
Birstal Gn *OXHEY* WD19 .... 230 E3
Birtley Cft *LTNE* LU2 .... 71 F8
Biscot Rd *LTNN/LIM* LU3 .... 4 A1
Bishops Av *BORE* WD6 .... 223 J5
BSF CM23 .... 105 J6
NTHWD HA6 .... 229 K3
Bishops Cl *BAR* EN5 .... 225 J6
HAT AL10 .... 170 E4
STALE/WH AL4 .... 168 D2
Bishopscote Rd *LTNN/LIM* LU3 ... 69 G6
Bishopsfield *HLWS* CM18 .... 180 A4
Bishops Md *HHW* HP1 .... 164 A8
Bishops Park Wy *BSF* CM23 .... 104 C2
Bishops Ri *HAT* AL10 .... 170 E5
Bishops Rd *WLYN* AL6 .... 123 K3
Biskra *WAT* WD17 .... 220 B1
Bisley Cl *CHES/WCR* EN8 .... 214 C1
Bittern Cl *CHESW* EN7 .... 195 K3
STVGE SG2 .... 76 C3
Bittern Wy *LWTH* SG6 .... 25 J8
The Bit *TRING* HP23 .... 135 J8
Blackberry Md *STVGE* SG2 .... 76 E6
Blackbirds La *CSTN* WD25 .... 205 K4

Black Boy Wd *LCOL/BKTW* AL2 ..... 188 C8
Blackbury Cl *POTB/CUF* EN6 .... 210 D1
Blackbushe *BSF* CM23 .... 86 B8
Blackbush Spring *HLW* CM20 ...... 7 F3
Black Cut *STAL* AL1 .... 11 D5
Blackdale *CHESW* EN7 .... 196 E5
Black Ditch Rd *WAB* EN9 .... 215 H6
Black Ditch Wy *WAB* EN9 .... 215 G6
Blacketts Wood Dr
RKW/CH/CXG WD3 ....⋯........ 216 E4
Black Fan Rd *WGCE* AL7 .... 148 A2
Blackford Rd *OXHEY* WD19 .... 230 E4
Blackhorse La *HTCHE/RSTV* SG4 ... 56 E4
Blackhorse La *HTCHE/RSTV* SG4 ... 56 E5
POTB/CUF EN6 .... 191 H8
STALW/RED AL3 .... 142 B3
Blackhorse Rd *LWTH* SG6 .... 42 C1
Blackley Cl *WAT* WD17 .... 204 A7
Black Lion Ct *HLWE* CM17 .... 157 F5
Black Lion Hl *RAD* WD7 .... 207 H2
Blackmoor La *WATW* WD18 .... 219 J5
Blackmore *LWTH* SG6 .... 42 B6
Blackmore Wy *STALW/WH* AL4 ..... 119 K3
Blacksmiths Cl *WARE* SG12 .... 153 F2
Blacksmiths Hl *STVGE* SG2 .... 78 B5
Blacksmith's La *ROY* SG8 .... 31 H4
STALW/RED AL3 .... 10 A4
Blacksmiths Wy *SBW* CM21 .... 131 K8
Black Swan La *LTNN/LIM* LU3 ..... 69 F4
Blackthorn Cl *GSTN* WD25 .... 204 C2
STALE/WH AL4 .... 169 F3
Blackthorn Dr *LTNE* LU2 .... 70 D5
Blackthorne Cl *HAT* AL10 .... 170 E7
Blackthorn Rd *WGCE* AL7 .... 148 B4
Blackwater La *HHS/BOV* HP3 ...... 186 E1
Blackwell Dr *OXHEY* WD19 .... 13 D5
Blackwell Rd *KGLGY* WD4 .... 186 A7
Bladon Cl *HTCHE/RSTV* SG4 .... 57 K6
Blair Cl *BSF* CM23 .... 105 F2
HHNE HP2 .... 141 C8
STVGE SG2 .... 76 A8
Blairhead Dr *OXHEY* WD19 .... 230 C2
Blake Cl *STAL* AL1 .... 189 J1
Blakelands *AMP/FLIT/B* MK45 ..... 36 D7
Blakemere Rd *WGCW* AL8 .... 147 J3
Blakemore End Rd
HTCHE/RSTV SG4 .... 57 H6
Blakeney Dr *LTNE* LU2 .... 69 H2
Blakeney Rd *STVG* SG1 .... 75 F2
Blakes Wy *WLYN* AL6 .... 122 C3
Blanche La *POTB/CUF* EN6 .... 208 E4
Blandford Av *LTNE* LU2 .... 69 J3
Blandford Rd *STAL* AL1 .... 11 F3
The Blanes *WARE* SG12 .... 127 G6
Blattner Cl *BORE* WD6 .... 223 H4
Blaydon Rd *LTNE* LU2 .... 5 E3
Blenheim Cl *OXHEY* WD19 .... 13 D6
SBW CM21 .... 156 A1
Blenheim Ct *BSF* CM23 .... 105 F2
WGCE AL7 .... 148 A3
Blenheim Crs *LTNN/LIM* LU3 ...... 4 A1
Blenheim Rd *BAR* EN5 .... 225 J3
STAL AL1 .... 11 E3
Blenheim Wy *KNEB* SG3 .... 96 D3
Blenheim Rd *STALW/RED* AL3 ..... 204 B3
Blenkin Cl *STALW/RED* AL3 .... 167 K2
Blind La *STVGE* SG2 .... 61 H4
Blindman's La *CHES/WCR* EN8 .... 197 H8
Bloomfield Av *LTNE* LU2 .... 5 E2
Bloomfield Rd *CHESW* EN7 .... 196 A3
HARP AL5 .... 118 B6
Bluebell Cl *HERT/BAY* SG13 .... 151 K3
HHW HP1 .... 163 H7
CHESW EN7 .... 196 B6
Bluebell Dr *ABLGY* WD5 .... 187 F5
Bluebells *WLYN* AL6 .... 122 E2
Bluebell Wood Cl *LTN* LU1 .... 88 E2
Blueberry Cl *STALW/RED* AL3 ..... 168 A2
Bluebridge Av *BRKMPK* AL9 ...... 192 E5
Blue Bridge Rd *BRKMPK* AL9 ..... 192 E5
Bluecoats Av *HERT/WAS* SG14 .... 151 G3
Bluecoat Yd *WARE* SG12 .... 127 H8
Bluehouse Hill
  Hemel Hempstead Rd
    STALW/RED AL3 .... 167 H7
Bluett Rd *LCOL/BKTW* AL2 .... 190 B5
Blundell Cl *STALW/RED* AL3 .... 168 A2
Blundell Rd *LTNN/LIM* LU3 .... 69 F6
Blunesfield *POTB/CUF* EN6 .... 210 E1
Blunts La *LCOL/BKTW* AL2 .... 187 K2
Blyth Cl *BORE* WD6 .... 223 J1
STVG SG1 .... 75 F2
Blythe Rd *HOD* EN11 .... 177 J5
Blythway *WGCE* AL7 .... 123 F8
Blythwood Gdns *STSD* CM24 ...... 86 C3
Blythwood Rd *PIN* HA5 .... 230 K1
Boardman Cl *BAR* EN5 .... 225 K5
Bockings *STVGE* SG2 .... 60 E8
Bodmin Rd *LTNW/LEA* LU4 .... 68 E5
Bodwell Cl *HHW* HP1 .... 163 K5
Bogmoor Rd *ROY* SG8 .... 33 F3
Bognor Gdns *OXHEY* WD19 .... 230 D4
Bogs Gap La *ROY* SG8 .... 15 J6
Bohemia *HHNE* HP2 .... 8 B4

Boissy Cl *STALE/WH* AL4 .... 169 H
Boleyn Cl *HHNE* HP2 .... 165 H
Boleyn Ct *BROX* EN10 .... 176 D
Boleyn Dr *STAL* AL1 .... 10 C
Bolingbroke Rd *LTN* LU1 .... 89 G
Bolingbrook *STALE/WH* AL4 .... 168 D2
Bolney Gn *LTNE* LU2 .... 70 E6
Bolton Rd *LTN* LU1 .... 5 D
Boniface Gdns
  KTN/HRWW/W HA3 231
Boniface Wk *KTN/HRWW/W* HA3 ... 231
Bonks Hl *SBW* CM21 .... 132 B
Bonneting La *BSF* CM23 .... 67 K
Bonney Gv *CHESW* EN7 .... 196 E
Bonnick Cl *LTN* LU1 .... 4 A
Booths Cl *BRKMPK* AL9 .... 192 D
Bornedene *POTB/CUF* EN6 .... 209 K
Borough Wy *POTB/CUF* EN6 .... 209 K
Borrell Cl *BROX* EN10 .... 176 D
Bosanquet Rd *HOD* EN11 .... 177 H1
Bosmore Rd *LTNN/LIM* LU3 .... 68 E
Boswell Cl *RAD* WD7 .... 207 H
Boswell Dr *HTCH/STOT* SG5 .... 40 C
Boswell Gdns *STVG* SG1 .... 58 E
Boswick La *BERK* HP4 .... 160 E
Botley La *CSHM* HP5 .... 182 C
Botley Rd *CSHM* HP5 .... 182 A
HHNE HP2 .... 165 F
Bottom House La *TRING* HP23 .... 136 B
Bottom La *KGLGY* WD4 .... 202 E
Bottom Rd *TRING* HP23 .... 158 E
The Boulevard *WATW* WD18 219
WGCE AL7 .... 148 A
Boulton Rd *STVG* SG1 59
The Bounce *HHNE* HP2 .... 8 A3
Boundary Dr *HERT/WAS* SG14 .... 151 C
Boundary La *WGCE* AL7 .... 147 K
Boundary Rd *BSF* CM23 .... 105 A
STAL AL1 .... 11 C
Boundary Wy *GSTN* WD25 .... 204 C
HHNE HP2 .... 9 F
Bourne Cl *BROX* EN10 .... 176 D
WARE SG12 .... 127 H7
Bourne End La *HHW* HP1 .... 163 F
Bourne End Rd *NTHWD* HA6 ...... 229 K3
Bournehall Av *BUSH* WD23 .... 221 J
Bournehall La *BUSH* WD23 .... 221 J
Bournehall Rd *BUSH* WD23 .... 221 J
Bourne Honour *WARE* SG12 .... 126 C
Bournemouth Rd *STVG* SG1 .... 75 G1
Bourne Rd *BERK* HP4 .... 161 G
BUSH WD23 .... 221 J
The Bourne *BSF* CM23 .... 106 A
HHW HP1 183
WARE SG12 .... 127 F
Bouvier Rd *PEND* EN3 .... 214 E
Bovingdon Crs *GSTN* WD25 .... 204 C
Bovingdon Green La
  HHS/BOV HP3 183
Bow Br *STALW/RED* AL3 .... 167 F
Bowbrook V *LTNE* LU2 .... 71 C
Bowcock Wk *STVG* SG1 .... 2 C5
Bower Heath La *HARP* AL5 .... 118 C
Bowershott *LWTH* SG6 .... 42 A
Bowers Wy *HARP* AL5 .... 118 C
Bowes Lyon Ms *STALW/RED* AL3 ... 10 C4
Bowgate *STAL* AL1 .... 11 J
Bowlers Md *BUNT* SG9 .... 63 H
Bowling Cl *BSF* CM23 .... 105 J3
HARP AL5 143
Bowling Gn *STVG* SG1 .... 75 H1
Bowling Green La *BUNT* SG9 ...... 63 J
LTNE LU2 .... 4 C
Bowling Rd *WARE* SG12 .... 127 J
Bowmans Av *HTCHE/RSTV* SG4 ... 57 J
Bowmans Cl *POTB/CUF* EN6 .... 210 A
WLYN AL6 .... 122 A
Bowmans Ct *HHNE* HP2 .... 8 B
Bowmans Gn *GSTN* WD25 .... 205 J
Bowring Gn *OXHEY* WD19 .... 230 C
Bowyers *HHNE* HP2 .... 8 A
Bowyer's Cl *HTCH/STOT* SG5 ..... 40 B
Boxberry Cl *STAL* AL1 .... 148 D
Boxfield *WGCE* AL7 148
Boxfield Gn *STVGE* SG2 .... 76 D
Boxgrove Cl *LTNE* LU2 .... 70 D
Boxhill *HHNE* HP2 .... 8 A3
Box La *HHW* HP1 184
HOD EN11 176
Boxted Cl *LTNW/LEA* LU4 .... 68 D
Boxted Rd *HHW* HP1 .... 163 K
Boxtree La *KTN/HRWW/W* HA3 ... 231
Boxwell Rd *BERK* HP4 .... 161 J3
Boyce Cl *BORE* WD6 .... 223 K
Boyd Cl *BSF* CM23 .... 106 A
Boyle Cl *LTNE* LU2 .... 4 C
Braceby Cl *LTNN/LIM* LU3 .... 68 E
Brace Cl *CHESW* EN7 .... 195 G
Brache *STALW/RED* AL3 .... 142 D
Brackendale *POTB/CUF* EN6 ...... 210 C
Brackendale Gv *HARP* AL5 .... 117 K
LTNN/LIM LU3 .... 69 J
Brackendene *LCOL/BKTW* AL2 ... 188 E

Bracken Hl *BERK* HP4 .... 162 B4
Bracken La *WLYN* AL6 .... 123 F2
The Brackens *HHNE* HP2 .... 8 A4 🔲
Bracklesham Gdns *LTNE* LU2 ...... 70 E6
Bracknell Pl *HHNE* HP2 .... 8 C1
Bradbury *RKW/CH/CXG* WD3 ...... 227 G4
Bradbury Cl *BORE* WD6 .... 224 A1
Bradden La *HHNE* HP2 .... 139 H2
Bradford Rd *RKW/CH/CXG* WD3 ... 217 F7
Bradford St *HTCH/STOT* SG5 ...... 56 B2
Bradgate *POTB/CUF* EN6 .... 195 F5
Bradgate Cl *POTB/CUF* EN6 .... 195 F6
Bradgers Hill *LTNE* LU2 .... 69 K5
Bradley Common *BSF* CM23 .... 86 B6
Bradley Rd *LTNW/LEA* LU4 .... 68 C8
   PEND EN3 .... 214 D8
Bradleys Cnr *HTCHE/RSTV* SG4 .... 57 G1
Bradman Wy *STVG* SG1 .... 59 G8
Bradmore Gn *BRKMPK* AL9 .... 192 E4
Bradmore La *BRKMPK* AL9 .... 192 D4
Bradmore Wy *BRKMPK* AL9 .... 192 E4
Bradshaw Rd *WATN* WD24 .... 220 D1
Bradshaws Hl *HAT* AL10 .... 170 E8
Bradway *HTCHE/RSTV* SG4 .... 93 H3
Braemar Cl *KNEB* SG3 .... 96 C2
Braeside Cl *PIN* HA5 .... 231 H6 🔲
Brain Cl *HAT* AL10 .... 171 G3 🔲
Brakynbery *BERK* HP4 .... 161 F2
Brallings La *CFSP/GDCR* SL9 ...... 226 D3
Bramble Cl *CFSP/GDCR* SL9 .... 226 B5 🔲
   CSTN WD25 .... 204 B4
   HARP AL5 .... 118 B6 🔲
   LTNW/LEA LU4 .... 68 B5
Bramble Ri *HLW* CM20 .... 6 B3
Bramble Rd *HAT* AL10 .... 170 B5
   LTNW/LEA LU4 .... 68 B5
The Brambles *BSF* CM23 .... 105 F4
   CHES/WCR EN8 .... 214 C1
   ROY SG8 .... 21 J4
   STAL AL1 .... 10 C6
   STVG SG1 .... 58 D7
   WARE SG12 .... 127 G6 🔲
   WLYN AL6 .... 122 E1 🔲
Brambling Cl *BUSH* WD23 .... 13 F5 🔲
Brambling Ri *HHNE* HP2 .... 8 B2
Bramfield *CSTN* WD25 .... 205 F4
   HTCHE/RSTV SG4 .... 57 F3 🔲
Bramfield La *HERT/WAS* SG14 ...... 125 G6
Bramfield Pl *HHNE* HP2 .... 141 F8
Bramfield Rd *HERT/WAS* SG14 .... 150 B1
   KNEB SG3 .... 96 E8
Bramhanger Acre *LTNN/LIM* LU3 .. 68 C2
Bramingham Rd *LTNN/LIM* LU3 .... 69 F2
Bramleas *WATW* WD18 .... 12 A4
Bramley Cl *BLDK* SG7 .... 27 F8 🔲
Bramley Ct *CSTN* WD25 .... 204 C2 🔲
Bramley Gdns *OXHEY* WD19 ...... 230 D5
Bramley Wy *STALE/WH* AL4 .... 119 F7
Brampton *CHESW* EN7 .... 196 E6
   HARP AL5 .... 118 C8
Brampton Park Rd *HTCH/STOT* SG5 .. 40 F5
Brampton Rd *OXHEY* WD19 .... 230 B2
   ROY SG8 .... 21 K3
   STAL AL1 .... 11 F3
Brampton Ter *BORE* WD6 .... 207 K8 🔲
Bramshaw Gdns *OXHEY* WD19 .... 230 E4
Bramshott La *HTCHE/RSTV* SG4 .... 56 D5
Branch Cl *HAT* AL10 .... 171 H2
Branch Rd *LCOL/BKTW* AL2 .... 189 F5
   STALW/RED AL3 .... 10 A3
Brandles Rd *LWTH* SG6 .... 42 A6
Brandon Cl *CHESW* EN7 .... 196 C4
Brand St *HTCH/STOT* SG5 .... 56 C2
Branksome Ave *HHNE* HP2 .... 9 D4
Branton Cl *LTNE* LU2 .... 71 F7 🔲
Brantwood Rd *LTN* LU1 .... 4 A4
Bray Cl *BORE* WD6 .... 224 B1
Brayes Mnr *HTCH/STOT* SG5 ...... 25 K3
Brays Md *CSHM* HP5 .... 7 E6
Brays Rd *LTNE* LU2 .... 70 C6
Brazier Cl *AMP/FLIT/B* MK45 ...... 36 B6
Braziers End *CSHM* HP5 .... 159 H7
Braziers Fld *HERT/BAY* SG13 ...... 151 J3 🔲
Braziers Quay *BSF* CM23 .... 105 J3
Bread And Cheese La *BROX* EN10 .. 196 C2
Breadcroft La *HARP* AL5 .... 118 D7
Breakmead *WCCE* AL7 .... 148 C5 🔲
Breakspear *STVG* SG2 .... 76 D6
Breakspear Av *STAL* AL1 .... 11 E5
Breakspear Ct *ABLGY* WD5 .... 187 F5
Breakspeare Rd *WATN* WD24 ...... 204 C8
Breakspeare Rd *ABLGY* WD5 ...... 203 K1
Breakspear Wy *HHNE* HP2 .... 9 F5
Breaks Rd *HAT* AL10 .... 171 G3 🔲
Brecken Cl *STALE/WH* AL4 .... 168 D2
Brecon Cl *LTN* LU1 .... 4 B5 🔲
Brendon Av *LTNE* LU2 .... 70 D8
Brett Pl *WATN* WD24 .... 204 B7
Brett Rd *BAR* EN5 .... 225 H5
Bretts Md *LTN* LU1 .... 4 A6

Brewers Cl *BSF* CM23 .... 105 F4
Brewery La *BLDK* SG7 .... 26 E8 🔲
   STSD CM24 .... 86 D2
Brewery Rd *HOD* EN11 .... 177 F3
Brewhouse Hl *STALE/WH* AL4 ...... 145 F1
Brewhouse La *HERT/WAS* SG14 .... 151 F3 🔲
Briants Cl *PIN* HA5 .... 231 F7
Briarcliff *HHW* HP1 .... 163 H5 🔲
Briar Cl *BERK* HP4 .... 162 D2
   CHES/WCR EN8 .... 197 G7
   LTNE LU2 .... 70 D5
Briardale *STVG* SG1 .... 2 C4
   WARE SG12 .... 127 G6
Briarley Cl *BROX* EN10 .... 176 E8
Briar Patch La *LWTH* SG6 .... 41 H6
Briar Rd *CSTN* WD25 .... 204 B4
   STALE/WH AL4 .... 169 F3
Briars Cl *HAT* AL10 .... 171 F4
Briars La *HAT* AL10 .... 171 F4
The Briars *CHES/WCR* EN8 .... 214 D1
   HERT/BAY SG13 .... 151 K3
   HLWS CM18 .... 180 A5 🔲
   RKW/CH/CXG WD3 .... 201 K6
Briars Wd *HAT* AL10 .... 171 F4
Briar Wy *BERK* HP4 .... 161 K6
Briarwood Dr *NTHWD* HA6 .... 230 B8
Briary La *ROY* SG8 .... 21 G4
Briary Wood End *WLYN* AL6 .... 123 F1
Briary Wood La *WLYN* AL6 .... 123 F1
Brickcroft *BROX* EN10 .... 197 J4 🔲
Brickendon La *HERT/BAY* SG13 .... 151 F6
   HERT/BAY SG13 .... 175 G4
Bricket Rd *STAL* AL1 .... 11 D4
Brickfield *HAT* AL10 .... 171 F1
Brickfield Av *HHS/BOV* HP3 .... 9 E6
Brickfield La *BAR* EN5 .... 224 E6
The Brickfields *WARE* SG12 ...... 127 F7
Brick Kiln Cl *BUSH* WD23 .... 13 F5 🔲
Brick Kiln La *HTCH/STOT* SG5 .... 56 C4
Bricklin Rd *STVG* SG1 .... 2 A2
Brick Knoll Pk *STALE/WH* AL4 .... 169 F7
Brickly Rd *LTNN/LEA* LU4 .... 68 A4
Brickmakers La *HHS/BOV* HP3 ...... 9 E6
Brickwall Cl *WGCW* AL8 .... 147 F1
Brickyard La *ROY* SG8 .... 31 J4
Bride Hall La *WLYN* AL6 .... 120 E5
Bridewell La *BUNT* SG9 .... 63 J1
Bridge End *BUNT* SG9 .... 63 J1
Bridge Pl *WAT* WD17 .... 13 E4 🔲
Bridger Cl *CSTN* WD25 .... 204 E3
Bridge Rd *KGLGY* WD4 .... 203 H3
   KNEB SG3 .... 96 B7
   LWTH SG6 .... 41 K3
   STVG SG1 .... 75 G3
   WGCE AL7 .... 147 K2
   WGCW AL8 .... 147 H2
Bridge Rd East *WGCE* AL7 .... 147 K2
Bridges Ct *HERT/WAS* SG14 ...... 151 F3 🔲
Bridge St *BERK* HP4 .... 162 A5
   BSF CM23 .... 105 J2
   HHW HP1 .... 164 B7
   HTCH/STOT SG5 .... 56 C3
   LTN LU1 .... 4 C4
Bridgewater Hl *BERK* HP4 .... 161 J3
Bridgewater Rd *BERK* HP4 .... 161 J3
Bridgewater Wy *BUSH* WD23 ...... 221 J6
Bridle Cl *HOD* EN11 .... 153 F7
   PEND EN3 .... 214 E7
   STALW/RED AL3 .... 11 D2
Bridle La *RKW/CH/CXG* WD3 ...... 218 B3
Bridle Pth *WAT* WD17 .... 12 C1
Bridle Wy *BERK* HP4 .... 161 H3
   HOD EN11 .... 153 F8 🔲
   WARE SG12 .... 155 F3
Bridle Wy (North) *HOD* EN11 ...... 153 F7
Bridle Wy (South) *HOD* EN11 ...... 153 F8
Bridlington Rd *OXHEY* WD19 ...... 230 E2
Brierley Cl *CHES/WCR* EN8 .... 214 C1
Briery Fld *RKW/CH/CXG* WD3 .... 217 K3
Briery Wy *HHNE* HP2 .... 9 D3
Brigadier Hl *ENC/FH* EN2 .... 213 F8
Brighton Rd *WATN* WD24 .... 204 B8
Brighton Wy *STVG* SG1 .... 75 F1
Brightview Cl *LCOL/BKTW* AL2 .... 188 A7 🔲
Brightwell Rd *WATW* WD18 .... 12 B4
Brill Cl *LTNE* LU2 .... 70 E7
Brimfield Cl *LTNE* LU2 .... 70 E7
Brimstone Wy *BERK* HP4 .... 161 F5
Brinklow Ct *STAL* AL1 .... 188 D1 🔲
Brinley Cl *CHES/WCR* EN8 .... 214 C1
Brinsmead *LCOL/BKTW* AL2 ...... 189 F5
Briscoe Cl *HOD* EN11 .... 176 E1
Briscoe Rd *HOD* EN11 .... 176 E1
Bristol Rd *LTNN/LIM* LU3 .... 69 F5
Britannia *STDN* SG11 .... 81 K7
Britannia Av *LTNN/LIM* LU3 .... 69 G4
Britannia Rd *CHES/WCR* EN8 ...... 214 E4
Brittain Wy *STVG* SG2 .... 3 F3
Britten Cl *BORE* WD6 .... 223 G6
Britton Av *STALW/RED* AL3 .... 10 C4 🔲
Brixham Cl *STVG* SG1 .... 75 G2

Brixton Rd *WATN* WD24 .... 220 C1
Broad Acre *LCOL/BKTW* AL2 ...... 188 A8
Broad Acres *HAT* AL10 .... 170 C1
Broadacres *LTNE* LU2 .... 69 J3 🔲
Broad Ct *WGCE* AL7 .... 147 K3
Broadcroft *HHNE* HP2 .... 8 A3 🔲
   LWTH SG6 .... 41 K7 🔲
Broadfield *BSF* CM23 .... 85 J7
   HLW CM20 .... 7 D5
Broadfield Cl *MHAD* SG10 .... 103 G8
Broadfield Pl *WGCW* AL8 .... 147 C4 🔲
Broadfield Rd *HHNE* HP2 .... 8 C5
   KNEB SG3 .... 96 C8
Broadfields *CHESW* EN7 .... 195 K7
   HARP AL5 .... 118 B7
   PIN HA5 .... 231 J8
   RYLN/HDSTN HA2 .... 231 J8
   SBW CM21 .... 131 K5
Broadfields La *OXHEY* WD19 ...... 220 C8
Broadfield Wy *MHAD* SG10 ...... 103 G8
Broad Gn *HERT/BAY* SG13 .... 174 C1
Broad Green Wd *HERT/BAY* SG13 .. 174 C1
Broadhall Wy *STVG* SG2 .... 3 E6
Broadlake Cl *LCOL/BKTW* AL2 .... 190 B5
Broadleaf Av *BSF* CM23 .... 105 F5
Broadleaf Gv *WLYN* AL6 .... 122 B8
Broadley Rd *HLWW/ROY* CM19 .... 179 G5
Broadmead *HTCHE/RSTV* SG4 ...... 56 E4
Broad Md *LTNN/LIM* LU3 .... 69 F6
Broadmead Cl *PIN* HA5 .... 231 F6 🔲
Broadmeadow Ride
   HTCHE/RSTV SG4 .... 56 E5
Broadmeads *WARE* SG12 .... 127 H8
Broadoak Av *PEND* EN3 .... 214 C5
Broad Oak Wy *STVG* SG2 .... 76 A8
Broadstone Rd *HARP* AL5 .... 143 K3
Broad St *HHNE* HP2 .... 8 A5
Broadview *STVG* SG1 .... 2 C2
The Broad Wk *NTHWD* HA6 .... 229 H8
Broadwater *BERK* HP4 .... 161 K4
   POTB/CUF EN6 .... 193 H8
Broadwater Av *LWTH* SG6 .... 41 J4
Broadwater Crs *STVG* SG2 .... 76 A8
   WGCE AL7 .... 147 J4
Broadwater Dl *LWTH* SG6 .... 41 J4
Broadwater La *STVG* SG2 .... 76 D8
Broadwater Rd *WGCE* AL7 .... 147 K4
   WGCW AL8 .... 147 J4
Broadway *LWTH* SG6 .... 41 J6
Broadway Av *HLWE* CM17 .... 156 C5
The Broadway *BRKMPK* AL9 ...... 171 H4
   PIN HA5 .... 231 G6
   STALE/WH AL4 .... 119 K4
   WAT WD17 .... 13 D2 🔲
Brocket Rd *HOD* EN11 .... 177 F3
   WGCW AL8 .... 146 E5
Brockett Cl *WGCW* AL8 .... 147 G3
Brocket Vw *STALE/WH* AL4 ...... 145 G1
Brocklesbury Cl *WATN* WD24 .... 13 A3
Brockles Md *HLWW/ROY* CM19 .. 179 K5
Brockswood La *WGCW* AL8 ...... 147 G2
Brockwell Shott *STVG* SG2 .... 60 D8
Brodewater Rd *BORE* WD6 ...... 224 A2 🔲
Brodie Rd *ENC/FH* EN2 .... 213 F8
Bromborough Gn *OXHEY* WD19 .. 230 D4 🔲
Bromet Cl *WAT* WD17 .... 204 A8
Bromleigh Cl *CHES/WCR* EN8 .... 197 J6 🔲
Bromley Cl *LTNN/LIM* LU3 .... 68 E1
Brompton Cl *LTNN/LIM* LU3 ...... 68 E1
Bronte Crs *HHNE* HP2 .... 141 G8 🔲
Brookbridge La *KNEB* SG3 .... 96 E7
Brookdene Av *OXHEY* WD19 ...... 12 C6
Brookdene Dr *NTHWD* HA6 ...... 230 A6
Brook Dr *RAD* WD7 .... 206 C3
   STVGE SG2 .... 96 C1
Brooke Cl *BUSH* WD23 .... 221 K7
Brooke End *STALW/RED* AL3 ...... 142 B5
Brooke Gdns *BSF* CM23 .... 106 B2
Brooke Rd *ROY* SG8 .... 15 K6
   SBW CM21 .... 132 B7
Brooke Wy *BUSH* WD23 .... 221 K7 🔲
Brook Fld *STVGE* SG2 .... 77 F7
Brookfield Cl *TRING* HP23 .... 135 G3
Brookfield Gdns *CHES/WCR* EN8 .. 197 H5
Brookfield La *CHES/WCR* EN8 .... 197 F6
   STVGE SG2 .... 77 G5
Brookfield La East
   CHES/WCR EN8 .... 197 H5
Brookfield La West
   CHES/WCR EN8 .... 197 G5
Brookfields *SBW* CM21 .... 132 B7
Brookhill *STVGE* SG2 .... 96 A1
Brooklands Cl *LTNW/LEA* LU4 .... 68 B5
Brooklands Gdns *POTB/CUF* EN6 .. 209 K2
Brook La *BERK* HP4 .... 161 J4
   SBW CM21 .... 132 B7
Brooklane Fld *HLWS* CM18 ...... 180 C4
Brookmans Av *BRKMPK* AL9 .... 193 F4
Brookmill Cl *OXHEY* WD19 ...... 12 C6 🔲
Brook Rd *BORE* WD6 .... 223 K1
   CHES/WCR EN8 .... 214 E4
   SBW CM21 .... 132 B8
   STSD CM24 .... 86 D3

Brooksfield WGCE AL7 .... 148 C2
Brookside HAT AL10 .... 170 C4
Brookside Cl BAR EN5 .... 225 J6
   HERT/BAY SG13 .... 151 H4
   HLWW/ROY CM19 .... 179 G3
   HOD EN11 .... 177 F3
   LWTH SG6 .... 41 K4
   POTB/CUF EN6 .... 209 F2
   WAB EN9 .... 215 K2
Brookside Cl BAR EN5 .... 225 J6
Brookside Crs POTB/CUF EN6 .... 195 G5
Brookside Gdns EN EN1 .... 214 A7
Brookside Rd OXHEY WD19 .... 12 C6
Brooksies SAFWS CB11 .... 35 H3
Brook St HTCH/STOT SG5 .... 25 J3
   LTN LU1 .... 4 B3
   TRING HP23 .... 135 G3
Brook Vw HTCHE/RSTV SG4 .... 57 G3
Broom Cl CHESW EN7 .... 196 E5
   HAT AL10 .... 170 C4
Broomer Pl CHESW EN8 .... 197 G7
Broomfield HLW CM20 .... 156 E6
   LCOL/BKTW AL2 .... 188 E5
Broomfield Av BROX EN10 .... 197 J4
Broomfield Cl WLYN AL6 .... 122 C5
Broomfield Ri ABLGY WD5 .... 203 J2
Broomfield Rd WLYN AL6 .... 122 C5
   WAT WD17 .... 204 B8
Broom Hl HHW HP1 .... 163 H7
   WLYN AL6 .... 123 J5
Broomhills WGCE AL7 .... 148 B2
Broomleys STALE/WH AL4 .... 169 F3
Brooms Cl WGCW AL8 .... 122 D8
Brooms Rd LTNE LU2 .... 5 D3
Broomstick Hall Rd WAB EN9 .... 215 K3
Broomstick La CSHM HP5 .... 182 C5
Broom Wk STVG SG1 .... 2 C3
Broughinge Rd BORE WD6 .... 224 A2
Broughton Av LTNN/LIM LU3 .... 69 H4
Broughton Hi LWTH SG6 .... 42 A3
Broughton Wy RKW/CH/CXG WD3 .... 217 K7
Brownfields WGCE AL7 .... 148 A2
Brownfield Wy STALE/WH AL4 .... 119 K3
Browning Dr HTCHE/RSTV SG4 .... 57 F1
Browning Rd ENC/FH EN2 .... 213 G8
   HARP AL5 .... 118 E7
Brownlow La LBUZ LU7 .... 109 K2
Brownlow Rd BERK HP4 .... 161 K4
   BORE WD6 .... 223 K4
Brown's Cl LTNW/LEA LU4 .... 68 C4
Brown's Ri TRING HP23 .... 135 E6
Browns Spring BERK HP4 .... 163 F2
The Brow CSTG HP8 .... 226 A2
   GSTN WD25 .... 204 C3
Brox Dell STVG SG1 .... 2 C1
Broxley Md LTNW/LEA LU4 .... 68 A4
Bruce Gv WATN WD24 .... 204 C8
Bruce Rd BAR EN5 .... 225 K3
Bruce Wy CHES/WCR EN8 .... 214 C1
Brunel Rd STVGE SG2 .... 3 E1
Brunswick Rd WAB EN9 .... 215 F8
Brunswick St LTNE LU2 .... 4 C3
Brushrise WATN WD24 .... 204 B6
Brushwood Dr RKW/CH/CXG WD3 .... 217 F4
Bryan Rd BSF CM23 .... 105 J1
Bryanstone Rd CHES/WCR EN8 .... 214 C1
Bryant Cl HARP AL5 .... 118 C6
Bryce Cl WARE SG12 .... 127 H6
Buchanan Ct BORE WD6 .... 224 B2
Buchanan Dr LTNE LU2 .... 5 F3
Buckettsland La BORE WD6 .... 208 C8
Buckingham Dr LTNE LU2 .... 70 D7
Buckingham Rd BORE WD6 .... 224 C4
   TRING HP23 .... 134 D2
   WATN WD24 .... 204 D7
Buckland Ri PIN HA5 .... 230 D7
Buckle Cl LTNN/LIM LU3 .... 68 E2
Bucklersbury HTCH/STOT SG5 .... 56 C7
Bucklers Cl HARP AL5 .... 176 E8
Bucknalls Cl GSTN WD25 .... 205 F5
Bucknalls Dr LCOL/BKTW AL2 .... 205 G1
Bucknalls La GSTN WD25 .... 205 F5
Bucks Aly HERT/BAY SG13 .... 174 A5
Bucks Av OXHEY WD19 .... 13 F6
Bucks HI KGLGY WD4 .... 202 B5
Buckthorn Av STVG SG1 .... 2 C4
Buckton Rd BORE WD6 .... 207 J8
Buckwood La DUN/WHIP LU6 .... 114 A2
Buckwood Rd DUN/WHIP LU6 .... 114 E3
Buddcroft WGCE AL7 .... 148 C2
Bude Crs STVG SG1 .... 75 F3
Building End Rd ROY SG8 .... 34 D1
Bulbourne Cl BERK HP4 .... 161 G3
   HHW HP1 .... 163 K7
Bulbourne Ct TRING HP23 .... 135 F2
Bulbourne Rd TRING HP23 .... 135 G2
Bullace Cl HHW HP1 .... 163 K5
Bullbeggars La BERK HP4 .... 162 D5
Bullen's Green La STALE/WH AL4 .... 191 J1
Bullfields SBW CM21 .... 132 C5
Bullhead Rd BORE WD6 .... 224 B5
Bull La BUNT SG9 .... 47 G5
   BUNT SG9 .... 62 E1
   SAFWS CB11 .... 34 D7
   STALE/WH AL4 .... 144 D5

Bullock's HI HTCHE/RSTV SG4 .... 73 K8
Bullock's La HERT/BAY SG13 .... 151 F5
Bull Pln HERT/WAS SG14 .... 151 G3
Bull Rd HARP AL5 .... 143 J1
Bullrush Cl HAT AL10 .... 171 G5
Bull's Cross ENC/FH EN2 .... 213 K6
Bulls Cross Ride CHESW EN7 .... 213 K4
Bullsland Gdns RKW/CH/CXG WD3 .... 216 E6
Bullsland La RKW/CH/CXG WD3 .... 216 E6
Bulls La BRKMPK AL9 .... 192 E2
Bullsmoor Cl CHES/WCR EN8 .... 214 B5
Bullsmoor Gdns
   CHES/WCR EN8 .... 214 A5
Bullsmoor La EN EN1 .... 214 A5
   PEND EN3 .... 214 C5
Bullsmoor Ride CHES/WCR EN8 .... 214 B5
Bullsmoor Wy CHES/WCR EN8 .... 214 A5
Bull Stag Gn BRKMPK AL9 .... 171 H2
Bullwell Crs CHES/WCR EN8 .... 197 J7
Bulstrode Cl KGLGY WD4 .... 184 C7
Bulstrode La KGLGY WD4 .... 184 C7
Bulwer Link STVG SG1 .... 2 C5
Bumbles Green La WAB EN9 .... 199 H3
Buncefield La HHNE HP2 .... 9 F7
The Bungalows HARP AL5 .... 118 E6
Bunkers La HHS/BOV HP3 .... 186 A3
Bunnsfield WGCE AL7 .... 148 D2
Bunstrux TRING HP23 .... 134 D3
Buntingford Rd STDN SG11 .... 81 J5
   TRING HP23 .... 135 G4
Bunyan Cl HTCH/STOT SG5 .... 39 F5
Bunyan Rd HTCH/STOT SG5 .... 56 D1
Bunyans Cl LTNN/LIM LU3 .... 69 F4
Burbage Cl CHES/WCR EN8 .... 214 D1
Burchell Ct BUSH WD23 .... 221 K7
Burfield Cl HAT AL10 .... 171 F2
Burfield Rd RKW/CH/CXG WD3 .... 216 E5
Burford Gdns HOD EN11 .... 177 F2
Burford St HOD EN11 .... 177 F2
Burford Wy HTCH/STOT SG5 .... 40 A7
Burge End La HTCH/STOT SG5 .... 38 E4
Burghley Av BORE WD6 .... 224 B5
   BSF CM23 .... 105 F2
Burghley Cl STVGE SG2 .... 96 B1
Burgundy Cft WGCE AL7 .... 148 A5
Burhill Gv PIN HA5 .... 231 F8
Burleigh Md BRKMPK AL9 .... 171 H2
Burleigh Rd CHES/WCR EN8 .... 214 D2
   HERT/BAY SG13 .... 151 K2
   HHS/BOV HP3 .... 9 F6
   STAL AL1 .... 168 E6
Burley LWTH SG6 .... 25 K3
Burley HI HLWE CM17 .... 181 G2
Burley Rd BSF CM23 .... 105 K5
Burnell Ri LWTH SG6 .... 41 H4
Burnells Wy STSD CM24 .... 86 D2
Burnell Wk LWTH SG6 .... 41 J4
Burnet Cl HHS/BOV HP3 .... 8 B6
Burnett Pk HLWW/ROY CM19 .... 179 J6
Burnett Sq HERT/WAS SG14 .... 150 C2
Burnham Cl ENC/FH EN2 .... 213 H8
   WLYN AL6 .... 123 K3
Burnham Green Rd WLYN AL6 .... 123 K5
Burnham Rd LTNE LU2 .... 5 F1
   STAL AL1 .... 11 F4
Burnley Cl OXHEY WD19 .... 230 D4
Burnsall Pl HARP AL5 .... 143 K5
Burns Cl HTCHE/RSTV SG4 .... 57 F1
   STVGE SG2 .... 76 C1
Burnside HERT/WAS SG14 .... 150 D4
   HOD EN11 .... 176 E3
   SBW CM21 .... 132 B7
   STAL AL1 .... 168 E8
Burns Rd ROY SG8 .... 21 G4
Burnt Cl LTNN/LIM LU3 .... 68 E2
Burntfarm Ride CHESW EN7 .... 212 E2
Burntmill Cl HLW CM20 .... 6 B1
Burntmill La HLW CM20 .... 6 B1
Burr Cl AMP/FLIT/B MK45 .... 36 C5
   LCOL/BKTW AL2 .... 190 D5
Burrowfield WGCE AL7 .... 147 J5
Burrs La ROY SG8 .... 32 C6
Burr's Pl LTN LU1 .... 4 C3
Burr St LTNE LU2 .... 4 C3
Bursland LWTH SG6 .... 41 H3
Burston Dr LCOL/BKTW AL2 .... 188 E6
Burton Av WATW WD18 .... 12 D3
Burton Cl STALE/WH AL4 .... 120 A4
Burton La CHESW EN7 .... 196 C6
Burton's La CSTG HP8 .... 216 B4
   RKW/CH/CXG WD3 .... 216 C5
Burwell Rd STVGE SG2 .... 3 F4
Burycroft WGCW AL8 .... 122 E8
Burydale STVGE SG2 .... 76 C2
Burydell La LCOL/BKTW AL2 .... 189 F5
Bury End HTCH/STOT SG5 .... 39 F5
Bury Gn HHW HP1 .... 164 B5
   STALE/WH AL4 .... 145 F1
Bury Green Rd CHESW EN7 .... 197 F8
Bury HI HHW HP1 .... 164 B5
Bury Hill Cl HHW HP1 .... 164 B5
Bury Holme BROX EN10 .... 197 K1
Bury La HERT/WAS SG14 .... 124 D5

KNEB SG3 .... 96 E6
LTNN/LIM LU3 .... 52 A4
RKW/CH/CXG WD3 .... 218 C6
WLYN AL6 .... 94 E8
Bury Lodge La RBSF CM22 .... 107 H1
   STSD CM24 .... 87 F6
Bury Md ARL/CHE SG15 .... 24 E2
Burymead STVG SG1 .... 58 C8
Bury Mdw RKW/CH/CXG WD3 .... 218 C6
Bury Mead Rd HTCH/STOT SG5 .... 40 D2
Bury Park Rd LTN LU1 .... 4 A2
Bury Ri HHS/BOV HP3 .... 184 B3
Bury Rd HAT AL10 .... 171 H3
   HHW HP1 .... 164 B5
   HLWE CM17 .... 157 F5
Burywick HARP AL5 .... 143 J4
Bushbarns CHESW EN7 .... 196 E2
Bushby Av BROX EN10 .... 176 E8
Bushel Whf TRING HP23 .... 135 F2
Bushey Cl WGCE AL7 .... 148 C4
   HLWS CM18 .... 7 D7
Bushey Cft HLWS CM18 .... 7 D7
Bushey Gn WGCE AL7 .... 148 C4
Bushey Grove Rd BUSH WD23 .... 13 E5
Bushey Hall Dr BUSH WD23 .... 13 E5
Bushey Hall Rd BUSH WD23 .... 13 E5
Bushey Ley WGCE AL7 .... 148 C4
Busheymill Br BUSH WD23 .... 205 F1
Bushey Mill Crs WATN WD24 .... 204 D2
Bushey Mill La BUSH WD23 .... 221 G2
   WATN WD24 .... 204 D3
Bushfield Rd HHS/BOV HP3 .... 184 A1
Bush Hall La BRKMPK AL9 .... 171 J5
Bushmead Rd LTNE LU2 .... 69 K4
Bush Spring BLDK SG7 .... 27 G5
Bushwood Cl BRKMPK AL9 .... 192 B1
Butchers La HTCHE/RSTV SG4 .... 73 G1
Butely Rd LTNW/LEA LU4 .... 68 A5
Bute Sq LTN LU1 .... 4 C4
Bute St LTN LU1 .... 4 C4
Butlers Dr CHING E4 .... 215 H8
Butlin Rd LTN LU1 .... 89 G3
Butterfield Green Rd LTNE LU2 .... 70 B3
Butterfield La STAL AL1 .... 189 G3
Butterfield Rd STALE/WH AL4 .... 145 F1
Butterfly La BORE WD6 .... 222 E1
Buttermere Cl STAL AL1 .... 168 E7
Buttersweet Ri SBW CM21 .... 132 C8
Butterwick GSTN WD25 .... 205 F6
Butt Field Vw LCOL/BKTW AL2 .... 188 E7
Buttlehide RKW/CH/CXG WD3 .... 227 G4
Buttondene Crs BROX EN10 .... 177 G8
Butts End HHW HP1 .... 163 K7
Buttsmead NTHWD HA6 .... 229 H5
The Butts BROX EN10 .... 197 J7
Buxton Cl STALE/WH AL4 .... 169 G2
Buxton Pth OXHEY WD19 .... 230 D2
Buxton Rd LTN LU1 .... 4 B4
Buxtons La ROY SG8 .... 15 G4
Byde St HERT/WAS SG14 .... 151 F2
Byers Cl POTB/CUF EN6 .... 210 D4
Byewaters WATW WD18 .... 219 H6
The Byeway RKW/CH/CXG WD3 .... 228 D5
Byfield WGCW AL8 .... 122 C6
Byfield Cl LTNW/LEA LU4 .... 68 A3
Bygrave Rd BLDK SG7 .... 27 J8
Bylands Cl BSF CM23 .... 105 G2
Byng Dr POTB/CUF EN6 .... 210 B3
Bynghams HLWW/ROY CM19 .... 179 G5
Byng Rd BAR EN5 .... 225 J2
Byrd Wk BLDK SG7 .... 43 F7
Byron Av BORE WD6 .... 223 K4
   WATN WD24 .... 220 E2
Byron Cl HTCHE/RSTV SG4 .... 57 F1
   STVGE SG2 .... 76 D1
Byron Pl HHNE HP2 .... 141 G2
Byron Rd HARP AL5 .... 118 C3
   LTNW/LEA LU4 .... 68 A4
   ROY SG8 .... 21 H4
Byslips Rd DUN/WHIP LU6 .... 114 B9
By the Wd OXHEY WD19 .... 230 E2
Byways BERK HP4 .... 162 B6
The Byway POTB/CUF EN6 .... 210 B1

C

Cabot Cl STVGE SG2 .... 3 E1
Caddington Common
   STALW/RED AL3 .... 115 J1
Cade Cl LWTH SG6 .... 26 C2
Cades Cl LTN LU1 .... 89 F7
Cades La LTN LU1 .... 89 F7
Cadmore La CHES/WCR EN8 .... 197 J5
Cadwell La HTCH/STOT SG5 .... 40 D7
Caernarvon Cl HHNE HP2 .... 8 A5
   STVGE SG2 .... 96 C1
Caesars Rd STALE/WH AL4 .... 145 G2
Cage Pond Rd RAD WD7 .... 207 K3
Caishowe Rd BORE WD6 .... 224 A4
Caister Cl HHS/BOV HP3 .... 8 B6
   STVG SG1 .... 58 A4
Calbury Cl STAL AL1 .... 168 E7
Caldbeck WAB EN9 .... 215 J4

Caldecot Av *CHESW* EN7 .... 196 D7 🅿
Caldecote Gdns *BUSH* WD23 ...... 222 B6
Caldecote La *BUSH* WD23 .... 222 C7
Caldecote Rd *BLDK* SG7 .... 16 D8
Caldecot Wy *BROX* EN10 .... 176 E8 🅿
Calder Av *BRKMPK* AL9 .... 193 G4
Caldwell Rd *OXHEY* WD19 .... 230 E3
Caleb Cl *LTNW/LEA* LU4 .... 68 E7
Caledon Rd *LCOL/BKTW* AL2 ...... 190 A4
California *BLDK* SG7 .... 27 F8
California La *BUSH* WD23 .... 222 A8
Callisto Ct *HHNE* HP2 .... 8 C2 🅿
Callowland Pl *WATN* WD24 .... 204 C3 🅿
Calnwood Rd *LTNW/LEA* LU4 ...... 68 A7
Calton Av *HERT/WAS* SG14 .... 150 C4
Calverley Cl *BSF* CM23 .... 105 H6
Calverton Rd *LTNN/LIM* LU3 .... 68 C3
Calvert Rd *BAR* EN5 .... 225 J2
Camberley Pl *HARP* AL5 .... 144 A3 🅿
Camborne Dr *HHNE* HP2 .... 8 B1
Cambrian Wy *HHNE* HP2 .... 8 B2
Cambridge Dr *CHES/WCR* EN8 .... 197 G7 🅿
Cambridge Dr *POTB/CUF* EN6 .... 209 K1
Cambridge Rd *HLW* CM20 .... 157 F3 🅿
  HTCHE/RSTV SG4 .... 41 G8
  ROY SG8 .... 23 C6
  ROY SG8 .... 32 D4
  SBW CM21 .... 132 C4
  STAL AL1 .... 168 E7
  STDN SG11 .... 81 H7
  STSD CM24 .... 86 D1
  WATW WD18 .... 13 G3 🅿
Cambridge St *LTN* LU1 .... 5 D6
Cambridge Ter *BERK* HP4 .... 162 A5 🅿
Cameron Dr *CHES/WCR* EN8 ...... 214 C4
Camfield *WCCE* AL7 .... 148 A7
Camlet Wy *STALW/RED* AL3 .... 10 A3
Campania Gv *LTNN/LIM* LU3 .... 69 F1
Campbell Cl *BUNT* SG9 .... 63 H2
  HLWE CM17 .... 180 E2 🅿
  HTCHE/RSTV SG4 .... 57 F1 🅿
Campers Av *LWTH* SG6 .... 41 J4
Campers Rd *LWTH* SG6 .... 41 J4
Campers Wk *LWTH* SG6 .... 41 J4
Campfield Rd *HERT/WAS* SG14 .... 150 C4
  STAL AL1 .... 11 F4
Campfield Wy *LWTH* SG6 .... 41 J4
Campine Cl *CHES/WCR* EN8 ...... 197 H6 🅿
Campion Cl *CSTN* WD25 .... 204 B3 🅿
Campion Rd *HHW* HP1 .... 163 H7
Campions Ct *BERK* HP4 .... 161 H7
The Campions *BORE* WD6 .... 207 J8 🅿
  STSD CM24 .... 86 D1 🅿
Campion Wy *ROY* SG8 .... 21 J4
Campkin Md *STVGE* SG2 .... 76 E6 🅿
Camp Rd *STAL* AL1 .... 11 E5
The Campus *WGCW* AL8 .... 147 J2
Camp View Rd *STAL* AL1 .... 168 E7
Canada La *BROX* EN10 .... 197 J3
The Canadas *BROX* EN10 .... 197 J3 🅿
Canberra Cl *STALW/RED* AL3 .... 168 C2
Canberra Gdns *LTNN/LIM* LU3 .... 69 G3
Candlefield Rd *HHS/BOV* HP3 .... 186 A1
Canes La *HLWE* CM17 .... 181 H8
Canfield *BSF* CM23 .... 105 H1
Cangelis Cl *HHW* HP1 .... 163 K8
Canham Cl *HTCHE/RSTV* SG4 .... 93 C8
Cannix Cl *STVGE* SG2 .... 3 E6
Cannon La *LTNE* LU2 .... 70 D4
Cannon Ms *WLYN* EN9 .... 215 G3
Cannon Rd *WATW* WD18 .... 13 D4 🅿
Cannons Cl *BSF* CM23 .... 85 K8
  ROY SG8 .... 15 C4
Cannons Cl *STDN* SG11 .... 81 J6
Cannons Md *STSD* CM24 .... 86 C2
Cannons Meadow *WLYN* AL6 .... 124 A8
Cannons Mill La *BSF* CM23 .... 85 K7
Cannon St *STALW/RED* AL3 .... 10 C3
Canons Brook *HLWW/ROY* CM19 .. 179 H1
Canons Cl *RAD* WD7 .... 206 E5
Canons Fld *STALE/WH* AL4 ...... 120 B8 🅿
  WLYN AL6 .... 122 E1
Canonsfield Rd *WLYN* AL6 .... 122 E1
Canons Ga *CHES/WCR* EN8 ...... 197 K4
  HLW CM20 .... 155 H7
Canopus Wy *NTHWD* HA6 .... 230 B3
Canterbury Cl *LTNW/LEA* LU4 .... 68 E5
  NTHWD HA6 .... 230 A3
Canterbury Rd *BORE* WD6 .... 223 K2
  WAT WD17 .... 12 C1 🅿
Canterbury Wy
  RKW/CH/CXG WD3 .... 219 G3
  STVG SG1 .... 59 F7
Capella Rd *NTHWD* HA6 .... 230 A4
Capell Av *RKW/CH/CXG* WD3 .... 217 G5
Capell Rd *RKW/CH/CXG* WD3 .... 217 G5
Capell Wy *RKW/CH/CXG* WD3 .... 217 G5
Capel Rd *EN* EN1 .... 214 A6
  OXHEY WD19 .... 13 C5
Capeverie Wk *WAT* WD17 .... 219 K1
Cape Rd *STAL* AL1 .... 168 E6
Caponfield *WCCE* AL7 .... 148 C5
Cappell La *WARE* SG12 .... 153 H4

Capron Rd *LTNW/LEA* LU4 .... 68 D5
Captains Wk *BERK* HP4 .... 162 A6 🅿
Caractacus Cottage Vw
  WATW WD18 .... 12 B6
Caractacus Gn *WATW* WD18 ...... 12 A5 🅿
Caravan La *RKW/CH/CXG* WD3 .. 218 D7
Carbone Hl *POTB/CUF* EN6 ...... 195 F4 🅿
Carde Cl *HERT/WAS* SG14 .... 150 C2
Cardiff Cl *STVGE* SG2 .... 96 C2
Cardiff Gv *LTN* LU1 .... 4 B4
Cardiff Rd *LTN* LU1 .... 4 B4
  WATW WD18 .... 12 C5
Cardiff Wy *ABLGY* WD5 .... 204 B2 🅿
Cardigan St *LTN* LU1 .... 4 B4
Cardinal Av *BORE* WD6 .... 224 A3
Cardinal Cl *CHESW* EN7 .... 196 D4 🅿
Cardinal Gv *STALW/RED* AL3 ...... 10 A6
Cardy Rd *HHW* HP1 .... 164 A7
Carew Rd *NTHWD* HA6 .... 229 K5
Carew Wy *OXHEY* WD19 .... 231 G2
Careys Cft *BERK* HP4 .... 161 G2
Carisbrooke Av *WATN* WD24 ...... 220 E1
Carisbrooke Rd *HARP* AL5 .... 118 E7
  LTNW/LEA LU4 .... 68 C3
Carisbrook Rd *LCOL/BKTW* AL2 .. 188 D4
Carleton Ri *WLYN* AL6 .... 122 B3 🅿
Carleton Rd *CHES/WCR* EN8 ...... 197 H5
Carlisle Av *STALW/RED* AL3 .... 10 C2
Carlton Cl *BORE* WD6 .... 224 C4 🅿
  LTNN/LIM LU3 .... 4 A1
Carlton Crs *LTNN/LIM* LU3 .... 69 H6
Carlton Rd *HARP* AL5 .... 118 C7
Carman Ct *TRING* HP23 .... 134 E6 🅿
Carmelite Rd *KTN/HRWW/W* HA3 .. 231 K7
Carnaby Rd *BROX* EN10 .... 176 D6
Carnarvon Rd *BAR* EN5 .... 225 K3
Carnegie Gdns *LTNN/LIM* LU3 .... 69 F1
Carnegie Rd *STALW/RED* AL3 ...... 168 A2
Caro La *HHS/BOV* HP3 .... 165 F8
Carol Cl *LTNN/LIM* LU3 .... 69 G5
Caroline Pl *OXHEY* WD19 .... 13 F5 🅿
Caroon Dr *RKW/CH/CXG* WD3 .. 202 A6
Carpenders Av *OXHEY* WD19 ...... 231 F2
Carpenders Cl *HARP* AL5 .... 117 K5 🅿
Carpenters Rd *EN* EN1 .... 214 B6
The Carpenters *BSF* CM23 .... 105 F5 🅿
Carpenters Wood Dr
  RKW/CH/CXG WD3 .... 216 E4
Carpenter Wy *POTB/CUF* EN6 .. 210 D3
Carrigans *BSF* CM23 .... 105 H1
Carrington Av *BORE* WD6 .... 224 A4
Carrington Cl *BAR* EN5 .... 225 F5
Carrington Pl *TRING* HP23 .... 135 G4
Carrington Sq
  KTN/HRWW/W HA3 .... 231 K6 🅿
Carsdale Cl *LTNN/LIM* LU3 .... 69 F3 🅿
Carteret Rd *LTNE* LU2 .... 70 D8
Carters Cft *BSF* CM23 .... 105 J3
  STVGE SG2 .... 76 E5
Carters Leys *BSF* CM23 .... 105 G3 🅿
Carters Md *HLWE* CM17 .... 180 E2
Carters Wy *ARL/CHE* SG15 .... 24 C5
Cart Pth *GSTN* WD25 .... 204 D3
Cartwright Rd *ROY* SG8 .... 21 H4 🅿
  STVG SG1 .... 59 J7
Carve Wk *LWTH* SG6 .... 26 A8
Carvers Cft *KNEB* SG3 .... 96 C3
Cary Wk *RAD* WD7 .... 206 E4
Cashio La *LWTH* SG6 .... 26 A8
Caslon Wy *LWTH* SG6 .... 25 K8
Cassandra Ga *CHES/WCR* EN8 .. 197 K5
Cassiobridge Rd *WATW* WD18 .. 219 K4
Cassiobury Dr *WAT* WD17 .... 12 B2
Cassiobury Park Av *WATW* WD18 .. 219 K3
Cassio Rd *WATW* WD18 .... 12 C3
Castle Cl *BUSH* WD23 .... 221 J6
  HOD EN11 .... 153 H8 🅿
Castle Croft Rd *LTN* LU1 .... 89 F3
Castle Gate Wy *BERK* HP4 .... 161 K3 🅿
Castle Hl *BERK* HP4 .... 161 K3
Castle Hill Av *BERK* HP4 .... 161 K4 🅿
Castle Hill Cl *BERK* HP4 .... 161 J4 🅿
Castle Md *HHW* HP1 .... 164 A8
Castle Ri *STALE/WH* AL4 .... 119 H7
Castle Rd *HOD* EN11 .... 153 G8
  STAL AL1 .... 168 E6 🅿
Castles Cl *HTCH/STOT* SG5 .... 25 K2
Castle St *BERK* HP4 .... 161 K5 🅿
  BSF CM23 .... 105 J3 🅿
  HERT/BAY SG13 .... 151 G4
  HERT/WAS SG14 .... 151 F3 🅿
  LTN LU1 .... 4 C4 🅿
Castle Vw *BSF* CM23 .... 105 K2
Catesby Gn *LTNN/LIM* LU3 .... 52 A8
Catham Cl *STAL* AL1 .... 168 E8
Catharall Rd *LTNN/LIM* LU3 .... 69 H3
Catherine Cl *HHNE* HP2 .... 165 G1 🅿
Catherine Rd *PEND* EN3 .... 214 D6
Catherine St *STALW/RED* AL3 ...... 10 C5
Catisfield Rd *PEND* EN3 .... 214 D7 🅿
Catkin Cl *HHW* HP1 .... 164 A5

Catlin St *HHS/BOV* HP3 .... 185 F1
Catsbrook Rd *LTNN/LIM* LU3 ...... 69 G3
Catsdell Bottom *HHS/BOV* HP3 .. 186 B1
Catsey La *BUSH* WD23 .... 221 K7
Catsey Wd *BUSH* WD23 .... 221 K7
Catterick Wy *BORE* WD6 .... 223 J1
Cattlegate Rd *POTB/CUF* EN6 .. 212 A1
Cattlegate Road Crews Hl
  ENC/FH EN2 .... 212 C4
Cattley Cl *BAR* EN5 .... 225 K4
Cattlins Cl *CHESW* EN7 .... 196 C7
Cattsdell *HHNE* HP2 .... 8 B3
Causeway Cl *POTB/CUF* EN6 .... 210 E1
The Causeway *BSF* CM23 .... 105 J2
  BUNT SG9 .... 50 C8
  BUNT SG9 .... 63 J1
  POTB/CUF EN6 .... 210 D1
  ROY SG8 .... 30 D1
  SAFWS CB11 .... 34 E6
  STDN SG11 .... 65 H8
  STDN SG11 .... 82 A2 🅿
Cautherly La *WARE* SG12 .... 152 E4
Cavalier Cl *LTNN/LIM* LU3 .... 69 F3
Cavalier Ct *BERK* HP4 .... 161 K5 🅿
Cavan Dr *STALW/RED* AL3 .... 168 A1
Cavan Rd *STALW/RED* AL3 .... 142 B3
Cavell Rd *CHESW* EN7 .... 196 D5
Cavell Wk *STVGE* SG2 .... 76 D3
Cavendish Crs *BORE* WD6 .... 223 K4
Cavendish Rd *BAR* EN5 .... 225 H3
  LTNN/LIM LU3 .... 69 G7
  STAL AL1 .... 11 E4
  STALW/RED AL3 .... 115 H3
  STVG SG1 .... 75 F3
Cavendish Wy *HAT* AL10 .... 170 D4
Cawkell Cl *STSD* CM24 .... 86 C2
Caxton Hl *HERT/BAY* SG13 .... 151 J3 🅿
Caxton Rd *HOD* EN11 .... 153 G7
Caxton Wy *STVG* SG1 .... 75 G5
  WATW WD18 .... 219 J7
Cecil Cl *BSF* CM23 .... 96 C2
Cecil Ct *BAR* EN5 .... 225 J3
  HLWS CM18 .... 179 K4
Cecil Crs *HAT* AL10 .... 171 G2
Cecil Rd *CHES/WCR* EN8 .... 214 C2
  HERT/BAY SG13 .... 151 F6
  HOD EN11 .... 177 H1
  POTB/CUF EN6 .... 209 G2
  STAL AL1 .... 11 E4
Cecil St *WATN* WD24 .... 204 C8
Cedar Av *CHES/WCR* EN8 .... 214 C3
  HTCH/STOT SG5 .... 40 C5
Cedar Cl *HERT/WAS* SG14 .... 150 C4
  POTB/CUF EN6 .... 193 G8
  SBW CM21 .... 132 C8
  WARE SG12 .... 152 C1
Cedar Ct *BSF* CM23 .... 85 J8
  STALE/WH AL4 .... 169 G6
Cedar Crs *ROY* SG8 .... 21 F3
Cedar Dr *PIN* HA5 .... 231 H5
Cedar Gn *HOD* EN11 .... 177 F4 🅿
Cedar Lawn Av *BAR* EN5 .... 225 K5
Cedar Pk *BSF* CM23 .... 105 G5
Cedar Park Rd *ENC/FH* EN2 ...... 213 F8
Cedar Rd *BERK* HP4 .... 162 A6 🅿
  ENC/FH EN2 .... 212 E8
  HAT AL10 .... 171 F5
  OXHEY WD19 .... 13 D5
Cedars Av *RKW/CH/CXG* WD3 .. 218 C2
Cedars Cl *BORE* WD6 .... 223 K4
  CFSP/GDCR SL9 .... 226 B4
Cedar Wk *HHS/BOV* HP3 .... 164 C8
Cedar Wy *BERK* HP4 .... 162 A6 🅿
Cedar Wood Dr *STALE/WH* AL4 .. 169 G6
Cedarwood Dr *STALE/WH* AL4 ... 169 G6
Celandine Dr *LTNN/LIM* LU3 ...... 69 F1
Cell Barnes Cl *STAL* AL1 .... 168 E8 🅿
Cell Barnes La *STAL* AL1 .... 11 F5
Cemetery Hl *HHW* HP1 .... 164 B7
Cemetery Rd *BSF* CM23 .... 105 J4
Cemmaes Court Rd *HHW* HP1 ... 164 B5
Cemmaes Meadow *HHW* HP1 ... 164 B6
Central Av *CHES/WCR* EN8 .... 214 D3
  DUN/WHIP LU6 .... 113 G1
Central Dr *STAL* AL1 .... 169 F5
  WCCE AL7 .... 148 A1
Central Rd *HLW* CM20 .... 156 D5
Central Wy *NTHWD* HA6 .... 229 K6 🅿
Centre Wy *WAB* EN9 .... 215 H5
Century Rd *HOD* EN11 .... 177 F2
  WARE SG12 .... 127 H7 🅿
Cervantes Ct *NTHWD* HA6 .... 230 A6 🅿
Chace Av *POTB/CUF* EN6 .... 210 E2
The Chace *STVGE* SG2 .... 76 A8
Chad La *STALW/RED* AL3 .... 116 C4
Chadwell *WARE* SG12 .... 152 B1
Chadwell Av *CHES/WCR* EN8 .... 197 G6
Chadwell Cl *LTNE* LU2 .... 5 D2 🅿
Chadwell Ri *WARE* SG12 .... 152 B1
Chadwell Rd *STVG* SG1 .... 75 G5
Chaffinches Gn *HHS/BOV* HP3 .. 186 A2 🅿
Chaffinch La *WATW* WD18 .... 12 A4 🅿
Chagney Cl *LWTH* SG6 .... 41 J3
Chain Wk *BLDK* SG7 .... 19 F7
  BUNT SG9 .... 29 K8

BUNT SG9 .... 45 K3
CHESW EN7 .... 196 A6
ENC/FH EN2 .... 212 D6
HERT/BAY SG13 .... 173 H1
HERT/WAS SG14 .... 98 A2
HERT/WAS SG14 .... 124 C7
HERT/WAS SG14 .... 149 H7
ROY SG8 .... 19 H6
ROY SG8 .... 30 C5
STVGE SG2 .... 78 B8
WARE SG12 .... 99 K8
Chalet CI *BERK* HP4 .... 161 G5
Chalfont Av *AMS* HP6 .... 216 A1
Chalfont CI *HHNE* HP2 .... 165 G1
Chalfont La *RKW/CH/CXG* WD3 .... 216 E5
RKW/CH/CXG WD3 .... 227 F6
Chalfont Rd *CFSP/GDCR* SL9 .... 226 E2
Chalfont Wy *LTNE* LU2 .... 70 D7
Chalgrove *WGCE* AL7 .... 148 E2
Chalk DI *WGCE* AL7 .... 148 C2
Chalkdell Flds *STAL* AL1 .... 11 F1
Chalkdell HI *HHNE* HP2 .... 8 B5 🄳
Chalkdown *LTNE* LU2 .... 69 J2
STVGE SG2 .... 76 E2
Chalk Fld *LWTH* SG6 .... 42 C6 🄳
Chalk HI *LTNE* LU2 .... 71 G5
OXHEY WD19 .... 13 F5
Chalk Hills *BLDK* SG7 .... 43 F4
Chalk La *HLWE* CM17 .... 157 K7
Chalks Av *SBW* CM21 .... 132 B6
Challinor *HLWW* CM18 .... 181 H1
Challney CI *LTNW/LEA* LU4 .... 68 C7
Chalton Rd *LTNW/LEA* LU4 .... 68 B4
Chamberlain CI *HLWE* CM17 .... 181 F1
Chamberlaines *HARP* AL5 .... 117 G4
Chambersbury La *HHS/BOV* HP3 .... 186 A3
Chambers Ga *STVG* SG1 .... 2 B1
Chambers La *HTCH/STOT* SG5 .... 40 C5
Chambers' St *HERT/WAS* SG14 .... 151 F3
Champions CI *BORE* WD6 .... 208 A2 🄳
Champions Wy *HOD* EN11 .... 153 F8 🄳
Chancellors Rd *STVG* SG1 .... 58 C8
Chancery CI *STALE/WH* AL4 .... 169 C11
Chandlers CI *BSF* CM23 .... 105 F5 🄳
Chandler's La *RKW/CH/CXG* WD3 .... 202 E3 🄳
Chandlers Rd *STALE/WH* AL4 .... 169 F3
Chandlers Wy *HERT/WAS* SG14 .... 150 D5 🄳
Chandos *BORE* WD6 .... 223 J2
LTNW/LEA LU4 .... 68 E8
Chantry CI *BSF* CM23 .... 105 H1
ENC/FH EN2 .... 213 F8
KGLGY WD4 .... 186 A7 🄳
Chantry La *HAT* AL10 .... 170 E5
HTCHE/RSTV SG4 .... 57 K7
LCOL/BKTW AL2 .... 190 A5 🄳
Chantry PI *RYLN/HDSTN* HA2 .... 231 J7
Chantry Rd *BSF* CM23 .... 105 H1
KTN/HRWW/W HA3 .... 231 J7
The Chantry *HLW* CM20 .... 7 F1 🄳
Chaomans *LWTH* SG6 .... 41 K6 🄳
Chapel CI *BERK* HP4 .... 138 A3
GSTN WD25 .... 204 A4
LTN LU1 .... 69 H1
STAL AL1 .... 189 F1
Chapel Cottages *HHNE* HP2 .... 8 A4 🄳
Chapel Cft *KGLGY* WD4 .... 201 K1
Chapel Crofts *BERK* HP4 .... 161 F3
Chapel End *BUNT* SG9 .... 63 J2
HOD EN11 .... 177 F4
Chapel End La *TRING* HP23 .... 134 B1
Chapel Flds *HLWE* CM17 .... 181 F3
Chapelfields *WARE* SG12 .... 153 J4
Chapel HI *STSD* CM24 .... 86 C2
Chapel La *HERT/WAS* SG14 .... 149 J7
HLWE CM17 .... 181 F3
STDN SG11 .... 103 H1
TRING HP23 .... 109 F5
Chapel PI *HTCH/STOT* SG5 .... 25 K4
Chapel Rd *HTCHE/RSTV* SG4 .... 72 B8 🄳
STALW/RED AL3 .... 116 B7
Chapel Rw *DEN/HRF* UB9 .... 228 B7
Chapel St *BERK* HP4 .... 161 K5
BLDK SG7 .... 16 D3
HHNE HP2 .... 8 C4 🄳
LTN LU1 .... 4 C4 🄳
TRING HP23 .... 134 E6
Chapel Viad *LTN* LU1 .... 4 B4
Chapel Wy *ABLGY* WD5 .... 187 F5 🄳
Chapman Rd *STVG* SG1 .... 58 B8
Chapmans End *STDN* SG11 .... 81 J6
Chapmans Yd *WAT* WD17 .... 13 D3 🄳
Chappell Ct *WARE* SG12 .... 126 C2
Chappel Meadow *TRING* HP23 .... 135 G3
Chard Dr *LTNN/LIM* LU3 .... 52 B8
Chardins CI *HHW* HP1 .... 163 J5 🄳
Charles St *BERK* HP4 .... 161 J5
HHW HP1 .... 164 B7
LTNE LU2 .... 5 D2
TRING HP23 .... 135 F6
Charlesworth CI *HHS/BOV* HP3 .... 164 C8 🄳
Charlock Wy *WATW* WD18 .... 12 A5
Charlotte CI *STALE/WH* AL4 .... 169 H6
Charlton CI *HOD* EN11 .... 177 F3 🄳
Charlton Mead La *HOD* EN11 .... 177 H4
Charlton Rd *HTCH/STOT* SG5 .... 56 B4

Charlton Wy *HOD* EN11 .... 177 F4
Charlwood Rd *LTNW/LEA* LU4 .... 68 A8
Charmbury Ri *LTNE* LU2 .... 70 B5 🄳
Charmouth Ct *STAL* AL1 .... 11 F1
Charmouth Rd *STAL* AL1 .... 11 F2
Charndon CI *LTNN/LIM* LU3 .... 52 B8
Charnwood Rd *EN* EN1 .... 214 A6 🄳
Charters Cross *HLWS* CM18 .... 180 A4 🄳
Chartridge CI *BAR* EN5 .... 225 F5
BUSH WD23 .... 221 K6 🄳
Chartridge Wy *HHNE* HP2 .... 9 F5 🄳
Chartwell CI *WAB* EN9 .... 215 K3
Chartwell Dr *LTNE* LU2 .... 69 K6
Chartwell Rd *NTHWD* HA6 .... 230 A6
Charwood CI *RAD* WD7 .... 207 H3 🄳
Chasden Rd *HHW* HP1 .... 163 J3
Chase CI *ARL/CHE* SG15 .... 24 E1
Chase Hill Rd *ARL/CHE* SG15 .... 24 E1
Chaseside CI *LBUZ* LU7 .... 110 A2 🄳
Chase St *LTN* LU1 .... 4 C6
The Chase *BSF* CM23 .... 105 J3
CHESW EN7 .... 195 K6
HERT/BAY SG13 .... 151 J4
HHNE HP2 .... 8 B6
RAD WD7 .... 206 C5
WARE SG12 .... 153 F5
WATW WD18 .... 219 K4
WLYN AL6 .... 123 F7
Chaseways *SBW* CM21 .... 156 E1
Chasten HI *LWTH* SG6 .... 41 H7
Chatsworth CI *BORE* WD6 .... 223 K3 🄳
BSF CM23 .... 105 F2
Chatsworth St *STVGE* SG2 .... 76 A8
Chatsworth Rd *LTNW/LEA* LU4 .... 69 C8
Chatteris CI *LTNW/LEA* LU4 .... 68 C5 🄳
Chatterton *LWTH* SG6 .... 42 B4
Chatton CI *LTNE* LU2 .... 71 F7
Chaucer CI *BERK* HP4 .... 161 G4
Chaucer CI *LTNN/LIM* LU3 .... 4 A1 🄳
ROY SG8 .... 21 C1
Chaucer Wk *HHNE* HP2 .... 141 C8
Chaucer Wy *HOD* EN11 .... 153 F7
HTCHE/RSTV SG4 .... 57 C2
Chaulden House Gdns *HHW* HP1 .... 163 J8
Chaulden La *HHW* HP1 .... 163 H8
Chaulden Ter *HHW* HP1 .... 163 J7
Chaul End La *LTNW/LEA* LU4 .... 68 D8
Chaul End Rd *LTN* LU1 .... 68 A8
Chauncy Av *POTB/CUF* EN6 .... 210 D3
Chauncy CI *WARE* SG12 .... 127 C6
Chauncy Gdns *BLDK* SG7 .... 27 H8 🄳
Chauncy Rd *STVG* SG1 .... 2 C2
Chaworth Gn *LTNW/LEA* LU4 .... 68 B4 🄳
Cheapside *LTN* LU1 .... 4 C4 🄳
Cheapside Sq *LTN* LU1 .... 4 C4 🄳
Chedburgh *WGCE* AL7 .... 148 E2 🄳
Cheddington La *TRING* HP23 .... 109 C4
Cheddington Rd *LBUZ* LU7 .... 110 B4
Cheffins Rd *HOD* EN11 .... 152 E8
Chells La *STVGE* SG2 .... 76 D1 🄳
Chells Wy *STVGE* SG2 .... 3 F1
Chelmsford Rd *HERT/WAS* SG14 .... 150 D4
Chelsea Flds *HOD* EN11 .... 153 C7 🄳
Chelsea Gdns *HLWE* CM17 .... 181 H2
Chelsing Ri *HHNE* HP2 .... 9 F6 🄳
Chelsworth CI *LTNE* LU2 .... 70 E8 🄳
Chelveston *WGCE* AL7 .... 148 E2
Chelwood Av *HAT* AL10 .... 171 F2
Chelwood CI *NTHWD* HA6 .... 229 H6 🄳
Cheney Av *LTNW/LEA* LU4 .... 68 B4
Chenies Av *AMS* HP6 .... 216 A1
Chenies CI *HHNE* HP2 .... 165 C1 🄳
Chenies Rd *RKW/CH/CXG* WD3 .... 217 C2
Chenies Wy *WATW* WD18 .... 219 K7
Chennells *HAT* AL10 .... 170 E5
Chennells CI *HTCHE/RSTV* SG4 .... 41 F7
The Chennies *HARP* AL5 .... 143 K2 🄳
Chepstow CI *STVG* SG1 .... 76 C1
Chequer La *STALW/RED* AL3 .... 142 B5
Chequers *BRKMPK* AL9 .... 171 J1
BSF CM23 .... 105 F1 🄳
WGCE AL7 .... 147 J5
Chequers Bridge Rd *STVG* SG1 .... 2 A2
Chequers CI *BUNT* SG9 .... 63 H1 🄳
HTCH/STOT SG5 .... 25 K3
LBUZ LU7 .... 110 C5
Chequers Fld *WGCE* AL7 .... 147 J6
Chequers HI *STALW/RED* AL3 .... 116 C7
Chequers La *CSTN* WD25 .... 187 H8
HTCHE/RSTV SG4 .... 73 C2
LBUZ LU7 .... 110 C5
Chequer St *LTN* LU1 .... 5 D5
STAL AL1 .... 10 C4
Cheriton CI *STALE/WH* AL4 .... 169 C2
Cherry Acre *CFSP/GDCR* SL9 .... 226 A3
Cherry CI *KNEB* SG3 .... 96 A5
Cherry Cft *WGCW* AL8 .... 122 D7
Cherry Croft Gdns *PIN* HA5 .... 231 G6 🄳
Cherrydale *WATW* WD18 .... 12 A3
Cherry Dr *ROY* SG8 .... 21 J2
Cherry Gdns *BSF* CM23 .... 105 K1
SBW CM21 .... 132 C5
Cherry HI *LCOL/BKTW* AL2 .... 188 C3
RKW/CH/CXG WD3 .... 218 A3
Cherry Hollow *ABLGY* WD5 .... 204 A1

Cherry Orch *HHW* HP1 .... 163 J7 🄳
Cherry Ri *CSTG* HP8 .... 226 A6
Cherry Rd *PEND* EN3 .... 214 B8
Cherry Tree Av *LCOL/BKTW* AL2 .... 190 B6
Cherry Tree CI *LTNE* LU2 .... 5 E2 🄳
Cherry Tree Gn *HERT/WAS* SG14 .... 150 C5
Cherrytree La *CFSP/GDCR* SL9 .... 226 A4
Cherry Tree La *HHNE* HP2 .... 9 F7
Cherrytree La *HHNE* HP2 .... 165 H4 🄳
Cherry Tree La *RKW/CH/CXG* WD3 .... 217 F5
STALE/WH AL4 .... 119 J3
Cherry Tree Ri *STVGE* SG2 .... 60 D7
Cherry Tree Rd *HOD* EN11 .... 177 F4
WATN WD24 .... 204 C2
Cherry Wk *RKW/CH/CXG* WD3 .... 218 B8
Cherry Wy *HAT* AL10 .... 171 F6 🄳
Chertsey CI *LTNE* LU2 .... 90 D7
Chertsey Ri *STVGE* SG2 .... 76 D3
Cherwell CI *RKW/CH/CXG* WD3 .... 219 F7
Chesfield CI *BSF* CM23 .... 105 J3
Chesford Rd *LTNE* LU2 .... 70 D7
Chesham La *CFSP/GDCR* SL9 .... 226 B4
Chesham Rd *BERK* HP4 .... 161 K3
CSHM HP5 .... 182 B8
HHS/BOV HP3 .... 183 C6
TRING HP23 .... 135 J2
Chesham Wy *WATW* WD18 .... 219 K6
Cheshunt Wash *CHES/WCR* EN8 .... 197 J3
Cheslyn CI *LTNE* LU2 .... 71 F7
Chess CI *CSHM* HP5 .... 200 A4
RKW/CH/CXG WD3 .... 218 C2
Chessfield Pk *AMS* HP6 .... 216 B8
Chess HI *RKW/CH/CXG* WD3 .... 218 C2
Chess La *RKW/CH/CXG* WD3 .... 218 C2
Chess Vale Ri *RKW/CH/CXG* WD3 .... 218 E6 🄳
Chess Valley Wk *CSHM* HP5 .... 200 B8
Chess Wy *RKW/CH/CXG* WD3 .... 217 K2
Chesswood Wy *PIN* HA5 .... 230 E8 🄳
Chester Av *LTNW/LEA* LU4 .... 68 C7
Chester CI *LTNW/LEA* LU4 .... 68 E1
Chesterfield Rd *BAR* EN5 .... 225 J3
PEND EN3 .... 214 C7
Chester Rd *BORE* WD6 .... 224 B1
NTHWD HA6 .... 230 A7
STVG SG1 .... 59 C8
WATW WD18 .... 12 B8
Chesterton Av *HARP* AL5 .... 118 E3
Chestnut Av *NTHWD* HA6 .... 230 A6
RKW/CH/CXG WD3 .... 217 K7
WARE SG12 .... 127 K6
Chestnut CI *BERK* HP4 .... 112 E4
BERK HP4 .... 162 E7
BSF CM23 .... 105 J3
CFSP/GDCR SL9 .... 226 C2
WARE SG12 .... 129 K1
Chestnut Ct *HTCH/STOT* SG5 .... 56 B1
Chestnut Dr *BERK* HP4 .... 162 A7
STAL AL1 .... 168 E7
Chestnut La *TRDG/WHET* N20 .... 225 H8
Chestnut Ri *BUSH* WD23 .... 221 K4
Chestnut Rd *PEND* EN3 .... 214 C8
The Chestnuts *HERT/BAY* SG13 .... 151 J3
HHS/BOV HP3 .... 184 C3
WLYN AL6 .... 94 E7
Chestnut Wk *CFSP/GDCR* SL9 .... 226 B6
HTCHE/RSTV SG4 .... 56 E5
STVG SG1 .... 58 C2
WATN WD24 .... 204 E3
WLYN AL6 .... 123 F7
Cheverells CI *STALW/RED* AL3 .... 115 H5
Cheviot CI *BUSH* WD23 .... 221 K6
Cheviot Rd *LTNN/LIM* LU3 .... 68 C3
Cheviots *HAT* AL10 .... 171 F2
HHNE HP2 .... 8 C5
Cheyne CI *LBUZ* LU7 .... 110 D5
WARE SG12 .... 127 K6
Cheyney CI *ROY* SG8 .... 15 J4
Cheyney St *ROY* SG8 .... 15 J4
Chicheley Rd *KTN/HRWW/W* HA3 .... 231 J7
Chichester Wy *GSTN* WD25 .... 205 F3
Chicken La *LCOL/BKTW* AL2 .... 190 E5 🄳
Chilcott Rd *WATN* WD24 .... 204 D1
Chilcourt *ROY* SG8 .... 21 J2
Childs Av *DEN/HRF* UB9 .... 228 E1
Childwick Ct *HHS/BOV* HP3 .... 186 A3 🄳
Chilham CI *HHS/BOV* HP3 .... 8 E5 🄳
Chiltern Av *BUSH* WD23 .... 221 J6
Chiltern CI *BERK* HP4 .... 161 H4
BORE WD6 .... 223 J2
BUSH WD23 .... 221 J6
CHESW EN7 .... 195 K6
WARE SG12 .... 127 J7
Chiltern Dr *RKW/CH/CXG* WD3 .... 217 K7
Chiltern Gdns *LTNW/LEA* LU4 .... 68 D2
Chiltern HI *CFSP/GDCR* SL9 .... 226 B5
Chiltern Park Av *BERK* HP4 .... 161 H4
Chiltern Ri *LTN* LU1 .... 4 A6
Chiltern Rd *AMP/FLIT/B* MK45 .... 36 C1 🄳
BLDK SG7 .... 43 F7
HTCHE/RSTV SG4 .... 56 E5
STALE/WH AL4 .... 169 J3
Chilterns *HAT* AL10 .... 171 F2
HHNE HP2 .... 8 B6
The Chilterns *DUN/WHIP* LU6 .... 114 C2
HTCHE/RSTV SG4 .... 56 E1

Chiltern Vw *LWTH* SG6 .... 41 H4
Chiltern Wy *TRING* HP23 .... 135 H4
Chilton Gn *WGCE* AL7 .... 148 D3
Chilvers Bank *BLDK* SG7 .... 42 E2
Chilwell Gdns *OXHEY* WD19 .... 230 D3
Chilworth Ga *BROX* EN10 .... 176 E8
Chindit Cl *BROX* EN10 .... 176 C6
Chinnery Hl *BAR* EN5 .... 105 J4
Chipperfield Rd *HHS/BOV* HP3 .... 183 K6
HHS/BOV HP3 .... 185 G2
KGLGY WD4 .... 185 H7
Chipping Cl *BAR* EN5 .... 225 K3 🔲
Chippingfield *HLWE* CM17 .... 157 F6
Chishill Rd *ROY* SG8 .... 23 G7
Chiswell Ct *WATN* WD24 .... 204 D8 🔲
Chiswellgreen La *LCOL/BKTW* AL2 .. 188 A3
Chittenden Cl *HOD* EN11 .... 153 G8 🔲
Chobham St *LTN* LU1 .... 5 D5 🔲
Cholesbury La *TRING* HP23 .... 159 F7
Chorleywood Bottom
RKW/CH/CXG WD3 .... 217 G5
Chorleywood Cl
RKW/CH/CXG WD3 .... 218 C7 🔲
Chorleywood Rd
RKW/CH/CXG WD3 .... 218 A5
Chouler Gdns *STVG* SG1 .... 58 D7
The Chowns *HARP* AL5 .... 143 H4
Christchurch Crs *RAD* WD7 .... 206 D6 🔲
Christ Church La *BAR* EN5 .... 225 K2
Christchurch Rd *HHNE* HP2 .... 8 A4
TRING HP23 .... 134 E5
Christie Cl *BROX* EN10 .... 176 E7
Christie Rd *STVGE* SG2 .... 76 D4
Christy's Yd *BLDK* SG7 .... 16 D3
Church Cl *NTHWD* HA6 .... 230 A6 🔲
POTB/CUF EN6 .... 195 G7
RAD WD7 .... 206 D6
WLYN AL6 .... 94 C7 🔲
Church Crs *STALW/RED* AL3 .... 10 E3
Church Crt *STALE/WH* AL4 .... 169 F8
Church Dr *BSF* CM23 .... 67 K1
Church End *ARL/CHE* SG15 .... 24 E2
HLWW/ROY CM19 .... 179 H3
ROY SG8 .... 23 C8
STALE/WH AL4 .... 145 F7
STALW/RED AL3 .... 115 H3
STALW/RED AL3 .... 116 C8
STALW/RED AL3 .... 142 B5
STDN SG11 .... 82 A2
STVGE SG2 .... 60 E7
Church Farm La *ROY* SG8 .... 15 J8
TRING HP23 .... 134 C5
Church Farm Wy *GSTN* WD25 .... 205 J8 🔲
Churchfield *HARP* AL5 .... 143 K1
HLW CM20 .... 7 F2
ROY SG8 .... 23 G8
Churchfield Rd *CFSP/GDCR* SL9 ...... 226 A7 🔲
WLYN AL6 .... 123 J8
Churchfields *BROX* EN10 .... 177 F6
HERT/BAY SG13 .... 151 G4
STDN SG11 .... 81 K7 🔲
STSD CM24 .... 86 E3
Churchfields La *BROX* EN10 .... 177 F6
Churchgate *CHES/WCR* EN8 .... 197 F6
Churchgate Rd *CHES/WCR* EN8 ...... 197 F7
Churchgate St *HLWE* CM17 .... 157 H5
Church Gn *HARP* AL5 .... 118 C8
Church Gv *AMS* HP6 .... 216 B1
Church Hl *ABLGY* WD5 .... 187 F4
HERT/BAY SG13 .... 152 A5
LBUZ LU7 .... 109 K1
Churchill Rd *AMP/FLIT/B* MK45 .... 36 C6 🔲
LTNN/LEA LU4 .... 69 F2
STAL AL1 .... 11 F2
Church La *ARL/CHE* SG15 .... 24 E1
BERK HP4 .... 161 K5
BLDK SG7 .... 17 K5
BRKMPR AL9 .... 171 H4
BROX EN10 .... 197 K1
BSF CM23 .... 105 G7
CFSP/GDCR SL9 .... 226 A7
CHES/WCR EN8 .... 197 G7
GSTN WD25 .... 205 J8
HERT/WAS SG14 .... 125 J3
HHS/BOV HP3 .... 183 K5
HTCHE/RSTV SG4 .... 43 K8
HTCHE/RSTV SG4 .... 58 C5
HTCHE/RSTV SG4 .... 73 G3
HTCHE/RSTV SG4 .... 93 G7
KGLGY WD4 .... 186 A8
LBUZ LU7 .... 110 A2
LWTH SG6 .... 26 C8
MHAD SG10 .... 103 G6
POTB/CUF EN6 .... 194 B8
RBSF CM22 .... 87 K1
RKW/CH/CXG WD3 .... 201 K7
RKW/CH/CXG WD3 .... 217 K8
ROY SG8 .... 15 G4
ROY SG8 .... 30 D2
ROY SG8 .... 31 J4
ROY SG8 .... 32 C5
STALE/WH AL4 .... 170 A6
STVG SG1 .... 2 A1

TRING HP23 .... 109 K8
TRING HP23 .... 158 E2
WARE SG12 .... 99 J1
Church Langley Wy *HLWE* CM17 .... 181 F1
Church Leys *HLWS* CM18 .... 7 E5
Church Md *DUN/WHIP* LU6 .... 113 K5
HLWW/ROY CM19 .... 154 C8
Church Pth *HTCHE/RSTV* SG4 .... 57 K6
Church Pl *WLYN* AL6 .... 122 C4 🔲
Church Rd *AMP/FLIT/B* MK45 .... 36 C7
BERK HP4 .... 137 K1
BERK HP4 .... 162 E3
DUN/WHIP LU6 .... 113 K5
HERT/BAY SG13 .... 173 K5
HERT/WAS SG14 .... 150 E2
HHS/BOV HP3 .... 9 F6 🔲
HLWE CM17 .... 181 F4
HTCH/STOT SG5 .... 25 K3
HTCHE/RSTV SG4 .... 72 D1
LBUZ LU7 .... 110 E4
LTN LU1 .... 89 H7
LTNN/LIM LU3 .... 52 A3
NTHWD HA6 .... 230 A6
POTB/CUF EN6 .... 193 H8
RBSF CM22 .... 106 B7
RBSF CM22 .... 107 F4
STALW/RED AL3 .... 116 B7
STSD CM24 .... 86 E4
WAT WD17 .... 220 B1
WGCW AL8 .... 147 J3 🔲
Church St *BLDK* SG7 .... 42 E1
BRKMPK AL9 .... 171 H3
BRKMPK AL9 .... 173 F3
BSF CM23 .... 105 J2
BUNT SG9 .... 63 J1
HERT/WAS SG14 .... 151 G3 🔲
HHNE HP2 .... 8 A3
HHS/BOV HP3 .... 183 K5
HTCH/STOT SG5 .... 38 A1
LTN LU1 .... 4 C8
RKW/CH/CXG WD3 .... 15 G5
ROY SG8 .... 15 J5
ROY SG8 .... 15 J8
SBW CM21 .... 132 C7 🔲
STALE/WH AL4 .... 145 G1
STALW/RED AL3 .... 10 C3
WAB EN9 .... 215 H3 🔲
WARE SG12 .... 127 H8
WATW WD18 .... 13 D3 🔲
WLYN AL6 .... 122 C4
Church Vw *BROX* EN10 .... 176 B6
TRING HP23 .... 108 E5 🔲
Church Wk *BUSH* WD23 .... 221 H6 🔲
SBW CM21 .... 132 D7
Church Yd *TRING* HP23 .... 135 F5
Cicero Dr *LTNN/LIM* LU3 .... 51 J5
Cillocks Cl *HOD* EN11 .... 177 F2
Claggy Rd *HTCHE/RSTV* SG4 .... 92 E7
Claggate Rd *BUSH* WD23 .... 221 J6
Clare Cl *BORE* WD6 .... 223 J6
Clare Ct *NTHWD* HA6 .... 229 J4
Clare Crs *BLDK* SG7 .... 43 F3 🔲
Claremont *CHESW* EN7 .... 196 D7
LCOL/BKTW AL2 .... 205 H1
Claremont Crs *RKW/CH/CXG* WD3 .. 219 H5
Claremont Rd *EBAR* EN4 .... 210 D8
LTNN/LEA LU4 .... 69 C8
Clarence Cl *BUSH* WD23 .... 222 C7
Clarence Rd *BERK* HP4 .... 161 K5 🔲
HARP AL5 .... 118 C7
STAL AL1 .... 11 F4
STSD CM24 .... 86 D2 🔲
Clarendon Cl *HHNE* HP2 .... 8 B4 🔲
Clarendon Ms *BORE* WD6 .... 223 K3 🔲
Clarendon Rd *BORE* WD6 .... 223 K3
CHES/WCR EN8 .... 197 H7
HARP AL5 .... 118 C7
LTNE LU2 .... 4 B2
WAT WD17 .... 12 C2 🔲
Clarion Cl *HTCH/STOT* SG5 .... 54 E7
Clarke's Rd *HAT* AL10 .... 171 G2
Clarke's Spring *TRING* HP23 .... 136 A4
Clarke Wy *GSTN* WD25 .... 204 B5
Clarkfield *RKW/CH/CXG* WD3 .... 217 K8
Clarkhill *HLWS* CM18 .... 180 B5
Clark Rd *ROY* SG8 .... 21 H2
Clarks Cl *WARE* SG12 .... 127 H6
Clarks Md *BUSH* WD23 .... 221 K7
Claudian Pl *STALW/RED* AL3 .... 167 H7
Claverhambury Rd *WAB* EN9 .... 199 F7
Claverley Gn *LTNE* LU2 .... 71 F7
Claverton Cl *HHS/BOV* HP3 .... 183 J6
Claybury *BUSH* WD23 .... 221 J7
Claybush Rd *BLDK* SG7 .... 17 K6
Claycroft *WGCE* AL7 .... 148 D3
Claydon Cl *LTNN/LIM* LU3 .... 69 H2
Claydown Wy *LTN* LU1 .... 89 G8
Claygate Av *HARP* AL5 .... 118 A7
Clay Hall Rd *DUN/WHIP* LU6 .... 114 D2
Clay Hl *ENC/FH* EN2 .... 213 F7
Clay La *BUSH* WD23 .... 222 B7
Claymore *HHNE* HP2 .... 8 B1
Claymore Dr *HTCH/STOT* SG5 .... 40 D4
Claymores *STVG* SG1 .... 2 C2
Claypit Hl *RBSF* CM22 .... 87 K4

Clayponds *BSF* CM23 .... 105 K2
Cleall Av *WAB* EN9 .... 215 H4
The Cleave *HARP* AL5 .... 119 F8
Clement Rd *CHES/WCR* EN8 .... 197 J5 🔲
Clements End Rd *DUN/WHIP* LU6 .. 114 C7
Clements Rd *RKW/CH/CXG* WD3 .... 217 G5
Clements St *WARE* SG12 .... 127 J8
Clevedon Rd *LTNE* LU2 .... 5 F1
Cleveland Crs *BORE* WD6 .... 224 B5
Cleveland Rd *HHNE* HP2 .... 9 E3
STALW/RED AL3 .... 115 J4
Cleves Rd *HHNE* HP2 .... 165 G1
Cleviscroft *STVG* SG1 .... 2 C4
Clifford Crs *LTNN/LEA* LU4 .... 68 B4
Clifton Cl *CHES/WCR* EN8 .... 197 J7
Clifton Hatch *HLWS* CM18 .... 180 D4 🔲
Clifton Rd *LTN* LU1 .... 89 G1
WATW WD18 .... 12 A5
Clifton St *STAL* AL1 .... 11 D3
Clifton Wy *BORE* WD6 .... 223 K1
WARE SG12 .... 127 H6
The Climb *RKW/CH/CXG* WD3 .... 218 A6
Clinton Av *LTNE* LU2 .... 70 A5
Clinton End *HHNE* HP2 .... 9 F5
Clitheroe Gdns *OXHEY* WD19 .... 230 E2
Clive Cl *POTB/CUF* EN6 .... 210 A1
Clive Wy *WATN* WD24 .... 220 D1
Cloister Garth *BERK* HP4 .... 161 K5
STAL AL1 .... 189 G2 🔲
Cloister Lawns *LWTH* SG6 .... 41 K5
Cloisters Rd *LTNN/LEA* LU4 .... 68 A6
LWTH SG6 .... 41 K5
The Cloisters *RKW/CH/CXG* WD3 .. 218 D7
WGCW AL8 .... 147 J3
Clonard Wy *PIN* HA5 .... 231 H5
Closemead Cl *NTHWD* HA6 .... 229 H5 🔲
The Close *BLDK* SG7 .... 42 E2
BRKMPK AL9 .... 192 E4
BUNT SG9 .... 45 F3
BUSH WD23 .... 221 J6 🔲
HARP AL5 .... 117 K5
LTNN/LIM LU3 .... 69 F4
POTB/CUF EN6 .... 210 B2
RAD WD7 .... 206 C3
RKW/CH/CXG WD3 .... 218 A8
ROY SG8 .... 21 K2
STAL AL1 .... 188 E1 🔲
STALW/RED AL3 .... 115 J4
WARE SG12 .... 127 J8
WLYN AL6 .... 94 E8
Clothall Rd *BLDK* SG7 .... 43 F1
Clovelly Wy *STVG* SG1 .... 75 F2
Clover Av *BSF* CM23 .... 104 E3
Clover Fld *HLWS* CM18 .... 180 D4
Cloverfield *WGCE* AL7 .... 123 F8
The Clover Fld *BUSH* WD23 .... 221 G6
Cloverland *HAT* AL10 .... 170 E7
Clover Wy *HHW* HP1 .... 164 A5
The Clump *RKW/CH/CXG* WD3 ...... 217 K5
Clusterbucks *HERT/WAS* SG14 ...... 125 J3
Clutterbucks *RKW/CH/CXG* WD3 .. 201 K6
Clyde Rd *HOD* EN11 .... 177 J5
Clydesdale Cl *BORE* WD6 .... 224 C5
Clydesdale Rd *ROY* SG8 .... 21 J3 🔲
Clyde Sq *HHNE* HP2 .... 164 E1 🔲
Clyde Ter *HERT/BAY* SG13 .... 151 K3
Clyfton Cl *BROX* EN10 .... 197 K1
Clyston Rd *WATW* WD18 .... 12 A5
Coach Dr *HTCHE/RSTV* SG4 .... 56 D4
The Coach House
AMP/FLIT/B MK45 .... 36 C6
Coachman's La *BLDK* SG7 .... 42 D1
Coalport Cl *HLWE* CM17 .... 181 F2
Coates Dell *GSTN* WD25 .... 205 F3
Coates Rd *BORE* WD6 .... 223 G7
Coates Wy *GSTN* WD25 .... 204 E3
Cobbett Cl *PEND* EN3 .... 214 B6
Cobbetts Ride *TRING* HP23 .... 134 E6
Cobb Gn *GSTN* WD25 .... 204 C2
Cobbinsend Rd *WAB* EN9 .... 199 K7
The Cobbins *WAB* EN9 .... 215 K2
Cobbins Wy *HLWE* CM17 .... 157 H5
Cobb Rd *BERK* HP4 .... 161 G5
Cob Cl *BORE* WD6 .... 224 B5
Cobden Hl *RAD* WD7 .... 206 E6
Cobden St *LTNE* LU2 .... 4 C2
Cobham Rd *WARE* SG12 .... 127 K7
Cobmead *HAT* AL10 .... 171 G2
Cockbush Av *HERT/BAY* SG13 .... 151 K2
Cocker Rd *EN* EN1 .... 214 A6
Cockfosters Rd *EBAR* EN4 .... 211 G8
Cock La *BROX* EN10 .... 176 B5
SAFWS CB11 .... 51 H6
Cockle Wy *RAD* WD7 .... 207 H3
Cockrobin La *HLWE* CM20 .... 155 H2
Codicote Dr *GSTN* WD25 .... 204 E4
Codicote Rd *HTCHE/RSTV* SG4 .... 93 J3
STALE/WH AL4 .... 120 B8
WLYN AL6 .... 120 D7
Codicote Rw *HHNE* HP2 .... 165 F1
Codmore Crs *CSHM* HP5 .... 182 A8
Cogmore *SAFWS* CB11 .... 35 K2
Cohen Cl *CHES/WCR* EN8 .... 214 D2
Colburn Av *PIN* HA5 .... 231 F5
Colchester Rd *NTHWD* HA6 .... 230 B8 🔲

Cold Christmas La WARE SG12 .... 127 H3
Coldham Gv PEND EN3 .... 214 D7 🔲
Coldharbour La BUSH WD23 .... 221 J6
  HARP AL5................................. 118 D5
Coldharbour Rd
  HLWW/ROY CM19 .... 179 H2
Colebrook Av LTNN/LIM LU3 .... 68 B2
Cole Green La WGCE AL7 .... 148 A5
Cole Green Wy HERT/WAS 150 B5
Coleman Green La STALE/WH AL4 .. 145 J4
Colemans La WAB EN9 .... 198 A4
Colemans Rd HTCHE/RSTV SG4 ...... 72 A8
Coleridge Cl CHESW EN7 .... 196 D5
  HTCHE/RSTV SG4 .... 57 F1
Coleridge Crs HHNE HP2 .... 141 G8
Cole Rd WAT WD17 .... 220 C1
Colesdale POTB/CUF EN6 .... 195 G8
Coles Gn BUSH WD23 .... 221 K8
Coles Hl HHW HP1 .... 163 K4
Colestrete STVG SG1 .... 3 D4
Colestrete Cl STVG SG1 .... 3 D5
Coleswood Rd HARP AL5 .... 143 K2
Colgrove WGCW AL8 .... 147 H4
Colindale Av STAL AL1 .... 11 E6
Colin Rd LTNE LU2 .... 5 D1
College Cl BSF CM23 .... 105 C3
  STALW/RED AL3 .... 116 B8
  WARE SG12 .... 152 C1 🔲
College Ct STALW/RED AL3 .... 10 C4
College La HAT AL10 .... 170 D5
College Rd ABLGY WD5 .... 204 B1
  CHES/WCR EN8 .... 197 G8
  CHESW EN7 .... 197 F8
  HERT/BAY SG13 .... 152 B7
  HOD EN11 .... 176 E1
  STAL AL1 .... 168 E7
College Sq HLW CM20 .... 6 C4 🔲
College St STALW/RED AL3............. 10 C4
College Wy NTHWD HA6 .... 229 J5
  WGCW AL8.............................. 147 J2
Collens Rd HARP AL5 .... 143 J4
Collenswood Rd STVGE SG2 .... 3 F4
Collet Cl CHES/WCR EN8 .... 197 H6
Collett Rd HHW HP1 .... 164 B6
  WARE SG12 .... 127 H7
Colley Land RKW/CH/CXG WD3 ..... 217 H4
Collingdon St LTN LU1 .... 4 B3
Collingtree LTNE LU2 .... 70 C5 🔲
Collingwood Dr
  LCOL/BKTW AL2 .... 190 B3 🔲
Collins Crs BSF CM23 .... 86 A8
Collins Meadow HLWW/ROY CM19 ... 6 A4
Collison Cl HTCHE/RSTV SG4 .... 41 G7
Collyer Rd LCOL/BKTW AL2 .... 190 B5
Colnbrook Cl LCOL/BKTW AL2 ...... 190 C5 🔲
Colne Av OXHEY WD19 .... 12 C5
  RKW/CH/CXG WD3 .... 227 K1
Colne Gdns LCOL/BKTW AL2 .... 190 C5
Colne Md RKW/CH/CXG WD3 .... 227 K1
Colne Valley Trail
  RKW/CH/CXG WD3 .... 228 B1
Colne Wy HHNE HP2 .... 164 C1
Colney Heath La STALE/WH AL4 .... 169 H7
Colonial Wy WATN WD24 .... 220 D1
The Colonnade CHES/WCR EN8 .... 197 H6 🔲
Colonsay HHS/BOV HP3 .... 165 H8
Colston Crs CHESW EN7 .... 195 K5
Colts Cnr STVGE SG2 .... 3 F4
Coltsfield STSD CM24 .... 86 D2
Coltsfoot WGCE AL7 .... 148 C5
Coltsfoot Dr ROY SG8 .... 21 J3
Coltsfoot La KNEB SG3 .... 123 K2
Coltsfoot Rd WARE SG12 .... 127 J6
The Coltsfoot HHW HP1 .... 163 H7
The Colts BSF CM23 .... 105 H6
Columbus Cl STVG SG1 .... 3 E1
Columbus Gdns NTHWD HA6 .... 230 B7 🔲
Colvin Gdns CHES/WCR EN8 .... 214 C5
Colwell Ri LTNE LU2 .... 71 F7
Colwell Rd STVGE SG2 .... 76 D6
Colwyn Cl STVG SG1 .... 75 C1
Colyer Cl WLYN AL6 .... 123 F6
Combe Rd WATW WD18 .... 12 A5
Combe St HHW HP1 .... 164 B6 🔲
Comet Cl GSTN WD25 .... 204 A4
Comet Rd HAT AL10 .... 170 E4
Comet Wy HAT AL10 .... 170 D4
Common Fld TRING HP23 .... 135 J8
Commonfields HLW CM20 .... 7 D3
Common Gdns BERK HP4 .... 162 D3
Common Gate Rd
  RKW/CH/CXG WD3 .... 217 G5
Common La BLDK SG7 .... 17 H3
  GSTN WD25 .... 206 D3
  HARP AL5................................ 119 F4
  HTCHE/RSTV SG4 .... 92 E4
  KGLGY WD4 .... 185 K6
  ROY SG8................................. 34 C1
Common Ri HTCHE/RSTV SG4 .... 40 E8
Common Rd DUN/WHIP LU6 .... 113 J6
  HTCH/STOT SG5 .... 25 J1
  RKW/CH/CXG WD3 .... 217 G4
  WAB EN9 .... 179 F7
Commonside Rd HLWS CM18 .... 180 C5

Commons La HHNE HP2................. 8 B4
The Commons WGCE AL7 .... 148 B6
The Common BERK HP4 .... 162 C5
  HARP AL5................................ 117 H5
  HAT AL10 .... 171 F7
  KGLGY WD4 .... 201 K2
Common Vw LWTH SG6 .... 42 A3
Common Whf WARE SG12 .... 127 J8 🔲
Compton Av LTNN/LEA LU4 .... 68 C5
Compton Gdns LCOL/BKTW AL2 .... 188 D4
Compton Pl OXHEY WD19 .... 231 F3
Comyne Rd WATN WD24 .... 204 A6
The Comyns BUSH WD23 .... 221 K8
Concorde Dr HHNE HP2 .... 8 A5 🔲
Concorde St LTNE LU2 .... 5 D3
Conduit La BUNT SG9 .... 49 J8 🔲
  HOD EN11 .... 177 F3
Conduit La East HOD EN11 .... 177 F3
Coney Cl HAT AL10 .... 171 G6 🔲
Coneydale WGCW AL8 .... 147 J1
Coney Gn SBW CM21 .... 132 B6
Congreve Rd WAB EN9 .... 215 K3
Conifer Cl CHESW EN7 .... 196 D7
The Conifers GSTN WD25 .... 204 D5 🔲
Conifer Wk STVGE SG2 .... 76 D2
Coningesby Dr WAT WD17 .... 219 K1
Coningsby Bank STAL AL1 .... 188 E2
Coningsby Cl BRKMPK AL9 .... 192 D2 🔲
Coningsby Dr POTB/CUF EN6 .... 210 E3
Coniston Cl HHS/BOV HP3 .... 9 F6 🔲
Coniston Rd KGLGY WD4 .... 185 K6
  LTNN/LIM LU3 .... 68 C3
Connaught Cl HHNE HP2 .... 9 D3
Connaught Gdns BERK HP4 .... 161 G2 🔲
Connaught Rd BAR EN5 .... 225 J6
  HARP AL5................................ 118 D7 🔲
  LTNN/LEA LU4 .... 68 E8
  STALW/RED AL3 .... 10 B2
Connemara Cl BORE WD6 .... 224 C6 🔲
Conner's Cl ROY SG8 .... 15 C5
Connop Rd PEND EN3 .... 214 C8
Conquerors Hl STALE/WH AL4 ...... 145 H1
Conquest Cl HTCHE/RSTV SG4 .... 56 D4
Constantine Cl STVG SG1 .... 59 F8 🔲
Constantine Pl BLDK SG7 .... 27 H8 🔲
Convent Cl HTCH/STOT SG5 .... 56 D1
Conway Gdns ENC/FH EN2 .... 213 H8
Conway Rd LTNN/LEA LU4 .... 69 C8
Conyers HLW CM20 .... 6 B2
Cook Rd STVGE SG2 .... 3 F1
Cook's Hole Rd ENC/FH EN2 .... 212 E8
Cooks Md BUSH WD23 .... 221 J6
Cooks Spinney HLW CM20 .... 7 F2
Cooks Vennel HHW HP1 .... 164 A4 🔲
Cooks Wy HAT AL10 .... 171 G6
  HTCHE/RSTV SG4 .... 40 E8
Coombe Gdns BERK HP4 .... 161 G4
Coombe Hill Rd
  RKW/CH/CXG WD3 .... 217 K7
Coombelands Rd ROY SG8............. 21 J1
Coombe Rd BUSH WD23 .... 221 K7
  ROY SG8.................................. 19 K8
Coombes Rd LCOL/BKTW AL2 .... 190 A4
Coopers Cl BSF CM23 .... 104 E5
  HTCHE/RSTV SG4 .... 119 K1
  STVGE SG2 .... 76 E5
Coopers Green La HAT AL10 .... 146 B8
  STALE/WH AL4 .... 169 J3
  WGCW AL8.............................. 146 E7
Cooper's Hl HTCHE/RSTV SG4 .... 92 E8
Coopers La POTB/CUF EN6 .... 194 A7
Coopers Lane Rd POTB/CUF EN6 ... 211 H5
Coopers Meadow STALW/RED AL3.. 142 B3
Coopers Rd POTB/CUF EN6 .... 193 J8
Cooters End La HARP AL5 .... 118 B5
Copenhagen Cl LTNE LU2 .... 68 C1
Copmans Wick RKW/CH/CXG WD3.. 217 G5
The Coppens HTCH/STOT SG5 .... 26 A4
Copper Beech Cl HHW HP1 .... 184 D1
Copper Beeches HARP AL5 .... 118 D8
  WLYN AL6 .... 122 D2 🔲
Copperfields LTNN/LEA LU4 .... 68 A5
  ROY SG8................................. 21 C3 🔲
  WGCE AL7 .... 148 D4 🔲
Coppermill La RKW/CH/CXG WD3.. 227 J6
Copper Rdg CFSP/GDCR SL9 .... 226 C5
Copperwood HERT/BAY SG13 .... 151 J3 🔲
Coppice Cl HAT AL10 .... 170 D8
Coppice Md HTCH/STOT SG5 .... 25 J4
The Coppice HHNE HP2 .... 9 E4
  OXHEY WD19 .... 13 D5 🔲
  TRING HP23 .... 135 J8
The Coppings HOD EN11 .... 153 F8 🔲
Coppins Cl BERK HP4 .... 161 F5
The Coppins STALW/RED AL3 .... 115 H4
Copse Cl NTHWD HA6 .... 229 H6
Copse Hl HLWW/ROY CM19 .... 179 J4
  WLYN AL6 .... 123 J1
Copse Hill Cl HHS/BOV HP3 .... 164 B8
The Copse BSF CM23 .... 106 B1 🔲
  HERT/BAY SG13 .... 151 K3
  HHW HP1................................ 163 H4
Copse Wy LTNN/LIM LU3 .... 68 C1
Copsewood Rd WATN WD24 .... 220 C1

Copse Wood Wy NTHWD HA6 ...... 229 H6
Copshall Cl HLWS CM18 .... 180 B5
Copthall Cl CFSP/GDCR SL9 .... 226 C5
Copthall Cnr CFSP/GDCR SL9........ 226 B5
Copthall La CFSP/GDCR SL9 .... 226 B5
Copthorne LTNE LU2 .... 70 E5
Copthorne Av BROX EN10 .... 176 E5
Copthorne Cl
  RKW/CH/CXG WD3 .... 218 E5 🔲
Copthorne Rd RKW/CH/CXG WD3 .. 218 E5
Coral Gdns HHNE HP2 .... 8 C4 🔲
Corals Md WGCE AL7 .... 147 J2
Coram Cl BERK HP4 .... 161 K4
Corbar Cl EBAR EN4 .... 210 E2
Corbridge Dr LTNE LU2 .... 71 F7
Corby Cl LCOL/BKTW AL2 .... 188 C6
Cordell Cl CHES/WCR EN8 .... 197 J6
Corder Cl STALW/RED AL3 .... 188 C2
Coreys Mill La STVG SG1 .... 58 B3
Corfe Cl HHS/BOV HP3 .... 8 B6
Corinium Gdns LTNN/LIM LU3 .... 69 F1
Corinium Ga STALW/RED AL3 .... 167 H1
Corncastle Rd LTN LU1 .... 4 A3
Corncrake Cl LTNE LU2 .... 70 D1
Corncroft HAT AL10 .... 171 G2
Cornel Cl LTN LU1 .... 89 F7
Cornerfield HAT AL10 .... 171 C2
Corner Hall HHS/BOV HP3 .... 164 C8
Corner Hall Av HHS/BOV HP3 .... 164 C8
Corner Meadow HLWS CM18 .... 180 C6
Corners WGCE AL7 .... 148 B2
Corner Wd STALW/RED AL3 .... 115 H4
Cornfield Crs BERK HP4 .... 160 E5
Cornfield Rd BUSH WD23 .... 221 J6
Cornfields HHW HP1 .... 164 A4 🔲
  STVGE SG2 .... 76 D2
Cornhill Dr PEND EN3 .... 214 D7
Corn Md WGCW AL8 .... 122 C4
Cornwall Cl CHES/WCR EN8 .... 214 C2
Cornwall Rd HARP AL5 .... 118 C2
  LTN HA5 .... 231 C1
  STAL AL1 .... 11 C4
Coronation Av ROY SG8 .... 21 C3
Coronation Rd BSF CM23 .... 105 J2
  WARE SG12 .... 127 J6
Corringham Ct STAL AL1 .... 11 E3
Corton Cl STVG SG1 .... 75 D7
Cory-wright Wy STALE/WH AL4 .... 120 C1
Cosgrove Wy LTN LU1 .... 88 C2
Cotefield LTNW/LEA LU4 .... 68 B6
Cotesmore Rd HHW HP1 .... 163 H7
Cotlandswick LCOL/BKTW AL2 ..... 190 A4
Cotney Cft STVGE SG2 .... 76 E3
Cotswold Av BUSH WD23 .... 221 K6
Cotswold Cl STALE/WH AL4 .... 169 F1
Cotswold Gdns LTNN/LIM LU3 .... 68 E3
Cotswolds HAT AL10 .... 171 F7
Cottage Cl RKW/CH/CXG WD3 ...... 218 E6
  WAT WD17 .... 12 A7
Cottage Gdns CHES/WCR EN8........ 197 J6
Cottered Rd BUNT SG9 .... 46 D2
Cotterells HHS/BOV HP3 .... 164 B8
  HHW HP1................................ 164 B8
Cotterells Hi HHW HP1 .... 164 B7
Cotton Dr HERT/BAY SG13 .... 152 A2
Cotton Fld HAT AL10 .... 171 C5
Cottonmill Crs STAL AL1 .... 10 C5
Cottonmill La STAL AL1 .... 10 C5
Cotton Rd POTB/CUF EN6 .... 210 D7
Coulser Cl HHW HP1 .... 163 K6
Coulter Cl POTB/CUF EN6 .... 195 F7
Council Rd BSF CM23 .... 106 A2
Counters Cl HHW HP1 .... 163 K6
Countess Cl DEN/HRF UB9 .... 228 B8
Coursers Rd STALE/WH AL4 .... 190 E1
Courtaulds KGLGY WD4 .... 185 F1
Courtenay Av KTN/HRWW/W HA3 . 231 C1
Courtfield Cl BROX EN10 .... 177 F6
Courtfields HARP AL5 .... 119 F7
Courtlands Cl WATN WD24 .... 203 K6
Courtlands Dr WAT WD17 .... 203 K6
Courtleigh Av EBAR EN4 .... 210 E1
The Courtway OXHEY WD19 .... 231 F2
The Courtyard STALE/WH AL4 ...... 169 J1
Covent Garden LTNW/LEA LU4 ...... 68 A5
Coventry Cl STVG SG1 .... 59 F1
Coverdale LTNW/LEA LU4 .... 68 A7
Covert Cl BERK HP4 .... 160 E5
Covert Rd BERK HP4 .... 160 E5
The Covert NTHWD HA6 .... 229 H6
Cowards La WLYN AL6 .... 121 K7
Cowbridge HERT/WAS SG14 .... 151 F2
Cowdray Cl LTNE LU2 .... 70 D6
Cow La BUSH WD23 .... 221 H6
  GSTN WD25 .... 204 C3
  TRING HP23 .... 135 C4
Cowles CHESW EN7 .... 196 C3
Cowley Hl BORE WD6 .... 207 J8
Cowlins HLWE CM17 .... 157 G5
Cowper Ct STALW/RED AL3 .... 115 H4
  WATN WD24 .... 204 D7
Cowper Crs HERT/WAS SG14 .... 125 J4
Cowper Ri STALW/RED AL3 .... 115 H4
Cowper Rd BERK HP4 .... 161 G4

HARP AL5................................ 118 D8
HHW HP1................................ 164 A7
STALW/RED AL3...................... 115 H4
WGCE AL7.............................. 148 A5
Cowper St *LTN* LU1........................ 4 C5
Cowpers Wy *WLYN* AL6............ 123 K4
Cowridge Crs *LTNE* LU2................. 5 E3
Cowslip Hl *LWTH* SG6................... 41 J2
Cox Cl *RAD* WD7........................ 207 H7
Cox's Wy *ARL/CHE* SG15........... 24 E4
Coyney Gn *LTNN/LIM* LU3........... 4 A2
Cozens La East *BROX* EN10....... 176 D8
Cozens La West *BROX* EN10...... 176 D8
Cozens Rd *WARE* SG9................ 127 K7
Crabb's La *BUNT* SG9.................. 67 C2
Crab La *GSTN* WD25................... 205 J4
Crabtree Cl *BUSH* WD23............. 221 J5
HHS/BOV HP3......................... 164 C8
Crabtree Dell *LWTH* SG6.............. 42 C6
Crabtree La *HARP* AL5................ 119 F8
HHS/BOV HP3......................... 164 C8
Crab Tree La *HTCH/STOT* SG5..... 39 F5
Crab Tree Rd *KNEB* SG3................ 96 A6
Crackley Meadow *HHNE* HP2..... 165 C1 🔢
Cradock Rd *LTNW/LEA* LU4........... 68 A8
Craft Wy *ROY* SG8....................... 15 J7
Cragg Av *RAD* WD7..................... 206 C6
Cragside *KNEB* SG3...................... 96 D2 🔢
Craigavon Rd *HHNE* HP2............... 8 C1
Craiglands *STALW/WH* AL4......... 169 G2
Craig Mt *RAD* WD7..................... 206 A5
Craigs Wk *CHES/WCR* EN8......... 197 H6
Craigweil Av *RAD* WD7............... 206 C5
Cranborne Av *HTCH/STOT* SG5.... 56 B3
Cranborne Cl *HERT/BAY* SG13... 151 F6
POTB/CUF EN6......................... 209 K1
Cranborne Crs *POTB/CUF* EN6.... 209 K1
Cranborne Gdns *WGCE* AL7....... 148 A4 🔢
Cranborne Rd *CHES/WCR* EN8.... 214 C2 🔢
HAT AL10.............................. 171 G3
HOD EN11.............................. 177 G2
POTB/CUF EN6....................... 192 E8
Cranbourne Dr *HARP* AL5.......... 143 K3
HOD EN11.............................. 177 G2
Cranbrook Cl *WARE* SG12.......... 127 H6 🔢
Cranbrook Rd *LTNN/LIM* LU3...... 68 C1
STALW/WH AL4...................... 169 H6
Cranefield Cl *WGCS* WD25......... 205 F2
Crane Md *WARE* SG12................ 152 D1
Cranes Wy *BORE* WD6................ 224 B5
Cranfield Crs *POTB/CUF* EN6..... 195 C7
Cranleigh Cl *CHESW* EN7............ 196 E6
Cranleigh Gdns *LTNN/LIM* LU3.... 69 H6
Cranmer Cl *POTB/CUF* EN6........ 193 J8
Cranwell Gdns *BSF* CM23............ 86 B8
Cravells Rd *HARP* AL5................ 143 K3
Crawford Rd *HAT* AL10............... 171 F2
Crawley Cl *LTN* LU1..................... 89 H8
Crawley Dr *HHNE* HP2................... 8 C1
Crawley Green Rd *LTNE* LU2......... 5 K3
Crawley Rd *LTN* LU1.................... 4 B3
Crawley's La *TRING* HP23.......... 159 K3
Creamery Ct *LWTH* SG6................ 42 C6
Crecy Gdns *STALW/RED* AL3...... 142 B3
Creighton Av *STAL* AL1.............. 189 F7
Crescent East *EBAR* EN4............ 210 D8
Crescent Ri *LTNE* LU2................... 5 D3
Crescent Rd *BSF* CM23............... 105 K3
HHNE HP2............................... 8 A5
LTNE LU2.............................. 5 D3
The Crescent *ABLGY* WD5.......... 187 F8 🔢
BUNT SG9............................... 62 A2
GSTN WD25........................... 205 J3
HLWE CM17........................... 157 F3
HTCH/STOT SG5..................... 40 B8
HTCHE/RSTV SG4.................... 56 E6
LBUZ LU7.............................. 110 C5
LCOL/BKTW AL2...................... 188 C5
LTN LU1................................ 88 D5
LWTH SG6.............................. 42 A4
RKW/CH/CXG WD3................... 219 C4
STVGE SG2............................. 61 H6
TRING HP23........................... 110 A8
WAT WD17............................ 13 D3 🔢
WLYN AL6.............................. 122 D1
Crescent West *EBAR* EN4........... 210 D8
Cress End *RKW/CH/CXG* WD3.... 217 K8
Cresset Cl *WARE* SG12............... 153 H6
Cresswick *HTCHE/RSTV* SG4...... 93 H2
Crest Dr *PEND* EN3.................... 214 D6
Crest Pk *HHNE* HP2...................... 9 F4
The Crest *CHESW* EN7................ 195 K5
LTNN/LIM LU3......................... 69 G2 🔢
SBW CM21............................. 132 B2
WARE SG12........................... 127 H5
WLYN AL6.............................. 122 D1
Creswick Ct *WGCE* AL7.............. 147 J4 🔢
Crew Curve *BERK* HP4................ 161 C2
Crib St *WARE* SG12.................... 127 H7
Cricketers *STAL* AL1.................... 11 D3
Cricketer's La *ARL/CHE* SG15...... 24 E4
Cricketfield La *BSF* CM23........... 105 C4
Crispin Fld *LBUZ* LU7................. 110 C5
Croasdaile Rd *STSD* CM24........... 86 D1
Croasdale Cl *STSD* CM24............. 86 D1

Croft Cl *KGLGY* WD4................. 184 E8
Croft End Rd *KGLGY* WD4.......... 184 E8
Crofters *SBW* CM21................... 132 C6
Crofters End *BSF* CM23............. 132 C5
Crofters Rd *NTHWD* HA6........... 229 K3
Croft Fld *HAT* AL10.................. 171 F4 🔢
KGLV WD4............................ 184 E8
Croft La *KGLGY* WD4................ 184 E8
LWTH SG6............................. 26 A8
Croft Meadow *KGLGY* WD4........ 184 E8
Croft Mdw *LBUZ* LU7................ 110 A2
Croft Rd *CFSP/GDCR* SL9.......... 226 B8
LTNE LU2.............................. 70 C6 🔢
WARE SG12........................... 127 C7
Crofts Pth *HHS/BOV* HP3.......... 165 G8
HTCH/STOT SG5..................... 25 K3
The Croft *BAR* EN5................... 225 K4
BROX EN10........................... 197 J1
LCOL/BKTW AL2..................... 188 C3
LTNN/LIM LU3........................ 68 C1
WARE SG12........................... 128 E5
WGCE AL7............................ 148 A6
Croftwell *HARP* AL5................... 144 C1
Cromer Cl *BERK* HP4................. 138 B5
Cromer Rd *WATN* WD24............ 204 D8 🔢
Cromer Wy *LTNE* LU2................. 69 J2
Crompton Rd *STVG* SG1............. 75 F3
Cromwell Av *CHESW* EN7.......... 197 H8
Cromwell Cl *BSF* CM23............. 104 E2
STALW/WH AL4...................... 169 H1
Cromwell Gn *LWTH* SG6............ 42 B1
Cromwell Hl *LTNE* LU2............... 4 B2
Cromwell Rd *AMP/FLIT/B* MK45.. 36 C5
BORE WD6............................ 223 H1
HERT/BAY SG13..................... 151 J2
LTNN/LIM LU3........................ 4 B2
LWTH SG6............................. 42 B1
STVGE SG2........................... 76 D4
WGCE AL7............................ 127 K8
Cromwell Wy *HTCH/STOT* SG5.... 39 F5
Crooked Mile *HOD* EN11........... 198 C8
Crooked Wy *WAB* EN9.............. 177 K8
Crookhams *WGCE* AL7.............. 148 B1
Crop Common *HAT* AL10........... 171 G2
Crosby Cl *LTNW/LEA* LU4........... 69 F7 🔢
STALW/WH AL4...................... 190 A1
Crossbrook *HAT* AL10............... 170 D5
Crossbrook St *CHES/WCR* EN8... 197 H8 🔢
Crosset Gn *HHS/BOV* HP3........ 165 H8 🔢
Crossfell Rd *HHS/BOV* HP3....... 165 G8
Crossfield Cl *BERK* HP4............. 161 G5
Crossfield Rd *HOD* EN11........... 177 C1
Crossfields *STALW/RED* AL3....... 188 D1
Crossgates *STVG* SG1................. 2 C3
Crosslands *STVG* SG1................ 2 C3
Cross La *HARP* AL5.................. 143 K4
HERT/WAS SG14.................... 150 E3 🔢
CFSP/GDCR SL9..................... 226 C4
Cross Lanes Cl *CFSP/GDCR* SL9.. 226 C4 🔢
Crossleys *LWTH* SG6................... 25 K7 🔢
Crossmead *OXHEY* WD19........... 12 C5
Cross Oak Rd *BERK* HP4............ 161 H6
Crossoaks La *BORE* WD6........... 208 C5
POTB/CUF EN6....................... 208 D4
Crosspaths *HARP* AL5............... 117 J5
The Crosspath *RAD* WD7........... 207 H3
Cross Rd *BUSH* WD23................ 13 F5
CHES/WCR EN8...................... 214 D3 🔢
HERT/WAS SG14.................... 151 F2
Cross St *LTNE* LU2...................... 4 C3
LWTH SG6.............................. 41 K2
STALW/RED AL3..................... 10 C5
WARE SG12........................... 127 J8
WAT WD17............................ 13 D2
Crossway *CSHM* HP5................ 182 A8 🔢
Cross Wy *HARP* AL5................. 118 E6
Crossway *PIN* HA5................... 230 D8 🔢
WGCW AL8............................ 122 B7
Crossways *BERK* HP4................ 161 G6
HHS/BOV HP3.......................... 9 F5
Crouchfield *HERT/WAS* SG14.... 126 B8 🔢
HHW HP1............................. 164 A7
Crouchfield La *WARE* SG12....... 126 C5 🔢
Crouch Hall Gdns *STALW/RED* AL3.. 142 B3
Crouch Hall La *STALW/RED* AL3... 142 B3
Crouch La *CHESW* EN7.............. 196 A5
Crowborough Pth
OXHEY WD19......................... 230 X1 🔢
Crow Furlong *HTCH/STOT* SG5.... 56 B3
Crowland Rd *LTNE* LU2.............. 70 D4
Crownfield *BROX* EN10.............. 177 F7
Crown Ga *HLW* CM20.................. 6 C4
Crown La *ROY* SG8..................... 31 J4
Crown Ri *GSTN* WD25................ 204 D2
Crown Rd *BORE* WD6................ 223 K1
Crown St *STALW/RED* AL3......... 142 C4
Crown Ter *BSF* CM23................. 105 K2 🔢
Croxdale Rd *BORE* WD6............ 223 H2
Croxley Vw *WATW* WD18........... 219 K6
Croxton Cl *LTNN/LIM* LU3.......... 69 F2 🔢
Crozier Av *BSF* CM23................ 105 F1
Crusader Wy *WATW* WD18.......... 12 A5
Cubbington Cl *LTNN/LIM* LU3...... 69 F2 🔢

Cubitt Cl *HTCHE/RSTV* SG4....... 57 G2
Cubitts Cl *WLYN* AL6................ 123 F6
Cuckmans Dr *LCOL/BKTW* AL2.. 188 C3
Cucumber La *BRKMPK* AL9....... 173 G7
Cuffley Av *GSTN* WD25............. 204 E4
Cuffley Cl *LTNN/LIM* LU3........... 68 E6
Cuffley Ct *HHNE* HP2................ 165 H1
Cuffley Hl *CHESW* EN7.............. 195 J7
Cullera Cl *NTHWD* HA6............. 230 A5
Culverden Rd *OXHEY* WD19...... 230 C2
Culverhouse Rd *LTNN/LIM* LU3.. 69 H5
Culver Rd *STAL* AL1................... 11 D3
Culworth Cl *LTN* LU1................. 88 D6
Cumberland Cl *HERT/WAS* SG14.. 151 F1 🔢
HHS/BOV HP3........................ 186 E2
Cumberland Dr *STALW/RED* AL3.. 142 C4
Cumberland St *LTN* LU1.............. 4 C5
Cumberlow Pl *HHS/BOV* HP3...... 9 F6 🔢
Cundalls Rd *WARE* SG12........... 127 J7
Cunningham Av *PEND* EN3........ 214 D6
STAL AL1.............................. 11 E6
Cunningham Hill Rd *STAL* AL1.... 11 C5
Cunningham Rd *CHES/WCR* EN8.. 197 J5
Cupid Green La *HHNE* HP2....... 140 D6
Curlew Cl *BERK* HP4................. 161 K6
LWTH SG6............................. 25 J8
Curlew Rd *LTNE* LU2................. 70 D4
Currie St *HERT/BAY* SG13......... 151 H2
Curteys *HLWE* CM17................ 157 G4
Curtis Cl *RKW/CH/CXG* WD3..... 217 K8
Curtis Rd *HHS/BOV* HP3........... 165 J7
Curtis Wy *HARP* AL5................ 162 A6
Curzon Rd *LTNN/LIM* LU3........... 4 A2
Cussons Rd *CHESW* EN7.......... 196 E7
Cutenhoe Rd *LTN* LU1................. 5 D6
Cutforth Rd *SBW* CM21............. 132 C6
Cuthbert Cl *CHESW* EN7........... 196 D7 🔢
Cutlers Gn *LTNE* LU2................. 71 G7
Cutmore Dr *STALW/WH* AL4..... 170 A8
Cuttsfield Ter *HHW* HP1............ 163 J7
Cutts La *STVG* SG1.................... 2 C3
Cuttys La *STVG* SG1................... 2 C3
Cwmbran Ct *HHNE* HP2............. 8 C1 🔢
Cygnet Cl *BORE* WD6............... 224 B1 🔢
NTHWD HA6.......................... 229 H6
Cygnet Ga *BSF* CM23............... 105 J3
Cylers Thicket *WLYN* AL6......... 122 C3 🔢
Cypress Av *ENC/FH* EN2........... 212 D5
WGCE AL7............................ 148 D4
Cypress Cl *WAB* EN9................ 215 J4 🔢
Cypress Wk *GSTN* WD25........... 204 C5 🔢
Cyrils Wy *STAL* AL1.................. 189 F1

D

Dacorum Wy *HHW* HP1............. 164 B6
Dacre Crs *HTCHE/RSTV* SG4...... 93 F8
Dacre Gdns *BORE* WD6............. 224 C5
Dacre Gn *ROY* SG8................... 21 K3
Dacre Rd *HTCH/STOT* SG5........ 56 E1
Dagger La *BORE* WD6............... 222 D6
Daggs Dell Rd *HHW* HP1........... 163 H4
Dagnall Rd *HHW* HP1............... 139 G4
Dagnalls *LWTH* SG6................... 41 K7 🔢
Dahlia Cl *CHESW* EN7............... 196 A3
LTNE LU2.............................. 70 C2
Daintrees *WARE* SG12.............. 130 A5
Dairyglen Av *CHES/WCR* EN8.... 214 C1
Dalby Cl *LTNW/LEA* LU4............ 68 A5
Dale Av *STALW/WH* AL4............ 119 K4
Dale Cl *HTCHE/RSTV* SG4.......... 56 D5
PIN HA5............................... 230 C7
Dale Ct *SBW* CM21.................. 132 B8 🔢
Dale Rd *LTN* LU1........................ 4 A4
Daleside Dr *POTB/CUF* EN6...... 210 A2
Dales Rd *BORE* WD6................ 224 C5
The Dale *LWTH* SG6.................. 41 J3
WAB EN9.............................. 215 K4
Dalewood *HARP* AL5................ 119 F8 🔢
WGCE AL7............................ 148 E4
Dalkeith Rd *HARP* AL5.............. 118 E7
Dallow Rd *LTN* LU1................... 88 D1
Dalton Cl *LTNN/LIM* LU3............ 52 B8
Dalton Gdns *BSF* CM23............ 105 H6
Dalton St *STALW/RED* AL3......... 10 C5
Dalton Wy *HTCHE/RSTV* SG4..... 93 H3
WAT WD17............................ 13 E5
Daltry Cl *STVG* SG1.................. 58 C7
Daltry Rd *STVG* SG1................. 58 C7
Damask Cl *WLYN* AL6............... 59 H1 🔢
TRING HP23.......................... 135 H1
Damask Gn *HHW* HP1............... 163 H7 🔢
Damask Green Rd
HTCHE/RSTV SG4.................... 59 H1
Dammersey Cl *STALW/RED* AL3.. 115 K5
Damson Wy *STALE/WH* AL4....... 169 G4
Dancers End La *TRING* HP23..... 134 B7
Dancers Hill Rd *BAR* EN5.......... 209 J6
Dancote *KNEB* SG3................... 96 A4
Dane Acres *BSF* CM23.............. 105 G1

Dane Br *MHAD* SG10 .... 103 J6
Dane Bridge La *MHAD* SG10 ...... 103 J7
Danebridge Rd *MHAD* SG10 ...... 103 H7
Dane Cl *HARP* AL5 .... 118 E5
  HTCH/STOT SG4 .... 25 K1
Dane End *ROY* SG8 .... 31 F4
Dane End La *HTCHE/RSTV* SG4 ...... 60 E1
Dane End Rd *STDN* SG11 .... 100 C5
Danefield Rd *HTCH/STOT* SG5 ...... 38 E5
Danemead *HOD* EN11 .... 153 F8
Dane O'coys Rd *BSF* CM23 ...... 85 H8
Dane Pk *BSF* CM23 .... 105 G1
Dane Rd *AMP/FLIT/B* MK45 ...... 36 C6
  LTNN/LIM LU3 .... 69 G7
Danesbury La *WLYN* AL6 .... 122 C1
Danesbury Pk *HERT/WAS* SG14 ...... 151 G2
Danesbury Park Rd *WLYN* AL6 ...... 122 C2
Danescroft *LWTH* SG6 .... 25 K8
Danesgate *STVG* SG1 .... 2 B4
The Danes *LCOL/BKTW* AL2 ...... 188 E6
Dane St *BSF* CM23 .... 105 K2
Danestrete *STVG* SG1 .... 2 B3
Daniells *WGCE* AL7 .... 148 B2
Danvers Cft *TRING* HP23 .... 135 H4
Danvers Dr *LTNN/LIM* LU3 ...... 52 C3
Danziger Wy *BORE* WD6 .... 224 D1
Darblay Cl *STALE/WH* AL4 ...... 145 J2
  WLYN AL6 .... 95 K6
Darcy Cl *CHES/WCR* EN8 .... 214 D1
Darkes La *POTB/CUF* EN6 .... 210 B2
Dark La *BUNT* SG9 .... 29 K8
  CHESW EN7 .... 196 E8
  HARP AL5 .... 144 A2
  WLYN AL6 .... 121 J1
Darley Cl *LTNE* LU2 .... 71 J8
Darnicle Hl *CHESW* EN7 .... 195 H3
Darrington Rd *BORE* WD6 .... 223 H1
Darr's La *BERK* HP4 .... 160 E4
The Dart *HHNE* HP2 .... 165 F1
Darwin Cl *HHNE* HP2 .... 141 G8
  STALE/WH AL4 .... 145 H2
Darwin Gdns *OXHEY* WD19 ...... 230 D4
Darwin Rd *STVGE* SG2 .... 3 F2
The Dashes *HLW* CM20 .... 7 D3
Datchet Cl *HHNE* HP2 .... 165 G1
Datchworth Turn *HHNE* HP2 ...... 9 F5
Davenham Av *NTHWD* HA6 ...... 230 A3
Davenport *HLWE* CM17 .... 181 G5
Davies St *HERT/BAY* SG13 ...... 151 H3
Davis Crs *HTCH/STOT* SG5 ...... 39 F4
Davison Cl *CHES/WCR* EN8 ...... 197 H6
Davison Dr *CHES/WCR* EN8 ...... 197 H6
Davis' Rw *ARL/CHE* SG15 ...... 24 E5
Davys Cl *STALE/WH* AL4 .... 145 H2
Dawes La *RKW/CH/CXG* WD3 ...... 201 J6
Dawley *WGCE* AL7 .... 123 F8
Dawley Ct *HHNE* HP2 .... 8 C1
Dawlish Cl *STVGE* SG2 .... 96 D2
Dawlish Rd *LTNW/LEA* LU4 ...... 68 E6
Dawson Cl *HNLW* SG16 .... 24 A4
Dayemead *WGCE* AL7 .... 148 C6
Days Cl *HAT* AL10 .... 170 E4
  ROY SG8 .... 21 G4
Days Md *HAT* AL10 .... 170 E4
Deacon Cl *STAL* AL1 .... 189 F2
Deacons Cl *BORE* WD6 .... 223 K4
  PIN HA5 .... 230 C8
Deaconsfield Rd *HHS/BOV* HP3 ...... 185 H1
Deacons Hts *BORE* WD6 .... 223 K6
Deacons Hl *OXHEY* WD19 .... 13 D5
Deacon's Hill Rd *BORE* WD6 ...... 223 J5
Deacons Wy *HTCH/STOT* SG5 ...... 40 B8
Deadhearn La *CSTG* HP8 .... 216 D8
Deadman's Ash La
  RKW/CH/CXG WD3 .... 202 A6
Dead Woman's La
  HTCHE/RSTV SG4 .... 73 F3
Deakin Cl *WATW* WD18 .... 219 K7
Deanacre Cl *CFSP/GDCR* SL9 ...... 226 B5
Deancroft Rd *CFSP/GDCR* SL9 ...... 226 B5
Dean Fld *HHS/BOV* HP3 .... 183 J5
Deans *ABLGY* WD5 .... 203 J2
  TRING HP23 .... 135 F5
Deanscroft *KNEB* SG3 .... 96 A4
Deans Furlong *TRING* HP23 ...... 135 F5
Dean's Gdns *STALE/WH* AL4 ...... 168 D2
Deans Meadow *BERK* HP4 .... 112 E4
Deansway *HHS/BOV* HP3 .... 185 K1
Deard's End La *KNEB* SG3 ...... 96 A3
Deards Wd *KNEB* SG3 .... 96 A4
Debenham Rd *CHESW* EN7 ...... 197 F5
Deepdene *POTB/CUF* EN6 .... 209 J1
Deep Denes *LTNE* LU2 .... 5 E1
Deeping Cl *KNEB* SG3 .... 96 A5
Deer Cl *HERT/BAY* SG13 .... 151 J5
Deerfield Cl *WARE* SG12 .... 127 H7
The Deerings *HARP* AL5 .... 143 H5
Deer Pk *HLWW/ROY* CM19 ...... 179 H4
Deer Park Wk *CSHM* HP5 .... 182 A6
Deerswood Av *HAT* AL10 .... 171 G6
The Dee *HHNE* HP2 .... 164 E1
Deeves Hall La *POTB/CUF* EN6 ...... 208 D3
De Havilland Cl *HAT* AL10 ...... 170 E3
De Havilland Ct *RAD* WD7 ...... 207 H2

De Havilland Wy *ABLGY* WD5 ...... 204 A2
Deimos Dr *HHNE* HP2 .... 9 D2
Delahay Ri *BERK* HP4 .... 161 J3
Delamare Rd *CHES/WCR* EN8 ...... 197 K7
Delamere Rd *BORE* WD6 .... 224 A5
Delfcroft *WARE* SG12 .... 127 G6
Delfield Gdns *LTN* LU1 .... 88 D5
Delius Cl *BORE* WD6 .... 223 F6
Dellcot Cl *LTNE* LU2 .... 70 C4
Dellcott Cl *WGCW* AL8 .... 147 G2
Dellcroft Wy *HARP* AL5 .... 143 H3
Dellcut Rd *HHNE* HP2 .... 9 D3
Dellfield *BERK* HP4 .... 161 H3
  STAL AL1 .... 11 E5
  WARE SG12 .... 127 H1
Dellfield Av *BERK* HP4 .... 161 J3
Dellfield Cl *RAD* WD7 .... 206 B5
  WAT WD17 .... 12 B1
Dellfield Rd *HAT* AL10 .... 171 F4
Dell La *BSF* CM23 .... 105 K2
  RBSF CM22 .... 132 C1
Dellmeadow *ABLGY* WD5 .... 186 E8
Dell Meadow *HHS/BOV* HP3 ...... 185 J2
Dellors Cl *BAR* EN5 .... 225 J5
Dell Ri *LCOL/BKTW* AL2 .... 188 C4
Dell Rd *BERK* HP4 .... 160 E2
  PEND EN3 .... 214 B8
  WATN WD24 .... 204 B7
Dell Side *WATN* WD24 .... 204 B7
Dellsome La *BRKMPK* AL9 ...... 191 K1
  STALE/WH AL4 .... 191 J1
Dell Springs *BUNT* SG9 .... 63 J1
The Dells *HHS/BOV* HP3 .... 9 E6
Dellswood Cl *HERT/BAY* SG13 ...... 151 H4
Dells Wood Cl *HOD* EN11 ...... 152 E8
The Dell *BLDK* SG7 .... 42 E5
  CFSP/GDCR SL9 .... 226 B5
  HERT/BAY SG13 .... 151 F6
  LTN LU1 .... 88 D6
  LTNE LU2 .... 71 J8
  NTHWD HA6 .... 229 K1
  PIN HA5 .... 230 E8
  RAD WD7 .... 206 D6
  ROY SG8 .... 21 G4
  STAL AL1 .... 11 F2
  STVG SG1 .... 2 C3
Dellwood Cl *RKW/CH/CXG* WD3 ...... 218 A8
Delmar Av *HHNE* HP2 .... 165 J7
Delmerend La *STALW/RED* AL3 ...... 116 C3
Delphine Cl *LTN* LU1 .... 89 J3
Delta Gain *OXHEY* WD19 .... 230 E1
Demontfort Ri *WARE* SG12 ...... 127 G6
Denbigh Cl *HHS/BOV* HP3 ...... 8 B6
Denbigh Rd *LTNN/LIM* LU3 ...... 69 G7
Denby *LWTH* SG6 .... 42 B5
Denby Gra *HLWE* CM17 .... 181 H1
Dencora Wy *LTNN/LIM* LU3 ...... 68 A1
Dendridge Cl *EN* EN1 .... 214 A7
Dene La *STVGE* SG2 .... 77 F2
Dene Rd *NTHWD* HA6 .... 229 H5
Denewood Cl *WAT* WD17 .... 204 A7
Denham Cl *HHNE* HP2 .... 165 F1
  LTNN/LIM LU3 .... 68 D1
Denham La *CFSP/GDCR* SL9 ...... 226 C5
Denham Wk *CFSP/GDCR* SL9 ...... 226 C5
Denham Wy *BORE* WD6 .... 224 B1
Denham Wy
(North Orbital Road)
  RKW/CH/CXG WD3 .... 217 H8
Denmark St *WAT* WD17 .... 12 C1
Denny Av *WAB* EN9 .... 215 J4
Denny Ct *BSF* CM23 .... 86 A7
Denny Ga *CHES/WCR* EN8 ...... 197 K5
Denny's La *BERK* HP4 .... 161 G7
Densley Cl *WGCW* AL8 .... 147 H1
Denton Cl *BAR* EN5 .... 225 H5
  LTNN/LEA LU4 .... 68 A5
Denton Rd *STVG* SG1 .... 2 C4
Dents Cl *LWTH* SG6 .... 42 C6
Derby Rd *HOD* EN11 .... 177 J5
  LTNN/LEA LU4 .... 68 B7
  WAT WD17 .... 13 D3
Derby Wy *STVG* SG1 .... 76 C1
Derwent Av *LTNN/LIM* LU3 ...... 69 G6
  PIN HA5 .... 231 F5
Derwent Rd *HARP* AL5 .... 117 J5
  HHS/BOV HP3 .... 9 F6
  LTNE LU2 .... 5 E3
Desborough Cl *HERT/WAS* SG14 ...... 126 A8
Desborough Dr *WLYN* AL6 ...... 123 J4
Desborough Rd *HTCHE/RSTV* SG4 ...... 57 G1
Desmond Rd *WATN* WD24 .... 204 A6
De Tany Ct *STAL* AL1 .... 10 C5
Deva Cl *STALW/RED* AL3 .... 167 H3
Devereux Dr *WAT* WD17 .... 203 K8
De Vere Wk *WAT* WD17 .... 219 K2
Devoils La *BSF* CM23 .... 105 J2
Devon Cl *STAL* AL1 .... 11 D5
Devon Rd *LTNE* LU2 .... 5 F4
  WATN WD24 .... 220 E1
Devonshire Cl *STVGE* SG2 ...... 96 B1
Devonshire Rd *HARP* AL5 ...... 118 D7
  PIN HA5 .... 231 G7
Dewars Cl *WLYN* AL6 .... 122 C3

Dewes Green Rd *BSF* CM23 ...... 51 H
Dewgrass Gv *CHES/WCR* EN8 ...... 214 C5
Dewhurst Rd *CHES/WCR* EN8 ...... 197 G
Dewpond Cl *STVG* SG1 .... 75 H
Dewsbury Rd *LTNN/LIM* LU3 ...... 69 G
Dexter Cl *LTNN/LIM* LU3 .... 52 B
  STAL AL1 .... 11 F
Dexter Rd *BAR* EN5 .... 225 J
  DEN/HRF UB9 .... 228 B
Diamond Rd *WATN* WD24 .... 204 B
Dickens Cl *STALW/RED* AL3 ...... 10 C
Dickens Ct *HHNE* HP2 .... 141 G
Dicket Md *WLYN* AL6 .... 122 C
Dickins Cl *CHESW* EN7 .... 196 E
Dickinson Av *RKW/CH/CXG* WD3 ...... 219 F
Dickinson Sq *RKW/CH/CXG* WD3 ...... 219 G
Dickson *CHESW* EN7 .... 196 D
Dig Dag Hl *CHESW* EN7 .... 196 D
Digswell Cl *BORE* WD6 .... 207 K
Digswell Hl *WLYN* AL6 .... 122 A
Digswell Park Rd *WGCW* AL8 ...... 122 D
Digswell Ri *WGCE* AL7 .... 123 F
Digswell Rd *WGCW* AL8 .... 122 E
Dimmocks La *RKW/CH/CXG* WD3 ...... 201 K
Dimsdale Crs *BSF* CM23 .... 106 A
Dimsdale St *HERT/WAS* SG14 ...... 151 F
Dinant Link Rd *HOD* EN11 ...... 177 F
Dingle Cl *BAR* EN5 .... 224 E
Dinmore *HHS/BOV* HP3 .... 183 H
Ditchfield Rd *HOD* EN11 ...... 153 F
Ditchling Cl *LTNE* LU2 .... 70 D
Ditton Gn *LTNE* LU2 .... 70 E
Divot Pl *HERT/BAY* SG13 .... 152 A2
Dixies Cl *BLDK* SG7 .... 17 K
Dixon Pl *BUNT* SG9 .... 63 J
Dixons Hill Cl *BRKMPK* AL9 ...... 192 B
Dixons Hill Rd *BRKMPK* AL9 ...... 192 B
Dobb's Weir Rd *HOD* EN11 ...... 177 J
Docklands *HTCH/STOT* SG5 ...... 39 F5
Doctor's Commons Rd *BERK* HP4 ...... 161 J
Dodds La *HHNE* HP2 .... 140 D
Dodwood *WGCE* AL7 .... 148 C
Doggetts Wy *STAL* AL1 .... 10 B
Dognell Gn *WGCW* AL8 .... 147 G
Dolesbury Dr *WLYN* AL6 .... 95 K
Dolphin Wy *BSF* CM23 .... 105 K
Doncaster Cl *STVG* SG1 .... 76 D
Doncaster Gn *OXHEY* WD19 ...... 230 D4
Donkey La *TRING* HP23 .... 134 D7
Donne Cl *ROY* SG8 .... 21 G1
Dorchester Av *HOD* EN11 ...... 177 F
Dordans Rd *LTNW/LEA* LU4 ...... 68 D
Dorel Cl *LTNE* LU2 .... 5 D
Dormans Cl *NTHWD* HA6 .... 229 J
Dormer Cl *BAR* EN5 .... 225 J
Dorrien's Cft *BERK* HP4 .... 161 G2
Dorrington Cl *LTNN/LIM* LU3 ...... 4 A
Dorrofield Cl *RKW/CH/CXG* WD3 ...... 219 H
Dorset Cl *BERK* HP4 .... 161 C
Douglas Av *WATN* WD24 .... 204 E
Douglas Dr *STVG* SG1 .... 76 B
Douglas Gdns *BERK* HP4 .... 161 H4
Douglas Rd *HARP* AL5 .... 118 B
  LTNW/LEA LU4 .... 69 F
Douglas Wy *WGCE* AL7 .... 148 D3
Doulton Cl *HLWE* CM17 .... 181 H
Dove Cl *BSF* CM23 .... 105 H
  STSD CM24 .... 86 D
Dove Ct *HAT* AL10 .... 171 F
Dovedale *LTNE* LU2 .... 69 K
  WARE SG12 .... 3 F
Dovedale Cl *DEN/HRF* UB9 ...... 228 B
Dovehouse Cft *HLW* CM20 ...... 7 F2
Dovehouse Hl *LTNE* LU2 .... 5 F
Dove House La *DUN/WHIP* LU6 ...... 114 A
Dove La *POTB/CUF* EN6 .... 210 C
Dove Pk *PIN* HA5 .... 231 G
  RKW/CH/CXG WD3 .... 216 E
Dover Cl *LTNN/LIM* LU3 .... 69 F
Doverfield *CHESW* EN7 .... 196 A
Dover Wy *RKW/CH/CXG* WD3 ...... 219 H
Dowling Ct *HHS/BOV* HP3 ...... 185 H
Downalong *BUSH* WD23 .... 222 A
Downedge *STALW/RED* AL3 ...... 10 A
Downer Dr *RKW/CH/CXG* WD3 ...... 201 J
Downes Rd *STALE/WH* AL4 ...... 168 E
Downfield Cl *HERT/BAY* SG13 ...... 152 B
Downfield Rd *CHES/WCR* EN8 ...... 214 D
  HERT/BAY SG13 .... 152 B
Downfields *WGCW* AL8 .... 147 C
Down Green La *STALE/WH* AL4 ...... 144 E
Downhall Ley *BUNT* SG9 .... 63 J
Downings *WB* RKW/CH/CXG* WD3 ...... 227 C
Downlands *BLDK* SG7 .... 27 G8
  LTNN/LIM LU3 .... 68 B2
  ROY SG8 .... 21 G
  STVGE SG2 .... 76 E
  WAB EN9 .... 215 K4

Downsfield HAT AL10 .... 171 G7
Downside HHNE HP2 .... 8 B4
Downs La HAT AL10 .... 171 F6
Downs Rd LTN LU1 .... 4 A4
The Downs HAT AL10 .... 171 F6
   HLW CM20 .... 7 D4
Dowry Wk WAT WD17 .... 204 A3
Drakes Cl CHES/WCR EN8 .... 197 H6
Drakes Dr NTHWD HA6 .... 229 G7
   STAL AL1 .... 189 K1
   STVGE SG2 .... 3 F1
Drakes Wy HAT AL10 .... 171 G6
Drapers Wy STVG SG1 .... 2 A1
Drayman's Cl BSF CM23 .... 104 E4
Drayson Cl WAB EN9 .... 215 J2
Drayton Av POTB/CUF EN6 .... 209 K2
Drayton Rd BORE WD6 .... 223 K4
The Drey CFSP/GDCR 226 B4
Driftway ROY SG8 .... 31 J5
The Driftway HHNE HP2 .... 8 C5
Driftwood Av LCOL/BKTW AL2 .... 188 C4
Driver's End La HTCHE/RSTV SG4 .. 94 E5
The Drive BAR EN5 .... 225 K3
   BRKMPK AL9 .... 193 C5
   CFSP/GDCR SL9 .... 226 B6
   CHESW EN7 .... 195 K6
   CHESW EN7 .... 197 F6
   HARP AL5 .... 118 C8
   HERT/WAS SG14 .... 151 F1
   HLW CM20 .... 7 D3
   HOD EN11 .... 177 F1
   LCOL/BKTW AL2 .... 189 J3
   NTHWD HA6 .... 229 K7
   POTB/CUF EN6 .... 210 A3
   RAD WD7 .... 206 D4
   RKW/CH/CXG WD3 .... 218 A5
   SBW CM21 .... 132 C7
   STALE/WH AL4 .... 119 K2
   WAT WD17 .... 203 J7
   WLYN AL6 .... 96 B8
The Driveway POTB/CUF EN6 ...... 195 G6
Drop La LCOL/BKTW AL2 .... 205 J1
Drovers Wy BSF CM23 .... 105 F5
   HAT AL10 .... 171 G1
   STALW/RED AL3 .... 10 C4
Drummond Ride TRING HP23 ...... 135 F4
Drury La WARE SG12 .... 129 K8
Drycroft WGCE AL7 .... 147 K7
Dryden Crs STVGE SG2 .... 76 D1
Drysdale Cl NTHWD HA6 .... 229 K6
Dubbs Knoll Rd ROY SG8 .... 15 G4
Dubrae Cl STALW/RED AL3 .... 167 H8
Duchess Cl BSF CM23 .... 104 E2
Duchy Rd EBAR EN4 .... 210 E8
Ducketts Md MHAD SG10 .... 104 A8
Ducketts Md HLWW/ROY CM19 .. 154 C8
Ducketts Wd WARE SG12 .... 127 H2
Duck La STVGE SG2 .... 78 B5
Duckling La SBW CM21 .... 132 C7
Duckmore La TRING HP23 .... 134 D8
Ducks Hill Rd NTHWD HA6 .... 229 F8
   NTHWD HA6 .... 229 C8
   NTHWD HA6 .... 229 C6
Dudley Av CHES/WCR EN8 .... 214 C2
Dudley Rd HLWW/ROY CM19 ...... 154 C8
Dudley St LTNE LU2 .... 4 C3
Dudswell La BERK HP4 .... 160 E4
Dugdale Hill La POTB/CUF EN6 .. 209 K3
Dugdales RKW/CH/CXG WD3 ..... 219 F4
Dukes Av DUN/WHIP LU6 .... 113 G5
Duke's La HTCH/STOT SG5 .... 56 C1
Dukes Ride BSF CM23 .... 105 F3
Duke Rd HOD EN11 .... 177 F2
   LTNE LU2 .... 4 C3
   WAT WD17 .... 13 D2
Dukes Wy BERK HP4 .... 161 H3
Dulwich Wy RKW/CH/CXG WD3 .. 219 F5
Dumbarton Av CHES/WCR EN8 ... 214 C4
Dumfries Cl OXHEY WD19 .... 230 B2
Dumfries St LTN LU1 .... 4 B5
Duncan Cl WGCE AL7 .... 147 K4
Duncan Wy BUSH WD23 .... 221 G2
Duncombe Cl HERT/WAS SG14 ... 151 F1
   LTNN/LIM LU3 .... 69 H3
Duncombe Rd BERK HP4 .... 161 G4
   HERT/WAS SG14 .... 151 F2
Duncots Cl HTCH/STOT SG5 .... 40 C6
Dundale Rd TRING HP23 .... 135 F5
Dunhams La LWTH SG6 .... 42 B3
Dunlin Cl LTNN/LIM LU3 .... 69 F3
Dunlin Rd HHNE HP2 .... 164 D1
Dunmow Rd BSF CM23 .... 106 A2
   RBSF CM22 .... 107 F2
Dunn Cl STVG SG1 .... 2 C5
Dunnock Rd BORE WD6 .... 223 K4
Dunny La KGLGY WD4 .... 201 J2
   RKW/CH/CXG WD3 .... 200 D3
Dunsby Rd LTNN/LIM LU3 .... 69 F3
Dunsley Pl TRING HP23 .... 135 G6
Dunsmore Cl BUSH WD23 .... 222 A6
Dunsmore Rd LTN LU1 .... 4 A5
Dunsmore Wy BUSH WD23 .... 221 K6
Dunstable Cl STALE/WH AL4 .... 69 F8
Dunstable Pl LTN LU1 .... 4 B3
Dunstable Rd DUN/WHIP LU6 ..... 112 E3

LTN LU1 .... 4 B4
LTNW/LEA LU4 .... 68 C7
STALW/RED AL3 .... 117 F8
Dunstall Rd AMP/FLIT/B MK45 ...... 36 C7
Dunstalls HLWW/ROY CM19 .... 179 H5
Dunster Cl BAR EN5 .... 225 J4
   DEN/HRF UB9 .... 228 A7
Dunster Rd HHNE HP2 .... 141 G8
Dunsters Md WGCE AL7 .... 148 B5
Dunston Hl TRING HP23 .... 135 F5
Durban Rd East WATW WD18 .... 12 B3
Durban Rd West WATW WD18 ...... 12 B3
Durbar Rd LTNW/LEA LU4 .... 69 F8
Durham Cl SBW CM21 .... 132 A8
   WARE SG12 .... 153 G4
Durham Rd LTNE LU2 .... 5 E5
   STVG SG1 .... 59 G8
Durley Gdns LTN LU1 .... 4 B6
Durrants Dr RKW/CH/CXG WD3 .. 219 H3
Durrants Hill Rd HHS/BOV HP3 ... 185 H1
Durrants La BERK HP4 .... 161 F5
Durrants Rd BERK HP4 .... 161 G4
Duxford Cl LTNW/LIM LU3 .... 69 G2
Duxons Turn HHNE HP2 .... 9 H5
Dwight Rd WATW WD18 .... 219 J7
Dyes La HTCHE/RSTV SG4 .... 74 D1
Dyke La STALE/WH AL4 .... 145 H2
Dylan Rd BORE WD6 .... 223 G7
Dymoke Gn STALE/WH AL4 .... 11 F1
Dymokes Wy HOD EN11 .... 153 F8
Dyrham La BAR EN5 .... 209 F6
Dysons Cl CHES/WCR EN8 .... 214 C3

E

Eagle Centre Wy LTNW/LEA LU4 ... 68 A2
Eagle Ct HERT/BAY SG13 .... 152 A2
Eagle Wy HAT AL10 .... 171 F6
Ealing LTNW/LEA LU4 .... 68 A2
Earls Cl BSF CM23 .... 105 G3
Earls Hill Gdns ROY SG8 .... 21 G3
Earls La POTB/CUF EN6 .... 208 D2
Earlsmead LWTH SG6 .... 41 K6
Earls St WAT WD17 .... 13 D2
Earls Meade LTNE LU2 .... 4 B2
Easington Rd WARE SG12 .... 99 H2
Easingwold Gdns LTN LU1 .... 88 E1
Eastbourne Av STVG SG1 .... 75 F3
Eastbrook Rd WAB EN9 .... 215 K3
Eastbrook Wy HHNE HP2 .... 8 B5
Eastbury Av NTHWD HA6 .... 229 K8
Eastbury Ct STAL AL1 .... 11 E3
Eastbury Rd NTHWD HA6 .... 229 K5
   OXHEY WD19 .... 13 D6
Eastcheap LWTH SG6 .... 41 K4
East Cl HTCHE/RSTV SG4 .... 41 F8
   LCOL/BKTW AL2 .... 188 D3
   STVG SG1 .... 3 D3
Eastcote Dr HARP AL5 .... 144 A3
Eastcott Cl LTNE LU2 .... 70 D8
East Dr GSTN WD25 .... 204 C6
   NTHWD HA6 .... 229 K1
   STAL AL1 .... 132 C8
Eastern Av CHES/WCR EN8 .... 214 E3
   HNLW SG16 .... 24 A6
Eastern Wy LWTH SG6 .... 26 A8
Eastfield Av WATN WD24 .... 220 E1
Eastfield Cl LTNE LU2 .... 70 D5
Eastfield Ct STALE/WH AL4 .... 169 G3
Eastfield Rd CHES/WCR EN8 .... 214 E2
   PEND EN3 .... 214 C8
   ROY SG8 .... 21 J2
East Flint HHW HP1 .... 163 H5
East Ga HLW CM20 .... 6 C3
Eastgate STVG SG1 .... 2 B4
Eastglade NTHWD HA6 .... 229 K4
East Hl LTNN/LIM LU3 .... 69 C3
Eastholm LWTH SG6 .... 42 A1
Eastholm Gn LWTH SG6 .... 42 A1
East La ABLGY WD5 .... 187 G6
   GSTN WD25 .... 187 H8
   STALE/WH AL4 .... 120 B8
Eastlea Av GSTN WD25 .... 205 F7
East Lodge La ENC/FH EN2 .... 212 A6
Eastman Wy HHNE HP2 .... 9 D2
East Md WGCE AL7 .... 148 C6
East Mimms HHNE HP2 .... 8 B4
Eastmoor Pk HARP AL5 .... 143 K3
East Mt STALE/WH AL4 .... 120 B8
Eastnor HHS/BOV HP3 .... 183 J6
Easton Gdns BORE WD6 .... 224 D4
Eastor WGCE AL7 .... 123 G8
East Pk HLWE CM17 .... 157 F6
   SBW CM21 .... 132 C8
East Reach STVGE SG2 .... 3 E2
East Ridgeway POTB/CUF EN6 ... 195 F6
East Riding WLYN AL6 .... 123 K4
East Rd BSF CM23 .... 106 A2
   HLW CM20 .... 156 E5
   PEND EN3 .... 214 B8
East St HHNE HP2 .... 8 A5

LTNE LU2 .... 53 K7
WARE SG12 .... 127 H8
East Vw BRKMPK AL9 .... 173 G3
   HTCHE/RSTV SG4 .... 57 G7
East Wy WAB EN9 .... 215 J5
Eastwick Crs RKW/CH/CXG WD3 .. 227 J1
Eastwick Hall La HLW CM20 .... 155 H3
Eastwick Rd HLW CM20 .... 155 J5
Eastwick Rw HHNE HP2 .... 9 D6
Eaton Ga HHNE HP2 .... 229 H5
Eaton Green Rd LTNE LU2 .... 90 D1
Eaton Pl LTNE LU2 .... 70 E8
Eaton Rd HHNE HP2 .... 9 E2
   STAL AL1 .... 168 E6
Eaton Valley Rd LTNE LU2 .... 5 F2
Ebberns Rd HHS/BOV HP3 .... 185 J1
Ebenezer St LTN LU1 .... 4 B5
Ebury Ap RKW/CH/CXG WD3 ...... 218 C8
Ebury Cl NTHWD HA6 .... 229 H4
Ebury Rd RKW/CH/CXG WD3 ...... 218 C8
   WAT WD17 .... 13 E2
Echo Hl ROY SG8 .... 21 G4
Eddy St BERK HP4 .... 161 H4
Edenhall Cl HHNE HP2 .... 165 J7
Edens Cl BSF CM23 .... 106 A2
Edgars Ct WGCE AL7 .... 147 K4
Edgbaston Dr RAD WD7 .... 207 H2
Edgcott Cl LTNN/LIM LU3 .... 52 B8
Edgecote Cl LTN LU1 .... 88 D6
Edgehill Gdns LTNN/LIM LU3 .... 68 B1
Edgewood Dr LTNE LU2 .... 70 D3
Edgeworth Cl STVGE SG2 .... 76 D8
Edgwarebury La BORE WD6 .... 223 J7
   EDGE HA8 .... 223 J8
Edinburgh Cl RKW/CH/CXG WD3 .. 217 K6
Edinburgh Crs CHES/WCR EN8 ... 214 D3
Edinburgh Dr GSTN WD25 .... 204 E2
Edinburgh Pl HLW CM20 .... 156 D5
Edinburgh Wy HLW CM20 .... 156 E5
   HLWE CM17 .... 157 F4
Edison Cl STALE/WH AL4 .... 169 F4
Edison Rd STVGE SG2 .... 3 F2
Edkins Cl LTNE LU2 .... 69 K4
Edlyn Cl BERK HP4 .... 161 G4
Edmonds Dr STVGE SG2 .... 76 E5
Edmund Beaufort Dr
   STALW/RED AL3 .... 10 C2
Edmunds Rd HERT/WAS SG14 .... 150 C2
Edridge Cl BUSH WD23 .... 221 K5
Edulf Rd BORE WD6 .... 224 A2
Edward Amey Cl GSTN WD25 ...... 204 D6
Edward Cl ABLGY WD5 .... 204 A2
   STAL AL1 .... 11 E5
Edward Ct HHS/BOV HP3 .... 185 H2
Edward St LTNE LU2 .... 5 D2
Edwyn Cl BAR EN5 .... 225 H5
Egdon Dr LTNE LU2 .... 69 J3
Egerton Rd BERK HP4 .... 161 H3
Eight Acres TRING HP23 .... 135 F5
Eighth Av LTNN/LIM LU3 .... 68 C2
Eisenberg Cl BLDK SG7 .... 27 H8
Elaine Gdns LTN LU1 .... 89 F8
Elbow La HERT/BAY SG13 .... 152 A8
   STVGE SG2 .... 76 C8
Eldefield LWTH SG6 .... 41 H2
Elderbeck Cl CHESW EN7 .... 196 E6
Elderberry Cl LTNE LU2 .... 70 C5
Elderberry Dr HTCHE/RSTV SG4 .. 56 E5
Elderberry Wy GSTN WD25 .... 204 C5
Elderfield HLWE CM17 .... 157 G5
Elder Rd WARE SG12 .... 127 K6
Elder Wy STVG SG1 .... 2 B5
Eldon Av BORE WD6 .... 223 K2
Eldon Rd HOD EN11 .... 177 J5
   LTNW/LEA LU4 .... 68 D7
Eleanor Av STALW/RED AL3 .... 10 C2
Eleanor Cross Rd CHES/WCR EN8 .. 214 D4
Eleanor Gdns BAR EN5 .... 225 J5
Eleanor Rd CHES/WCR EN8 .... 214 D5
   HERT/WAS SG14 .... 151 F2
Eleanor Wy CHES/WCR EN8 .... 214 E4
Elfrida Rd WATW WD18 .... 13 D4
Elgar Cl BORE WD6 .... 223 F7
Elgin Dr NTHWD HA6 .... 229 K6
Elgin Rd BROX EN10 .... 197 K2
   CHES/WCR EN8 .... 197 G8
Elgood Av NTHWD HA6 .... 230 B5
Eliot Rd ROY SG8 .... 21 H1
   STVGE SG2 .... 76 D3
Elizabeth Cl BAR EN5 .... 225 J3
   WAB EN9 .... 177 J8
   WGCE AL7 .... 148 D3
Elizabeth Ct STALE/WH AL4 .... 169 G3
Elizabeth Dr TRING HP23 .... 135 G3
Elizabeth Rd BSF CM23 .... 105 H4
Elizabeth St LTN LU1 .... 4 B5
Elizabeth Wy HLW CM20 .... 155 H3
   HLWW/ROY CM19 .... 179 G2
Ellenborough Cl BSF CM23 .... 105 G4
Ellenbrook Cl WATN WD24 .... 220 D1
Ellenbrook Crs HAT AL10 .... 170 C4
Ellenbrook La HAT AL10 .... 170 C4
Ellen Cl HHNE HP2 .... 9 C5
Ellenhall Cl LTNN/LIM LU3 .... 4 A2
Ellerdine Cl LTNN/LIM LU3 .... 69 G5

Ellesborough Cl OXHEY WD19 ...... 230 D4
Ellesfield WLYN AL6 ...... 122 B4
Ellesmere Rd BERK HP4 ...... 162 A5
Ellingham Cl HHNE HP2 ...... 9 D3
Ellingham Rd HHNE HP2 ...... 8 C1
Elliott Cl WGCE AL7 ...... 147 J6
Ellis Av CFSP/GDCR SL9 ...... 226 C7
  STVG SC1 ...... 75 K1
Elliswick Rd HARP AL5 ...... 118 D3
Ellwood Gdns GSTN WD25 ...... 204 C4
Elm Av LTN LU1 ...... 88 D6
  OXHEY WD19 ...... 13 F6
Elmbank Av BAR EN5 ...... 225 H4
Elmbridge HLWE CM17 ...... 157 J6
Elmbrook Dr BSF CM23 ...... 105 H5
Elm Cl WAB EN9 ...... 215 J4
Elmcote Wy RKW/CH/CXG WD3 ...... 218 E6
Elm Dr CHES/WCR EN8 ...... 197 J6
  HAT AL10 ...... 171 F5
  STALE/WH AL4 ...... 169 F6
Elmfield PIN HA5 ...... 231 G6
Elmfield Cl BSF CM23 ...... 105 H2
Elm Gdns ENC/FH EN2 ...... 213 G8
  WGCW AL8 ...... 147 G3
Elm Gn HHW HP1 ...... 163 H4
Elm Gv BERK HP4 ...... 161 K5
  BSF CM23 ...... 106 A2
  WATN WD24 ...... 204 B7
Elm Hatch PIN HA5 ...... 231 G6
Elmhurst Cl BSF CM23 ...... 105 J6
Elmhurst Rd PEND EN3 ...... 214 B7
Elmoor Av WLYN AL6 ...... 122 B4
Elmoor Cl WLYN AL6 ...... 122 B5
Elmore Rd LTNE LU2 ...... 5 E2
Elm Pk BLDK SG7 ...... 43 F1
Elm Park Rd PIN HA5 ...... 230 D8
Elm Rd BSF CM23 ...... 105 H1
Elmroyd Av POTB/CUF EN6 ...... 210 A3
Elmroyd Cl POTB/CUF EN6 ...... 210 A3
Elms Cl HTCHE/RSTV SG4 ...... 57 J6
Elmscroft Gdns POTB/CUF EN6 ...... 210 A2
Elmside DUN/WHIP LU6 ...... 114 B1
Elmside Wk HTCH/STOT SG5 ...... 56 C2
Elms Rd CFSP/GDCR SL9 ...... 226 B6
  WARE SG12 ...... 128 A7
The Elms HERT/BAY SG13 ...... 151 K3
  WLYN AL6 ...... 94 E7
Elmtree Av LTNE LU2 ...... 71 F6
Elm Tree Wk RKW/CH/CXG WD3 ...... 217 J4
  TRING HP23 ...... 135 F4
Elm Wk RAD WD7 ...... 206 C6
  ROY SG8 ...... 21 K2
  STVGE SG2 ...... 3 F5
Elm Wy RKW/CH/CXG WD3 ...... 218 A8
Elmwood SBW CM21 ...... 132 D8
  WGCW AL8 ...... 147 G4
Elmwood Av BLDK SG7 ...... 43 F2
  BORE WD6 ...... 224 A4
Elmwood Crs LTNE LU2 ...... 69 K6
Elsinge Rd EN EN1 ...... 214 A6
Elstree Hl North BORE WD6 ...... 223 G5
Elstree Hl South BORE WD6 ...... 223 F7
Elstree Rd BORE WD6 ...... 222 D6
  BUSH WD23 ...... 222 A8
  HHNE HP2 ...... 141 F8
  STAN HA7 ...... 222 C7
Elstree Wy BORE WD6 ...... 224 B2
Elton Rd HERT/WAS SG14 ...... 151 F7
Elveden Cl LTNE LU2 ...... 71 J4
Elvington Gdns LTNN/LIM LU3 ...... 52 B8
Elwood HLWE CM17 ...... 181 K7
Ely Cl HAT AL10 ...... 170 E3
  STVG SG1 ...... 59 H7
Ely Gdns BORE WD6 ...... 224 C5
Ely Rd STAL AL1 ...... 168 E7
Ely Wy LTNW/LEA LU4 ...... 68 C5
Embleton Rd OXHEY WD19 ...... 230 B2
Emerton Ct BERK HP4 ...... 161 E1
Emerton Garth BERK HP4 ...... 161 F2
Emmanuel Rd NTHWD HA6 ...... 230 A6
Emma Rothschild Ct
  TRING HP23 ...... 135 F4
Emma's Crs WARE SG12 ...... 153 G5
Emmer Gn LTNE LU2 ...... 71 G7
Emmitt Cl RAD WD7 ...... 207 H3
Emperor Cl BERK HP4 ...... 161 G2
Emperors Ga STVGE SG2 ...... 76 D1
Empress Rd LTNE LU2 ...... 68 D5
Endeavour Rd CHES/WCR EN8 ...... 197 H5
Enderby Rd LTNN/LIM LU3 ...... 68 A5
Endersby Rd BAR EN5 ...... 225 H5
Endymion Ct HAT AL10 ...... 171 H3
Endymion Ms HAT AL10 ...... 171 H3
Endymion Rd HAT AL10 ...... 171 H3
Englehurst HARP AL5 ...... 119 F8
Enid Cl LCOL/BKTW AL2 ...... 205 G1
Ennerdale Cl STAL AL1 ...... 168 E8
Ennis Cl HARP AL5 ...... 144 A3
Ennismore Cl LWTH SG6 ...... 42 C6
Ennismore Gn LTNE LU2 ...... 71 G8
Enslow Cl LTN LU1 ...... 88 D6
Enterprise Wy LTNN/LIM LU3 ...... 69 G1
Epping Gn HHNE HP2 ...... 165 G1
Epping Gn WAB EN9 ...... 179 G6
Ereswell Rd LTNN/LIM LU3 ...... 69 F2

Erin Cl LTNW/LEA LU4 ...... 69 F7
Ermine Cl CHESW EN7 ...... 214 A1
  ROY SG8 ...... 21 H1
  STALW/RED AL3 ...... 167 H7
Ermine Ct BUNT SG9 ...... 63 J1
Ermine St BUNT SG9 ...... 47 H6
  WARE SG12 ...... 127 H2
Escarpment Av DUN/WHIP LU6 ...... 113 F1
Escot Wy BAR EN5 ...... 225 F5
Esdaile La HOD EN11 ...... 177 F4
Eskdale LCOL/BKTW AL2 ...... 190 D5
  LTNW/LEA LU4 ...... 68 A4
Essendon Gdns WCCE AL7 ...... 148 A3
Essendon Hl BRKMPK AL9 ...... 173 F3
Essex Cl LTN LU1 ...... 4 C5
Essex La ABLGY WD5 ...... 203 J3
Essex Md HHNE HP2 ...... 140 E8
Essex Rd BORE WD6 ...... 223 K3
  HOD EN11 ...... 177 G2
  STVG SG1 ...... 75 G1
  WAT WD17 ...... 12 B1
Essex St STAL AL1 ...... 11 D5
Estcourt Rd WAT WD17 ...... 13 D2
Estfeld Cl HOD EN11 ...... 153 G8
Ethelred Cl WGCE AL7 ...... 148 A4
Etna Rd STALW/RED AL3 ...... 10 C3
Europa Rd HHNE HP2 ...... 8 C2
Euston Av WATW WD18 ...... 12 A4
Evans Av GSTN WD25 ...... 204 A5
Evan's Cl RKW/CH/CXG WD3 ...... 219 H5
Evans Gv STALE/WH AL4 ...... 169 F2
Evans Wy TRING HP23 ...... 135 G5
Evedon Cl LTNN/LIM LU3 ...... 68 E3
Evelyn Dr PIN HA5 ...... 230 E6
Evensyde WATW WD18 ...... 219 H6
Everard Cl STAL AL1 ...... 10 C6
Everest Cl ARL/CHE SG15 ...... 25 F4
Everest Wy HHNE HP2 ...... 9 D5
Everett Cl BUSH WD23 ...... 222 B8
  CHESW EN7 ...... 196 C3
Evergreen Cl KNEB SG3 ...... 96 B7
Evergreen Rd WARE SG12 ...... 127 K6
Evergreen Wk HHS/BOV HP3 ...... 164 D8
Evergreen Wy LTNN/LIM LU3 ...... 69 F1
Everlasting La STALW/RED AL3 ...... 10 E2
Exchange Rd STVG SG1 ...... 3 C3
  WATW WD18 ...... 12 C3
Exeter Cl STVG SG1 ...... 59 H7
  WATN WD24 ...... 13 D1
Explorer Dr WATW WD18 ...... 12 A5
Extension Rd HERT/BAY SG13 ...... 151 J3
Exton Av LTNE LU2 ...... 5 E2
Eynsford Ct HTCHE/RSTV SG4 ...... 56 D3
Eynsford Rd LTNW/LEA LU4 ...... 68 C6
Eywood Rd STAL AL1 ...... 10 B6

F

Faggots Cl RAD WD7 ...... 207 F5
Faints Cl CHESW EN7 ...... 196 C7
Fairacre HHS/BOV HP3 ...... 185 K2
Fairacres POTB/CUF EN6 ...... 210 A3
Fair Cl BUSH WD23 ...... 221 J7
Faircross Wy STAL AL1 ...... 11 F3
Fairfax Av LTNN/LIM LU3 ...... 68 C2
Fairfax Rd HERT/BAY SG13 ...... 151 J2
Fairfield BUNT SG9 ...... 63 J3
Fairfield Av OXHEY WD19 ...... 230 B1
Fairfield Cl HARP AL5 ...... 119 F8
  RAD WD7 ...... 206 B7
Fairfield Dr BROX EN10 ...... 197 K2
Fairfield Rd HOD EN11 ...... 177 F1
Fairfield Wy HTCHE/RSTV SG4 ...... 57 G1
Fairfolds GSTN WD25 ...... 205 F5
Fairford Av LTNE LU2 ...... 69 K4
Fairgreen Rd LTN LU1 ...... 88 E6
Fairhaven Crs OXHEY WD19 ...... 230 A1
Fairhill HHS/BOV HP3 ...... 185 K2
Fairlands Wy STVG SG1 ...... 2 A3
  STVGE SG2 ...... 76 C1
Fairlawns WAT WD17 ...... 220 A1
Fairley Wy CHESW EN7 ...... 197 F6
Fairmead Av HARP AL5 ...... 143 K1
Fair Oak Dr LTNE LU2 ...... 70 A6
Fairoaks Gv PEND EN3 ...... 214 C7
Fairthorn Cl TRING HP23 ...... 134 D6
Fair Vw POTB/CUF EN6 ...... 193 H8
Fairview Dr WAT WD17 ...... 203 K6
Fairview Rd STVG SG1 ...... 75 G1
Fairway BSF CM23 ...... 106 B3
  HHS/BOV HP3 ...... 185 K2
  SBW CM21 ...... 132 D7
  WARE SG12 ...... 152 B1
Fairway Av BORE WD6 ...... 224 A2
Fairway Cl HARP AL5 ...... 143 H4
  LCOL/BKTW AL2 ...... 188 E5
Fairways CHES/WCR EN8 ...... 197 H4
The Fairway ABLGY WD5 ...... 203 J2
  HLWS CM18 ...... 180 C4
  NTHWD HA6 ...... 229 K3
Falcon Cl HAT AL10 ...... 171 F6

  NTHWD HA6 ...... 229 K
  SBW CM21 ...... 132 A
  STVGE SG2 ...... 76 E
Falconer Rd BUSH WD23 ...... 221 K
Falconers Fld HARP AL5 ...... 117 K
Falconers Pk SBW CM21 ...... 132 E
Falconers Rd LTNE LU2 ...... 5 E
Falconer St BSF CM23 ...... 105 H
Falcon Rdg BERK HP4 ...... 161 K
Falcon Wy GSTN WD25 ...... 205 F
  WGCE AL7 ...... 147 K
Faldo Rd AMP/FLIT/B MK45 ...... 36 A
Falkirk Gdns OXHEY WD19 ...... 230 E4
Falkland Rd BAR EN5 ...... 225 H
Fallowfield LTNN/LIM LU3 ...... 69 G
  STVGE SG2 ...... 76 D
  WGCE AL7 ...... 123 J
Fallowfield Cl DEN/HRF UB9 ...... 228 A
Fallow Ri HERT/BAY SG13 ...... 151 K
Fallows Gn HARP AL5 ...... 118 B
Falstaff Gdns STAL AL1 ...... 188 C
Falstone Gn LTNE LU2 ...... 71 F
Fanhams Hall Rd WARE SG12 ...... 127 K
Fanhams Rd WARE SG12 ...... 127 J
Fanshaw Crt HERT/WAS SG14 ...... 150 E
Fanshawe Crs WARE SG12 ...... 127 J
Fanshawe St HERT/WAS SG14 ...... 150 E
Fanshaws La HERT/BAY SG13 ...... 175 H
Fantail La TRING HP23 ...... 134 B
Faraday Cl LTNW/LEA LU4 ...... 68 B8
  WATW WD18 ...... 219 H
Faraday Rd STVGE SG2 ...... 3 C
Far End HAT AL10 ...... 171 H
Faringdon Rd LTNW/LEA LU4 ...... 68 B
Faringford Cl POTB/CUF EN6 ...... 210 E
Farland Rd HHNE HP2 ...... 9 F
Farley Farm Rd LTN LU1 ...... 89 H
Farley Hl LTNE LU2 ...... 4 D
Farm Av HARP AL5 ...... 117 K
Farmbrook LTNE LU2 ...... 69 K
Farm Cl AMS HP6 ...... 216 D
  BAR EN5 ...... 225 G
  BORE WD6 ...... 207 H8
  CHES/WCR EN8 ...... 197 J
  HERT/WAS SG14 ...... 150 B
  LWTH SG6 ...... 42 D
  POTB/CUF EN6 ...... 195 G
  STVG SG1 ...... 2 B
  WGCW AL8 ...... 147 F
Farmers Cl GSTN WD25 ...... 204 E
Farm Gn LTN LU1 ...... 4 E
Farm Hill Rd WAB EN9 ...... 215 H
Farmhouse Cl BROX EN10 ...... 197 K3
Farmhouse La HHNE HP2 ...... 9 F
Farm La RKW/CH/CXG WD3 ...... 218 E
  STDN SG11 ...... 101 H
Farm Pl BERK HP4 ...... 161 G
Farm Rd LTN LU1 ...... 117 J
  NTHWD HA6 ...... 229 G
  RKW/CH/CXG WD3 ...... 216 C
  STAL AL1 ...... 189 F
Farm Wy BUSH WD23 ...... 221 J
  NTHWD HA6 ...... 229 H
Farnham Cl HHS/BOV HP3 ...... 183 K
  SBW CM21 ...... 132 E
Farquhar St HERT/WAS SG14 ...... 151 F
Farraline Rd WATW WD18 ...... 12 C
Farrant Wy BORE WD6 ...... 223 H
Farrer Top STALW/RED AL3 ...... 115 H
Farriday Cl STALW/RED AL3 ...... 168 B
Farriers WARE SG12 ...... 153 F
Farriers Cl BLDK SG7 ...... 26 E
  WLYN AL6 ...... 94 E
Farriers End BROX EN10 ...... 197 K
Farriers Wy BORE WD6 ...... 224 A
Farringford Cl LCOL/BKTW AL2 ...... 188 D
Farrow Cl LTNN/LIM LU3 ...... 52 B
Farr's La LTNE LU2 ...... 91 F
Farthing Dr LWTH SG6 ...... 42 E
The Farthings HHW HP1 ...... 164 A
Faverolle Gn CHES/WCR EN8 ...... 197 H
Faversham Cl TRING HP23 ...... 135 F
Fawcett Rd STVGE SG2 ...... 76 D
Fawn Ct BRKMPK AL9 ...... 171 J
Fay Gn ABLGY WD5 ...... 203 F
Feacey Down HHW HP1 ...... 163 J
Fearney Md RKW/CH/CXG WD3 ...... 217 J
Fearnley Rd WGCW AL8 ...... 147 F
Fearnley St WATW WD18 ...... 12 C
  WATW WD18 ...... 12 C
Featherbed La HHS/BOV HP3 ...... 185 G
Feather Dell HAT AL10 ...... 170 E
Featherstone Gdns BORE WD6 ...... 224 E
Featherston Rd STVGE SG2 ...... 76 D
Federal Wy WATN WD24 ...... 220 D
Felbrigg Cl LTNE LU2 ...... 71 G
Felden Cl GSTN WD25 ...... 204 A
Felden Dr HHS/BOV HP3 ...... 184 B
Felden La HHS/BOV HP3 ...... 184 B
Feldon Cl PIN HA5 ...... 231 G
Felix Av LTNE LU2 ...... 5 F
Fellowes La STALE/WH AL4 ...... 191 H
Fellowes Wy STVGE SG2 ...... 3 F
Fells Cl HTCH/STOT SG5 ...... 56 D
Felmersham Ct LTN LU1 ...... 89 G

Felmersham Rd LTN LU1 .... 89 F2
Felmongers HMW CM20 .... 156 E7
elstead Cl LTNE LU2 .... 70 A6
elstead Cl HERT/WAS EN8 .... 214 D2
elstead Wy LTNE LU2 .... 5 D1
elton Cl BORE WD6 .... 207 H8
  BROX EN10 .... 197 K5
  LTNE LU2 .... 70 E8
en End HTCH/STOT SG5 .... 25 K1
ennells HLWW/ROY CM19 .... 179 J6
ennycroft Rd HHW HP1 .... 163 J3
ensomes Aly HHNE HP2 .... 8 A4
ensom's Ct HHNE HP2 .... 8 A4
enton Gra HLWE CM17 .... 181 F2
enwick Cl LTNN/LIM LU3 .... 69 C4
ermor Crs LTNE LU2 .... 70 D8
ern Cl BROX EN10 .... 197 K5
erndale MHAD SG10 .... 103 C7
erndale Rd LTN LU1 .... 89 C2
  PEND EN3 .... 214 D7
ern Dells HAT AL10 .... 170 E5
erndene LCOL/BKTW AL2 .... 205 C3
erndown NTHWD HA6 .... 230 B8
erndown Cl PIN HA5 .... 231 F6
ern Dr OXHEY WD19 .... 230 D2
ern Dr HHS/BOV HP3 .... 8 B6
ernecroft STAL AL1 .... 188 C1
ern Gv WGCW AL8 .... 122 D7
ernheath LTNN/LIM LU3 .... 52 A8
ernhill HLWS CM18 .... 180 B5
ern Hill La HLWS CM18 .... 180 C5
ernhills ABLGY WD5 .... 203 J4
ernleigh Ct RYLN/HDSTN HA2 .... 231 J8
ernleys LTNW/LEA LU4 .... 169 F3
erns Cl PEND EN3 .... 214 D6
ernsleigh Cl CFSP/GDCR SL9 .... 226 B5
ernville La HHNE HP2 .... 8 A5
ern Wy GSTN WD25 .... 204 C5
erny Hl EBAR EN4 .... 211 C8
errars Cl LTNW/LEA LU4 .... 68 A8
errers La STALE/WH AL4 .... 144 D4
errier Rd STVGE SG2 .... 76 D3
erryhills Cl OXHEY WD19 .... 230 D2
esants Cft HLW CM20 .... 156 E6
etherstone Cl POTB/CUF EN6 .... 210 E3
ddle Bridge La HAT AL10 .... 170 E3
dler Pl BUSH WD23 .... 221 J6
eld Cl CSHM HP5 .... 182 A6
  HARP AL5 .... 144 A2
  STALE/WH AL4 .... 168 D2
eld Crs ROY SG8 .... 21 K2
eld End Cl LTNE LU2 .... 70 D5
  OXHEY WD19 .... 13 F6
elders Wy RAD WD7 .... 207 H3
eldfare LWTH SG6 .... 25 J8
  STVGE SG2 .... 76 E6
eldfares LCOL/BKTW AL2 .... 190 B5
eldgate Rd LTNW/LEA LU4 .... 68 C6
eldings Rd CHES/WCR EN8 .... 197 K7
eld La LWTH SG6 .... 41 K5
eld Rd HHNE HP2 .... 9 D6
  OXHEY WD19 .... 13 F5
elds End Cl TRING HP23 .... 135 F3
elds End La HHW HP1 .... 163 C4
eld Vw BAR EN5 .... 225 C4
eld View Ri LCOL/BKTW AL2 .... 188 A7
eld View Rd POTB/CUF EN6 .... 210 B3
eldway BERK HP4 .... 162 B7
eld Wy CFSP/GDCR SL9 .... 226 A6
  HHW HP1 .... 183 J5
  HOD EN11 .... 153 C7
  RKW/CH/CXG WD3 .... 218 A8
eldway TRING HP23 .... 135 J8
  WARE SG12 .... 153 C5
fth Av GSTN WD25 .... 204 E5
  LWTH SG6 .... 42 C3
fth Avenue Allende Av HLW CM20 .... 6 C3
gtree Hl HHNE HP2 .... 8 A4
ey Cl STVG SG1 .... 75 F2
mer Rd LTNW/LEA LU4 .... 68 D5
nch Cl HAT AL10 .... 171 C5
nchdale Rd HHNE HP2 .... 163 K6
nches End STVGE SG2 .... 77 J1
e Fishers HERT/BAY SG13 .... 152 A3
  HTCHE/RSTV SG4 .... 56 E4
nch La BUSH WD23 .... 221 H4
nchmoor HLWS CM18 .... 180 A4
nch Rd BERK HP4 .... 161 H5
nley Rd HARP AL5 .... 119 F6
nsbury Pk LTNW/LEA LU4 .... 68 A3
nucane Ri BUSH WD23 .... 231 K1
nway LTN LU1 .... 89 F1
nway Rd HHNE HP2 .... 9 E1
rbank Cl LTNN/LIM LU3 .... 68 B1
rbank Rd OXHEY WD19 .... 13 F6
rbank Rd STALW/RED AL3 .... 168 C2
r St Cl STVGE SG2 .... 76 A8
recrest LWTH SG6 .... 25 J8
lands BSF CM23 .... 105 H3
r Pk HLWW/ROY CM19 .... 179 J4
rs Cl HAT AL10 .... 171 C5
  HTCH/STOT SG5 .... 56 B1
rs Dr STALE/WH AL4 .... 120 A4
rs La POTB/CUF EN6 .... 210 C3

First Av GSTN WD25 .... 204 D5
First Avenue Mandela Av HLW CM20 .... 6 C3
  HLWE CM17 .... 156 E6
The Firs CHESW EN7 .... 196 C4
  STAL AL1 .... 189 K2
  TRING HP23 .... 135 J8
  WGCW AL8 .... 122 C7
Firs Wk HHNE HP2 .... 229 J5
  WLYN AL6 .... 123 K4
Fir Tree Cl HHS/BOV HP3 .... 9 D6
Fir Tree Ct BORE WD6 .... 223 J4
Fir Tree Hl RKW/CH/CXG WD3 .... 203 F7
Firway WLYN AL6 .... 123 F2
Firway Cl WLYN AL6 .... 123 F2
Firwood Av STALE/WH AL4 .... 169 H6
Fisher Cl KGLGY WD4 .... 186 A7
Fishers Cl CHES/WCR EN8 .... 215 F4
  STDN SG11 .... 81 J6
Fishers Gn STVG SG1 .... 58 A8
Fisher's Green Rd STVG SG1 .... 75 C1
Fishers Md STDN SG11 .... 81 J6
Fishery Rd HHW HP1 .... 163 K8
Fish Farm St STALW/RED AL3 .... 142 C4
Fish Hl ROY SG8 .... 21 H3
Fishponds Rd HTCH/STOT SG5 .... 56 C1
Fishpool St STALW/RED AL3 .... 10 B4
Fish St STALW/RED AL3 .... 142 C4
Fitzjohn Av BAR EN5 .... 225 K5
Fitzroy Av LTNN/LIM LU3 .... 69 C6
Fitzwarin Cl LTNN/LIM LU3 .... 68 D2
Fitzwilliams Ct HLWE CM17 .... 157 H5
Five Acres HLWS CM18 .... 180 B5
  KGLGY WD4 .... 185 K7
  LCOL/BKTW AL2 .... 190 B3
  STSD CM24 .... 86 D1
Five Acres Av LCOL/BKTW AL2 .... 188 B7
Five Fields Cl OXHEY WD19 .... 231 C1
Five Oaks LTN LU1 .... 88 E5
Five Springs LTNN/LIM LU3 .... 68 D3
Flagstaff Cl WAB EN9 .... 215 C3
Flagstaff Rd WAB EN9 .... 215 C2
The Flags HHNE HP2 .... 9 E5
Flamsteadbury La
  STALW/RED AL3 .... 142 B5
Flamstead End Rd
  CHES/WCR EN8 .... 197 F6
Flash La ENC/FH EN2 .... 213 F7
Flatfield Rd HHS/BOV HP3 .... 165 F8
Flaunden Bottom CSHM HP5 .... 200 B7
Flaunden Hl HHS/BOV HP3 .... 200 D7
Flaunden La HHS/BOV HP3 .... 200 E2
  RKW/CH/CXG WD3 .... 201 H3
Flavian Cl STALW/RED AL3 .... 167 C8
Flecks La ROY SG8 .... 15 K2
The Fleet ROY SG8 .... 21 C5
Fleetwood Crs STVG SG1 .... 75 C2
Fleetwood Wy OXHEY WD19 .... 230 D3
Fleming Cl CHESW EN7 .... 196 E4
Fleming Crs HERT/WAS SG14 .... 150 D3
Fletcher Wy HHNE HP2 .... 164 B4
Flexley Wd WGCE AL7 .... 123 F8
Flex Meadow HLWW/ROY CM19 .... 179 F2
Flinders Cl STAL AL1 .... 11 F6
  STVGE SG2 .... 76 C3
Flint Cl LTNN/LIM LU3 .... 68 D2
Flint Copse STALW/RED AL3 .... 142 D3
The Flintings HHNE HP2 .... 139 J1
Flint Rd LWTH SG6 .... 42 C1
Flint Wy STALW/RED AL3 .... 167 K2
Flitch Wy RBSF CM22 .... 107 J2
Flora Gv STAL AL1 .... 11 E5
Floral Dr LCOL/BKTW AL2 .... 190 B4
Florence Av LTNN/LIM LU3 .... 68 C3
Florence Cl GSTN WD25 .... 204 B5
  STAL AL1 .... 181 F3
Florence St HTCH/STOT SG5 .... 56 D7
Flowers Wy LTN LU1 .... 4 C4
Flowton Gv HARP AL5 .... 143 H2
Fold Cft HLW CM20 .... 155 H8
Foldingshott KNEB SG3 .... 96 E6
Follett Dr ABLGY WD5 .... 204 A1
Folly Av STALW/RED AL3 .... 10 B3
Folly Cl HTCHE/RSTV SG4 .... 56 E4
  RAD WD7 .... 206 C6
Folly Flds STALE/WH AL4 .... 119 K7
Folly La LTN LU1 .... 88 C5
  STALW/RED AL3 .... 10 B3
Folly Pathway RAD WD7 .... 206 C5
The Folly BUNT SG9 .... 63 H2
  HERT/WAS SG14 .... 151 C3
Folly Vw WARE SG12 .... 153 C4
Fontmell Cl STALW/RED AL3 .... 11 D1
Football Cl BLDK SG7 .... 26 E3
Forbes Av POTB/CUF EN6 .... 210 C3
Ford Cl BUSH WD23 .... 221 K4
Ford Fld STDN SG11 .... 103 H1
Fordham Cl BLDK SG7 .... 17 K4
Fordham Rd ROY SG8 .... 21 J4
Ford Hl STDN SG11 .... 103 J1
Ford St STDN SG11 .... 81 K3
Fordwich Cl HERT/WAS SG14 .... 150 D3
Fordwich Ri HERT/WAS SG14 .... 150 D3
Fordwich Ri HERT/WAS SG14 .... 150 D3
Fordwich Rd WGCW AL8 .... 147 H4
Forebury Av SBW CM21 .... 132 D7

The Forebury SBW CM21 .... 132 D7
Forefield LCOL/BKTW AL2 .... 188 C5
Forest Av HHS/BOV HP3 .... 164 C8
Foresters Cl CHESW EN7 .... 196 C5
Foresthall Rd STSD CM24 .... 86 C5
Fore St BRKMPK AL9 .... 171 H3
  HERT/WAS SG14 .... 151 C3
  HLWE CM17 .... 157 F5
  HTCHE/RSTV SG4 .... 43 H8
Forest Rd CHES/WCR EN8 .... 197 H7
  GSTN WD25 .... 204 C3
  PEND EN3 .... 214 D6
Forest Rw STVGE SG2 .... 76 A8
Forest Wy HLWE CM17 .... 180 E5
  RBSF CM22 .... 107 H3
Forge Cl HTCH/STOT SG5 .... 56 D1
  KGLGY WD4 .... 201 K1
Forge End LCOL/BKTW AL2 .... 188 C4
Forge La NTHWD HA6 .... 229 K6
  WLYN AL6 .... 122 B4
Forres Cl HOD EN11 .... 177 F1
Forrest Crs LTNE LU2 .... 70 B5
Forresters Dr WGCE AL7 .... 148 D4
Fortuna Cl STVGE SG2 .... 76 D1
Fortune La BORE WD6 .... 223 C6
The Fortunes HLWS CM18 .... 7 E6
Forty Hl EN EN1 .... 213 J7
Foster Cl CHES/WCR EN8 .... 197 J8
  STVG SG1 .... 58 C8
Foster Dr HTCHE/RSTV SG4 .... 56 E4
Foster Rd HHW HP1 .... 164 A8
Foster St HLWE CM17 .... 181 J5
Foston Cl LTNN/LIM LU3 .... 68 E4
Fotherley Rd RKW/CH/CXG WD3 .... 227 J1
Founceley Av WARE SG12 .... 99 J1
Founders Rd HOD EN11 .... 153 C8
Fountain Farm HLWS CM18 .... 7 E6
Fountain Pl WAB EN9 .... 215 H4
Fountains Rd LTNN/LIM LU3 .... 69 H6
Fouracres LWTH SG6 .... 42 A7
Four Acres STVG SG1 .... 2 B1
  WGCE AL7 .... 147 K5
Fouracres Dr HHS/BOV HP3 .... 164 E8
The Four Acres SBW CM21 .... 132 E7
Fouracres Wk HHS/BOV HP3 .... 164 E8
Four Limes STALE/WH AL4 .... 145 G1
Fourth Av GSTN WD25 .... 204 E5
  HLW CM20 .... 6 B3
  HLWW/ROY CM19 .... 179 H1
  LTNN/LIM LU3 .... 68 C2
  LWTH SG6 .... 42 C2
The Four Tubs BUSH WD23 .... 222 A7
  BUSH WD23 .... 222 A7
Fovant Cl HARP AL5 .... 143 K3
Fowley Cl CHES/WCR EN8 .... 214 E4
Foxbury Cl LTNE LU2 .... 69 J3
Fox Cl BORE WD6 .... 223 G6
  BUSH WD23 .... 221 J5
  TRING HP23 .... 135 H8
Fox Cnr ROY SG8 .... 15 G4
Foxcroft STAL AL1 .... 11 F6
Foxdell NTHWD HA6 .... 229 J5
Foxdells HERT/WAS SG14 .... 149 K6
Foxdells La BSF CM23 .... 85 J7
Foxdell Wy CFSP/GDCR SL9 .... 226 B4
Foxes Cl HERT/BAY SG13 .... 152 A3
Foxes Dr CHESW EN7 .... 196 D7
Foxes La POTB/CUF EN6 .... 195 G6
Foxfield STVGE SG2 .... 76 D6
Foxfield Cl NTHWD HA6 .... 230 A5
Foxglove Bank ROY SG8 .... 21 K4
Foxglove Cl BSF CM23 .... 105 F3
  HAT AL10 .... 171 G5
The Foxgloves HHW HP1 .... 163 H7
Foxglove Wy WLYN AL6 .... 122 E1
Foxgrove Pth OXHEY WD19 .... 230 E4
Foxhill LTNE LU2 .... 69 K4
Fox Hl ROY SG8 .... 15 G4
Foxhill WD24 .... 204 B6
Fox Hill Rd ROY SG8 .... 15 G4
Foxholes Av HERT/BAY SG13 .... 151 K3
Foxhollows HAT AL10 .... 171 G2
Foxlands Cl GSTN WD25 .... 204 A4
Foxley Dr BSF CM23 .... 105 K1
Foxley Gv WLYN AL6 .... 122 E5
Foxleys OXHEY WD19 .... 231 F2
Fox Rd STVG SG1 .... 2 C3
  TRING HP23 .... 135 H7
Fox's La BRKMPK AL9 .... 192 C3
Foxton Rd HOD EN11 .... 176 E3
Frampton Rd POTB/CUF EN6 .... 193 J8
Frampton St HERT/WAS SG14 .... 151 C3
Francis Av STALW/RED AL3 .... 10 C1
Francis Cl HTCH/STOT SG5 .... 25 J3
  HTCHE/RSTV SG4 .... 56 E4
Francis Rd BLDK SG7 .... 16 C3
  WARE SG12 .... 127 H7
  WATW WD18 .... 12 C5
Francis St LTN LU1 .... A3
Frankland Cl RKW/CH/CXG WD3 .... 219 F7
Frankland Rd RKW/CH/CXG WD3 .... 219 G6
Franklin Av AMP/FLIT/B MK45 .... 36 B6
  CHESW EN7 .... 196 E8
Franklin Cl HTCH/STOT SG5 .... 39 F5
  STALE/WH AL4 .... 170 D8

Franklin Gdns *HTCHE/RSTV* SG4 ...... 41 F8
Franklin's Rd *WAT* WD17 .... 12 C1 ⊡
Franklin's Rd *STVG* SG1 .... 75 H1
Frank Martin Ct *CHESW* EN7 .... 196 E8
Fraser Av *CHES/WCR* EN8 .... 197 J6 ⊡
Frederick St *LTNE* LU2 .... 4 C3
Frederick Street Pas *LTNE* LU2 .... 4 B3
Freeman Av *LTNN/LIM* LU3 .... 69 G1
Freemans Cl *HTCH/STOT* SG5 .... 40 A8
Freewaters Cl *HTCH/STOT* SG5 ...... 40 C5
Freman Dr *BUNT* SG9 .... 63 H1 ⊡
French Horn La *HAT* AL10 .... 171 G3 ⊡
French Rw *STAL* AL1 .... 10 C4 ⊡
French's Cl *WARE* SG12 .... 153 F4
Frensham *CHESW* EN7 .... 196 D5
Frensham Dr *HTCHE/RSTV* SG4 ...... 41 G7
Freshwater Cl *LTNN/LIM* LU3 .... 68 E2 ⊡
Freshwaters *HLW* CM20 .... 7 D3 ⊡
Fretherne Rd *WGCW* AL8 .... 147 J3
Friars Cl *LTN* LU1 .... 89 G4
Friarscroft *BROX* EN10 .... 177 F6
Friars Fld *BERK* HP4 .... 161 F2
Friars Rd *HTCHE/RSTV* SG4 .... 43 H8
STDN SG11 .... 82 B3
Friars Wk *TRING* HP23 .... 135 F5
Friars Wy *BUSH* WD23 .... 221 G1
KGLGY WD4 .... 186 A8
LTN LU1 .... 89 G4
Friars Wd *BSF* CM23 .... 106 B1
Friday Furlong *HTCH/STOT* SG5 ...... 56 A1 ⊡
Friedberg Av *BSF* CM23 .... 105 G4
Friendless La *STALW/RED* AL3 ...... 115 J6
Friends Av *CHES/WCR* EN8 .... 214 C2
Frimley Rd *HHW* HP1 .... 163 H5
Fringewood Cl *NTHWD* HA6 .... 229 G7
Frinton Cl *OXHEY* WD19 .... 230 C1
Friston Gn *LTNE* LU2 .... 70 E8 ⊡
Fridsnden Copse *BERK* HP4 .... 162 C1
Frithwood Av *NTHWD* HA6 .... 230 A5
Frobisher Cl *BUSH* WD23 .... 221 H6
HARP AL5 .... 143 H4
ROY SG8 .... 21 J2
STAL AL1 .... 168 E5
WAT WD17 .... 12 A1
Frobisher Dr *STVGE* SG2 .... 3 F1
Frobisher Rd *STAL* AL1 .... 169 F8 ⊡
Frobisher Wy *HAT* AL10 .... 170 C1
Froghall La *STVGE* SG2 .... 60 D8
Frogmoor La *RKW/CH/CXG* WD3 ... 228 C3
Frogmore *LCOL/BKTW* AL2 .... 189 G5
Frogmore Hl *HERT/WAS* SG14 .... 97 H3
Frogmore Rd *HHS/BOV* HP3 .... 185 H2 ⊡
Frogmore *TRING* HP23 .... 135 F5
Frogs Hall La *STDN* SG11 .... 79 J6
Frome Cl *LTNW/LEA* LU4 .... 68 D5
Frome Sq *HHNE* HP2 .... 165 F1 ⊡
Front St *LTN* LU1 .... 89 H1
The Front *BERK* HP4 .... 162 E2
Frowick Rd *BRKMPK* AL9 .... 192 B1
Frowyke Crs *POTB/CUF* EN6 .... 209 F2
Fry Rd *STVGE* SG2 .... 76 D4
Fryth Md *STALW/RED* AL3 .... 10 A3
Fulbeck Wy *RYLN/HDSTN* HA2 .... 231 K8
Fulbourne Cl *LTNW/LEA* LU4 .... 68 D7
Fulford Gv *OXHEY* WD19 .... 230 C1
Fuller Ct *BSF* CM23 .... 105 K2 ⊡
Fuller Gdns *WATN* WD24 .... 204 C7
Fuller Rd *WATN* WD24 .... 204 C7
Fullers Ct *LWTH* SG6 .... 41 J2
Fullers Md *HLWE* CM17 .... 181 J7
Fuller Wy *RKW/CH/CXG* WD3 ...... 219 F5
Fulling Mill La *WLYN* AL6 .... 122 B3
Fulmar Crs *HHW* HP1 .... 163 K1
Fulmore Ct *HARP* AL5 .... 119 G5
Fulton Cl *STVG* SG1 .... 2 A3
Fulton Crs *BSF* CM23 .... 86 B8
Furham Fld *PIN* HA5 .... 231 H6
Furlay Cl *LWTH* SG6 .... 41 H2
Furlongs *HHW* HP1 .... 163 K5
Furlong Wy *WARE* SG12 .... 152 E2
Furriers Ct *BSF* CM23 .... 105 F4
The Furrows *LTNN/LIM* LU3 .... 69 G2
Furse Av *STALW/RED* AL4 .... 11 F1
Furtherfield *ABLGY* WD5 .... 203 K2 ⊡
Furtherground *HHNE* HP2 .... 8 B6 ⊡
Furzebushes La *LCOL/BKTW* AL2 ... 188 A3
Furze Cl *LTNE* LU2 .... 69 J2
OXHEY WD19 .... 230 D4
Furzedown *STVGE* SG2 .... 3 F4
Furzedown Ct *HARP* AL5 .... 143 J1
Furzefield Rd *WGCE* AL7 .... 147 K4
Furze Gv *ROY* SG8 .... 21 J4 ⊡
Furzehill Rd *BORE* WD6 .... 224 B5
Furzen Crs *HAT* AL10 .... 170 E7
Furze Rd *HHW* HP1 .... 163 H7
Furze Vw *RKW/CH/CXG* WD3 ...... 217 F6

G

Gable Cl *ABLGY* WD5 .... 203 K2
PIN HA5 .... 231 H6
Gables Av *BORE* WD6 .... 223 J3
Gables Cl *CFSP/GDCR* SL9 .... 226 B3
Gaddesden Crs *WATN* WD24 .... 204 E4
Gaddesden Gv *WGCE* AL7 .... 148 C3 ⊡
Gaddesden La *STALW/RED* AL3 ... 141 F5

Gaddesden Rw *HHNE* HP2 .... 139 K1
Gade Av *WATW* WD18 .... 219 K4
Gade Bank *RKW/CH/CXG* WD3 ... 219 J4
Gadebridge La *HHW* HP1 .... 164 A4
Gadebridge Rd *HHW* HP1 .... 164 A5
Gade Cl *HHW* HP1 .... 164 A3
WATW WD18 .... 219 K4
Gade Valley Cl *KGLGY* WD4 .... 186 A6
Gade View Rd *HHS/BOV* HP3 ...... 185 H3
Gadmore La *TRING* HP23 .... 158 D2
Gadswell Cl *GSTN* WD25 .... 205 F6
Gage Cl *ROY* SG8 .... 21 H1
Gainsborough Av *STAL* AL1 .... 11 E5
Gainsford Crs *HTCHE/RSTV* SG4 ... 41 C7
Gainswood *WGCE* AL7 .... 147 K4
Gall End La *STSD* CM24 .... 86 E2 ⊡
Galley Gn *HERT/BAY* SG13 .... 153 F7 ⊡
Galley Hl *HHW* HP1 .... 163 K4 ⊡
Galleyhill Rd *WAB* EN9 .... 215 K2 ⊡
Galley La *BAR* EN5 .... 209 F8
Galliard Cl *LTNN/LIM* LU3 .... 69 G5
Galloway Cl *BROX* EN10 .... 197 K4
BSF CM23 .... 105 J1
Galloway Rd *BSF* CM23 .... 105 J1
Gallows Hl *KGLGY* WD4 .... 203 H1
Gallows Hill La *ABLGY* WD5 .... 203 H2
Galston Rd *LTNW/LIM* LU3 .... 68 C1
Gammon Cl *HHS/BOV* HP3 .... 9 D6
Gammons La *WATN* WD24 .... 204 B7
Ganders Ash *GSTN* WD25 .... 204 B3 ⊡
Gandhi Ct *WATN* WD24 .... 13 E1 ⊡
Gangies Hl *SBW* CM21 .... 131 J5
Ganton Wk *OXHEY* WD19 .... 231 F5 ⊡
Ganymede Pl *HHNE* HP2 .... 8 C2 ⊡
Gaping La *HTCH/STOT* SG5 .... 56 B2
Garden Av *HAT* AL10 .... 171 F7
Garden Cl *BAR* EN5 .... 225 H4
HARP AL5 .... 143 H4
ROY SG8 .... 21 J2
STAL AL1 .... 168 E5
WAT WD17 .... 12 A1
Garden Ct *STALE/WH* AL4 .... 120 B8
Garden Field La *BERK* HP4 .... 162 C1
Gardenia Av *LTNN/LIM* LU3 .... 69 F5
Garden La *ROY* SG8 .... 21 H4
Garden Reach *CSTG* HP8 .... 216 A3
Garden Rd *ABLGY* WD5 .... 203 K1 ⊡
BUNT SG9 .... 63 J1
KNEB SG3 .... 96 C7
Garden Rw *HTCH/STOT* SG5 .... 56 D1
The Gardens *BLDK* SG7 .... 42 E1 ⊡
BRKMPK AL9 .... 192 E5
HTCH/STOT SG5 .... 25 J3
WAT WD17 .... 12 A1
Garden Terrace Rd *HLWE* CM17 ... 157 F5
Garden Wk *ROY* SG8 .... 21 J2
STVG SG1 .... 2 C3
Gardiners La *BLDK* SG7 .... 17 K5
The Gardiners *HLWE* CM17 .... 180 E2
Garfield St *WATN* WD24 .... 204 C6
Garland Cl *CHES/WCR* EN8 .... 214 D1 ⊡
HHNE HP2 .... 8 A1 ⊡
Garland Rd *WARE* SG12 .... 127 J8
Garnault Rd *EN* EN1 .... 213 J8
Garner Dr *BROX* EN10 .... 197 J4
Garners End *CFSP/GDCR* SL9 ..... 226 B5
Garners End *CFSP/GDCR* SL9 ..... 226 B5
Garners Rd *CFSP/GDCR* SL9 .... 226 B5
Garnett Cl *WATN* WD24 .... 204 E6
Garnett Dr *LCOL/BKTW* AL2 .... 188 C3
Garrard Wy *STALE/WH* AL4 .... 145 G1
Garratts Rd *BUSH* WD23 .... 221 K7
Garretts Md *LTNE* LU2 .... 70 C6
Garsmouth Wy *GSTN* WD25 .... 204 E4
Garston Crs *GSTN* WD25 .... 204 D4 ⊡
Garston Dr *GSTN* WD25 .... 204 D4
Garston La *GSTN* WD25 .... 204 E4
Garthland Dr *BAR* EN5 .... 225 C5
Garth Rd *LWTH* SG6 .... 41 J6
The Garth *ABLGY* WD5 .... 203 J3
Gartlet Rd *WAT* WD17 .... 12 C3
Gascoyne Wy *HERT/BAY* SG13 ... 151 G4
Gas La *ROY* SG8 .... 32 C6
Gate Cl *BORE* WD6 .... 224 B1
Gatecroft *HHS/BOV* HP3 .... 164 E8
Gate End *NTHWD* HA6 .... 230 B6
Gatehill Gdns *LTNN/LIM* LU3 .... 52 B8 ⊡
Gatehill Rd *NTHWD* HA6 .... 230 A6
Gatesbury Rd *STDN* SG11 .... 81 K6 ⊡
Gatesdene Cl *BERK* HP4 .... 137 K1
Gateshead Rd *BORE* WD6 .... 223 J2
Gates Wy *STVG* SG1 .... 2 A2
Gateway Cl *NTHWD* HA6 .... 229 H5
The Gateways *CHESW* EN7 .... 196 B6
Gatwick Cl *BSF* CM23 .... 86 A8 ⊡
Cauldie Wy *STDN* SG11 .... 81 J7
Gaumont Ap *WATW* WD18 .... 12 C7
Gaundy Wy *LWTH* SG6 .... 25 K7
Gaveston Dr *BERK* HP4 .... 161 J3
Gayland Av *LTNE* LU2 .... 5 F3
Gayton Cl *LTNN/LIM* LU3 .... 69 F5
Gaywood Av *CHES/WCR* EN8 ..... 197 H8
Geddes Rd *BUSH* WD23 .... 221 K4 ⊡
Geddings Rd *HOD* EN11 .... 177 G3
The Generals Wk *PEND* EN3 .... 214 D7 ⊡

Gentlemens Fld *WARE* SG12 127
George La *ROY* SG8 .... 21 H3
George Leighton Ct *STVGE* SG2 3
Georges Md *BORE* WD6 .... 223 G6
George St *BERK* HP4 162
HERT/WAS SG14 151
HHNE HP2 8
LTN LU1 4
STALW/RED AL3 10
STALW/RED AL3 115
WATW WD18 219
George St West *LTN* LU1 .... 4 C4
George's Wood Rd *BRKMPK* AL9 ... 193
George V Av *PIN* HA5 231
George V Wy *RKW/CH/CXG* WD3 ... 201
George Wk *WARE* SG12 .... 127 H8
Georgewood Rd *HHS/BOV* HP3 ... 185
Gerard Av *BSF* CM23 105
Gernon Rd *LWTH* SG6 41
Gernon Wk *LWTH* SG6 41
Gew's Cnr *CHES/WCR* EN8 197
Ghibert Wy *BERK* HP4 161
Gibb Cft *HLWS* CM18 180
Gibbons Cl *BORE* WD6 223
STALE/WH AL4 145
Gibbons Wy *KNEB* SG3 96
Gibbs Cl *CHES/WCR* EN8 197
Gibbs Couch *OXHEY* WD19 230
Gibbs Fld *BSF* CM23 105
Gibson Cl *HTCHE/RSTV* SG4 57
Gifford's La *STDN* SG11 79
Gilbert Rd *DEN/HRF* UB9 228
Gilbert's Hl *TRING* HP23 158
Gilbert St *PEND* EN3 214
Gilbey Av *BSF* CM23 106
Gilbey Crs *STSD* CM24 86
Gildea Cl *PIN* HA5 231
Gilden Cl *HLWE* CM17 .... 157 H5
Gilden Wy *HLWE* CM17 157
Gilder Cl *LTNN/LIM* LU3 69
Gilderdale *LTNW/LEA* LU4 68
Gilders *SBW* CM21 132
Giles Cl *STALE/WH* AL4 145
Gillam St *LTNE* LU2 4
Gillan Gn *BUSH* WD23 .... 231 K1
Gillian Av *STAL* AL1 188
Gilliat's Gn *RKW/CH/CXG* WD3 ... 217
Gillison Cl *LWTH* SG6 42
Gills Hl *RAD* WD7 206
Gills Hill La *RAD* WD7 206
Gills Hollow *RAD* WD7 206
Gilmour Cl *ENC/FH* EN2 213
Gilpin Gn *HARP* AL5 118
Gilpin Rd *WARE* SG12 152
Gilpin's Gallop *WARE* SG12 153
Gilpin's Ride *BERK* HP4 162
Gilsland *WAB* EN9 215
Ginns Rd *BUNT* SG9 67
Gippeswyck Cl *PIN* HA5 .... 230 E2
Gipsy La *BSF* CM23 86
KNEB SG3 95
LTN LU1 5
Girdle Rd *HTCHE/RSTV* SG4 40
Girons Ct *HTCHE/RSTV* SG4 57
Girtin Rd *BUSH* WD23 221
Girton Ct *CHES/WCR* EN8 197
Girton Wy *RKW/CH/CXG* WD3 219
Gisburne Wy *WATN* WD24 204
Gladden Ct *HLWS* CM18 .... 180 B3
Gladding Rd *CHESW* EN7 195
Gladeside *STALE/WH* AL4 169
The Glades *HHW* HP1 163
The Glade *BLDK* SG7 42
LWTH SG6 41
WCCW AL8 .... 147 H
The Gladeway *WAB* EN9 215
Gladsmuir Rd *BAR* EN5 225
Gladstone Rd *HOD* EN11 177
WARE SG12 99
WARE SG12 127
WAT WD17 13
Glaisdale *LTNW/LEA* LU4 68
Glamis Cl *CHESW* EN7 196
HHNE HP2 141
Gleave Cl *STAL* AL1 168
Glebe Av *ARL/CHE* SG15 24
Glebe Cl *BRKMPK* AL9 .... 173 G
CFSP/GDCR SL9 226
HERT/WAS SG14 98
HERT/WAS SG14 .... 151 G
HHS/BOV HP3 185
LBUZ LU7 110
Glebe Cottages *BRKMPK* AL9 173
Glebe Ct *BSF* CM23 106
Glebelands *HLW* CM20 7
Glebe La *BAR* EN5 225
Glebe Rd *HERT/WAS* SG14 151
LWTH SG6 42
WLYN AL6 122
The Glebe *GSTN* WD25 204
KGLGY WD4 .... 186 A
Glemsford Cl *LTNW/LEA* LU4 .... 68 A
Glemsford Dr *HARP* AL5 119
Glencoe Rd *BUSH* WD23 221
Glencorse Gn *OXHEY* WD19 .... 230 E

Glendale HHW HP1 ..... 164 A6
Gleneagles Cl OXHEY WD19 ..... 230 E4 🔲
Gleneagles Dr LTNE LU2 ..... 69 J5
Glenester Cl HHNE HP1 ..... 153 F8
Glen Faba Rd HLWW/ROY CM19 ..... 178 A3
Glenferrie Rd STAL AL1 ..... 11 F4
The Gowers HLW CM20 ..... 7 F2
Glenfield Ct HERT/WAS SG14 ..... 150 C2 🔲
Glenfield Rd LTNW/LIM LU3 ..... 69 H3
Glengall Pl STAL AL1 ..... 189 G1 🔲
Glenhaven Av BORE WD6 ..... 223 K3
Glenlyn Av STAL AL1 ..... 168 E7 🔲
The Glen HHNE HP2 ..... 165 F1 🔲
    LTN LU1 ..... 88 D6
    NTHWD HA6 ..... 229 J6
Glenview Rd HHW HP1 ..... 164 A6
Glenville Av ENC/FH EN2 ..... 213 F8
Glen Wy WAT WD17 ..... 203 K8
Glenwood BROX EN10 ..... 176 E5
    WCCE AL7 ..... 148 D4 🔲
Glenwood Cl STVGE SG2 ..... 76 D7
Glevum Cl STALW/RED AL3 ..... 167 G8
Globe Cl HARP AL5 ..... 118 E8
Globe Crs BSF CM23 ..... 85 G3
Gloucester Av CHES/WCR EN8 ..... 214 D3
Gloucester Cl STVGE SG1 ..... 58 E7 🔲
Gloucester Rd ENC/FH EN2 ..... 213 F8
    LTN LU1 ..... 4 B4 🔲
Glover Cl CHESW EN7 ..... 196 D5 🔲
Glovers Cl HERT/BAY SG13 ..... 151 F5 🔲
Glovers La HLWE CM17 ..... 181 H6
The Glynde STVGE SG2 ..... 96 C1
Glynswood CFSP/GDCR SL9 ..... 226 C5
Goat La EN EN1 ..... 213 J8
Goblins Gn WGCE AL7 ..... 147 J4
Goddard End STVGE SG2 ..... 76 D8
Goddards Cl HERT/BAY SG13 ..... 173 K5
Godfrey Rd STVGE SG2 ..... 3 F5
Godfreys Cl LTN LU1 ..... 89 C3
Godfries Cl WLYN AL6 ..... 124 A6
Godwin Cl CHING E4 ..... 215 H3
Goffs Crs CHESW EN7 ..... 196 A7
Goff's La CHESW EN7 ..... 196 A7
Goff's Oak Av CHESW EN7 ..... 195 K6
Golda Cl BAR EN5 ..... 225 J6
Gold Cl BROX EN10 ..... 176 D6
Goldcrest Wy BUSH WD23 ..... 221 K8
Goldcroft HHS/BOV HP3 ..... 165 F8
Golden Dell WGCE AL7 ..... 148 A7
Goldfield Rd TRING HP23 ..... 134 E6
Goldfinch Wy BORE WD6 ..... 223 K4 🔲
Gold Hl East CFSP/GDCR SL9 ..... 226 A8
Goldings BSF CM23 ..... 106 A1
Goldings Crs HAT AL10 ..... 171 G3
Goldings La HERT/WAS SG14 ..... 125 J8
Goldington Ct HOD EN11 ..... 152 E8 🔲
Goldon LWTH SG6 ..... 42 B5
Goldstone Cl WARE SG12 ..... 127 H7 🔲
Golf Cl BUSH WD23 ..... 13 G6
Golf Club Rd BRKMPK AL9 ..... 193 G4
Gold Ride ENC/FH EN2 ..... 212 D5
Gombards STALW/RED AL3 ..... 10 C3 🔲
Gomer Cl HTCHE/RSTV SG4 ..... 94 D8
Gonville Av RKW/CH/CXG WD3 ..... 219 G6
Gonville Crs STVGE SG2 ..... 76 D7
Goodey Mead STVGE SG2 ..... 78 C7
Goodliffe Pk BSF CM23 ..... 86 A7
Goodrich Cl GSTN WD25 ..... 204 B5
Goodwin Ct CHES/WCR EN8 ..... 197 J6 🔲
Goodwins Md LBUZ LU7 ..... 110 A3
Goodwin Stile BSF CM23 ..... 105 G4
Goodwood Av PEND EN3 ..... 214 B7
    WATN WD24 ..... 203 K5
Goodwood Cl HOD EN11 ..... 176 E2
Goodwood Rd ROY SG8 ..... 21 K3 🔲
Goodyers Rd RAD WD7 ..... 206 C3
Goose Acre CSHM HP5 ..... 182 C8
    LBUZ LU7 ..... 110 C2
Gooseacre WGCE AL7 ..... 148 A5
Gooseberry Hl LTNW/LIM LU3 ..... 69 C3
Goosecroft HHW HP1 ..... 163 J6 🔲
Goosefields RKW/CH/CXG WD3 ..... 218 B6
Goose La RBSF CM22 ..... 133 H2
Goral Md RKW/CH/CXG WD3 ..... 218 C8
Gordian Wy STVGE SG1 ..... 59 J8
Gordon St STAL AL1 ..... 168 E7 🔲
Gordon Rd CHES/WCR EN8 ..... 215 F4
Gordon St LTN LU1 ..... 4 B4 🔲
Gordons Wk HARP AL5 ..... 143 K1 🔲
Gorelands La CSTG HP8 ..... 226 B1
Gore La STDN SG11 ..... 101 H6
Gorham Dr STAL AL1 ..... 189 G1
Gorle Cl GSTN WD25 ..... 204 B4
Gorleston Cl STVGE SG1 ..... 58 A8
Gorse Cl HAT AL10 ..... 170 E7
Gorse Cnr STALW/RED AL3 ..... 10 C2
Gorselands HARP AL5 ..... 143 K2 🔲
Gorst Cl LWTH SG6 ..... 41 J4
Gosforth La OXHEY WD19 ..... 230 B2
Gosforth Pth OXHEY WD19 ..... 230 B2 🔲
Gosling Av HTCH/STOT SG5 ..... 54 E7
Gosmore Ley Cl HTCHE/RSTV SG4 ..... 56 D6
Gosmore Rd HTCHE/RSTV SG4 ..... 56 D7
The Gossamers GSTN WD25 ..... 205 F5
Gosselin Rd HERT/WAS SG14 ..... 151 F1
Gossoms Ryde BERK HP4 ..... 161 H4

Gothic Wy ARL/CHE SG15 ..... 24 E4
Gould Cl BRKMPK AL9 ..... 192 B2
Government Rw PEND EN3 ..... 215 F7
Gowar Fld POTB/CUF EN6 ..... 209 F1
Gower Rd ROY SG8 ..... 21 G2
The Gowers HLW CM20 ..... 7 F2
Grace Av RAD WD7 ..... 207 G5
Grace Cl BORE WD6 ..... 224 C1
Grace Gdns BSF CM23 ..... 105 J5
Grace Wy STVG SG1 ..... 75 K1
Graemes Dyke Rd BERK HP4 ..... 161 H6
Grafton Cl STALE/WH AL4 ..... 69 G7
Graham Av BROX EN10 ..... 176 D6
Graham Cl STAL AL1 ..... 189 F1
Graham Gdns LTNW/LIM LU3 ..... 69 H5
Grailands BSF CM23 ..... 105 G1
Grammar School Wk
    HTCH/STOT SG5 ..... 56 C2
Grampian Wy LTNW/LIM LU3 ..... 68 B1
The Granaries WAB EN9 ..... 215 K3 🔲
Granary Cl STALE/WH AL4 ..... 145 C1 🔲
Granary La HARP AL5 ..... 118 D8
The Granary HLWW/ROY CM19 ..... 154 C8
    WARE SG12 ..... 153 H6
Granby Av HARP AL5 ..... 118 E7
Granby Park Rd CHESW EN7 ..... 196 D6
Granby Rd LTNW/LEA LU4 ..... 68 C6
    STVG SG1 ..... 58 C7
Grand Union Canal Wk BERK HP4 ..... 161 F2
    HHW HP1 ..... 163 F8
    LBUZ LU7 ..... 110 A5
    RKW/CH/CXG WD3 ..... 227 K3
    TRING HP23 ..... 110 A7
Grange Av LTNW/LIM LU3 ..... 68 D4
    LTNW/LEA LU4 ..... 68 C5
    TRDG/WHET N20 ..... 225 K7
Grange Bottom ROY SG8 ..... 21 J4
Grange Cl CFSP/GDCR SL9 ..... 226 B7
    HERT/WAS SG14 ..... 150 E3 🔲
    HHNE HP2 ..... 9 D6 🔲
    HTCHE/RSTV SG4 ..... 56 E5
    STALW/RED AL3 ..... 115 H5
    WAT WD17 ..... 220 B1
Grange Ct WAB EN9 ..... 215 H4
Grange Court Rd HARP AL5 ..... 143 K3
Grangedale Cl NTHWD HA6 ..... 229 K7 🔲
Grange Dr HTCH/STOT SG5 ..... 25 K3
Grange Flds CFSP/GDCR SL9 ..... 226 B7
Grange Gdns WARE SG12 ..... 152 D1
Grange Hl WLYN AL6 ..... 122 C5
Grange La LBUZ LU7 ..... 110 D5
    HLWW/ROY CM19 ..... 178 D1
Grange Pk BSF CM23 ..... 85 J8
Grange Ri WLYN AL6 ..... 94 E8
Grange Rd AMP/FLIT/B MK45 ..... 36 B6
    BORE WD6 ..... 223 J5
    BSF CM23 ..... 105 K2
    BUSH WD23 ..... 13 F4
    CFSP/GDCR SL9 ..... 226 A7
    LBUZ LU7 ..... 110 D5
    LWTH SG6 ..... 41 K1
    TRING HP23 ..... 109 G8
Grangeside BSF CM23 ..... 85 J7
Grange St STALW/RED AL3 ..... 10 C3
Grange Wk BERK HP4 ..... 105 K2
Grangewood POTB/CUF EN6 ..... 193 H8
Gransden Cl LTNW/LIM LU3 ..... 69 J2
Grant Gdns HARP AL5 ..... 118 D7
Grantham Cl ROY SG8 ..... 21 J1
Grantham Gdns WARE SG12 ..... 127 J7
Grantham Gn BORE WD6 ..... 224 B5
Grantham Rd LTNW/LEA LU4 ..... 69 F8
Granville Dene HHS/BOV HP3 ..... 183 J5
Granville Gdns HOD EN11 ..... 153 F7
Granville Rd BAR EN5 ..... 225 H4
    HTCHE/RSTV SG4 ..... 41 F8
    LTN LU1 ..... 89 G1
    STAL AL1 ..... 11 E4
    WATW WD18 ..... 13 D3 🔲
Grasmere Av HARP AL5 ..... 118 E7
    LTNW/LIM LU3 ..... 69 C2
Grasmere Cl GSTN WD25 ..... 204 C2
    HHS/BOV HP3 ..... 165 C8 🔲
Grasmere Rd LTNW/LIM LU3 ..... 69 C2
    STAL AL1 ..... 168 E8
    WARE SG12 ..... 127 J6 🔲
Grassingham End CFSP/GDCR SL9 ..... 226 B6
Grassingham Rd CFSP/GDCR SL9 ..... 226 B6
Grassington Cl LCOL/BKTW AL2 ..... 188 C3 🔲
Grass Mdw STVGE SG2 ..... 76 E2
Grass Warren ARL/CHE AL6 ..... 124 A8
Grassy Cl HHW HP1 ..... 163 K5
Gravel Dr TRING HP23 ..... 134 E6
Graveley Av BORE WD6 ..... 224 B4
Graveley Dell WGCE AL7 ..... 148 C4 🔲
Graveley La HTCHE/RSTV SG4 ..... 57 K4
Gravel Hl CFSP/GDCR SL9 ..... 226 A5
Gravelhill Ter HHW HP1 ..... 163 K7
Gravel La HHW HP1 ..... 163 K6
Gravelly La STDN SG11 ..... 81 K2
Gravel Pth BERK HP4 ..... 162 A5
Gravely Ct HHS/BOV HP3 ..... 9 F6 🔲

The Graylings ABLGY WD5 ..... 203 K3
Grays Cl AMP/FLIT/B MK45 ..... 36 C6
    ROY SG8 ..... 21 G1
Grays Ct BSF CM23 ..... 105 H1
Graysfield WCCE AL7 ..... 148 B6
Gray's La HTCH/STOT SG5 ..... 56 B2
The Grazings HHNE HP2 ..... 8 C3
Great Ashby Wy STVG SG1 ..... 59 G6
Great Braitch La HAT AL10 ..... 146 D7
Great Brays HLWS CM18 ..... 7 F5
Great Break WCCE AL7 ..... 148 C4
Great Cambridge Rd BROX EN10 ..... 197 J4
    CHES/WCR EN8 ..... 214 B1
Great Conduit WCCE AL7 ..... 148 D2
Great Dell WGCW AL8 ..... 147 J1
Great Eastern Cl BSF CM23 ..... 105 K3 🔲
Great Elms Rd HHS/BOV HP3 ..... 185 K2
Greatfield Cl HARP AL5 ..... 117 J5
Great Ganett WCCE AL7 ..... 148 C5
Great Gn HTCH/STOT SG5 ..... 39 F5
Great Gv BUSH WD23 ..... 221 J8
Great Groves CHESW EN7 ..... 196 C6
Great Hadham Rd BSF CM23 ..... 104 C4
Greatham Rd BUSH WD23 ..... 13 G2
Great Heart HHNE HP2 ..... 8 B3
Great Heath HAT AL10 ..... 171 G1
Great Innings North
    HERT/WAS SG14 ..... 98 A6
Great Innings South
    HERT/WAS SG14 ..... 98 A6 🔲
Great Lawne KNEB SG3 ..... 96 E7
Great Ley WGCE AL7 ..... 147 K5
Great Leylands HLWS CM18 ..... 7 F5
Great Meadow BROX EN10 ..... 177 F8
Great Molewood HERT/WAS SG14 ..... 125 K8
Great North Rd BRKMPK AL9 ..... 147 G8
    HAT AL10 ..... 171 H1
    WCCW AL8 ..... 147 F3
    WLYN AL6 ..... 122 D3
Great Palmers HHNE HP2 ..... 164 E1 🔲
Great Pk KGLGY WD4 ..... 186 A8
Great Plumtree HLW CM20 ..... 7 E2
Great Rd HHNE HP2 ..... 8 C4
Great Slades POTB/CUF EN6 ..... 210 A3
Great Sturgess Rd HHW HP1 ..... 163 J6 🔲
Great Whites Rd HHS/BOV HP3 ..... 164 E8
Greenacre Cl BAR EN5 ..... 210 A8
Greenacres HHS/BOV HP3 ..... 165 J8
    LBUZ LU7 ..... 110 C5 🔲
Green Acres LTNE LU2 ..... 53 K7
    STVGE SG2 ..... 76 D8
    WCCE AL7 ..... 148 A6 🔲
Greenall Cl CHES/WCR EN8 ..... 197 J8
Greenbank CHESW EN7 ..... 197 F6
Greenbank Rd WAT WD17 ..... 203 J6
Greenbury Cl RKW/CH/CXG WD3 ..... 217 F3
    ROY SG8 ..... 23 F8
Green Cl BRKMPK AL9 ..... 192 E4
    CHES/WCR EN8 ..... 214 D2
    LTNW/LEA LU4 ..... 68 A4
    STVGE SG2 ..... 76 A8
Greencoates HERT/BAY SG13 ..... 151 H4 🔲
Green Cft HAT AL10 ..... 171 F1
Green Dell Wy HHS/BOV HP3 ..... 9 E5
Green Drift ROY SG8 ..... 21 F3
Greene Field Rd BERK HP4 ..... 161 K5 🔲
Green End BRKMPK AL9 ..... 192 E4
Green End La HHW HP1 ..... 163 J6
Green End Rd HHW HP1 ..... 163 K6
Greenes Ct BERK HP4 ..... 161 K4 🔲
Greene Wk BERK HP4 ..... 162 A6
Greenfield BRKMPK AL9 ..... 171 J1
    ROY SG8 ..... 21 F2
    WGCW AL8 ..... 122 D8 🔲
Greenfield Av HTCH/STOT SG5 ..... 40 B5
    OXHEY WD19 ..... 231 F1 🔲
Greenfield End CFSP/GDCR SL9 ..... 226 C6 🔲
Greenfield La HTCH/STOT SG5 ..... 40 C5 🔲
Greenfield Rd STVG SG1 ..... 2 C1
Greenfields STSD CM24 ..... 86 D2
Greenfield St WAB EN9 ..... 215 H4
Greengate LTNW/LIM LU3 ..... 68 B1
Greenheys Cl NTHWD HA6 ..... 229 K7
Greenhill Av LTNE LU2 ..... 69 J6
Green Hill Cl STDN SG11 ..... 82 A3 🔲
Greenhill Crs WATW WD18 ..... 219 K6
Greenhill Pk BSF CM23 ..... 105 C4
Greenhills HLW CM20 ..... 7 D4
    WARE SG12 ..... 127 C6
Greenhills Cl RKW/CH/CXG WD3 ..... 218 A5
Greenland Rd BAR EN5 ..... 225 H6
Green La BLDK SG7 ..... 18 A4
    BROX EN10 ..... 198 B1
    DUN/WHIP LU6 ..... 114 C1
    HHNE HP2 ..... 9 F6
    HHS/BOV HP3 ..... 183 J6
    HTCHE/RSTV SG4 ..... 41 F8
    LBUZ LU7 ..... 110 E4 🔲
    LCOL/BKTW AL2 ..... 189 J2
    LTNE LU2 ..... 70 C5
    LWTH SG6 ..... 26 B8
    NTHWD HA6 ..... 229 J6
    OXHEY WD19 ..... 220 D8

RKW/CH/CXG WD3......................... 218 E5
STALW/RED AL3.............................. 10 B1
STALW/RED AL3............................. 115 K5
STDN SG11...................................... 82 A2
WGCE AL7..................................... 148 D5
Green Lane La HARP AL5............... 144 B1
Green La HAT AL10....................... 170 E1
WGCW AL8................................... 146 E5
Green Meadow POTB/CUF EN6.... 193 G8
Green Milverton LTNN/LIM LU3.. 69 E2
Green Oaks LTNE LU2.................... 70 A6
Green Pth TRING HP23................. 134 D5
Greenriggs LTNE LU2.................... 71 G7
Greenside BORE WD6................... 207 K8
Greenside Dr HTCH/STOT SG5...... 56 B1
Greenside Pk LTNE LU2................. 69 K6
Greensleeves CI STALE/WH AL4... 169 F7
Greenstead SBW CM21................. 132 C8
Green St RAD WD7........................ 207 K5
RKW/CH/CXG WD3...................... 217 F2
ROY SG8... 21 H1
STVG SG1... 2 A1
Greensward BUSH WD23.............. 221 J6
The Green BSF CM23..................... 105 J6
CHES/WCR EN8............................ 197 C6
HTCH/STOT SG5............................ 25 K2
KNEB SG3.. 95 G4
LTNE LU2... 91 K6
LTNW/LEA LU4................................ 68 B4
RKW/CH/CXG WD3...................... 218 G4
ROY SG8.. 15 K8
ROY SG8.. 21 H3
WARE SG12................................... 127 H6
WLYN AL6.. 94 D9
WLYN AL6...................................... 122 B4
Green V WGCE AL7....................... 148 B4
Green View CI HHS/BOV HP3...... 183 J7
Greenway BERK HP4..................... 161 H5
BSF CM23....................................... 106 B3
HARP AL5...................................... 144 A1
HLWW/ROY CM19........................ 179 F1
LWTH SG6....................................... 42 A7
PIN HA5... 230 E8
STVGE SG2...................................... 77 J1
Greenways ABLGY WD5............... 203 J3
BUNT SG9.. 63 H1
CHESW EN7.................................. 195 K7
HERT/WAS SG14........................... 150 E3
LTNE LU2... 70 C4
STVG SG1.. 2 C2
The Greenway PEND EN3............ 214 C5
POTB/CUF EN6.............................. 210 B3
RKW/CH/CXG WD3...................... 217 K7
TRING HP23................................... 134 E4
Greenwood CI STALE/WH AL4.... 214 A1
RAD WD7....................................... 207 H2
Greenwood Dr GSTN WD25......... 204 C4
Greenwood Gdns RAD WD7........ 207 H3
Greenyard WAB EN9..................... 215 H3
Greer Rd KTN/HRWW/W HA3...... 231 K7
Gregories CI LTNE LU2..................... 4 B2
Gregory Av POTB/CUF EN6.......... 210 D3
Gregson CI BORE WD6................. 224 B2
Grenadier CI STALE/WH AL4........ 169 F7
Grenadine CI CHESW EN7............ 196 D5
Grenadine Wy TRING HP23.......... 135 F4
Grenfell CI BORE WD6.................. 224 B1
Grenville Av BROX EN10............... 176 E7
Grenville CI CHES/WCR EN8........ 214 C2
Grenville Wy STVGE SG2............... 76 B8
Gresford CI STALE/WH AL4.......... 169 G6
Gresham CI LTNE LU2.................... 70 E8
Gresham Ct BERK HP4.................. 161 J6
Gresley CI WGCW AL8................... 147 K2
Gresley Wy STVGE SG2................... 59 K8
Greville CI BRKMPK AL9............... 192 B2
Greycaine Rd WATN WD24........... 204 E7
Greydells Rd STVG SG1.................... 2 C1
Greyfriars WARE SG12.................. 127 F6
Greyfriars La HARP AL5................ 143 H2
Greygoose Pk HLWW/ROY CM19.. 179 J4
Greyhound La POTB/CUF EN6...... 209 F3
Greystoke CI BERK HP4................ 161 H6
Griffiths Wy STAL AL1.................... 10 B6
Grimaldi Av LTNN/LIM LU3............ 69 F6
Grimsdyke Crs BAR EN5............... 225 H3
Grimsdyke Rd PIN HA5................. 231 F6
TRING HP23................................... 135 J8
Grimstone Rd HTCHE/RSTV SG4.. 57 J3
Grimston Rd STAL AL1................... 11 E4
STAL AL1... 11 E5
Grimthorpe CI STALW/RED AL3... 10 B1
Grindcobbe CI STAL AL1.............. 189 F1
Grinstead La RBSF CM22.............. 133 G3
Groom Rd BROX EN10.................. 197 K4
Groomsby Dr LBUZ LU7................ 110 E4
Grooms Cottages CSHM HP5....... 182 D8
Grosvenor CI RBSF CM23............. 105 G6
Grosvenor Rd BLDK SG7............... 27 F8
BORE WD6..................................... 223 K3
BROX EN10.................................... 176 E6
LTNN/LIM LU3................................ 69 G4
NTHWD HA6................................. 230 A4
STAL AL1... 11 D5

WAT WD17....................................... 13 D3
Grosvenor Rd West BLDK SG7....... 27 F8
Grosvenor Ter HHW HP1............. 163 K7
The Grotto WARE SG12................ 152 C1
Ground La HAT AL10..................... 171 G2
Grove Av HARP AL5...................... 144 A2
Grovebury Gdns
    LCOL/BKTW AL2........................ 188 E5
Grove Ct WAB EN9....................... 215 G3
Grove Crs RKW/CH/CXG WD3..... 219 F4
Grovedale CI CHESW EN7............ 196 D8
Grove End LTN LU1......................... 89 G4
Grove Farm Pk NTHWD HA6....... 229 J4
Grove Gdns TRING HP23............. 135 G4
Grove Hall Rd BUSH WD23........... 13 F5
Grove HI STSD CM24..................... 86 D2
Grovelands HHNE HP2.................... 9 F3
Grovelands
    LCOL/BKTW AL2........................ 188 D5
Grovelands Av HTCHE/RSTV SG4.. 41 C7
Groveland Wy HTCH/STOT SG5.... 26 A4
Grove La CSHM HP5.................... 182 D5
Grove Lea HAT AL10..................... 171 F7
Grove Md HAT AL10..................... 170 E4
Grove Meadow WGCE AL7.......... 148 D3
Grove Mill La RKW/CH/CXG WD3.. 203 H8
Grove Pk TRING HP23.................. 135 G4
Grove Park Rd LTN LU1.................. 89 F6
Grove Pl BRKMPK AL9................. 192 C2
Grover CI HHNE HP2....................... 8 A4
Grove Rd BORE WD6.................... 223 K1
    HARP AL5.................................... 144 A2
    HHW HP1.................................... 163 K8
    HTCH/STOT SG5........................... 56 D1
    LTN LU1.. 4 B4
    NTHWD HA6................................ 229 J4
    RKW/CH/CXG WD3..................... 227 K1
    STAL AL1....................................... 10 C5
    STVG SG1... 2 A1
    TRING HP23................................. 135 G4
    WARE SG12................................. 127 K7
Grove Rd West PEND EN3........... 214 B7
Grover Rd OXHEY WD19.............. 13 E5
The Grove BRKMPK AL9............... 193 C5
    CSHM HP5.................................. 200 A6
    LTN LU1... 89 C4
    POTB/CUF EN6............................. 210 D2
    RAD WD7....................................... 206 D4
    RBSF CM22................................... 106 E5
    STDN SG11................................... 104 D2
Grove Wk HERT/WAS SG14......... 151 F1
Grove Wy RKW/CH/CXG WD3.... 216 E4
Grovewood CI RKW/CH/CXG WD3.. 216 E5
Grubbs La BRKMPK AL9................ 172 C8
Guessens Gv WGCW AL8............. 147 H3
Guessens Rd WGCW AL8............. 147 H3
Guessens Wk WGCW AL8............. 147 H2
Guildford CI STVG SG1.................... 58 E7
Guildford St STAL AL1.................. 168 E7
Guildford St LTN LU1........................ 4 C5
The Guilfords HLWE CM17........... 157 F1
Guinery Gv HHS/BOV HP3.......... 185 K2
Guinevere Gdns CHES/WCR EN8.. 197 J8
Gulland CI BUSH WD23................ 221 K5
Gullbrook HHW HP1.................... 163 K6
Gullet Wood Rd GSTN WD25...... 204 B5
The Gulphs HERT/BAY SG13....... 151 G3
Gun La KNEB SG3............................ 96 B5
Gun Meadow Av KNEB SG3.......... 96 B5
Gunnels Wood Rd STVG SG1.......... 2 A5
Gun Rd KNEB SG3.......................... 96 B5
Gun Road Gdns KNEB SG3............ 96 A5
Gurney Court Rd STAL AL1............ 11 E2
Gurney's La HTCH/STOT SG5......... 39 K2
Gwent CI GSTN WD25................. 204 E4
Gwynfa CI WLYN AL6.................... 122 D2
Gwynne CI TRING HP23............... 135 F4
Gwynns Wk HERT/BAY SG13...... 151 H3
Gypsy CI WARE SG12.................... 152 E5
Gypsy La BRKMPK AL9.................. 148 A5
    GSTN WD25.................................. 203 J5
    WARE SG12.................................. 152 E5

H

Hackforth CI BAR EN5.................. 225 G5
Hackney CI BORE WD6................. 224 C5
Haddestoke Ga BROX EN10......... 197 K4
Haddon CI BORE WD6.................. 223 K2
    HHS/BOV HP3................................ 9 D6
    STVGE SG2..................................... 96 D2
Haddon La LTNE LU2....................... 5 D3
    RKW/CH/CXG WD3..................... 217 F5
Hadham CI BSF CM23................... 105 G1
Hadham Gv BSF CM23.................. 105 F1
Hadham Rd BSF CM23................... 84 C8
    STDN SG11..................................... 82 A8
Hadland CI HHW HP1................... 183 J4
Hadleigh Ct BROX EN10.............. 176 E8
    HARP AL5...................................... 144 B3
Hadley Gv BAR EN5...................... 225 K2
Hadley Rd EBAR EN4.................... 211 H1
    ENC/FH EN2.................................. 212 B2
Hadlow Down CI LTNN/LIM LU3... 69 F6
Hadrian CI STALW/RED AL3........ 167 G3
Hadrians Wk STVGE SG2................ 76 D1
Hadrian Wy LWTH SG6.................. 42 D7
Hadwell CI STVGE SG2...................... 3 E7
Hagdell Rd LTN LU1........................... 4 A4
Haggden La WATW WD18.............. 12 A4
Haggerston Rd BORE WD6........... 207 H4
Haig CI STAL AL1.......................... 168 E7
Hailey Av HOD EN11.................... 177 F2
Hailey La HOD EN11.................... 152 C6
Haines Wy GSTN WD25............... 204 B6
Haldens WGCE AL7...................... 123 F5
Hale Rd HERT/BAY SG13.............. 151 G3
Hales Meadow HARP AL5............ 118 C2
Hales Pk HHNE HP2......................... 9 F1
Hales Park CI HHNE HP2................. 9 F4
Haleswood Rd HHNE HP2............... 9 D1
Half Acre STVG SG1........................ 56 B1
Halfacre HI CFSP/GDCR SL9........ 226 C2
Half Acres La BUNT SG9................. 49 G8
Half Acres BSF CM23................... 105 J1
Halfhide La CHES/WCR EN8........ 197 H6
Halfhides WAB EN9..................... 215 J3
Half Moon La LTN LU1................. 116 C2
Half Moon Meadow HHNE HP2.. 165 H1
Halfway Av LTNW/LEA LU4............ 68 C8
Halifax Rd RKW/CH/CXG WD3.... 217 F5
Halifax Wy WGCE AL7.................. 148 C9
Hallam CI WATN WD24................... 13 D2
Hallam Gdns PIN HA5.................. 231 F6
Halland Wy NTHWD HA6.............. 229 J3
Hall CI RKW/CH/CXG WD3.......... 217 K8
Hall Dr DEN/HRF UB9................... 228 B3
Halleys Rdg HERT/WAS SG14...... 150 D4
Hall Gdns STALE/WH AL4............. 191 H1
Hall Gv WGCE AL7....................... 148 C5
Hall Heath CI STAL AL1................ 168 E4
Halliday CI RAD WD7.................... 207 H2
Hallingbury CI RBSF CM22.......... 106 A4
Hallingbury Rd RBSF CM23......... 106 A4
    SBW CM21.................................. 132 E5
Halling HI HLW CM20...................... 7 E1
Hall La BUNT SG9........................... 49 G8
    HTCHE/RSTV SG4........................ 120 A1
    KNEB SG3....................................... 96 B2
Hall Md LWTH SG6......................... 41 G3
Hallmores BROX EN10................. 177 F5
Hallowell Rd NTHWD HA6........... 229 K4
Hallowes Crs OXHEY WD19........ 230 B2
Hall Pk BERK HP4......................... 162 B6
Hall Park Ga BERK HP4................ 162 B3
Hall Park HI BERK HP4.................. 162 B2
Hall Place Gdns STAL AL1.............. 11 D3
Halls CI WLYN AL6........................ 122 C5
Hallside Rd EN EN1....................... 213 J8
Hallwicks Rd LTNE LU2.................. 70 C6
Hallworth Dr HTCH/STOT SG5...... 25 J3
Halsey Dr HHW HP1..................... 163 J4
    HTCHE/RSTV SG4........................... 57 G2
Halsey PL LCOL/BKTW AL2......... 190 D5
Halsey Rd WATW WD18................. 12 C2
Halstead HI CHESW EN7.............. 196 C8
Halter CI BORE WD6.................... 224 C5
Haltside HAT AL10....................... 170 C5
Halwick CI HHW HP1................... 164 A2
Halyard CI LTNN/LIM LU3.............. 69 G3
Hamberlins La BERK HP4............. 160 C2
Hamblings CI RAD WD7............... 207 G2
Hambridge Wy HTCH/STOT SG5.. 39 F1
Hambro CI LTNE LU2.................... 118 B2
Hamburgh Ct CHES/WCR EN8.... 197 H8
Hamels Dr HERT/BAY SG13........ 152 A2
Hamels La BUNT SG9..................... 80 C2
Hamer CI HHS/BOV HP3.............. 183 J6
Hamilton Av HOD EN11............... 177 F2
Hamilton CI LCOL/BKTW AL2..... 188 C2
    POTB/CUF EN6............................. 209 F2
Hamilton Ct STAL AL1.................. 171 G6
Hamilton Md HHS/BOV HP3....... 183 J5
Hamilton Rd BERK HP4................ 161 J5
    KGLGY WD4.................................. 203 H3
    OXHEY WD19.................................. 230 C2
    STAL AL1... 11 F3
Hamilton St WATW WD18.............. 13 D4
Hamlet HI HLWW/ROY CM19...... 178 D5
The Hamlet BERK HP4.................. 162 D2
Hammarskjold Rd HLW CM20......... 6 B3
Hammer La HHNE HP2.................... 8 C4
Hammers Ga LCOL/BKTW AL2.... 188 C4
Hammond CI CHESW EN7........... 196 D4
    STVG SG1... 2 B2
Hammonds HI HARP AL5............. 143 G4
Hammonds La HAT AL10.............. 146 A6
    STALE/WH AL4............................. 145 K6
Hammondstreet Rd CHESW EN7.. 195 K3
Hammondswick HARP AL5........... 143 G5
Hampden HTCHE/RSTV SG4.......... 93 F8
Hampden CI LWTH SG6.................. 42 B7
Hampden Crs CHESW EN7........... 214 A7

Hampden HI *WARE* SG12 .... 127 K8
Hampden Hill CI *WARE* SG12 .... 127 K7 ⊡
Hampden PI *LCOL/BKTW* AL2 .... 189 G7
Hampden Dr *HTCHE/RSTV* SC4 .... 41 G8
  KTN/HRWW/W HA3 .... 231 H7
Hampden Wy *WAT* WD17 .... 203 K6
Hampermill La *OXHEY* WD19 .... 220 B8
Hampton CI *STVGE* SG2 .... 96 D2
Hampton Gdns *SBW* CM21 .... 156 E2
Hampton Rd *LTNW/LEA* LU4 .... 69 C8
Hamstel Rd *HLW* CM20 .... 6 A2
Hanaper Dr *ROY* SG8 .... 23 F8
Hanbury CI *CHES/WCR* EN8 .... 197 H8
Hanbury Dr *WARE* SG12 .... 127 H7
Hanbury Dr *WARE* SG12 .... 127 G3
Hancock CI *BORE* WD6 .... 224 B1
Hancock Dr *LTNE* LU2 .... 69 K3
Hancroft Rd *HHS/BOV* HP3 .... 164 B8
Handa CI *HHS/BOV* HP3 .... 186 B1
Handcross Rd *LTNE* LU2 .... 70 E6
Hand La *SBW* CM21 .... 132 A8
Handside CI *WGCW* AL8 .... 147 H3 ⊡
Handside Gn *WGCW* AL8 .... 147 H2
Handside La *WGCW* AL8 .... 147 G4
Handsworth CI *OXHEY* WD19 .... 230 B2
Hangar Ruding *OXHEY* WD19 .... 231 G2
Hanger CI *HHW* HP1 .... 164 A7
Hangmans La *WLYN* AL6 .... 123 F1
Hanover CI *STVGE* SG2 .... 76 A8
Hanover Gn *HHW* HP1 .... 163 K8
Hanover PI *AMP/FLIT/B* MK45 .... 36 C5
Hanover Wk *HAT* AL10 .... 170 E7 ⊡
Hanscombe End Rd
  HTCH/STOT SG5 .... 37 K1
Hansells Md *HLWW/ROY* CM19 ..... 178 B1
Hanswick CI *LTNE* LU2 .... 5 F1
Hanworth CI *LTNE* LU2 .... 69 J2 ⊡
Hanyards La *POTB/CUF* EN6 .... 195 F6
Harbert Gdns *LCOL/BKTW* AL2 .... 188 D7
Harberts Rd *HLWW/ROY* CM19 .... 6 A5
Harborne CI *OXHEY* WD19 .... 230 C1 ⊡
Harbury Dell *LTNN/LIM* LU3 .... 69 G2
Harcamlow Wy *RBSF* CM22 .... 107 C5
  STDN SG11 .... 82 A8
  WARE SG12 .... 154 B1
Harcourt Rd *BUSH* WD23 .... 221 K5
  TRING HP23 .... 135 H5
Harcourt St *LTN* LU1 .... 4 C6
Harding CI *GSTN* WD25 .... 204 D3
  LTNN/LIM LU3 .... 68 D2 ⊡
  STALW/RED AL3 .... 142 C4 ⊡
Hardings *WGCE* AL7 .... 148 D2
Hardwick CI *STVGE* SG2 .... 96 D2
Hardwicke Rd *LCOL/BKTW* AL2 ... 190 B5
Hardwick Gn *LTNN/LIM* LU3 .... 69 F2
Hardy CI *BAR* EN5 .... 225 K5
  HTCHE/RSTV SC4 .... 41 G7
Hardy Dr *ROY* SG8 .... 21 H1
Hardy Rd *HHNE* HP2 .... 8 C1 ⊡
Harebell *WGCE* AL7 .... 147 K6 ⊡
Harebell CI *HERT/BAY* SG13 .... 152 A3
The Harebreaks *WATN* WD24 .... 204 B7
Hare Crs *GSTN* WD25 .... 204 B2
Harefield *HLW* CM20 .... 7 F3
  STVGE SG2 .... 76 D5
Harefield PI *STALE/WH* AL4 .... 169 G3
Harefield Rd *LTN* LU1 .... 88 E1 ⊡
  RKW/CH/CXG WD3 .... 228 C3
Hare La *HAT* AL10 .... 171 G6
Harepark CI *HHW* HP1 .... 163 J5 ⊡
Hare St *HLWW/ROY* CM19 .... 6 A4
Hare Street Rd *BUNT* SG9 .... 63 K2
Hare Street Springs
  HLWW/ROY CM19 .... 6 B4
Harewood *RKW/CH/CXG* WD3 ..... 218 B5
Harewood Rd *OXHEY* WD19 .... 230 C1
Harford Dr *WAT* WD17 .... 203 K8
Hargrave CI *STSD* CM24 .... 86 D1
Hargreaves Av *CHESW* EN7 .... 214 A1
Hargreaves CI *CHESW* EN7 .... 214 A1 ⊡
Hargreaves CI *ROY* SG8 .... 21 H4 ⊡
Harkness Wy *HTCHE/RSTV* SC4 ...... 41 C7
Harlech Rd *ABLGY* WD5 .... 204 B1
Harlesden Rd *STAL* AL1 .... 11 F4
Harlestone CI *LTNN/LIM* LU3 .... 52 A8
Harley Ct *STALE/WH* AL4 .... 169 G2 ⊡
The Harlings *HERT/BAY* SG13 .... 152 B7
Harlow Common *HLWE* CM17 ...... 181 G4
Harlow Rd *HHNE* HP2 .... 8 C1
Harlow Rd *HLWW/ROY* CM19 ...... 154 D8
  SBW CM21 .... 157 F1
Harmer End La *WLYN* AL6 .... 123 C5
Harmer Green La *WLYN* AL6 .... 123 F5
Harmony CI *HAT* AL10 .... 171 F2
Harness Wy *STALE/WH* AL4 .... 169 C3
Harold Crs *WAB* EN9 .... 215 H2
Harold Rd *AMP/FLIT/B* MK45 .... 36 C6
Harolds Rd *HLWW/ROY* CM19 ..... 179 G2
Harpenden La *STALW/RED* AL3 ... 142 C3
Harpenden Ri *HARP* AL5 .... 118 A6
Harpenden Rd *HARP* AL5 .... 143 J2
  STALE/WH AL4 .... 144 E1
  STALW/RED AL3 .... 143 K5
Harper La *RAD* WD7 .... 206 D1
Harpsfield Broadway *HAT* AL10 ..... 170 E3

Harptree Wy *STAL* AL1 .... 11 E2
Harriet Walker Wy
  RKW/CH/CXG WD3 .... 217 J7 ⊡
Harriet Wy *BUSH* WD23 .... 222 A7
Harris Ct *AMP/FLIT/B* MK45 .... 36 B5
Harris La *HTCH/STOT* SG5 .... 55 F7
  RAD WD7 .... 207 K4
Harrison CI *HTCHE/RSTV* SC4 .... 56 D2 ⊡
  NTHWD HA6 .... 229 H5
Harrisons *BSF* CM23 .... 86 C7
Harrison Wk *CHES/WCR* EN8 .... 197 H8
Harrison Rd *ROY* SG8 .... 204 B5
Harris's La *WARE* SG12 .... 127 G8
Harrowdene Rd *STVGE* SG2 .... 76 D5
Harrowden Rd *LTNE* LU2 .... 5 F3
Harrow Wy *OXHEY* WD19 .... 231 F2 ⊡
Harrow Yd *TRING* HP23 .... 135 F6
Harry Scott Ct *LTNW/LEA* LU4 .... 68 B3
Harston Dr *PEND* EN3 .... 215 F8
Hartfield Av *BORE* WD6 .... 223 K4
Hartfield CI *BORE* WD6 .... 223 K5
Hartforde Rd *BORE* WD6 .... 223 K2
Harthall La *KGLGY* WD4 .... 186 B6
Hartham La *HERT/WAS* SG14 ...... 151 F3
Hart Hill Dr *LTNE* LU2 .... 5 D3
Hart Hill La *LTNE* LU2 .... 5 E4 ⊡
Hartland Rd *CHES/WCR* EN8 .... 197 H8
Hart La *LTNE* LU2 .... 5 E2
Hartley Rd *LTNE* LU2 .... 5 D3
Hartmoor Ms *PEND* EN3 .... 214 C7 ⊡
Hart La *LTNE* LU2 .... 5 E2
Hartsbourne Av *BUSH* WD23 .... 231 K1
Hartsbourne Wy *HHNE* HP2 .... 9 F6 ⊡
Harts CI *BUSH* WD23 .... 221 H2 ⊡
Hartsfield Rd *LTNE* LU2 .... 5 E1
Hartspring La *GSTN* WD25 .... 221 H2
Hart Wk *LTNE* LU2 .... 5 E2 ⊡
Hartwell Gdns *HARP* AL5 .... 118 A8
Harvest CI *STALE/WH* AL4 .... 169 F2
  WLYN AL6 .... 122 E2
Harvest End *GSTN* WD25 .... 204 E5
Harvest La *STVGE* SG2 .... 76 D2
Harvest Md *HAT* AL10 .... 171 G3
Harvest Rd *BORE* WD6 .... 223 J4
Harveyfields *WAB* EN9 .... 215 H4
Harvey Rd *LCOL/BKTW* AL2 .... 190 A4
  RKW/CH/CXG WD3 .... 219 F6
  STVGE SG2 .... 3 F2
Harvey's HI *LTNE* LU2 .... 70 A4
Harwood CI *WCCW* AL8 .... 122 E7 ⊡
  WLYN AL6 .... 124 A7
Harwood Rd *WAB* EN9 .... 122 E8
Harwoods Rd *WATW* WD18 .... 12 B3
Hasedines Rd *HHW* HP1 .... 163 K5
Haseldine Mdw *HAT* AL10 .... 170 C5
Haseldine Rd *LCOL/BKTW* AL2 .... 190 B4
Haselfoot *LWTH* SG6 .... 41 J3
Hasketon Dr *LTNN/LEA* LU4 .... 68 A3
Haslemere *BSF* CM25 .... 105 K5
Haslewood Av *HOD* EN11 .... 177 F2
Haslingden CI *HARP* AL5 .... 117 K6
Hastings CI *STVG* SG1 .... 75 F1
Hastings Rd *AMP/FLIT/B* MK45 ...... 36 C6
Hastings St *LTN* LU1 .... 4 B4 ⊡
Hastings Wy *BUSH* WD23 .... 13 F5 ⊡
  RKW/CH/CXG WD3 .... 219 G4
Hastingwood Rd *HLWE* CM17 ...... 181 H6
Hastoe HI *TRING* HP23 .... 135 F8
Hastoe La *TRING* HP23 .... 135 F7
Hatch Gn *RBSF* CM22 .... 133 F1
Hatching Green CI *HARP* AL5 .... 143 H3
Hatch La *BLDK* SG7 .... 43 F4
Hatfield Av *HAT* AL10 .... 170 E1
Hatfield Crs *HHNE* HP2 .... 8 C1
Hatfield Rd *BRKMPK* AL9 .... 148 B8
  POTB/CUF EN6 .... 210 D1
  STAL AL1 .... 168 A6
  STALE/WH AL4 .... 169 H6
  WATN WD24 .... 220 C1
Hathaway CI *LTNN/LEA* LU4 .... 68 A7 ⊡
Hathaway CI *STALE/WH* AL4 .... 169 H6
Hatherleigh Gdns *POTB/CUF* EN6 . 210 E2
Hatters La *WATW* WD18 .... 219 F5 ⊡
Hatters Wy *LTN* LU1 .... 68 E8
Hatton Rd *CHES/WCR* EN8 .... 197 H7
Havelock Ri *LTNE* LU2 .... 4 C2
Havelock Rd *KGLGY* WD4 .... 185 K6
  LTNE LU2 .... 4 C2
Haven CI *HAT* AL10 .... 170 E3
Havenfield *KGLGY* WD4 .... 202 A1
Havercroft CI *STAL* AL1 .... 10 B6
Haverdale *LTNN/LEA* LU4 .... 68 B5 ⊡
Havers La *BSF* CM23 .... 105 J4
Haward Rd *HOD* EN11 .... 177 H1
Hawbush CI *WLYN* AL6 .... 122 B5 ⊡
Hawbush Ri *WLYN* AL6 .... 122 B4
Hawes CI *NTHWD* HA6 .... 230 A6
Hawes La *WAB* EN9 .... 215 H3
Haweswater Dr *GSTN* WD25 .... 204 D4 ⊡
Hawfield Gdns *LCOL/BKTW* AL2 ... 189 F4
Hawkenbury *HLWW/ROY* CM19 ... 179 H3
Hawkesworth CI *NTHWD* HA6 ..... 229 K6 ⊡
Hawkfields *LTNE* LU2 .... 69 K3

Hawkings Wy *HHW* HP1 .... 183 J4
Hawkins CI *BORE* WD6 .... 224 B2 ⊡
Hawkins Hall La *KNEB* SG3 .... 97 F7
Hawkshead La *BRKMPK* AL9 .... 192 E6
Hawkshill Dr *HHW* HP1 .... 184 C1
Hawksmead CI *PEND* EN3 .... 214 C5 ⊡
Hawksmoor *RAD* WD7 .... 207 K3
Hawkswood Wy *HTCH/PR* HP23 .. 135 H5 ⊡
Hawridge V *CSHM* HP5 .... 160 A8
Hawsley Rd *HARP* AL5 .... 143 H5
Hawthorn Av *LTNE* LU2 .... 70 C5
Hawthorn CI *ABLGY* WD5 .... 204 A2
  HARP AL5 .... 144 A2
  HERT/WAS SG14 .... 150 D2 ⊡
  HTCH/STOT SG5 .... 56 B3
  ROY SG8 .... 21 K2 ⊡
  WAT WD17 .... 204 A8
Hawthorn Crs *LTN* LU1 .... 88 D6
Hawthorne Av *CHESW* EN7 .... 197 F8
Hawthorne CI *CHESW* EN7 .... 214 A1
Hawthorne Rd *RAD* WD7 .... 206 D4 ⊡
Hawthorn Gv *ENC/FH* EN2 .... 213 G8
Hawthorn HI *LWTH* SG6 .... 41 J2
Hawthorn La *HHW* HP1 .... 163 J5
Hawthorn Ri *BSF* CM23 .... 105 J6
Hawthorn Rd *HOD* EN11 .... 177 G1
Hawthorns *HLWS* CM18 .... 180 C5
  WGCW AL8 .... 147 J1 ⊡
The Hawthorns *BERK* HP4 .... 161 H4
  HHS/BOV HP3 .... 184 D2
  RKW/CH/CXG WD3 .... 227 G4
  STVG SG1 .... 3 D4
  WARE SG12 .... 127 F6
Hawthorn Wy *LCOL/BKTW* AL2 ... 188 C2
  ROY SG8 .... 21 K2
Hawtrees *RAD* WD7 .... 206 C5
Haybourn Md *HHW* HP1 .... 164 A7
Hay CI *BORE* WD6 .... 224 B2
Haycroft *BSF* CM23 .... 106 B3
  LTNE LU2 .... 69 G3 ⊡
Haycroft Rd *STVG* SG1 .... 2 B1
Haydens Rd *HLWW/ROY* CM19 .... 6 B4
Haydock Rd *ROY* SG8 .... 21 K3 ⊡
Haydon Rd *OXHEY* WD19 .... 13 F5
Hayes CI *LTNE* LU2 .... 70 C4
Hayfield *STVGE* SG2 .... 76 E2
Hayfield CI *BUSH* WD23 .... 221 J4
Haygarth *KNEB* SG3 .... 96 B5
Hayhurst Rd *LTNW/LEA* LU4 .... 68 A7
Hay La *HARP* AL5 .... 118 C2
Hayley Bell Gdns *BSF* CM23 .... 105 J6
Hayley Common *STVGE* SG2 .... 76 D5
Hayling Dr *LTNE* LU2 .... 70 D6
Hayling Rd *OXHEY* WD19 .... 230 A2
Haymeads *WGCW* AL8 .... 122 E8
Haymeads La *BSF* CM23 .... 106 B5
Haymoor *LWTH* SG6 .... 41 J2
Haynes CI *WGCE* AL7 .... 148 B4
Haynes Md *BERK* HP4 .... 161 H3
Haysman CI *LWTH* SG6 .... 42 A2
Hay St *ROY* SG8 .... 15 J7
Hayton CI *LTNN/LIM* LU3 .... 52 B7
Haywood CI *PIN* HA5 .... 230 E8
Haywood La *ROY* SG8 .... 30 E3
Haywood Pk *RKW/CH/CXG* WD3 ... 217 J5
Haywoods Dr *HHW* HP1 .... 184 D1
Haywoods La *ROY* SG8 .... 21 J2
Hazelbury Av *ABLGY* WD5 .... 203 H2
Hazelbury Crs *LTN* LU1 .... 4 A3
Hazel CI *CHESW* EN7 .... 196 C4 ⊡
  WLYN AL6 .... 122 E6
Hazelcroft *PIN* HA5 .... 231 H5
Hazeldell Link *HHW* HP1 .... 163 H7 ⊡
Hazeldell Rd *HHW* HP1 .... 163 H7
Hazeldene *CHES/WCR* EN8 .... 214 D2
Hazelend Rd *BSF* CM23 .... 86 A6
Hazel Gv *GSTN* WD25 .... 204 C5
  HAT AL10 .... 170 E7
  HTCH/STOT SG5 .... 25 J4
  WCCE AL7 .... 148 C2
Hazel Md *BAR* EN5 .... 225 G5
Hazelmere Rd *STALE/WH* AL4 ..... 169 F3
  STVGE SG2 .... 96 B1
Hazel Rd *BERK* HP4 .... 162 A6
  LCOL/BKTW AL2 .... 188 D6
The Hazels *WLYN* AL6 .... 124 A7 ⊡
Hazel Tree Rd *WATN* WD24 .... 204 C1
Hazelwood CI *HTCH/STOT* SG5 ...... 56 D1 ⊡
  LTNE LU2 .... 70 C5
Hazelwood Dr *PIN* HA5 .... 230 C8
  STALE/WH AL4 .... 169 F4
Hazelwood La *ABLGY* WD5 .... 203 J2
Hazelwood Rd *RKW/CH/CXG* WD3 219 H6
Hazely *TRING* HP23 .... 135 H5
Heacham CI *LTNN/LEA* LU4 .... 68 A5
Headingley CI *CHESW* EN7 .... 196 D4 ⊡
  RAD WD7 .... 207 H2
  STVG SG1 .... 75 K1
Headstone La *KTN/HRWW/W* HA3 231 J7
  RYLN/HDSTN HA2 .... 231 J8
Healey Rd *WATW* WD18 .... 12 A5
Heath Av *ROY* SG8 .... 21 G3
  STALW/RED AL3 .... 10 C2

WAT WD17 .... 12 C2
WATW WD18 .... 12 C2
WLYN AL6 .... 94 E8
WLYN AL6 .... 122 C4
High Street Gn HHNE HP2 .... 9 D2
High Town Rd LTNE LU2 .... 5 D3
High Vw BSF CM23 .... 86 B6
CSTG HP8 .... 226 A1
HAT AL10 .... 170 E6
HTCH/STOT SG5 .... 56 B3
RKW/CH/CXG WD3 .... 217 K4
STALW/RED AL3 .... 115 J5
WATW WD18 .... 12 C2
Highview Cl POTB/CUF EN6 ...... 210 D3
Highview Gdns POTB/CUF EN6.. 210 D3
STALE/WH AL4 .... 169 F1
High Wickfield WGCE AL7 ...... 148 D4
Highwood Av BUSH WD23 .... 221 G1
High Wood Cl LTN LU1 .... 88 E2
Highwoodhall La HHS/BOV HP3 .. 186 A5
High Wood Rd HOD EN11 .... 152 E8
High Wych La HLW CM20 .... 136 B3
SBW CM21 .... 131 J7
High Wych Wy HHNE HP2 .... 141 F8
Hilbury HAT AL10 .... 170 E5
Hilfield La GSTN WD25 .... 221 J1
Hiljon Crs CFSP/GDCR SL9 ...... 226 D3
Hillary Cl LTNW/LEA LU4 .... 68 C2
Hillary Crs LTN LU1 .... 4 A5
Hillary Ri ARL/CHE SG15 .... 25 F4
Hillary Rd HHNE HP2 .... 9 D4
Hillborough Rd LTN LU1 .... 4 B5
Hillbrow LWTH SG6 .... 41 H4
Hill Cl BAR EN5 .... 225 H5
HARP AL5.
LTNN/LIM LU3 .... 69 H2
Hill Common HHS/BOV HP3 .... 186 A1
Hill Ct BERK HP4 .... 162 A4
Hill Crest HTCHE/RSTV SG4.... 93 H3
POTB/CUF EN6 .... 210 D2
Hillcrest BLDK SG7 .... 43 F2
HAT AL10 .... 171 F5
STVG SG1 .... 3 D4
Hillcrest Av LTNE LU2 .... 69 H1
Hillcrest Rd RAD WD7 .... 207 K3
Hill Croft CI LTNW/LEA LU4...... 68 C3
Hillcroft Crs OXHEY WD19 ...... 220 C8
Hilldown Rd HHW WD1 .... 163 H4
Hill Dyke Rd STALE/WH AL4 .... 145 G2
Hill End La STAL AL1 .... 189 K1
STALE/WH AL4 .... 190 A1
Hill End Rd DEN/HRF UB9 ...... 228 A2
Hill Farm Av GSTN WD25 .... 204 B3
Hill Farm La STALW/RED AL3 .. 142 C8
WLYN AL6 .... 121 G4
Hill Farm Rd CFSP/GDCR SL9.. 226 B6
Hillfield HAT AL10 .... 171 G1
Hillfield Av HTCHE/RSTV SG4 .. 40 E7
Hillfield Ct HHNE HP2 .... 8 B5
Hillfield La South BUSH WD23.. 222 B6
Hillfield Sq CFSP/GDCR SL9 .... 226 B6
HHNE HP2.......................... 8 A5
Hillgate HTCHE/RSTV SG4........ 40 E6
Hilliard Rd NTHWD HA6 .... 230 B7
Hillingdon Rd GSTN WD25 ...... 204 B4
Hillingdon Trail DEN/HRF UB9.. 227 K6
Hill Ley HAT AL10 .... 170 E4
Hill Leys POTB/CUF EN6 .... 195 C6
Hill Md BERK HP4 .... 161 H6
Hillmead STVG SG1 .... 3 E2
Hill Milford HARP AL5 .... 119 F6
Hill Pickford HARP AL5 .... 119 F5
Hill Ri CFSP/GDCR SL9 .... 226 A8
LTNN/LIM LU3 .... 68 B2
POTB/CUF EN6 .... 195 F5
POTB/CUF EN6 .... 210 D8
RKW/CH/CXG WD3 .... 218 A7
Hillrise Av WATN WD24 .... 204 E8
Hill Rise Crs CFSP/GDCR SL9.. 226 B8
Hill Rd HTCHE/RSTV SG4 .... 94 D8
NTHWD HA6 .... 229 J7
Hillsborough Gn OXHEY WD19 .. 230 B2
Hillshott LWTH SG6 .... 42 A3
Hill Side LBUZ LU7 .... 109 K3
Hillside HAT AL10 .... 171 F4
HLWE CM17 .... 181 J3
HOD EN11 .... 176 E2
ROY SG8 .... 21 H4
STVG SG1 .... 3 D4
WARE SG12 .... 152 C1
WGCE AL7 .... 148 C6
WLYN AL6 .... 94 E8
Hillside Av BORE WD6 .... 224 B3
BSF CM23 .... 105 K2
CHES/WCR EN8.................. 214 C1
Hillside Cl ABLGY WD5.......... 203 K2
CFSP/GDCR SL9 .... 226 B5
Hillside Crs CHES/WCR EN8 .... 214 C1
ENC/FH EN2 .... 213 G8
NTHWD HA6 .... 230 B7
OXHEY WD19 .... 13 F5
WARE SG12 .... 153 G5
Hillside Gdns BAR EN5 .... 225 K4

BERK HP4 .... 162 A6
NTHWD HA6 .... 230 B6
Hillside La WARE SG12 .... 153 F4
Hillside Ri NTHWD HA6 .... 230 B6
Hillside Rd BUSH WD23............ 13 F4
HARP AL5........................ 118 B6
LTNN/LIM LU3 .... 4 B2
NTHWD HA6 .... 230 B6
PIN HA5 .... 230 B6
RAD WD7 .... 206 E5
RKW/CH/CXG WD3 .... 217 F5
STAL AL1 .... 11 D3
Hillside Ter HERT/BAY SG13 .... 151 F5
Hillside Wy WLYN AL6 .... 123 G1
Hills La NTHWD HA6 .... 229 K7
Hill St STALW/RED AL3 .... 10 B4
The Hill HLWE CM17 .... 157 F5
STALE/WH AL4 .... 145 G1
Hill Top BLDK SG7 .... 42 A3
Hilltop STALW/RED AL3.......... 142 A3
Hilltop Cl CHESW EN7 .... 196 D4
Hilltop Rd BERK HP4 .... 161 K6
KGLGY WD4 .... 186 D5
Hill Tree Cl SBW CM21 .... 132 B8
Hill Vw BERK HP4 .... 161 H5
BUNT SG9 .... 47 H1
HTCHE/RSTV SG4 .... 93 H3
Hillview Cl PIN HA5 .... 231 G5
Hillview Crs LTNE LU2 .... 69 H2
Hillview Gdns CHES/WCR EN8.. 197 J5
Hillview Rd PIN HA5 .... 231 G6
Hilly Fld HLWS CM18 .... 180 C5
Hilly Flds WGCE AL7 .... 148 D2
Hilmay Dr HHW HP1 .... 164 A7
Hilton Cl STVG SG1 .... 75 G2
Himalayan Wy WATW WD18 .... 12 A5
Hindhead Gn OXHEY WD19 .... 230 D4
Hine Wy HTCH/STOT SG5 .... 40 A8
Hinxworth Rd BLDK SG7 .... 16 B7
Hipkins BSF CM23 .... 105 H5
Hitchens Cl HHW HP1 .... 163 J5
Hitchin La HARP AL5.............. 118 C7
Hitchin Rd ARL/CHE SG15 ...... 24 E6
HTCH/STOT SG5 .... 25 H6
HTCH/STOT SG5 .... 37 K8
HTCHE/RSTV SG4 .... 43 H8
HTCHE/RSTV SG4 .... 56 D5
HTCHE/RSTV SG4 .... 93 G7
LTNE LU2 .... 5 D3
LWTH SG6 .... 41 J6
STVG SG1 .... 58 B7
Hitchin St BLDK SG7 .... 42 E1
Hitherbaulk WCCE AL7 .... 147 J5
Hither Fld WARE SG12 .... 127 J6
Hitherfield La HARP AL5.......... 118 C7
Hither Meadow CFSP/GDCR SL9 .. 226 B8
Hitherway WGCW AL8 .... 122 D7
Hobbs Cl CHES/WCR EN8 ...... 197 H7
STALE/WH AL4 .... 169 H7
Hobbs Cross Rd HLWE CM17 .. 157 J6
Hobbs Hill Rd HHS/BOV HP3 .. 185 J2
Hobbs Wy WGCW AL8 .... 147 H3
Hobletts Rd HHNE HP2.............. 8 C4
Hobsons Cl HOD EN11 .... 152 E8
Hobsons Wk TRING HP23 ...... 134 E4
Hobtoe Rd HLW CM20 .... 155 H8
Hockerill HERT/WAS SG14 ...... 98 B6
Hockerill St BSF CM23 .... 105 K2
Hocklands WGCE AL7 .... 148 D2
Hockwell Ring LTNW/LEA LU4.. 68 A4
Hoddesdon Rd WARE SG12 .... 153 H6
Hodges Wy WATW WD18 .... 12 B5
Hodings Rd HLW CM20 .... 6 A3
Hodwell BLDK SG7 .... 17 K5
Hoecroft WAB EN9 .... 178 A8
Hoe La EN EN1 .... 214 A8
PEND EN3 .... 214 A8
WAB EN9 .... 178 A8
WARE SG12 .... 152 C3
Hoestock Rd SBW CM21.......... 132 B7
The Hoe OXHEY WD19 .... 230 E1
Hogg End La STALW/RED AL3 .. 166 B4
Hogg La BORE WD6................ 222 D4
Hogg Hall La BERK HP4 .... 112 C4
Hog La CSHM HP5 .... 160 C8
Hogpits Bottom HHW HP3...... 200 D2
Hogsdell La HERT/BAY SG13 .. 152 A5
Holbeck La CHESW EN7 .... 196 D4
Holbein Ga NTHWD HA6 ...... 229 K4
Holborn Cl STALE/WH AL4 ...... 169 G1
Holcroft Rd HARP AL5 .... 119 F6
Holdbrook HTCHE/RSTV SG4.... 57 F2
Holden Cl HERT/BAY SG13 .... 151 H2
HTCHE/RSTV SG4 .... 57 G2
Holders La STVGE SG2 .... 77 F4
The Holdings BRKMPK AL9 .... 171 J2
Holecroft WAB EN9................ 215 K4
Holford Wy LTNN/LIM LU3 ...... 52 B8
Holgate Dr LTNW/LEA LU4 ...... 68 A6
Holland Gdns GSTN WD25 .... 204 D5
Holland La LTNN/LIM LU3 ...... 69 G7
Holland's Cft WARE SG12 ...... 129 K8
Holliday St BERK HP4 .... 162 A5
Holliers Wy HAT AL10 .... 171 F4
Hollies Cl ROY SG8 .... 21 J3

The Hollies HHS/BOV HP3 .... 183 J7
RKW/CH/CXG WD3 .... 217 F7
TRING HP23 .... 135 J8
Hollies Wy POTB/CUF EN6 .... 210 D1
Holloway La RKW/CH/CXG WD3 .. 200 E8
Holloways La BRKMPK AL9 .... 192 D1
The Holloway RAYLNE/WEN HP22 .. 134 B5
Hollow La HTCHE/RSTV SG4...... 56 D2
Hollybush Av LCOL/BKTW AL2.. 188 C2
Hollybush Cl BERK HP4 .... 163 G2
OXHEY WD19 .... 13 D6
WLYN AL6 .... 122 F1
Hollybush Hl LTNE LU2 .... 54 B8
Hollybush La BRKMPK AL9...... 148 A7
HARP AL5........................ 118 B6
HHW HP1 .... 163 J5
HTCHE/RSTV SG4 .... 92 F1
KNEB SG3 .... 96 B6
STALW/RED AL3 .... 116 A6
WGCE AL7 .... 147 K6
Hollybush Rd LTNE LU2 .... 70 D8
Hollybush Wy CHESW EN7 .... 196 E6
Holly Cl HAT AL10 .... 170 E5
Holly Copse STVG SG1.............. 3 D4
Holly Cft HERT/WAS SG14 .... 150 C2
Hollycross Rd WARE SG12 ...... 152 E1
Holly Dell HERT/BAY SG13 .... 151 F5
Holly Dr BERK HP4 .... 162 A6
POTB/CUF EN6 .... 210 C3
Holly Farm Cl LTN LU1 .... 88 D5
Hollyfield HAT AL10 .... 171 F7
Holly Fld HLWW/ROY CM19 .... 179 K4
Hollyfield Cl TRING HP23 ...... 135 H4
Hollyfields BROX EN10 .... 197 J4
Hollygrove BUSH WD23 .... 222 A7
Holly Gv PIN HA5 .... 231 F7
Holly Grove Rd HERT/WAS SG14 .. 124 E6
Holly Hall Ct WLYN AL6 .... 122 C4
Holly Hedges La HHS/BOV HP3.. 184 A8
Holly La HARP AL5 .... 119 G2
Holly Leys STVGE SG2 .... 96 C1
Holly Rd KNEB SG3 .... 96 B8
PEND EN3 .... 214 C6
Holly Shaws STVGE SG2............ 3 F6
Holly St LTN LU1 .... 4 C5
Hollytree Cl CFSP/GDCR SL9 .. 226 B8
Holly Tree Ct HHNE HP2............ 9 E5
Holly Wk HARP AL5 .... 119 F8
WGCW AL8........................ 122 C7
Holmbrook La LTNN/LIM LU3 .. 69 H4
Holmdale LWTH SG6 .... 42 A4
Holmdale Rd BORE WD6 ...... 223 J2
Holme Cl CHES/WCR EN8 ...... 214 D1
HAT AL10 .... 170 E1
Holme Lea GSTN WD25 .... 204 D4
Holme Pk BORE WD6 .... 223 J2
Holme Rd HAT AL10 .... 170 E1
Holmesdale CHES/WCR EN8 .. 214 B5
Holmes Meadow EPP CM16 .. 179 J7
Holmfield Cl LTN LU1 .... 4 B6
Holmscroft Rd LTNN/LIM LU3 .. 68 E3
Holmshill La BORE WD6 .... 208 E7
Holmside Ri OXHEY WD19 .... 230 C2
Holmwood Rd PEND EN3 ...... 214 C6
Holroyd Crs BLDK SG7 .... 42 E2
Holt Cl BORE WD6 .... 223 J4
Holts Meadow STALW/RED AL3 .. 142 C3
Holtsmere Cl GSTN WD25 ...... 204 D5
LTNE LU2 .... 70 D8
Holtsmere End La HHNE HP2 .. 141 G7
The Holt HHNE HP2................ 8 B6
WCCE AL7 .... 148 E4
Holwell Hyde WGCE AL7 ...... 148 D4
Holwell Hyde La BRKMPK AL9.. 148 D7
Holwell La BRKMPK AL9 ...... 149 F8
Holwell Rd HTCH/STOT SG5 .. 39 H3
WGCE AL7 .... 148 D4
Holy Cross Hl BROX EN10 ...... 196 E1
Holyfield Rd WAB EN9 .... 198 C7
Holyrood Crs STAL AL1 .... 189 F2
Holywell Cl DUN/WHIP LU6 .. 113 K3
Holywell Hl STAL AL1 .... 10 B6
Holywell Rd DUN/WHIP LU6 .. 113 K2
WATW WD18 .... 12 B4
Home Cl BROX EN10 .... 197 K2
HLW CM20 .... 7 E4
HTCH/STOT SG5 .... 25 K3
LTNW/LEA LU4 .... 68 B5
Homedale Dr LTNW/LEA LU4 .. 68 C7
Home Farm Rd BERK HP4 ...... 160 E2
RKW/CH/CXG WD3 .... 229 F3
Homefield BERK HP4 .... 162 E2
BLDK SG7 .... 16 D3
HHS/BOV HP3 .... 183 K6
Homefield La HTCHE/RSTV SG4.. 74 E7
Homefield Rd BUSH WD23...... 221 H5
HHNE HP2.......................... 9 E5
RAD WD7 .... 206 D7
RKW/CH/CXG WD3 .... 217 G4
WARE SG12 .... 127 J7
Homeleigh Ct CHES/WCR EN8 .. 197 J5
Home Ley WCCE AL7 .... 147 K3
Home Meadow WGCE AL7 .... 148 A3

Home Park Mill Link Rd
  KGLGY WD4 .... 203 G1
Home Pastures *RBSF* CM22 .... 133 K6
Homerfield *WGCW* AL8 .... 147 H3
Homerswood La *WLYN* AL6 .... 122 A7
Homerton Rd *LTNN/LIM* LU3 .... 69 F3
Homestead *LCOL/BKTW* AL2 .... 188 E5
Homestead La *WGCE* AL7 .... 148 A6
Homestead Moat *STVC* SG1 .... 2 C3
Homestead Rd *HAT* AL10 .... 171 F1
  RKW/CH/CXG WD3 .... 218 C7
Homestead Wy *LTN* LU1 .... 4 A6
Homewood Av *POTB/CUF* EN6 .... 195 G5
Homewood La *POTB/CUF* EN6 .... 194 E5
Homewood Rd *STAL* AL1 .... 168 E3
Honeybourne *BSF* CM23 .... 105 H5
Honey Brook *WAB* EN9 .... 215 K3
Honeycroft *WCCW* AL8 .... 147 H4
Honeycroft Dr *STALE/WH* AL4 .... 190 A1
Honeycross Rd *HHW* HP1 .... 163 H7
Honeygate *LTNE* LU2 .... 69 K5
Honey La *BUNT* SG9 .... 63 J1
  CHES/WCR EN8 .... 214 E4
  SAFWS CB11 .... 51 H6
  WAB EN9 .... 215 K4
Honeymeade *HLW* CM20 .... 157 F2
Honeysuckle Cl *BSF* CM23 .... 105 F3
  HERT/BAY SG13 .... 151 K3
Honeysuckle Gdns *HAT* AL10 .... 171 G5
Honeyway *ROY* SG8 .... 21 J2
Honeywood Cl *POTB/CUF* EN6 .... 210 E3
Hook Fld *HLWS* CM18 .... 7 D6
Hook Ga *EN* EN1 .... 214 A7
Hook La *POTB/CUF* EN6 .... 211 G2
Hoops La *STVG* SG2 .... 30 D3
Hook St *LTN* LU1 .... 4 C6
The Hoo *HLWE* CM17 .... 157 F4
Hope Gn *GSTN* WD25 .... 204 B3
Hopewell Rd *BLDK* SG7 .... 42 D1
Hopground Cl *STAL* AL1 .... 11 F6
Hopkins Crs *STALE/WH* AL4 .... 144 E8
Hopkins Yd *STAL* AL1 .... 11 D5
Hopton Rd *STVG* SG2 .... 75 F2
Horace Gay Gdns *LWTH* SG6 .... 41 J4
Horbeam Cl *BORE* WD6 .... 223 K1
Hordle Gdns *STAL* AL1 .... 11 E5
Hornbeam La *BRKMPK* AL9 .... 173 F7
Hornbeams *LCOL/BKTW* AL2 .... 188 B8
Hornbeams Av *EN* EN1 .... 214 B5
Hornbeam Spring *KNEB* SG3 .... 96 A5
The Hornbeams *HLW* CM20 .... 6 B2
  STVGE SG2 .... 3 F4
Hornbeam Wy *CHESW* EN7 .... 196 D7
The Hornets *WATW* WD18 .... 12 C3
Horn Hl *HTCHE/RSTV* SG4 .... 93 H3
Hornhill Rd *RKW/CH/CXG* WD3 .... 227 J5
Hornsby Cl *LTNE* LU2 .... 70 D8
Horns Cl *HERT/BAY* SG13 .... 151 J3
Hornsfield *WGCE* AL7 .... 148 D2
Horns Mill Rd *HERT/BAY* SG13 .... 150 E6
Horns Rd *HERT/BAY* SG13 .... 151 F4
Horrocks Cl *WARE* SG12 .... 127 H6
Horsecroft Rd *HHW* HP1 .... 163 K8
  HLWW/ROY CM19 .... 179 F2
Horse Hl *CSHM* HP5 .... 200 A4
Horselers *HHS/BOV* HP3 .... 186 A1
Horsemans Dr *LCOL/BKTW* AL2 .... 188 C4
Horseshoe Hl *BUNT* SG9 .... 65 G1
Horseshoe La *BUNT* SG9 .... 65 F3
  GSTN WD25 .... 204 C2
  TRDG/WHET N20 .... 225 J8
Horseshoes Cl *LBUZ* LU7 .... 109 K2
The Horseshoe *HHS/BOV* HP3 .... 165 H8
Horsham Cl *LTNE* LU2 .... 70 E6
Horsler Cl *AMP/FLIT/B* MK45 .... 36 C2
Horsleys *RKW/CH/CXG* WD3 .... 227 J2
Horton Gdns *HHNE* HP2 .... 141 F8
Hospital Rd *ARL/CHE* SG15 .... 24 D6
Housden Cl *STALE/WH* AL4 .... 145 H2
Housefield Wy *STALE/WH* AL4 .... 190 A1
House La *ARL/CHE* SG15 .... 24 E2
  STALE/WH AL4 .... 145 F8
Housewood End *HHNE* HP2 .... 164 A3
Howard Agne Cl *HHW* HP1 .... 183 J5
Howard Cl *BUSH* WD23 .... 222 B7
  HTCH/STOT SG5 .... 25 J4
  LTNN/LIM LU3 .... 69 F3
  STALE/WH AL4 .... 190 A1
  WAB EN9 .... 215 H1
  WATN WD24 .... 204 B7
Howard Ga *LWTH* SG6 .... 42 B6
Howard La *PIN* HA5 .... 230 C8
Howards Dr *HHW* HP1 .... 163 J3
Howardsgate *WCCW* AL8 .... 147 J3
Howards Wd *LWTH* SG6 .... 42 B6
Howard Wy *BAR* EN5 .... 225 J5
  HLW CM20 .... 7 E1
Howe Cl *RAD* WD7 .... 207 H2
Howe Dell *HAT* AL10 .... 171 G4
Howe Rd *HHS/BOV* HP3 .... 165 F8
Howe Fld *HARP* AL5 .... 118 A6
Howfield Gn *HOD* EN11 .... 152 E8

Howicks Gn *WGCE* AL7 .... 148 B6
Howland Garth *STAL* AL1 .... 188 E2
Howlands *WGCE* AL7 .... 148 B6
Howton Pl *BUSH* WD23 .... 222 A8
How Wd *LCOL/BKTW* AL2 .... 188 D6
Hoylake Gdns *OXHEY* WD19 .... 230 E3
Hubbards Rd *RKW/CH/CXG* WD3 .... 217 G5
Huckleberry Cl *LTNN/LIM* LU3 .... 69 F1
Hudnall La *BERK* HP4 .... 138 A3
Hudson Cl *STAL* AL1 .... 188 E1
  WATN WD24 .... 204 A6
Hudson Rd *STVGE* SG2 .... 3 F1
Huggins La *BRKMPK* AL9 .... 192 B1
Hughenden Rd *STALE/WH* AL4 .... 168 E3
Hull Gv *HLWW/ROY* CM19 .... 179 H6
Hull La *STDN* SG11 .... 81 K2
Humberstone Cl *LTNW/LEA* LU4 .... 68 D7
Humberstone Rd *LTNW/LEA* LU4 .... 68 D7
Humphrey Talbot Av
  DUN/WHIP LU6 .... 113 H2
Hunsdon *WGCE* AL7 .... 148 C8
Hunsdon Rd *STALE/WH* AL4 .... 165 J1
Hunston Cl *LTNW/LEA* LU4 .... 68 A4
Hunt Cl *STALE/WH* AL4 .... 169 C1
Hunter Cl *BORE* WD6 .... 224 B5
  POTB/CUF EN6 .... 210 C3
Huntercrombe Gdns
  OXHEY WD19 .... 230 D4
Hunters Cl *HHS/BOV* HP3 .... 183 J7
  HTCH/STOT SG5 .... 25 J3
  STVGE SG2 .... 76 E2
  TRING HP23 .... 135 G4
Hunter's La *GSTN* WD25 .... 204 A4
Hunters Oak *HHNE* HP2 .... 165 C1
Hunters Pk *BERK* HP4 .... 162 B4
Hunters Reach *CHESW* EN7 .... 196 D5
Hunters Ride *LCOL/BKTW* AL2 .... 205 H1
Hunters Wy *ROY* SG8 .... 21 J3
  WGCE AL7 .... 147 K6
Huntingdon Cl *BROX* EN10 .... 197 J2
Huntingdon Rd *STVG* SG1 .... 75 G1
Hunting Ga *HHNE* HP2 .... 8 B1
  HTCHE/RSTV SG4 .... 40 E6
Hunton Bridge Hl *KGLGY* WD4 .... 203 H3
Hunts Cl *LTN* LU1 .... 4 A5
Huntsman Cl *STDN* SG11 .... 81 J6
Huntsmans Cl *BERK* HP4 .... 112 E4
Huntsmill Rd *HHW* HP1 .... 163 H7
Hurlock Wy *LTNW/LEA* LU4 .... 68 B4
Hurricane Wy *GSTN* WD25 .... 204 B2
Hurst Cl *BLDK* SG7 .... 27 C8
  WGCE AL7 .... 148 D4
Hurst Dr *CHES/WCR* EN8 .... 214 C4
Hurstlings *WGCE* AL7 .... 148 C5
Hurst Pl *NTHWD* HA6 .... 229 G7
Hurst Wy *LTNN/LIM* LU3 .... 68 D4
Hutton Cl *HERT/WAS* SG14 .... 150 D3
Hutton La *KTN/HRWW/W* HA3 .... 231 K6
Hutton Wk *KTN/HRWW/W* HA3 .... 231 K6
Hyburn Cl *HHS/BOV* HP3 .... 9 E6
  LCOL/BKTW AL2 .... 188 B8
Hydean Wy *STVGE* SG2 .... 3 E5
Hyde Av *HTCH/STOT* SG5 .... 25 J4
  POTB/CUF EN6 .... 210 C3
Hyde Cl *HARP* AL5 .... 118 D5
Hyde Gn East *STVGE* SG2 .... 3 F5
Hyde Gn North *STVGE* SG2 .... 3 F5
Hyde Gn South *STVGE* SG2 .... 3 F5
Hyde La *HHS/BOV* HP3 .... 183 J5
  KGLGY WD4 .... 186 B5
  LCOL/BKTW AL2 .... 188 E6
  LTNE LU2 .... 91 J7
Hyde Md *WAB* EN9 .... 198 E1
Hyde Mdw *HHS/BOV* HP3 .... 183 J6
Hyde Rd *LTN* LU1 .... 69 K2
  WAT WD17 .... 12 B2
The Hyde *WARE* SG12 .... 127 F7
Hyde Va *WGCE* AL7 .... 148 A5
Hyde View Rd *HARP* AL5 .... 118 D5
Hyde Wy *WGCE* AL7 .... 147 K3
Hyperion Ct *HHNE* HP2 .... 8 C2
Hyver Hl *MLHL* NW7 .... 224 D1

Ibberson Wy *HTCHE/RSTV* SG4 .... 56 D1
Iceni Ct *LWTH* SG6 .... 42 B2
Ickleford Rd *HTCH/STOT* SG5 .... 56 D1
Ickley Cl *LTNW/LEA* LU4 .... 68 A4
Icknield Cl *HTCH/STOT* SG5 .... 40 C5
  STALW/RED AL3 .... 167 G8
Icknield Gn *LWTH* SG6 .... 41 J5
  TRING HP23 .... 135 F3
Icknield Rd *LTNN/LIM* LU3 .... 69 F3
Icknield Wk *ROY* SG8 .... 21 J2
Icknield Wy *BERK* HP4 .... 113 G4
  BLDK SG7 .... 26 E8
  BUNT SG9 .... 30 A7
  LTNN/LIM LU3 .... 69 G1
  LWTH SG6 .... 41 G3
  ROY SG8 .... 30 D2
  TRING HP23 .... 134 C6

Icknield Wy East *BLDK* SG7 .... 27 F8
Icknield Way Pth
  AMP/FLIT/B MK45 .... 52 A1
  BLDK SG7 .... 26 E6
  HTCH/STOT SG5 .... 38 E6
  HTCH/STOT SG5 .... 40 D4
  HTCH/STOT SG5 .... 53 K3
  LTNN/LIM LU3 .... 69 F3
  LTNW/LEA LU4 .... 68 B6
  ROY SG8 .... 18 D3
  ROY SG8 .... 23 F2
Ilford Cl *LTNE* LU2 .... 70 D7
Ilkley Rd *OXHEY* WD19 .... 230 E4
Imberfield *LTNW/LEA* LU4 .... 68 B6
Imperial Wy *WATN* WD24 .... 220 D3
Indells *HAT* AL10 .... 170 E5
Ingelheim Ct *STVG* SG1 .... 2 B1
Ingersoll Rd *PEND* EN3 .... 214 E8
Inglefield *POTB/CUF* EN6 .... 193 G8
Ingles *WGCW* AL8 .... 122 E6
Ingleside Dr *STVG* SG1 .... 58 B8
Ingram Gdns *LTNE* LU2 .... 69 J3
Inkerman Rd *STAL* AL1 .... 11 D5
Inkerman St *LTN* LU1 .... 4 B4
Innes Ct *HHS/BOV* HP3 .... 164 C8
Inn's Cl *STVG* SG1 .... 2 B2
Inskip Crs *STVG* SG1 .... 2 C3
Iona Cl *STVG* SG1 .... 59 F2
Iredale Vw *BLDK* SG7 .... 27 G8
Iron Dr *HERT/BAY* SG13 .... 152 A2
Irving Cl *BSF* CM23 .... 105 G5
Irving Crs *LBUZ* LU7 .... 110 A1
Isabel Ga *CHES/WCR* EN8 .... 197 K4
Isabelle Cl *CHESW* EN7 .... 196 A2
Isenburg Wy *HHNE* HP2 .... 164 C1
Isherwood Cl *ROY* SG8 .... 21 G1
Islington Wy *STVG* SG1 .... 59 F2
Iveagh Cl *NTHWD* HA6 .... 229 G2
Ivel Cl *AMP/FLIT/B* MK45 .... 36 D6
Ivel Rd *STVG* SG1 .... 2 A1
Ivel Wy *BLDK* SG7 .... 43 G3
  HTCH/STOT SG5 .... 25 K1
Ives Rd *HERT/WAS* SG14 .... 150 E1
Ivinghoe Br *LBUZ* LU7 .... 110 C1
Ivinghoe Cl *GSTN* WD25 .... 204 E1
  STALE/WH AL4 .... 169 F1
Ivinghoe Rd *BUSH* WD23 .... 222 A4
  RKW/CH/CXG WD3 .... 217 J2
Ivory Cl *STALE/WH* AL4 .... 169 F1
Ivory Ct *HHS/BOV* HP3 .... 185 J1
Ivybridge *BROX* EN10 .... 177 F5
Ivy House La *BERK* HP4 .... 162 A5
Ivy Lea *RKW/CH/CXG* WD3 .... 217 K8
Ivy Rd *LTN* LU1 .... 4 A3
Ivy Ter *HOD* EN11 .... 177 H1

Jackdaw Cl *STVGE* SG2 .... 76 E2
Jackdaws *WGCE* AL7 .... 148 D3
Jackets La *DEN/HRF* UB9 .... 229 F6
Jacketts Fld *ABLGY* WD5 .... 187 F2
Jackman's Pl *LWTH* SG6 .... 42 B3
Jacks La *DEN/HRF* UB9 .... 227 K7
Jacksons Dr *CHESW* EN7 .... 196 E3
Jackson's La *ROY* SG8 .... 31 J3
Jackson St *BLDK* SG7 .... 26 E8
Jack Stevens Cl *HLWE* CM17 .... 181 F3
James Cl *BUSH* WD23 .... 13 F1
James Ct *LTN* LU1 .... 4 C5
Jameson Rd *HARP* AL5 .... 118 D7
James Wy *STVG* SG1 .... 2 A5
Jane Cl *HHNE* HP2 .... 165 G1
Jarden *LWTH* SG6 .... 42 C1
Jarman Cl *HHS/BOV* HP3 .... 164 C8
Jarman Wy *ROY* SG8 .... 21 F1
Jarvis Cleys *CHESW* EN7 .... 196 D4
Jarvis Cl *BAR* EN5 .... 225 J3
Jasmin Cl *BSF* CM23 .... 105 F2
  NTHWD HA6 .... 230 A3
Jasmine Dr *HERT/BAY* SG13 .... 151 K3
Jasmine Gdns *HAT* AL10 .... 170 E2
Jasmin Wy *HHW* HP1 .... 163 H5
Jasons Hl *CSHM* HP5 .... 182 D5
Jasper Cl *PEND* EN3 .... 214 B6
Jay Cl *LWTH* SG6 .... 41 J4
Jaywood *LTNE* LU2 .... 70 D7
Jeans La *BSF* CM23 .... 105 H4
Jeffrey Cl *ROY* SG8 .... 21 G1
Jellicoe Rd *WATW* WD18 .... 12 B3
Jenkins Av *LCOL/BKTW* AL2 .... 188 A4
Jenkins La *BSF* CM23 .... 106 A1
  TRING HP23 .... 158 D2
Jennings Cl *STVG* SG1 .... 2 C3
Jennings Rd *STAL* AL1 .... 11 E8
Jennings Wy *BAR* EN5 .... 225 H6
  HHS/BOV HP3 .... 164 D3
Jenning Wd *WLYN* AL6 .... 123 F7
Jepps La *ROY* SG8 .... 21 H3
Jerome Dr *STALW/RED* AL3 .... 167 H6
Jerounds *HLWW/ROY* CM19 .... 6 A5

Jersey CI *HOD* EN11 .... 177 F2
Jersey La *STAL* AL1 .... 168 E4
  STALE/WH AL4 .... 145 F8
Jervis Av *PEND* EN3 .... 214 D5
Jervis Rd *CM23* 105 J3
Jessop Rd *STVG* SG1 .... 59 G8
Jeve CI *BLDK* SG7 .... 27 G1
Jill Grey PI *HTCH/STOT* SG5 .... 56 D3
The Jinnings *WGCE* AL7 .... 148 C6
Jocelyns *HLWE* CM17 .... 157 F5
Jocketts HI *HHW* HP1 .... 163 J6
Jocketts Rd *HHW* HP1 .... 163 J7
Joel St *NTHWD* HA6 .... 230 B8
John Barker PI *HTCH/STOT* SG5 .... 40 A8
John Bunyan Trail *HTCH/STOT* SG5 .. 37 G6
  LTNE LU2 .... 53 J7
  LTNN/LIM LU3 .... 52 B7
Johnby CI *PEND* EN3 .... 214 D7
John Eliot CI *WAB* EN9 .... 177 K8
John Howland CI *HNLW* SG16 .... 24 B1
Johns La *CSHM* HP5 .... 160 E8
Johnson Ct *HHS/BOV* HP3 .... 164 D8
Johns Rd *CM23* 85 K8
John St *LTN* LU1 .... 4 C4
  ROY SG8 .... 21 H3
John Tate Rd *HERT/BAY* SG13 .... 151 J4
Joiner's CI *CFSP/GDCR* SL9 .... 226 C6
Joiners La *CFSP/GDCR* SL9 .... 226 B5
Joiners Wy *CFSP/GDCR* SL9 .... 226 B6
The Joint *ROY* SG8. .... 32 A3
Jones Rd *CHESW* EN7 .... 195 K8
Jonquil CI *WGCE* AL7 .... 148 C5
Jordan CI *WD25* 204 A5
Jordans Rd *RKW/CH/CXG* WD3 .... 217 K2
Jordan's Wy *LCOL/BKTW* AL2 .... 188 A8
Joslyn CI *PEND* EN3 .... 215 G4
Joyce CI *WAB* EN9 .... 215 J4
Joyners Fld *HLWS* CM18 .... 179 K5
Jubilee Av *LCOL/BKTW* AL2 .... 190 B4
  WARE SG12 .... 127 K7
Jubilee CI *PIN* HA5 .... 230 D8
Jubilee Crs *ARL/CHE* SG15 .... 24 D7
Jubilee End *ROY* SG8 .... 15 J7
Jubilee Rd *LWTH* SG6 .... 42 C2
  STVG SG1 .... 75 C1
  WATN WD24 .... 204 B8
Jubilee St *LTNE* LU2 .... 5 D2
Jubilee Wy *ROY* SG8 .... 15 J7
Judge's HI *POTB/CUF* EN6 .... 194 B7
Judge St *WATN* WD24 .... 204 C8
Julia Ga *STVG* SG1 .... 76 D1
Julian's Ct *STVG* SG2 .... 75 H1
Julian's Rd *STVG* SG1 .... 75 G1
Julius Gdns *LTNN/LIM* LU3 .... 68 E2
Juniper Av *LCOL/BKTW* AL2 .... 205 H1
Juniper CI *BAR* EN5 .... 225 J5
  BROX EN10 .... 197 K3
  LTNW/LEA LU4 .... 68 D7
Juniper Gdns *RAD* WD7 .... 207 H3
Juniper Ga *RKW/CH/CXG* WD3. .... 228 C3
Juniper Gn *HHW* HP1 .... 163 H6
Juniper Gv *WAT* WD17 .... 204 B3
Jupiter CI *HHNE* HP2 .... 8 C3
Juxon CI *RYLN/HDSTN* HA2 .... 231 J7

K

Kardwell CI *HTCHE/RSTV* SG4 .... 56 E3
Katescroft *WGCE* AL7 .... 147 K2
Katherine PI *ABLGY* WD5 .... 204 B2
Katherine's Wy *HLWW/ROY* CM19 .... 179 H4
Katrine Sq *HHNE* HP2 .... 8 A1
Keats CI *HHNE* HP2 .... 141 G8
  ROY SG8 .... 21 C1
  STVGE SG2 .... 76 C1
Keats Wy *HTCHE/RSTV* SG4 .... 57 G2
Keble Ter *ABLGY* WD5 .... 204 A2
Kecksy's *SBW* CM21 .... 132 D5
Keeble CI *LTNE* LU2 .... 71 F8
Keele CI *WATN* WD24 .... 13 D1
Keepers CI *LBUZ* LU7 .... 110 A2
  LTNE LU2 .... 70 D7
Keiths Rd *HHS/BOV* HP3. .... 9 D6
Keiths Wd *KNEB* SG3. .... 96 A4
Kelbys *WGCE* AL7 .... 148 D2
Keller CI *STVGE* SG2 .... 3 F4
Kelling CI *LTNE* LU2 .... 69 H1
Kelly CI *BORE* WD6 .... 224 C2
Kelman CI *CHES/WCR* EN8 .... 214 C1
Kelmscott CI *WATW* WD18 .... 12 B5
Kelmscott Crs *WATW* WD18 .... 12 B4
Kelshall *GSTN* WD25 .... 205 F6
Kelshall St *ROY* SG8 .... 30 C4
Kelvin CI *LTN* LU1 .... 4 C5
Kemble CI *POTB/CUF* EN6 .... 210 C5
Kempe CI *STAL* AL1 .... 188 E2
Kempe Rd *EN* EN1 .... 214 A6
Kemp PI *BUSH* WD23 .... 221 H6
Kemprow *GSTN* WD25 .... 206 A5
Kemps Dr *NTHWD* HA6 .... 230 A6
Kempsey CI *LTNE* LU2 .... 70 E2
Kendal CI *LTNN/LIM* LU3 .... 68 C1

Kendale *HHS/BOV* HP3. .... 9 E6
Kendale Rd *HTCHE/RSTV* SG4 .... 56 D3
  LTNW/LEA LU4 .... 68 A7
Kendall CI *WGCE* AL7. .... 148 A7
Kendals CI *RAD* WD7 .... 206 B6
Kenerne Dr *BAR* EN5 .... 225 K5
Kenford CI *GSTN* WD25 .... 204 D2
Kenilworth CI *HHS/BOV* HP3 .... 8 B6
  STVGE SG2 .... 96 D2
Kenilworth Ct *WAT* WD17 .... 220 B1
Kenilworth Dr *BORE* WD6 .... 224 B3
  RKW/CH/CXG WD3 .... 219 G4
Kenilworth Gdns *OXHEY* WD19 . ... 230 D4
Kenilworth Rd *LTN* LU1 .... 4 A3
Kennedy Av *HOD* EN11 .... 176 E3
Kennedy CI *CHES/WCR* EN8. .... 197 J6
  PIN HA5 .... 231 G5
Kennedy Rd *WARE* SG12 .... 99 H2
Kennel La *HARP* AL5 .... 117 G4
Kennelwood La *HAT* AL10 .... 171 G3
Kenneth Rd *LTNE* LU2 .... 5 E2
Kenning Rd *HOD* EN11 .... 177 H5
Kennington Rd *LTNN/LIM* LU3 .... 69 G7
Kensington Av *WATW* WD18 .... 12 A3
Kensington CI *STAL* AL1 .... 11 F6
Kensington Wy *BORE* WD6 .... 224 C3
Kensworth Rd *DUN/WHIP* LU6 .... 114 A5
Kent CI *BORE* WD6. .... 208 C8
Kent Crs *BSF* CM23 .... 105 H5
Kentish La *BRKMPK* AL9 .... 193 J2
Kenton Gdns *STAL* AL1 .... 11 E5
Kent Rd *LTN* LU1 .... 88 E1
Kents Av *HHS/BOV* HP3 .... 185 H2
Kent's La *STDN* SG11 .... 81 K7
Kenwood Dr *RKW/CH/CXG* WD3 .... 227 J1
Kenworth CI *CHES/WCR* EN8. .... 197 J6
Kerdistone CI *POTB/CUF* EN6 .... 193 H8
Kerr CI *KNEB* SG3. .... 96 A4
Kerri CI *BAR* EN5 .... 225 H4
Kerril Cft *HLW* CM20 .... 155 H8
Kershaw CI *LTNN/LIM* LU3 .... 69 F1
Kershaw's HI *HTCHE/RSTV* SG4 .... 56 D3
Kessingland Av *STVG* SG1 .... 58 A8
Keston Ms *WAT* WD17 .... 12 C1
Kestrel CI *BERK* HP4 .... 161 K6
  GSTN WD25 .... 205 F4
  STVGE SG2 .... 76 E7
Kestrel Gdns *BSF* CM23 .... 105 F3
Kestrel Gn *HAT* AL10 .... 171 F5
The Kestrels *LCOL/BKTW* AL2 .... 205 F1
Kestrel Wk *LWTH* SG6 .... 42 B6
Kestrel Wy *WGCE* AL7 .... 148 A5
Keswick CI *STAL* AL1 .... 168 E7
Keswick Dr *PEND* EN3 .... 214 B6
Kettering Rd *PEND* EN3 .... 214 C7
Kettle Green Rd *MHAD* SG10 .... 103 F7
Ketton CI *LTNE* LU2 .... 5 F4
Kewferry Dr *NTHWD* HA6 .... 229 G4
Kewferry Rd *NTHWD* HA6 .... 229 H5
Keyfield Ter *STAL* AL1 .... 10 C5
Keymer CI *LTNE* LU2 .... 70 D8
Keynton Rd *HERT/WAS* SG14 .... 150 C2
Keysers Rd *BROX* EN10 .... 177 F8
Kibes La *WARE* SG12 .... 127 H8
Kidner CI *LTNE* LU2 .... 69 K4
Kilbride CI *HHNE* HP2 .... 8 C1
Kilby CI *WD25* 204 E5
Kilfillan Gdns *BERK* HP4 .... 161 H6
Kilmarnock Dr *LTNE* LU2 .... 69 K4
Kilmarnock Rd *OXHEY* WD19 .... 230 E3
Kilncroft *HHS/BOV* HP3 .... 165 G8
Kilnfield *WCCE* AL7 .... 123 F8
Kiln Gnd *HHS/BOV* HP3 .... 165 F8
Kiln House CI *WARE* SG12 .... 127 J7
Kiln La *HLWE* CM17 .... 181 F2
Kiln Wy *NTHWD* HA6 .... 229 K5
Kilsmore La *CHES/WCR* EN8 .... 197 H6
Kilvinton Dr *ENC/FH* EN2 .... 213 G8
Kilworth CI *WGCE* AL7 .... 148 C5
Kimberley *LWTH* SG6 .... 25 K7
Kimberley CI *BSF* CM23 .... 105 K4
Kimberley Rd *STALW/RED* AL3 .... 10 B3
Kimble CI *WATW* WD18 .... 219 K6
Kimble Crs *BUSH* WD23 .... 221 K7
Kimps Wy *HHS/BOV* HP3 .... 186 A1
Kimpton Bottom *HARP* AL5 .... 119 G2
Kimpton CI *HHNE* HP2 .... 165 G1
Kimpton PI *GSTN* WD25 .... 204 E4
Kimpton Rd *HTCHE/RSTV* SG4 .... 94 B8
  LTN LU1 .... 5 E5
  LTNE LU2 .... 92 B7
  STALE/WH AL4 .... 120 A3
  WLYN AL6 .... 121 J3
Kimptons CI *POTB/CUF* EN6 .... 209 J3
Kimptons Md *POTB/CUF* EN6 .... 209 J3
Kinderscout *HHS/BOV* HP3 .... 165 F8
Kindersley CI *WLYN* AL6 .... 122 C3
Kindersley Wy *ABLGY* WD5 .... 203 H1
King Arthur Ct *CHES/WCR* EN8 .... 214 D1
King Charles Rd *RAD* WD7 .... 207 H3
King Croft Rd *HARP* AL5 .... 144 A2
King Edward Rd *CHES/WCR* EN8 .... 214 D3
  OXHEY WD19 .... 13 F5

RAD WD7 .... 207 J3
King Edward's Rd *WARE* SG12 .... 127 J7
King Edward St *HHS/BOV* HP3 .... 185 H2
Kingfisher CI *NTHWD* HA6 .... 229 G7
  STALE/WH AL4 .... 120 B8
  WARE SG12 .... 127 J7
Kingfisher Ct *HTCHE/RSTV* SG4 .... 56 E3
Kingfisher Dr *HHS/BOV* HP3 .... 185 K3
Kingfisher Lure
  RKW/CH/CXG WD3 .... 218 A4
Kingfisher Ri *STVGE* SG2. .... 76 E7
Kingfisher Wy *BSF* CM23 .... 105 K2
King George Av *BUSH* WD23 .... 221 J6
King George CI *STVG* SG1 .... 2 C2
King George Rd *WAB* EN9 .... 215 H4
  WARE SG12 .... 127 J7
King Georges Av *WATW* WD18 .... 219 K5
King Georges CI *HTCH/STOT* SG5 .... 40 B7
King George's Wy *HTCHE/RSTV* SG4.. 93 H3
Kingham Rd *WARE* SG12 .... 128 E4
Kinghamway *LTNE* LU2 .... 4 C2
King Harry La *STALW/RED* AL3 .... 167 H7
King Harry St *HHNE* HP2 .... 8 A5
King Henry's Ms *PEND* EN3 .... 215 F7
King James Av *POTB/CUF* EN6 .... 195 G7
King James Wy *ROY* SG8 .... 21 H3
Kings Av *HHS/BOV* HP3 .... 185 K2
  WATW WD18 .... 12 B3
Kingsbridge Rd *BSF* CM23 .... 105 K1
Kingsbury Av *STALW/RED* AL3. .... 10 A3
Kings CI *CSTG* HP8 .... 226 A1
  KGLGY WD4 .... 202 A1
  NTHWD HA6 .... 230 A5
  WATW WD18 .... 13 D3
Kings Ct *BSF* CM23 .... 105 K1
Kingscroft *WGCE* AL7 .... 148 C2
Kingsdale Rd *BERK* HP4 .... 161 H6
Kingsdon La *HLWE* CM17 .... 181 F2
Kingsdown *HTCHE/RSTV* SG4 .... 57 F2
Kingsdown Av *LTNE* LU2 .... 69 J5
Kings Farm Rd *RKW/CH/CXG* WD3 .. 217 G6
Kingsfield *HOD* EN11 .... 177 F1
Kingsfield Ct *OXHEY* WD19 .... 13 E5
Kingsfield Dr *PEND* EN3 .... 214 C5
Kingsfield Rd *OXHEY* WD19 .... 13 E6
  WARE SG12 .... 99 H2
Kingsfield Wy *PEND* EN3 .... 214 C5
Kingsgate *STALW/RED* AL3 .... 10 A6
Kingshill Av *STALE/WH* AL4 .... 168 E3
Kingshill Wy *BERK* HP4. .... 161 H7
Kingsland Rd *HHW* HP1 .... 163 K8
  LTN LU1 .... 5 D5
Kingsland Wy *BLDK* SG7. .... 18 A6
King's La *KGLGY* WD4 .... 201 K1
Kingsley Av *BORE* WD6 .... 223 J2
  CHES/WCR EN8. .... 197 F7
Kingsley CI *BRKMPK* AL9 .... 148 A7
Kingsley Rd *LTNN/LIM* LU3 .... 69 F4
Kingsley Wk *TRING* HP23 .... 135 F3
Kingsmead *CHES/WCR* EN8. .... 197 H6
  POTB/CUF EN6 .... 195 G6
  SBW CM21 .... 132 C8
  STALE/WH AL4 .... 169 G3
Kingsmead CI *HLWW/ROY* CM19...... 178 C2
Kings Meadow *KGLGY* WD4 .... 186 A6
Kingsmill Ct *HAT* AL10 .... 171 G6
Kingsmoor Rd *HLWW/ROY* CM19 .... 179 J4
Kings Rd *BAR* EN5 .... 225 H3
  BERK HP4 .... 161 J6
  CHES/WCR EN8. .... 214 D4
  HERT/BAY SG13 .... 151 K2
  HTCH/STOT SG5 .... 56 D1
  LCOL/BKTW AL2 .... 190 A4
  STALW/RED AL3 .... 10 A3
  STVG SG1. .... 2 B4
Kingston Rd *LTNE* LU2 .... 5 D1
Kingston V *ROY* SG8 .... 21 J4
King St *BSF* CM23 .... 105 J2
  LTN LU1 .... 4 B4
  STALW/RED AL3 .... 115 J4
  TRING HP23 .... 135 F6
  WATW WD18 .... 13 D3
Kings Walden Ri *STVGE* SG2 .... 76 D2
King's Walden Rd *HTCH/STOT* SG5 .. 54 E7
Kingsway *HTCH/STOT* SG5 .... 25 J2
  LTN LU1 .... 89 F1
  LTNW/LEA LU4 .... 69 F8
  POTB/CUF EN6 .... 195 G8
  ROY SG8 .... 21 G1
  WARE SG12 .... 127 H6
Kingsway North Orbital Rd
  GSTN WD25 .... 204 B4
Kingswell Ride *POTB/CUF* EN6 .... 195 G8
Kingswood Av *HTCHE/RSTV* SG4 .... 57 H1
Kingswood Rd *GSTN* WD25 .... 204 C4
Kingwell Rd *EBAR* EN4 .... 210 E8
King William CI *AMP/FLIT/B* MK45 .... 36 D5
Kinmoor CI *LTNN/LIM* LU3 .... 68 C1
Kinross Crs *LTNN/LIM* LU3 .... 68 C1
Kinsbourne CI *HARP* AL5 .... 117 J5
Kinsbourne Crs *HARP* AL5 .... 117 H6
Kinsbourne Green La *HARP* AL5 .... 117 H6
Kipling CI *HTCHE/RSTV* SG4 .... 57 G2
Kipling Gv *HHNE* HP2 .... 141 G8

The Kipling *LTNN/LIM* LU3 .... 69 G3 🔲
Kipling Wy *HARP* AL5 .... 118 D8
Kirby Cl *NTHWD* HA6 .... 230 A5
Kirkcaldy Gn *OXHEY* WD19 .... 230 D2 🔲
Kirkdale Rd *HARP* AL5 .... 118 C7
Kirklands *WGCW* AL8 .... 122 E7
Kirkwick Av *HARP* AL5 .... 118 B8
Kitchener Cl *STAL* AL1 .... 11 F5
Kitcheners La *STVGE* SG2 .... 60 D8
Kitching La *STVG* SG1 .... 74 E4
Kite Fld *BERK* HP4 .... 161 F2
Kite Wy *LWTH* SG6 .... 41 J1
Kitsbury Rd *BERK* HP4 .... 161 J5
Kitsbury Ter *BERK* HP4 .... 161 J5
Kit's La *BLDK* SG7 .... 44 E1
Kitson Wy *HLW* CM20 .... 6 B5 🔲
Kitswell Wy *RAD* WD7 .... 206 C3
Kitt's End Rd *BAR* EN5 .... 209 K7
Knap Cl *LWTH* SG6 .... 42 C1
Knebworth Pth *BORE* WD6 .... 224 C4 🔲
Kneesworth St *ROY* SG8 .... 21 C2
Knella Gn *WGCE* AL7 .... 148 B3
Knella Rd *WGCE* AL7 .... 148 A3
Knights Cl *BSF* CM23 .... 104 E1
   BUNT SG9 .... 63 J3
Knights Fld *LTNE* LU2 .... 4 B2
Knightsfield *WGCW* AL8 .... 122 D7
Knights Orch *HHW* HP1 .... 163 J4
Knights Templars Gn *STVGE* SG2 .. 76 D1
Knight St *SBW* CM21 .... 132 C2
Knole La *SAFWS* CB11 .... 35 J2
Knoll Crs *NTHWD* HA6 .... 229 K8
Knolles Crs *BRKMPK* AL9 .... 192 B2
Knoll Ri *LTNE* LU2 .... 69 K5
The Knoll *HERT/BAY* SG13 .... 152 A2
Knowle Dr *HARP* AL5 .... 144 A2
The Knowle *HOD* EN11 .... 177 F4 🔲
Knowl Piece *HTCHE/RSTV* SG4 ...... 40 E6
Knowl Wy *BORE* WD6 .... 223 H5
Knutsford Av *WATN* WD24 .... 204 E3
Koh-i-noor Av *BUSH* WD23 .... 221 H6
Kristiansand Wy *LWTH* SG6 .... 42 C1
Kymswell Rd *STVGE* SG2 .... 76 D5
Kynance Cl *LTNE* LU2 .... 70 B6
Kyrkeby *LWTH* SG6 .... 42 C1
Kytes Dr *GSTN* WD25 .... 204 E3

L

Laburnum Cl *CHES/WCR* EN8 .... 214 C1
   LTNN/LIM LU3 .... 69 H2
Laburnum Gv *LCOL/BKTW* AL2 .... 188 C3
   LTNN/LIM LU3 .... 69 G2
Laburnum Rd *HOD* EN11 .... 177 G1 🔲
Lachbury Cl *LTN* LU1 .... 89 F3
Lackmore Rd *EN* EN1 .... 214 B5 🔲
Lacre Wy *LWTH* SG6 .... 42 C2
Ladbrooke Cl *POTB/CUF* EN6 ...... 210 B2 🔲
Ladbrooke Dr *POTB/CUF* EN6 ...... 210 B2
Ladies Gv *STALW/RED* AL3 .... 10 A2
Lady Gv *WGCE* AL7 .... 147 K7
Ladyhill *LTNN/LEA* LU4 .... 68 A3
Ladymeadow *HHS/BOV* HP3 .... 185 H5
Lady's Cl *WATW* WD18 .... 13 D3
Ladyshot *HLW* CM20 .... 7 F3
Ladysmith Rd *LBUZ* LU7 .... 110 E4
   STALW/RED AL3 .... 10 C3
Ladywalk *RKW/CH/CXG* WD3 ...... 227 H4
Ladywood Cl *RKW/CH/CXG* WD3 .. 218 A3
Ladywood Rd *HERT/WAS* SG14 .... 150 C3
Laidon Sq *HHW* HP2 .... 8 A1
Lake Dr *BUSH* WD23 .... 231 K1
Laker Ct *LTNE* LU2 .... 4 B2
Lake Rd *WAB* EN9 .... 177 K7
Lakeside *TRING* HP23 .... 135 F4
Lakeside Pl *LCOL/BKTW* AL2 ...... 190 B6
Lakeside Rd *CHES/WCR* EN8 .... 197 G6
The Lake *BUSH* WD23 .... 222 A8
Lake Vw *POTB/CUF* EN6 .... 210 D3 🔲
Lalleford Rd *LTNE* LU2 .... 70 D8
Lamb Cl *GSTN* WD25 .... 204 D4
   HAT AL10 .... 171 G5 🔲
Lambert Cl *BUSH* WD23 .... 13 E3
Lamb La *STALW/RED* AL3 .... 142 C4
Lamb Meadow *ARL/CHE* SG15 ...... 24 D6
Lambourn Cha *RAD* WD7 .... 206 C6 🔲
Lambourn Dr *LTNE* LU2 .... 69 K3
Lambourn Gdns *HARP* AL5 .... 118 B6 🔲
Lambs Cl *POTB/CUF* EN6 .... 195 H4
Lambton Av *CHES/WCR* EN8 .... 214 C3 🔲
Lamer La *STALW/RED* AL3 .... 120 B5
Lamers Rd *LTNE* LU2 .... 5 F1
Lammasmead *BROX* EN10 .... 197 K4
Lammas Md *HTCH/STOT* SG5 .... 40 C7
Lammas Rd *HERT/WAS* SG14 .... 98 A3
   LBUZ LU7 .... 110 A2
   WATW WD18 .... 13 D4 🔲
Lammas Wy *LWTH* SG6 .... 41 K1
Lamorna Cl *LTNN/LIM* LU3 .... 68 E3 🔲
   RAD WD7 .... 206 E4

Lampits *HOD* EN11 .... 177 C3
Lampitts Cross *LTNN/LIM* LU3 ...... 69 F4 🔲
Lamsey Rd *HHS/BOV* HP3 .... 164 C8
Lancaster Av *EBAR* EN4 .... 210 E8
   LTNE LU2 .... 69 H1 🔲
Lancaster Cl *AMP/FLIT/B* MK45 .... 36 D5 🔲
   STVG SG1 .... 58 E7
Lancaster Dr *HHW* HP1 .... 183 H5
Lancaster Rd *HTCH/STOT* SG5 ...... 56 C1
   STAL AL1 .... 11 E2
Lancaster Wy *ABLGY* WD5 .... 204 A1 🔲
   BSF CM23 .... 104 E1
Lancing Rd *LTNE* LU2 .... 70 E6
Lancing Wy *RKW/CH/CXG* WD3 .... 219 G5
Landau Wy *BROX* EN10 .... 197 K4
Landford Cl *RKW/CH/CXG* WD3 .... 228 D1
Landmead Rd *CHES/WCR* EN8 ...... 197 J7
Lands' End *BORE* WD6 .... 223 G6
Lane End *BERK* HP4 .... 160 E7
   HAT AL10 .... 170 E7
   HLWE CM17 .... 181 H2
Lanefield Wk *WGCW* AL8 .... 147 H3 🔲
Lane Gdns *BUSH* WD23 .... 222 B8
Lanercost Cl *WLYN* AL6 .... 123 F2
Langbridge Cl *HTCHE/RSTV* SG4 .... 56 E4
Langdale Av *HARP* AL5 .... 119 F7
Langdale Gdns *PEND* EN3 .... 214 C5
Langdon St *TRING* HP23 .... 135 F6
Langfield Cl *WAB* EN9 .... 177 K8 🔲
Langford Dr *LTNE* LU2 .... 70 B6
Langham Cl *LTNE* LU2 .... 69 J2
   STALW/RED AL3 .... 169 F1
Langholme *BUSH* WD23 .... 221 K8 🔲
Langland Cl *NTHWD* HA6 .... 229 H6
Langland Dr *PIN* HA5 .... 231 F6
Langley Av *HHS/BOV* HP3 .... 185 J1
Langleybury La *KGLGY* WD4 .... 203 G4
   WAT WD17 .... 203 G7
Langley Crs *KGLGY* WD4 .... 186 A8
   STALW/RED AL3 .... 10 B2
Langley Gv *STALE/WH* AL4 .... 145 F7
Langley Hl *KGLGY* WD4 .... 185 K7
Langley Hill Cl *KGLGY* WD4 .... 186 A7 🔲
Langley La *ABLGY* WD5 .... 204 A1
   HTCHE/RSTV SG4 .... 74 C7
Langley Lodge La *KGLGY* WD4 .... 202 D1
Langley Rd *ABLGY* WD5 .... 203 K1
   KGLGY WD4 .... 185 F8
   WAT WD17 .... 220 A1
Langley St *LTN* LU1 .... 4 C5 🔲
Langley Wy *WAT* WD17 .... 220 A1
Langmead Dr *BUSH* WD23 .... 222 A8
Langthorne Av *STVG* SG1 .... 2 C1
Langton Gv *NTHWD* HA6 .... 229 H4
Langton Rd *HOD* EN11 .... 176 E5
   KTN/HRWW/W HA3 .... 231 K6
Langwood Gdns *WAT* WD17 .... 220 B1 🔲
Lankester Rd *ROY* SG8 .... 21 G4
Lannock *LWTH* SG6 .... 42 C5
Lannock Hl *HTCHE/RSTV* SG4........ 42 D7
Lanrick Copse *BERK* HP4 .... 162 B4
Lansdowne Rd *LTNN/LIM* LU3 .... 4 A2
Lansdown Rd *CFSP/GDCR* SL9 .... 226 A7 🔲
Lanterns La *STVGE* SG2 .... 76 E3
Laporte Wy *LTNW/LEA* LU4 .... 68 E8
Lapwing Cl *HHNE* HP2 .... 8 B1
Lapwing Dell *LWTH* SG6 .... 42 B7
Lapwing Ri *STVGE* SG2 .... 76 E7
Lapwing Wy *ABLGY* WD5 .... 204 B1 🔲
Larch Av *HTCHE/RSTV* SG4............ 56 E5
   LCOL/BKTW AL2 .... 188 A8
Larch Cl *CHESW* EN7 .... 196 C5 🔲
Larches Av *EN* EN1 .... 214 B5
The Larches *BERK* HP4 .... 160 E4
   BUSH WD23 .... 13 F4
   LTNE LU2 .... 4 B2
   STALW/RED AL3 .... 169 G2
   WARE SG12 .... 127 G5
Larch Ri *BERK* HP4 .... 161 H4
Larchwood *BSF* CM23 .... 105 G4
Larchwood Rd *HHNE* HP2 .... 8 C3
Larken Cl *BUSH* WD23 .... 221 K8
Larken Dr *BUSH* WD23 .... 221 K8
Larkens Cl *STDN* SC11 .... 81 J6
Larkins Cl *BLDK* SG7 .... 27 F8
Larkinson *STVG* SG1 .... 2 A1
Lark Ri *HAT* AL10 .... 171 H4
Larksfield *WARE* SG12 .... 127 J6
Larkspur Cl *BSF* CM23 .... 105 G4
   HHW HP1 .... 163 H5
Larkspur Gdns *LTNW/LEA* LU4........ 68 E7
Larks Rdg *LCOL/BKTW* AL2 .... 188 C3
Larksway *BSF* CM23 .... 105 F3
Larkswood *HLWE* CM17 .... 181 F3 🔲
Larkswood Ri *STALE/WH* AL4 .... 169 F1
Larmans Rd *PEND* EN3 .... 214 B6 🔲
Larsen Dr *WAB* EN9 .... 215 J4 🔲
Larwood Gv *STVG* SG1 .... 76 B1
Latchmore Bank *RBSF* CM22........ 106 A7
Latchmore Cl *HTCHE/RSTV* SG4.... 56 D4
Latimer Cl *HHNE* HP2 .... 165 C1
   PIN HA5 .... 230 D7
   WATW WD18 .... 219 K7
Latimer Gdns *PIN* HA5 .... 230 D7
   WGCE AL7 .... 148 C3

Latimer Rd *AMS* HP6......................... 200 C🔲
   LTN LU1 .... 4 C
Latium Cl *STAL* AL1 .... 10 C
Lattimore Rd *STAL* AL1 .... 11 D🔲
   STALE/WH AL4 .... 145 F
Latton Gn *HLWS* CM18 .... 180 C
Latton Hall Cl *HLW* CM20 .... 7 F
Latton House *HLWS* CM18 .... 180 E
Latton St *HLW* CM20 .... 180 E
   HLWE CM17 .... 180 E
Lauderdale Rd *ABLGY* WD5 .... 203 H
Laundry La *WAB* EN9 .... 199 F
Launton Cl *LTNN/LIM* LU3 .... 52 B
Laureate Wy *HHW* HP1 .... 164 A
Laurel Av *POTB/CUF* EN6 .... 210 A
Laurel Bank *HHS/BOV* HP3 .... 184 D
Laurel Cl *HHNE* HP2 .... 8 C
Laureldene *MHAD* SG10 .... 103 G8 🔲
Laurel Flds *POTB/CUF* EN6 .... 210 A
Laurel Rd *CFSP/GDCR* SL9 .... 226 A
   STAL AL1 .... 11 E
Laurels Cl *STALW/RED* AL3 .... 188 D
The Laurels *BERK* HP4 .... 162 E
   CHESW EN7 .... 196 C
Laurel Wy *HTCH/STOT* SG5............ 40 C
Lauries Cl *HHW* HP1 .... 162 E
Laurino Pl *BUSH* WD23 .... 231 K
Lavender Cl *BSF* CM23 .... 105 G
   CHESW EN7 .... 196 D5 🔲
   HLW CM20 .... 7 D
   LTNE LU2 .... 69 K
Lavender Ct *BLDK* SG7 .... 26 E8
Lavender Gdns *ENC/FH* EN2 .... 212 E
Lavender Wy *HTCH/STOT* SG5 ...... 56 B
Lavinia Av *GSTN* WD25 .... 204 C
Lavrock La *RKW/CH/CXG* WD3 .... 218 E
Lawford Av *RKW/CH/CXG* WD3 .... 217 F
Lawford Cl *LTN* LU1 .... 4 A3 🔲
   RKW/CH/CXG WD3 .... 217 F
Law Hall La *HTCHE/RSTV* SG4 .... 92 C
Lawn Av *HTCHE/RSTV* SG4 .... 93 F
Lawn Gdns *LTN* LU1 .... 4 B
Lawn La *HHS/BOV* HP3 .... 164 C
Lawns Cl *HTCH/STOT* SG5 .... 54 E
The Lawns Dr *BROX* EN10 .... 176 E
The Lawns *HHW* HP1 .... 163 H
   PIN HA5 .... 231 J
   RAD WD7 .... 207 H3 🔲
   STALW/RED AL3 .... 10 B3
   STVGE SG2 .... 76 E
   WGCW AL8 .... 122 C
Lawn V *PIN* HA5 .... 230 E
Lawrance Gdns *CHES/WCR* EN8 .... 197 H
Lawrance Rd *STALW/RED* AL3 ...... 167 K
Lawrence Av *LWTH* SG6 .... 42 A
   SBW CM21 .... 132 C
   STVG SG1 .... 2 C
   WARE SG12 .... 153 H
Lawrence Cl *HERT/WAS* SG14 ...... 150 E
Lawrence End Rd *LTNE* LU2 .... 91 H
Lawrence Moorings *SBW* CM21 .... 132 C
Laxton Cl *LTNE* LU2 .... 71 F
Laxton Gdns *BLDK* SG7 .... 43 C
Lay Brook *STALE/WH* AL4 .... 168 D2
Layham Dr *LTNE* LU2 .... 70 E
Layhill *HHNE* HP2 .... 8 A
Layston Meadow *BUNT* SG9 .... 63 H
Layston Pk *ROY* SG8 .... 21 H
Lea Bushes *GSTN* WD25 .... 205 F
Lea Cl *BSF* CM23 .... 86 A
   BUSH WD23 .... 221 J5
Leaf Cl *NTHWD* HA6 .... 229 F
Leafield *LTNN/LIM* LU3 .... 68 E
Leaford Crs *WATN* WD24 .... 204 A
Leaforis Rd *CHESW* EN7 .... 196 E
Leafy La *TRING* HP23 .... 134 C2
Leagrave Rd *LTNN/LIM* LU3 .... 69 F
Lea Gv *BSF* CM23 .... 86 A
Leamington Rd *LTNN/LIM* LU3 .... 69 F
Lea Mt *CHESW* EN7 .... 196 C
Leander Gdns *GSTN* WD25 .... 205 F7
Lea Rd *HARP* AL5 .... 118 D
   HOD EN11 .... 177 F
   LTN LU1 .... 5 D
   WAB EN9 .... 215 F
   WATN WD24 .... 204 C8
Leasey Bridge La *STALE/WH* AL4 .... 119 H
Leasey Dell Dr *STALE/WH* AL4 ...... 119 J
Leaside *HHNE* HP2 .... 9 F
The Leas *BLDK* SG7 .... 42 E
   BUSH WD23 .... 221 C
   HHS/BOV HP3 .... 186 A
Leat Cl *SBW* CM21 .... 132 C
Leathwaite Cl *LTNN/LIM* LU3 .... 68 E
Lea Valley Wk *BRKMPK* AL9 .... 147 H
   BRKMPK AL9 .... 149 C
   BRKMPK AL9 .... 171 H
   HERT/BAY SG13 .... 151 H
   HERT/WAS SG14 .... 98 C
   LTNE LU2 .... 90 C
   LTNE LU2 .... 198 A
   WAB EN9 .... 198 A
   WAB EN9 .... 215 H
   WARE SG12 .... 153 H
   WGCW AL8 .... 146 E
Leavesden Rd *WATN* WD24 .... 204 C

Leaves Spring *STVGE* SG2 .... 3 D6
Leaview *WAB* EN9 .... 215 G3
Lea Wk *HARP* AL5 .... 118 E5
Lebanon Cl *WAT* WD17 .... 203 J6
Le Corte Cl *KGLGY* WD4 .... 185 K7
Lectern La *STAL* AL1 .... 189 C2 ⬚
Ledgemore La *HHNE* HP2 .... 139 J3
Ledwell Rd *LTN* LU1 .... 88 E6
Leeches Wy *LBUZ* LU7 .... 110 A2
Lee Cl *HERT/BAY* SG13 .... 151 F5
WARE SG12 .... 153 H5 ⬚
Leecroft Rd *BAR* EN5 .... 225 K4
Leefe Wy *POTB/CUF* EN6 .... 195 F6
Leeming Rd *BORE* WD6 .... 223 J1
Lees Av *NTHWD* HA6 .... 230 A7
Leeside *BAR* EN5 .... 225 K4
POTB/CUF EN6 .... 210 E2
Leete Pl *ROY* SG8 .... 21 G2
Leggatts Cl *WATN* WD24 .... 204 A6
Leggatts Ri *CSTN* WD25 .... 204 B5
Leggatts Wy *WATN* WD24 .... 204 B6
Leggatts Wood Av *WATN* WD24 .... 204 C6
Leggett Gv *STVG* SG1 .... 75 K1
Leggfield Ter *HHW* HP1 .... 163 J6 ⬚
Legions Wy *BSF* CM23 .... 105 K1
Legra Av *HOD* EN11 .... 177 F3 ⬚
Leicester Rd *LTNW/LEA* LU4 .... 68 D8
Leigh Common *WGCE* AL7 .... 147 K5
Leigh Ct *BORE* WD6 .... 224 C2 ⬚
Leigh Rodd *OXHEY* WD19 .... 231 F2
Leighton Buzzard Rd *HHW* HP1 .... 139 H7
Lemon Field Dr *CSTN* WD25 .... 205 F3 ⬚
Lemsford Cl *BORE* WD6 .... 224 B4
Lemsford La *WGCW* AL8 .... 147 C4
Lemsford Rd *HAT* AL10 .... 171 F2 ⬚
STAL AL1 .... 11 E4
Lemsford Village *WGCW* AL8 .... 147 H4
Lennox Gn *LTNE* LU2 .... 71 G7 ⬚
Lensbury Ct *CHES/WCR* EN8 .... 197 J6 ⬚
Leonard's Cl *WLYN* AL6 .... 122 E1
Lesbury Cl *LTNE* LU2 .... 71 F8
Leslie Cl *STVGE* SG2 .... 76 D7
Letchmore Rd *RAD* WD7 .... 206 D6
STVG SG1 .... 2 B1
Letchworth Cl *OXHEY* WD19 .... 230 E4 ⬚
HHS/BOV HP3 .... 9 F6
Letchworth Ga *LWTH* SG6 .... 42 B4
Letchworth La *LWTH* SG6 .... 41 K6
Letchworth Rd *BLDK* SG7 .... 42 D3
LTNN/LIM LU3 .... 68 C3
LWTH SG6 .... 42 D2
Levenage La *WARE* SG12 .... 130 A6
Leven Cl *CHES/WCR* EN8 .... 214 C3 ⬚
OXHEY WD19 .... 230 E4 ⬚
Levendale *LTNW/LEA* LU4 .... 68 B4 ⬚
Leven Dr *CHES/WCR* EN8 .... 214 C3
Leven Wy *HHNE* HP2 .... 8 A1 ⬚
Leveret Cl *WATN* WD25 .... 204 B4
Leverstock Green Rd *HHNE* HP2 .... 9 D4
HHS/BOV HP3 .... 9 F6
Leverton Wy *WAB* EN9 .... 215 H3
Lewes Wy *RKW/CH/CXG* WD3 .... 219 G4
Lewis Cl *DEN/HRF* UB9 .... 228 B8
Lewis La *ARL/CHE* SG15 .... 24 E3
CFSP/GDCR SL9 .... 226 B7
Lewsey Rd *LTNW/LEA* LU4 .... 68 A6
Lexington Cl *BORE* WD6 .... 223 K3 ⬚
Lexington Wy *BAR* EN5 .... 225 J4
Leyburne Rd *LTNN/LIM* LU3 .... 69 G3
Leycroft Wy *HARP* AL5 .... 144 B3
Leyden Rd *STVG* SG1 .... 2 B5
Leygreen Cl *LTNE* LU2 .... 5 E3
Leyhill Dr *LTN* LU1 .... 89 C5
Leyland Av *STAL* AL1 .... 10 C6
Leyland Cl *CHES/WCR* EN8 .... 197 G6 ⬚
Leys Av *LWTH* SG6 .... 41 K3
Leys Cl *DEN/HRF* UB9 .... 228 C7
Leysdown *WGCE* AL7 .... 148 C3
Leys Rd *HHS/BOV* HP3 .... 164 E8
The Leys *STALE/WH* AL4 .... 169 J1
TRING HP23 .... 135 H5
Leyton Gn *HARP* AL5 .... 118 C8
Leyton Rd *HARP* AL5 .... 118 C8
Ley Wk *WGCE* AL7 .... 148 D5
Liberty Cl *HERT/BAY* SG13 .... 151 F5
Library Rd *LTN* LU1 .... 4 C4 ⬚
Lichfield Wy *BROX* EN10 .... 176 E8 ⬚
Liddel Cl *LTNN/LIM* LU3 .... 69 F6
Lidgate Cl *LTNW/LEA* LU4 .... 68 A3
Lieutenant Ellis Wy *CHESW* EN7 .... 213 J1
Lighthorne Ri *LTNN/LIM* LU3 .... 69 C2
Lilac Av *LTN* LU1 .... 214 B6
Lilac Cl *CHESW* EN7 .... 214 A1 ⬚
Lilac Rd *HOD* EN11 .... 177 G1
Lilac Wy *HARP* AL5 .... 144 A3 ⬚
Lilley Bottom *LTNE* LU2 .... 54 A8
Lilley Bottom Rd *HTCHE/RSTV* SG4 .... 72 B7
Lilleyhoo La *LTNE* LU2 .... 54 B7
Lilliard Cl *HOD* EN11 .... 153 G7
Lilly La *HHW* HP1 .... 165 J2
The Limberlost *WLYN* AL6 .... 122 E5
Limbrick Rd *HARP* AL5 .... 143 J3
Limbury Rd *LTNN/LIM* LU3 .... 68 E5
Lime Av *LTNW/LEA* LU4 .... 68 A6
STALE/WH AL4 .... 119 K3

Lime Cl *AMP/FLIT/B* MK45 .... 36 C6
OXHEY WD19 .... 13 E6 ⬚
STVGE SG2 .... 76 E5
WARE SG12 .... 127 J7
Limedene Cl *PIN* HA5 .... 230 E7
Lime Gv *ROY* SG8 .... 21 J1
TRDG/WHET N20 .... 225 K8
Limekiln La *BLDK* SG7 .... 43 F2
STSD CM24 .... 86 B3
Limes Ct *HOD* EN11 .... 177 F3 ⬚
Limes Crs *BSF* CM23 .... 105 K2
Limes Rd *CHES/WCR* EN8 .... 214 C2
The Limes *ARL/CHE* SG15 .... 24 E1
HTCH/STOT SG5 .... 56 B3
STALW/RED AL3 .... 11 D2
WGCE AL7 .... 148 B5
Limetree Av *LTN* LU1 .... 117 C2
Lime Tree Pl *STAL* AL1 .... 11 D5 ⬚
ENC/FH EN2 .... 213 F8
RKW/CH/CXG WD3 .... 218 A5
Lime Wk *HHS/BOV* HP3 .... 164 E8
Linacres *LTNN/LEA* LU4 .... 68 C5
Linbridge Wy *LTNE* LU2 .... 71 F7
Linces Wy *WGCE* AL7 .... 148 C5
Lincoln Cl *BSF* CM23 .... 105 G4
WGCE AL7 .... 148 D2
Lincoln Ct *BERK* HP4 .... 161 J5
BORE WD6 .... 224 C5 ⬚
Lincoln Dr *OXHEY* WD19 .... 230 D2
RKW/CH/CXG WD3 .... 219 G4
Lincoln Rd *CFSP/GDCR* SL9 .... 226 B7
LTNW/LEA LU4 .... 69 G8
STVG SG1 .... 59 J7
Lincoln's Cl *STALE/WH* AL4 .... 169 F1
Lincoln Wy *RKW/CH/CXG* WD3 .... 219 G4
Lincot La *HTCHE/RSTV* SG4 .... 94 B2
Lindbergh Av *WGCE* AL7 .... 148 D5 ⬚
Linden Cl *CHESW* EN7 .... 197 F8 ⬚
Linden Ct *HARP* AL5 .... 143 J1
Linden Crs *STAL* AL1 .... 169 F6
Lindencroft *LWTH* SG6 .... 26 A8
Linden Dr *CFSP/GDCR* SL9 .... 226 D7
Linden Gld *HHW* HP1 .... 164 A7 ⬚
Linden Lea *GSTN* WD25 .... 204 B3
Linden Rd *LTNW/LEA* LU4 .... 68 D5
STALW/RED AL3 .... 142 B3
The Lindens *BSF* CM23 .... 105 J3
HHS/BOV HP3 .... 184 C1
STVG SG1 .... 2 C4 ⬚
Lindley Cl *HARP* AL5 .... 118 C5
Lindlings *HHW* HP1 .... 163 H7
Lindsay Av *HTCHE/RSTV* SG4 .... 57 F4
Lindsay Pl *CHESW* EN7 .... 197 F8 ⬚
Lindsey Cl *BSF* CM23 .... 85 J8
LTNE LU2 .... 70 E8
Lindsey Rd *STALW/RED* AL3 .... 85 J8
Lindum Pl *STALW/RED* AL3 .... 167 G8
Linford Cl *HLWW/ROY* CM19 .... 6 B6
Linford End *HLWW/ROY* CM19 .... 6 B6
Lingfield Cl *NTHWD* HA6 .... 229 K6
Lingfield Rd *ROY* SG8 .... 21 J5 ⬚
STVG SG1 .... 59 J8
Lingholm Wy *BAR* EN5 .... 225 J5
Lingmoor Dr *CSTN* WD25 .... 204 B3
Linington Av *CSHM* HP5 .... 182 C8
Link Cl *HAT* AL10 .... 171 G4
Link Dr *HAT* AL10 .... 171 G4
Linkfield *WGCE* AL7 .... 147 K7
Link Rd *BSF* CM23 .... 105 J1
WATN WD24 .... 13 E1
WLYN AL6 .... 123 F2 ⬚
Links Av *HERT/BAY* SG13 .... 152 A2
Links Dr *BORE* WD6 .... 223 J4 ⬚
RAD WD7 .... 206 C4
The Links *CHES/WCR* EN8 .... 197 H4 ⬚
Links Vw *STALW/RED* AL3 .... 10 A2 ⬚
Links Wy *RKW/CH/CXG* WD3 .... 219 H3
LTNE LU2 .... 69 J3
NTHWD HA6 .... 229 H7
Linksway *NTHWD* HA6 .... 229 J7
Link Wy *BSF* CM23 .... 105 H3
Linkway *PIN* HA5 .... 230 E7
Linkways East *STVG* SG1 .... 3 D3
Linkways West *STVG* SG1 .... 3 D3
Linnet Cl *BUSH* WD23 .... 221 K8
LWTH SG6 .... 41 J1
Linnet Rd *ABLGY* WD5 .... 204 B1
Linsey Cl *HHS/BOV* HP3 .... 186 A2
Linster Gv *BORE* WD6 .... 224 B5
Linten Cl *HTCHE/RSTV* SG4 .... 57 G3
Linton Av *BORE* WD6 .... 223 J4
Lintott Cl *STVG* SG1 .... 2 B6
Linwood *SBW* CM21 .... 132 C7 ⬚
Linwood Rd *HARP* AL5 .... 143 K2 ⬚
WARE SG12 .... 127 K6
Lion Ct *BORE* WD6 .... 224 B1
Liphook Rd *OXHEY* WD19 .... 230 E3
Lippitts Hl *LTNE* LU2 .... 69 K4
Lismore *HHS/BOV* HP3 .... 165 H4 ⬚
STVGE SG2 .... 76 D8
Lister Av *HTCHE/RSTV* SG4 .... 56 C4
Liston Cl *LTNW/LEA* LU4 .... 68 A4
Litlington Rd *ROY* SG8 .... 15 K8

Little Acre *STALW/RED* AL3 .... 10 C1
Little Acres *WARE* SG12 .... 152 C1
Little Berries *LTNN/LIM* LU3 .... 68 D2
Little Brays *HLWS* CM18 .... 7 F5
Little Bridge Rd *BERK* HP4 .... 162 A5 ⬚
Littlebrook Gdns *CHES/WCR* EN8 .... 197 H8
Little Brook Rd *HLWW/ROY* CM19 .... 178 D3
Little Burrow *WGCE* AL7 .... 147 J5
Little Bushey La *BUSH* WD23 .... 221 H3
Little Catherells *HHW* HP1 .... 163 J4 ⬚
Little Cattins *HLWW/ROY* CM19 .... 179 C5
Little Chishill Rd *ROY* SG8 .... 33 J1
Little Church Rd *LTNE* LU2 .... 70 C6
Littlecote Pl *PIN* HA5 .... 231 G7 ⬚
Little Dell *WGCW* AL8 .... 147 J1
Littlefield Rd *LTNE* LU2 .... 70 C6
Little Ganett *WGCE* AL7 .... 148 C5
Little Graylings *ABLGY* WD5 .... 203 K3
Littlegreen La *LTNN* LU1 .... 88 D7
Little Green La *RKW/CH/CXG* WD3 .... 218 E3
Little Gv *BUSH* WD23 .... 221 J4
Little Grove Fld *HLWW/ROY* CM19 .... 6 E4 ⬚
Little Hardings *WGCE* AL7 .... 148 D2
Little Hayes *KGLGY* WD4 .... 186 A7 ⬚
Little Heath *RBSF* CM22 .... 133 K6
Little Heath La *BERK* HP4 .... 162 E4
Little Hl *RKW/CH/CXG* WD3 .... 217 F6
Little Hoo *TRING* HP23 .... 134 E3
Little How Cft *ABLGY* WD5 .... 203 H1
Little Lake *WGCE* AL7 .... 148 C6
Little La *HARP* AL5 .... 143 K3
HTCH/STOT SG5 .... 39 F4
Little Ley *WGCE* AL7 .... 147 K6 ⬚
Little Martins *BUSH* WD23 .... 221 J5
Little Md *HAT* AL10 .... 171 G1 ⬚
Little Mimms *HHNE* HP2 .... 8 A4
Little Moss La *PIN* HA5 .... 231 F8
Little Mundells *WGCE* AL7 .... 148 B3
Little Orchard Cl *ABLGY* WD5 .... 203 J1
PIN HA5 .... 231 F8 ⬚
Little Oxhey La *OXHEY* WD19 .... 231 F4
Little Pk *HHS/BOV* HP3 .... 183 J6
Little Piper's Cl *CHESW* EN7 .... 195 K7
Little Potters *BUSH* WD23 .... 222 A7
Little Pynchons *HLWS* CM18 .... 180 C4
Little Rdg *WGCE* AL7 .... 148 B3
Little Rivers *WGCE* AL7 .... 148 B2
Little Rd *HHNE* HP2 .... 8 B4
Little Stream Cl *NTHWD* HA6 .... 229 K4
Little Thistle *WGCE* AL7 .... 148 D5
Little Tring Rd *TRING* HP23 .... 134 E3
Little Twye Rd *TRING* HP23 .... 158 E5
Little Wade *WGCE* AL7 .... 148 A6
Little Widbury *WARE* SG12 .... 127 K8
Little Widbury La *WARE* SG12 .... 127 K8
Little Windmill Hl *KGLGY* WD4 .... 201 H2
Little Wood Cft *LTNN/LIM* LU3 .... 68 D2
Little Youngs *WGCW* AL8 .... 147 H3
Liverpool Rd *LTN* LU1 .... 4 B4
STAL AL1 .... 11 D4
WATW WD18 .... 12 C4
Livingstone Link *STVGE* SG2 .... 76 C1
Llanbury Cl *CFSP/GDCR* SL9 .... 226 B6
Lloyd-taylor Cl *STDN* SG11 .... 83 J7
Lloyd Wy *HTCHE/RSTV* SG4 .... 93 F8
Loates La *WAT* WD17 .... 13 D2
Local Board Rd *WAT* WD17 .... 13 D4 ⬚
Locarno Av *LTNW/LEA* LU4 .... 68 B4
Lochnell Rd *BERK* HP4 .... 161 G3
Lockers Park La *HHW* HP1 .... 164 B5 ⬚
Lockley Crs *HAT* AL10 .... 171 G2
Lockleys Dr *WLYN* AL6 .... 122 C4
Lodge Av *BORE* WD6 .... 223 J5
Lodge Cl *HERT/WAS* SG14 .... 151 F1
Lodge Ct *HTCH/STOT* SG5 .... 40 C5
Lodge Crs *CHES/WCR* EN8 .... 214 D8 ⬚
Lodge Dr *BRKMPK* AL9 .... 171 J1
RKW/CH/CXG WD3 .... 218 B4
Lodge End *RAD* WD7 .... 206 E4
RKW/CH/CXG WD3 .... 219 J4
Lodge Fld *WGCE* AL7 .... 122 E8
Lodge Gdns *HARP* AL5 .... 118 C2
Lodge Hall *HLWS* CM18 .... 180 B5
Lodge La *CSTG* HP8 .... 216 C2
WAB EN9 .... 215 J5
Lodge Rd *RKW/CH/CXG* WD3 .... 219 J4
Lodge Wy *STVGE* SG2 .... 76 B8
Loftus Cl *LTNW/LEA* LU4 .... 68 A5
Lombardy Cl *HHNE* HP2 .... 165 J7
Lombardy Dr *BERK* HP4 .... 162 A6
Lombardy Wy *BORE* WD6 .... 223 H1
Lomond Rd *HHNE* HP2 .... 8 A1
Lomond Wy *STVG* SG1 .... 59 J2
London Loop *BORE* WD6 .... 224 A6
ENC/FH EN2 .... 212 C1
MLHL NW7 .... 224 B7
London Rd *BERK* HP4 .... 162 A5
BLDK SG7 .... 43 F3
BSF CM23 .... 105 J2
BUNT SG9 .... 63 K3
BUSH WD23 .... 13 G5
EPP CM16 .... 180 E8
HARP AL5 .... 117 G3
HERT/BAY SG13 .... 151 H3
HHS/BOV HP3 .... 185 F1

HHW HP1	162	E8
HLWE CM17	157	F6
HTCHE/RSTV SG4	56	D4
HTCHE/RSTV SG4	74	A1
KNEB SG3	96	B4
LTN LU1	4	C6
RAD WD7	207	J3
RKW/CH/CXG WD3	218	D8
ROY SG8	21	H4
SBW CM21	132	C7
STAL AL1	11	D5
STALW/RED AL3	115	J4
STVG SG1	2	B5
TRING HP23	135	G6
WARE SG12	152	C1
WLYN AL6	122	C5
London Rw ARL/CHE SG15	24	E4
Long Acre HLWE CM17	156	F5
Longacres STALE/WH AL4	169	G6
Long Arrotts HHW HP1	164	A4
Long Banks HLWS CM18	180	A4
Long Barn CI GSTN WD25	204	B2
Long Border Rd BRKMPK CM22	87	K8
Longbridge CI TRING HP23	135	F3 ⊡
Long Buftlers HARP AL5	144	C1
Long Chaulden HHW HP1	163	H7
Longcliffe Pth OXHEY WD19	230	B2 ⊡
Long CI LTNE LU2	70	D6
Long Cft OXHEY WD19	12	C6
STSD CM24	86	C1
Longcroft Av HARP AL5	118	B8
Long Croft Dr CHES/WCR EN8	214	E4
Longcroft Gdns WGCW AL8	147	J4 ⊡
Longcroft Gn WGCW AL8	147	J4 ⊡
Longcroft La HHS/BOV HP3	184	A6
WGCW AL8	147	J4
Longcroft Rd AMP/FLIT/B MK45	36	B7
RKW/CH/CXG WD3	227	G4
Longcroft Rd STVG SG1	2	C1
Long Cutt STALW/RED AL3	142	E3
Longdean Pk HHS/BOV HP3	186	A2
Long Elmes KTN/HRWW/W HA3	231	J7
Long Elms ABLGY WD5	203	J3
Long Elms CI ABLGY WD5	203	J3 ⊡
Long Fallow LCOL/BKTW AL2	188	C5
Longfield HHS/BOV HP3	165	G8
HLWS CM18	7	F6
Longfield Av PEND EN3	214	B7
Longfield Dr LTNW/LEA LU4	68	C3
Longfield Gdns TRING HP23	134	C3
Longfield La CHESW EN7	196	D5
Longfield Rd HARP AL5	143	K2
TRING HP23	134	D6
Longfields STVGE SG2	76	D8
Long John HHS/BOV HP3	164	E8
Longlands HHNE HP2	8	C4
Longlands CI CHES/WCR EN8	214	C2 ⊡
Longlands Rd WGCE AL7	148	A5
Long La HHS/BOV HP3	200	C1
HTCHE/RSTV SG4	92	D2
RKW/CH/CXG WD3	217	J8
RKW/CH/CXG WD3	217	F6
STVGE SG2	77	F4
Long Leaves STVGE SG2	3	E6
Long Ley HLW CM20	7	E4
LBUZ LU7	110	A2
WGCE AL7	148	D3
Long Marston La LBUZ LU7	109	J3
Long Marston Rd TRING HP23	109	J3
Longmead BUNT SG9	63	H2
HAT AL10	171	G1
KNEB SG3	96	B7 ⊡
LWTH SG6	41	J2
Long Meadow BSF CM23	105	G3
STALW/RED AL3	115	J4
Longmeadow Dr HTCH/STOT SG5	40	C4
Long Mimms HHNE HP2	8	B4 ⊡
Long Moor CHES/WCR EN8	197	J7
Longmore CI RKW/CH/CXG WD3	227	J3
Longmore Gdns WGCE AL7	148	A5
Long Rdg STVGE SG2	76	E8
Long Spring STALW/RED AL3	168	C2
Longspring WATN WD24	204	C7
Long Vw BERK HP4	161	H3
Long Wk CSTG HP8	216	B3
Long Wd HLWS CM18	180	A4
Longwood Rd HERT/WAS SG14	150	C2
The Loning PEND EN3	214	B8
Lonsdale HHNE HP2	8	B2
Lonsdale CI LTNN/LIM LU3	69	F4
Lonsdale Rd STVG SG1	3	D1
Loom La RAD WD7	206	C7
Loom PI RAD WD7	206	D6
Loop Rd WAB EN9	215	G2
Lord Mead La WLYN AL6	121	G2
Lords Av BSF CM23	104	E2
Lords CI RAD WD7	207	H2
Lordship La LWTH SG6	42	B5
Lordship Rd CHESW EN7	197	F8
Lords Meadow STALW/RED AL3	142	B4
Lord St HOD EN11	176	D5
WAT WD17	13	D2 ⊡
Lords Wd WGCE AL7	148	D3
Loring Rd BERK HP4	161	K6
Lorrimer CI LTNE LU2	69	K3
Lothair Rd LTNE LU2	70	B5
Loudhams Wood La CSTG HP8	216	A2
Loudwater Dr RKW/CH/CXG WD3	218	B4
Loudwater Hts RKW/CH/CXG WD3	218	A3
Loudwater La RKW/CH/CXG WD3	218	B5
Loudwater Rdg		
RKW/CH/CXG WD3	218	B4 ⊡
Louise Wk HHS/BOV HP3	183	J6
Louvain Wy GSTN WD25	204	C2
Lovatts RKW/CH/CXG WD3	219	F4
Love La ABLGY WD5	187	F8
BLDK SG7	17	C4
KGLGY WD4	185	J7
Lovel CI HHW HP1	163	K6
Lovell CI HTCHE/RSTV SG4	56	E5 ⊡
Lovell Rd EN EN1	214	A5
Lovering Rd CHESW EN7	196	A3
Lovet Rd HLWW/ROY CM19	179	H2
Lowbell La LCOL/BKTW AL2	190	C5
Lower Adeyfield Rd HHNE HP2	8	B4
Lower Barn HHS/BOV HP3	185	K1
Lower Bourne Gdns WARE SG12	127	G6
Lower Clabdens WARE SG12	127	K8
Lower Dagnall St STALW/RED AL3	10	B4
Lower Derby Rd WAT WD17	13	D3 ⊡
Lower Emms HHNE HP2	165	H1 ⊡
Lowerfield WGCE AL7	148	B4
Lower Gower Rd STAL AL1	11	H1
Lower Harpenden Rd LTN LU1	5	F6
Lower Hatfield Rd		
HERT/BAY SG13	150	C8
Lower High St WAT WD17	13	D3
Lower Icknield Wy TRING HP23	109	K8
Lower Innings HTCH/STOT SG5	56	A1
Lower Island Wy WAB EN9	215	G5
Lower Kings Rd BERK HP4	161	K4
Lower King St ROY SG8	21	H3
Lower Luton Rd HARP AL5	118	E6 ⊡
HARP AL5	119	F6 ⊡
LTNE LU2	118	D3
STALE/WH AL4	119	H7
Lower Mardley HI WLYN AL6	123	F1
Lower Meadow CHES/WCR EN8	197	H5
HLWS CM18	180	B5
Lower Paddock Rd OXHEY WD19	13	F5
Lower Park Crs BSF CM23	105	J4
Lower Paxton Rd STAL AL1	11	D5 ⊡
Lower Plantation		
RKW/CH/CXG WD3	218	B3
Lower Rd CFSP/GDCR SL9	226	A7
HHS/BOV HP3	186	A4
HTCHE/RSTV SG4	72	C8
RBSF CM22	133	G2
RKW/CH/CXG WD3	217	G4
WARE SG12	152	E3
Lower Sales HHW HP1	163	J7
Lower Sean STVGE SG2	3	E5
Lower St STSD CM24	86	E2 ⊡
Lower Tail OXHEY WD19	231	F2
Lower Tub BUSH WD23	222	A7 ⊡
Lower Yott HHNE HP2	8	B6
Lowestoft Rd WATN WD24	220	C1 ⊡
Loweswater CI GSTN WD25	204	D3 ⊡
Lowfield SBW CM21	132	C8
Lowfield La HOD EN11	177	F3
Lowgate La WARE SG12	99	K5
Low Hill Rd HLWW/ROY CM19	178	A3
Lowlands BRKMPK AL9	171	H1 ⊡
Low Rd BRKMPK AL9	173	G1
Lowson Gv OXHEY WD19	13	F6
Lowswood CI NTHWD HA6	229	H7
Lowther CI BORE WD6	223	J5 ⊡
Loxley Rd BERK HP4	161	F3
Lucan Rd BAR EN5	225	K3
Lucas Gdns LTNN/LIM LU3	69	G1
Lucas La BLDK SG7	18	A5
HTCH/STOT SG5	56	B2
Lucerne Wy LTNN/LIM LU3	69	H5
Lucks HI HHW HP1	163	H6
Ludlow Av LTN LU1	89	K5
Ludlow Md OXHEY WD19	230	C2
Ludlow Wy RKW/CH/CXG WD3	219	H4
Ludwick Wy WGCE AL7	148	A5
Lukes La TRING HP23	109	H6
Lukes Lea TRING HP23	110	A8
Lullington CI LTNE LU2	70	D6
Lullington Garth BORE WD6	224	A6 ⊡
Lulworth Av CHESW EN7	195	K7
Lumbards WGCE AL7	123	G8
Lumen Rd ROY SG8	21	H2
Lunardi CI STDN SG11	81	H6
Lundin Wk OXHEY WD19	230	E3 ⊡
Luther King Rd HLW CM20	6	B4
The Luton Dr LTN LU1	5	E6
Luton La STALW/RED AL3	142	E1
Luton Rd AMP/FLIT/B MK45	36	B8
HARP AL5	118	A5
HTCHE/RSTV SG4	92	D7
LTN LU1	88	E5
LTNE LU2	54	C7
LTNN/LIM LU3	52	B4
STALW/RED AL3	115	J2
Luton White HI LTNE LU2	71	H1
Luxembourg CI LTNN/LIM LU3	68	C⁷
Luxford PI SBW CM21	132	D6
Luynes Ri BUNT SG9	63	J8
Lybury La STALW/RED AL3	141	K2
Lycaste CI STAL AL1	11	E5
Lych Ga GSTN WD25	204	E³
Lycrome Rd CSHM HP5	182	A6
Lydia Ms BRKMPK AL9	192	C2
Lye Green Rd CSHM HP5	182	A8
Lye HI HTCHE/RSTV SG4	92	A2
Lye La LCOL/BKTW AL2	188	C6
The Lye BERK HP4	138	A3
Lygean Av WARE SG12	127	J8
Lygetun Dr LTNN/LIM LU3	68	C2
Lygrave STVGE SG2	96	D⁷
Lyles La WGCW AL8	147	K¹
Lyle's Rw HTCHE/RSTV SG4	56	D3
Lymans Rd ARL/CHE SG15	24	E3
Lyme Av BERK HP4	160	E²
Lymington Rd STVG SG1	75	G³
Lynch HI OUN/WHIP LU6	114	E1
The Lynch HOD EN11	177	G3
Lyndale STVG SG1	2	C⁴
Lyndhurst Av PIN HA5	230	C7
Lyndhurst CI HARP AL5	118	E7 ⊡
Lyndhurst Dr HARP AL5	118	E7
Lyndhurst Gdns PIN HA5	230	C7
Lyndhurst Rd LTN LU1	4	A4
Lyndon Av PIN HA5	231	F5
Lyndon Md STALE/WH AL4	145	F7
Lyneham Rd LTNE LU2	70	D8
Lyne Wy HHW HP1	163	J4
Lynmouth Rd WGCE AL7	148	A3
Lynsey CI STALW/RED AL3	142	B2
Lynton Av ARL/CHE SG15	24	E4
STAL AL1	169	F8
Lynwood Av LTNE LU2	70	B6
Lynwood Dr NTHWD HA6	229	K7
Lynwood Hts RKW/CH/CXG WD3	218	A5
Lyon Wy STALE/WH AL4	169	K6
Lyrical Wy HHW HP1	164	A4
Lysander CI HHW HP1	183	H5
Lysander Wy ABLGY WD5	204	B2 ⊡
WGCE AL7	148	C2 ⊡
Lys Hill Gdns HERT/WAS SG14	150	E1
Lytham Av OXHEY WD19	230	E4
Lytton Av PIN HA5	231	F6
PEND EN3	214	D8
Lytton Flds KNEB SG3	96	A5 ⊡
Lytton Gdns WGCW AL8	147	J3
Lytton Rd PIN HA5	231	F6
Lyttons Wy HOD EN11	153	F8 ⊡
Lyttons Wy STVG SG1	2	A3

M

Mabbutt CI LCOL/BKTW AL2	188	A8
Mabey's Wk SBW CM21	131	K8
Macdonnell Gdns GSTN WD25	204	A1 ⊡
Macer's La BROX EN10	197	K2
Macintosh CI CHESW EN7	196	B4 ⊡
Mackenzie Sq STVGE SG2	3	F5
Mackerel Hall ROY SG8	21	F3
Maddesfield Ct RAD WD7	207	H3 ⊡
Maddles LWTH SG6	42	D5
Maddox Rd HHNE HP2	9	E5
HLW CM20	7	D5
Made Feld STVG SG1	3	D5 ⊡
Madgeways CI WARE SG12	152	E4 ⊡
Madgeways La WARE SG12	152	E4
Magellan CI STVGE SG2	76	E4 ⊡
Magna CI HARP AL5	144	A3
Magnaville Rd BSF CM23	105	H5
BUSH WD23	222	B7
Magnolia Av ABLGY WD5	204	A2
Magnolia CI HERT/BAY SG13	151	K3
LCOL/BKTW AL2	189	F4 ⊡
Magpie Crs STVGE SG2	76	E5
The Magpies LTNE LU2	69	J3
Maidenhall Rd LTNW/LEA LU4	69	F7
Maidenhead St HERT/WAS SG14	151	G3 ⊡
Maidenhead Yd		
HERT/WAS SG14	151	G3 ⊡
Maiden St HTCHE/RSTV SG4	43	J8
Main Av NTHWD HA6	229	H2
Main Rd HERT/WAS SG14	124	E6
Main Rd North BERK HP4	112	C2
Main Rd South BERK HP4	112	E4
Maitland Rd STSD CM24	86	D3
Malborough Rd WATW WD18	12	C5
Malden Flds BUSH WD23	13	E4
Malden Rd BORE WD6	223	K3
WAT WD17	12	B1 ⊡
Maldon Ct HARP AL5	118	D7 ⊡
Malham CI LTNW/LEA LU4	68	C3
Malins CI BAR EN5	225	H5 ⊡
Mallard Gdns LTNN/LIM LU3	69	F4
Mallard Rd ABLGY WD5	204	B1 ⊡
ROY SG8	21	G3
STVGE SG2	76	E7
Mallards Ri HLWE CM17	181	F1
The Mallards HHS/BOV HP3	185	K3

Mallard Wy *GSTN* WD25 .... 205 F6 🔲
   NTHWD HA6 .... 229 H6
Mallows Gn *HLWW/ROY* CM19 .. 179 H5
Mallow Wk *ROY* SG8 .... 21 J4 🔲
The Mall *LCOL/BKTW* AL2 .... 188 E5
Malm Cl *RKW/CH/CXG* WD3 .... 228 C1
Malmes Cft *HHS/BOV* HP5 .... 165 H8
Malmsdale *WGCW* AL8 .... 122 D7
Maltby Dr *EN* EN1 .... 214 A8
Malthouse Cl *LTNE* LU2 .... 71 G8
Malthouse La *HTCH/STOT* SG5 ..... 26 A2
Malting La *MHAD* SG10 .... 103 C7
   STDN SG11 .... 81 K2
   TRING HP23 .... 136 E4
Maltings Cl *BLDK* SG7 .... 27 H8 🔲
   ROY SG8 .... 21 G2 🔲
Maltings Dr *STALE/WH* AL4 .... 145 F2
Maltings Orch *HTCH/STOT* SG5 .... 39 F6
The Maltings *KGLGY* WD4 .... 203 H3
   STAL AL1 .... 10 C4 🔲
   STVGE SG2 .... 77 J1
Malus Cl *HHNE* HP2 .... 9 D5
Malvern Cl *STALE/WH* AL4 .... 168 E2
Malvern Rd *LTN* LU1 .... 89 G2
   PEND EN3 .... 214 D7
Malvern Wy *HHNE* HP2 .... 8 B3
   RKW/CH/CXG WD3 .... 219 G5
Malzeard Rd *LTNN/LIM* LU3 .... 4 A2
Manan Cl *HHS/BOV* HP3 .... 165 H8 🔲
Manchester Cl *STVG* SG1 .... 59 F6
Manchester St *LTN* LU1 .... 4 B4
Mancroft Rd *LTN* LU1 .... 88 C6
Mandela Pl *WATN* WD24 .... 13 E1 🔲
Mandelyns *BERK* HP4 .... 161 F2
Mandeville *STVGE* SG2 .... 76 D8
Mandeville Cl *BROX* EN10 .... 176 E6
   HERT/BAY SG13 .... 151 F6 🔲
   WAT WD17 .... 220 A8
Mandeville Dr *STAL* AL1 .... 189 F1
Mandeville Ri *WGCW* AL8 .... 147 J1
Mandeville Rd *HERT/BAY* SG13 .. 151 F6
   PEND EN3 .... 214 D7
   POTB/CUF EN6 .... 210 D2
Mangrove La *HERT/BAY* SG13 .... 151 H5
Mangrove La *HERT/BAY* SG13 .... 151 H6
Mangrove Rd *HERT/BAY* SG13 ... 151 H5
   LTNE LU2 .... 70 D6
Manland Av *HARP* AL5 .... 118 E7
Manland Wy *HARP* AL5 .... 118 E7
Manley Hwy *HTCH/STOT* SG5 ..... 55 K2
Manley Rd *HHNE* HP2 .... 8 B4 🔲
Manly Dixon Dr *PEND* EN3 .... 214 D7
Mannicotts *WGCW* AL8 .... 147 G3
Manning Pl *LTNE* LU2 .... 71 F7 🔲
Manor Av *HHS/BOV* HP3 .... 185 H1 🔲
Manor Cl *BAR* EN5 .... 225 K4
   BERK HP4 .... 161 K5 🔲
   HAT AL10 .... 170 E1
   HERT/WAS SG14 .... 151 G1
   HTCH/STOT SG5 .... 40 C6
   LWTH SG6 .... 41 K6
Manor Cottages *NTHWD* HA6 .... 230 A7 🔲
Manor Ct *DEN/HRF* UB9 .... 228 B8
   EN EN1 .... 214 A6
   RAD WD7 .... 206 C7
Manor Crs *HTCHE/RSTV* SG4 ...... 57 J7
Manor Dr *LCOL/BKTW* AL2 .... 188 C5
Manor Farm Cl *LTNN/LEA* LU4 ... 68 B6
Manor Farm Rd *EN* EN1 .... 214 A5
Manor Hatch *HLWS* CM18 .... 7 F5
Manor Hatch Cl *HLWS* CM18 ..... 180 E2
Manor House Dr *NTHWD* HA6 ... 229 G6
Manor House Gdns *ABLGY* WD5 .. 203 J1
Manor Links *BSF* CM23 .... 106 B2
Manor Pde *HAT* AL10 .... 170 E1 🔲
Manor Rd *AMP/FLIT/B* MK45 .... 36 D7
   BAR EN5 .... 225 K4
   BSF CM23 .... 105 K2
   HAT AL10 .... 170 E1
   HLWE CM17 .... 157 F4
   HOD EN11 .... 177 F1
   LBUZ LU7 .... 109 K2
   LCOL/BKTW AL2 .... 190 A4
   LTN LU1 .... 5 D5
   POTB/CUF EN6 .... 210 A1
   STAL AL1 .... 11 D3
   STALE/WH AL4 .... 119 H7
   STSD CM24 .... 86 A4
   TRING HP23 .... 135 F4
   WAB EN9 .... 215 J3
   WAT WD17 .... 220 C1
Manorside *BAR* EN5 .... 225 K4
Manor St *BERK* HP4 .... 162 A5 🔲
Manor Vw *STVGE* SG2 .... 76 C8
Manorville Rd *HHS/BOV* HP3 ..... 185 G2
Manor Wy *BORE* WD6 .... 224 B5
   KNEB SG3 .... 95 H3
   LWTH SG6 .... 41 K6
   POTB/CUF EN6 .... 193 G8
   RKW/CH/CXG WD3 .... 219 F4
Mansard Cl *TRING* HP23 .... 135 F6 🔲
Manscroft Rd *HHW* HP1 .... 164 A4
Mansdale Rd *STALW/RED* AL3 ... 142 A5
Mansfield *SBW* CM21 .... 131 J8

Mansfield Gdns
   HERT/WAS SG14 .... 151 F1 🔲
Mansfield Rd *BLDK* SG7 .... 42 E2
   LTNN/LEA LU4 .... 69 G8
Mansion Dr *TRING* HP23 .... 135 G6
Manston Cl *CHES/WCR* EN8 ...... 197 G8 🔲
Manston Dr *BSF* CM23 .... 86 A8
Manston Rd *HLW* CM20 .... 7 D4
Manton Dr *LTNE* LU2 .... 69 J5
Manton Rd *HTCHE/RSTV* SG4 ..... 57 G3
Manx Cl *LTNN/LEA* LU4 .... 69 G1
Maple Av *BSF* CM23 .... 105 G1
   STALW/RED AL3 .... 167 K2
Maple Cl *BSF* CM23 .... 105 G1
   BUSH WD23 .... 13 F1
   HHW HP1 .... 171 F5 🔲
Maplecroft La *WAB* EN9 .... 177 K7
Maplefield *LCOL/BKTW* AL2 ...... 188 D7
Maple Gn *HHW* HP1 .... 163 H4
   WAT WD17 .... 220 B1 🔲
   WGCE AL7 .... 123 F8
Maple Leaf Cl *ABLGY* WD5 .... 204 B2 🔲
Maple Lodge Cl
   RKW/CH/CXG WD3 .... 227 H3
Maple Rd *HARP* AL5 .... 118 B8
Maple Rd East *LTN* LU1 .... 89 G1
Maple Rd West *LTNN/LEA* LU4 ... 89 G1
Maple Spring *BSF* CM23 .... 105 F1
The Maples *CHESW* EN7 .... 196 C6
   HLWW/ROY CM19 .... 179 J6
   HTCHE/RSTV SG4 .... 56 D4
Mapleton Crs *PEND* EN3 .... 214 B8
Maple Wy *DUN/WHIP* LU6 .... 114 C1
   ROY SG8 .... 21 J1
Maplewood *WARE* SG12 .... 127 G6 🔲
Maran Av *WLYN* AL6 .... 122 C5 🔲
Marconi Wy *STALE/WH* AL4 .... 169 G6
Mardlebury Rd *KNEB* SG3 .... 96 B8
Mardley Av *WLYN* AL6 .... 123 F1
Mardley Dell *WLYN* AL6 .... 96 A8
Mardley Hts *WLYN* AL6 .... 123 F1
Mardley Hl *WLYN* AL6 .... 123 F1 🔲
Mardley Wd *WLYN* AL6 .... 123 F1 🔲
Mardyke Rd *HLW* CM20 .... 7 F2
Marford Rd *STALE/WH* AL4 .... 145 J1
   WGCW AL8 .... 146 C2
Margaret Av *STALW/RED* AL3 ..... 10 C2
Margaret Cl *ABLGY* WD5 .... 204 A2 🔲
   POTB/CUF EN6 .... 210 D3
   WAB EN9 .... 215 J3 🔲
Margeholes *OXHEY* WD19 .... 231 F1
Margery Wd *WGCE* AL7 .... 123 G7
Marguerite Wy *BSF* CM23 .... 105 J3
Marian Gdns *GSTN* WD25 .... 204 C3
Marigold Pl *HLWE* CM17 .... 156 E5 🔲
Marina Gdns *CHES/WCR* EN8 .... 197 G8
Mariner Wy *HHNE* HP2 .... 9 D6 🔲
Marion Cl *BUSH* WD23 .... 221 G1
Mark Dr *CFSP/GDCR* SL9 .... 226 A3
Markeston Gn *OXHEY* WD19 ...... 230 E3 🔲
Market Hl *BUNT* SG9 .... 63 J2 🔲
   ROY SG8 .... 21 H3
Market Oak La *HHS/BOV* HP3 .... 186 A2
Market Pl *CFSP/GDCR* SL9 .... 226 A7
   HERT/WAS SG14 .... 151 G3 🔲
   STAL AL1 .... 10 C4
   WATW WD18 .... 13 D3 🔲
Market Sq *BSF* CM23 .... 105 J2
   STVG SG1 .... 2 B3
Market St *BSF* CM23 .... 105 J2 🔲
   HERT/WAS SG14 .... 151 G3 🔲
   HLWE CM17 .... 157 F5
   WATW WD18 .... 12 C3
Markfield Cl *LTNN/LIM* LU3 .... 69 H3 🔲
Mark Hall Moors *HLW* CM20 ..... 156 E6
Markham Rd *CHESW* EN7 .... 196 A4
   LTNN/LIM LU3 .... 69 H1
Mark Rd *HHNE* HP2 .... 9 D3
Markwell Wd *EPP* CM16 .... 179 J7
Markyate Rd *LTN* LU1 .... 89 G8
Marlborough Cl *BSF* CM23 .... 105 J4
   HTCHE/RSTV SG4 .... 59 H1
   WLYN AL6 .... 123 F1 🔲
Marlborough Ga *STAL* AL1 .... 11 D4
Marlborough Ri *HHNE* HP2 .... 8 B2
Marlborough Rd *LTNN/LIM* LU3 .... 4 A2 🔲
   STAL AL1 .... 11 D4 🔲
   STVGE SG2 .... 76 D4
Marle Gdns *WAB* EN9 .... 215 H2
Marley Rd *WGCE* AL7 .... 148 B5
Marlin Cl *BERK* HP4 .... 161 H6 🔲
Marlin Copse *BERK* HP4 .... 161 H6 🔲
Marlin Hl *TRING* HP23 .... 135 F8
Marlins Cl *RKW/CH/CXG* WD3 ... 217 H2
Marlins Meadow *WATW* WD18 ... 219 J6
Marlin Sq *ABLGY* WD5 .... 204 A1
The Marlins *NTHWD* HA6 .... 230 A5
Marlins Turn *HHW* HP1 .... 164 A3
Marlowe Cl *STVGE* SG2 .... 76 D1
Marlowes *HHNE* HP2 .... 8 A5
Marnham Ri *HHW* HP1 .... 163 K4 🔲
Marquis Cl *BSF* CM23 .... 104 C2
   HARP AL5 .... 119 F7

Marquis La *HARP* AL5 .... 119 F7
Marrilyne Av *PEND* EN3 .... 214 E8
Marriott Rd *BAR* EN5 .... 225 J3
   LTNN/LIM LU3 .... 69 G3
Marriotts Wy *HHS/BOV* HP3 ...... 164 C8
Marriott Ter *RKW/CH/CXG* WD3 . 217 J4
Marryat Rd *EN* EN1 .... 214 A5
Marschefield *HTCH/STOT* SG5 .... 25 J3
Marsden Cl *WGCW* AL8 .... 147 G5 🔲
Marsden Gn *WGCW* AL8 .... 147 G4
Marsden Rd *WGCW* AL8 .... 147 G4
Marshall Av *STALW/RED* AL3 ...... 11 D1
Marshall Rd *LTNE* LU2 .... 70 D7
Marshalls Heath La *HARP* AL5 ... 119 J4
Marshalls Wy *STALE/WH* AL4 .... 119 H7
Marshal's Dr *STAL* AL1 .... 11 F1
Marshalswick La *STAL* AL1 .... 11 F1
Marshbarns *BSF* CM23 .... 105 F1
Marsh Cl *CHES/WCR* EN8 .... 214 E3
Marshcroft Dr *CHES/WCR* EN8 .. 197 J8
Marshcroft La *TRING* HP23 .... 135 J3
Marshe *POTB/CUF* EN6 .... 210 E2
Marshgate *STVG* SG1 .... 2 B3
Marshgate Dr *HERT/BAY* SG13 .. 151 H2
Marsh Hl *WAB* EN9 .... 198 E5
Marsh La *HLWE* CM17 .... 157 H4
   WARE SG12 .... 152 D1
   WARE SG12 .... 153 J6
Marshmoor Crs *BRKMPK* AL9 ... 171 J6
Marshmoor La *BRKMPK* AL9 ..... 171 H8
Marsh Rd *LTNN/LIM* LU3 .... 68 D4
Marsom Gv *LTNN/LIM* LU3 .... 69 G1
Marston Cl *HHS/BOV* HP3 .... 9 D6 🔲
Marston Gdns *LTNE* LU2 .... 69 J5
Marsworth Av *PIN* HA5 .... 230 E7
Marsworth Cl *WATW* WD18 ...... 219 K7 🔲
Marsworth Rd *LBUZ* LU7 .... 110 D5
Marten Ga *STALE/WH* AL4 .... 168 D2
Martian Av *HHNE* HP2 .... 8 C2
Martin Cl *HAT* AL10 .... 171 F6
Martindale Rd *HHW* HP1 .... 163 J4
Martinfield *WGCE* AL7 .... 148 A2 🔲
Martingale Rd *ROY* SG8 .... 21 J3 🔲
Martins Cl *RAD* WD7 .... 206 B6 🔲
Martins Dr *CHES/WCR* EN8 .... 197 J6
   HERT/BAY SG13 .... 152 A3
Martins Wy *STVG* SG1 .... 59 H8
Martin Wy *LWTH* SG6 .... 41 H4
Martlesham *WGCE* AL7 .... 149 F3
Martyr Cl *STAL* AL1 .... 189 F2 🔲
Marwood Cl *KGLGY* WD4 .... 185 K7 🔲
Maryland *HAT* AL10 .... 171 F4 🔲
Marymead Cl *STVGE* SG2 .... 96 B1
Marymead Dr *STVGE* SG2 .... 96 B1
Mary Park Gdns *BSF* CM23 .... 105 J5
Maryport Rd *LTNN/LEA* LU4 .... 69 F7
Mary Proud Cl *WLYN* AL6 .... 122 E2 🔲
Masefield *HTCHE/RSTV* SG4 .... 57 G2
Masefield Av *BORE* WD6 .... 224 B5
Masefield Cl *HARP* AL5 .... 118 D5 🔲
Masefield Rd *HARP* AL5 .... 118 D6
Mason Cl *BORE* WD6 .... 224 C2
Masons Ct *BSF* CM23 .... 105 H2
   HHNE HP2 .... 9 E4
Masons Rd *EN* EN1 .... 214 A6
   HHNE HP2 .... 9 E4
Mason Wy *WAB* EN9 .... 215 K3
Masters Cl *LTN* LU1 .... 89 G4
Matching La *BSF* CM23 .... 105 G1
Mathams Dr *BSF* CM23 .... 105 J1
Mathews Cl *STVG* SG1 .... 58 D8
Matlock Cl *BAR* EN5 .... 225 J5
Matlock Crs *LTNN/LEA* LU4 .... 68 D3
   OXHEY WD19 .... 230 D2
Matthew Ga *HTCHE/RSTV* SG4 ... 56 E4
Mattocke Rd *HTCH/STOT* SG5 .... 40 A8
Maude Crs *WATN* WD24 .... 204 C2
Maud Jane's Cl *LBUZ* LU7 .... 110 E4
Maulden Cl *LTNE* LU2 .... 70 D8
Maunds Hatch *HLWS* CM18 ...... 180 A5
Maxted Rd *HHNE* HP2 .... 9 E3
Maxwell Cl *RKW/CH/CXG* WD3 .. 227 K1
Maxwell Ri *OXHEY* WD19 .... 13 F8 🔲
Maxwell Rd *BORE* WD6 .... 224 A3
   NTHWD HA6 .... 229 J6
   STAL AL1 .... 168 E7
   STVG SG1 .... 75 G4
Maybury Av *CHES/WCR* EN8 ..... 197 F6
   CHESW EN7 .... 197 F6 🔲
May Cl *STALW/RED* AL3 .... 10 C2
Maycock Gv *NTHWD* HA6 .... 230 C4
Maycroft *LWTH* SG6 .... 26 A8
   PIN HA5 .... 230 D2
Maycroft Rd *CHESW* EN7 .... 196 C4
Maydencroft La *HTCH/STOT* SG5 .. 56 B5
Maydwell Ldg *BORE* WD6 .... 223 J2
Mayes Cl *BSF* CM23 .... 106 C1
Mayfair Cl *STALE/WH* AL4 .... 169 F1
Mayfare *RKW/CH/CXG* WD3 ...... 219 J5
Mayfield *WGCW* AL8 .... 122 C7
Mayfield Cl *HARP* AL5 .... 118 A6
   HLWE CM17 .... 157 J5
Mayfield Pk *BSF* CM23 .... 105 G6 🔲

Mayfield Rd *LTNE* LU2.......................... 70 C5
Mayflower Av *HHNE* HP2....................... 8 A5
Mayflower Cl *HERT/WAS* SG14 .... 150 B5
  WAB EN9 .... 215 G1
  WLYN AL6 .... 94 E8
Mayflower Gdns *BSF* CM23 .... 104 E3
Mayflower Rd *LCOL/BKTW* AL2........ 188 D5
May Gdns *BORE* WD6 .... 223 G6
Mayhill Rd *BAR* EN5......................... 225 K6
Maylands Av *HHNE* HP2...................... 9 E3
Maylands Rd *OXHEY* WD19 .... 230 D3
Maylin Cl *HTCHE/RSTV* SG4 .... 57 G1
Maylins Dr *SBW* CM21 .... 132 B3
Maynard Dr *STAL* AL1 .... 189 F1
Maynard Pl *POTB/CUF* EN6 .... 195 G7
Maynard Rd *STAL* AL1 .... 8 A6
Mayne Av *LTNW/LEA* LU4.................. 68 E5
  STALW/RED AL3............................ 167 G8
Mayo Cl *CHES/WCR* EN8.................. 197 G6
Mayo Gdns *HHW* HP1....................... 164 A7
Mayshades Cl *KNEB* SG3................... 96 B7
Mays La *BAR* EN5.............................. 225 G5
May St *LTN* LU1 .... 4 C5
Maythorne Cl *WATW* WD18 .... 219 K4
Maytree Crs *WATN* WD24 .... 204 A6
Maytrees *HTCHE/RSTV* SG4 .... 56 C5
  RAD WD7 .... 206 D7
Maze Green Hts *BSF* CM23 .... 105 F3
Maze Green Rd *BSF* CM23 .... 105 G2
Mazoe Cl *BSF* CM23.......................... 105 J4
Mazoe Rd *BSF* CM23 .... 105 J4
Mcadam Cl *HOD* EN11..................... 177 F1
Mcdonald Ct *HAT* AL10 .... 171 F6
  HAT AL10 .... 171 F7
Mc Kellar Cl *BUSH* WD23 .... 231 K1
Mc Kenzie Rd *BROX* EN10 .... 177 F6
Mead Cl *STVG* SG1............................. 3 D2
Mead Ct *WAB* EN9 .... 215 G4
Meadgate Rd *HOD* EN11.................. 177 J6
Mead La *HERT/BAY* SG13 .... 151 H2
Meadowbank *HTCHE/RSTV* SG4 ...... 41 F8
  KGLGY WD4 .... 186 A8
  OXHEY WD19 .... 13 D6
Meadowbanks *BAR* EN5................... 225 J5
Meadowbrook *TRING* HP23............ 135 G3
Meadow Cl *BERK* HP4 .... 161 H7
  BRKMPK AL9 .... 192 D2
  HERT/BAY SG13 .... 151 J2
  KNEB SG3 .... 96 E7
  LCOL/BKTW AL2 .... 188 C8
  LCOL/BKTW AL2 .... 190 A5
  STALE/WH AL4 .... 169 F3
  TRING HP23 .... 135 G3
Meadowcroft *BERK* HP4 .... 160 E2
  BUSH WD23 .... 221 J6
  CFSP/GDCR SL9............................ 226 A8
Meadow Cft *HAT* AL10 .... 170 E4
Meadowcroft *STAL* AL1 .... 189 J2
  STSD CM24 .... 86 D2
Meadowcross *WAB* EN9................... 215 K4
Meadow Dell *HAT* AL10 .... 170 E4
Meadow Gn *WGCW* AL8 .... 147 H3
Meadowlands *BSF* CM23 .... 105 H4
  BSF CM23 .... 85 K4
Meadow La *LBUZ* LU7...................... 110 E6
Meadow Rd *BERK* HP4 .... 161 H7
  BORE WD6 .... 224 A2
  BUSH WD23 .... 221 J5
  GSTN WD25 .... 204 B4
  HHS/BOV HP3 .... 186 A5
  LTNN/LIM LU3 .... 69 G5
Meadow Road Cl *BERK* HP4 .... 161 H7
The Meadows *BSF* CM23 .... 105 H4
  HTCHE/RSTV SG4 .... 72 B8
  SBW CM21 .... 132 E7
Meadowsweet Cl *BSF* CM23 .... 105 F3
The Meadow *HERT/BAY* SG13 .... 152 D7
  WGCE AL7 .... 148 D3
Meadow Vw *BUNT* SG9.................... 63 H3
Meadow Wk *HARP* AL5..................... 143 K1
  STDN SG11 .... 81 K7
Meadow Wy *ABLGY* WD5................. 187 F5
  HHS/BOV HP3 .... 184 D1
  HTCH/STOT SG5 .... 25 J3
  HTCH/STOT SG5 .... 54 E6
  HTCH/STOT SG5 .... 56 B3
  HTCHE/RSTV SG4 .... 94 D8
  KGLGY WD4 .... 186 A8
  LTN LU1 .... 88 D5
  LWTH SG6 .... 41 K4
  POTB/CUF EN6 .... 210 B4
  RKW/CH/CXG WD3 .... 218 D7
  ROY SG8 .... 30 E5
  SBW CM21 .... 132 E8
  STVG SG1 .... 3 D3
Mead Pl *RKW/CH/CXG* WD3 .... 218 A8
Mead Rd *RAD* WD7 .... 207 K3
Meads La *STALE/WH* AL4 .... 120 B8
The Meads *BERK* HP4 .... 161 G3
  LCOL/BKTW AL2 .... 188 D7
  LTNN/LIM LU3 .... 69 F6
  LWTH SG6 .... 41 J5
Mead Temple *HHNE* HP2 .... 8 A3
The Mead *CHES/WCR* EN8 .... 197 G7
  HTCH/STOT SG5 .... 40 C7

Mead Vw *BUNT* SG9.......................... 67 G3
Meadview Rd *WARE* SG12 .... 152 B1
Meadway *BERK* HP4 .... 162 B4
Mead Wy *BUSH* WD23...................... 13 F1
Meadway *HARP* AL5.......................... 144 B2
  HOD EN11 .... 177 F5
  KNEB SG3...................................... 96 A5
  PEND EN3 .... 214 C6
  STALE/WH AL4 .... 191 H1
  STVG SG1.. 75 F3
  WCCE AL7 .... 148 A5
Meadway Cl *PIN* HA5 .... 231 J5
The Meadway *POTB/CUF* EN6........ 195 H6
Meautys *STALW/RED* AL3................. 167 G8
Medalls Link *STVGE* SG2..................... 3 E5
Medalls Pth *STVGE* SG2...................... 3 E5
Medcalf Rd *PEND* EN3 .... 214 E7
Medina Rd *LTNW/LEA* LU4 .... 69 F8
Medlows *HARP* AL5........................... 118 A7
Medow Md *RAD* WD7 .... 206 C3
Medway Cl *GSTN* WD25 .... 204 D4
Medway Rd *HHNE* HP2.................... 164 E1
Medwick Ms *HHNE* HP2 .... 165 G1
Meeting House La *BLDK* SG7 .... 26 E8
Megg La *KGLGY* WD4....................... 185 F7
Melbourn Cl *HTCH/STOT* SG5 .... 25 K4
Melbourn Rd *STALW/RED* AL3......... 168 C2
Melbourne Ct *WGCW* AL8................ 147 G4
Melbourne Rd *BUSH* WD23............. 221 J5
Melbourn Rd *ROY* SG8 .... 21 J2
Melbourn St *ROY* SG8....................... 21 H3
Melford Cl *LTNE* LU2 .... 70 E8
The Melings *HHNE* HP2................... 165 G1
Melne Rd *STVGE* SG2......................... 96 C1
Melrose Av *BORE* WD6 .... 224 A5
  POTB/CUF EN6 .... 210 C3
Melrose Pl *WAT* WD17...................... 204 A8
Melson St *LTN* LU1............................. 4 C4
Melsted Rd *HHW* HP1...................... 164 A6
Melvern Cl *STVGE* SG2....................... 96 C2
Melvyn Cl *CHESW* EN7 .... 195 K6
Memorial Rd *LTNN/LIM* LU3............ 68 E5
Memorial Wy *WAT* WD17 .... 12 B2
Mendip Cl *STALE/WH* AL4 .... 169 F1
Mendip Rd *BUSH* WD23 .... 221 K6
Mendip Wy *HHNE* HP2 .... 8 B2
  LTNN/LIM LU3 .... 68 B1
Mendlesham *WGCE* AL7 .... 149 F3
Mentley La *STDN* SG11 .... 80 D5
Mentley La East *STDN* SG11 .... 81 J5
Mentley La West *STDN* SG11 .... 81 G5
Mentmore Rd *LBUZ* LU7................. 109 K1
  STAL AL1 .... 10 C3
Mentmore Vw *TRING* HP23............ 134 E4
Mepham Crs *KTN/HRWW/W* HA3 .. 231 K6
Mepham Gdns
  KTN/HRWW/W HA3 .... 231 K6
Mercer Pl *PIN* HA5 .... 230 D8
  HLWW/ROY CM19 .... 179 H4
Mercers Av *BSF* CM23 .... 104 E5
Mercers Rw *STAL* AL1 .... 10 B6
Merchant Dr *HERT/BAY* SG13 .... 151 J2
Merchants Wk *BLDK* SG7 .... 27 H8
Mercia Rd *BLDK* SG7......................... 43 G1
Meredith Cl *PIN* HA5 .... 230 E6
Meredith Rd *STVG* SG1....................... 3 E1
Merefield *SBW* CM21 .... 132 C8
Meriden Wy *GSTN* WD25................ 205 F7
Meridian Wy *WARE* SG12 .... 153 G4
Merle Av *DEN/HRF* UB9.................. 228 B8
Merling Cft *BERK* HP4...................... 161 F5
Mermaid Cl *HTCHE/RSTV* SG4 .... 57 F2
Merritt Wk *BRKMPK* AL9 .... 192 B2
Merrow Dr *HHW* HP1 .... 163 H5
Merryfield Cl *BORE* WD6 .... 223 J2
Merryfields *STALE/WH* AL4 .... 169 H6
Merry Hill Mt *BUSH* WD23 .... 221 J8
Merry Hill Rd *BUSH* WD23.............. 221 H7
Mersey Pl *HHNE* HP2 .... 164 E1
  LTN LU1 .... 4 B4
Merton Rd *ENC/FH* EN2 .... 213 G8
  WATW WD18 .... 12 C3

Middlefields *LWTH* SG6..................... 41 K1
Middle Furlong *BUSH* WD23 .... 221 J4
Middlehill *HHW* HP1 .... 163 H6
Middleknights Hl *HHW* HP1........... 163 K4
Middle La *HHS/BOV* HP3.................. 183 J7
Middle Ope *WATN* WD24 .... 204 C7
Middle Rd *BERK* HP4 .... 161 J5
  WAB EN9 .... 215 G2
Middle Rw *BSF* CM23 .... 105 J3
Middlesborough Cl *STVG* SG1 .... 59 F7
Middle St *WAB* EN9 .... 199 F1
Middleton Rd *LTNE* LU2 .... 70 E5
  RKW/CH/CXG WD3 .... 217 K8
Middle Wy *WATN* WD24 .... 204 C7
Midhurst *LWTH* SG6.......................... 41 J3
Midhurst Gdns *LTNN/LIM* LU3 .... 69 H4
Midland Rd *HHNE* HP2 .... 8 A5
  LTN LU1 .... 4 C3
Midway *STALW/RED* AL3 .... 188 D1
Milburn Cl *LTNN/LIM* LU3 .... 52 B8
Mildmay Rd *STVG* SG1....................... 76 C1
Mildred Av *BORE* WD6 .... 223 K4
  WATW WD18 .... 12 B3
Mile Cl *WAB* EN9 .... 215 H3
Mile House Cl *STAL* AL1 .... 189 J1
Mile House La *STAL* AL1 .... 189 H2
Miles Cl *HLWW/ROY* CM19 .... 6 A5
Milestone Cl *STVGE* SG2 .... 76 E5
Milestone Rd *HTCH/STOT* SG5 ...... 40 B8
  KNEB SG3 .... 96 B4
Milford Cl *STALE/WH* AL4 .... 169 G2
Milford Hl *HARP* AL5........................ 119 F5
Milksey La *HTCHE/RSTV* SG4 .... 58 B4
Milland Ct *BORE* WD6 .... 224 C1
Millard Wy *HTCHE/RSTV* SG4 .... 41 G7
Millbank *HHS/BOV* HP3 .... 185 H2
Mill Br *HERT/WAS* SG14 .... 151 F3
Millbrook Rd *BUSH* WD23 .... 221 G1
Mill Cl *BUNT* SG9................................ 63 J2
  HHS/BOV HP3 .... 186 A3
  HHW HP1 .... 164 A2
  HTCH/STOT SG5 .... 26 A3
  WARE SG12 .... 127 H8
  WGCW AL8 .... 147 F4
Millcrest Rd *CHESW* EN7 .... 195 K6
Millcroft *BSF* CM23 .... 85 K8
Mill End *STDN* SG11 .... 82 A7
Millers Cl *BSF* CM23 .... 105 F4
Millersdale *HLWW/ROY* CM19 ...... 179 J5
Millers La *WARE* SG12 .... 153 H5
Millers Ri *STAL* AL1............................ 11 D5
Millers Vw *MHAD* SG10 .... 103 F8
Millers Yd *HERT/WAS* SG14 .... 151 G3
Mill Farm Cl *PIN* HA5...................... 230 D8
Mill Fld *HLWE* CM17 .... 157 F5
Millfield *BERK* HP4 .... 160 E2
  WARE SG12 .... 127 J1
  WGCE AL7 .... 148 D2
Millfield La *HTCHE/RSTV* SG4 .... 56 D5
  LTN LU1 .... 88 B6
  STDN SG11 .... 104 A1
Millfield Rd *LTNN/LIM* LU3 .... 69 G6
Millfields *SBW* CM21 .... 132 D6
  STSD CM24 .... 86 D3
Millfield Wk *HHS/BOV* HP3............. 186 A1
Millfield Wy *LTN* LU1 .... 88 C6
Mill Gdns *TRING* HP23 .... 135 G3
Mill Green La *BRKMPK* AL9 .... 147 K8
Mill Green Rd *WGCE* AL7 .... 147 K4
Mill Hl *BSF* CM23 .... 85 H4
  ROY SG8 .... 21 J5
  STSD CM24 .... 86 C3
Millhouse La *ABLGY* WD5............... 187 G5
Millhurst Ms *HLWE* CM17 .... 157 H5
Milliners Wy *BSF* CM23 .... 105 F5
  LTNN/LIM LU3 .... 4 A2
Mill La *AMP/FLIT/B* MK45 .... 36 B6
  ARL/CHE SG15.............................. 24 D5
  BROX EN10 .... 176 E7
  BUNT SG9 .... 50 C4
  CHES/WCR EN8............................ 197 J6
  HERT/WAS SG14 .... 98 C4
  HLWE CM17 .... 157 H5
  HTCH/STOT SG5 .... 26 A3
  HTCH/STOT SG5 .... 37 H6
  HTCHE/RSTV SG4 .... 43 J8
  HTCHE/RSTV SG4 .... 56 D6
  KGLGY WD4 .... 186 A7
  RBSF CM22 .... 133 K5
  ROY SG8 .... 30 D1
  SBW CM21 .... 132 D6
  STALW/RED AL3 .... 116 A8
  STDN SG11 .... 84 A3
  WLYN AL6 .... 122 C4
Mill Lane Cl *BROX* EN10 .... 176 E7
Mill Race *WARE* SG12 .... 153 J5
Mill Rd *HERT/BAY* SG13 .... 151 G2
  HERT/WAS SG14 .... 151 G2
  HTCHE/RSTV SG4 .... 56 D6
  ROY SG8 .... 21 H2
Mill Side *STSD* CM24 .... 86 C3
Millstream Cl *HERT/WAS* SG14 ...... 150 E3
  HTCHE/RSTV SG4 .... 40 E7
Mill St *BERK* HP4 .... 161 K5
  BLDK SG7 .... 17 K5

BSF CM23 .... 105 K4
HHS/BOV HP3 .... 185 H2
HLWE CM17 .... 181 H4
LTN LU1 .... 4 B3
Millthorne Cl RKW/CH/CXG WD3 .. 218 E5 ▣
Mill View Rd TRING HP23 ...... 134 E5
Millwards HAT AL10 .... 171 G7
Mill Wy BUSH WD23 .... 13 F1
Millway HTCHE/RSTV SG4 .... 72 A7
Mill Wy RKW/CH/CXG WD3 ...... 217 J3 ▣
Milne Cl LWTH SG6 .... 42 B6
Milne Fld PIN HA5 .... 231 H6
Milner Cl GSTN WD25 .... 204 C4 ▣
Milner Ct BUSH WD23 .... 221 J6
Milner Wy DEN/HRF UB9 ...... 228 A7
Milton Ct WAB EN9 .... 215 H4 ▣
Milton Dene HHNE HP2 .... 165 G1
Milton Dr BORE WD6 .... 224 A5 ▣
Milton Rd HARP AL5 .... 118 D8
    LTN LU1 .... 4 A3
    WARE SG12 .... 127 H7
Milton St WATN WD24 .... 220 C1
Milton Vw HTCHE/RSTV SG4 ... 57 G2
Milverton Gn LTNN/LIM LU3 ... 69 F2
Milwards HLWW/ROY CM19 .... 179 J5 ▣
Mimms Hall Rd POTB/CUF EN6 .. 209 J1
Mimms La BORE WD6 .... 208 C3
    RAD WD7 .... 207 K3
Mimram Cl HTCHE/RSTV SG4 ... 93 H2
Mimram Rd HERT/WAS SG14 ... 150 E4
    WLYN AL6 .... 122 C4 ▣
Minchen Rd HLW CM20 .... 7 F3
Minehead Wy STVG SG1 .... 75 F2
Minerva Cl STVG SG1 .... 59 J8
Minerva Dr WAT WD17 .... 203 K6
The Minims HAT AL10 .... 171 F5
Minsden Rd STVGE SG2 .... 76 E6
Minster Cl HAT AL10 .... 171 F6
Minster Rd ROY SG8 .... 21 G1
Minstrel Cl HHW HP1 .... 164 A5 ▣
Minton Cl HLWE CM17 .... 181 F1
Misbourne Av CFSP/GDCR SL9 .. 226 B4
Misbourne Cl CFSP/GDCR SL9 .. 226 B4 ▣
Missden Dr HHS/BOV HP3 ..... 165 H8
Miss Joans Ride DUN/WHIP LU6 .. 113 G2
Mistletoe HI LTNE LU2 .... 90 D1
Mistley Rd HLW CM20 .... 7 H2
Miswell La TRING HP23 .... 134 E6
Mitchell Cl ABLGY WD5 .... 204 B2 ▣
    HHW HP1 .... 183 H5
    STAL AL1 .... 189 F2
    WGCE AL7 .... 148 D3 ▣
Mitre Gdns BSF CM23 .... 105 K3 ▣
Mixes Hill Rd LTNE LU2 .... 70 A6
The Mixies HTCH/STOT SG5 .... 25 J3
The Moakes LTNN/LIM LU3 .... 68 D2
Moat Cl BUSH WD23 .... 221 J5 ▣
Moatfield Rd BUSH WD23 ..... 221 J5
Moat La LTNN/LIM LU3 .... 69 G5
Moatside BUNT SG9 .... 49 G2
The Moat STDN SG11 .... 81 J6
Moatwood Gn WGCE AL7 ...... 147 K4 ▣
Mobbsbury Wy STVGE SG2 .... 3 F1
Mobley Gn LTNE LU2 .... 70 D5
Moffats Cl BRKMPK AL9 ...... 193 G4
Moffats La BRKMPK AL9 ...... 192 E5
Moira Cl LTNN/LIM LU3 .... 68 D3
Molescroft HARP AL5 .... 117 K5
Moles La BUNT SG9 .... 48 A6
Molewood Rd HERT/WAS SG14 . 150 E2
Mollison Av PEND EN3 .... 214 D5
Molteno Rd WAT WD17 .... 220 B1
Momples Rd HLW CM20 .... 7 H4
Monarch's Wy CHES/WCR EN8 .. 214 C3 ▣
Monastery Cl STALW/RED AL3 .. 10 B4 ▣
Money Hill Rd RKW/CH/CXG WD3 . 218 B8
Money Hole La WLYN AL6 ..... 149 F2
Monica Cl WATN WD24 .... 13 E1
Monklands LWTH SG6 .... 41 H3
Monksbury HLWS CM18 .... 180 D1
Monks Cl BROX EN10 .... 177 F6
    LWTH SG6 .... 41 J5
    STAL AL1 .... 11 D6
    STALW/RED AL3 .... 142 C4
Monks Horton Wy STAL AL1 ... 11 F2
Monksmead BORE WD6 .... 224 B4
Monks Ri WGCW AL8 .... 122 D7
Monks Vw STVGE SG2 .... 3 D6
Monks Wk BUNT SG9 .... 63 J2
Monkswick Rd HLW CM20 ..... 7 H1
Monkswood WGCW AL8 ...... 122 C7
Monkswood Dr BSF CM23 ..... 105 G3
Monkswood Gdns BORE WD6.... 224 C5
Monkswood Wy STVG SG1 ..... 2 C4
    STVGE SG2 .... 2 C6
Monmouth Rd WAT WD17 ..... 12 C2 ▣
Mons Av BLDK SG7 .... 43 F3
Mons Cl HARP AL5 .... 144 A3
Monson Rd BROX EN10 ...... 176 E6 ▣
Montacute Rd BUSH WD23 .... 222 D3
Montague Av LTNW/LEA LU4.... 68 D3
Montague Hall Pl BUSH WD23 .. 221 H6 ▣
Montague Rd BERK HP4 .... 161 J5

Montayne Rd CHES/WCR EN8 ... 214 C2
Montfitchet Wk STVGE SG2 .... 76 E2
Montgomerie Cl BERK HP4 ..... 161 H3 ▣
Montgomery Av HHNE HP2 .... 9 D4
Montgomery Dr CHES/WCR EN8 .. 197 J6
Monton Cl LTNN/LIM LU3 ...... 68 E3
Montrose Av LTNN/LIM LU3 .... 69 H6
Monument La CFSP/GDCR SL9 .. 226 B5
Moorend SG4 .... 148 B6
Moor End Rd HHW HP1 .... 164 B7
Moore Rd BERK HP4 .... 161 G3
Moorfields HLWS CM18 .... 179 K6
Moor Hall Rd HLWE CM17 ..... 157 J5
Moorhead Cl HTCH/STOT SC5 .. 56 B3
Moorhurst Av CHESW EN7 ..... 195 K7
The Moorings BSF CM23 ...... 105 K3
Moorland Gdns LTNE LU2 ...... 4 B3 ▣
Moorland Rd HARP AL5 .... 118 D5
    HHW HP1 .... 163 J8
Moorlands LCOL/BKTW AL2 .... 189 G6 ▣
    WGCE AL7 .... 148 B6
Moor La RKW/CH/CXG WD3 .... 201 H6
    RKW/CH/CXG WD3 .... 228 D1
Moor Lane Crossing WATW WD18 . 219 H7
Moormead HI HTCH/STOT SC5 .. 56 A3
Moor Mill La LCOL/BKTW AL2... 189 C7
Moor Park Rd NTHWD HA6 .... 229 J5
Moorside WGCE AL7 .... 148 B6
Moors Ley STVGE SG2 .... 60 C8
The Moors WGCE AL7 .... 148 B2
Moor St LTN LU1 .... 4 A3
Moortown Rd OXHEY WD19 .... 230 D3
Moor Vw WATW WD18 .... 12 B6
Moorymead Cl HERT/WAS SG14 . 98 A5
Morecambe Cl STVG SG1 ...... 75 C2
Morefields TRING HP23 .... 135 F3
Moremead WAB EN9 .... 215 J3
Moreton Av HARP AL5 .... 118 B7
Moreton Cl CHESW EN7 ...... 197 F5
Moreton End Cl HARP AL5 .... 118 B7 ▣
Moreton End La HARP AL5 .... 118 B7
Moreton Pl HARP AL5 .... 118 B6 ▣
Moreton Rd LTNE LU2 .... 5 E1
Morgan Cl NTHWD HA6 .... 230 A4
    STVG SG1 .... 58 D8
Morgan Gdns GSTN WD25 ..... 205 J3 ▣
Morgans Cl HERT/BAY SG13 ... 151 C5 ▣
Morgan's Rd HERT/BAY SG13 .. 151 C5
Morgan's Wk HERT/BAY SG13 .. 151 C6
Morice Rd HOD EN11 .... 176 E1
Morland Wy CHES/WCR EN8 ... 197 J6
Morley Gv HLW CM20 .... 6 B3
Morley HI ENC/FH EN2 .... 213 G8
Mornington HLW CM20 .... 123 C5
Mornington Rd RAD WD7 ..... 206 D4
Morningtons HLWW/ROY CM19 . 179 J5
Morpeth Av BORE WD6 .... 207 J8
Morrell Cl LTNN/LIM LU3 ...... 69 F2
Morris Cl CFSP/GDCR SL9 ..... 226 C7
    HNLW SG16 .... 24 A4
    LTNN/LIM LU3 .... 68 D1
Morriston Cl OXHEY WD19 .... 230 D4 ▣
Morris Wy LCOL/BKTW AL2 .... 190 B4
Morse Cl HERT/WAS UB9 ..... 228 B8
Mortain Dr BERK HP4 .... 161 G3
Mortimer Cl BUSH WD23 ...... 221 J6 ▣
    LTN LU1 .... 88 E3
Mortimer Ga CHES/WCR EN8 .. 197 K5
Mortimer HI TRING HP23 ..... 135 C5 ▣
Mortimer Ri TRING HP23 ..... 135 C5 ▣
Mortimer Rd ROY SG8 .... 21 J3
Morton Cl LBUZ LU7 .... 110 C5
Morton St ROY SG8 .... 21 H1
Morven Cl POTB/CUF EN6 ..... 210 D1
Mossbank Av LTNE LU2 .... 90 D1
Moss Cl PIN HA5 .... 231 C8
    RKW/CH/CXG WD3 .... 228 C1
Mossendew Cl DEN/HRF UB9 .. 228 C7
Moss Gn WGCE AL7 .... 147 K5
Moss La PIN HA5 .... 231 F8
Mossman Dr LTN LU1 .... 88 D5
Moss Rd GSTN WD25 .... 204 D8
Moss Side LCOL/BKTW AL2 .... 188 B8
Moss Wy HTCH/STOT SC5 ..... 40 A8
Mostyn Rd BUSH WD23 .... 221 K5
    LTNW/LEA LU4 .... 68 D1
Motts Cl HERT/WAS SG14 ..... 97 K5
Moulton Ri LTNE LU2 .... 5 D3
Mountbatten Cl STAL AL1 ..... 189 K1 ▣
Mount Cl HHW HP1 .... 163 H6
Mount Dr LCOL/BKTW AL2 .... 189 F3
    STSD CM24 .... 86 D4
Mounteagle ROY SG8 .... 21 H4
Mountfield Rd HHNE HP2 ..... 8 B5
    LTNE LU2 .... 4 C1
Mountfitchet Rd STSD CM24 .. 86 D4
Mount Garrison HTCHE/RSTV SC4 . 56 D2
Mount Grace Rd LTNE LU2 .... 70 D3
    POTB/CUF EN6 .... 210 D1
Mountjoy HTCHE/RSTV SG4 .... 41 G8 ▣
Mount Pleasant DEN/HRF UB9 . 227 K7
    HTCH/STOT SC5 .... 56 B3
    STALW/RED AL3 .... 10 B3
Mount Pleasant Cl BRKMPK AL9 . 171 H1

Mount Pleasant La BRKMPK AL9 .. 171 H1
    LCOL/BKTW AL2 .... 187 K8 ▣
Mount Pleasant Rd LTNN/LIM LU3 . 68 D4
Mount Rd HERT/WAS SG14 .... 150 D4
    STALE/WH AL4 .... 120 B8
Mountsorrel HERT/BAY SG13 .. 151 J3 ▣
The Mount CHESW EN7 .... 196 B4 ▣
    POTB/CUF EN6 .... 193 H8
    RKW/CH/CXG WD3 .... 218 B6
    ROY SG8 .... 22 E8
Mount Vw ENC/FH EN2 .... 212 C8
    LCOL/BKTW AL2 .... 190 C5
Mountview NTHWD HA6 .... 230 B5
Mount Vw RKW/CH/CXG WD3 .. 218 A8
Mountview Rd CHESW EN7 .... 196 C4
Mountway POTB/CUF EN6 ..... 193 G8
Mount Wy WGCE AL7 .... 148 A6
Mountway La WGCE AL7 ...... 148 A6
Mowbray Crs HTCH/STOT SC5 .. 25 K3
Mowbray Gdns HTCHE/RSTV SG4 . 56 E4
Mowbray Rd HLW CM20 .... 7 E2
Moxes Wd LTNN/LIM LU3 ..... 68 D2
Moxom Av CHES/WCR EN8 .... 197 J8
Mozart St STVG SG1 .... 2 A3
Muddy La LWTH SG6 .... 41 K6
Muirfield LTNE LU2 .... 69 K3
Muirfield Cl OXHEY WD19 .... 230 D4 ▣
    OXHEY WD19 .... 230 D4 ▣
Muirfield Gn OXHEY WD19 .... 230 D3 ▣
Muirfield Rd OXHEY WD19 .... 230 C3
Muirhead Wy KNEB SG3 ...... 96 A4 ▣
Mulberry Cl BROX EN10 ...... 197 K2
    LCOL/BKTW AL2 .... 188 D6 ▣
    LTN LU1 .... 89 G2
    TRING HP23 .... 135 F4 ▣
Mulberry Ct BSF CM23 ...... 105 K4
Mulberry Gdns RAD WD7 ..... 207 H3
Mulberry Gn HLWE CM17 ..... 157 G5
Mulberry Wy HTCH/STOT SC5 .. 40 B7
Mullion Cl KTN/HRWW/W HA3 . 231 J7
    LTNE LU2 .... 70 C5
Mullion Wk OXHEY WD19 ..... 230 E3 ▣
Mullway LWTH SG6 .... 41 G3
Mundells CHESW EN7 .... 196 E5
    WGCE AL7 .... 148 A2
Munden Gv WATN WD24 ...... 204 D8
Munden Rd WARE SG12 ...... 99 H2
Mundesley Cl STVG SG1 ...... 58 B8
Mundesly Cl OXHEY WD19 .... 230 D3 ▣
Mungo-park Cl BUSH WD23 ... 231 K1 ▣
Munro Rd BUSH WD23 .... 221 J5
The Muntings STVGE SG2 ..... 3 F5
Munts Meadow HTCHE/RSTV SC4 . 43 J8
Murchison Rd HOD EN11 ..... 177 C1
Muriel Av WATW WD18 .... 13 D4
Murray Crs PIN HA5 .... 230 E1
Murray Rd BERK HP4 .... 161 K4
    NTHWD HA6 .... 229 K7
Murrell La HTCH/STOT SC5 .... 26 A4
Murton Ct STAL AL1 .... 11 D3
Musgrave Cl CHESW EN7 ..... 196 D5 ▣
Muskalls Cl CHESW EN7 ...... 196 E5 ▣
Muskham Rd HLW CM20 .... 7 F1
Musk HI HHW HP1 .... 163 H7
Musleigh Mnr WARE SG12 .... 127 K8 ▣
Musley HI WARE SG12 .... 127 J7
Musley La WARE SG12 .... 127 J7
Mussons Pth LTNE LU2 .... 4 C3
Muswell Cl LTNN/LIM LU3 ..... 69 G3
Mutchetts Cl GSTN WD25 ..... 205 F3
Mutford Cft LTNE LU2 .... 70 E2 ▣
Mutton La POTB/CUF EN6 ..... 209 J1
Myddelton Av ENC/FH EN1 .... 213 H8 ▣
Myddleton Rd WARE SG12 .... 152 C1
Myers Cl RAD WD7 .... 207 H2 ▣
Myles Ct CHESW EN7 .... 196 A7
Mylne Cl CHES/WCR EN8 ..... 197 J8
Mymms Dr BRKMPK AL9 ...... 193 C5
Myrtle Gv ENC/FH EN2 .... 213 C8
Myrtleside Cl NTHWD HA6 .... 229 J6

N

Nails La BSF CM23 .... 105 J2 ▣
Nairn Cl HARP AL5 .... 144 A3
Nairn Gn OXHEY WD19 .... 230 B2
Nancy Downs OXHEY WD19 ... 13 D6
Napier Cl LCOL/BKTW AL2 .... 190 B3
Napier Dr BUSH WD23 .... 13 F5
Napier Rd LTN LU1 .... 4 B4 ▣
Nappsbury Rd LTNW/LEA LU4.. 68 C3
Napsbury Av LCOL/BKTW AL2 . 190 A4
Napsbury La LCOL/BKTW AL2 . 189 J3
    STAL AL1 .... 189 J1
The Nap KGLGY WD4 .... 186 A2
Nascot Pl WAT WD17 .... 12 C1
Nascot Rd WAT WD17 .... 12 C1
Nascot St WAT WD17 .... 12 C1
Nascot Wood Rd WAT WD17 .. 204 A3
Naseby Rd LTN LU1 .... 89 G2
Nash Cl BORE WD6 .... 223 J4
    BRKMPK AL9 .... 192 D1

STVGE SG2 .... 3 F2
Nash Mills La HHS/BOV HP3........ 185 K4
Nash Rd ROY SG8 .... 21 H4 ⊡
Nathaniel Wk TRING HP23 .... 135 F4
Nathans Cl WLYN AL6 .... 122 C2 ⊡
Nayland Cl LTNE LU2 .... 71 F8 ⊡
Nazeingbury Cl WAB EN9 .... 177 J8 ⊡
Nazeing Common WAB EN9 .... 199 J1
Neal Cl NTHWD HA6............................ 230 B7
Neal Ct HERT/WAS SG14 .... 151 F3
Neal St WATW WD18 .... 13 D4
Neaole Cl BORE WD6 .... 224 B1 ⊡
Necton Rd STALE/WH AL4 .... 145 H1
Needham Rd LTNW/LEA LU4 .... 68 A3
Neil Wy RKW/CH/CXG WD3 .... 217 J7
Neil Gwynn Cl RAD WD7 .... 207 H2
Nelson Av STAL AL1 .... 189 K1
Nelson Rd BERK HP4 .... 112 E4
    BSF CM23 .... 105 K4
Nelson St HERT/WAS SG14 .... 150 E2 ⊡
Neptune Dr HHNE HP2 .... 8 B3
Neptune Ga STVGE SG2 .... 59 H8 ⊡
Neston Rd WATN WD24 .... 204 D7
Netherby Cl TRING HP23 .... 135 G3
Nethercott Cl LTNE LU2 .... 70 B8 ⊡
Nethercott Ri LTNE LU2 .... 70 B8 ⊡
Netherfield La WARE SG12............... 153 J6
Netherfield Rd HARP AL5 .... 143 J5
Netherhall Rd HLWW/ROY CM19 .... 178 A3
Netherstones HTCH/STOT SG5 .... 25 K2 ⊡
Nether St STVGE SG12 .... 130 A4
Netherway STALE/RED AL3 .... 188 C1
Netley Dell LWTH SG6 .... 42 B6
Nettleswellbury Farm HLWS CM18 .. 7 F5 ⊡
Netteswell Orch HLW CM20 .... 6 C3
Netteswell Rd HLW CM20 .... 7 D2
Nettlecroft HHW HP1 .... 164 A7
    WGCE AL7 .... 148 C2 ⊡
Nettleden Rd BERK HP4 .... 137 K2
Nevell's Gn LWTH SG6 .... 41 K2
Nevells Rd LWTH SG6 .... 41 K3
Nevil Cl NTHWD HA6 .... 229 J4
Neville Cl POTB/CUF EN6 .... 210 A1
Neville Rd LTNN/LIM LU3 .... 69 G2
Nevill Gv WATN WD24 .... 220 C1
Newark Gn BORE WD6 .... 224 D3
Newark Rd LTNW/LEA LU4 .... 69 F7
New Barnes Av STAL AL1 .... 189 J1
New Barn La RBSF CM22 .... 106 B8
New Barns La MHAD SG10 .... 103 F5
New Bedford Rd LTN LU1 .... 4 B3 ⊡
Newberries Av RAD WD7 .... 206 E5
Newbiggin Pth OXHEY WD19 .... 230 D3 ⊡
Newbold Rd LTNN/LIM LU3 .... 69 G2
Newbury Av PEND EN3 .... 214 E7
Newbury Cl BSF CM23 .... 105 H1
    LTNW/LEA LU4 .... 68 D7
    STVG SG1 .... 58 D8 ⊡
Newcastle Cl STVG SG1 .... 59 F7 ⊡
New Cl KNEB SG3 .... 96 A3
Newcombe Rd LTN LU1 .... 4 A4
Newcome Rd RAD WD7 .... 207 K4
New Cottages BRKMPK AL9 .... 192 D6
New Ct KNEB SG3 .... 96 B7 ⊡
Newdigate Gn DEN/HRF UB9 .... 228 C7
Newdigate Rd DEN/HRF UB9 .... 228 C7
Newdigate Rd East DEN/HRF UB9 .. 228 C7
Newell La STVGE SG2 .... 60 E2
Newell Ri HHS/BOV HP3 .... 185 J1
Newell Rd HHS/BOV HP3 .... 185 J1
Newells LWTH SG6 .... 42 D5
Newells Hedge LBUZ LU7 .... 110 D4 ⊡
New England Cl
    HTCHE/RSTV SG4 .... 56 D5 ⊡
New England St STALW/RED AL3 ..... 10 B4
New Farm La NTHWD HA6 .... 229 K7
Newfield La HHNE HP2 .... 8 C5
Newfields WGCW AL8 .... 147 G4
New Ford Rd WATN WD24 .... 169 G8 ⊡
Newford Cl HHNE HP2 .... 9 E4
Newgate STVGE SG2 .... 3 E5
Newgate St HERT/BAY SG13 .... 195 F1 ⊡
Newgate St STALE/WH AL4 .... 169 G8 ⊡
Newgatestreet Rd CHESW EN7 .... 195 K4
Newgate Street Village
    HERT/BAY SG13 .... 195 G3
New Greens Av HERT/WAS SG14 ... 168 A1 ⊡
Newground Rd TRING HP23 .... 136 C6
Newhall Cl HHS/BOV HP3 .... 183 J5 ⊡
Newhouse Crs GSTN WD25 .... 204 C3
New House Pk STAL AL1 .... 189 J1
Newhouse Rd HHW HP1 .... 183 J4
New Inn Rd BLDK SG7 .... 16 D5
New Kent Rd STAL AL1 .... 10 C3
Newland Cl PIN HA5 .... 231 F5 ⊡
    STAL AL1 .... 189 J1
Newlands LWTH SG6 .... 42 A6
Newlands Av RAD WD7 .... 206 C4
Newlands Cl East
    HTCHE/RSTV SG4 .... 56 D5 ⊡
Newlands Cl West
    HTCHE/RSTV SG4 .... 56 D5 ⊡
Newlands La HTCHE/RSTV SG4 .... 56 D5 ⊡
Newlands Pl BAR EN5 .... 225 J5

Newlands Rd HHW HP1 .... 163 H5
    LTN LU1 .... 89 H6
Newlands Wk GSTN WD25 .... 204 E3
Newlands Wy POTB/CUF EN6 .... 193 H8 ⊡
Newlyn Cl LCOL/BKTW AL2 .... 188 A8
    STVG SG1 .... 75 F3
Newman Av ROY SG8 .... 21 K3
Newmans Dr HARP AL5 .... 118 B7
Newmarket Rd ROY SG8 .... 21 J3
Newnham Cl LTNE LU2 .... 70 E8
Newnham Rd BLDK SG7 .... 26 D4
Newnham Wy BLDK SG7 .... 17 G8
New Park Dr HHNE HP2 .... 9 E4
New Park La DEN/HRF UB9 .... 228 B7
    HERT/BAY SG13 .... 194 E2
New Park La STVGE SG2 .... 77 F7
New Pl WLYN AL6 .... 122 B5 ⊡
Newport Cl PEND EN3 .... 214 D7 ⊡
Newport Md OXHEY WD19 .... 230 E3 ⊡
Newports SBW CM21 .... 132 A8
Newquay Gdns OXHEY WD19 .... 230 C1 ⊡
New River Av WARE SG12 .... 153 G5
New River Cl HOD EN11 .... 177 G2
New Rd BERK HP4 .... 161 G2
    BERK HP4 .... 162 A4
    BROX EN10 .... 176 E5
    CSTG EN8 .... 216 B3
    GSTN WD25 .... 222 B1
    HERT/WAS SG14 .... 151 G1
    HLWE CM17 .... 157 G5
    KGLGY WD4 .... 184 D8
    KNEB SG3 .... 96 C6
    POTB/CUF EN6 .... 209 F3
    RAD WD7 .... 206 B6
    RAD WD7 .... 207 K4
    RKW/CH/CXG WD3 .... 217 J1
    RKW/CH/CXG WD3 .... 219 F5
    ROY SG8 .... 15 H4
    STDN SG11 .... 103 H2
    TRING HP23 .... 109 G8
    TRING HP23 .... 135 G3
    WARE SG12 .... 127 J8
    WAT WD17 .... 13 D3
    WGCW AL8 .... 147 F6
    WLYN AL6 .... 123 F6
Newstead HAT AL10 .... 170 E7
New St BERK HP4 .... 162 A5
    LBUZ LU7 .... 109 K2
    LTN LU1 .... 4 C5 ⊡
    SBW CM21 .... 132 C6
    WATW WD17 .... 13 D3 ⊡
Newteswell Dr WAB EN9 .... 215 J2
Newton Cl HARP AL5 .... 144 A3 ⊡
    HOD EN11 .... 153 G7
Newton Crs BORE WD6 .... 224 B4 ⊡
Newtondale LTNW/LEA LU4 .... 68 B4 ⊡
Newton Dr SBW CM21 .... 132 B8
Newton Rd STVGE SG2 .... 3 F2
Newtons Wy HTCHE/RSTV SG4 .... 56 D5 ⊡
New Town WLYN AL6 .... 94 E8
Newtown Rd BSF CM23 .... 105 J3
New Town St LTN LU1 .... 4 C5 ⊡
New Town St LTN LU1 .... 4 C5 ⊡
New Wd WGCE AL7 .... 148 D2
Niagara Cl CHES/WCR EN8 .... 197 H7 ⊡
Nicholas Cl STALW/RED AL3 .... 10 C1
    WATN WD24 .... 204 C7
Nicholas La HERT/WAS SG14 .... 151 G3 ⊡
Nicholas Pl STVG SG1 .... 58 D8
Nicholas Rd BORE WD6 .... 223 J6
Nicholas Wy HHNE HP2 .... 8 C3 ⊡
    NTHWD HA6 .... 229 H7
Nicholls Cl AMP/FLIT/B MK45 .... 36 B6
    STALW/RED AL3 .... 142 A4
Nicholls Fld HLWS CM18 .... 180 E2 ⊡
Nichols Cl LTNE LU2 .... 5 F1
Nicholson Dr BUSH WD23 .... 221 K8
Nicky Line HHNE HP2 .... 8 B5
    STALW/RED AL3 .... 141 K8
Nicoll Wy BORE WD6 .... 224 D3
Nightingale Cl ABLGY WD5 .... 204 B1 ⊡
    LTNE LU2 .... 70 D3
    RAD WD7 .... 206 C4
Nightingale La STAL AL1 .... 190 A2
    STALE/WH AL4 .... 190 A1
Nightingale Pl
    RKW/CH/CXG WD3 .... 218 C7 ⊡
Nightingale Rd BUSH WD23 .... 221 H5
    CHESW EN7 .... 196 A3
    HTCH/STOT SG5 .... 56 D1
    RKW/CH/CXG WD3 .... 218 B7
Nightingales La CHIG HP8 .... 216 A5
Nightingale Wk STVGE SG2 .... 76 D3
Nightingale Wy STALE/WH AL4 .... 190 A1
Nimbus Wy HTCHE/RSTV SG4 .... 57 G2 ⊡
Nimrod Cl STALE/WH AL4 .... 169 F4
Ninesprings Wy HTCHE/RSTV SG4 .. 57 G3
Ninian Rd HHNE HP2 .... 164 D1
Ninning's La WLYN AL6 .... 95 J7
Ninnings Rd CFSP/GDCR SL9 .... 226 C6
Ninnings Wy CFSP/GDCR SL9 .... 226 C6 ⊡
Ninth Av LTNN/LIM LU3 .... 68 C2
Niton Cl BAR EN5 .... 225 J6
Niven Cl BORE WD6 .... 224 B1 ⊡
The Nobles BSF CM23 .... 105 G3 ⊡

Nodes Dr STVGE SG2 .... 76 B6
Noke La LCOL/BKTW AL2 .... 188 A4
Noke Shot HARP AL5 .... 118 E5
Noke Side LCOL/BKTW AL2 .... 188 C5 ⊡
Nokeside STVGE SG2 .... 96 C1
The Nokes HHW HP1 .... 163 K4 ⊡
The Noke WARE SG12 .... 153 G5 ⊡
Norbury Av WATN WD24 .... 220 D3
Norcott Av WATN WD24 .... 204 D8
Norfolk Gdns BORE WD6 .... 224 C4 ⊡
Norfolk Rd BUNT SG9 .... 63 H7
    LTNE LU2 .... 5 E1
    RKW/CH/CXG WD3 .... 218 D8
Norfolk Wy BSF CM23 .... 105 J4
Norman Av BSF CM23 .... 105 G3
Norman Cl WAB EN9 .... 215 J3
Norman Ct POTB/CUF EN6 .... 193 J8
Norman Crs PIN HA5 .... 230 D7
Normandy Ct HHNE HP2 .... 8 A4 ⊡
Normandy Dr BERK HP4 .... 161 H4
Normandy Rd STALW/RED AL3 .... 10 C3
    AMP/FLIT/B MK45 .... 36 C6
Norman Rd AMP/FLIT/B MK45 .... 36 C6
    LTNN/LIM LU3 .... 69 G7
    WLYN AL6 .... 122 B6 ⊡
Normans Cl LWTH SG6 .... 25 K8
Normansfield Cl BUSH WD23 .... 221 J7 ⊡
Normans La WLYN AL6 .... 95 K7
Norman's Wy STSD CM24 .... 86 D2
Norris Cl BSF CM23 .... 106 B2
Norris Gv BROX EN10 .... 176 D6
Norris La HOD EN11 .... 177 F2
Norris Ri HOD EN11 .... 176 E2
Norris Rd HOD EN11 .... 177 F3
North Ap GSTN WD25 .... 204 B6
    RKW/CH/CXG WD3 .... 229 H1
North Av HLW CM20 .... 42 B2
    RAD WD7 .... 207 H2
Northaw Cl HHNE HP2 .... 165 C7
Northaw Rd West POTB/CUF EN6 .. 194 C8
North Barn BROX EN10 .... 177 G8
North Bridge Rd BERK HP4 .... 161 G2
Northbrook Dr NTHWD HA6 .... 229 K7
North Brook End ROY SG8 .... 15 J7
Northbrook Rd BAR EN5 .... 225 K6
Northbrooks HLWW/ROY CM19 .... 6 A5
Northchurch La CSHM HP5 .... 160 D7
North Cl BAR EN5 .... 225 H5
    LCOL/BKTW AL2 .... 188 D7
    ROY SG8 .... 21 G2
North Common Rd
    STALW/RED AL3 .... 142 B5 ⊡
Northcourt RKW/CH/CXG WD3 .... 217 K8 ⊡
Northdown Rd CFSP/GDCR SL9 ..... 226 B5
    HAT AL10 .... 171 F7
North Drift Wy LTN LU1 .... 89 G2
North Dr STDN SG11 .... 100 E8
Northend HHS/BOV HP3 .... 165 G8
Northfield STDN SG11 .... 82 A2 ⊡
Northfield Gdns WATN WD24 .... 204 D7
Northfield Rd BLDK SG7 .... 17 J1
    BORE WD6 .... 224 A1
    CHES/WCR EN8 .... 214 D2
    HARP AL5 .... 118 E5
    SBW CM21 .... 132 C5
    TRING HP23 .... 135 K1
Northfields LWTH SG6 .... 25 K8
North Ga HLW CM20 .... 6 B3 ⊡
Northgate End BSF CM23 .... 105 J1
Northgate Pth BORE WD6 .... 207 J8 ⊡
North Gv HLWS CM18 .... 7 F5
North Hl RKW/CH/CXG WD3 .... 217 H2
North Orbital Rd LCOL/BKTW AL2 .. 188 A8
    STALE/WH AL4 .... 170 B7
North Orbital Road St Albans Rd
    GSTN WD25 .... 204 E3
North Pl HLW CM20 .... 156 D4
    WAB EN9 .... 215 G3 ⊡
North Ride WLYN AL6 .... 122 C3
Northridge Wy HHW HP1 .... 163 J7
North Riding LCOL/BKTW AL2 .... 188 C5
North Rd BERK HP4 .... 161 G3
    BLDK SG7 .... 26 E7
    CHES/WCR EN8 .... 214 D3
    HERT/WAS SG14 .... 150 E3
    HOD EN11 .... 177 F2
    RKW/CH/CXG WD3 .... 217 G5
    STVG SG1 .... 58 C7
North Road Av HERT/WAS SG14 ..... 150 D2
North Road Gdns HERT/WAS SG14.. 150 E3
North St BSF CM23 .... 105 J1
    LTNE LU2 .... 4 C2
    WAB EN9 .... 177 K8
North Ter BSF CM23 .... 105 J1
Northumberland Av EN EN1 .... 214 A5
Northview Rd LTNE LU2 .... 5 F3
Northway RKW/CH/CXG WD3 .... 218 C7
    WGCE AL7 .... 123 F8 ⊡
Northwell Dr LTNN/LIM LU3 .... 68 D1
North Western Av GSTN WD25 .... 204 B5
    WATN WD24 .... 204 A5

North Western Avenue Colne Wy
  WATN WD24 .... 204 D6
North Western Avenue Elton Wy
  GSTN WD25 .... 221 J2
North Western Avenue Gade Side
  KGLGY WD4 .... 203 H5
  WAT WD17 .... 203 J5
North Western Avenue Otterspool Wy GSTN WD25 .... 205 C8
North Western Avenue (Tylers Way) BUSH WD23 ..... 221 K4
North Western Avenue (Watford By-pass) STAN HA7 .. 222 D6
Northwick Rd OXHEY WD19 .... 230 D3
Northwood WGCE AL7 .... 148 E3
Northwood Cl CHESW EN7 .... 196 D5
Northwood Rd DEN/HRF UB9 .... 228 D7
Northwood Wy DEN/HRF UB9 .... 228 C7
  NTHWD HA6 .... 230 B6
Nortoft Rd CFSP/GDCR SL9 .... 226 C5
Norton Bury La LWTH SG6 .... 26 C7
Norton Cl BORE WD6 .... 223 K1
Norton Crs BLDK SG7 .... 42 E1
Norton Green Rd STVG SG1 .... 2 A5
Norton Mill La LWTH SG6 .... 26 D6
Norton Rd HTCH/STOT SG5 .... 26 A4
  LTNN/LIM LU3 .... 68 E5
  LWTH SG6 .... 42 A1
  STVG SG1 .... 2 A5
Nortonstreet La HTCHE/RSTV SG4 .... 94 B2
Norton Wy North LWTH SG6 .... 42 A1
Norton Wy South LWTH SG6 .... 42 A1
Norvic Rd TRING HP23 .... 110 A3
Norwich Cl STVG SG1 .... 59 H8
Norwich Wy RKW/CH/CXG WD3 ...... 219 G3
Norwood Cl HERT/WAS SG14 .... 150 C2
Norwood Rd CHES/WCR EN8 .... 197 J8
Nottingham Ga GSTN WD25 .... 204 B3
Nottingham Rd
  RKW/CH/CXG WD3 .... 217 F8
Novello Wy BORE WD6 .... 224 C1
Nugent's Pk PIN HA5 .... 231 F7
Nunnery Cl STAL AL1 .... 11 D6
Nunnery La LTNN/LIM LU3 .... 69 C4
Nunnery Stables STAL AL1 .... 10 C6
Nunsbury Dr BROX EN10 .... 197 J3
Nun's Cl HTCH/STOT SG5 .... 56 C2
Nuns La STAL AL1 .... 189 G2
Nupton Dr BAR EN5 .... 225 H6
Nurseries Rd STALE/WH AL4 .... 145 H2
Nursery Cl STVGE SG2 .... 96 B3
Nursery Flds SBW CM21 .... 132 B7
Nursery Gdns TRING HP23 .... 135 G5
  WGCE AL7 .... 122 E8
Nursery HI WGCE AL7 .... 123 F8
Nursery Rd BROX EN10 .... 197 J3
  BSF CM23 .... 105 J3
  HOD EN11 .... 153 C8
  LTNW/LIM LU3 .... 68 E4
  WAB EN9 .... 177 J8
Nutcroft KNEB SG3 .... 96 E7
Nutfield WGCE AL7 .... 123 C8
Nut Gv WGCW AL8 .... 122 D8
Nuthampstead Rd ROY SG8 .... 32 D7
Nutleigh Gv HTCH/STOT SG5 .... 40 B8
Nut Slip BUNT SG9 .... 63 J3
Nuttfield Cl RKW/CH/CXG WD3 ...... 219 G6
Nye Wy HHS/BOV HP3 .... 183 J6
Nymans Cl LTNE LU2 .... 70 E6

O

Oak Av LCOL/BKTW AL2 .... 188 D5
Oak Cl HHS/BOV HP3 .... 185 K2
  WAB EN9 .... 215 J4
Oakcroft Cl PIN HA5 .... 230 C8
Oakdale ABLGY AL8 .... 122 D8
Oakdale Av NTHWD HA6 .... 230 B8
Oakdale Cl OXHEY WD19 .... 230 D3
Oakdale Rd OXHEY WD19 .... 230 D3
Oakdene CHES/WCR EN8 .... 197 J8
Oakdene Rd HHS/BOV HP3 .... 185 K2
  WATN WD24 .... 204 D4
Oakdene Wy STAL AL1 .... 169 F6
Oak Dr BERK HP4 .... 162 A6
  SBW CM21 .... 157 F1
Oak End BUNT SG9 .... 63 H3
  HLWS CM18 .... 7 E6
Oaken Gv WGCE AL7 .... 147 K6
Oak Farm BORE WD6 .... 224 B5
Oakfield RKW/CH/CXG WD3 .... 217 K2
Oakfield Av HTCHE/RSTV SG4 ...... 57 F4
Oakfield Cl POTB/CUF EN6 .... 210 A1
Oakfield Rd HARP AL5 .... 143 G4
Oakfields STVGE SG2 .... 76 C8
Oakfields Av KNEB SG3 .... 96 B3
Oakfields Cl STVGE SG2 .... 76 D8
Oakfields Rd KNEB SG3 .... 96 B3
Oak Gdns NTHWD HA6 .... 229 G7
Oak Gn ABLGY WD5 .... 203 G2
Oak Gv HAT AL10 .... 170 E4

  HERT/BAY SG13 .... 151 H5
Oakhill LWTH SG6 .... 42 D5
Oakhill Av PIN HA5 .... 231 F8
Oakhill Cl RKW/CH/CXG WD3 ...... 227 H3
Oakhill Dr WLYN AL6 .... 122 A3
Oakhill Rd RKW/CH/CXG WD3 ..... 227 G3
Oakhurst Av HARP AL5 .... 143 G3
Oakhurst Rd PEND EN3 .... 214 C6
Oakington WGCE AL7 .... 148 E3
Oakington Av AMS HP6 .... 216 B1
Oaklands BERK HP4 .... 161 H5
Oaklands Av BRKMPK AL9 .... 192 E5
  OXHEY WD19 .... 220 D8
Oaklands Cl BSF CM23 .... 86 A7
Oaklands Ct WAT WD17 .... 220 D8
Oaklands Dr BSF CM23 .... 86 A8
  HLWE CM17 .... 181 F2
Oaklands Ga NTHWD HA6 .... 229 K5
Oaklands Gv BROX EN10 .... 197 J2
Oaklands La BAR EN5 .... 225 G4
  STALE/WH AL4 .... 169 J4
Oaklands Pk BSF CM23 .... 86 A7
Oaklands Ri WLYN AL6 .... 123 F1
Oaklands Rd CHESW EN7 .... 196 C4
Oak La HTCHE/RSTV SG4 .... 58 B5
  POTB/CUF EN6 .... 195 H6
  TRING HP23 .... 159 F7
Oaklea WLYN AL6 .... 122 F2
Oaklea Cl WLYN AL6 .... 122 E1
Oaklea Wd WLYN AL6 .... 122 E2
Oakleigh Dr RKW/CH/CXG WD3 .... 219 H6
Oakleigh Rd PIN HA5 .... 231 G5
Oakley Cl LTNW/LEA LU4 .... 68 C5
Oakley Rd HARP AL5 .... 144 A2
  LTNW/LEA LU4 .... 68 C5
Oakmeade PIN HA5 .... 231 H5
Oakmere Av POTB/CUF EN6 ...... 210 D3
Oakmere Cl POTB/CUF EN6 ...... 210 E1
Oakmere La POTB/CUF EN6 ...... 210 D2
Oak Piece WLYN AL6 .... 122 D2
Oakridge LCOL/BKTW AL2 .... 188 B7
Oakridge Av WD7 .... 206 C3
Oakridge La GSTN WD25 .... 206 B4
Oak Rd KNEB SG3 .... 96 C8
  LTN LU1 .... 4 A3
Oakroyd Av POTB/CUF EN6 .... 210 A3
Oakroyd Cl POTB/CUF EN6 .... 210 A4
Oaks Cl HTCHE/RSTV SG4 .... 56 D4
  RAD WD7 .... 206 C5
Oaks Cross STVGE SG2 .... 96 C1
The Oaks BERK HP4 .... 161 H5
  LTN LU1 .... 89 H8
  OXHEY WD19 .... 220 D8
Oak St BSF CM23 .... 105 J3
  HHS/BOV HP3 .... 185 K2
Oak Tree Cl ABLGY WD5 .... 203 J2
Oaktree Cl BSF CM23 .... 105 J2
Oak Tree Cl HAT AL10 .... 171 F5
  HERT/BAY SG13 .... 152 B6
  STVGE SG2 .... 78 C5
Oak Tree Ct BORE WD6 .... 223 G6
Oaktree Garth WGCE AL7 .... 147 K2
Oakview Cl CHESW EN7 .... 197 F6
Oakway Dr DUN/WHIP LU6 .... 113 K2
Oak Wy HARP AL5 .... 143 H4
Oakwell Dr POTB/CUF EN6 ...... 211 J3
Oak Wd BERK HP4 .... 161 G6
Oakwood Av BORE WD6 .... 224 A4
Oakwood Cl STVGE SG2 .... 76 D7
Oakwood Dr LTNN/LIM LU3 ...... 68 B1
  STALE/WH AL4 .... 169 K5
Oakwood Rd LCOL/BKTW AL2 .... 188 B7
  PIN HA5 .... 230 C8

Old Farm LBUZ LU7 .... 110 D5
Old Field Cl AMS HP6 .... 216 B1
Oldfield Ri HTCHE/RSTV SG4 ..... 93 H2
Oldfield Rd HHW HP1 .... 163 H7
  LCOL/BKTW AL2 .... 190 B3
Old Fishery La HHW HP1 .... 163 J8
Old Fold Vw BAR EN5 .... 225 H3
Old Forge Cl GSTN WD25 .... 204 B3
  WCCE AL7 .... 123 F7
Old Forge Rd EN EN1 .... 213 J8
Old French Horn La HAT AL10 ... 171 G3
Old Gannon Cl NTHWD HA6 ..... 229 H3
Old Hale Wy HTCH/STOT SG5 .... 40 C8
Old Hall Cl PIN HA5 .... 231 F7
Old Hall Dr PIN HA5 .... 231 F7
Old Hall Ri HLWE CM17 .... 181 H1
Oldhall St HERT/WAS SG14 ..... 151 G3
Old Harpenden Rd
  STALW/RED AL3 .... 168 B2
Old Herns La WGCE AL7 .... 148 D1
Old Hertford Rd BRKMPK AL9 ... 171 H2
Old Hwy HOD EN11 .... 177 G5
Oldhouse Cft HLW CM20 .... 7 D2
Old House La HLWW/ROY CM19 .. 178 E4
  KGLGY WD4 .... 203 F5
Old House Rd HHNE HP2 .... 8 C5
Oldings Cnr HAT AL10 .... 147 G8
Old Knebworth La KNEB SG3 .... 95 H3
Old La KNEB SG3 .... 96 C4
Old Leys HAT AL10 .... 171 F8
Old London Rd HERT/BAY SG13 .. 151 H3
  STAL AL1 .... 11 D5
The Old Maltings BSF CM23 .... 105 K2
Old Maple HHNE HP2 .... 140 E8
Old Md CFSP/GDCR SL9 .... 226 B5
Old Mill Gdns BERK HP4 .... 162 A5
Old Mill La RBSF CM22 .... 133 F3
Old Mill Rd KGLGY WD4 .... 203 H4
Old Nazeing Rd BROX EN10 ..... 177 J7
  WAB EN9 .... 177 H8
Old North Rd ROY SG8 .... 21 G1
Old Oak STAL AL1 .... 189 G1
Old Oak Cl ARL/CHE SG15 ...... 24 E1
Old Oaks WAB EN9 .... 215 K2
Old Orch HLWS CM18 .... 6 C6
  LCOL/BKTW AL2 .... 189 F4
  LTN LU1 .... 4 B6
Old Orchard Ms BERK HP4 ...... 161 K6
Old Parkbury La LCOL/BKTW AL2 . 189 H7
Oldpark Ride CHESW EN7 .... 213 G2
Old Park Rd HTCH/STOT SG5 .... 56 C2
Old Rectory Cl HARP AL5 ...... 118 C7
Old Rectory Dr HAT AL10 ...... 171 G4
Old Rectory Gdns STALE/WH AL4 . 120 B8
Old Redding KTN/HRWW/W HA3 .. 231 J4
Old River La BSF CM23 .... 105 J2
Old Rd AMP/FLIT/B MK45 .... 36 C8
  HLWE CM17 .... 157 F3
Old's Ap WATW WD18 .... 219 H8
Old School Cl HTCHE/RSTV SG4 .. 94 E8
Old School Gdns
  AMP/FLIT/B MK45 .... 36 C7
Old School Gn STVGE SG2 ...... 78 B4
Old School Wk ARL/CHE SG15 ... 24 E5
Old's Cl WATW WD18 .... 219 G8
Old Shire La CFSP/GDCR SL9 .... 226 E2
  RKW/CH/CXG WD3 .... 216 D6
Old Shire Lane Circular Wk
  RKW/CH/CXG WD3 .... 217 F7
Old Sopwell Gdns STAL AL1 .... 11 D6
Old South Cl PIN HA5 .... 230 E7
Old Uxbridge Rd
  RKW/CH/CXG WD3 .... 227 H6
Old Vicarage Gdns
  STALW/RED AL3 .... 115 H3
The Old Walled Gdn STVG SG1 .. 58 C8
Old Watford Rd LCOL/BKTW AL2 . 188 A8
Old Watling St STALW/RED AL3 .. 116 B5
Oldwood WLYN AL6 .... 122 E2
Oliver Cl HHS/BOV HP3 .... 185 J2
  LCOL/BKTW AL2 .... 189 F5
Oliver Ri HHS/BOV HP3 .... 185 J2
Oliver Rd HHS/BOV HP3 .... 185 K2
Olivers Cl BERK HP4 .... 163 F2
Oliver's La HTCH/STOT SG5 .... 25 K2
Olivia Gdns DEN/HRF UB9 ...... 228 B7
Olleberrie La RKW/CH/CXG WD3 . 201 H3
Olwen Ms PIN HA5 .... 230 E8
Onslow Cl HAT AL10 .... 171 G4
Onslow Rd LTNW/LEA LU4 ...... 68 C4
On the HI OXHEY WD19 .... 231 F1
The Opening WLYN AL6 .... 121 K1
Openshaw Wy LWTH SG6 .... 42 A3
Oram Pl HHS/BOV HP3 .... 185 H1
Orbital Crs GSTN WD25 .... 204 A5
Orchard BUSH? Orchard Av BERK HP4 . 161 H5
Orchard Av BERK HP4 .... 161 H5
  GSTN WD25 .... 204 C3
  HARP AL5 .... 118 B8
Orchard Cl AMP/FLIT/B MK45 ... 36 C7
  BORE WD6 .... 223 J2
  HHNE HP2 .... 8 C3
  HTCHE/RSTV SG4 .... 56 D6
  LWTH SG6 .... 41 K1
  POTB/CUF EN6 .... 195 G6

RAD WD7 .... 206 B7
RKW/CH/CXG WD3 .... 217 C3
STAL AL1 .... 11 E5
WARE SG12 .... 127 H7 🖪
WARE SG12 .... 153 H5
WAT WD17 .... 12 A1
Orchard Crs STVG SG1 .... 2 A1
Orchard Cft HLW CM20 .... 7 F2
Orchard Dr LCOL/BKTW AL2 .... 188 D4
RKW/CH/CXG WD3 .... 217 F3
WAT WD17 .... 220 A1
Orchard Gdns WAB EN9 .... 215 G4
Orchard House La STAL AL1 .... 10 C5
Orchard Md HAT AL10 .... 170 E4
The Orchard on the Gn
RKW/CH/CXG WD5 .... 218 E5
Orchard Rd BAR EN5 .... 225 K4
BLDK SG7 .... 42 E1
BSF CM23 .... 86 A8
HTCHE/RSTV SG4 .... 41 F8
ROY SG8 .... 21 F2
STVG SG1 .... 75 C1
WLYN AL6 .... 122 C4 🖪
Orchard Sq BROX EN10 .... 197 K2 🖪
The Orchards LTN LU1 .... 89 H7
SBW CM21 .... 132 C7 🖪
TRING HP23 .... 134 E6
Orchard St HHS/BOV HP3 .... 185 H1 🖪
STALW/RED AL3 .... 10 B5
The Orchard BLDK SG7 .... 43 F1
HERT/WAS SG14 .... 125 K8
KGLGY WD4 .... 186 A7
WARE SG12 .... 126 C2
WGCW AL8 .... 147 J1
WLYN AL6 .... 94 D8
Orchard Wy CHESW EN7 .... 195 K5
HHS/BOV HP3 .... 183 J6
HTCHE/RSTV SG4 .... 72 B8
KNEB SG3 .... 95 K4
LBUZ LU7 .... 110 E4
LTNW/LEA LU4 .... 68 B5
LWTH SG6 .... 41 K4
POTB/CUF EN6 .... 193 H6
RKW/CH/CXG WD3 .... 217 K7
ROY SG8 .... 21 G1
Ordelmere LWTH SG6 .... 25 K8
Ordnance Rd PEND EN3 .... 214 C7
Oregon Wy LTNN/LIM LU3 .... 69 F1
Organ Hall Rd BORE WD6 .... 223 H1
Orient Cl STAL AL1 .... 11 D6
Oriole Cl ABLGY WD5 .... 204 B1 🖪
Oriole Wy BSF CM23 .... 105 F3
Orion Wy NTHWD HA6 .... 230 A3
Orlando Cl HTCHE/RSTV SG4 .... 56 E3 🖪
Ormesby Dr POTB/CUF EN6 .... 209 J2
Ormonde Rd NTHWD HA6 .... 229 J3
Ormsby Cl LTN LU1 .... 4 C6
Ormskirk Rd OXHEY WD19 .... 230 E3
Oronsay HHS/BOV HP3 .... 165 G8
Orphanage Rd WAT WD17 .... 13 D1 🖪
Orton Cl STALE/WH AL4 .... 168 D2
Orwell Ct WATN WD24 .... 13 E1 🖪
Orwell Vw BLDK SG7 .... 43 G7
Osborne Gdns POTB/CUF EN6 .... 193 H8 🖪
Osborne Rd BROX EN10 .... 177 F5
CHES/WCR EN8 .... 197 J5 🖪
LTN LU1 .... 5 D5
POTB/CUF EN6 .... 193 H8
WATN WD24 .... 204 D8 🖪
Osborne Wy TRING HP23 .... 135 J8
Osborn Rd AMP/FLIT/B MK45 .... 36 D6
Osborn Wy WGCW AL8 .... 147 J2 🖪
Osbourne Wy KGLGY WD4 .... 185 K6
Osmington Pl TRING HP23 .... 134 E5
Osprey Gdns STVGE SG2 .... 76 E7
Osterley Cl STVGE SG2 .... 96 D2
Oster St STALW/RED AL3 .... 10 B3
Ostler Cl BSF CM23 .... 105 F5 🖪
Ostler's Gn SAFWS CB11 .... 35 K4
Oswald Rd STAL AL1 .... 11 D5
Otley Wy OXHEY WD19 .... 230 D2
Otter Gdns HAT AL10 .... 171 G5
Otterspool La GSTN WD25 .... 205 F8
Otterspool Wy WATN WD25 .... 221 G1
Otterton Cl HARP AL5 .... 118 B6 🖪
Ottoman Ter WAT WD17 .... 13 D2 🖪
Ottway Wk WLYN AL6 .... 122 B5
Otway Gdns BUSH WD23 .... 222 B7
Otways Cl POTB/CUF EN6 .... 210 C3 🖪
Oudle La MHAD SG10 .... 103 G6
Oughtonhead La HTCH/STOT SG5 .... 55 K1
Oughton Head Wy HTCH/STOT SG5 .... 56 B1
Oulton Crs POTB/CUF EN6 .... 209 J2
Oulton Ri HARP AL5 .... 118 E6
Oulton Wy OXHEY WD19 .... 231 G3
Oundle Av BUSH WD23 .... 221 K6
Oundle Ct STVGE SG2 .... 96 D1
Oundle Pth STVGE SG2 .... 96 D1
The Oundle STVGE SG2 .... 76 D8
Ousden Cl CHES/WCR EN8 .... 197 J8
Ousden Dr CHES/WCR EN8 .... 197 J8
Ouseley Cl LTNW/LEA LU4 .... 68 C6
Outfield Rd CFSP/GDCR SL9 .... 226 A6 🖪
Outlook Dr CSTG HP8 .... 226 A2
The Oval BROX EN10 .... 197 J3

HNLW SG16 .... 24 A6
Overfield Rd LTNE LU2 .... 70 D8
Overlord Cl BROX EN10 .... 176 D6 🖪
Overstone Rd HARP AL5 .... 118 E8 🖪
LTNW/LEA LU4 .... 68 C8
Overstream RKW/CH/CXG WD3 .... 218 A4
Oving Cl LTNE LU2 .... 70 E7
Owen Jones Cl HNLW SG16 .... 24 A4
Owens Wy RKW/CH/CXG WD3 .... 219 F5
Owles La BUNT SG9 .... 63 K3
Oxcroft BSF CM23 .... 105 J6
Oxendon Dr HOD EN11 .... 177 F4
Oxen Rd LTNE LU2 .... 5 D2
Oxfield Cl BERK HP4 .... 161 H6
Oxford Av STAL AL1 .... 169 F7
Oxford Cl CHES/WCR EN8 .... 197 G7
NTHWD HA6 .... 229 H3
Oxford Rd HTCHE/RSTV SG4 .... 72 B8
LTN LU1 .... 4 C5 🖪
Oxford St WATW WD18 .... 12 C4
Oxhey Av OXHEY WD19 .... 13 E6
Oxhey Dr OXHEY WD19 .... 230 C3
Oxhey La OXHEY WD19 .... 13 D6
PIN HA5 .... 231 H4
Oxhey Ridge Cl OXHEY WD19 .... 230 B4
Oxhey Rd OXHEY WD19 .... 13 D6
Ox La HARP AL5 .... 118 D6
Oxlease Dr HAT AL10 .... 171 G5
Oxleys Rd STVGE SG2 .... 3 F5
The Oxleys HLWE CM17 .... 157 G5
Oysterfields STALW/RED AL3 .... 10 A3

P

Pacatian Wy STVGE SG2 .... 76 D1
Packhorse Cl STALE/WH AL4 .... 169 F3
Packhorse La RAD WD7 .... 208 C1
Paddick Cl HOD EN11 .... 176 E2
Paddock Cl LWTH SG6 .... 41 K4
OXHEY WD19 .... 13 F5
WARE SG12 .... 129 K8
Paddock La BAR EN5 .... 224 D4
Paddock Md HLWS CM18 .... 179 K6
Paddock Rd BUNT SG9 .... 63 J1
Paddocks Cl STVGE SG2 .... 3 F5
The Paddocks HERT/BAY SG13 .... 152 A6 🖪
RKW/CH/CXG WD3 .... 217 J3
STALE/WH AL4 .... 119 K3
STVGE SG2 .... 3 F5
WGCE AL7 .... 148 C3 🖪
WLYN AL6 .... 94 E8 🖪
The Paddock BROX EN10 .... 177 F6
BSF CM23 .... 105 G6 🖪
CFSP/GDCR SL9 .... 226 B4
HAT AL10 .... 171 F3 🖪
HTCHE/RSTV SG4 .... 56 E4 🖪
Paddock Wd HARP AL5 .... 144 B2
Pageant Rd STAL AL1 .... 10 C5
Page Cl BLDK SG7 .... 43 F3
Page Hl WARE SG12 .... 127 F7
Page Rd HERT/BAY SG13 .... 151 K3
Pages Cl BSF CM23 .... 105 J4 🖪
Pages Cft BERK HP4 .... 161 H3 🖪
Paignton Cl LTNW/LEA LU4 .... 68 C5 🖪
Paine's La PIN HA5 .... 231 H3
Paines Cl LBUZ LU7 .... 110 A1
Painters La PEND EN3 .... 214 D5
Palace Cl KGLGY WD4 .... 185 K8
Palace Gdns BSF CM23 .... 105 H4 🖪
ROY SG8 .... 21 G3
Palfrey Cl STALW/RED AL3 .... 10 C2
Pallas Rd HHNE HP2 .... 8 C3
Palmer Av BUSH WD23 .... 221 J6
Palmer Cl HERT/WAS SG14 .... 151 F1
Palmer Gdns BAR EN5 .... 225 J5 🖪
Palmers Gv WAB EN9 .... 178 A8
Palmers Rd BORE WD6 .... 224 B1 🖪
Palmerston Cl WGCW AL8 .... 147 H3 🖪
Palmers Wy CHES/WCR EN8 .... 197 J7
Pamela Av HHS/BOV HP3 .... 185 K1
Pamela Gdns BSF CM23 .... 105 J6
Pams La HTCHE/RSTV SG4 .... 93 G8
Pancake La HHS/BOV HP3 .... 165 J7
Pankhurst Crs STVGE SG2 .... 76 E6
Pankhurst Pl WATN WD24 .... 13 E2 🖪
Panshanger Dr WGCE AL7 .... 148 C3
The Pantiles BUSH WD23 .... 222 A7
Panxworth Rd HHS/BOV HP3 .... 164 C8
Paper Mill La STDN SG11 .... 81 K8
Paradise HHNE HP2 .... 8 A6
Paradise Cl CHESW EN7 .... 197 F6
Paradise Rd WAB EN9 .... 215 H4 🖪
Paringdon Rd HLWW/ROY CM19 .... 179 J5
Parish Cl GSTN WD25 .... 204 D4 🖪
Parishes Md STVGE SG2 .... 76 D1 🖪
Park Av BSF CM23 .... 105 J6
BUSH WD23 .... 13 E1
HLWE CM17 .... 181 F4
LTNN/LIM LU3 .... 68 D2
POTB/CUF EN6 .... 210 D3
RAD WD7 .... 206 E3

RKW/CH/CXG WD3 .... 217 K
STAL AL1 .... 11 F
WATW WD18 .... 12 B
Park Av North HARP AL5 .... 118 B
Park Av South HARP AL5 .... 118 A
Park Cl BLDK SG7 .... 42 E
BRKMPK AL9 .... 171 H
BRKMPK AL9 .... 193 F
BUSH WD23 .... 13 E
RKW/CH/CXG WD3 .... 229 G
STALW/RED AL3 .... 115 H
STVGE SG2 .... 76 C
Park Ct HLW CM20 .... 6 C
Park Crs BLDK SG7 .... 42 E2
BORE WD6 .... 223 🖪
Park Dr BLDK SG7 .... 42 E
POTB/CUF EN6 .... 210 C
STDN SG11 .... 81 J
Parker Av HERT/WAS SG14 .... 151 G
Parker Cl LWTH SG6 .... 41 J
Parker's Fld STVGE SG2 .... 76 D
Park St WATN WD24 .... 220 C
Park Farm Cl HNLW SG16 .... 24 B
Park Farm La ROY SG8 .... 33 J
Parkfield LWTH SG6 .... 42 D 🖪
RKW/CH/CXG WD3 .... 217 J
Parkfield Av RYLN/HDSTN HA2 .... 231 K
RYLN/HDSTN HA2 .... 231 K
Parkfield Crs HTCHE/RSTV SG4 .... 93 G
RYLN/HDSTN HA2 .... 231 K
Parkfield Rd STALW/RED AL3 .... 115 H
Park Flds HLWW/ROY CM19 .... 178 B3
Parkfields WGCW AL8 .... 147 J
Park Gdns BLDK SG7 .... 42 E2 🖪
Park Ga HTCHE/RSTV SG4 .... 56 D
Parkgate Rd WATN WD24 .... 204 D
Park Gv CSTG HP8 .... 216 A
Park Hi HARP AL5 .... 118 B
HLWE CM17 .... 156 E
Park Hill Rd HHW HP1 .... 164 A6
Parkhurst Rd HERT/WAS SG14 .... 150 E
Parkins Cl STDN SG11 .... 101 F3 🖪
Parkinson Cl STALE/WH AL4 .... 145 G
Parkland Cl HOD EN11 .... 153 G8 🖪
Parkland Dr LTN LU1 .... 4 B 🖪
Parklands HHW HP1 .... 163 J4 🖪
ROY SG8 .... 21 J
WAB EN9 .... 215 K
Parklands Cl EBAR EN4 .... 210 E
Parklands Dr STALW/RED AL3 .... 167 H
Park La BROX EN10 .... 176 D 🖪
BSF CM23 .... 105 J
CHES/WCR EN8 .... 214 C
CHESW EN7 .... 196 E
DEN/HRF UB9 .... 227 K
HHNE HP2 .... 8 A
HLW CM20 .... 6 C
HTCHE/RSTV SG4 .... 93 F
KNEB SG3 .... 95 J
SAFWS CB11 .... 34 C
STALE/WH AL4 .... 191 C
STDN SG11 .... 81 J
Park Lane Paradise BROX EN10 .... 196 E2
Park Md HLW CM20 .... 6 A
Park Meadow BRKMPK AL9 .... 171 H
Park Mt HARP AL5 .... 118 A
Park Nook Gdns ENC/FH EN2 .... 213 G
Park Pl LCOL/BKTW AL2 .... 189 F
Park Ri BERK HP4 .... 161 F
HARP AL5 .... 118 A
Park Rise Cl HARP AL5 .... 118 A
Park Rd BUSH WD23 .... 221 H
CHES/WCR EN8 .... 214 C
HERT/BAY SG13 .... 151 H
HHW HP1 .... 164 B
HOD EN11 .... 177 F
PEND EN3 .... 214 D
POTB/CUF EN6 .... 194 C
RAD WD7 .... 206 D
RKW/CH/CXG WD3 .... 218 D
STSD CM24 .... 86 D
TRING HP23 .... 134 E
WARE SG12 .... 127 F
WAT WD17 .... 220 B
Parkside Dr WAT WD17 .... 219 K
Parkside Rd NTHWD HA6 .... 230 A
Park St BERK HP4 .... 161 J
BLDK SG7 .... 42 E
BRKMPK AL9 .... 171 H
HTCHE/RSTV SG4 .... 56 C
LCOL/BKTW AL2 .... 189 F
LTN LU1 .... 4 C4 🖪
TRING HP23 .... 135 F
Park Street La LCOL/BKTW AL2 .... 188 D
Park St West LTN LU1 .... 4 C
Park Ter LTN LU1 .... 5 D5
The Park STAL AL1 .... 11 E
STALW/RED AL3 .... 142 C
Park Viad LTN LU1 .... 5 D
Park Vw BRKMPK AL9 .... 171 H
HOD EN11 .... 177 F
PIN HA5 .... 231 G
POTB/CUF EN6 .... 210 D
STVGE SG2 .... 76 C

Park View Cl *LTNN/LIM* LU3 .... 68 C3
  STAL AL1 .... 11 F5
Park View Dr *STALW/RED* AL3 .... 115 H3
Park View Rd *BERK* HP4 .... 161 J5
  PIN HA5 .... 230 C5
Park Wy *HTCH/STOT* SG5 .... 56 C3
  RKW/CH/CXG WD3 .... 218 B8
Parkway *HLWW/ROY* CM19 .... 179 F1
  SBW CM21 .... 132 C8
  STVGE SG2 .... 76 B8
  WGCW AL8 .... 147 H4
Parkway Cl *WGCW* AL8 .... 147 H3
Parkway Cl *STAL* AL1 .... 189 K1 🗊
Parkway Gdns *WGCW* AL8 .... 147 H4
Parkwood Cl *HOD* EN11 .... 176 D5
Parkwood Dr *HHW* HP1 .... 163 J6
Parliament Sq
  HERT/WAS SG14 .... 151 G3 🗊
Parnall Rd *HLWS* CM18 .... 180 A5
Parndon Mill La *HLW* CM20 .... 6 A1
Parndon Wood Rd
  HLWW/ROY CM19 .... 179 K6
Parnell Cl *ABLGY* WD5 .... 187 F8
Parnel Rd *WARE* SG12 .... 127 K7
Parr Crs *HHNE* HP2 .... 165 G1
Parrotts *RKW/CH/CXG* WD3 .... 219 F4
Parrotts Fld *HOD* EN11 .... 177 G2
Parrott's La *TRING* HP23 .... 159 F6
Parsloe Rd *EPP* CM16 .... 179 H7
Parsonage Cl *ABLGY* WD5 .... 186 E8
  TRING HP23 .... 135 F5 🗊
Parsonage La *BRKMPK* AL9 .... 192 B1
  BSF CM23 .... 106 A1
  SAFWS CB11 .... 51 K6
  STDN SG11 .... 83 G3
  STSD CM24 .... 86 E5
Parsonage Leys *HLW* CM20 .... 7 E4
Parsonage Pl *TRING* HP23 .... 135 F6 🗊
Parsonage La *BRKMPK* AL9 .... 192 B1
  RKW/CH/CXG WD3 .... 218 C7
Parson's Cl *STALW/RED* AL3 .... 116 B8
Parthia Cl *ROY* SG8 .... 21 J3
Partridge Cl *BAR* EN5 .... 225 H6
  BUSH WD23 .... 221 K8 🗊
  CSHM HP5 .... 182 A6
Partridge Cl *HLWS* CM18 .... 7 D6
Partridge Hl *BLDK* SG7 .... 17 J6
Partridge Rd *HLWS* CM18 .... 6 C6
  STALW/RED AL3 .... 168 A2
Parva Cl *HARP* AL5 .... 144 A3
Parvills *WAB* EN9 .... 215 J3
Parys Rd *LTNN/LIM* LU3 .... 69 G3
Pascal Wy *LWTH* SG6 .... 42 B2
Pasfield *WAB* EN9 .... 215 J3 🗊
Passingham Av *HTCHE/RSTV* SG4 .... 56 E3
Paston Rd *HHNE* HP2 .... 8 A3
Pasture Cl *BUSH* WD23 .... 221 K7
Pasture La *HTCHE/RSTV* SG4 .... 82 B1
Pasture Loates *STSD* CM24 .... 86 C1
Pasture Rd *LWTH* SG6 .... 41 J6
The Pastures *HAT* AL10 .... 171 G5
  HHW HP1 .... 163 H5
  LCOL/BKTW AL2 .... 188 C2 🗊
  OXHEY WD19 .... 13 D6
  STVGE SG2 .... 76 E1
  WARE SG12 .... 127 C6
  WGCE AL7 .... 148 B5
Path Stort Valley Wy
  HERT/BAY SG13 .... 174 E8
The Pathway *OXHEY* WD19 .... 220 E8
  RAD WD7 .... 206 C6
Patmore Cl *BSF* CM23 .... 105 F1
Patmore Link Rd *HHNE* HP2 .... 9 F6
Patmore Rd *WAB* EN9 .... 215 K4 🗊
Patricia Gdns *BSF* CM23 .... 105 H4
Patrixbourne Av *HTCHE/RSTV* SG4 .... 56 E3
Paxton Rd *BERK* HP4 .... 162 B5 🗊
  STAL AL1 .... 11 D5
Paycock Rd *HLWW/ROY* CM19 .... 179 H3
Payne End *BUNT* SG9 .... 29 K8
Paynes Cl *LWTH* SG6 .... 26 A8 🗊
Paynesfield Rd *BUSH* WD23 .... 222 C7
Paynes La *WAB* EN9 .... 198 C2
Payne's Pk *HTCH/STOT* SG5 .... 56 C2
Peace Gv *WLYN* AL6 .... 123 G2
Peace Prospect *WAT* WD17 .... 12 B2 🗊
Peacocks *HLWW/ROY* CM19 .... 179 G3
Peacocks Cl *BERK* HP4 .... 161 G3 🗊
Peakes La *CHESW* EN7 .... 196 D5
Peakes Wy *CHESW* EN7 .... 196 D5
Pea La *BERK* HP4 .... 160 E3
Pearman Dr *WARE* SG12 .... 99 H2
Pearsall Cl *LWTH* SG6 .... 42 B4
Pearson Av *HERT/BAY* SG13 .... 151 F3
Pearsons Cl *HERT/BAY* SG13 .... 151 F5 🗊
Peartree Cl *HHW* HP1 .... 163 K5 🗊
  WGCE AL7 .... 147 K3
Peartree Cl *WGCE* AL7 .... 147 K4 🗊
Pear Tree Dell *LWTH* SG6 .... 42 B7
Peartree La *WGCE* AL7 .... 147 K4
Pear Tree Md *HLWS* CM18 .... 7 F6
Peartree Rd *HHW* HP1 .... 163 K5
  LTNE LU2 .... 70 D5
Pear Tree Wk *CHESW* EN7 .... 196 B4
Peartree Wy *STVGE* SG2 .... 3 E5

Peascroft Rd *HHS/BOV* HP3 .... 186 A1
Peasmead *BUNT* SG9 .... 63 J3 🗊
Peck Cl *AMP/FLIT/B* MK45 .... 36 B5
Peck's Hl *WAB* EN9 .... 177 K7
Pedlars La *ROY* SG8 .... 30 C2
Pedley Hl *DUN/WHIP* LU6 .... 114 A8
Peel Crs *HERT/WAS* SG14 .... 125 K8
Peel Pl *LTN* LU1 .... 4 B4
Pegmire La *GSTN* WD25 .... 221 K5
Pegrams Rd *HLWS* CM18 .... 179 K4
Pegsdon Cl *LTNN/LIM* LU3 .... 69 G2
Pegsdon Wy *HTCH/STOT* SG5 .... 37 K8
Peg's La *HERT/BAY* SG13 .... 151 G2 🗊
  WARE SG12 .... 129 K4
Peldon Rd *HLWW/ROY* CM19 .... 179 H3
Pelham Ct *HHNE* HP2 .... 9 F5 🗊
  WGCE AL7 .... 148 D4 🗊
Pelham Rd *SAFWS* CB11 .... 51 K5
  STDN SG11 .... 82 A2
The Pelhams *GSTN* WD25 .... 204 E5
Pelican Wy *LWTH* SG6 .... 25 K8 🗊
Pemberton Cl *STAL* AL1 .... 189 F1
Pembridge Cl *HHS/BOV* HP3 .... 183 H6
Pembridge La *BROX* EN10 .... 175 J7
Pembridge Rd *HHS/BOV* HP3 .... 183 J6 🗊
Pembroke Av *LTNN/LEA* LU4 .... 68 D6
Pembroke Cl *BROX* EN10 .... 197 J2
Pembroke Dr *CHESW* EN7 .... 195 K7
Pembroke Rd *BLDK* SG7 .... 43 F1
  NTHWD HA6 .... 229 H2
Pemsel Ct *HHS/BOV* HP3 .... 164 D8
Penda Cl *LTNN/LIM* LU3 .... 68 C3
Pendennis Ct *HARP* AL5 .... 144 A2 🗊
Penfold Cl *BLDK* SG7 .... 43 G2
Pengelly Cl *CHESW* EN7 .... 197 F8 🗊
Penhill *LTNN/LIM* LU3 .... 68 D2
Penlow Rd *HLWS* CM18 .... 179 K4
Penman Cl *LCOL/BKTW* AL2 .... 188 C5
Penn Cl *RKW/CH/CXG* WD3 .... 217 G6
Penne Cl *RAD* WD7 .... 206 D4
Penn Gaskell La *CFSP/GDCR* SL9 .... 226 C4
Pennine Av *LTNN/LIM* LU3 .... 68 B1
Pennine Wy *HHNE* HP2 .... 8 C2
Pennington La *STSD* CM24 .... 86 C1
Pennington Rd *CFSP/GDCR* SL9 .... 226 A6
Penningtons *BSF* CM23 .... 105 F4
Pennington Rd *CFSP/GDCR* SL9 .... 226 A6
Penn Rd *LWTH* SG6 .... 42 B6
  RKW/CH/CXG WD3 .... 217 G6
Penny Cft *HARP* AL5 .... 143 H5
Pennyfather Cl *KNEB* SG3 .... 97 F7 🗊
Pennyfathers La *WLYN* AL6 .... 123 C5
Pennymead *HLW* CM20 .... 7 F4
Penrose Av *OXHEY* WD19 .... 231 F1
Penrose Ct *HHNE* HP2 .... 8 B1
Penscroft Gdns *BORE* WD6 .... 224 C4
Penshurst *HLWE* CM17 .... 156 E6
Penshurst Cl *CFSP/GDCR* SL9 .... 226 A8
  HARP AL5 .... 117 K5 🗊
Penshurst Rd *POTB/CUF* EN6 .... 210 E1
Pentland *HHNE* HP2 .... 8 C2 🗊
Pentland Rd *BUSH* WD23 .... 221 K6
Pentley Pk *WGCW* AL8 .... 147 J1 🗊
Penton Dr *CHES/WCR* EN8 .... 197 H7
Pentrich Av *EN* EN1 .... 213 K8
Penzance Cl *DEN/HRF* UB9 .... 228 C8 🗊
Peplins Cl *BRKMPK* AL9 .... 192 E3
Peplins Wy *BRKMPK* AL9 .... 192 E3
Peppercorn Wk
  HTCHE/RSTV SG4 .... 57 F2 🗊
Pepper Hl *WARE* SG12 .... 152 E4
Pepsal End *STVGE* SG2 .... 76 C8
Pepsal End Rd *LTN* LU1 .... 89 F7
Pepys Crs *BAR* EN5 .... 225 H5
Pepys Wy *BLDK* SG7 .... 42 D1
Percheron Rd *BORE* WD6 .... 224 C6
Percival Wy *LTNE* LU2 .... 90 D2
Percy Rd *WATW* WD18 .... 12 C3 🗊
Peregrine Cl *BSF* CM23 .... 105 G3
  GSTN WD25 .... 205 F4
Perham Wy *LCOL/BKTW* AL2 .... 190 B4
Perimeter Rd *HAT* AL10 .... 170 D1
Perivale Gdns *GSTN* WD25 .... 204 C4
Periwinkle Cl *ROY* SG8 .... 32 C4
Periwinkle La *HTCHE/RSTV* SG5 .... 40 D8
Permain Cl *RAD* WD7 .... 207 H3
Perowne Wy *STDN* SG11 .... 81 K6
Perram Cl *BROX* EN10 .... 197 J4 🗊
Perriors Cl *CHESW* EN7 .... 196 E5
Perry Dr *ROY* SG8 .... 21 J2
Perry Gn *HHNE* HP2 .... 141 F8
Perry Hl *WAB* EN9 .... 199 F1
Perry Md *BUSH* WD23 .... 221 K6
Perrymead *LTNE* LU2 .... 71 G7
Perry Rd *HLWS* CM18 .... 179 K4
Perrysfield Rd *CHES/WCR* EN8 .... 197 J5
Perry Spring *HLWE* CM17 .... 181 F5
Perrywood La *HERT/WAS* SG14 .... 124 C3
Pescot Hl *HHW* HP1 .... 164 A4
Peterhill Cl *CFSP/GDCR* SL9 .... 226 B4
Peterlee Ct *HHNE* HP2 .... 8 C1 🗊
Peters Av *LCOL/BKTW* AL2 .... 190 A4
Petersfield *STALW/RED* AL3 .... 168 B2

Peter's Pl *BERK* HP4 .... 161 F3
Peters Wy *KNEB* SG3 .... 96 A3
Peterswood *HLWS* CM18 .... 180 A5
Peters Wood Hl *WARE* SG12 .... 152 C2
Pettys Cl *CHES/WCR* EN8 .... 197 H7
Petunia Ct *LTNW/LEA* LU4 .... 4 A2 🗊
Petworth Cl *STVGE* SG2 .... 96 D2
Pevensey Cl *LTNE* LU2 .... 70 E5 🗊
Pewterers Av *BSF* CM23 .... 105 F5
Pheasant Cl *BERK* HP4 .... 161 K6 🗊
  TRING HP23 .... 135 F2 🗊
Pheasant Wk *CFSP/GDCR* SL9 .... 226 A3
Phelips Rd *EPP* CM16 .... 179 H6
Phillimore Pl *RAD* WD7 .... 206 B6
Phillipers *GSTN* WD25 .... 205 F5 🗊
Phillips Av *ROY* SG8 .... 21 G1
Phipps Hatch La *ENC/FH* EN2 .... 213 F8
Phoenix Cl *NTHWD* HA6 .... 230 A3
The Phygtle *CFSP/GDCR* SL9 .... 226 B5
Piccotts End La *HHW* HP1 .... 164 B2
Piccotts End La *HHNE* HP2 .... 164 B3
Piccotts End Rd *HHW* HP1 .... 164 A2
Pickets Cl *BUSH* WD23 .... 222 A8
Picketts *WGCW* AL8 .... 122 D8
Pickford Hl *HARP* AL5 .... 118 E6
Pickford Rd *STALW/RED* AL3 .... 115 G7
Picknage Rd *ROY* SG8 .... 23 G7
Pie Cnr *STALW/RED* AL3 .... 116 B8
Pie Gdn *STALW/RED* AL3 .... 116 C8
Pierian Spring *HHW* HP1 .... 164 A4 🗊
Pietley Hl *STALW/RED* AL3 .... 116 A8
Pigeonwick *HARP* AL5 .... 118 C6
Piggottshill La *HARP* AL5 .... 143 K2
Piggotts La *LTNW/LEA* LU4 .... 68 C5
Piggotts Wy *BAR* EN5 .... 105 H4
Pightle Cl *ROY* SG8 .... 21 G2
Pig La *BSF* CM23 .... 105 K6
Pike End *STVGE* SG1 .... 2 B2
Pilgrim Cl *GSTN* WD25 .... 204 E3 🗊
  LCOL/BKTW AL2 .... 188 E5
Pilgrims Wy *STVGE* SG1 .... 59 H7
Pilkingtons *HLWE* CM17 .... 181 G1
Piltdown Rd *OXHEY* WD19 .... 230 E3 🗊
  OXHEY WD19 .... 230 E3 🗊
Pinceybrook Rd *HLWS* CM18 .... 179 K5
Pinchfield *RKW/CH/CXG* WD3 .... 227 G4
Pindar Rd *HOD* EN11 .... 177 G2
Pine Cl *BERK* HP4 .... 161 J5
  CHES/WCR EN8 .... 197 G6
  NTHWD HA6 .... 229 K5
Pine Crest *WLYN* AL6 .... 122 E1
Pinecroft *HHS/BOV* HP3 .... 185 K2
Pinecroft Crs *BAR* EN5 .... 225 K4
Pine Gv *BRKMPK* AL9 .... 193 H3
  BSF CM23 .... 106 A3
  BUSH WD23 .... 13 F1
  LCOL/BKTW AL2 .... 188 B8
Pinehurst Cl *ABLGY* WD5 .... 203 K2
Pinelands *BSF* CM23 .... 85 J8
Pine Rd *DUN/WHIP* LU6 .... 112 B1
Pines Av *EN* EN1 .... 214 B6
Pines Hl *STSD* CM24 .... 86 C4
The Pines *BORE* WD6 .... 223 J2 🗊
  HHW HP1 .... 184 D2
Pine Tree Cl *HHNE* HP2 .... 8 A4 🗊
Pine Wk *BERK* HP4 .... 160 E2
Pinewood *WGCE* AL7 .... 147 K5
Pinewood Cl *PIN* HA5 .... 231 J5
Pinewood Cl *BORE* WD6 .... 224 C1
  HLWE CM17 .... 181 F3
  PIN HA5 .... 231 J5
  STAL AL1 .... 169 F6
  WAT WD17 .... 220 B1 🗊
Pinewood Dr *POTB/CUF* EN6 .... 210 A1
Pinewood Gdns *HHS/BOV* HP3 .... 8 B6 🗊
  HHW HP1 .... 164 A6
Pinfold Rd *BUSH* WD23 .... 221 G2
Pinford Dell *LTNE* LU2 .... 70 E8 🗊
Pinnacles *WAB* EN9 .... 215 K4
Pinnate Pl *WGCE* AL7 .... 147 K7
Pinner Gn *PIN* HA5 .... 230 D8
Pinner Hl *PIN* HA5 .... 230 C6
Pinner Hill Rd *PIN* HA5 .... 230 D7
Pinner Park Av *RYLN/HDSTN* HA2 .... 231 K8
Pinner Park Gdns
  RYLN/HDSTN HA2 .... 231 K8
Pinner Rd *NTHWD* HA6 .... 230 A7
  OXHEY WD19 .... 13 E5
  PIN HA5 .... 230 E8
Pinnocks La *BLDK* SG7 .... 43 F2
Pinto Cl *BORE* WD6 .... 224 C6 🗊
Pioneer Wy *WATW* WD18 .... 12 A5
Pipers Av *HARP* AL5 .... 144 A2
Pipers Cl *STALW/RED* AL3 .... 142 B3
Pipers Hl *HHW* HP1 .... 139 F7
Pipers La *HARP* AL5 .... 144 B2
  STALW/RED AL3 .... 115 J1
Pippens *WGCW* AL8 .... 122 E8
Pippin Cl *RAD* WD7 .... 207 H3
Pirton Cl *HTCH/STOT* SG5 .... 56 B2
  STALE/WH AL4 .... 169 F1
Pirton Rd *HTCH/STOT* SG5 .... 39 J3
  HTCH/STOT SG5 .... 55 K2
  LTNW/LEA LU4 .... 68 A3
Pishiobury Dr *SBW* CM21 .... 157 G1

Pitsfield WGCW AL8 ..... 122 D8
Pitstone Cl STALE/WH AL4 ..... 169 F1
Pitt Dr STAL/WH AL4 ..... 190 A1
Pittman's Fld HLW CM20 ..... 7 E3
Pix Cl ARL/CHE SG15 ..... 24 E1
Pix Farm La HHW HP1 ..... 162 E7
Pixies Hill Crs HHW HP1 ..... 163 J8
Pixies Hill Rd HHW HP1 ..... 163 J7
Pixmore Av LWTH SG6 ..... 42 A5
Pixmore Wy LWTH SG6 ..... 41 K4
Pix Rd HTCH/STOT SG5 ..... 25 J4
  LWTH SG6 ..... 42 A3
Plaiters Cl TRING HP23 ..... 135 F5
Plaitford Cl RKW/CH/CXG WD3 ..... 228 D1
Plantaganet Pl WAB EN9 ..... 215 G3
Plantation Rd LTNN/LIM LU3 ..... 68 C2
Plantation Wk HHW HP1 ..... 163 K5
  HHW HP1 ..... 163 K4
Plash Dr STVG SG1 ..... 2 C3
Plashes Cl STDN SG11 ..... 81 J7
Plashets RBSF CM22 ..... 133 C8
Platt Cl LTNW/LEA LU4 ..... 68 C5
Plaw Hatch Cl BSF CM23 ..... 106 A1
Playhouse Sq HLW CM20 ..... 6 B4
The Pleasance HARP AL5 ..... 117 K5
Pleasant Mt HERT/BAY SG13 ..... 152 B5
Pleasant Pl BRKMPK AL9 ..... 171 H1
Pleasant Rd BSF CM23 ..... 105 H1
Plewes Cl DUN/WHIP LU6 ..... 114 C1
Plough Hl POTB/CUF EN6 ..... 195 G1
Plough La BERK HP4 ..... 162 E2
  DEN/HRF UB9 ..... 228 B5
  HTCHE/RSTV SG4 ..... 72 D4
  RKW/CH/CXG WD3 ..... 201 J3
Ploughmans Cl BSF CM23 ..... 105 F4
Ploughmans End WCCE AL7 ..... 148 D4
Plover Cl BERK HP4 ..... 161 K6
Ployters Rd HLWW/ROY CM19 ..... 179 K5
Plummers La LTNE LU2 ..... 92 A8
Plumpton Cl LTNE LU2 ..... 70 E6
Plumpton Rd HOD EN11 ..... 177 H1
Pluto Ri HHNE HP2 ..... 8 B3
Poets Cha HHW HP1 ..... 164 A4
Poets Cl HHW HP1 ..... 164 A5
Poets Ct HARP AL5 ..... 118 D8
Poets Ga CHESW EN7 ..... 196 B6
Polayn Garth WCCW AL8 ..... 147 J2
Polegate LTNE LU2 ..... 70 E7
Polehanger La HHW HP1 ..... 163 H1
Poles Hl RKW/CH/CXG WD3 ..... 201 H3
Poles La WARE SG12 ..... 127 G3
Police Rw ROY SG8 ..... 30 D2
Pollard Gdns STVG SG1 ..... 76 A1
Pollard Hatch HLWW/ROY CM19 ..... 179 J4
Pollards Cl CHESW EN7 ..... 196 A7
Pollards Ct CHESW EN7 ..... 196 A7
Pollards Wy HTCH/STOT SG5 ..... 38 E5
Pollywick Rd TRING HP23 ..... 135 J8
Polzeath Cl LTNE LU2 ..... 90 A1
Pomeroy Gv LTNE LU2 ..... 69 K4
Pomfret Av LTNE LU2 ..... 5 D3
Pond Cl DEN/HRF UB9 ..... 228 B8
  LTNN/LEA LU4 ..... 68 A4
Pond Cft HAT AL10 ..... 170 E3
  WCCE AL7 ..... 147 K4
Pondcroft Rd KNEB SG3 ..... 96 B4
Pondfield Crs STALE/WH AL4 ..... 168 E3
Pond La BLDK SG7 ..... 42 E1
Pond Rd HHS/BOV HP3 ..... 186 A4
Pondside HTCHE/RSTV SG4 ..... 58 C5
Pondsmeade STALW/RED AL3 ..... 142 C4
Pondwick Rd HARP AL5 ..... 118 A4
Pondwicks Cl STALW/RED AL3 ..... 10 B5
Pondwicks Rd LTN LU1 ..... 5 D4
Pooleys La BRKMPK AL9 ..... 192 C1
Popes La WATN WD24 ..... 204 C3
Popes Rd ABLGY WD5 ..... 203 K1
Popes Rw ROY SG8 ..... 21 H6
  WARE SG12 ..... 127 H6
Popis Gdns WARE SG12 ..... 127 J7
Poplar Av HAT AL10 ..... 170 C4
  LTNN/LIM LU3 ..... 69 H1
Poplar Cl HTCHE/RSTV SG4 ..... 56 E4
  PIN HA5 ..... 230 E7
  ROY SG8 ..... 21 J2
  STDN SG11 ..... 100 E8
Poplar Dr DUN/WHIP LU6 ..... 114 C1
Poplars ROY SG8 ..... 21 J2
Poplar Rd DUN/WHIP LU6 ..... 114 C1
Poplars WCCE AL7 ..... 148 C2
Poplars Cl GSTN WD25 ..... 204 C2
  HAT AL10 ..... 170 C4
  LTNE LU2 ..... 70 C6
The Poplars ARL/CHE SG15 ..... 24 E1
  CHESW EN7 ..... 196 C4
  HHW HP1 ..... 164 A7
  HTCH/STOT SG5 ..... 40 D4
  STAL AL1 ..... 189 K2
Popple Wy STVG SG1 ..... 2 C2
Poppy Cl HHW HP1 ..... 163 H5
Poppyfields WCCE AL7 ..... 148 D4
Poppy Md STVG SG1 ..... 3 D4
Poppy Wk CHESW EN7 ..... 196 B6
Porlock Dr LTNE LU2 ..... 70 D8
Porters Cl BUNT SG9 ..... 63 J1
Porters Hl HARP AL5 ..... 118 E5

Porters Park Dr RAD WD7 ..... 207 H2
Porters Wd STALW/RED AL3 ..... 168 C2
Portland Av HERT/WAS SG14 ..... 151 F5
Portland Dr CHESW EN7 ..... 213 K1
  ENC/FH EN2 ..... 213 H8
  HERT/BAY SG13 ..... 152 B5
Portland Pl BSF CM23 ..... 105 J2
  LTNW/LEA LU4 ..... 69 F8
Portland St STALW/RED AL3 ..... 10 B4
Port La RBSF CM22 ..... 106 A7
Portman Cl HTCH/STOT SG5 ..... 40 B7
  STALE/WH AL4 ..... 169 F1
Portmill La HTCH/STOT SG5 ..... 56 D2
Port V HERT/WAS SG14 ..... 150 E2
Postfield WCCE AL7 ..... 123 G8
Post Office Rd HLW CM20 ..... 6 B3
Post Office Rw HTCHE/RSTV SG4 ..... 43 H8
Postwood Gn HERT/BAY SG13 ..... 152 B6
Post Wood Rd WARE SG12 ..... 152 D2
Potash La TRING HP23 ..... 108 D5
Potten End Hl HHW HP1 ..... 163 H1
Potterscrouch La LCOL/BKTW AL2 ..... 187 K2
Potters Fld HLWE CM17 ..... 181 G5
  STALW/RED AL3 ..... 168 D2
Pottersheath Rd WLYN AL6 ..... 95 J8
Potters Heights Cl PIN HA5 ..... 230 C6
Potters La BORE WD6 ..... 224 B1
  STVG SG1 ..... 75 C5
Potter St BSF CM23 ..... 105 J2
  HLWE CM17 ..... 181 F2
  NTHWD HA6 ..... 230 B7
Potter Street Hl NTHWD HA6 ..... 230 C5
Pottery Cl LTNN/LIM LU3 ..... 68 C2
Potton Rd ROY SG8 ..... 15 F3
Pouchen End La HHW HP1 ..... 163 D1
Poulteney Rd STSD CM24 ..... 86 D1
Poultney Cl RAD WD7 ..... 207 H2
Pound Av STVG SG1 ..... 2 B2
Pound Cl WAB EN9 ..... 198 E1
Pound Fld GSTN WD25 ..... 204 A5
Pound Gn ROY SG8 ..... 15 G4
Pound La RAD WD7 ..... 207 J3
Poundwell WCCE AL7 ..... 148 B4
Powdermill La WAB EN9 ..... 215 G3
Powdermill Ms WAB EN9 ..... 215 G3
Powdermill Wy WAB EN9 ..... 215 G3
Power Ct LTN LU1 ..... 5 D4
Powis Rd POTB/CUF EN6 ..... 210 D4
Poynders Hl HHNE HP2 ..... 9 F6
Poynders Meadow WLYN AL6 ..... 121 K3
Poynings Cl HARP AL5 ..... 144 C1
Prae Cl STALW/RED AL3 ..... 10 A3
Praetorian Ct STAL AL1 ..... 188 E1
Prebendal Dr LTN LU1 ..... 89 G7
Prentice Wy LTNE LU2 ..... 90 E2
Prescott Rd CHES/WCR EN8 ..... 197 J5
Presdales Dr WARE SG12 ..... 152 C1
President Wy LTNE LU2 ..... 90 E1
Prestatyn Cl STVG SG1 ..... 75 G2
Preston Gdns LTNE LU2 ..... 5 D1
  PEND EN3 ..... 214 D7
Preston Rd HTCHE/RSTV SG4 ..... 73 H2
Prestwick Cl LTNE LU2 ..... 69 K4
Prestwick Dr BSF CM23 ..... 86 A8
Prestwick Rd OXHEY WD19 ..... 230 E2
Pretoria Rd WATW WD18 ..... 12 B3
Priestleys LWTN LU1 ..... 89 F2
Primary Wy ARL/CHE SG15 ..... 24 E5
Primett Rd STVG SG1 ..... 2 A1
Primley La RBSF CM22 ..... 133 G8
Primrose Cl ARL/CHE SG15 ..... 24 E5
  BSF CM23 ..... 105 F3
  HAT AL10 ..... 171 G5
Primrose Dr HERT/BAY SG13 ..... 152 A3
Primrose Fld HLWS CM18 ..... 180 C4
Primrose Gdns BUSH WD23 ..... 221 J7
Primrose Hl KGLGY WD4 ..... 186 B6
Primrose Hill Rd STVG SG1 ..... 2 B1
Primrose La ARL/CHE SG15 ..... 24 E5
Primrose Pth CHESW EN7 ..... 213 K1
Primrose Vw ROY SG8 ..... 21 K4
Prince Andrew's Cl ROY SG8 ..... 21 H4
Prince Edward St BERK HP4 ..... 161 K5
Prince Pk HHW HP1 ..... 163 K7
Princes Av PEND EN3 ..... 214 D6
  WATW WD18 ..... 12 B4
Princes Cl BERK HP4 ..... 161 H3
Princes Ct BSF CM23 ..... 105 F2
Princes Ga RBSF CM22 ..... 105 F2
Princes Ms ROY SG8 ..... 21 G4
Princess Diana Dr STALE/WH AL4 ..... 169 F7
Princess St LTN LU1 ..... 4 B5
Prince's St HTCH/STOT SG5 ..... 25 K2
  WARE SG12 ..... 127 K1
Prince St WAT WD17 ..... 13 D2
Prince Wy LTNE LU2 ..... 90 E1
Printers Wy HLW CM20 ..... 156 D4
Priors Cl HERT/BAY SG13 ..... 152 A6
Priors Hl HTCH/STOT SG5 ..... 38 E5
Priors Wood Rd HERT/BAY SG13 ..... 152 B6
Priory Av HLWE CM17 ..... 157 J2
Priory Cl BROX EN10 ..... 197 J2
  HOD EN11 ..... 177 F4
  ROY SG8 ..... 21 J3

Priory Ct BSF CM23 ..... 105 H
  HLWS CM18 ..... 180 D
Priory Dell STVG SG1 ..... 2 C
Priory Dr STSD CM24 ..... 86 C
Priory End HTCHE/RSTV SG4 ..... 56 C
Priory Gdns BERK HP4 ..... 161 K
  LTNE LU2 ..... 69 K
Priory Ga CHES/WCR EN8 ..... 197 K5
Priory La HTCHE/RSTV SG4 ..... 57 N
  ROY SG8 ..... 21 H
Priory Orch STALW/RED AL3 ..... 116 D
Priory St HERT/WAS SG14 ..... 151 C
  WARE SG12 ..... 127 C
Priory Vw BUSH WD23 ..... 222 E
  HTCHE/RSTV SG4 ..... 57 N
Priory Wk STAL AL1 ..... 189 C
Priory Wy HTCHE/RSTV SG4 ..... 56 C
Priory Wood Rbt RBSF CM22 ..... 107 F
Proctors Wy BSF CM23 ..... 105 H
Proctor Wy LTNE LU2 ..... 90 D
Progress Wy LTNW/LEA LU4 ..... 68 A
Prospect La HARP AL5 ..... 143 C
Prospect Pl WLYN AL6 ..... 122 C4
Prospect Rd CHES/WCR EN8 ..... 197 C
  STAL AL1 ..... 90 C
Prospect Vw LTNE LU2 ..... 90 C
Protea Wy LWTH SG6 ..... 42 E
Providence Gv STVG SG1 ..... 75 N
Providence Wy BLDK SG7 ..... 43 F2
Provost Wy LTNE LU2 ..... 90 C
Prowse Av BUSH WD23 ..... 231 N
Pryor Cl ABLGY WD5 ..... 204 A
Pryor Rd BLDK SG7 ..... 43 N
Pryors Cl BSF CM23 ..... 105 H
Pryor Wy LWTH SG6 ..... 42 C
Puddephat's La STALW/RED AL3 ..... 140 C
Pudding La HHW HP1 ..... 163 H
  ROY SG8 ..... 23 C
Pulham Av BROX EN10 ..... 176 D
Puller Rd BAR EN5 ..... 225 N
  HHW HP1 ..... 163 N
Pulleys Cl HHW HP1 ..... 163 N
Pulleys La HHW HP1 ..... 163 N
Pullman Dr HTCHE/RSTV SG4 ..... 57 F2
Pulter's Wy HTCHE/RSTV SG4 ..... 56 N
Pump Hl BUNT SG9 ..... 50 N
Punch Bowl La HHNE HP2 ..... 165 N
  STALW/RED AL3 ..... 166 E
Purbrook Av GSTN WD25 ..... 204 D
Purcell Cl BORE WD6 ..... 223 C4
  WLYN AL6 ..... 123 N
Purford Gn HLWS CM18 ..... 7 N
Purkiss Rd HERT/BAY SG13 ..... 151 F
Purlings Rd BUSH WD23 ..... 221 N
Pursley Gdns BORE WD6 ..... 207 K8
Purway Cl LTNN/LIM LU3 ..... 68 C
Purwell La HTCHE/RSTV SG4 ..... 57 C
Putney Rd PEND EN3 ..... 214 C
Puttenham Cl OXHEY WD19 ..... 230 N
Putteridge Rd LTNE LU2 ..... 70 N
Putters Cft HHNE HP2 ..... 164 N
Puttocks Cl BRKMPK AL9 ..... 192 C1
Puttocks Dr BRKMPK AL9 ..... 192 C1
Pyenest Rd HLWW/ROY CM19 ..... 179 N
The Pyghtle BUNT SG9 ..... 63 N
  LTN LU1 ..... 89 N
Pyms Cl LWTH SG6 ..... 42 N
Pynchbek BSF CM23 ..... 105 N
Pynchon Paddocks RBSF CM22 ..... 133 N
Pytchley Cl LTNE LU2 ..... 69 N
Pytt Fld HLWE CM17 ..... 180 N

Q

The Quadrangle WGCW AL8 ..... 147 H2
The Quadrant LWTH SG6 ..... 41 N
  ROY SG8 ..... 21 G
  STALE/WH AL4 ..... 168 N
  STVG SG1 ..... 2 N
Quaker La WAB EN9 ..... 215 N
Quaker Rd WARE SG12 ..... 127 N
Quakers La POTB/CUF EN6 ..... 193 N
Quantock Cl LTNN/LIM LU3 ..... 68 N
  STALE/WH AL4 ..... 169 F2
Quantock Ri LTNN/LIM LU3 ..... 69 N
Quantocks HHNE HP2 ..... 8 N
Quarry Springs HLW CM20 ..... 7 N
Quartermass Cl HHW HP1 ..... 163 K5
Quartermass Rd HHW HP1 ..... 163 N
Queen Anne's Cl HTCH/STOT SG5 ..... 25 N
Queen Hoo La WLYN AL6 ..... 124 N
Queen Mary's Av WATW WD18 ..... 219 N
Queens Av WATW WD18 ..... 12 N
Queens Cl LTN LU1 ..... 5 D
  SBW CM21 ..... 132 N
  STSD CM24 ..... 86 N
Queens Crs BSF CM23 ..... 105 N
  STALE/WH AL4 ..... 168 N
Queens Dr ABLGY WD5 ..... 204 N
  CHES/WCR EN8 ..... N
The Queen's Dr RKW/CH/CXG WD3 ..... 217 N

Queen's Pl *WAT* WD17 .... 13 D2
Queens Rd *BAR* EN5 .... 225 J3
  BERK HP4 .... 161 H4
  CHES/WCR EN8 .... 214 D4
  HARP AL5 .... 143 J2
  HERT/BAY SG13 .... 151 G4
  ROY SG8 .... 21 H2
  WARE SG12 .... 127 K7
  WAT WD17 .... 13 D2
The Queen's Sq *HHNE* HP2 .... 8 C5
  HTCHE/RSTV SG4 .... 56 D3
  KGLGY WD4 .... 201 K1
  LBUZ LU7 .... 110 D5
  STALW/RED AL3 .... 10 B4
  TRING HP23 .... 135 F6
Queens Wy *HOD* WD7 .... 207 H1
  CHES/WCR EN8 .... 214 E4
Queensway *HAT* AL10 .... 171 F4
  HHW HP1 .... 164 B5
  ROY SG8 .... 21 H2
Queenswood Crs *GSTN* WD25 .... 204 B3
Queenswood Dr *HTCHE/RSTV* SG4 .... 41 C8
Quendon Dr *WAB* EN9 .... 215 J3
Quickbeams *WGCE* AL7 .... 123 C8
Quickley La *RKW/CH/CXG* WD3 .... 217 F6
Quickley Ri *RKW/CH/CXG* WD3 .... 216 E6
Quickly Brow *RKW/CH/CXG* WD3 .... 216 E6
Quickmoor La *KGLGY* WD4 .... 202 A3
Quickswood *LTNN/LIM* LU3 .... 69 F2
Quickwood Cl *RKW/CH/CXG* WD3 .... 217 J6
Quills La *HLWS* SG6 .... 42 D5
Quinter Cl *LTNN/LIM* LU3 .... 68 E5
Quinces Cft *HHW* HP1 .... 163 K4
Quincey Rd *WARE* SG12 .... 127 J5
Quin Ct *STDN* SG11 .... 82 A2
Quinn Wy *LWTH* SG6 .... 42 C4
Quinta Dr *BAR* EN5 .... 225 C5
Quinton Wy *WAB* EN9 .... 215 H5

R

Raban Cl *STVGE* SG2 .... 76 D8
Rabley Heath Rd *WLYN* AL6 .... 95 F8
Rackman Dr *LTNN/LIM* LU3 .... 69 H4
Radburn Cl *HLWS* CM18 .... 180 D5
Radburn Wy *LWTH* SG6 .... 42 B5
Radcliffe Rd *HTCH/STOT* SC5 .... 56 E1
Radlett La *RAD* WD7 .... 207 J4
Radlett Park Rd *RAD* WD7 .... 206 E4
Radlett Rd *GSTN* WD25 .... 205 K8
  LCOL/BKTW AL2 .... 189 C7
  WATN WD24 .... 13 D2
Radstone Pl *LTNE* LU2 .... 71 F3
Radwell La *BLDK* SG7 .... 26 C5
Raebarn Gdns *BAR* EN5 .... 225 C5
Raffin Cl *KNEB* SG3 .... 96 E6
Raffin Green La *HERT/WAS* SG14 .... 97 C4
  KNEB SG3 .... 97 F6
Raffin Pk *KNEB* SG3 .... 97 F6
Ragged Hall La *LCOL/BKTW* AL2 .... 187 K2
Raglan Av *CHES/WCR* EN8 .... 214 C4
Raglan Gdns *OXHEY* WD19 .... 220 C8
Rags La *CHESW* EN7 .... 196 C5
Railway Pl *HERT/BAY* SG13 .... 151 H3
Railway Rd *CHES/WCR* EN8 .... 214 E3
Railway St *HERT/WAS* SG14 .... 151 G3
Railway Ter *KGLGY* WD4 .... 186 A5
Rainbow Cl *STALW/RED* AL3 .... 142 A4
Rainbow Ct *OXHEY* WD19 .... 13 D5
Rainer Cl *CHES/WCR* EN8 .... 197 H7
Rainsford Rd *STSD* CM24 .... 86 C1
Raleigh Crs *STVGE* SG2 .... 3 E1
Raleigh Gv *LTNW/LEA* LU4 .... 68 C3
The Rally *ARL/CHE* SG15 .... 24 E2
Ralston Wy *OXHEY* WD19 .... 230 E1
Ramblers Wy *WCCE* AL7 .... 148 C4
Rambling Wy *BERK* HP4 .... 162 B3
Rammerick Gdns *ARL/CHE* SG15 .... 24 D7
Ram Gorse *HLW* CM20 .... 6 A2
Ramney Dr *PEND* EN3 .... 214 D6
Ramridge Rd *LTNE* LU2 .... 5 E1
Ramsay Cl *BROX* EN10 .... 176 D7
Ramsbury Rd *STAL* AL1 .... 11 D5
Ramsdell *STVGE* SG1 .... 3 F5
Ramsey Cl *BRKMPK* AL9 .... 193 K5
  STAL AL1 .... 11 F6
Ramsey Lodge Ct *STAL* AL1 .... 11 D3
Ramsey Rd *AMP/FLIT/B* MK45 .... 36 C6
Ramson Ri *HHW* HP1 .... 163 H7
Randalls Ride *HHNE* HP2 .... 8 B3
Randals Hl *STVGE* SG2 .... 3 F5
Randon Cl *PIN* HA5 .... 231 J3
Rand's Meadow *HTCH/STOT* SG5 .... 39 K2
Raneleagh Rd *HHNE* HP2 .... 9 E5
Ranleigh Wk *HARP* AL5 .... 144 A3
Ranock Cl *LTNN/LIM* LU3 .... 68 C1
Ranskill Rd *BORE* WD6 .... 223 K1
Ransom Cl *HTCHE/RSTV* SG4 .... 56 D5
  OXHEY WD19 .... 13 D6

Rant Meadow *HHS/BOV* HP3 .... 9 D6
Ranulf Cl *HHW* CM17 .... 157 F3
Ranston Av *HOD* EN11 .... 153 G7
  STVGE SG2 .... 96 D2
Ranworth Cl *HHS/BOV* HP3 .... 164 C8
Raphael Cl *RAD* WD7 .... 207 H2
Raphael Dr *WATN* WD24 .... 13 E1
Rasehill Cl *RKW/CH/CXG* WD3 .... 218 B5
Rathlin *HHS/BOV* HP3 .... 165 C8
Ratty's La *HOD* EN11 .... 177 J3
Ravenbank Rd *LTNE* LU2 .... 70 D4
Raven Cl *RKW/CH/CXG* WD3 .... 218 B7
Raven Ct *HAT* AL10 .... 171 F6
Ravensburgh Cl
  AMP/FLIT/B MK45 .... 36 B6
Ravenscroft *GSTN* WD25 .... 205 F5
  HARP AL5 .... 144 A3
Ravenscroft Pk *BAR* EN5 .... 225 J3
Ravensdell *HHW* HP1 .... 163 J5
Ravens La *BERK* HP4 .... 162 A5
Ravensmead *CFSP/GDCR* SL9 .... 226 C4
Ravensthorpe *LTNE* LU2 .... 70 C5
Ravenswood Pk *NTHWD* HA6 .... 230 B5
Rawdon Dr *HOD* EN11 .... 177 H4
Rayburn Rd *HHW* HP1 .... 163 K4
Rayfield *WGCW* AL8 .... 122 D8
Raymer Cl *STAL* AL1 .... 11 D3
Raymond Cl *ABLGY* WD5 .... 203 J2
Raymonds Cl *WGCE* AL7 .... 147 K5
Raymonds Pln *WGCE* AL7 .... 147 K5
Raynham Cl *BSF* CM23 .... 106 B2
Raynham Rd *BSF* CM23 .... 106 A1
Raynham St *HERT/BAY* SG13 .... 151 H2
Raynham Wy *LTNE* LU2 .... 70 E8
Raynsford Rd *WARE* SG12 .... 127 J8
Rayton Rd *PEND* EN3 .... 214 C7
Ray's Hi *CSHM* HP5 .... 159 H7
The Readings *HLWS* CM18 .... 180 C4
  RKW/CH/CXG WD3 .... 217 J3
Recreation Gnd *STSD* CM24 .... 86 C3
Rectory Cl *BRKMPK* AL9 .... 173 J5
  WARE SG12 .... 154 C1
Rectory Fld *HLWW/ROY* CM19 .... 6 A6
Rectory Gdns *HAT* AL10 .... 171 G4
Rectory La *BERK* HP4 .... 161 K5
  BSF CM23 .... 85 F3
  HERT/WAS SG14 .... 98 A6
  HLWW/ROY CM19 .... 6 A6
  KGLGY WD4 .... 186 A6
  KNEB SG3 .... 96 D7
  LTNE LU2 .... 53 F7
  RAD WD7 .... 207 J3
  RAD WD7 .... 208 B1
  RKW/CH/CXG WD3 .... 218 C8
  STVG SG1 .... 58 C8
Rectory Rd *RKW/CH/CXG* WD3 .... 218 C7
  WGCW AL8 .... 122 B8
Rectory Wd *HLW* CM20 .... 6 B3
Redan Rd *WARE* SG12 .... 127 J6
Redbournbury La *STALW/RED* AL3 .... 142 E7
Redbourn La *HARP* AL5 .... 143 F3
Redbourn Rd *HHNE* HP2 .... 9 D1
  STALW/RED AL3 .... 167 F2
Redcar Dr *STVC* SG1 .... 75 F3
Redding La *STALW/RED* AL3 .... 116 E8
Reddings *HHS/BOV* HP3 .... 164 E8
  WGCW AL8 .... 147 H2
Reddings Av *BUSH* WD23 .... 221 J5
The Reddings *BORE* WD6 .... 223 J3
Redferns Cl *LTN* LU1 .... 89 F3
Redgrave Gdns *LTNN/LIM* LU3 .... 68 E1
Redhall Cl *HAT* AL10 .... 170 E1
Redhall Dr *HAT* AL10 .... 170 E7
Redhall La *RKW/CH/CXG* WD3 .... 218 D1
Redheath Cl *GSTN* WD25 .... 204 A5
Redhill Rd *HTCH/STOT* SC5 .... 56 A1
Redhoods Wy East *LWTH* SG6 .... 41 J3
Redhoods Wy West *LWTH* SG6 .... 41 J3
Red House Ct *WARE* SG12 .... 152 D2
Red Lion Cl *GSTN* WD25 .... 205 J7
Red Lion Crs *HLWE* CM17 .... 181 J7
Red Lion La *HHS/BOV* HP3 .... 185 K4
  HLWE CM17 .... 181 J7
  RKW/CH/CXG WD3 .... 201 K5
Red Lodge Gdns *BERK* HP4 .... 161 H6
Redmire Cl *LTNW/LEA* LU4 .... 68 A3
Red Rails *LTN* LU1 .... 4 A6
Redricks La *HLW* CM20 .... 156 C3
Red Rd *BORE* WD6 .... 223 J3
Redvers Cl *BSF* CM23 .... 85 K7
Red White And Blue Rd *BSF* CM23 .... 86 A7
Red Willow *HLWW/ROY* CM19 .... 179 G4
Redwing Cl *STVGE* SG2 .... 76 D5
Redwing Gv *ABLGY* WD5 .... 204 B1
Redwood Dr *HHS/BOV* HP3 .... 164 E8
  LTNN/LIM LU3 .... 68 B1
Redwood Ri *BORE* WD6 .... 207 K7
Redwoods *HERT/WAS* SG14 .... 151 F2
  WGCW AL8 .... 122 D8
Redwood Wy *BAR* EN5 .... 225 J5
Reed Cl *LCOL/BKTW* AL2 .... 190 B5
Reedham Cl *LCOL/BKTW* AL2 .... 188 C7
Reedings Wy *SBW* CM21 .... 132 D5
Reeds Crs *WATN* WD24 .... 13 D1

Reedsdale *LTNE* LU2 .... 71 G7
The Reeds *WGCE* AL7 .... 147 J4
Reeves Av *LTNN/LIM* LU3 .... 69 C5
Reeves La *HLWW/ROY* CM19 .... 178 D5
Regal Cl *STDN* SG11 .... 81 K7
Regal Wy *WATN* WD24 .... 204 D8
Regency Cl *BSF* CM23 .... 105 H2
Regency Ct *HLWS* CM18 .... 180 C4
Regent Cl *KGLGY* WD4 .... 186 A7
  STALE/WH AL4 .... 169 F2
  WGCE AL7 .... 147 K4
Regent Ct *HTCH/STOT* SC5 .... 25 K2
Regents Cl *RAD* WD7 .... 206 D4
Regent St *HTCH/STOT* SC5 .... 25 K3
  LTN LU1 .... 4 B4
  WATN WD24 .... 204 C8
Reginald Rd *NTHWD* HA6 .... 230 A7
Reginald St *LTNE* LU2 .... 4 C2
Rendlesham Av *RAD* WD7 .... 206 C7
Rendlesham Cl *WARE* SG12 .... 127 K7
Rendlesham Wy
  RKW/CH/CXG WD3 .... 217 F6
Rennison Cl *CHESW* EN7 .... 196 D5
Renshaw Cl *LTNE* LU2 .... 71 F7
Repton Cl *LTNN/LIM* LU3 .... 68 E3
Repton Gn *STALW/RED* AL3 .... 10 C1
Repton Wy *RKW/CH/CXG* WD3 .... 219 F5
Reson Wy *HHW* HP1 .... 164 A7
Reston Cl *BORE* WD6 .... 207 K8
Retford Cl *BORE* WD6 .... 207 K8
The Retreat *AMS* HP6 .... 216 B1
Revels Cl *HERT/WAS* SG14 .... 151 G1
Revels Rd *HERT/WAS* SG14 .... 151 G1
Reynard Copse *BSF* CM23 .... 85 J8
Reynards Rd *WLYN* AL6 .... 122 B2
Reynard's Wy *LCOL/BKTW* AL2 .... 188 B7
Reynard Wy *HERT/BAY* SG13 .... 151 K3
Reynolds Cl *HHW* HP1 .... 163 K4
Reynolds Crs *STALE/WH* AL4 .... 168 E1
Rhee Spring *BLDK* SG7 .... 27 H8
Rhodes Av *BSF* CM23 .... 105 J4
Rhodes Wy *WATN* WD24 .... 13 E1
Rhymes *HHW* HP1 .... 164 A4
Ribbledale *LCOL/BKTW* AL2 .... 190 D5
Ribblesdale *HHNE* HP2 .... 8 B2
Rib Cl *STDN* SG11 .... 81 K7
Ribocon Wy *LTNW/LEA* LU4 .... 68 A2
Ribston Cl *RAD* WD7 .... 207 G3
Rib Vw *HERT/WAS* SG14 .... 126 B8
Rice Cl *HHNE* HP2 .... 8 C4
Richards Cl *BUSH* WD23 .... 222 A7
  LTN LU1 .... 89 G3
Richardson Cl *LCOL/BKTW* AL2 .... 190 C5
Richardson Crs *CHESW* EN7 .... 195 K4
Richardson Pl *STALE/WH* AL4 .... 170 A8
Richard Stagg Cl *STAL* AL1 .... 168 E8
Richfield Rd *BUSH* WD23 .... 222 A8
Richmond Cl *BSF* CM23 .... 105 F2
  WARE SG12 .... 127 F6
Richmond Ct *BROX* EN10 .... 176 E8
  HAT AL10 .... 171 G7
  POTB/CUF EN6 .... 210 D1
Richmond Dr *WAT* WD17 .... 219 K2
Richmond Hl *LTNE* LU2 .... 5 D1
Richmond Rd *POTB/CUF* EN6 .... 210 D1
Richmond Wy *RKW/CH/CXG* WD3 .... 219 H4
Rickfield Cl *HAT* AL10 .... 171 F6
Rickmansworth La
  CFSP/GDCR SL9 .... 226 B5
Rickmansworth Rd *DEN/HRF* UB9 .... 228 B7
  NTHWD HA6 .... 229 G5
  PIN HA5 .... 230 C8
  RKW/CH/CXG WD3 .... 217 H3
  WATW WD18 .... 219 K4
Rickyard Cl *LTNE* LU2 .... 70 C6
Rickyard Meadow
  STALW/RED AL3 .... 142 B4
The Rickyard *BLDK* SG7 .... 17 K6
Riddell Gdns *BLDK* SG7 .... 43 F1
Riddings La *HLWS* CM18 .... 180 D5
Riddy Hill Cl *HTCHE/RSTV* SG4 .... 56 E3
Riddy La *LTNN/LIM* LU3 .... 69 C4
The Riddy *WLYN* AL6 .... 121 K1
Ridge Av *HARP* AL5 .... 118 A5
  LWTH SG6 .... 42 A3
Ridgedown *STALW/RED* AL3 .... 142 B4
Ridgefield *WAT* WD17 .... 203 K7
Ridgehurst Av *GSTN* WD25 .... 204 A3
Ridge La *WAT* WD17 .... 203 K6
Ridge Lea *HHW* HP1 .... 163 J7
Ridgemount End
  CFSP/GDCR SL9 .... 226 B4
Ridge Rd *LWTH* SG6 .... 42 A3
Ridge St *WATN* WD24 .... 204 C8
Ridgeview *LCOL/BKTW* AL2 .... 190 D6
Ridge Vw *TRING* HP23 .... 135 H4
Ridgeview Cl *BAR* EN5 .... 225 J6
Ridge Wy *RKW/CH/CXG* WD3 .... 218 A7
Ridgeway *BERK* HP4 .... 161 G5
  DUN/WHIP LU6 .... 114 C1
  HARP AL5 .... 118 A5
  LBUZ LU7 .... 111 J3
  STDN SG11 .... 83 J8
  STVC SG1 .... 3 D3
  TRING HP23 .... 111 G7

WGCE AL7 .... 148 C4
Ridgeway Cl HHS/BOV HP3 .... 185 K3
Ridgeways HLWE CM17 .... 181 H1
The Ridgeway ENC/FH EN2 .... 211 K6
  HERT/WAS SG14 .... 150 C2
  HTCH/STOT SG5 .... 56 B3
  POTB/CUF EN6 .... 194 C5
  POTB/CUF EN6 .... 211 G5
  RAD WD7 .... 206 C7
  STALE/WH AL4 .... 168 D2
  WARE SG12 .... 127 G6
  WAT WD17 .... 203 K7
  WLYN AL6 .... 94 E8
Ridgewood Dr HARP AL5 .... 118 A6
Ridgewood Gdns HARP AL5 .... 118 A5 🗓
Ridgmont Rd STAL AL1 .... 11 D5
The Ridings BSF CM23 .... 105 G5
  CSHM HP5 .... 200 A6
  HERT/WAS SG14 .... 150 D4
  LTNN/LIM LU3 .... 4 A2
  STALW/RED AL3 .... 115 J3
  STVGE SG2 .... 3 F5
Ridler Rd EN EN1 .... 213 H8 🗓
Ridlins End STVGE SG2 .... 76 D7
Rigery La STDN SG11 .... 100 E3
Riley Rd PEND EN3 .... 214 B8
Ringshall Dr BERK HP4 .... 137 J1
Ringshall Rd BERK HP4 .... 112 D6
Ringtale Pl BLDK SG7 .... 27 H8 🗓
Ringway Rd LCOL/BKTW AL2 .... 188 D5
Ringwood Rd LTNW/LEA LU4 .... 69 J3
Ripley Rd LTNW/LEA LU4 .... 68 B8
Ripley Wy CHESW EN7 .... 197 F8
  HHW HP1 .... 163 H5
Ripon Ct POTB/CUF EN6 .... 210 B1 🗓
Ripon Rd STVG SG1 .... 59 F7
Ripon Wy BORE WD6 .... 224 B5
  STALE/WH AL4 .... 169 G2
Risdens HLWS CM18 .... 179 K4 🗓
Risedale Cl HHS/BOV HP3 .... 185 J1 🗓
Risedale Hl HHS/BOV HP3 .... 185 J1
Risedale Rd HHS/BOV HP3 .... 185 J1
The Rise BLDK SG7 .... 42 E2
  BORE WD6 .... 223 J5
  LCOL/BKTW AL2 .... 189 F5
Rising Hill Cl NTHWD HA6 .... 229 H5 🗓
Risingholme Cl BUSH WD23 .... 221 J7
Ritcroft Cl HHS/BOV HP3 .... 9 E6
Ritcroft Dr HHS/BOV HP3 .... 9 E6
Ritcroft St HHS/BOV HP3 .... 9 E6
Ritz Ct POTB/CUF EN6 .... 210 B1 🗓
Rivenhall End WGCE AL7 .... 148 D3
River Av HOD EN11 .... 177 G2
River Cl CHES/WCR EN8 .... 215 F4
River Ct HTCH/STOT SG5 .... 40 D5
Riverfield La SBW CM21 .... 132 C6 🗓
Riverford Cl HARP AL5 .... 118 D5
River Hl STALW/RED AL3 .... 116 B7
River Md HTCH/STOT SG5 .... 40 A7
River Meads WARE SG12 .... 153 H4
Rivermill WAT CM20 .... 6 B2
River Pk HHW HP1 .... 163 K8
Riversend Rd HHS/BOV HP3 .... 185 G1
Rivershill HERT/WAS SG14 .... 98 B6
Riverside BSF CM23 .... 105 J2
  BUNT SG9 .... 63 J2
  LCOL/BKTW AL2 .... 190 C5 🗓
  WLYN AL6 .... 122 B4
Riverside Av BROX EN10 .... 177 F8
Riverside Cl KGLGY WD4 .... 186 B7
  STAL AL1 .... 11 D6 🗓
Riverside Ct HLW CM20 .... 157 F3
Riverside Dr RKW/CH/CXG WD3 ... 218 C8
Riverside Gdns BERK HP4 .... 161 H4
Riverside Rd LTNN/LIM LU3 .... 69 F4
  OXHEY WD19 .... 12 C5
  STAL AL1 .... 11 D5
Rivett Cl BSF CM23 .... 27 G8 🗓
Robbery Bottom La WLYN AL6 ...... 123 F1
Robbs Cl HHW HP1 .... 163 K4 🗓
Robe End HHW HP1 .... 163 J4
Robert Av LCOL/BKTW AL2 .... 188 E2
Robert Cl POTB/CUF EN6 .... 209 K3
Roberts Cl CHES/WCR EN8 .... 197 J8 🗓
Roberts La CFSP/GDCR SL9 .... 226 D4
Robertson Cl BROX EN10 .... 197 J4 🗓
Roberts Rd WATW WD18 .... 13 D4 🗓
Roberts Wy HAT AL10 .... 170 E6
Roberts Wood Dr CFSP/GDCR SL9 .. 226 D4
Robert Wallace Cl BSF CM23 .... 85 J8
Robeson Wy BORE WD6 .... 224 B1
Robina Cl NTHWD HA6 .... 230 A8
Robin Cl WARE SG12 .... 153 H6
Robin Hl BERK HP4 .... 161 K6
Robin Hood Dr BUSH WD23 .... 221 G1
Robin Hood La HAT AL10 .... 171 F3
Robin Hood Meadow
  HHNE HP2 .... 164 E1 🗓
Robin Md WGCE AL7 .... 123 G8
Robins Cl LCOL/BKTW AL2 .... 190 C5 🗓

Robinsfield HHW HP1 .... 163 K6
Robins Nest Hl HERT/BAY SG13 ... 173 K6
Robinson Av CHESW EN7 .... 195 K6
Robinson Cl BSF CM23 .... 105 J4
Robinson Crs BUSH WD23 .... 221 K8
Robins Orch CFSP/GDCR SL9 ...... 226 B5 🗓
Robins Rd HHS/BOV HP3 .... 165 F8
Robins Wy HAT AL10 .... 170 E7
Robinswood LTNE LU2 .... 69 K4
Robin Wy POTB/CUF EN6 .... 195 G6
Robson Cl CFSP/GDCR SL9 .... 226 B4
Robsons Cl CHES/WCR EN8 .... 197 G7 🗓
Rochester Av LTNE LU2 .... 70 D5
Rochester Dr GSTN WD25 .... 204 D5 🗓
Rochester Rd RKW/CH/CXG WD3 .. 219 G4
  ROY SG8 .... 21 H1 🗓
Rochford Av WAB EN9 .... 215 J4
Rochford Cl BROX EN10 .... 197 J4
Rochford Dr LTNE LU2 .... 71 F7
Rochford Rd BSF CM23 .... 86 A8
Rockcliffe Av KGLGY WD4 .... 186 B8
Rockfield Av WARE SG12 .... 127 H6
Rockingham Wy STVG SG1 .... 2 C5
Rockleigh HERT/WAS SG14 .... 150 E3
Rockley Rd LTN LU1 .... 89 F3
Rock Rd ROY SG8 .... 21 C1
Rockways BAR EN5 .... 224 E6
Rodeheath LTNW/LEA LU4 .... 68 C6
Roden Cl HLWE CM17 .... 157 J5
Rodgers Cl BORE WD6 .... 223 G6
Rodney Av STAL AL1 .... 11 F6
Rodney Crs HOD EN11 .... 177 F1
Roebuck Cl HERT/BAY SG13 .... 151 K3
  LTN LU1 .... 89 F3
Roebuck Ga STVGE SG2 .... 76 A8
Roe Cl HTCH/STOT SG5 .... 25 J4
Roedean Cl LTNE LU2 .... 70 E6
Roe End La STALW/RED AL3 .... 114 E5
Roefields Cl HHS/BOV HP3 .... 184 C2
Roe Green Cl HAT AL10 .... 170 D5
Roe Green La HAT AL10 .... 170 E4
Roe Hill Cl HAT AL10 .... 170 E5
Roehyde Wy HAT AL10 .... 170 D6
Roestock Gdns STALE/WH AL4 ..... 191 H1
Roestock La STALE/WH AL4 .... 191 H1
Rofant Rd NTHWD HA6 .... 229 K5
Rogate Rd LTNE LU2 .... 70 D4
Rogers Ruff NTHWD HA6 .... 229 H7
Roland St STAL AL1 .... 11 H4
Rolleston Cl WARE SG12 .... 127 G6 🗓
Rollswood WGCE AL7 .... 147 K6
Rollswood Rd WLYN AL6 .... 122 A2
Rollys La BLDK SG7 .... 17 K5
Roman Gdns KGLGY WD4 .... 186 B8
  LWTH SG6 .... 41 J3
Roman La BLDK SG7 .... 43 F1
Roman Ri SBW CM21 .... 132 B7
Roman Rd AMP/FLIT/B MK45 .... 36 D6
  LTNW/LEA LU4 .... 68 D6
  RAD WD7 .... 206 D5
Roman St HOD EN11 .... 177 F2 🗓
Roman V HLWE CM17 .... 157 F4
Roman Wy STALW/RED AL3 .... 115 J3
  STDN SG11 .... 81 J6 🗓
  WLYN AL6 .... 122 C4
Romany Cl LWTH SG6 .... 41 G3
Romany Ct HHNE HP2 .... 9 F4 🗓
Romeland BORE WD6 .... 223 G6 🗓
  STALW/RED AL3 .... 10 B4
  WAB EN9 .... 215 H3
Romeland Hl STALW/RED AL3 ...... 10 B4
Romilly Dr OXHEY WD19 .... 231 F3
Rondini Av LTNN/LIM LU3 .... 69 G7
Ronsons Wy STALW/RED AL3 ...... 168 C2
Rookery Dr LTNE LU2 .... 69 K3
Rookery Wd STSD CM24 .... 86 D1 🗓
Rookery Yd STVG SG1 .... 2 A1 🗓
Rookes Cl LWTH SG6 .... 42 B6
Rooks Hl RKW/CH/CXG WD3 ...... 218 B4
  WGCW AL8 .... 147 H4
Rooks Nest La ROY SG8 .... 30 D2
Rook Tree Cl HTCH/STOT SG5 ..... 26 A3 🗓
Rook Tree La HTCH/STOT SG5 ..... 25 K2
Rookwood Dr STVGE SG2 .... 76 C8
Rosary Ct POTB/CUF EN6 .... 193 H8 🗓
Rosary Gdns BUSH WD23 .... 221 J7
Roseacre Gdns WGCE AL7 .... 148 E3 🗓
Roseacres SBW CM21 .... 132 B6
Rosebank WAB EN9 .... 215 K4
Rosebarn La TRING HP23 .... 109 H8
Roseberry Ct WAT WD17 .... 220 B1 🗓
Rosebery BSF CM23 .... 106 B3
Rosebery Av HARP AL5 .... 118 B7
Rosebery Rd BUSH WD23 .... 221 J8
Rosebery Wy TRING HP23 .... 135 G4
Rosebriar Wk WATN WD24 .... 204 A6
Rose Ct CHESW EN7 .... 196 E5
Rosecroft Dr WAT WD17 .... 203 K7
Rosecroft La WLYN AL6 .... 123 G1
Rosedale WGCE AL7 .... 123 F7
Rosedale Av CHESW EN7 .... 196 E5
Rosedale Cl LCOL/BKTW AL2 ...... 188 A8
  LTNW/LEA LU4 .... 68 B2
Rosedale Wy CHESW EN7 .... 196 E5
Rose Gdns WATW WD18 .... 12 B4

Roseheath HHW HP1 .... 163 🗓
Rosehill BERK HP4 .... 161 J5 🗓
Rosehill Cl HOD EN11 .... 176 ▢
Rosehill Gdns ABLGY WD5 .... 203 ▢
Roselands Av HOD EN11 .... 176 ▢
Rose La STALE/WH AL4 .... 120 ▢
Rose Lawn BUSH WD23 .... 221 ▢
Rose Md POTB/CUF EN6 .... 193 ▢
Rose Meadow STDN SG11 .... 64 ▢
Rosemont Cl LWTH SG6 .... 41 J2 🗓
Rosemount HLWW/ROY CM19 ..... 179 ▢
Rose V HOD EN11 .... 177 ▢
Rose Wk ROY SG8 .... 21 G2 🗓
  STALE/WH AL4 .... 168 ▢
The Rose Wk RAD WD7 .... 206 ▢
Rose Wood Cl LTNE LU2 .... 5 ▢
Rosewood Ct HHW HP1 .... 163 H 🗓
Rosewood Dr ENC/FH EN2 .... 212 ▢
Roslyn Cl BROX EN10 .... 176 ▢
Ross Cl KTN/HRWW/W HA3 .... 231 ▢
  LTN LU1 .... 89 ▢
Ross Crs GSTN WD25 .... 204 ▢
Rossfold Rd LTNN/LIM LU3 .... 68 ▢
Rossington Av BORE WD6 .... 207 ▢
Rossiter Flds BAR EN5 .... 225 ▢
Rosslyn Crs LTNN/LIM LU3 .... 69 ▢
Rosslyn Rd WATW WD18 .... 12 ▢
Rossway LTN LU1 .... 89 ▢
Ross Wy NTHWD HA6 .... 230 ▢
Rossway Dr BUSH WD23 .... 221 ▢
Rossway La TRING HP23 .... 160 ▢
Roswell Cl CHES/WCR EN8 .... 197 ▢
Rothamsted Av HARP AL5 .... 118 ▢
Rotheram Av LTN LU1 .... 89 ▢
Rother Cl GSTN WD25 .... 204 ▢
Rother Fld LTNE LU2 .... 70 ▢
Rotherfield Rd PEND EN3 .... 214 ▢
Rothesay Rd LTN LU1 .... 4 B ▢
Roughdown Av HHS/BOV HP3 ...... 184 ▢
Roughdown Rd HHS/BOV HP3 ..... 185 ▢
Roughdown Villas Rd
  HHS/BOV HP3 .... 184 ▢
The Roughs NTHWD HA6 .... 229 ▢
Roughwood Cl WAT WD17 .... 203 ▢
Roughwood La CSTG HP8 .... 216 ▢
Roundabout La WLYN AL6 .... 123 ▢
Round Coppice Rd RBSF CM22 ... 107 ▢
Roundcroft CHESW EN7 .... 196 ▢
Roundfield Av HARP AL5 .... 119 ▢
Roundhaye STDN SG11 .... 81 ▢
Roundhedge Wy ENC/FH EN2 ...... 212 C ▢
Roundhills WAB EN9 .... 215 ▢
The Roundings HERT/BAY SG13 ... 152 ▢
Roundmoor Dr CHES/WCR EN8 ... 197 ▢
The Roundway WATW WD18 .... 12 ▢
Roundwood HHS/BOV HP3 .... 185 ▢
Roundwood Cl HTCHE/RSTV SG4 .. 41 ▢
  WLYN AL6 .... 122 ▢
Roundwood Dr WCCW AL8 .... 147 ▢
Roundwood Gdns HARP AL5 .... 118 ▢
Roundwood La HARP AL5 .... 117 ▢
Roundwood Pk HARP AL5 .... 118 ▢
Rounton Rd WAB EN9 .... 215 ▢
Rosebarn La RKW/CH/CXG WD3 .. 202 ▢
Rowan Cl HTCHE/RSTV SG4 .... 59 ▢
  LCOL/BKTW AL2 .... 205 ▢
  LTN LU1 .... 89 ▢
  STALE/WH AL4 .... 169 ▢
Rowan Crs LWTH SG6 .... 41 ▢
  STVG SG1 .... 2 ▢
Rowan Dr BROX EN10 .... 197 ▢
Rowan Gv HTCHE/RSTV SG4 .... 56 ▢
Rowans WGCE AL7 .... 123 ▢
The Rowans BLDK SG7 .... 42 ▢
  BROX EN10 .... 176 ▢
  HHW HP1 .... 163 k ▢
Rowan Wk SBW CM21 .... 132 ▢
Rowan Wy HARP AL5 .... 143 ▢
Rowcroft HHW HP1 .... 163 ▢
Rowelfield LTNE LU2 .... 70 ▢
Rowington Cl LTNE LU2 .... 71 ▢
Rowland Rd STVG SG1 .... 2 ▢
Rowlands Av PIN HA5 .... 231 ▢
Rowlands Cl CHES/WCR EN8 ...... 197 ▢
Rowland Wy LWTH SG6 .... 41 k ▢
Rowlatt Dr STALW/RED AL3 .... 168 ▢
Rowley Cl OXHEY WD19 .... 13 F ▢
Rowley Green Rd BAR EN5 .... 225 ▢
Rowley La BAR EN5 .... 224 ▢
  BORE WD6 .... 224 ▢
Rowley's Rd HERT/BAY SG13 ...... 151 ▢
Rowley Wk HHNE HP2 .... 165 k ▢
Rowney Gdns SBW CM21 .... 157 ▢
Rowney La WARE SG12 .... 100 ▢
Rowney Wd SBW CM21 .... 132 ▢
Royal Av CHES/WCR EN8 .... 214 ▢
Royal Cl HHS/BOV HP3 .... 185 ▢
Royal Oak Cl BUNT SG9 .... 47 ▢
Royal Oak Gdns BSF CM23 .... 105 ▢
Royal Oak La HTCH/STOT SG5 ..... 39 ▢
Royal Rd STAL AL1 .... 168 ▢
Royce Cl BROX EN10 .... 176 L ▢
Roydon Cl HHNE HP2 .... 141 ▢
Roydon Rd HLWW/ROY CM19 ...... 155 ▢
  WARE SG12 .... 153 ▢

oyle Cl CFSP/GDCR SL9 ... 226 C6
oy Rd NTHWD HA6 ... 230 A6
Gose Gv ROY SG8 ... 21 H5
oyston Cl STALE/WH SG14 ... 150 E3 🖬
oyston Gv PIN HA5 ... 231 D5
oyston Park Rd PIN HA5 ... 231 C5
oyston Rd BLDK SG7 ... 27 G8
  ROY SG8 ... 23 F6
  ROY SG8 ... 32 C4
  STAL AL1 ... 168 E7
ucklers La KGLGY WD4 ... 184 E6
uckles Cl STVG SG1 ... 2 C3
udd Cl STVGE SG2 ... 3 F5
udham Cl LWTH SG6 ... 42 C6 🖬
udolph Rd BUSH WD23 ... 221 H6
udyard Cl LTNW/LEA LU4 ... 68 C6
ue De St Lawrence WAB EN9 ... 215 H4 🖬
ugley Dell Rd LTNE LU2 ... 53 K7
ugby Wy RKW/CH/CXG WD3 ... 219 C5
he Ruins STALW/RED AL3 ... 142 C4
umballs Rd HHS/BOV HP3 ... 186 A1
umbold Rd HOD EN11 ... 177 H1
umsley CHESW EN7 ... 196 E5
uncie Cl STALE/WH AL4 ... 168 D2
uncorn Crs HHNE HP2 ... 8 C1
undells HLWS CM18 ... 180 D5
  LWTH SG6 ... 42 D5
unfold Av LTNW/LIM LU3 ... 69 F4
unham Cl LTNW/LEA LU4 ... 68 A5
unham Rd HHS/BOV HP3 ... 164 D8
unley Rd LTN LU1 ... 88 E2
unnalow LWTH SG6 ... 41 H2
unsley WCCE AL7 ... 45 G...
uscombe Dr LCOL/BKTW AL2 ... 188 E4 🖬
ushall Gn LTNE LU2 ... 70 E7
ushby Md LWTH SG6 ... 42 A4
ushby Pl LWTH SG6 ... 42 A3
ushby Wy LWTH SG6 ... 42 A3
ush Cl WARE SG12 ... 153 H5
ushden Rd LTNN SG9 ... 45 K1
ushendon Furlong LBUZ LU7 ... 110 E4 🖬
ushen Dr HERT/BAY SG13 ... 152 B6
ushes Md HLWS CM18 ... 7 D6
ushfield POTB/CUF EN6 ... 209 J3
  SBW CM21 ... 132 C7 🖬
ushfield Rd WARE SG12 ... 127 K6 🖬
ush La RBSF CM22 ... 87 H1
ushleigh Av CHES/WCR EN8 ... 197 H8
ushleigh Gn BSF CM23 ... 105 G5
ushmere La HHNE HP5 ... 182 C6
ushmoor Cl RKW/CH/CXG WD3 ... 228 C1 🖬
ushton Av GSTN WD25 ... 204 B5
ushton Gv HLWE CM17 ... 181 C5
uskin Av WAB EN9 ... 215 K4
uskin Cl LHTCE/RSTV SG4 ... 196 C4
uskin La HTCHE/RSTV SG4 ... 57 C2
usper Gn LTNE LU2 ... 70 E1
ussell Av STALW/RED AL3 ... 10 C4
ussell Cl AMS HP6 ... 216 A1
  DUN/WHIP LU6 ... 114 C1
  NTHWD HA6 ... 229 H4
  ROY SG8 ... 15 J7
  STVGE SG2 ... 3 F5
ussell Ct LCOL/BKTW AL2 ... 188 C8 🖬
ussell Crs GSTN WD25 ... 204 A5 🖬
ussellcroft Rd WGCW AL8 ... 147 H2
ussell La WAT WD17 ... 203 J6
ussell Pl HHS/BOV HP3 ... 185 F1
ussell Ri LTN LU1 ... 4 B5
ussell Rd EN EN1 ... 213 J8
  NTHWD HA6 ... 229 H4
ussell's Dr CHES/WCR EN8 ... 214 D1 🖬
ussell's Ride CHES/WCR EN8 ... 214 C1
ussell St HERT/WAS SG14 ... 151 F5
  LTN LU1 ... 4 B5
ussell Wy OXHEY WD19 ... 12 C6
usset Cl CHESW EN7 ... 196 C4 🖬
usset Dr RAD WD7 ... 207 H2
  STALE/WH AL4 ... 169 F7
he Russets CFSP/GDCR SL9 ... 226 A8 🖬
ussett Wd WCCE AL7 ... 148 C4
utherford Cl BORE WD6 ... 224 B2
  STVG SG1 ... 75 F3
utherford Wy BUSH WD23 ... 222 A8
uthin Cl LTN LU2 ... 4 B6
uthven Av CHES/WCR EN8 ... 214 C3
utland Crs LTNE LU2 ... 5 E4
he Rutts BUSH WD23 ... 222 A8
yall Cl LCOL/BKTW AL2 ... 188 A7
yan Wy WATN WD24 ... 220 D1
ydal Wy LTNN/LIM LU3 ... 68 E4
yder Rd HTCH/STOT SG5 ... 40 B6
yder Cl BUSH WD23 ... 221 J6
  HERT/BAY SG13 ... 152 A2
  HHS/BOV HP3 ... 183 J6
yders Av STALE/WH AL4 ... 170 D6
he Ryde BRKMPK AL9 ... 171 H1
Rye Cl HARP AL5 ... 118 D5 🖬
yecroft HAT AL10 ... 170 E6 🖬
  HLWW/ROY CM19 ... 6 A1
  STVG SG1 ... 2 C1
Ryecroft Cl HHNE HP2 ... 9 F6 🖬
yecroft Crs BAR EN5 ... 225 G5
yecroft Wy LTNE LU2 ... 70 B6

Ryefield Cl HOD EN11 ... 153 G7
Ryefield LTNN/LIM LU3 ... 52 A8 🖬
Ryefield Crs NTHWD HA6 ... 230 B8 🖬
Rye Gdns BLDK SG7 ... 27 H8 🖬
Rye Hl HARP AL5 ... 118 D5
Rye Hill Rd HLWS CM18 ... 180 A6
Ryelands WGCE AL7 ... 148 A6 🖬
Rye Rd HOD EN11 ... 153 J8
Rye St BSF CM23 ... 85 J8
Rylands Heath LTNE LU2 ... 71 G7
Rymill Cl HHS/BOV HP3 ... 183 J6
Ryton Cl LTN LU1 ... 89 G2

S

Saberton Cl STALW/RED AL3 ... 142 A5
Sacombe Gn LTNN/LIM LU3 ... 52 B8
Sacombe Green Rd WARE SG12 ... 99 H5
Sacombe Pound WARE SG12 ... 99 G3
Sacombe Rd HERT/WAS SG14 ... 125 K5
  HHW HP1 ... 163 J4
Scombs Ash La SBW CM21 ... 131 G2
Saddlers Cl BLDK SG7 ... 42 E1 🖬
  BORE WD6 ... 224 C5 🖬
  PIN HA5 ... 231 H4
Saddlers Pl ROY SG8 ... 21 G2 🖬
Sadleir Rd STAL AL1 ... 11 D6
Sadlers Md HLWS CM18 ... 7 F5
Sadlers Wy HERT/WAS SG14 ... 151 J7 🖬
Sadlier Cl STDN SG11 ... 81 J7 🖬
Saffron Cl ARL/CHE SG15 ... 24 E2
  HOD EN11 ... 176 E2
  LTNE LU2 ... 69 J2 🖬
  LTNE LU2 ... 69 J8 🖬
Saffron Hl LWTH SG6 ... 41 J3
Saffron La HHW HP1 ... 164 A5 🖬
Saffron Mdw STDN SG11 ... 81 K7
Saffron St ROY SG8 ... 21 K4
Sainfoin End HHNE HP2 ... 9 D3 🖬
St Agnells Ct HHNE HP2 ... 9 D1
St Agnells La HHNE HP2 ... 164 E1 🖬
St Albans Dr STVG SG1 ... 58 E8
St Albans Hl HHS/BOV HP3 ... 185 J1
St Albans La ABLGY WD5 ... 187 F4
St Albans Link STVG SG1 ... 58 C6 🖬
St Albans Rd BAR EN5 ... 225 K1
  GSTN WD25 ... 204 D6
  HARP AL5 ... 143 J3
  HHNE HP2 ... 8 C6 🖬
  HHS/BOV HP3 ... 8 A6
  POTB/CUF EN6 ... 208 D1
  STALE/WH AL4 ... 168 D2
  STALW/RED AL3 ... 142 D5
  WAT WD17 ... 12 C1
  WATN WD24 ... 204 C8
  WLYN AL6 ... 121 J3
St Albans Rd East HAT AL10 ... 171 G3
St Albans Rd West HAT AL10 ... 170 B4
St Andrew's Av HARP AL5 ... 118 B8 🖬
St Andrew's Cl LTN LU1 ... 89 H8
St Andrews Dr STVG SG1 ... 59 F6
St Andrew's Pl HTCHE/RSTV SG4 ... 56 D1 🖬
St Andrew's Rd HHS/BOV HP3 ... 185 H2 🖬
St Andrew St HERT/WAS SG14 ... 151 F5
St Anna Rd BAR EN5 ... 225 J5 🖬
St Anne's Cl CHESW EN7 ... 196 E6 🖬
  OXHEY WD19 ... 230 D3
St Anne's Pk BROX EN10 ... 177 F6
St Anne's Rd HTCH/STOT SG5 ... 56 D1 🖬
  LCOL/BKTW AL2 ... 190 B5
St Ann's Rd LTN LU1 ... 5 D4
St Anthonys Av HHS/BOV HP3 ... 165 J8
St Audreys Cl HAT AL10 ... 171 G7
St Audreys Gn WGCE AL7 ... 148 A4
St Augusta Ct STALW/RED AL3 ... 10 C2 🖬
St Augustine Av LTNN/LIM LU3 ... 69 G6
St Augustine Cl HTCH/STOT SG5 ... 56 D1 🖬
St Augustines Cl BROX EN10 ... 176 E6 🖬
St Augustines Dr BROX EN10 ... 176 E6
St Bernard's Cl LTNN/LIM LU3 ... 69 H6
St Bernard's Rd STALW/RED AL3 ... 10 C1
St Catharine's Av LTNN/LIM LU3 ... 69 G5
St Catharine's Cl HOD EN11 ... 177 F5
St Catherines Av LTNN/LIM LU3 ... 69 G5
St Cross Cl HOD EN11 ... 177 F5 🖬
St Cuthberts Gdns PIN HA5 ... 231 G6 🖬
St Cuthberts Rd HOD EN11 ... 153 H8
St David's Cl HHS/BOV HP3 ... 165 J8
  STVG SG1 ... 59 F6
St David's Dr BROX EN10 ... 176 E6
St Dunstan's Rd WARE SG12 ... 154 E1 🖬
St Edmunds BERK HP4 ... 161 K6
St Edmunds Wk STALE/WH AL4 ... 169 G7 🖬
St Edmund's Wy HLWE CM17 ... 157 F5 🖬
St Elmo Cl HTCHE/RSTV SG4 ... 56 D4 🖬
St Ethelbert Av LTNN/LIM LU3 ... 69 G5
St Etheldreda's Dr HAT AL10 ... 171 H4 🖬
St Faiths Cl HTCHE/RSTV SG4 ... 41 J1
St Francis Cl BUNT SG9 ... 63 K3
  OXHEY WD19 ... 220 D3 🖬
  POTB/CUF EN6 ... 210 D3
St George's Dr OXHEY WD19 ... 231 F2
St George's Rd EN EN1 ... 213 J8

  HHS/BOV HP3 ... 185 G2 🖬
  WATN WD24 ... 204 C7 🖬
  WATN WD24 ... 204 C8 🖬
St George's Wy STVG SG1 ... 2 B3
St Giles' Av POTB/CUF EN6 ... 209 F3
St Giles Rd HTCHE/RSTV SG4 ... 94 E7
St Helen's Cl STALE/WH AL4 ... 145 G1 🖬
St Heliers Rd STALE/WH AL4 ... 168 E1
St Ives Cl LTNN/LIM LU3 ... 69 G6
  WLYN AL6 ... 123 F6
St James Rd HARP AL5 ... 118 D6
  LTNN/LIM LU3 ... 69 G6
  WATW WD18 ... 12 C4
St James's Rd CHESW EN7 ... 196 A6
St James Wy BSF CM23 ... 104 E4
St John Cl LTN LU1 ... 89 G4
St Johns STDN SG11 ... 81 K6
St John's Av HLWE CM17 ... 157 F5
St John's Cl POTB/CUF EN6 ... 210 D3
  WLYN AL6 ... 122 C3
St John's Ct HARP AL5 ... 143 K2 🖬
  STAL AL1 ... 168 E5
St John's Crs STSD CM24 ... 86 D2
St John's La STSD CM24 ... 86 D2 🖬
  WARE SG12 ... 153 F3
St John's Rd ARL/CHE SG15 ... 24 E5
  HARP AL5 ... 143 K2
  HHW HP1 ... 164 A8
  HTCHE/RSTV SG4 ... 56 D4 🖬
  STSD CM24 ... 86 D2
  WAT WD17 ... 12 C1
St John's Ter ENC/FH EN2 ... 213 G1 🖬
St Johns Wk HLWE CM17 ... 157 F5 🖬
St John's Well Cl BERK HP4 ... 161 J4 🖬
St John's Well La BERK HP4 ... 161 J4
St Joseph's Cl LTNN/LIM LU3 ... 69 F5
St Julian's Rd STAL AL1 ... 10 C6
St Katharines Cl HTCH/STOT SG5 ... 40 B6
St Katherine's Wy BERK HP4 ... 161 G2
St Laurence Dr BROX EN10 ... 197 J1
St Lawrence Cl ABLGY WD5 ... 186 E8
  HHS/BOV HP3 ... 183 J5
St Lawrences Av LTNN/LIM LU3 ... 69 H5
St Lawrence Wy LCOL/BKTW AL2 ... 188 C8 🖬
St Leonards Cl BUSH WD23 ... 13 F3 🖬
  HERT/WAS SG14 ... 151 H1 🖬
St Leonard's Ct STALE/WH AL4 ... 145 F8 🖬
St Leonards Crs STALE/WH AL4 ... 145 F8
St Leonard's Rd HERT/WAS SG14 ... 151 G1 🖬
  WAB EN9 ... 198 D2
St Luke's Av ENC/FH EN2 ... 213 G8
St Luke's Cl LTNW/LEA LU4 ... 68 D7
St Margarets STVGE SG2 ... 3 D6
St Margarets Av LTNN/LIM LU3 ... 69 G5
St Margaret's Cl BERK HP4 ... 162 A6
St Margaret's Rd WARE SG12 ... 153 F7
St Margarets Wy HHNE HP2 ... 165 J6 🖬
St Marks Cl STALE/WH AL4 ... 170 A8
St Martin's Av LTNE LU2 ... 5 D1
St Martins Cl HARP AL5 ... 118 C5 🖬
  OXHEY WD19 ... 230 D3 🖬
St Martin's Rd KNEB SG3 ... 96 B4
St Mary's Av BERK HP4 ... 160 E3
  HTCH/STOT SG5 ... 25 K3
  NTHWD HA6 ... 229 K4
St Mary's Cl HTCH/STOT SG5 ... 39 F5 🖬
  LWTH SG6 ... 41 K7
  STALW/RED AL3 ... 142 B4
  STVGE SG2 ... 77 F7
  WLYN AL6 ... 122 C3
St Mary's Dr STSD CM24 ... 86 D2
St Mary's La HERT/WAS SG14 ... 150 C5
St Mary's Ri HTCHE/RSTV SG4 ... 72 A8
St Mary's Rd CHES/WCR EN8 ... 197 G7
  HHNE HP2 ... 8 A4
  LTN LU1 ... 4 C4
  STDN SG11 ... 81 J7
  WATW WD18 ... 12 C3
St Marys Wk STALE/WH AL4 ... 168 E2
St Mary's Wy BLDK SG7 ... 42 E3
  CFSP/GDCR SL9 ... 226 A8
St Matthews Cl LTNE LU2 ... 4 C3 🖬
  OXHEY WD19 ... 13 E5 🖬
St Michael's Av HHS/BOV HP3 ... 9 G6 🖬
  HHS/BOV HP3 ... 165 G8 🖬
St Michael's Cl HLW CM20 ... 7 D3 🖬
St Michael's Crs LTNN/LIM LU3 ... 69 H6
St Michaels Dr GSTN WD25 ... 204 C3
St Michael's Mt HTCHE/RSTV SG4 ... 56 E1 🖬
St Michael's Rd BROX EN10 ... 176 E6
  HTCHE/RSTV SG4 ... 57 F1
St Michael's St STALW/RED AL3 ... 10 A4
St Michaels Wy POTB/CUF EN6 ... 193 H8 🖬
St Mildreds Av LTNN/LIM LU3 ... 69 G5
St Monicas Av LTNN/LIM LU3 ... 69 G6
St Neots Cl BORE WD6 ... 207 K8 🖬
St Nicholas Av HARP AL5 ... 118 C8
St Nicholas Cl BORE WD6 ... 223 C6
St Nicholas Fld BSF CM23 ... 67 K1
St Nicholas Mt HHW HP1 ... 163 J6
St Olam's Cl LTNN/LIM LU3 ... 69 G3 🖬
St Olives HTCH/STOT SG5 ... 25 J3
St Pauls Pl STAL AL1 ... 11 F4

St Paul's Rd *HHNE* HP2.................. 8 B4
  LTN LU1 .... 4 C6
St Pauls Wy *WAB* EN9 .... 215 J5 ▣
  WATN WD24 .... 13 D1 ▣
St Peter's Av *ARL/CHE* SG15 .... 24 E2
St Peter's Cl *BAR* EN5 .... 225 G5
  BUSH WD23............................ 222 A8
  HAT AL10 .... 171 F3 ▣
  RKW/CH/CXG WD3 .... 228 A1
  STALW/RED AL3 .... 10 C3
St Peters Hl *TRING* HP23 .... 135 F5
St Peters Rd *LTN* LU1 .... 89 G2
  STAL AL1 .... 11 D4
St Peter's St *STAL* AL1 .... 10 C3
St Peters Wy *RKW/CH/CXG* WD3 216 E4
St Ronans Cl *EBAR* EN4 .... 210 E8
St Saviours's Crs *LTN* LU1............ 4 B5
St Stephen's Av *STALW/RED* AL3 ... 10 A6
St Stephen's Cl *STALW/RED* AL3 188 D1 ▣
St Stephen's Hl *STAL* AL1 .... 10 B6
St Stephens Rd *BAR* EN5 .... 225 J5
  PEND EN3 .... 214 C7
St Thomas' Dr *PIN* HA5 .... 231 F7
St Thomas Pl *STALE/WH* AL4 ... 145 G1
St Vincent Dr *STAL* AL1 .... 11 F6
St Vincent's Wy *POTB/CUF* EN6 210 D3 ▣
St Winifreds Av *LTN/LIM* LU3 ...... 69 H5
St Yon Ct *STALE/WH* AL4 .... 169 G6
Sakins Cft *HLWS* CM18 .... 180 C4
Sale Dr *BLDK* SG7...................... 27 F8
Salisbury Av *HARP* AL5 .... 118 B7
  STAL AL1 .... 168 E5
Salisbury Cl *BAR* CM23 .... 105 J3
  POTB/CUF EN6.......................... 210 D2
Salisbury Crs *CHES/WCR* EN8 ... 214 C2
Salisbury Gdns *WCCE* AL7 .... 148 A4
Salisbury Rd *BAR* EN5............... 225 K3
  BLDK SG7 .... 26 E8
  HARP AL5............................... 119 F6
  HOD EN11 .... 177 H2
  LTN LU1 .... 4 B5
  PEND EN3 .... 214 E7
  STVG SG1 .... 59 G7
  WATN WD24 .... 204 C8
  WCCE AL7 .... 148 A4
Salisbury Rd *HERT/WAS* SG14 ... 151 G3 ▣▣
Sally Deards La *WLYN* AL6 .... 95 G5
Salmon Cl *WCCE* AL7 .... 123 C8
Salmons Cl *WARE* SG12 .... 127 H6
Saltdean Cl *LTNE* LU2 .... 70 E5
Salters *BSF* CM23 .... 105 F5
Salter's Cl *BERK* HP4 .... 161 G3 ▣
  RKW/CH/CXG WD3................ 218 D8
Saltfield Crescent *LTNN/LEA* LU4... 68 B5
Salusbury La *HTCH/STOT* SG5 .... 54 E7
Salwey Crs *BROX* EN10............. 176 E6
Samian Ga *STALW/RED* AL3 ...... 167 G8
Sampson Av *BAR* EN5 .... 225 J5
Sanctuary Cl *DEN/HRF* UB9 ...... 228 B6
Sandalls Spring *HHW* HP1 .... 163 J4
Sandalwood Cl *LTNN/LIM* LU3 ... 69 G2 ▣
Sanday Cl *HHS/BOV* HP3 .... 165 H3
Sandbrook La *TRING* HP23 .... 109 G8
Sandell Cl *LTNE* LU2.................... 5 D1
Sanderling Cl *LWTH* SG6............ 41 J1
Sanders Cl *LCOL/BKTW* AL2 ...... 190 B5
Sanders Rd *HHS/BOV* HP3 .... 185 K1
Sandfield Rd *STAL* AL1 .... 11 F4
Sandgate Rd *LTNW/LEA* LU4 ...... 68 C7
Sandhurst Ct *HARP* AL5 .... 144 A3 ▣
Sandifield *HAT* AL10 .... 171 C7
Sand La *AMP/FLIT/B* MK45 .... 36 B2
Sandle Rd *BSF* CM23................. 105 K2
Sandmere Cl *HHNE* HP2.............. 9 D6 ▣
Sandon Cl *TRING* HP23 .... 134 E5
Sandon Rd *CHES/WCR* EN8 ...... 197 G8
Sandover Cl *HTCHE/RSTV* SG4 ... 57 F3
Sandown Rd *STVG* SG1............... 59 J8
  WATN WD24 .... 204 D8
Sandpit La *STAL* AL1 .... 11 E3
Sandpit Rd *WCGE* AL7 .... 147 K5
Sandridgebury La
  STALW/RED AL3 .... 144 E7
Sandridge Cl *HHNE* HP2 .... 141 F8
Sandridge Rd *STAL* AL1 .... 11 D2
Sandringham Av
  HLWW/ROY CM19 .... 179 F1
Sandringham Crs *STALE/WH* AL4 168 D2
Sandringham Rd
  POTB/CUF EN6........................ 193 H8 ▣
  WATN WD24 .... 204 C2
Sandringham Wy *CHES/WCR* EN8 214 B4
Sandy Cl *HERT/WAS* SG14......... 150 C5
Sandy Gv *HTCHE/RSTV* SG4 .... 56 D3
Sandy La *BUSH* WD23................ 221 K3
  NTHWD HA6.......................... 230 A1
Sandy Lodge La *NTHWD* HA6 ... 229 J1
Sandy Lodge Rd
  RKW/CH/CXG WD3 .... 229 G1
Sandy Lodge Wy *NTHWD* HA6.. 229 K4
Sandy Ri *CFSP/GDCR* SL9 .... 226 B7
Sanfoine Cl *HTCHE/RSTV* SG4 .... 57 J7
Santers La *POTB/CUF* EN6 .... 209 K3
Santingfield North *LTN* LU1 .... 89 G3
Santingfield South *LTN* LU1 .... 89 G4

Sappers Cl *SBW* CM21.............. 132 D7
Saracens Head *HHNE* HP2 .... 9 D4 ▣
Sarratt Av *HHNE* HP2................ 165 F1
Sarratt La *RKW/CH/CXG* WD3 ... 218 A2
Sarratt Rd *RKW/CH/CXG* WD3 ... 202 A7
Sarum Pl *HHNE* HP2.................... 8 B1
Sarum Rd *LTNN/LIM* LU3 .... 68 D5
Satinwood Ct *HHS/BOV* HP3 .... 164 D8 ▣
Saturn Wy *HHNE* HP2.................. 8 C2
Sauncey Av *HARP* AL5 .... 118 D6
Sauncey Wd *HARP* AL5.............. 119 D5
Sauncey Wood La *HARP* AL5 .... 119 G4
Saunders Cl *CHES/WCR* EN8 .... 197 G6
  LWTH SG6 .... 42 B2
Savill Cl *CHESW* EN7................. 196 A3 ▣
Saville Cl *SAFWS* CB11 .... 51 K5
Savoy Cl *DEN/HRF* UB9............ 228 C8
Savoy Wd *EPP* CM16 .... 179 J7 ▣
Sawbridgeworth Rd *RBSF* CM22 133 F4
  SBW CM21.............................. 133 C6
Sawells *BROX* EN10.................. 176 E7
Sawtry Cl *LTNN/LIM* LU3............ 69 F3
Sawtry Wy *BORE* WD6 .... 207 K8 ▣
Sawyers La *POTB/CUF* EN6 ...... 209 J4
Sawyers Wy *HHNE* HP2 .... 8 C5 ▣
Saxon Av *HTCH/STOT* SG5 .... 25 K1
Saxon Cl *HARP* AL5 .... 118 E5
  LWTH SG6 .... 25 K8
Saxon Ct *BORE* WD6 .... 223 H1 ▣
Saxon Crs *AMP/FLIT/B* MK45 ...... 36 C5
Saxon Rd *LTNN/LIM* LU3............ 69 C7
  STALE/WH AL4 .... 145 G2
  WLYN AL6 .... 122 B6
Saxon Wy *BLDK* SG7 .... 27 H8
Saxtead Cl *LTNE* LU2.................. 70 E8
Sayers Gdns *BERK* HP4............. 161 H2
Sayer Wy *KNEB* SG3 .... 96 A5
Sayesbury Av *SBW* CM21.......... 132 B6
Sayesbury Rd *SBW* CM21......... 132 C7
Sayes Gdns *SBW* CM21............ 132 D7
Saywell Rd *LTNE* LU2 .... 5 F2
Scammell Wy *WATW* WD18 .... 12 A5
Scarborough Av *STVG* SG1.......... 75 F3
Scatterdells La *KGLGY* WD4...... 184 D8
Scholar's Hl *WARE* SG12........... 129 F5
Scholars Ms *WGCW* AL8 .... 147 J2
Scholars Wk *CFSP/GDCR* SL9 ... 226 B5
School Cl *BRKMPK* AL9.............. 173 G3 ▣
  STVGE SG2.............................. 3 F5
Schoolfields *LWTH* SG6.............. 42 C4
School La *BRKMPK* AL9............. 173 G3
  BUSH WD23............................ 221 J7
  CFSP/GDCR SL9..................... 226 A7
  HAT AL10 .... 171 G3
  HERT/WAS SG14 .... 98 B6
  HLW CM20............................. 7 D1
  HTCH/STOT SG5 .... 54 E7
  HTCHE/RSTV SG4 .... 73 H3
  LCOL/BKTW AL2 .... 205 G4
  LTNW/LEA LU4 .... 68 A6
  ROY SG8 .... 23 G8
  SAFWS CB11 .... 35 J2
  STVGE SG2.............................. 61 H6
  STVGE SG2.............................. 77 F7
  WLYN AL6 .... 122 B6
  WLYN AL6 .... 124 A8
School Md *ABLGY* WD5 .... 203 J2
School Rd *POTB/CUF* EN6 .... 193 J8
School Rw *HHW* HP1 .... 163 J7
School Wk *LWTH* SG6 .... 42 B3
Schubert Rd *BORE* WD6 .... 223 C6
Scot Gv *PIN* HA5 .... 230 E6
Scotscraig *RAD* WD7.................. 206 C5
Scots Hl *RKW/CH/CXG* WD3 ...... 218 E6
Scots Hill Cl *RKW/CH/CXG* WD3 218 E6
Scots Mill La *RKW/CH/CXG* WD3 218 E6
Scott Av *WARE* SG12 .... 153 C5
Scott Rd *BSF* CM23................... 105 H3
  LTN LU3 .... 4 B6
  STVGE SG2.............................. 3 F2
Scotts Cl *WARE* SG12............... 152 C1
Scott's Rd *WARE* SG12............. 152 C1
Scotts Vw *WGCW* AL8............... 147 H4
Scottswood Cl *BUSH* WD23 ...... 13 F1 ▣
Scottswood Rd *BUSH* WD23 ...... 13 F1
Scriveners Cl *HHNE* HP2............. 8 B5
Scrubbits Sq *RAD* WD7 .... 206 D5 ▣
Scrubbitts Park Rd *RAD* WD7 ... 206 D5
Seabrook *LTNW/LEA* LU4 .... 68 A6
Seabrook Rd *KGLGY* WD4......... 186 A6
Seacroft Gdns *OXHEY* WD19 .... 230 E2
Seaford Cl *LTNE* LU2.................. 70 C6
Seaforth Dr *CHES/WCR* EN8 .... 214 C4
Seal Cl *LTNN/LEA* LU4 .... 68 C6
Seaman Cl *LCOL/BKTW* AL2 ..... 189 F3
Searches La *ABLGY* WD5........... 187 H5
  HHS/BOV HP3 .... 187 J5
Seaton Rd *HHS/BOV* HP3.......... 185 H1
  LCOL/BKTW AL2 .... 190 B5
  LTNN/LEA LU4....................... 68 E2
Sebright Rd *BAR* EN5................ 225 J2 ▣
  HHW HP1................................ 163 K8
  STALW/RED AL3 .... 115 J4
Secker Crs *KTN/HRWW/W* HA3 ... 231 K7

Second Av *GSTN* WD25.............. 204 ▣
  HLWE CM17............................ 180 ▣
  HLWS CM18............................... 7 ▣
  LWTH SG6 .... 42 ▣
Sedbury Cl *LTNN/LIM* LU3........... 69 ▣
Sedge Gn *HLWW/ROY* CM19 .... 178 ▣
  WAB EN9 .... 177 ▣
Sedgwick Rd *LTNW/LEA* LU4 ..... 68 ▣
Seebohm Cl *HTCH/STOT* SG5 ... 40 ▣
Seeleys *HLWE* CM17 .... 157 ▣
Sefton Cl *STAL* AL1 .... 11 E3
Sefton Rd *STVG* SG1 .... 59 H▣
Selbourne Rd *LTNW/LEA* LU4.... 68 ▣
Selby Av *STALW/RED* AL3 .... 10 C4
Selden Hl *HHNE* HP2.................... 8 ▣
Sele Ml *HERT/WAS* SG14 .... 150 E3
Sele Rd *HERT/WAS* SG14.......... 150 ▣
Selina Cl *LTNN/LIM* LU3.............. 68 ▣
Sells Rd *WARE* SG12................... 127 ▣
Sellwood Dr *BAR* EN5 .... 225 ▣
Selsey Dr *LTNE* LU2 .... 70 ▣
Selwyn Av *HAT* AL10 .... 170 ▣
Selwyn Crs *HAT* AL10 .... 170 ▣
Selwyn Dr *HAT* AL10 .... 170 ▣
Semphill Rd *HHS/BOV* HP3 .... 185 ▣
Senate Pl *STVG* SG1................... 59 ▣
Sequoia Cl *BUSH* WD23 .... 222 A8▣
Sequoia Pk *PIN* HA5................. 231 ▣
Serby Av *ROY* SG8 .... 21 ▣
Sergehill La *ABLGY* WD5 .... 187 ▣
Serpentine Cl *STVG* SG1............. 59 ▣
The Service Rd *POTB/CUF* EN6 .. 210 ▣
Seven Acres *NTHWD* HA6.......... 230 E▣
The Severalls *LTNE* LU2 .... 70 C6
Severn Dr *EN* EN1...................... 213 ▣
Severnmead *HHNE* HP2................ 8 ▣
Severnvale *LCOL/BKTW* AL2 ..... 190 D5
Severn Wy *GSTN* WD25.............. 204 ▣
Sewardstone Rd *WAB* EN9 .... 215 ▣
Sewardstone St *WAB* EN9 .... 215 ▣
Sewardstone Wy *WAB* EN9 .... 215 ▣
Sewell Cl *STALE/WH* AL4............ 169 ▣
Sewell Harris Cl *HLW* CM20 .... 7 ▣
Sewells *WGCW* AL8 .... 122 ▣
Sexton Cl *CHESW* EN7............... 195 K3
Seymour Av *LTN* LU1 .... 5 ▣
Seymour Cl *PIN* HA5 .... 231 ▣
Seymour Crs *HHNE* HP2.............. 8 ▣
Seymour Rd *BERK* HP4.............. 161 ▣
  LTN LU1 .... 5 ▣
  STALW/RED AL3 .... 11 ▣
Seymours *HLWW/ROY* CM19 ... 179 ▣
Shackledell *STVGE* SG2................ 3 ▣
Shacklegate La *HTCHE/RSTV* SG4 ... 93 ▣
Shackleton Spring *STVGE* SG2...... 3 ▣
Shackleton Wy *ABLGY* WD5 ..... 204 B2▣
  WGCE AL7 .... 148 ▣
Shady Bush Cl *BUSH* WD23 ...... 221 K7
Shady La *WAT* WD17 .... 12 C1
Shaftenbre End Rd *ROY* SG8 ...... 23 ▣
Shaftesbury Rd *LTNW/LEA* LU4... 89 ▣
  WAT WD17 .... 13 D2
Shaftesbury Wy *ROY* SG8 .... 21 ▣
Shakespeare Rd *HARP* AL5 .... 118 ▣
  LTNW/LEA LU4....................... 68 ▣
Shakespeare St *WATN* WD24 .... 204 ▣
Shalcross Dr *CHES/WCR* EN8..... 197 ▣
Shallcross Crs *HAT* AL10 .... 170 ▣
Shambrook Rd *CHESW* EN7....... 195 ▣
Shangani Rd *BSF* CM23 .... 105 ▣
Shanklin Cl *CHESW* EN7............ 196 ▣
  LTNN/LIM LU3........................ 69 ▣
Shanklin Gdns *OXHEY* WD19 ... 230 ▣
Shantock Hall La *HHS/BOV* HP3 ... 183 ▣
Shantock La *HHS/BOV* HP3 .... 183 ▣
Sharmans Cl *WLYN* AL6............. 123 ▣
Sharose Ct *STALW/RED* AL3 ...... 115 ▣
Sharpcroft *HHNE* HP2................. 8 A3 ▣
Sharpecroft *HLWW/ROY* CM19 .... 6 ▣
Sharpenhoe Rd *AMP/FLIT/B* MK45 ... 36 ▣
  LTNN/LIM LU3........................ 52 ▣
Sharpes La *HHW* HP1 .... 162 ▣
Sharples Cl *LTNN/LIM* LU3 .... 69 ▣
Sharps Wy *HTCHE/RSTV* SG4...... 56 ▣
Shawbridge *HLWW/ROY* CM19 .. 179 ▣
Shaw Cl *CHES/WCR* EN8............ 197 ▣
The Shaws *WGCE* AL7............... 148 ▣
The Shearers *BSF* CM23 .... 104 ▣
Sheares Hoppit *WARE* SG12...... 129 ▣
Shearwater Cl *STVGE* SG2 .... 76 ▣
Sheepcot Dr *GSTN* WD25 .... 204 ▣
Sheepcote *WGCE* AL7 .... 148 ▣
Sheepcote La *STALE/WH* AL4 .... 120 ▣
Sheepcote Rd *HHNE* HP2............ 8 C5
Sheepcot La *GSTN* WD25 .... 204 ▣
Sheepcroft Hl *STVGE* SG2 .... 76 ▣
Sheephouse Rd *HHS/BOV* HP3 .. 164 ▣
Sheering Dr *HLWE* CM17 .... 157 ▣
Sheering Lower Rd *SBW* CM21... 157 ▣
Sheering Mill La *SBW* CM21....... 132 ▣
Sheering Rd *HLWE* CM17........... 157 ▣
Sheethanger La *HHS/BOV* HP3 .. 184 ▣
Shefton Ri *NTHWD* HA6 .... 230 ▣
Sheldon Cl *CHESW* EN7............. 196 ▣

HLWE CM17 .... 181 H1
helford Rd *BAR* EN5 .... 225 H6
helley Cl *HTCHE/RSTV* SC4 .... 57 C2
   NTHWD HA6 .... 230 A4
helley La *DEN/HRF* UB9 .... 227 K6
helton Wy *LTNE* LU2 .... 70 B6
henfield Ct *HLWS* CM18 .... 179 K4 🄳
henleybury *RAD* WD7 .... 190 C8
henleybury Cottages *RAD* WD7 . 207 H1
henley Hl *RAD* WD7 .... 206 E4
henley La *LCOL/BKTW* AL2 .... 189 K3
henley Rd *BORE* WD6 .... 223 K8
   HHNE HP2 .... 141 G8
   RAD WD7 .... 207 C5
henstone Hl *BERK* HP4 .... 162 B4
henwood Cr *BORE* WD6 .... 207 K7 🄳
   BORE WD6 .... 208 A7 🄳
hephall Gn *STVGE* SG2 .... 3 F6
hephall La *STVGE* SG2 .... 76 A8
hephall Vw *STVGE* SG1 .... 3 E3
hephall Wy *STVGE* SG2 .... 3 F4
hepherd La *ROY* SG8 .... 21 J4
hepherds Ct *BSF* CM23 .... 105 F5 🄳
hepherds Gn *HHW* HP1 .... 163 H7 🄳
   HHW HP1 .... 163 H7 🄳
hepherd's La *RKW/CH/CXG* WD3 . 217 G6 🄳
   STVG SG1 .... 74 E3
hepherds Md *HTCH/STOT* SG5 ..... 40 C7
hepherds Rd *WATW* WD18 .... 12 A2
hepherds Wy *BRKMPK* AL9 .... 193 J5
   HARP AL5 .... 117 K5 🄳
   RKW/CH/CXG WD3 .... 218 A7
hepley Ms *HTCH/STOT* SG5 .... 40 C7
heppard Cl *EN* EN1 .... 214 A8
sheppards Cl *STVG* SG1 .... 105 F5 🄳
sheppards La *RKW/ROY* CM19 .... 179 G4
sheppards Pl *STALW/RED* AL3 .... 11 D1
shepperton Cl *BORE* WD6 .... 224 C1 🄳
sheppey's La *KGLY* WD4 .... 186 E6
sheraton Cl *BORE* WD6 .... 223 J5
sherborne Av *LTNE* LU2 .... 69 J3
sherborne Cl *NTHWD* HA6 .... 229 J5
sherborne Wy *RKW/CH/CXG* WD3 . 219 G4
sherbourne Cl *HHS/BOV* HP3 .... 8 B6
sherd Cl *LTNN/LIM* LU3 .... 68 E2
sheredes Dr *HOD* EN11 .... 176 E4 🄳
sherfield Av *RKW/CH/CXG* WD3 .. 228 C2
sheridan Cl *HHW* HP1 .... 164 A7
sheridan Rd *LTNN/LIM* LU3 .... 4 A1 🄳
   OXHEY WD19 .... 13 E6
sheriden Wk *BROX* EN10 .... 176 D6
sheriff Wy *STVGE* SG1 .... 58 B8
sheringham Av *STVG* SG1 .... 58 B8
sheringham Cl *LTNE* LU2 .... 69 H2 🄳
sherington Av *PIN* HA5 .... 231 H6
sherrardspark Rd *WGCW* AL8 ..... 147 J1 🄳
sherwood *LWTH* SG6 .... 41 K1
sherwood Av *POTB/CUF* EN6 .... 209 K2
   STALE/WH AL4 .... 168 E3
sherwood Pl *HHNE* HP2 .... 8 C1 🄳
sherwood Rd *LTNW/LEA* LU4 .... 69 F7
sherwoods Rd *OXHEY* WD19 .... 13 F6
shetland Cl *BORE* WD6 .... 224 C6
shillington Rd *HTCH/STOT* SG5 .... 38 A3
shillitoe Av *POTB/CUF* EN6 .... 209 J2
shingle Cl *LTNN/LIM* LU3 .... 69 F1
shire Cl *BROX* EN10 .... 197 K4 🄳
shire La *CFSP/GDCR* SL9 .... 226 E4
   RKW/CH/CXG WD3 .... 216 C5
   TRING HP23 .... 158 D2
shiremeade *BORE* WD6 .... 223 J5
   ROY SG8 .... 4 B3
shires The *LTNE* LU2 .... 2 A1
   ROY SG8 .... 6 E1
shire Rd *ABLGY* WD5 .... 204 A2
shirley *LTN* LU1 .... 4 A3
   STAL AL1 .... 11 E5
shooters Dr *WAB* EN9 .... 177 K8
shooters Rd *ENC/FH* EN2 .... 212 D8
shootersway *BERK* HP4 .... 160 C3
shootersway La *BERK* HP4 .... 161 G6
shootersway Pk *BERK* HP4 .... 161 G5 🄳
shoplands *WGCW* AL8 .... 122 D8
shoreham Cl *STVG* SG1 .... 75 F1
shortcroft *BSF* CM23 .... 106 C1
shortcroft Ct *AMP/FLIT/B* MK45 ... 36 B7 🄳
shortlands Gn *WGCE* AL7 .... 148 A4 🄳
shortlands Pl *BSF* CM23 .... 105 J1 🄳
short La *LCOL/BKTW* AL2 .... 188 A7
   STVGE SG2 .... 77 F5
shortmead Dr *CHES/WCR* EN8 .. 214 D1
shothanger Wy *HHS/BOV* HP3 ... 184 B3
shottfield Cl *STALE/WH* AL4 .... 145 F7
shott La *LWTH* SG6 .... 42 A3
shott Lower *CHESW* EN7 .... 196 D4
shrubbery Gv *ROY* SG8 .... 21 H5
The Shrubbery *HHW* HP1 .... 163 H5
shrub Hill Rd *HHW* HP1 .... 163 J7
shrublands *BRKMPK* AL9 .... 193 H4
shrublands Av *BERK* HP4 .... 161 H5
shrublands Rd *BERK* HP4 .... 161 H4
The Shrublands *POTB/CUF* EN6 .. 209 K3

Shugars Gn *TRING* HP23 .... 135 G4
Sibley Av *HARP* AL5 .... 144 A2
Sibley Cl *LTNE* LU2 .... 70 C6
Sibneys Gn *HLWS* CM18 .... 180 B5
Sibthorpe Rd *BRKMPK* AL9 .... 192 D2 🄳
Siccut Rd *HTCHE/RSTV* SG4 .... 57 J5
Sicklefield Cl *CHESW* EN7 .... 196 D4 🄳
Siddons Rd *STVGE* SG2 .... 76 D3
Sidford Cl *HHW* HP1 .... 163 J6
The Sidings *BROX* EN10 .... 170 D5 🄳
   HAT AL10 .... 170 D5 🄳
   HHNE HP2 .... 8 A5
Sidmouth Cl *OXHEY* WD19 .... 230 C1
Sidney Ter *BSF* CM23 .... 105 J3
Silam Rd *STVG* SG1 .... 2 C3
Silecroft Cl *LTNE* LU2 .... 5 E3
Silk Mill Rd *OXHEY* WD19 .... 12 C6 🄳
   STALW/RED AL3 .... 142 C5
Silk Mill Wy *TRING* HP23 .... 135 F4
Silverbirch Av *HTCH/STOT* SG5 .... 25 K1
Silverdale Rd *BUSH* WD23 .... 13 F4
Silver Dell *WATN* WD24 .... 204 A5
Silverfield *BROX* EN10 .... 176 E8
Silver Hl *BORE* WD6 .... 208 B6
Silver St *BLDK* SG7 .... 196 B8
   CHESW EN7 .... 4 C4
   LTN LU1 .... 15 C6
   ROY SG8 .... 86 C3
   STSD CM24 .... 86 C3
   WAB EN9 .... 215 H4 🄳
Silverthorn Dr *HHS/BOV* HP3 ..... 186 B2
Silver Trees *LCOL/BKTW* AL2 ..... 188 B3
Silverwood Cl *NTHWD* HA6 .... 229 H7
Simmonds Rl *HHS/BOV* HP3 ...... 164 C8
Simon Dean *HHS/BOV* HP3 .... 183 J5
Simpkins Dr *AMP/FLIT/B* MK45 ... 36 C5
Simpson Cl *LTNW/LEA* LU4 .... 68 C7
Simpson Dr *BLDK* SG7 .... 43 F1
Sinderby Cl *BORE* WD6 .... 223 H4
Sinfield Cl *STVG* SG1 .... 3 E3
Singlets La *STALW/RED* AL3 .... 116 C5
Sir Joseph's Wk *HARP* AL5 .... 143 H1
Sir Peter's Wy *DUN/WHIP* LU6 ... 113 G3
Sirus Rd *NTHWD* HA6 .... 230 B4
Sish Cl *STVG* SG1 .... 2 B2
Sish La *STVG* SG1 .... 2 B2
Siskin Cl *BORE* WD6 .... 223 K4
   BUSH WD23 .... 13 F5 🄳
Sisson Cl *STVGE* SG2 .... 76 D7
Six Acres *HHS/BOV* HP3 .... 186 A1
Six Hills Wy *STVG* SG1 .... 2 A4
Sixth Av *GSTN* WD25 .... 204 E5
   LWTH SG6 .... 42 C3
   STSD CM24 .... 87 H6
Skegness Rd *STVG* SG1 .... 75 F1
Skegsbury La *HTCHE/RSTV* SG4 .. 92 C8
Skelton Cl *LTNN/LIM* LU3 .... 52 B8
Skidmore Wy *RKW/CH/CXG* WD3 . 218 C5
Skimpans Cl *BRKMPK* AL9 .... 192 D2
Skinners Cl *BSF* CM23 .... 105 F5
Skipton Cl *STVG* SG1 .... 96 A1
Skylark Cnr *STVGE* SG2 .... 76 E6
Skys Wood Rd *STALE/WH* AL4 .... 168 E2
Slade Cl *RAD* WD7 .... 206 E2
Sleaford Gn *STALE/WH* AL4 .... 230 E2
Sleapcross Gdns *STALE/WH* AL4 . 170 D8
Sleaps Hyde *STVGE* SG2 .... 76 D8
Sleapshyde La *STALE/WH* AL4 .... 170 D7
Sledale *HHNE* HP2 .... 8 B2
Sleets End *HHNE* HP1 .... 164 A4
Slimmons Dr *STALE/WH* AL4 ..... 168 D2
Slipe La *BROX* EN10 .... 197 K2
The Slipe *LBUZ* LU7 .... 110 A2
Slip La *KNEB* SG3 .... 95 G4
Slippers Hl *HHNE* HP2 .... 8 A4
Sloansway *WGCE* AL7 .... 123 F8
The Slype *STALE/WH* AL4 .... 119 J4
Small Acre *HHW* HP1 .... 163 J6 🄳
Smallcroft *WGCE* AL7 .... 148 C3
Smallford La *STALE/WH* AL4 ...... 145 H2 🄳
Smarts Gn *CHESW* EN7 .... 196 D4
Smeaton Cl *WAB* EN9 .... 215 K2 🄳
Smeaton Rd *WAB* EN9 .... 215 F8
Smithfield *HHNE* HP2 .... 8 A3
Smith's End La *ROY* SG8 .... 23 F8
Smiths Ga *CHESW* EN7 .... 196 B4
Smith St *WATW* WD18 .... 13 D3 🄳
Smug Oak La *LCOL/BKTW* AL2 ... 188 D8
Snailswell La *HTCH/STOT* SG5 ...... 40 C4
Snatchup *STALW/RED* AL3 .... 142 B4
Snells Md *BUNT* SG9 .... 63 J2
The Snipe *HTCHE/RSTV* SG4 .... 43 G8
Snowdrop Cl *BSF* CM23 .... 105 F3
Snowford Cl *LTNN/LIM* LU3 .... 69 G2
Snowhill Cottages *CSHM* HP5 .... 182 B2
Soham Rd *PEND* EN3 .... 214 E7
Solesbridge Cl *RKW/CH/CXG* WD3 .. 217 J3
Solesbridge La *RKW/CH/CXG* WD3 . 217 J2
Sollershott East *LWTH* SG6 .... 41 K5
Sollershott West *LWTH* SG6 .... 41 J5
Solomon's Hl
   RKW/CH/CXG WD3 .... 218 C7 🄳
Solway Rd *HHNE* HP2 .... 8 C3

Solway Rd North *LTNN/LIM* LU3 .. 69 F5
Solway Rd South *LTNN/LIM* LU3 .. 69 F6
Somerby Cl *BROX* EN10 .... 177 F7
Someries Rd *HARP* AL5 .... 118 E5 🄳
   HHW HP1 .... 163 J4
Somersby Cl *LTN* LU1 .... 4 C6 🄳
Somerset Av *LTNE* LU2 .... 5 E1
Somerset Rd *PEND* EN3 .... 215 F8 🄳
Somersham *WGCE* AL7 .... 148 E3
Somers Rd *BRKMPK* AL9 .... 192 C2
Somers Sq *BRKMPK* AL9 .... 192 C1 🄳
Somers Wy *BUSH* WD23 .... 221 K7
Sonia Cl *OXHEY* WD19 .... 13 D6
Soothouse Spring
   STALW/RED AL3 .... 168 C2
Soper Ms *PEND* EN3 .... 215 F8 🄳
Sopers Rd *POTB/CUF* EN6 .... 195 H7
Sopwell La *STAL* AL1 .... 10 C5
Sorrel Cl *LTNN/LIM* LU3 .... 69 F1
   ROY SG8 .... 21 K4
Sorrel Garth *HTCHE/RSTV* SG4 ... 56 E3
Sotheron Rd *WAT* WD17 .... 13 D1
Souberie Av *LWTH* SG6 .... 41 K4
Souldern St *WATW* WD18 .... 12 C4
Southacre Wy *PIN* HA5 .... 230 D7
Southall Cl *WARE* SG12 .... 127 H7
South Ap *NTHWD* HA6 .... 229 J2
South Bank Rd *BERK* HP4 .... 161 G3
Southbrook *SBW* CM21 .... 132 C8
Southbrook Dr *CHES/WCR* EN8 .. 197 H6 🄳
South Bucks Wy *CFSP/GDCR* SL9 . 226 D8
South Charlton Mead La
   HOD EN11 .... 177 J4 🄳
Southcliffe Dr *CFSP/GDCR* SL9 .. 226 B4
South Cl *BLDK* SG7 .... 43 F2 🄳
   LCOL/BKTW AL2 .... 188 D3
   ROY SG8 .... 21 F2
South Cottage Dr
   RKW/CH/CXG WD3 .... 217 J5
South Cottage Gdns
   RKW/CH/CXG WD3 .... 217 J5
Southdown Ct *HAT* AL10 .... 171 F7 🄳
Southdown Rd *HARP* AL5 .... 118 D8
   HAT AL10 .... 171 F7
South Drift Wy *LTN* LU1 .... 69 G8
South Dr *POTB/CUF* EN6 .... 195 G8
   STALE/WH AL4 .... 169 H5
Southend Cl *STVG* SG1 .... 2 A1
Southern Ri *LTNE* LU2 .... 118 B2
Southern Wy *DUN/WHIP* LU6 ..... 114 A5
   HLWE CM17 .... 181 F3
   HLWS CM18 .... 7 F6
   RKW/ROY CM19 .... 179 H4
   LWTH SG6 .... 41 J1
Southernwood Cl *HHNE* HP2 .... 9 D4 🄳
Southerton Wy *RAD* WD7 .... 207 H3
Southfield *BAR* EN5 .... 225 J6 🄳
   STDN SG11 .... 82 A4 🄳
   WGCE AL7 .... 147 J5
Southfield Av *WATN* WD24 .... 204 D8
Southfield Rd *CHES/WCR* EN8 ... 214 D2
   HOD EN11 .... 177 F1
Southfields *LWTH* SG6 .... 25 K8
   STVG SG1 .... 81 K7
Southfield Wy *STALE/WH* AL4 .... 169 G3
South Ga *HLW* CM20 .... 6 C4
Southgate *STVG* SG1 .... 2 B4
Southgate Rd *POTB/CUF* EN6 ... 210 D3
South Hill Cl *HTCHE/RSTV* SG4 .... 56 E3 🄳
South Hill Rd *HHW* HP1 .... 164 B6
South Ley *WGCE* AL7 .... 147 K6
Southmead Crs *CHES/WCR* EN8 . 197 J8
Southmill Rd *BSF* CM23 .... 105 K3
South Ordnance Rd *PEND* EN3 .. 215 F7
South Park Av *RKW/CH/CXG* WD3 . 217 J5
South Park Gdns *BERK* HP4 .... 161 J4
South Pl *HLW* CM20 .... 7 F1
   HTCH/STOT SG5 .... 56 B1
South Riding *LCOL/BKTW* AL2 .... 188 C3
South Rd *BLDK* SG7 .... 43 F2
   BSF CM23 .... 105 K4
   HLW CM20 .... 7 F1
   LTN LU1 .... 4 B5
   RKW/CH/CXG WD3 .... 217 J5
   STDN SG11 .... 81 J7
Southsea Av *WATW* WD18 .... 12 B3
Southsea Rd *STVG* SG1 .... 75 G1
South St *BSF* CM23 .... 105 J3
   HERT/WAS SG14 .... 151 G3
   WARE SG12 .... 153 H5
South Vw *LWTH* SG6 .... 41 K4
Southview Cl *CHESW* EN7 .... 196 C4
Southview Rd *HARP* AL5 .... 118 E6
South View Rd *PIN* HA5 .... 230 D5
Southwark Cl *STVG* SG1 .... 59 H8
Southway *WGCE* AL7 .... 203 J3
   GSTN WD25 .... 203 K3
   HAT AL10 .... 171 F8
   WAB EN9 .... 215 G7
South Weald Dr *WAB* EN9 .... 215 J3
Southwold Rd *WATN* WD24 .... 204 D7 🄳
Sowerby Av *LTNE* LU2 .... 70 D6
Sparhawke *LWTH* SG6 .... 26 A8
Sparrow Dr *STVGE* SG2 .... 76 D5
Sparrows Herne *BUSH* WD23 ..... 221 J7

Sparrows Wy BUSH WD23 .... 221 K7 ◳
Sparrowswick Ride
   STALW/RED AL3 .... 167 K1
Spayne Cl LTNN/LIM LU3 .... 69 G1
Spear Cl LTNN/LIM LU3 .... 68 D3
Speedwell Cl LTNN/LIM LU3.......... 69 F1
Speke Cl STVGE SG2 .... 76 E4 ◳
Spellbrook HTCH/STOT SG5 ..... 56 B1 ◳
Spellbrook La East BSF CM23 ...... 132 C3
Spellbrook La West SBW CM21..... 132 B2
Spencer Av CHESW EN7 .... 196 C4
Spencer Ct STSD CM24 .... 86 D3 ◳
Spencer Ga STAL AL1 .... 11 D2
Spencer Ms STAL AL1 .... 11 D3
Spencer Pl STALW/WH AL4 .... 145 F7 ◳
Spencer Rd LTNN/LIM LU3 .... 4 A2
Spencers Cft LHLWS CM18............ 7 F6
Spencer Wk RKW/CH/CXG WD3 .... 218 B5
Spencer Wy HHW HP1 .... 163 K3 ◳
Spenser Wy HARP AL5 .... 118 E8
Sperberry HI HTCHE/RSTV SG4 .... 57 F7
Spicersfield CHESW EN7 .... 196 C4
Spicer St STALW/RED AL3........... 10 B4
Spindle Berry Cl WLYN AL6 .... 123 G2 ◳
Spinney La WLYN AL6 .... 95 J7
Spinney Rd LTNN/LIM LU3 .... 68 C3
Spinney St HERT/BAY SG13 .... 151 K3 ◳
The Spinney BERK HP4............... 161 C6
   BLDK SG7 .... 42 E2
   BROX EN10 .... 176 E5 ◳
   HARP AL5 .... 118 A6 ◳
   HERT/BAY SG13 .... 151 J3
   POTB/CUF EN6 .... 210 E1 ◳
   STSD CM24 .... 86 D4
   STVGE SG2 .... 76 E2 ◳
   WAT WD17 .... 220 B1
   WGCE AL7 .... 147 K4
Spinning Wheel Md HLWS CM18.... 180 D4
Spooners Dr LCOL/BKTW AL2 ..... 188 C5 ◳
Spring Cl BAR EN5 .... 225 J5
   BORE WD6 .... 223 K1 ◳
   CSHM HP5 .... 200 A6
   DEN/HRF UB9 .... 228 C7
Spring Court Rd ENC/FH EN2 ...... 212 D4
Spring Crofts BUSH WD23 .... 221 H5
Spring Dr STVGE SG2 .... 96 B1
Springfield BUSH WD23 .... 222 A8
Springfield Cl POTB/CUF EN6 ...... 210 E1 ◳
   RKW/CH/CXG WD3 .... 219 G5
Springfield Crs HARP AL5 .... 118 C5
Spring Field Rd BERK HP4........... 161 G2
Springfield Rd CHES/WCR EN8 ...... 214 D2
   GSTN WD25 .... 204 C3 ◳
   HHNE HP2 .... 8 C4
   LTNN/LIM LU3 .... 69 H3
   STAL AL1 .... 11 F5
   STALE/WH AL4 .... 170 A6
Springfields BROX EN10............. 176 D4
   WGCW AL8 .... 147 G5
Spring Gdns GSTN WD25 .... 204 D5
Spring Gln HAT AL10 .... 170 E5
Springhall La SBW CM21 .... 132 C8
Springhall St SBW CM21 .... 132 C7
Springhead BLDK SG7 .... 17 K5
Spring Hills LTN LU20 .... 155 H7
   HHW HP1 .... 163 K5
Springle La HERT/BAY SG13 .... 152 E6
Spring Pl LTN LU1 .... 4 B5 ◳
Spring Rd HARP AL5 .... 117 C5 ◳
   LWTH SG6 .... 41 J4
Springshott LWTH SG6 .... 41 J4
The Springs BROX EN10.............. 197 J3
Spring View Rd WARE SG12 .... 127 J8
Spring Wk BROX EN10 .... 176 B7
Springwell Av RKW/CH/CXG WD3.. 227 K1
Springwell La RKW/CH/CXG WD3 .. 227 G2
Springwood CHESW EN7 .... 196 C4
Springwood Wk STALE/WH AL4 ... 169 F3 ◳
Spruce HI HLWS CM18 .... 180 B5
Spruce Wy LCOL/BKTW AL2 .... 188 C5 ◳
Spur Cl ABLGY WD5 .... 203 J5 ◳
Spurcroft LTNN/LIM LU3 .... 52 C8 ◳
Spurrs Cl HTCHE/RSTV SG4 .... 57 F2 ◳
The Spur CHES/WCR EN8 .... 197 H6 ◳
   STVG SG1 .... 2 C4
The Square BROX EN10 .... 197 K3 ◳
   BUNT SG9 .... 47 G4
   SBW CM21 .... 132 C7 ◳
   STALW/RED AL3 .... 142 A3
   WATN WD24........................... 204 C7
Squires Cl BSF CM23 .... 105 F1
Squires Ride HHNE HP2 .... 140 E8 ◳
Squirrel Cha HHW HP1 .... 163 H5
Squirrels Cl BSF CM23 .... 105 J1 ◳
The Squirrels BUSH WD23 .... 222 A6
   HERT/BAY SG13 .... 152 A3 ◳
Stackfield HLW CM20 .... 156 E6
Stacklands WGCW AL8 .... 147 G5
Staddles RBSF CM22 .... 106 A8
Stadium Wy HLWW/ROY CM19 .... 155 G8
Stafford Cl CHES/WCR EN8 .... 197 F7

Stafford Dr BROX EN10 .... 177 F6 ◳
Stafford Rd KTN/HRWW/W HA3 ... 231 K6
Staffords HLWE CM17................ 157 H5 ◳
Stagg HI POTB/CUF EN6 .... 210 E5
Stag Green Av BRKMPK AL9 .... 171 K3
Stag La BERK HP4 .... 161 H4
   RKW/CH/CXG WD3 .... 217 F6
Stainer Rd BORE WD6 .... 223 G1 ◳
Stainers BSF CM23 .... 105 G4
Stains Cl CHES/WCR EN8 .... 197 J6
Stake Piece Rd ROY SG8 .... 21 C3
Stakers Ct HARP AL5.................. 118 D8
Stamford Av ROY SG8 .... 21 K2
Stamford Cl POTB/CUF EN6 .... 210 E2
Stamford Rd WAT WD17 .... 12 C1
Stanborough Av BORE WD6 .... 207 K8
Stanborough Cl WCCW AL8 .... 147 H4 ◳
Stanborough Gn WGCW AL8 .... 147 H5
Stanborough La WGCW AL8 .... 147 H5
Stanborough Rd WGCW AL8 .... 147 G6
Stanbury Av WAT WD17 .... 203 K7
Standard Rd PEND EN3 .... 214 D8
Standfield ABLGY WD5 .... 203 K1 ◳
Standhill Cl HTCHE/RSTV SG4..... 56 D3
Standhill Rd HTCHE/RSTV SG4..... 56 D3
Standingford EPP CM16 .... 179 J6 ◳
Standon HI STDN SG11 .... 81 H7
Standon Rd STDN SG11 .... 83 F6
Standring Ri HHS/BOV HP3 .... 185 F1 ◳
Stane Cl BSF CM23 .... 105 J1
Stane Fld LWTH SG6 .... 42 B6
Stanelow Crs STDN SG11 .... 81 J7
Stane St BLDK SG7 .... 27 G8
Stanford Rd LTNE LU2 .... 5 E2
Stangate Crs BORE WD6 .... 224 D5
Stanhope Rd BAR EN5 .... 225 J6
   CHES/WCR EN8 .... 214 D3
   STAL AL1 .... 11 E5
Stanier Ri BERK HP4 .... 161 C2
Stanley Av LCOL/BKTW AL2 .... 188 C3
Stanley Dr HAT AL10 .... 171 G6
Stanley Gdns BORE WD6 .... 223 H1
   TRING HP23 .... 134 E6 ◳
Stanley Rd HERT/BAY SG13 .... 151 H4
   LTNN/LIM LU3 .... 52 A4
   NTHWD HA6 .... 230 B7 ◳
   STVGE SG2 .... 3 F1
   WAT WD17 .... 13 D2 ◳
Stanley St LTN LU1 .... 4 B5
Stanmore Crs LTNN/LIM LU3 ...... 68 E5
Stanmore Rd STVG SG1 .... 2 A1
Stanmount Rd LCOL/BKTW AL2 ... 188 C3 ◳
Stansted Dr HOD EN11............... 177 G1
Stansted Rd HERT/BAY SG13....... 151 K2
   HOD EN11 .... 155 G8
   WARE SG12 .... 152 C4
Stansted HI MHAD SG10 .... 103 H8
Stansted Rd BSF CM23 .... 86 B6
   RBSF CM22 .... 87 G1
Stanton Cl STALE/WH AL4 .... 169 C2
Stanton Rd LTNW/LEA LU4 .... 68 B7
Staplefield Cl PIN HA5 .... 231 F6
Stapleford WGCE AL7 .... 148 E3 ◳
Stapleford Rd LTNE LU2 .... 70 C5
Stapleton Cl POTB/CUF EN6 .... 210 E1
Stapleton Rd BORE WD6 .... 207 K8
Stapley Rd STALW/RED AL3 .... 10 C3 ◳
Staplyton Rd BAR EN5 .... 225 K3
Star Holme Ct WARE SG12 .... 127 J8
Starkey Cl CHESW EN7 .... 196 A3 ◳
Starling La POTB/CUF EN6.......... 195 H6
Star St WARE SG12 .... 127 J8
Statham Cl LTNN/LIM LU3 .... 52 B8
Station Ap CHES/WCR EN8 .... 214 D4 ◳
   HARP AL5............................. 118 D8
   HTCHE/RSTV SG4 .... 56 E1 ◳
   KNEB SG3 .... 96 A4
   NTHWD HA6 .... 229 K6 ◳
   OXHEY WD19 .... 230 E2 ◳
   RAD WD7 .... 206 D5
   RKW/CH/CXG WD3 .... 217 F4
Station Cl BRKMPK AL9 .... 192 E4 ◳
   POTB/CUF EN6 .... 210 A1
Station Footpath KGLGY WD4...... 186 B8
Station Pl LWTH SG6 .... 41 K3 ◳
Station Rd ARL/CHE SG15 .... 24 E5
   BERK HP4 .... 162 A4
   BLDK SG7 .... 18 B5
   BLDK SG7 .... 19 F7
   BLDK SG7 .... 27 F8
   BORE WD6 .... 223 K4
   BRKMPK AL9 .... 192 D5
   BROX EN10 .... 176 E6
   BSF CM23 .... 105 K3 ◳
   BUNT SG9 .... 63 J2
   CHES/WCR EN8....................... 215 F4
   HARP AL5 .... 118 D8
   HERT/WAS SG14 .... 150 A3
   HERT/WAS SG14 .... 149 H6
   HHS/BOV HP3 .... 164 A8
   HLWE CM17 .... 157 F5
   KGLGY WD4 .... 186 B7
   KNEB SG3 .... 96 A5
   LBUZ LU7 .... 110 E4

Station Wy LWTH SG6................. 41 ◳
Staveley Rd LTNW/LEA LU4 .... 68 ◳
Steeplands BUSH WD23 221
Steeple Vw BSF CM23................ 105 ◳
Stephens Cl LTNE LU2 .... 70 ◳
Stephenson Cl ROY SG8 .... 21 F2
Stephenson Wy BUSH WD23....... 220 ◳
Stephens Wy STALW/RED AL3 ..... 142 ◳
Stepnells TRING HP23 .... 110 ◳
Sterling Av CHES/WCR EN8 .... 214 ◳
Stevenage Crs BORE WD6 .... 223 ◳
Stevenage Ri HHNE HP2 .... 8 ◳
Stevenage Rd HTCHE/RSTV SG4 ... 56 ◳
   KNEB SG3 .... 96 ◳
   STVGE SG2 .... 77 ◳
Stevens Gn BUSH WD23 .... 221 K8 ◳
Steward Cl CHES/WCR EN8 .... 197 ◳
Stewart Cl ABLGY WD5 .... 204 ◳
Stewart Rd HARP AL5................. 118 ◳
The Stewarts BSF CM23 .... 105 ◳
Stile Cft HLWS CM18 .... 7 ◳
Stilton Pth BORE WD6 .... 207 K8
Stirling Cl HTCHE/RSTV SG4 .... 57 ◳
   STVGE SG2 .... 96 ◳
Stirling Wy ABLGY WD5 .... 204 ◳
   BORE WD6............................. 224 ◳
   WGCE AL7 .... 149 ◳
Stoat Cl HERT/BAY SG13 .... 151 ◳
Stobarts Cl KNEB SG3 .... 96 ◳
Stockbreach Cl HAT AL10 .... 171 ◳
Stockbreach Rd HAT AL10 .... 171 ◳
Stockens Dell KNEB SG3 .... 96 ◳
Stockens Gn KNEB SG3 .... 96 A5
Stockers Farm Rd
   RKW/CH/CXG WD3 .... 228 ◳
Stockfield Av HOD EN11 .... 177 ◳
Stockholm Wy LTNN/LIM LU3 ...... 68 ◳
Stocking La ROY SG8 .... 33 ◳
Stockings La HERT/BAY SG13 ...... 174 ◳
Stockingstone Rd LTNE LU2 .... 69 ◳
Stockmen Fld BSF CM23 .... 105 ◳
Stockport Rd RKW/CH/CXG WD3 .. 217 ◳
Stocks Meadow HHNE HP2 .... 9 ◳
Stocks Rd TRING HP23 .... 136 ◳
Stockwell Cl CHESW EN7 .... 196 ◳
Stockwood Crs LTN LU1.............. 4 ◳
Stonecroft KNEB SG3 .... 96 ◳
Stonecroft Cl BAR EN5 .... 225 ◳
Stonecross STAL AL1.................. 11 ◳
   STALW/RED AL3 .... 11 ◳
Stonecross Rd HAT AL10 .... 171 ◳
Stonehills WGCW AL8 .... 147 ◳
Stonelea Rd HHS/BOV HP3 .... 185 ◳
Stoneleigh Av EN EN1 .... 214 ◳
Stoneleigh Av CHES/WCR EN8 .... 214 C3
   LTNN/LIM LU3 .... 69 ◳
Stoneleigh Dr HOD EN11............. 153 ◳
Stoneley LWTH SG6 .... 25 ◳
Stonemason Cl HARP AL5 .... 118 C6
Stonemead WGCW AL8 .... 122 ◳
Stonesdale LTNW/LEA LU4 .... 68 B5
Stoneways Cl LTNW/LEA LU4 .... 68 ◳
Stoney Cl BERK HP4 .... 161 G3
Stoney Common STSD CM24 .... 86 ◳
Stoney Common Rd STSD CM24 ... 86 C
Stoney Cft TRING HP23 .... 136 ◳
Stoneycroft WGCE AL7................ 148 ◳
Stoneyfield Dr STSD CM24.......... 86 ◳
Stoneygate Rd LTNW/LEA LU4 ..... 68 ◳
Stoney La HHS/BOV HP3 .... 183 ◳
   HHW HP1.............................. 183 ◳
   KGLGY WD4 .... 184 ◳
Stonnells Cl LWTH SG6 .... 41 ◳
Stony Cft STVG SG1 .... 2 ◳
Stony Hills WARE SG12 .... 126 ◳
Stony La CSHM HP5 .... 200 ◳
   LTNN/LIM LU3 .... 71 ◳
Stonyshotts WAB EN9 .... 215 ◳
Stony Wd HLWS CM18 .... 6 ◳
Stopsley Wy LTNE LU2 .... 70 ◳
Storehouse La HTCHE/RSTV SG4 .. 56 D2 ◳
Storey St HHS/BOV HP3 .... 185 ◳
Stormont Rd HTCH/STOT SG5 ..... 40 D

Stornoway *HHS/BOV* HP3 ..... 165 G8
Stortford Hall Pk *BSF* CM23 ..... 106 A1
Stortford Hall Rd *BSF* CM23 ..... 106 A1
Stortford Rd *HOD* EN11 ..... 177 G2
  RBSF CM22 ..... 133 J3
  STDN SC11 ..... 82 A8
  STDN SC11 ..... 83 K7
Stort Ldg *BSF* CM23 ..... 105 G1
Stort Ml *HLW* CM20 ..... 156 E3
Stort Rd *BSF* CM23 ..... 105 J3
Stort Valley Wy *HLW* CM20 ..... 157 G2
  HLWW/ROY CM19 ..... 154 B8
  SBW CM21 ..... 133 G7
Stotfold Rd *ARL/CHE* SG15 ..... 24 E1
  BLDK SG7 ..... 26 C1
  HTCHE/RSTV SG4 ..... 41 G5
  LWTH SG6 ..... 41 G2
The Stow *HLW* CM20 ..... 7 E2
Strafford Cl *POTB/CUF* EN6 ..... 210 B2
Strafford Ct *KNEB* SG3 ..... 96 B4
Strafford Ga *POTB/CUF* EN6 ..... 210 B2
Strafford Rd *BAR* EN5 ..... 225 K3
The Straits *BSF* EN9 ..... 215 G2
strangers Wy *LTNW/LEA* LU4 ..... 68 B5
strangeways *WAT* WD17 ..... 203 K6
stratfield Dr *BROX* EN10 ..... 176 D5
stratfield Rd *BORE* WD6 ..... 223 J3
stratford Rd *LTNW/LEA* LU4 ..... 69 G8
  WAT WD17 ..... 12 B1
stratford Wy *HHS/BOV* HP3 ..... 185 F1
  LCOL/BKTW AL2 ..... 188 D7
  WAT WD17 ..... 12 A1
strathmore Av *HTCH/STOT* SG5 ..... 40 C8
  LTN LU1 ..... 4 C6
strathmore Rd *HTCHE/RSTV* SG4 ..... 93 H3
strathmore Wk *LTN* LU1 ..... 5 D5
stratton Av *ENC/FH* EN2 ..... 213 G7
stratton Gdns *LTNE* LU2 ..... 69 J5
strawberry Fieds *WARE* SG12 ..... 127 F3
strawberry Fld *LTNN/LIM* LU3 ..... 68 D2
strawfields *WCGE* AL7 ..... 148 C2
strawmead *HAT* AL10 ..... 171 G2
straw Plait *ARL/CHE* SG15 ..... 24 D5
strayfield Rd *ENC/FH* EN2 ..... 212 D6
the Street *BLDK* SG7 ..... 44 E1
  BSF CM23 ..... 67 K2
  BUNT SG9 ..... 65 G3
  BUNT SG9 ..... 66 C5
  KGLGY WD4 ..... 201 K1
  RBSF CM22 ..... 107 F4
  STDN SC11 ..... 79 J6
  STDN SC11 ..... 82 A2
stretton Wy *BORE* WD6 ..... 207 H8
stringers La *STVGE* SG2 ..... 77 F8
stripling Wy *WATW* WD18 ..... 12 B5
stroma Cl *HHS/BOV* HP3 ..... 165 H8
stronnell Cl *LTNE* LU2 ..... 70 B6
stronsay *HHS/BOV* HP3 ..... 165 H8
stuart Ct *BORE* WD6 ..... 223 G6
stuart Dr *HTCHE/RSTV* SG4 ..... 57 F2
  ROY SG8 ..... 21 H1
stuart Rd *AMP/FLIT/B* MK45 ..... 36 C5
  WLYN AL6 ..... 122 B5
stuarts Cl *HHS/BOV* HP3 ..... 164 C8
stuart St *LTN* LU1 ..... 4 C4
stuart Wy *CHESW* EN7 ..... 214 A1
stud Gn *WD25* 204 B2
studham La *BERK* HP4 ..... 113 G5
the Studios *BUSH* WD23 ..... 221 H6
studlands Ri *ROY* SG8 ..... 21 J3
studley Rd *LTNN/LIM* LU3 ..... 68 B3
sturgeon's Rd *HTCHE/RSTV* SG4 ..... 41 F7
sturlas Wy *CHES/WCR* EN8 ..... 214 C3
sturmer Rd *STALE/WH* AL4 ..... 169 F7
sturrock Wy *HTCHE/RSTV* SG4 ..... 57 C3
styles Cl *LTNE* LU2 ..... 70 D7
such Cl *LWTH* SG6 ..... 42 B2
sudbury Rd *LTNW/LEA* LU4 ..... 68 A3
suffolk Cl *BORE* WD6 ..... 224 C5
  LCOL/BKTW AL2 ..... 190 A3
suffolk Rd *POTB/CUF* EN6 ..... 209 K2
  ROY SG8 ..... 21 J3
sugar La *HHW* HP1 ..... 162 E8
sulgrave Crs *TRING* HP23 ..... 135 H4
sullivan Crs *DEN/HRF* UB9 ..... 228 C3
sullivan Wy *BORE* WD6 ..... 223 F6
summer Dl *WGCW* AL8 ..... 122 D7
summerfield *HAT* AL10 ..... 171 F7
summerfield Cl *LCOL/BKTW* AL2 ..... 190 A4
summerfield Rd *GSTN* WD25 ..... 204 B6
  LTN LU1 ..... 88 E1
summer Gv *BORE* WD6 ..... 223 G6
summer Hl *BORE* WD6 ..... 223 K5
summerhouse La *DEN/HRF* UB9 ..... 227 K6
  GSTN WD25 ..... 221 K1
summerhouse Wy *ABLGY* WD5 ..... 187 F8
summersland Rd
  STALE/WH AL4 ..... 169 F2
summers Rd *LTNE* LU2 ..... 70 D8
summer St *LTN* LU1 ..... 89 H7
summerswood La *BORE* WD6 ..... 208 D5
summer Wk *STALE/WH* AL4 ..... 115 J4
summit Rd *POTB/CUF* EN6 ..... 192 E8
sumners Farm Cl *EPP* CM16 ..... 179 H6

Sumpter Yd *STAL* AL1 ..... 10 C5
Sunderland Av *STAL* AL1 ..... 11 F3
Sundew Rd *HHW* HP1 ..... 163 H7
Sundon Park Rd *LTNN/LIM* LU3 ..... 68 B1
Sun Hl *ROY* SG8 ..... 21 G4
Sun La *HARP* AL5 ..... 118 C7
Sunmead Rd *HHNE* HP2 ..... 8 A3
Sunningdale *BSF* CM23 ..... 105 H5
  LTNE LU2 ..... 70 A6
Sunningdale Ms *WGCE* AL7 ..... 123 F7
Sunny Bank *LBUZ* LU7 ..... 109 K2
Sunnybank Rd *POTB/CUF* EN6 ..... 210 B3
Sunny Cft *HLWS* CM18 ..... 180 C4
Sunnydell *LCOL/BKTW* AL2 ..... 188 D4
Sunnyfield *BRKMPK* AL9 ..... 171 J1
Sunny Hl *BUNT* SG9 ..... 63 J2
Sunnyhill Rd *HHW* HP1 ..... 164 A6
  RKW/CH/CXG WD3 ..... 227 C5
Sunnymede Av *CSHM* HP5 ..... 182 A6
Sunnyside *STSD* CM24 ..... 86 D3
  WAB EN9 ..... 178 A8
Sunnyside Rd *HTCHE/RSTV* SG4 ..... 56 E3
Sunridge Av *LTNE* LU2 ..... 4 C1
Sunrise Crs *HHS/BOV* HP3 ..... 185 K3
Sunset Dr *LTNE* LU2 ..... 70 A6
Sunset Vw *BAR* EN5 ..... 225 K2
Sun St *BLDK* SG7 ..... 42 E1
  HTCH/STOT SG5 ..... 56 C3
  SBW CM21 ..... 132 D8
  WAB EN9 ..... 215 H8
Surrey Pl *TRING* HP23 ..... 135 F6
Surrey St *LTN* LU1 ..... 4 C5
Sursham Ct *STALW/RED* AL3 ..... 115 J4
Sussex Cl *HOD* EN11 ..... 177 F2
Sussex Pl *LTNE* LU2 ..... 70 E7
Sussex Rd *WATN* WD24 ..... 204 B8
Sutcliffe Cl *BUSH* WD23 ..... 221 K4
  STVG AL1 ..... 76 B1
Sutherland Av *POTB/CUF* EN6 ..... 195 F6
Sutherland Cl *BAR* EN5 ..... 225 J5
Sutherland Ct *WGCE* AL7 ..... 148 A2
Sutherland Pl *LTN* LU1 ..... 4 B6
Sutherland Wy *POTB/CUF* EN6 ..... 195 F6
Sutton Acres *RBSF* CM22 ..... 133 H2
Sutton Cl *BROX* EN10 ..... 176 D6
  TRING HP23 ..... 135 G3
Sutton Crs *BAR* EN5 ..... 225 J5
Sutton Gdns *LTNN/LIM* LU3 ..... 68 C3
Sutton Rd *SDY/GAM/PO* SG19 ..... 14 A1
  WAT WD17 ..... 13 D2
Swallow Cl *BUSH* WD23 ..... 221 J5
  RKW/CH/CXG WD3 ..... 218 D8
Swallowdale La *HHNE* HP2 ..... 9 D2
Swallowfield *WCCE* AL7 ..... 148 A3
Swallowfields *WCCE* AL7 ..... 148 A5
Swallow Gdns *HAT* AL10 ..... 171 F6
Swallow La *STAL* AL1 ..... 189 K1
Swallow Oaks *ABLGY* WD5 ..... 204 A2
Swallows *HLWE* CM17 ..... 157 F5
The Swallows *WCCE* AL7 ..... 123 F7
Swan and Pike Rd *PEND* EN3 ..... 215 F8
Swan Cl *RKW/CH/CXG* WD3 ..... 218 C7
Swan Ct *BSF* CM23 ..... 105 J3
Swanells Wd *DUN/WHIP* LU6 ..... 113 K5
Swanfield Rd *CHES/WCR* EN8 ..... 214 D3
Swangley's La *KNEB* SG3 ..... 96 B4
Swanhill *WCCE* AL7 ..... 123 G8
Swanland Rd *BRKMPK* AL9 ..... 209 G3
  POTB/CUF EN6 ..... 209 J3
Swan La *ROY* SG8 ..... 15 G5
Swanley Bar La *POTB/CUF* EN6 ..... 193 H6
Swanley Crs *POTB/CUF* EN6 ..... 193 H7
Swan Md *HHS/BOV* HP3 ..... 185 K3
Swans Cl *STALE/WH* AL4 ..... 169 H7
Swans Rd *CHES/WCR* EN8 ..... 214 C4
Swanstand *LWTH* SG6 ..... 42 D5
Swanston Pth *OXHEY* WD19 ..... 230 D2
Swan St *BLDK* SG7 ..... 17 K5
Swasedale Rd *LTNN/LIM* LU3 ..... 68 B3
Sweet Briar *BSF* CM23 ..... 104 C3
  WCCE AL7 ..... 148 B5
Sweetbriar Cl *HHW* HP1 ..... 163 K3
Sweyne *HLWE* CM17 ..... 181 F4
Sweyns Md *STVGE* SG2 ..... 76 D1
Swift Cl *LWTH* SG6 ..... 41 J1
  WARE SG12 ..... 153 H6
Swiftfields *WCCE* AL7 ..... 148 A2
Swifts Green Cl *LTNE* LU2 ..... 70 C4
Swifts Green Rd *LTNE* LU2 ..... 70 C4
Swinburne Av *HTCH/STOT* SG5 ..... 40 A8
Swingate *STVG* SG1 ..... 2 B3
Swing Br *LBUZ* LU7 ..... 110 B4
Swing Gate La *BERK* HP4 ..... 162 A6
Swiss Av *WATW* WD18 ..... 219 K4
Swiss Cl *WATW* WD18 ..... 219 K3
Sworders Yd *BSF* CM23 ..... 105 J2
Sycamore Ap *RKW/CH/CXG* WD3 ..... 219 H5
Sycamore Av *HAT* AL10 ..... 171 F5
Sycamore Cl *BUSH* WD23 ..... 13 F1
  CHESW EN7 ..... 196 D5
  GSTN WD25 ..... 204 C5
  HTCHE/RSTV SG4 .....
Sycamore Dr *LCOL/BKTW* AL2 ..... 189 F5
  TRING HP23 ..... 135 G5

Sycamore Fld *HLWW/ROY* CM19 ..... 179 H5
Sycamore Ri *BERK* HP4 ..... 162 A6
Sycamore Rd *RKW/CH/CXG* WD3 ..... 219 H5
The Sycamores *BLDK* SG7 ..... 26 E8
  BSF CM23 ..... 106 A3
  HHS/BOV HP3 ..... 184 D1
  RAD WD7 ..... 206 E4
Sydney Rd *WATW* WD18 ..... 219 K5
Sylam Cl *LTNN/LIM* LU3 ..... 68 D2
Sylvan Cl *HHS/BOV* HP3 ..... 9 D6
Sylvandale *WGCE* AL7 ..... 148 D4
Sylvan Wy *WCCE* AL7 ..... 148 E3
Sylvesters *HLWW/ROY* CM19 ..... 179 G3
Sylvia Av *PIN* HA5 ..... 231 G5
Symonds Ct *CHES/WCR* EN8 ..... 197 H6
Symonds Green La *STVG* SG1 ..... 75 F2
Symonds Green Rd *STVG* SG1 ..... 75 F2
Symonds Rd *HTCH/STOT* SG5 ..... 56 B1

T

Tabbs Cl *LWTH* SG6 ..... 42 B1
Tacitus Cl *STVGE* SG2 ..... 76 D1
Tailors *BSF* CM23 ..... 104 E4
Takeley Cl *LWTH* SG6 ..... 215 J3
Talbot Av *OXHEY* WD19 ..... 13 F6
Talbot Ct *HHS/BOV* HP3 ..... 164 C8
Talbot Rd *HAT* AL10 ..... 171 F1
  LTNE LU2 ..... 5 D2
  RKW/CH/CXG WD3 ..... 218 D8
Talbot St *HERT/BAY* SG13 ..... 151 H3
  HTCH/STOT SG5 ..... 56 B1
Talbot Wy *LWTH* SG6 ..... 42 B1
Talisman St *HTCHE/RSTV* SG4 ..... 57 G2
Tallents Crs *HARP* AL5 ..... 119 F6
Tallis Wy *BORE* WD6 ..... 223 G1
Tall Trees *HTCHE/RSTV* SG4 ..... 56 E5
  ROY SG8 ..... 21 J3
Tamar Cl *STVG* SG1 ..... 59 C6
Tamar Gn *HHNE* HP2 ..... 164 E1
Tamarisk Cl *STALW/RED* AL3 ..... 168 B2
Tameton Cl *LTNE* LU2 ..... 71 F7
Tamworth Rd *HERT/BAY* SG13 ..... 151 J2
Tancred Rd *LTNE* LU2 ..... 70 B5
Tanfield Cl *CHESW* EN7 ..... 196 E5
Tanfield Gn *LTNE* LU2 ..... 71 F8
Tanglewood *WLYN* AL6 ..... 123 G2
Tanners Cl *STALW/RED* AL3 ..... 10 B3
Tanners Crs *HERT/BAY* SG13 ..... 151 F5
Tanners Hl *ABLGY* WD5 ..... 204 A1
Tanners Wy *WARE* SG12 ..... 129 J8
Tanners Wood La *ABLGY* WD5 ..... 203 K2
Tannery Cl *ROY* SG8 ..... 21 G3
Tannery Drift *ROY* SG8 ..... 21 G2
The Tannery *BUNT* SG9 ..... 63 J2
Tannsfield Dr *HHNE* HP2 ..... 8 C3
Tannsmore Cl *HHNE* HP2 ..... 8 C3
Tansycroft *WGCE* AL7 ..... 148 C2
Tanworth Cl *NTHWD* HA6 ..... 229 H5
Tanworth Gdns *PIN* HA5 ..... 230 C8
Tanyard La *HTCHE/RSTV* SG4 ..... 121 G1
Tany's Dell *HLW* CM20 ..... 7 F1
Taransey *HHS/BOV* HP3 ..... 165 G8
Tarpan Wy *BROX* EN10 ..... 197 K4
Tarrant Dr *HARP* AL5 ..... 143 K2
Tassell Hall *STALW/RED* AL3 ..... 142 A3
Tate Gdns *BUSH* WD23 ..... 222 B7
Tate Rd *CFSP/GDCR* SL9 ..... 226 C4
Tatlers La *STVGE* SG2 ..... 76 E4
Tatsfield Av *WAB* EN9 ..... 198 D1
Tattershall Dr *HHNE* HP2 ..... 141 F8
Tattle Hl *HERT/WAS* SG14 ..... 125 G7
Tauber Cl *BORE* WD6 ..... 223 J4
Taunton Rd *LTNE* LU2 ..... 5 F2
Taverners *HHNE* HP2 ..... 8 B3
Taverners Wy *HOD* EN11 ..... 177 F3
Tavistock Av *STAL* AL1 ..... 188 E1
Tavistock Cl *POTB/CUF* EN6 ..... 210 E1
  STAL AL1 ..... 189 F1
Tavistock Crs *LTN* LU1 ..... 4 C6
Tavistock Rd *WATN* WD24 ..... 220 E1
Tawneys Rd *HLWS* CM18 ..... 7 E6
Taylifers *HLWW/ROY* CM19 ..... 179 H6
Taylor Cl *STALE/WH* AL4 ..... 168 D1
Taylors Av *HOD* EN11 ..... 177 F4
Taylors End Rd *STSD* CM24 ..... 87 K8
Taylor's Rd *HTCH/STOT* SG5 ..... 25 K1
Taylor St *LTNE* LU2 ..... 5 D3
Taywood Cl *STVGE* SG2 ..... 3 F6
Teal Dr *NTHWD* HA6 ..... 229 H6
Teasel Cl *ROY* SG8 ..... 21 J4
Tedder Rd *HHNE* HP2 ..... 9 D4
Teesdale *HHNE* HP2 ..... 8 B2
  LTNW/LEA LU4 ..... 68 B4
Tee Side *HERT/BAY* SG13 ..... 152 A2
Telford Av *STVGE* SG2 ..... 3 E2
Telford Cl *GSTN* WD25 ..... 204 E5
Telford Rd *LCOL/BKTW* AL2 ..... 190 A5
Telford Wy *LTN* LU1 ..... 4 B3
Telscombe Wy *LTNE* LU2 ..... 70 D6
Temperance St *STALW/RED* AL3 ..... 10 B4
Tempest Av *POTB/CUF* EN6 ..... 210 D2

Templar Av *BLDK* SG7 .... 43 F3
Templars La *HTCHE/RSTV* SG4 .... 73 G3
Temple Bank *HLW* CM20 .... 156 E4
Temple Cl *CHESW* EN7 .... 213 K1
  HTCHE/RSTV SG4 .... 55 H5
  LTNE LU2 .... 69 K4
  WAT WD17 .... 12 A1
Temple Flds *HERT/WAS* SG14 .... 126 A8
Temple Gdns *RKW/CH/CXG* WD3 .... 229 G7
Temple La *WARE* SG12 .... 126 C2
Templepan La *RKW/CH/CXG* WD3... 202 D7
Temple Vw *STALW/RED* AL3 .... 10 B2
Templewood *WGCW* AL8 .... 122 D8
Tempsford Av *BORE* WD6 .... 224 C4
Tempsford Cl *RYLN/HDSTN* HA2 .. 231 K8
Tenby Dr *LTNW/LEA* LU4 .... 68 C6
Tenby Ms *LTNW/LEA* LU4 .... 68 D6
Tendring Rd *HLWS* CM18 .... 6 B6
The Tene *BLDK* SG7 .... 43 F1
Tennand Cl *CHESW* EN7 .... 196 B4
Tennison Av *BORE* WD6 .... 224 A5
Tennyson Av *HTCHE/RSTV* SG4 ...... 57 G2
  WAB EN9 .... 215 K4
Tennyson Rd *HARP* AL5 .... 118 C6
  LCOL/BKTW AL2 .... 188 C4
  LTN LU1 .... 4 C6
Tenth Av *LTN/LIM* LU3 .... 68 E2
Tenzing Gv *LTN* LU1 .... 4 A5
Tenzing Rd *HHNE* HP2 .... 9 D5
Teresa Gdns *WAT* WD17 .... 12 C1
Tethys Rd *HHNE* HP2 .... 8 C2
Tewin Cl *STALE/WH* AL4 .... 169 F2
  WLYN AL6 .... 123 J4
Tewin Ct *WGCE* AL7 .... 148 A2
Tewin Hl *WLYN* AL6 .... 124 A6
Tewin Rd *HHNE* HP2 .... 9 F5
  WGCE AL7 .... 148 A2
Thames Av *HHNE* HP2 .... 164 E1
Thamesdale *LCOL/BKTW* AL2 .... 190 D5
Thatchers Cft *HHNE* HP2 .... 8 B1
Thatchers End *HTCHE/RSTV* SG4 .... 57 H1
The Thatchers *BSF* CM23 .... 105 F4
Thaxted Cl *LTNE* LU2 .... 71 G7
Thaxted Wy *WAB* EN9 .... 215 J3
Thaynesfield *POTB/CUF* EN6 .... 210 E2
Thelby Cl *LTNN/LIM* LU3 .... 68 E3
Thele Av *WARE* SG12 .... 153 J5
Theleway Cl *HOD* EN11 .... 153 G8
Thellusson Wy
  RKW/CH/CXG WD3 .... 217 K7
Thelusson Cl *RAD* WD7 .... 206 D5
Theobald Crs *KTN/HRWW/W* HA3.. 231 J7
Theobald's Cl *POTB/CUF* EN6 .... 195 H8
Theobald's Gv *CHES/WCR* EN8 ...... 214 C2
Theobald's La *CHES/WCR* EN8 ..... 214 A2
Theobalds Park Rd *ENC/FH* EN2 .. 212 E5
Theobald's Rd *POTB/CUF* EN6 .... 195 G8
Theobald St *RAD* WD7 .... 206 C8
Therfield Rd *STALW/RED* AL3 .... 10 C1
Thetford Gdns *LTNE* LU2 .... 69 J3
Thieves La *HERT/WAS* SG14 .... 150 C3
  HERT/WAS SG14 .... 150 C2
Third Av *GSTN* WD25 .... 204 E5
  HLWS CM18 .... 6 C4
  HLW/ROY CM19 .... 6 A5
  LTNN/LIM LU3 .... 68 C2
  LWTH SG6 .... 42 C2
Thirlestane *STAL* AL1 .... 11 D3
Thirlestone Rd *LTNW/LEA* LU4...... 68 C8
Thirlmere *STVG* SG1 .... 59 J7
Thirlmere Dr *STAL* AL1 .... 168 E8
Thirlmere Gdns *NTHWD* HA6 .... 229 G4
Thirsk Rd *BORE* WD6 .... 207 K8
Thistle Cl *HHW* HP1 .... 163 H7
Thistlecroft *HHW* HP1 .... 164 A7
Thistle Gv *WGCE* AL7 .... 148 D6
Thistle Rd *LTN* LU1 .... 5 D4
The Thistles *HHW* HP1 .... 164 A5
Thistley La *HTCHE/RSTV* SG4 .... 56 D1
Thomas Rochford Wy
  CHES/WCR EN8 .... 197 K5
Thompsons Cl *CHESW* EN7 .... 196 B4
Thompsons Meadow *ROY* SG8 .... 15 H5
Thompson Wy *RKW/CH/CXG* WD3 .. 217 K7
Thorley Hl *BSF* CM23 .... 105 H5
Thorley La *BSF* CM23 .... 104 E4
Thorley Park Rd *BSF* CM23 .... 105 J5
Thornage Cl *LTNE* LU2 .... 69 J2
Thorn Av *BUSH* WD23 .... 221 K8
Thornbera Cl *BSF* CM23 .... 105 J5
Thornbera Gdns *BSF* CM23 .... 105 J5
Thornbera Rd *BSF* CM23 .... 105 J5
Thornbury *HARP* AL5 .... 119 F8
Thornbury Cl *HOD* EN11 .... 153 G7
  STVG SG2 .... 96 B3
Thornbury Gdns *BORE* WD6 .... 224 B4
Thorncroft *HHS/BOV* HP3 .... 165 G8
Thorndyke Ct *PIN* HA5 .... 231 G6
Thorne Cl *HHW* HP1 .... 164 A8
Thornfield Rd *BSF* CM23 .... 105 H1

Thorn Gv *BSF* CM23 .... 106 A3
Thornhill Rd *LTNW/LEA* LU4 .... 68 E8
  NTHWD HA6 .... 229 H3
Thorntondale *LTNW/LEA* LU4 .... 68 B4
Thornton Gv *PIN* HA5 .... 231 H5
Thornton Rd *BAR* EN5 .... 225 K3
  POTB/CUF EN6 .... 193 J8
Thornton St *HERT/WAS* SG14 ...... 151 G3
  STALW/RED AL3 .... 10 B3
Thorn Tree Dr *TRING* HP23 .... 134 E5
Thorpe Crs *OXHEY* WD19 .... 12 C6
Thorpefield Cl *STALE/WH* AL4 ..... 169 G3
Thorpe Rd *STAL* AL1 .... 10 C5
Thrales Cl *LTNN/LIM* LU3 .... 68 D2
Three Cherrytrees La *HHNE* HP2 ..... 9 E1
Three Close La *BERK* HP4 .... 161 K6
Three Closes *HTCH/STOT* SG5 ...... 38 E5
Three Corners *HHS/BOV* HP3 ...... 165 F8
Three Forests Wy
  HLWW/ROY CM19 .... 178 A1
  RBSF CM22 .... 107 F8
  SBW CM21 .... 132 C8
  WAB EN9 .... 178 E7
Three Forest Wy *RBSF* CM22 ...... 107 C2
Three Horseshoes Rd
  HLWW/ROY CM19 .... 6 A6
Three Houses La *HTCHE/RSTV* SG4.. 94 B6
Three Stiles *STVGE* SG2 .... 78 B5
Three Valleys Wy *BUSH* WD23 ...... 13 E4
Thresher Cl *BSF* CM23 .... 105 F4
Thricknells Cl *LTNN/LIM* LU3 .... 68 D2
Thrift Farm La *BORE* WD6 .... 224 E1
Thristers Cl *LWTH* SG6 .... 42 B6
Throcking La *BUNT* SG9 .... 47 G8
Throcking Rd *BUNT* SG9 .... 62 B1
Thrums *WATN* WD24 .... 204 C7
Thrush Av *HAT* AL10 .... 171 F6
Thrush Gn *RKW/CH/CXG* WD3 ..... 218 B7
Thrush La *POTB/CUF* EN6 .... 195 C6
Thumbswood *WGCE* AL7 .... 148 B6
Thumpers *HHNE* HP2 .... 8 B1
Thundercourt *WARE* SG12 .... 127 H7
Thundridge Cl *WGCE* AL7 .... 148 C4
Thurgood Rd *HOD* EN11 .... 177 F1
Thurlow St *STVG* SG1 .... 58 D8
Thurnall Av *ROY* SG8 .... 21 H4
Thurnall Rd *BLDK* SG7 .... 43 F1
Thurstans *HLWW/ROY* CM19 .... 179 J6
Tibbles Ct *GSTN* WD25 .... 205 F5
Tibbs Hill Rd *ABLGY* WD5 .... 187 F8
Tiberius Rd *LTN/LIM* LU3 .... 68 E3
Tichborne *RKW/CH/CXG* WD3 ..... 227 C4
Tickenhall Dr *HLWE* CM17 .... 181 C1
Tilbury Rd *HAT* AL10 .... 7 F5
Tilecroft *WGCW* AL8 .... 122 D8
Tilegate Rd *HLWS* CM18 .... 7 F6
Tilehouse Cl *BORE* WD6 .... 223 J3
Tilehouse La *RKW/CH/CXG* WD3 .. 227 H7
Tilehouse St *HTCH/STOT* SG5 .... 56 C2
Tile Kiln Cl *HHS/BOV* HP3 .... 9 E6
Tile Kiln Crs *HHS/BOV* HP3 .... 9 E6
Tile Kiln La *HHS/BOV* HP3 .... 9 E6
Tilgate *LTNE* LU2 .... 70 E6
Tillers Link *STVGE* SG2 .... 3 E6
Tillotson Rd *KTN/HRWW/W* HA3... 231 J6
Tillwicks Rd *HLWS* CM18 .... 7 F5
Tilsworth Wk *STALE/WH* AL4 .... 169 F1
Timbercroft *WGCE* AL7 .... 148 C3
Timber Orch *HERT/WAS* SG14 ..... 125 J7
Timber Rdg *RKW/CH/CXG* WD3 .... 218 B4
Timbers Ct *HARP* AL5 .... 118 B7
Times Cl *HTCH/STOT* SG5 .... 40 B7
Timplings Rw *HHW* HP1 .... 164 A4
Timworth Cl *LTNE* LU2 .... 70 D7
Tingeys Cl *STALW/RED* AL3 .... 142 B4
Tinkers La *TRING* HP23 .... 160 B3
Tinsley Cl *LTN* LU1 .... 89 C4
Tintagel Cl *HHNE* HP2 .... 164 C1
  LTNN/LIM LU3 .... 69 C5
Tintern Cl *HARP* AL5 .... 117 J5
  KNEB SG3 .... 96 B2
Tinwell Ms *BORE* WD6 .... 224 C5
Tippendell La *LCOL/BKTW* AL2 .... 188 C3
Tippet Ct *STVG* SG1 .... 2 B5
Titan Ct *LTNW/LEA* LU4 .... 68 B3
Titan Rd *HHNE* HP2 .... 8 C2
Titchfield Rd *PEND* EN3 .... 214 D7
Tithe Barn Cl *STAL* AL1 .... 188 E1
Tithe Cl *WLYN* AL6 .... 94 B3
Tithelands *HLWW/ROY* CM19 ...... 179 G4
Titian Av *BUSH* WD23 .... 222 B7
Titmus Cl *STVG* SG1 .... 3 E2
Tiverton Ct *HARP* AL5 .... 144 B3
Tiverton Rd *POTB/CUF* EN6 .... 210 E1
Toddbrook *HLWW/ROY* CM19 .... 6 A5
Toddington Rd *LTNW/LEA* LU4 ...... 68 C4
Toland Cl *LTNW/LEA* LU4 .... 68 B8
Tolcarne Dr *PIN* HA5 .... 230 E1
Tollgate Cl *RKW/CH/CXG* WD3 .... 217 J4
Tollgate Rd *BRKMPK* AL9 .... 192 A3
  CHES/WCR EN8 .... 214 C5
  STALE/WH AL4 .... 191 J2
Tollpit End *HHW* HP1 .... 163 K3
Tollsworth Wy *STDN* SG11 .... 81 H6
Tolmers Av *POTB/CUF* EN6 .... 195 C6

Tolmers Gdns *POTB/CUF* EN6 ...... 195 C6
Tolmers Rd *POTB/CUF* EN6 .... 195 C6
Tolpits Cl *WATW* WD18 .... 12 A7
Tolpits La *WATW* WD18 .... 12 A7
Tomkins Cl *BORE* WD6 .... 223 H1
Toms Cft *HHNE* HP2 .... 8 B1
Toms Fld *HAT* AL10 .... 170 D2
Tom's Hl *KGLGY* WD4 .... 202 D1
Toms Hill Cl *TRING* HP23 .... 136 E4
Toms Hill Rd *TRING* HP23 .... 136 E1
Tom's La *KGLGY* WD4 .... 186 C2
Tooke Cl *PIN* HA5 .... 231 J1
Tooveys Mill Cl *KGLGY* WD4 .... 186 A7
Topland Rd *CFSP/GDCR* SL9 .... 226 A6
Topstreet Wy *HARP* AL5 .... 143 H5
Torquay Crs *STVG* SG1 .... 75 J5
Torquay Dr *LTNW/LEA* LU4 .... 68 B7
Torrington Dr *POTB/CUF* EN6 ..... 210 E3
Torrington Rd *BERK* HP4 .... 161 H6
Tortoiseshell Wy *BERK* HP4 .... 161 G6
Torwood Cl *BERK* HP4 .... 161 G6
Torworth Rd *BORE* WD6 .... 223 K1
Tot La *BSF* CM23 .... 86 E4
Totteridge Rd *PEND* EN3 .... 214 D8
Totton Ms *STALW/RED* AL3 .... 142 C4
Totts La *STVGE* SG2 .... 60 D3
Toulmin Dr *STALW/RED* AL3 .... 167 J2
Tovey Av *HOD* EN11 .... 177 F3
Tovey Cl *LCOL/BKTW* AL2 .... 190 E6
  WAB EN9 .... 198 A5
Tower Cl *BERK* HP4 .... 161 H6
  HTCHE/RSTV SG4 .... 57 G2
Tower Hl *KGLGY* WD4 .... 184 E5
  MHAD SG10 .... 115 H8
Tower Hill La *STALE/WH* AL4 .... 145 H6
Tower Rd *HTCHE/RSTV* SG4 .... 94 D2
  LTNE LU2 .... 5 E4
  WARE SG12 .... 127 J7
Towers Rd *HHNE* HP2 .... 8 E2
  PIN HA5 .... 231 K1
Tower St *HERT/WAS* SG14 .... 151 G3
Tower Vw *HTCHE/RSTV* SG4 .... 93 J4
Tower Wy *LTNE* LU2 .... 5 F4
Towne Rd *ROY* SG8 .... 21 J1
Town Farm *LBUZ* LU7 .... 110 A2
Town Farm Crs *STDN* SG11 .... 82 A6
Townfield *RKW/CH/CXG* WD3 ..... 218 E1
Town Flds *HAT* AL10 .... 171 F3
Town La *STVGE* SG2 .... 78 B3
Townley *LWTH* SG6 .... 42 C6
Town Mead Rd *WAB* EN9 .... 215 H5
Townsend *HHNE* HP2 .... 8 A1
Townsend Av *STAL* AL1 .... 11 C4
Townsend Cl *HARP* AL5 .... 118 E6
  ROY SG8 .... 15 F4
Townsend Dr *STALW/RED* AL3 ...... 10 C1
Townsend La *HARP* AL5 .... 117 K7
Townsend Rd *HARP* AL5 .... 118 E6
Townsend Wy *NTHWD* HA6 .... 230 A8
Townshend St *HERT/WAS* SG14 ... 151 H3
Townsley Cl *LTN* LU1 .... 4 E3
Tracyes Rd *HLWS* CM18 .... 180 E4
Trafalgar Av *BROX* EN10 .... 176 E7
Trafford Cl *RAD* WD7 .... 207 H2
  STVG SG1 .... 58 E4
Traherne Cl *HTCHE/RSTV* SG4 ...... 56 D4
Trajan Ga *STVG* SG1 .... 59 K4
Trap Rd *ROY* SG8 .... 15 K7
Trapstyle Rd *WARE* SG12 .... 126 B7
Travellers Cl *BRKMPK* AL9 .... 192 C3
Travellers La *BRKMPK* AL9 .... 171 K6
  HAT AL10 .... 171 K6
Treacle La *BUNT* SG9 .... 45 J4
Treacy Cl *BUSH* WD23 .... 231 J1
Trebellan Dr *HHNE* HP2 .... 8 B4
Tree Cl *HHS/BOV* HP3 .... 165 G8
Treehanger Cl *TRING* HP23 .... 135 C5
Treetops Cl *NTHWD* HA6 .... 229 F6
Trefusis Wk *WAT* WD17 .... 219 F4
Tregelles Rd *HOD* EN11 .... 177 F1
Tremaine Gv *HHNE* HP2 .... 8 D3
Trent Cl *RAD* WD7 .... 207 J2
  STVG SG1 .... 58 E2
Trent Rd *LTNN/LIM* LU3 .... 69 F2
Tresco Rd *BERK* HP4 .... 161 H7
Trescott Cl *LTNE* LU2 .... 71 F7
Trevalga Wy *HHNE* HP2 .... 164 C1
Trevelliance Wy *GSTN* WD25 ...... 204 E3
Trevelyan Wy *BERK* HP4 .... 161 J5
Trevor Rd *HTCHE/RSTV* SG4 .... 56 D4
Trevose Wy *OXHEY* WD19 .... 230 E1
Trewenna Dr *POTB/CUF* EN6 ...... 210 C3
Trident Rd *GSTN* WD25 .... 204 A4
Triggs Wy *LTNE* LU2 .... 71 J6
Trimley Cl *LTNW/LEA* LU4 .... 68 B7
Trinder Rd *BAR* EN5 .... 225 K4
Tring Ford Rd *TRING* HP23 .... 135 F4
Tring Hl *TRING* HP23 .... 134 E3
Tring Rd *BERK* HP4 .... 160 E6
  DUN/WHIP LU6 .... 112 A4
  TRING HP23 .... 109 J5
Trinity Cl *BSF* CM23 .... 105 J5
  NTHWD HA6 .... 229 J6
Trinity Gv *HERT/WAS* SG14 .... 151 G3
Trinity Hall Cl *WATN* WD24 .... 13 D2

Trinity La *CHES/WCR* EN8 .... **214** D2
Trinity Ms *HHS/BOV* HP3 .... **165** J7 🔲
Trinity Rd *HERT/BAY* SG13 .... **152** B6
　HTCHE/STOT SG5 .... **25** J2
　LTNN/LIM LU3 .... **69** F5
　STVG SG1 .... **2** A1
　WARE SG12 .... **127** J7
Trinity St *BSF* CM23 .... **105** J3 🔲
Trinity Wk *HERT/BAY* SG13 .... **152** B6
Trinity Wy *BSF* CM23 .... **105** J3
Tripton Rd *HLWS* CM18 .... **7** D5
Tristram Rd *HTCHE/RSTV* SG4 .... **40** E7
Triton Wy *HHW* HP2 .... **8** C3 🔲
Troon Gdns *LTNE* LU2 .... **69** K3
Trooper Rd *TRING* HP23 .... **136** D4
Trotters Bottom *BAR* EN5 .... **209** F7
Trotter's Gap *WARE* SG12 .... **153** K5
Trotters Rd *HLWS* CM18 .... **180** D4
Trout Ri *HLWS* CM18 .... **218** A3
Troutstream Wy
　RKW/CH/CXG WD3 .... **218** A4
Trouvere Pk *HHW* HP1 .... **164** A4
Trowbridge Gdns *LTNE* LU2 .... **69** K6
Trowley Bottom *STALW/RED* AL3 ... **141** C4
Trowley Hill Rd *STALW/RED* AL3 .. **116** B7
Trowley Ri *ABLGY* WD5 .... **203** K1
Truemans Rd *HTCH/STOT* SG5 .... **40** B7
Trumper Rd *STVG* SG1 .... **76** A1
Trumpington Dr *STAL* AL1 .... **189** F1
Trundlers Wy *BUSH* WD23 .... **222** B8 🔲
Truro Gdns *LTNN/LIM* LU3 .... **69** G4
Trust Rd *CHES/WCR* EN8 .... **214** D4 🔲
Tucker's Rw *BSF* CM23 .... **105** J3
Tucker St *WATW* WD18 .... **13** D4 🔲
Tudor Av *CHESW* EN7 .... **214** A1
　WATN WD24 .... **204** E7
Tudor Cl *AMP/FLIT/B* MK45 .... **36** C5 🔲
　CHESW EN7 .... **214** A1
　HAT AL10 .... **170** D7
　STVG SG1 .... **58** C8
　WARE SG12 .... **154** E1
Tudor Ct *BORE* WD6 .... **223** H2 🔲
　HTCH/STOT SG5 .... **56** B3 🔲
Tudor Dr *WATN* WD24 .... **204** E8
Tudor Manor Gdns *GSTN* WD25 .. **204** E2
Tudor Rd *BROX* EN10 .... **176** D7
Tudor Ri *LTNN/LIM* LU3 .... **69** G7
　PIN HA5 .... **230** D1
　STALE/WH AL4 .... **145** H1
　STALW/RED AL3 .... **168** B2
　WLYN AL6 .... **122** B6
Tudor Wk *WATN* WD24 .... **204** E7
Tudor Wy *HERT/WAS* SG14 .... **150** D3
　RKW/CH/CXG WD3 .... **217** K8
　WAB EN9 .... **215** J3
Tuffnells Wy *HARP* AL5 .... **117** K5
Tumbler Rd *HLWS* CM18 .... **7** F5
Tunfield Rd *HOD* EN11 .... **153** C8
Tunnel Wood Cl *WAT* WD17 ...... **204** A7
Tunnel Wood Rd *WAT* WD17 ..... **204** A7
　WATN WD24 .... **204** A7
Tunnmeade *HLW* CM20 .... **7** F3
Turf La *HTCHE/RSTV* SG4 .... **58** B5
Turkey St *EN* EN1 .... **213** K6
Turmore Dl *WGCW* AL8 .... **147** H4
Turnberry Cl *OXHEY* WD19 .... **230** D2 🔲
Turnberry Dr *LCOL/BKTW* AL2 ... **188** A3
Turner Cl *STVG* SG1 .... **58** C7
Turner Rd *BUSH* WD23 .... **221** K4
Turners Cl *HARP* AL5 .... **118** E5
　HERT/WAS SG14 .... **124** F5
Turners Crs *BSF* CM23 .... **105** F5
Turners Rd North *LTNE* LU2 .... **5** E1
Turners Rd South *LTNE* LU2 .... **5** E1
Turners Wood Dr *CSTG* HP8 ...... **226** A2
Turneys Orch *RKW/CH/CXG* WD3 ... **217** C5
Turnors *HLWW/ROY* CM19 .... **6** B4
Turnpike Dr *LTNN/LIM* LU3 .... **52** C3
Turnpike Gn *HHW* HP2 .... **8** C1
Turnpike La *HTCH/STOT* SG5 .... **40** B6
The Turnstones *GSTN* WD25 ..... **205** F6
Turpins Cha *WLYN* AL6 .... **123** F2
Turpins Cl *HERT/WAS* SG14 ...... **150** C3
Turpin's Ride *ROY* SG8 .... **21** H4
　WLYN AL6 .... **122** E2
Turpin's Ri *STVG* SG2 .... **75** K8
Turpin's Wy *BLDK* SG7 .... **43** F2
Tuxford Cl *BORE* WD6 .... **207** H8 🔲
Tweed Cl *BERK* HP4 .... **161** J4
Twelve Acres *WGCE* AL7 .... **147** K5
Twin Foxes *KNEB* SG3 .... **96** B8
Twinwoods *STVG* SG1 .... **3** D4
The Twist *TRING* HP23 .... **135** J5
The Twitchell *BLDK* SG7 .... **43** F1 🔲
Two Acres *WGCE* AL7 .... **148** A5
Two Dells La *CSHM* HP5 .... **182** B2
Two Oaks Dr *WLYN* AL6 .... **123** J3
Two Waters Rd *HHS/BOV* HP3 ... **185** G1
Twyford Bury La *BSF* CM23 .... **105** K5
Twyford Cl *BSF* CM23 .... **105** K4
Twyford Dr *LTNE* LU2 .... **70** E8
Twyford Gdns *BSF* CM23 .... **105** J5

Twyford Rd *BSF* CM23 .... **105** K4
　STALE/WH AL4 .... **169** F2
Tye End *STVGE* SG2 .... **96** C1
Tye Green Rd *RBSF* CM22 .... **87** H2
Tye Green Village *HLWS* CM18 .. **180** C4 🔲
Tyfield Cl *CHES/WCR* EN8 .... **197** G8 🔲
Tylers *HARP* AL5 .... **119** F8
Tylers Cswy *HERT/BAY* SG13 ..... **173** K8
Tylers Cl *BUNT* SG9 .... **63** H2 🔲
　KGLGY WD4 .... **185** K7
Tylersfield *ABLGY* WD5 .... **204** A1
Tylers Hill Rd *CSHM* HP5 .... **182** B8
Tylers Md *LTNE* LU2 .... **69** K4
Tylers Rd *HLWW/ROY* CM19 ..... **178** E6
Tylers Wd *WLYN* AL6 .... **123** J4
Tilney Cft *HLWW/ROY* CM19 .... **6** A4
Tynedale *LCOL/BKTW* AL2 .... **190** D5 🔲
Tynemouth Dr *EN* EN1 .... **213** K8
Tysea Cl *HLWS* CM18 .... **180** C4
Tysea Rd *HLWS* CM18 .... **180** C4
Tysoe Av *PEND* EN3 .... **214** E6
Tythe Rd *LTNW/LEA* LU4 .... **68** D3
Tyttenhanger Gn *STALE/WH* AL4 ... **190** B1

U

Uckfield Rd *PEND* EN3 .... **214** C7
Ufford Cl *KTN/HRWW/W* HA3 ..... **231** H1
Ufford Rd *KTN/HRWW/W* HA3 .... **231** H1
Ullswater Cl *STVG* SG1 .... **59** J7
Ullswater Dr *LTNE* LU2 .... **180** A4
Underacres Cl *HHNE* HP2 .... **9** D4
Underwood Rd *STVG* SG1 .... **58** C7
Union Gn *HHNE* HP2 .... **8** A4 🔲
　LTN LU1 .... **4** C5
Union Ter *BUNT* SG9 .... **63** J2
Unity Rd *PEND* EN3 .... **214** B7
Unwin Cl *LWTH* SG6 .... **41** J5
Unwin Rd *STVGE* SG2 .... **76** B1
Updale Cl *POTB/CUF* EN6 .... **209** K3
Upland Dr *BRKMPK* AL9 .... **193** H5
Uplands *LTNN/LIM* LU3 .... **68** C1
　RKW/CH/CXG WD3 .... **218** E6
　STDN SG11 .... **82** A3
　STVGE SG2 .... **76** E1
　WARE SG12 .... **127** K7
　WGCW AL8 .... **122** C7
Uplands Av *HTCHE/RSTV* SG4 ...... **57** F3
The Uplands *HARP* AL5 .... **143** H5
　LCOL/BKTW AL2 .... **188** A4
Upper Ashlyns Rd *BERK* HP4 ..... **161** J6
Upper Barn *HHS/BOV* HP3 .... **185** K1
Upper Bourne End La *HHW* HP1 ... **183** K1
Upper Clabdens *WARE* SG12 ...... **127** K8
Upper Culver St *STAL* AL1 .... **11** D2
Upper Dagnall St
　STALW/RED AL3 .... **10** C4 🔲
Upperfield Rd *WGCE* AL7 .... **148** A4
Upper George St *LTN* LU1 .... **4** B4
Upper Gn *WLYN* AL6 .... **123** K5
Upper Green Rd *WLYN* AL6 .... **124** A6
Upper Hall Pk *BERK* HP4 .... **162** B7
Upper Heath Rd *STAL* AL1 .... **11** E2
Upper Hwy *ABLGY* WD5 .... **203** K5
Upper Hill Ri *RKW/CH/CXG* WD3 ... **218** A6
Upper Hitch *OXHEY* WD19 .... **221** H5
Upper Hook *HLWS* CM18 .... **7** E6
Upper Icknield Wy *TRING* HP23 ... **135** J1
Upper King St *ROY* SG8 .... **21** H3
Upper Lattimore Rd *STAL* AL1 .... **11** D4
Upper Lea Valley Wk *LTNE* LU2 ... **69** J6
Upper Marlborough Rd
　STAL AL1 .... **11** D4 🔲
Upper Marsh La *HOD* EN11 ...... **177** F4
Upper Maylins *LWTH* SG6 .... **42** C5
Upper Mealines *HLWS* CM18 ..... **180** D4
Upper Paddock Rd *OXHEY* WD19 ... **13** F5
Upper Pk *HLW* CM20 .... **6** A5
Upper Sales *STVGE* SG2 .... **3** E5
Upper Sean *STVGE* SG2 .... **3** E5
Upper Shot *WGCE* AL7 .... **148** B7
Upper Shott *CHESW* EN7 .... **196** D4
Upper Station Rd *RAD* WD7 ...... **206** D5
Upperstone Cl *HTCH/STOT* SG5 ... **25** K3 🔲
Upper Stonyfield *HLWW/ROY* CM19 ... **6** A4
Upper Tail *OXHEY* WD19 .... **231** F2
Upper Tilehouse St
　HTCH/STOT SG5 .... **56** B3 🔲
Upton Av *STALW/RED* AL3 .... **10** C3
Upton Cl *LCOL/BKTW* AL2 .... **189** F3
　LTNE LU2 .... **69** J2
Upton Lodge Cl *BUSH* WD23 ..... **221** K7 🔲
Upton Rd *WATW* WD18 .... **12** C3
Upway *CFSP/GDCR* SL9 .... **226** C7
Upwell Rd *LTNE* LU2 .... **5** F1
Uranus Rd *HHNE* HP2 .... **8** B3
Urban Rd *BSF* CM23 .... **106** A2
Uxbridge Rd *RKW/CH/CXG* WD3 ... **218** A8
Uxbridge Road (Harrow Weald)
　KTN/HRWW/W HA3 .... **231** J6

Uxbridge Road (Hatch End)
　PIN HA5 .... **231** G6 🔲
Uxbridge Road (Pinner) *PIN* HA5 ... **230** E8

V

Vadis Cl *LTNN/LIM* LU3 .... **68** D2 🔲
Valance Rd *SAFWS* CB11 .... **51** J2
Vale Cl *CFSP/GDCR* SL9 .... **226** A7 🔲
　HARP AL5 .... **117** K5
Vale Ct *STALE/WH* AL4 .... **145** G2
Valence Dr *CHESW* EN7 .... **196** E6
Valency Cl *NTHWD* HA6 .... **230** A3
Valerian Wy *STVGE* SG2 .... **76** E1
Valerie Cl *STAL* AL1 .... **168** E6
Vale Rd *BUSH* WD23 .... **13** F4
Valeside *HERT/WAS* SG14 .... **150** D4
The Vale *CFSP/GDCR* SL9 .... **226** A7
Vallans Cl *WARE* SG12 .... **127** H6
Vallansgate *STVGE* SG2 .... **76** C8
Valley Cl *DUN/WHIP* LU6 .... **113** K5
　DUN/WHIP LU6 .... **113** G2
　HERT/BAY SG13 .... **151** G4
　PIN HA5 .... **230** C8
　WAB EN9 .... **215** H2
　WARE SG12 .... **127** F7 🔲
Valley Gn *HHNE* HP2 .... **141** G8
The Valley Gn *WGCW* AL8 .... **147** H2
Valley La *STALW/RED* AL3 .... **115** J8
Valley Ri *GSTN* WD25 .... **204** C3
　ROY SG8 .... **21** J4
　STALE/WH AL4 .... **119** H7
Valley Rd *BERK* HP4 .... **161** G3
　DUN/WHIP LU6 .... **113** K5
　LWTH SG6 .... **41** H2
　RKW/CH/CXG WD3 .... **217** K5
　STALW/RED AL3 .... **168** C3
　WGCW AL8 .... **147** C3
　WLYN AL6 .... **122** D1
Valley Rd South *WLYN* AL6 .... **121** K1 🔲
Valleyside *HHW* HP1 .... **163** J6
The Valley *HTCHE/RSTV* SG4 .... **93** H2
Valley Vw *BAR* EN5 .... **225** K6
　CHESW EN7 .... **196** A6
Valley Wk *RKW/CH/CXG* WD3 ... **219** H5
Valley Wy *STVGE* SG2 .... **3** D5
Vanda Crs *STAL* AL1 .... **11** E5
Vantorts Cl *SBW* CM21 .... **132** C7
Vantorts Rd *SBW* CM21 .... **132** C8
Vardon Rd *STVG* SG1 .... **76** A1
Varna Cl *LTNN/LIM* LU3 .... **69** F6
Varney Cl *CHESW* EN7 .... **196** E5
　HHW HP1 .... **163** J6
Varney Rd *HHW* HP1 .... **163** J6
Vaughan Md *STALW/RED* AL3 ... **142** B5 🔲
Vaughan Rd *HARP* AL5 .... **118** D8
　HTCHE/STOT SG5 .... **25** J3
Vauxhall Rd *HHNE* HP2 .... **9** D5
　LTNE LU2 .... **5** F6
Vega Crs *NTHWD* HA6 .... **230** A4
Vega Rd *BUSH* WD23 .... **221** K7
Velizy Av *HLW* CM20 .... **6** C3
Venetia Rd *LTNE* LU2 .... **70** B5
Ventnor Gdns *LTNN/LIM* LU3 ...... **68** G2
Ventura Pk *LCOL/BKTW* AL2 ..... **189** H7
Venus Hl *HHS/BOV* HP3 .... **200** D1
Vera Ct *OXHEY* WD19 .... **13** E6
Ver-colne Valley Wk *BUSH* WD23 ... **13** J7
　HHS/BOV HP3 .... **183** F6
　STAL AL1 .... **11** D5
　STALW/RED AL3 .... **142** C5
Verdure Cl *GSTN* WD25 .... **205** F2
Verity Cl *HAT* AL10 .... **171** F4
Verity Wy *STVG* SG1 .... **76** C8
Verlum Cl *WGCE* AL7 .... **148** A3 🔲
Verney Cl *BERK* HP4 .... **161** G4
　TRING HP23 .... **135** H4
Vernon Av *PEND* EN3 .... **214** D6
Vernon Dr *DEN/HRF* UB9 .... **228** B7
Vernon Rd *BUSH* WD23 .... **13** F4
　LTN LU1 .... **4** A3
Vernon's Cl *STAL* AL1 .... **11** D5
Ver Rd *STALW/RED* AL3 .... **10** B4
Verulam Gdns *LTNN/LIM* LU3 ..... **68** D3
Verulam Rd *HTCH/STOT* SG5 ...... **56** D1
　STALW/RED AL3 .... **10** A3
Verwood Rd *RYLN/HDSTN* HA2 ... **231** K8
Vesta Av *STAL* AL1 .... **188** C1
Veysey Cl *HHW* HP1 .... **164** A8 🔲
Viaduct Est *WARE* SG12 .... **152** D1
Viaduct Wy *WGCE* AL7 .... **123** F8
Vian Av *PEND* EN3 .... **214** D5
Vicarage Cswy *HERT/BAY* SG13 ... **152** A5
Vicarage La *ARL/CHE* SG15 .... **24** E1
　HHW HP1 .... **164** B7 🔲
　HHW HP1 .... **164** B8 🔲
　HTCH/STOT SG5 .... **38** B1
　POTB/CUF EN6 .... **194** B8
　STAL AL1 .... **188** E1
　STDN SG11 .... **81** K7
Vicarage Gdns *BERK* HP4 .... **162** E2

STALW/RED AL3 .... 116 B8
TRING HP23 .... 110 A7 🔢
Vicarage La BSF CM23 .... 67 K1
HERT/WAS SG14 .... 125 J6
HHS/BOV HP3 .... 183 J4
KGLGY WD4 .... 185 K7
LBUZ LU7 .... 111 F3
Vicarage Rd BERK HP4 .... 162 D2
BUNT SG9 .... 63 J1
LBUZ LU7 .... 110 D6
TRING HP23 .... 109 D7
TRING HP23 .... 135 J8
WARE SG12 .... 127 J8
WATW WD18 .... 12 B6
WATW WD18 .... 12 C3
Vicarage St LTN LU1 .... 5 D4
Vicarage Wd HLW CM20 .... 7 E3
Vicerons PI BSF CM23 .... 105 G5
Victoria Cl RKW/CH/CXG WD3 .... 218 C7
STVG SG1 .... 2 B1
Victoria Crs ROY SG8 .... 21 H2
Victoria Ga HLWE CM17 .... 180 E1
Victoria Rd BERK HP4 .... 161 K6
BUSH WD23 .... 221 J8
HARP AL5 .... 118 D8 🔢
WAB EN9 .... 215 H4
WATN WD24 .... 204 C8
Victoria St LTN LU1 .... 4 C5 🔢
STAL AL1 .... 11 D4
Victoria Wy HTCH/STOT SG5 .... 56 B1
Victory Rd BERK HP4 .... 161 H4 🔢
View Rd POTB/CUF EN6 .... 210 D2
Vigors Cft HAT AL10 .... 170 E5
Village St HTCHE/RSTV SG4 .... 74 E8
Village Wy AMSS HP7 .... 216 A2
Villa Rd LTN LU2 .... 4 B3
Villiers Crs STALE/WH AL4 .... 169 G3
Villiers Rd OXHEY WD19 .... 13 F5
Villiers-sur-marne Av BSF CM23 ...... 105 G4
Vincent LWTH SG6 .... 42 C5
Vincent Cl CHES/WCR EN8 .... 197 J6
Vincent Rd LTNW/LEA LU4 .... 68 C4
Vincenzo Cl BRKMPK AL9 .... 192 C1
Vine Cl WCCW AL8 .... 147 K1
Vine Gv HLW CM20 .... 156 A4
Vineyards Rd POTB/CUF EN6 .... 194 D7
The Vineyard WARE SG12 .... 127 K7
WGCW ALB .... 147 J1 🔢
Vinters Av STVG SG1 .... 3 D3
Violet Av ENC/FH EN2 .... 213 G8 🔢
Violets La BUNT SG9 .... 66 D5
Violet Wy RKW/CH/CXG WD3 .... 218 B4
Virgil Dr BROX EN10 .... 197 K1 🔢
Virginia Cl LTNE LU2 .... 70 A6
Viscount Cl LTNN/LIM LU3 .... 69 F3
Vivian Cl OXHEY WD19 .... 230 B1
Vivian Gdns OXHEY WD19 .... 220 B8
Vixen Dr HERT/BAY SG13 .... 151 K3
Vyse Cl BAR EN5 .... 225 H4

W

Wacketts CHESW EN7 .... 196 E5 🔢
Waddesdon Cl LTNE LU2 .... 70 E7 🔢
Waddington Rd STAL AL1 .... 10 C4 🔢
Wadesmill Rd HERT/WAS SG14 ...... 126 B8
WARE SG12 .... 127 G6
The Wades HAT AL10 .... 171 F7
Wadham Rd ABLGY WD5 .... 204 A1
Wadhurst Av LTNN/LIM LU3 .... 69 H5
Wadley Cl HHNE HP2 .... 8 C6 🔢
Wadnall Wy KNEB SG3 .... 96 A5
Wagon Rd BAR EN5 .... 210 B5
EBAR EN4 .... 210 C7
Wagon Wy RKW/CH/CXG WD3 ...... 218 D3
Walcot Av LTN LU2 .... 5 E1
Waldeck Rd LTN LU1 .... 4 A3
Waldegrave Rd HARP AL5 .... 119 F8
Walden End STVG SG1 .... 2 C4
Walden PI WGCW AL8 .... 147 J1
Walden Rd WGCW AL8 .... 147 J1
Waleys Cl LTNN/LIM LU3 .... 68 D1
Walfords Cl HLWE CM17 .... 157 F6
Walkern Rd HERT/WAS SG14 .... 97 K3
STVG SG1 .... 75 J1
STVGE SG2 .... 77 H5
Walkers Cl HARP AL5 .... 143 K2 🔢
Walkers Rd HARP AL5 .... 143 J2
The Walk POTB/CUF EN6 .... 210 B2
Wallace Av HTCHE/RSTV SG4 .... 40 E6
Waller Av LTNW/LEA LU4 .... 68 A6
Waller Dr NTHWD HA6 .... 230 B8 🔢
Wallers Wy HOD EN11 .... 153 G8
Wallingford Wk STAL AL1 .... 189 F1
Wallington Rd BLDK SG7 .... 43 G1
Walnut Av BLDK SG7 .... 43 G2
Walnut Cl HTCH/STOT SG5 .... 25 K3 🔢
HTCHE/RSTV SG4 .... 56 E3
LCOL/BKTW AL2 .... 188 D5

LTNE LU2 .... 70 C6
MHAD SG10 .... 103 G7
Walnut Ct WGCE AL7 .... 147 K6 🔢
Walnut Dr BSF CM23 .... 105 G6
Walnut Gn BUSH WD23 .... 221 G2 🔢
Walnut Gv HHNE HP2 .... 8 A5
WGCE AL7 .... 147 K6
Walnut Tree Av SBW CM21 .... 132 C5
Walnut Tree Cl CHES/WCR EN8 ...... 214 C1
HOD EN11 .... 177 F3 🔢
STVGE SG2 .... 76 D3
Walnut Tree Crs SBW CM21 .... 132 C6 🔢
Walnut Tree Rd HTCH/STOT SG5 ..... 39 F6
Walnut Tree Wk WARE SG12 .... 152 C3
Walnut Wy HTCH/STOT SG5 .... 40 C5
Walpole Cl PIN HA5 .... 231 H6
Walsham Cl STVGE SG2 .... 96 D2
Walsh Cl HTCH/STOT SG5 .... 56 B2
Walshford Wy BORE WD6 .... 207 K8
Walsingham Cl HAT AL10 .... 170 A3
LTNE LU2 .... 69 J2 🔢
Walsingham Wy LCOL/BKTW AL2 ... 190 A5
Walsworth Rd HTCH/STOT SG4 .... 56 E2
Waltham Gdns PEND EN3 .... 214 B7 🔢
Waltham Ga CHES/WCR EN8 .... 197 J4
Waltham Rd HTCHE/RSTV SG4 .... 56 D3
WAB EN9 .... 198 E4
Walton Gdns WAB EN9 .... 215 G3
Walton Rd BUSH WD23 .... 13 E5
HODN EN11 .... 177 G1
WARE SG12 .... 152 C1
Walton St STAL AL1 .... 11 E3
Walverns Cl OXHEY WD19 .... 13 D5 🔢
Wandon Cl LTNE LU2 .... 70 D5
Wannions Cl CSHM HP5 .... 182 C3
Wansbeck Cl HTCHE/RSTV SG4 .... 59 G6
Wansford Pk BORE WD6 .... 224 C4
Ward Cl CHESW EN7 .... 196 E5 🔢
WARE SG12 .... 127 G7
Ward Crs BSF CM23 .... 105 H3
Warden Hill Cl LTNE LU2 .... 69 H1 🔢
Warden Hill Gdns LTNE LU2 .... 69 H1
Warden Hill Rd LTNE LU2 .... 69 H1
Ward Hatch HLW CM20 .... 156 E6 🔢
Wardown Crs LTNE LU2 .... 4 C1
Warenford Wy BORE WD6 .... 223 K1
Ware Park Rd HERT/WAS SG14 ...... 151 G1
Ware Rd HERT/BAY SG13 .... 151 H3
HERT/WAS SG14 .... 98 B7
HOD EN11 .... 177 F1
HOD EN11 .... 177 F1
WARE SG12 .... 126 C2
WARE SG12 .... 29 J5
WARE SG12 .... 153 F6
Wareside HHNE HP2 .... 141 F8 🔢
Wareside Cl WGCE AL7 .... 148 C4 🔢
Warmark Rd HHW HP1 .... 163 H4 🔢
Warminster Cl LTNE LU2 .... 71 G8
Warneford Pl OXHEY WD19 .... 13 F5 🔢
Warner Rd WARE SG12 .... 152 C1
Warners Av HOD EN11 .... 176 E5
Warners Cl STVGE SG2 .... 3 F5
Warners End Rd HHW HP1 .... 163 K6
Warren Cl HAT AL10 .... 171 G1
LWTH SG6 .... 41 H2
Warren Rd WDGW AL8 .... 122 D8
Warrender Rd CSHM HP5 .... 182 A7
The Warren Dr LTN LU1 .... 90 C8
Warrenfield Cl CHESW EN7 .... 213 H1
Warrengate La POTB/CUF EN6 ...... 209 H1
Warrengate Rd BRKMPK AL9 .... 192 C6
Warren Gn HAT AL10 .... 171 G1
Warren Gv BORE WD6 .... 224 C4
Warren La BLDK SG7 .... 43 H2
BUNT SG9 .... 61 K3
Warren Park Rd HERT/WAS SG14 ... 151 F2
Warren Rd BUSH WD23 .... 221 K8
LCOL/BKTW AL2 .... 188 E2
LTN LU1 .... 88 E1
Warrensgreen La HTCHE/RSTV SG4 .. 59 K4
Warren Ter HERT/WAS SG14 .... 151 G1
The Warren CFSP/GDCR SL9 .... 226 C3
HARP AL5 .... 143 H4
KGLGY WD4 .... 185 K7
RAD WD7 .... 206 D3
ROY SG8 .... 21 H4
Warren Wy WLYN AL6 .... 122 E6
Warton Gn LTNE LU2 .... 71 F7
Warwick Av POTB/CUF EN6 .... 195 F5
Warwick Cl BUSH WD23 .... 222 B7
HERT/BAY SG13 .... 151 F5
POTB/CUF EN6 .... 195 F5
Warwick Ct RKW/CH/CXG WD3 .... 217 J3
Warwick Dr CHES/WCR EN8 .... 197 H6
Warwick Rd BORE WD6 .... 224 C3
BSF CM23 .... 106 A3
PEND EN3 .... 214 E7
STAL AL1 .... 11 E2
STVGE SG2 .... 76 D3
Warwick Rd East LTNW/LEA LU4 ..... 89 G1 🔢
Warwick Rd West LTNW/LEA LU4 .... 69 G8
Warwick Wy RKW/CH/CXG WD3 .... 219 H4
Washbrook Cl AMP/FLIT/B MK45 ..... 36 C1
Washington Av HHNE HP2 .... 164 D1
Wash La BAR EN5 .... 209 H5
POTB/CUF EN6 .... 209 H5

The Wash BUNT SG9 .... 67 F5
HERT/WAS SG14 .... 151 G3 🔢
Watchlytes WGCE AL7 .... 148 D3
Watchmead WCCE AL7 .... 148 B3 🔢
Waterbeach WGCE AL7 .... 148 B3 🔢
Watercress Cl STVGE SG2 .... 76 E4
Waterdale HERT/BAY SG13 .... 151 F5 🔢
Waterdell La HTCHE/RSTV SG4 .... 56 D7
Waterend La STALE/WH AL4 .... 146 B7
STALW/RED AL3 .... 142 C4
Water End Rd BERK HP4 .... 162 E3 🔢
Waterfield WGCE AL7 .... 148 C2 🔢
Waterfields Wy WAT WD17 .... 13 E3
Waterford Common
HERT/WAS SG14 .... 125 K7
Waterford Gn WGCE AL7 .... 148 C3
The Watergate OXHEY WD19 .... 230 E1 🔢
Waterhoose Moor HLWS CM18 .... 7 D5
Waterhouse St HHW HP1 .... 164 B6
Water La BERK HP4 .... 161 K5
BSF CM23 .... 105 J3
HHS/BOV HP3 .... 183 K7
HLWW/ROY CM19 .... 179 F5
HTCH/STOT SG5 .... 56 D1 🔢
KGLGY WD4 .... 186 B7
STSD CM24 .... 86 D3
WAT WD17 .... 13 D5 🔢
Waterloo La HTCH/STOT SG5 .... 39 J7
Waterman Cl OXHEY WD19 .... 12 C5
Watermark Wy HERT/BAY SG13 ..... 151 J5 🔢
Watermead Rd LTNN/LIM LU3 .... 68 E3
Watermill La HERT/WAS SG14 ...... 126 B6
Waters Dr RKW/CH/CXG WD3 .... 218 D8 🔢
Waters End HTCH/STOT SG5 .... 25 J3
Waterside KGLGY WD4 .... 186 A7
LCOL/BKTW AL2 .... 190 C5
RAD WD7 .... 206 E4 🔢
STSD CM24 .... 86 D3 🔢
WGCE AL7 .... 148 B1
Waterside Ct KGLGY WD4 .... 186 B7 🔢
Waterslade Gn LTNN/LIM LU3 .... 69 G3 🔢
Watersmeet HLWW/ROY CM19 ..... 179 J5
Waterwick Hl SAFWS CB11 .... 34 C8 🔢
Watery La HAT AL10 .... 170 D5
STALW/RED AL3 .... 116 D6
TRING HP23 .... 109 KE
Watford Field Rd WAT WD17 .... 13 D3 🔢
WATW WD18 .... 13 D4
Watford Heath OXHEY WD19 .... 13 G6
Watford Rd BORE WD6 .... 223 F6
KGLGY WD4 .... 186 A8
LCOL/BKTW AL2 .... 188 C3
NTHWD HA6 .... 230 A6
RAD WD7 .... 206 B6
RKW/CH/CXG WD3 .... 219 F6
STAL AL1 .... 188 D1
Watling Cl HHNE HP2 .... 8 B2 🔢
Watling Knoll RAD WD7 .... 206 C3
Watling St LCOL/BKTW AL2 .... 189 F3
STAL AL1 .... 188 E1
Watlington Rd HLWE CM17 .... 157 G5
Watling Vw STAL AL1 .... 188 E1
Watson Av STALW/RED AL3 .... 11 E1
Watson's Wk STAL AL1 .... 11 E5
Watton Rd KNEB SG3 .... 96 B4
WARE SG12 .... 127 G7
Watts Cl STDN SG11 .... 83 J7
Wauluds Bank Dr LTNN/LIM LU3 ..... 68 D2
Wavell Cl CHES/WCR EN8 .... 197 J5
Waveney HHNE HP2 .... 164 E1
Waveney Rd HARP AL5 .... 118 E6
Waverley Cl STVGE SG2 .... 96 B1
Waverley Gdns NTHWD HA6 .... 230 B7 🔢
Waverley Rd STALW/RED AL3 .... 10 B2
Waxwell La PIN HA5 .... 230 E8
Wayre St HLWE CM17 .... 157 F5
Waysbrook LWTH SG6 .... 42 B5
Wayside KGLGY WD4 .... 185 F8
POTB/CUF EN6 .... 210 E3 🔢
RAD WD7 .... 207 G3
Wayside Av BUSH WD23 .... 222 A6
The Wayside HHS/BOV HP3 .... 9 F6
Waysmeet LWTH SG6 .... 42 A5
Waytemore Rd BSF CM23 .... 105 H3
Wealmoor Gdns PIN HA5 .... 231 J5 🔢
Weall Gn GSTN WD25 .... 204 C2
Weatherby Rd LTNW/LEA LU4 .... 68 C7
Weavers Rd TRING HP23 .... 134 D5 🔢
Weaver St BSF CM23 .... 105 F5
Weavers Wy BLDK SG7 .... 43 G1 🔢
Webb Cl LWTH SG6 .... 42 A4
Webber Cl BORE WD6 .... 225 G6 🔢
Webb Ri STVG SG1 .... 3 D1
Wedgewood Cl HTCHE/RSTV SG4 ... 57 G2
NTHWD HA6 .... 229 H5 🔢
Wedgewood Dr HLWE CM17 .... 181 G2
Wedgewood Pk STVG SG1 .... 59 J7
Wedgewood Rd HTCHE/RSTV SG4 ... 57 F2
Wedgwood Ct STVG SG1 .... 59 J7
Wedgwood Ga STVG SG1 .... 59 H7
Wedgwood Wy STVG SG1 .... 59 H7
Wedhey HLWW/ROY CM19 .... 6 B4
Wedmore Rd HTCHE/RSTV SG4 ...... 56 E3
Wedon Wy BLDK SG7 .... 27 J5
Weedon Cl HNLW SG16 .... 24 A4

Welbeck Cl *BORE* WD6 .... 223 K3 ▣
Welbeck Ri *HARP* AL5 .... 144 A3
Welbeck Rd *LTNE* LU2 .... 4 C3 ▣
Welbury Av *LTNN/LIM* LU3 .... 69 H7
Welch Pl *PIN* HA5 .... 230 D7 ▣
Welclose St *STALW/RED* AL3 .... 10 B4
Weldon Cl *LTNE* LU2 .... 71 F8
Welham Ct *BRKMPK* AL9 .... 192 C2
Welham Mnr *BRKMPK* AL9 .... 192 C2
Welkin Gn *HHNE* HP2 .... 9 F4 ▣
Wellands *HAT* AL10 .... 171 F2 ▣
Well Ap *BAR* EN5 .... 225 H5 ▣
Well Cft *HHW* HP1 .... 164 A5
Wellcroft *LBUZ* LU7 .... 111 F4
Wellcroft Cl *WGCE* AL7 .... 148 B5
Wellcroft Rd *WGCE* AL7 .... 148 B4
Well End Rd *BORE* WD6 .... 208 B7
Wellen Ri *HHS/BOV* HP3 .... 185 J1
Wellers Gv *CHESW* EN7 .... 196 E6 ▣
Wellesley *EPP* CM16 .... 179 H6
Wellesley Av *NTHWD* HA6 .... 230 A4
Wellesley Crs *POTB/CUF* EN6 .... 209 F8
Wellfield Av *LTNN/LIM* LU3 .... 68 B1
Wellfield Rd *HAT* AL10 .... 171 F3
Wellfield Rd *HAT* AL10 .... 171 G3 ▣
Well Garth *WGCE* AL7 .... 147 K4
Wellgate Rd *LTNW/LEA* LU4 .... 68 C7
Well Gn *HERT/WAS* SG14 .... 124 C5
Wellhouse Cl *LTN* LU1 .... 89 F2
Wellhouse La *BAR* EN5 .... 225 H4
Wellingham Av *HTCH/STOT* SG5 .... 40 B8
Wellington Av *PIN* HA5 .... 231 G7 ▣
Wellington Cl *OXHEY* WD19 .... 231 G1
Wellington Dr *WGCE* AL7 .... 148 D3
Wellington Rd *LCOL/BKTW* AL2 .... 190 B4
   PIN HA5 .... 231 G7
   STAL AL1 .... 168 E7
   STVGE SG2 .... 76 D4
   WAT WD17 .... 12 C1 ▣
Wellington St *HERT/WAS* SG14 .... 150 E2 ▣
   LTN LU1 .... 4 B4
Well La *WARE* SG12 .... 127 F7 ▣
Wenlock St *LTNE* LU2 .... 4 C3 ▣
Wensley Cl *HARP* AL5 .... 144 A3
Wensleydale *HHNE* HP2 .... 8 B2
Wensley Di *LTNE* LU2 .... 4 C2
Wensum Wy *RKW/CH/CXG* WD3 .... 218 C3 ▣
Wentbridge Pth *BORE* WD6 .... 207 K8 ▣
Wentworth Av *BORE* WD6 .... 223 J5
   LTNW/LEA LU4 .... 68 B4
Wentworth Cl *POTB/CUF* EN6 ...... 210 B1 ▣
   WAT WD17 .... 204 A8
Wentworth Dr *BSF* CM23 .... 105 C3
Wentworth Rd *BAR* EN5 .... 225 J2
   HERT/BAY SG13 .... 151 F6
Wesley Cl *ARL/CHE* SG15 .... 24 E5
   CHESW EN7 .... 196 A6
Wesley Rd *STALW/RED* AL3 .... 115 J4
Wessex Dr *PIN* HA5 .... 231 F6
Westall Ct *HERT/WAS* SG14 .... 151 F4
Westbourne Rd *LTNW/LEA* LU4 .... 69 C8
Westbrook Cl *ROY* SG8 .... 18 C1
West Burrowfield *WGCE* AL7 .... 147 J5 ▣
Westbury *CHES/WCR* EN8 .... 197 H8 ▣
Westbury Cl *HTCH/STOT* SG5 .... 56 A1
Westbury Gdns *LTNE* LU2 .... 69 J6
Westbury Pl *LWTH* SG6 .... 41 J4
Westbury Ri *HLWE* CM17 .... 181 G2
Westbury Rd *NTHWD* HA6 .... 229 K3
   WATW WD18 .... 12 C4 ▣
Westbush Cl *HOD* EN11 .... 152 E8
West Chantry *RYLN/HDSTN* HA2 .. 231 J7 ▣
West Cl *BAR* EN5 .... 225 G5
   HOD EN11 .... 177 J1
   HTCHE/RSTV SG4 .... 41 F7
   STVG SG1 .... 3 D3
West Common *HARP* AL5 .... 143 J2
West Common Cl *HARP* AL5 .... 143 J4 ▣
West Common Gv *HARP* AL5 .... 143 J3

West Common Wy *HARP* AL5 .... 143 H4
Westcott *WGCE* AL7 .... 148 E2
Westcroft Cl *PEND* EN3 .... 214 B8 ▣
Westcroft Ct *BROX* EN10 .... 177 F5 ▣
West Dene *DUN/WHIP* LU6 .... 139 J1
West Dr *ARL/CHE* SG15 .... 24 E5
   GSTN WD25 .... 204 C6
   HTCH/STOT SG5 .... 25 F6
Westell Cl *BLDK* SG7 .... 43 G1
West End *BLDK* SG7 .... 17 J6
West End La *BAR* EN5 .... 225 J4
   BRKMPK AL9 .... 172 D4
West End Rd *BROX* EN10 .... 196 D1
   LBUZ LU7 .... 109 K2
Westerdale *HHNE* HP2 .... 8 B2
   LTNW/LEA LU4 .... 68 A4
Western Cl *LWTH* SG6 .... 25 J8
Western Rd *LTN* LU1 .... 4 B5 ▣
   TRING HP23 .... 134 E6
   WAB EN9 .... 177 K8
Western Wy *LWTH* SG6 .... 25 J8
Westfield *BRKMPK* AL9 .... 193 C6
   HLWS CM18 .... 7 D5
   WGCE AL7 .... 148 B2
Westfield Av *HARP* AL5 .... 118 C6
   WATN WD24 .... 204 E8
Westfield Ct *BSF* CM23 .... 105 H1
   CHES/WCR EN8 .... 214 C1
   HTCH/STOT SG5 .... 56 B2
Westfield Dr *HARP* AL5 .... 118 D5
Westfield La *HTCH/STOT* SG5 .... 56 B2
Westfield Pk *PIN* HA5 .... 231 G6
Westfield Pl *HARP* AL5 .... 118 D5
Westfield Rd *BERK* HP4 .... 161 F3
   BSF CM23 .... 105 H1
   HARP AL5 .... 118 D5
   HERT/WAS SG14 .... 151 F1
   HOD EN11 .... 176 E2
Westfields *STALW/RED* AL3 .... 167 H8
West Ga *HLW* CM20 .... 6 B4
West Hl *HTCH/STOT* SG5 .... 56 B2
West Hill Rd *HOD* EN11 .... 176 E1
   LTN LU1 .... 4 C6
Westholme *LWTH* SG6 .... 41 K1
West Hyde La *CFSP/GDCR* SL9 ...... 226 C5
Westland Dr *BRKMPK* AL9 .... 192 E5
Westland Rd *KNEB* SG3 .... 96 B4
   WAT WD17 .... 12 C1 ▣
West La *HTCH/STOT* SG5 .... 39 F4
   HTCH/STOT SG5 .... 54 F7
Westlea Av *WD25 .... 205 F7
Westlea Cl *BROX* EN10 .... 197 K2 ▣
Westlea Rd *BROX* EN10 .... 197 K1
Westlecote Gdns *LTNE* LU2 .... 69 J5
West Lieth *TRING* HP23 .... 134 D8
Westly Wd *WGCE* AL7 .... 148 B2
West Md *WGCE* AL7 .... 148 C6
Westmeade Cl *CHESW* EN7 .... 197 F7
Westmill *HTCH/STOT* SG5 .... 40 A7
Westmill Lawns *HTCH/STOT* SG5 .. 40 B8 ▣
Westmill Rd *HTCH/STOT* SG5 .... 40 A7
   WARE SG12 .... 126 D4
Westminster Ct *STALW/RED* AL3 .. 10 B6 ▣
Westmorland Av *LTNN/LIM* LU3 .... 68 E4
Weston Av *ROY* SG8 .... 21 G2
Weston Cl *POTB/CUF* EN6 .... 210 A2 ▣
Weston Rd *STVG* SG1 .... 58 E8
Weston Wy *BLDK* SG7 .... 42 E1
Westray *HHS/BOV* HP3 .... 165 H8 ▣
West Reach *STVGE* SG2 .... 3 D6
Westridge Cl *HHW* HP1 .... 163 J6 ▣
West Riding *LCOL/BKTW* AL2 .... 188 B8
   WLYN AL6 .... 123 K4
West Rd *BERK* HP4 .... 161 H4
   BSF CM23 .... 105 H3
   HLW CM20 .... 156 C5
   SBW CM21 .... 131 K6
   STSD CM24 .... 86 D1
Westron Gdns *TRING* HP23 .... 135 G5
West Side *BROX* EN10 .... 197 J3
West St *HERT/BAY* SG13 .... 151 F4
   LTNE LU2 .... 53 K8
   WARE SG12 .... 127 H8
   WAT WD17 .... 12 C1 ▣
West Valley Rd *HHS/BOV* HP3 ...... 185 G2
West Vw *HAT* AL10 .... 171 F2
   LWTH SG6 .... 41 H5
Westview *BORE* WD6 .... 223 G6 ▣
West View Gdns *BORE* WD6 .... 223 G6
Westview Rd *HHNE* HP2 .... 8 A4
West Vw Rd *STALW/RED* AL3 .... 10 C3
West Wy *HARP* AL5 .... 118 E7
   LTNE LU2 .... 70 D5
West Wy *RKW/CH/CXG* WD3 .... 218 A8
   WAB EN9 .... 215 G7
Westwick Cl *HHNE* HP2 .... 165 J7
Westwick Pl *CSTN* WD25 .... 204 D4
Westwick Rw *HHNE* HP2 .... 165 J7
Westwood Av *HTCHE/RSTV* SG4 .... 56 E3
Westwood Cl *AMS* HP6 .... 216 A1
   POTB/CUF EN6 .... 193 C8
Westwood Dr *AMS* HP6 .... 216 A1
Wetherby Cl *STVG* SG1 .... 76 D1
Wetherby Rd *BORE* WD6 .... 223 H1

Wetherfield *STSD* CM24 .... 86 C2
Wetherly Cl *HLWE* CM17 .... 157 F6
Wetherne Link *LTNW/LEA* LU4 .... 68 B4
Wexham Cl *LTNN/LIM* LU3 .... 68 D1
Weybourne Cl *HARP* AL5 .... 119 F7
Weybourne Dr *LTNE* LU2 .... 69 H2
Weymouth St *HHS/BOV* HP3 .... 185 H2
Whaley Rd *POTB/CUF* EN6 .... 210 D3
Wharfdale *LTNW/LEA* LU4 .... 68 B4 ▣
Wharfedale *HHNE* HP2 .... 8 B2
Wharf La *BERK* HP4 .... 136 D8
   RKW/CH/CXG WD3 .... 218 D7
Wharf Rd *BROX* EN10 .... 197 K2
   BSF CM23 .... 105 J3
   HHW HP1 .... 164 A8
Wharley Hook *HLWS* CM18 .... 180 C4
Wheatbarn *WGCE* AL7 .... 148 C2 ▣
Wheat Cl *STALE/WH* AL4 .... 168 D2
Wheatcotes *KNEB* SG3 .... 96 D8
Wheat Cft *BSF* CM23 .... 105 H5 ▣
Wheatfield *HAT* AL10 .... 171 C3 ▣
   HHNE HP2 .... 8 A3
Wheatfield Av *HARP* AL5 .... 143 H4 ▣
Wheatfield Crs *ROY* SG8 .... 21 J3 ▣
Wheatfield Rd *HARP* AL5 .... 143 G4
Wheatfields *HLWE* CM17 .... 157 C3 ▣
Wheathampstead Rd *HARP* AL5 .... 144 A1
Wheat Hl *LWTH* SG6 .... 41 J2
Wheatlands *STVGE* SG2 .... 76 D2
Wheatley Cl *SBW* CM21 .... 132 A8
   WCCE AL7 .... 148 B5
Wheatley Rd *WGCE* AL7 .... 148 A4
Wheatsheaf *STALE/WH* AL4 .... 169 F4 ▣
Wheatley Wy *CFSP/GDCR* SL9 ...... 226 B5
Wheatlock Md *STALW/RED* AL3 .... 142 B4
Wheatsheaf Dr *WARE* SG12 .... 127 F6
Wheatsheaf La *WARE* SG12 .... 129 K7
Wheelers Cl *WAB* EN9 .... 177 K8
Wheelers La *HHS/BOV* HP3 .... 164 D8
Wheelers Orch *CFSP/GDCR* SL9 .... 226 B5
Wheelwright Cl *BUSH* WD23 .... 221 J6 ▣
Wheelwrights Cl *BSF* CM23 .... 105 F5 ▣
Whetstone Cl *WLYN* AL6 .... 122 F3 ▣
Whinbush Gv *HTCH/STOT* SG5 ...... 56 D1 ▣
Whinbush Rd *HTCH/STOT* SG5 ...... 56 D2
Whippendell Rd *WATW* WD18 ...... 12 B4
Whippendell Rd *WATW* WD18 ...... 12 B4
Whipperley Ring *LTN* LU1 .... 89 F3
Whipperley Wy *LTN* LU1 .... 89 C3
Whisper Wd *RKW/CH/CXG* WD3 .... 218 A3
Whitby Rd *LTNN/LIM* LU3 .... 4 A2
Whitebarns *LBUNT* SG9 .... 96 C2
Whitebeam Cl *CHESW* EN7 .... 196 C4 ▣
Whitebeams *HAT* AL10 .... 171 F7 ▣
   LCOL/BKTW AL2 .... 188 D6
White Bear *STSD* CM24 .... 86 D1 ▣
Whitebroom Rd *HHW* HP1 .... 163 H4 ▣
Whitechurch Cl *LTNE* LU2 .... 70 E7 ▣
Whitechurch Gdns *LWTH* SG6 ...... 42 C6
White Craig Cl *PIN* HA5 .... 231 H4 ▣
Whitecroft *STAL* AL1 .... 189 K1
Whitecroft Rd *LTNE* LU2 .... 5 E3
White Crofts *HTCH/STOT* SG5 ...... 25 J2
Whitefield Av *LTNN/LIM* LU3 .... 68 B3
Whitefields Rd *CHES/WCR* EN8 .... 197 G6
Whitegale Cl *HTCHE/RSTV* SG4 .... 56 E3
Whitegates Cl *RKW/CH/CXG* WD3 .. 219 F4
Whitehall Cl *WAB* EN9 .... 177 K8 ▣
Whitehall La *BSF* CM23 .... 85 J8
Whitehall Rd *BSF* CM23 .... 85 H8
Whitehands Cl *HOD* EN11 .... 176 E5 ▣
White Hart Cl *BUNT* SG9 .... 63 H1
White Hart Dr *HHNE* HP2 .... 8 C6
White Hart Rd *HHNE* HP2 .... 8 C6
White Hedge Dr *STALW/RED* AL3 .. 10 B2
Whitehicks *LWTH* SG6 .... 26 A8
Whitehill *BERK* HP4 .... 162 A4
White Hl *HHW* HP4 .... 182 E2
   HHW HP1 .... 163 J7
   NTHWD HA6 .... 229 H5
   STALW/RED AL3 .... 141 G1
   STVGE SG2 .... 60 E6
   WLYN AL6 .... 122 A7
Whitehill Av *LTN* LU1 .... 4 B6
Whitehill Cl *BERK* HP4 .... 162 A4
White Hill Rd *AMP/FLIT/B* MK45 .. 36 C6
Whitehill Rd *HTCHE/RSTV* SG4 .... 56 E3
White Horse La *KNEB* SG3 .... 96 C8
   LCOL/BKTW AL2 .... 190 B4
Whitehorse St *BLDK* SG7 .... 43 F1
Whitehouse Av *BORE* WD6 .... 224 A4
White House Cl *CFSP/GDCR* SL9 .. 226 B6
Whitehouse La *ABLGY* WD5 .... 187 H4
Whitehurst Av *HTCH/STOT* SG5 .... 40 D8
Whitelands Av *RKW/CH/CXG* WD3 .. 216 E3
Whiteley Cl *WARE* SG12 .... 99 F1 ▣
White Lion Ct *HHNE* HP2 .... 47 G2
White Lion St *HHS/BOV* HP3 .... 185 H2 ▣
White Post Fld *SBW* CM21 .... 132 B7
White Shack La
   RKW/CH/CXG WD3 .... 202 E7

Whitesmead Rd *STVG* SG1 .... 2 C1
Whitestone Wk *HHW* HP1 .... 163 K3 🔲
White Stubbs La *BROX* EN10 .... 175 J7
Whitethorn Ct *WCCE* AL7 .... 148 B4
Whitethorn La *LWTH* SG6 .... 42 A6
Whitethorn Wy *LTN* LU1 .... 89 F3
Whitewaits *HLW* CM20 .... 7 D3
Whitewaybottom La *LTNE* LU2... 92 C3
The White Wy *STVGE* SG2 .... 76 D2
Whitewebbs La *ENC/FH* EN2 ...... 213 J5
Whitewebbs Rd *ENC/FH* EN2 ...... 212 E5
Whitewood Rd *BERK* HP4 .... 161 H5 🔲
Whitfield Wy *RKW/CH/CXG* WD3 ... 217 J8
Whit Hern Ct *CHES/WCR* EN8 ...... 197 G8
Whitings Cl *HARP* AL5 .... 119 F5
Whitings Rd *BAR* EN5 .... 225 H5
Whitlars Dr *KGLGY* WD4 .... 186 A6 🔲
Whitley Cl *ABLGY* WD5 .... 204 B2
Whitley Rd *HOD* EN11 .... 177 G1
Whitmores Wd *HHNE* HP2 .... 9 E4
Whitney Dr *STVG* SG1 .... 58 C8
Whittingham Cl *LTNE* LU2 ...... 71 G8 🔲
Whittingstall Rd *HOD* EN11 .... 177 G1
Whittington La *STVG* SG1 .... 2 C4
Whittington Wy *BAR* CM23 ..... 105 H6
Whittlesea Rd *KTN/HRWW/W* HA3.. 231 K6
Whitwell Cl *LTNN/LIM* LU3 ...... 69 G1
Whitwell Rd *GSTN* WD25 .... 204 E5
Whitworth Jones Av *HNLW* SG16 ..... 24 A4
Whitworth Rd *STVG* SG1 .... 59 H6
Whomerley Rd *STVG* SG1 .... 2 C4
Whydale Rd *ROY* SG8 .... 21 J4 🔲
Whytingham Rd *TRING* HP23 .... 135 H5
Wick Av *STALE/WH* AL4 .... 145 G1
Wicken Flds *WARE* SG12 .... 127 G6
The Wickets *LTNE* LU2 .... 4 B2
Wickfield Cl *KNEB* SG3 .... 96 B7 🔲
Wickham Cl *DEN/HRF* UB9 .... 228 C7
Wickhams Whf *WARE* SG12 ...... 127 J8 🔲
Wickham Wy *STDN* SG11 .... 81 K6 🔲
Wick Hi *DUN/WHIP* LU6 .... 114 D1
Wicklands Rd *WARE* SG12 .... 154 E1
Wickmere Cl *LTNE* LU2 .... 69 H2 🔲
Wick Rd *TRING* HP23 .... 159 H1
Wickstead Av *LTNW/LEA* LU4... 68 D6
The Wick *HERT/WAS* SG14 .... 125 K8
Widbury Gdns *WARE* SG12 ...... 127 K8 🔲
Widbury Hi *WARE* SG12 .... 128 A8
Widford Rd *MHAD* SG10 .... 130 A2
   WARE SG12 .... 129 K7
   WCCE AL7 .... 148 C3
Widford Ter *HHNE* HP2 .... 141 F8 🔲
Widgeon Wy *GSTN* WD25 .... 205 F6 🔲
Widmore Dr *HHNE* HP2 .... 9 D3
Wieland Rd *NTHWD* HA6 .... 230 B6
Wiggenhall Rd *WATW* WD18 ...... 12 C4
Wiggington Bottom *TRING* HP23 ... 159 J1
Wigmore La *LTNE* LU2 .... 70 E7
Wigmore Pl *LTNE* LU2 .... 71 F8
Wigmores North *WGCW* AL8 ... 147 J2 🔲
Wigram Wy *STVGE* SG2 .... 3 F4
Wilbury Cl *LWTH* SG6 .... 41 G2
Wilbury Hills Rd *LWTH* SG6 ...... 41 G3
Wilbury Rd *LWTH* SG6 .... 41 H2
Wilbury Wy *HTCHE/RSTV* SG4 ..... 40 E6
Wilcot Av *OXHEY* WD19 .... 13 F6
Wilcot Cl *OXHEY* WD19 .... 13 F6
Wilcox Cl *BORE* WD6 .... 224 B1
Wild Cherry Dr *LTN* LU1 .... 4 A5
The Wilderness *BERK* HP4 ...... 161 K5 🔲
Wildhill Rd *BRKMPK* AL9 .... 172 A7
Wild Oaks Cl *NTHWD* HA6 .... 230 A5
Wildwood *NTHWD* HA6 .... 229 J5
Wildwood Av *LCOL/BKTW* AL2... 188 B8
Wildwood La *STVG* SG1 .... 2 C5
Wilford Cl *NTHWD* HA6 .... 229 J6
Wilga Rd *WLYN* AL6 .... 122 B4
Wilkin's Green La *HAT* AL10 .... 170 B5
   STALE/WH AL4 .... 170 B6
Wilkins Gv *WGCW* AL8 .... 147 J4
Wilkinson Wy *HHS/BOV* HP3 ... 185 K2
Willenhall Cl *LTNN/LIM* LU3 ..... 69 F2 🔲
William Ct *HHS/BOV* HP3 .... 185 H2 🔲
William Covell Cl *ENC/FH* EN2 ... 212 C8 🔲
William Pl *STVGE* SG2 .... 3 E5
Williamson Wy *RKW/CH/CXG* WD3.. 217 K8
William St *BERK* HP4 .... 162 A5
   BUSH WD23 .... 13 E2
   LTNE LU2 .... 4 C2
   STALW/RED AL3 .... 115 J4 🔲
Williams Wy *RAD* WD7 .... 207 F5
Willian Church Rd *LWTH* SG6 .... 42 A7
Willian Rd *HTCHE/RSTV* SG4.... 41 F8
Willian Wy *BLDK* SG7 .... 42 E3 🔲
   LWTH SG6 .... 42 A5
Willinghall Cl *WAB* EN9 .... 215 J2 🔲
Williton Rd *LTNE* LU2 .... 5 F1
Willoughby Cl *BROX* EN10 ..... 176 D7 🔲
Willoughby Rd *HARP* AL5 .... 118 E6
Willoughby Wy *HTCHE/RSTV* SG4.. 56 E3 🔲
Willowby Ct *LCOL/BKTW* AL2.. 190 B4
Willow Cl *BSF* CM23 .... 105 H1
   BUNT SG9 .... 65 G1
   CHESW EN7 .... 196 C4
   ROY SG8 .... 31 H4

Willow Crs *STAL* AL1 .... 169 F6
Willow Dean *PIN* HA5 .... 230 E8 🔲
Willow Dene *BUSH* WD23........ 222 B7
Willowdene *CHES/WCR* EN8 .... 197 J5
Willow Dene *PIN* HA5 .... 230 E8
Willow Dr *BAR* EN5 .... 225 K4
Willow Edge *KGLGY* WD4 .... 186 A7 🔲
Willow End *NTHWD* HA6 .... 230 B5
Willowfield *HLWS* CM18 .... 6 C5
Willow Gv *WCCW* AL8 .... 122 D6
Willow La *HTCH/STOT* SG5 ...... 56 B3
   WATW WD18 .... 12 B4
Willowmead *HERT/WAS* SG14 ... 150 D4
Willow Md *SBW* CM21 .... 132 C8
Willow Pl *HLWE* CM17 .... 181 J5
Willow Rd *PIN* HA5 .... 230 D8
Willowside *LCOL/BKTW* AL2 ... 190 C5
Willowside Wy *ROY* SG8 .... 21 G1 🔲
Willows Link *STVGE* SG2 .... 76 B6
Willow Springs *BSF* CM23 ...... 105 G1
The Willows *HTCHE/RSTV* SG4.. 56 E4
   OXHEY WD19 .... 12 C6 🔲
   RKW/CH/CXG WD3 .... 227 K1
   STAL AL1 .... 189 K2
   STVGE SG2 .... 96 B1
Willow Tree Wy *HTCH/STOT* SG5... 40 C7
Willow Wk *WLYN* AL6 .... 122 C1
Willow Wy *HARP* AL5 .... 118 E5 🔲
   HAT AL10 .... 170 E7
   HHW HP1 .... 164 A4 🔲
   LCOL/BKTW AL2 .... 188 C5
   LTNN/LIM LU3 .... 68 D4
   POTB/CUF EN6 .... 210 C3
   RAD WD7 .... 206 B6
Wilsden Av *LTN* LU1 .... 4 A5
Wilshere Av *STAL* AL1 .... 188 C1
Wilshere Crs *HTCHE/RSTV* SG4 ... 57 C1
Wilshere Rd *WLYN* AL6 .... 122 A4
Wilson Cl *BSF* CM23 .... 105 J4
   STVG SG1 .... 58 D8
Wilsons La *BLDK* SG7 .... 17 J5
Wilstone Br *TRING* HP23 .... 109 H8
Wilstone Dr *STALE/WH* AL4 ..... 169 F1
Wilton Cl *BSF* CM23 .... 106 A2
Wilton Crs *HERT/BAY* SG13 ..... 151 F6
Wilton Rd *HTCH/STOT* SG5 .... 40 A8
Wilton Wy *HERT/BAY* SG13 ..... 151 F5 🔲
Wiltshire Rd *STVGE* SG2 .... 3 E4
Wimborne Cl *SBW* CM21 .... 132 B7 🔲
Wimborne Gv *WAT* WD17 ...... 203 K7
Wimborne Rd *LTN* LU1 .... 89 C1
Winch Cl *WLYN* AL6 .... 121 K1 🔲
Winchdells *HHS/BOV* HP3 ...... 186 A1
Winchester Cl *BSF* CM23 .... 105 G5
   STVG SG1 .... 59 G7
Winchester Wy
   RKW/CH/CXG WD3 .... 219 G5
Winchfield Wy *RKW/CH/CXG* WD3 .. 218 D7
Winch St *LTNE* LU2 .... 5 D2
Windermere Av *STAL* AL1 .... 168 E8
Windermere Cl *HHS/BOV* HP3..... 9 F6
   RKW/CH/CXG WD3 .... 217 G5
Windermere Crs *LTNN/LIM* LU3 ... 68 E4
Windhill *BSF* CM23 .... 105 H2
   WCCE AL7 .... 148 B2
Windhill Old Rd *BSF* CM23 ..... 105 H2
Winding Hi *MHAD* SG10 .... 103 H5
Winding Shot *HHW* HP1 .... 163 K5
Winding Shott *HERT/WAS* SG14 ... 124 E5
Windmill Av *STALE/WH* AL4 .... 169 F2
Windmill Cl *LBUZ* LU7 .... 111 F4
   ROY SG8 .... 32 C4
   WAB EN9 .... 215 K4
Windmill Dr *RKW/CH/CXG* WD3... 218 E6
Windmill Fld *WARE* SG12 .... 152 C1
Windmill Flds *HLWE* CM17 ...... 157 J5
Windmill Hi *BUNT* SG9 .... 63 K3
   HTCHE/RSTV SG4 .... 56 D2
   KGLGY WD4 .... 201 J2
Windmill La *BAR* EN5 .... 224 E6
   BUSH WD23 .... 222 B8
   CHES/WCR EN8 .... 197 J8
Windmill Rd *CFSP/GDCR* SL9... 226 A6 🔲
   HHNE HP2 .... 8 B5
   HTCHE/RSTV SG4 .... 72 A7
   LTN LU1 .... 5 E5
Windmills *WARE* SG12 .... 99 H1
Windmill St *BUSH* WD23 .... 222 B8
Windmill Wy *MHAD* SG10 .... 103 F8
   TRING HP23 .... 134 E5
Windmore Av *POTB/CUF* EN6 ... 209 H1
Windridge Cl *STALW/RED* AL3 .. 167 H8
Winds End *HHNE* HP2 .... 9 D3 🔲
Windsor Cl *CHESW* EN7 .... 196 E8
   HHS/BOV HP3 .... 164 D8
   HHS/BOV HP3 .... 183 J6 🔲
   NTHWD HA6 .... 230 B8
   STVGE SG2 .... 96 C2
   WLYN AL6 .... 122 B6
Windsor Dr *HERT/WAS* SG14 ... 150 C5
Windsor Gdns *BSF* CM23 .... 105 F2
Windsor Rd *AMP/FLIT/B* MK45 ... 36 C5
   BAR EN5 .... 225 J6
   KTN/HRWW/W HA3 .... 231 K5
   PEND EN3 .... 214 C6

ROY SG8 .... 21 K
WATN WD24.......................... 204 D
WLYN AL6 .... 122 B
Windsor St *LTN* LU1 .... 4 C5 🔲
Windsor Wk *LTN* LU1 .... 4 B5 🔲
Windsor Wy *RKW/CH/CXG* WD3 ... 217 K
Windward Cl *PEND* EN3............ 214 C
Windy Ri *WARE* SG12 .... 99 J2 🔲
Winford Dr *BROX* EN10 .... 176 E8
Wingate Gdns *WLYN* AL6 ...... 122 B4 🔲
Wingate Rd *LTNW/LEA* LU4 ...... 68 E
Wingate Wy *STAL* AL1 .... 171 F
Wingrave Rd *TRING* HP23 .... 109 H
Winifred Rd *HHS/BOV* HP3 ..... 185 H
Winkers Cl *CFSP/GDCR* SL9 ... 226 D
Winkers La *CFSP/GDCR* SL9 .... 226 C
Winkfield Cl *LTNW/LEA* LU4 ..... 68 A8 🔲
Winnington Rd *PEND* EN3........ 214 B
Winsdon Rd *LTN* LU1 .... 4 B
Winslow Cl *LTNN/LIM* LU3 ...... 69 H
Winston Churchill Wy
   CHES/WCR EN8 .... 214 B
Winston Cl *HTCH/STOT* SG5 ...... 56 B
Winston Ct *PIN* HA5 .... 231 J
Winston Gdns *BERK* HP4 .... 161 G
Winston Wy *POTB/CUF* EN6 .... 210 B3 🔲
Winstre Rd *BORE* WD6 .... 223 K
Winterscroft Rd *HOD* EN11 .... 176 E2
Winters La *STVGE* SG2 .... 60 D
Winton Ap *RKW/CH/CXG* WD3... 219 H
Winton Cl *LTNE* LU2................. 69 K
   LWTH SG6 .... 42 C
Winton Crs *RKW/CH/CXG* WD3 .. 219 G
Winton Dr *CHES/WCR* EN8....... 197 J
   RKW/CH/CXG WD3 .... 219 H
Winton Rd *WARE* SG12 .... 127 K
Wisden Rd *STVG* SG1 .... 76 A
Wiseman Cl *LTNE* LU2 .... 69 K2 🔲
Wisemans Gdns *SBW* CM21 .... 132 A
Wistlea Crs *STALE/WH* AL4 ..... 170 A
Wistow Rd *LTNN/LIM* LU3 .... 69 H
Witchford Wy *WCCE* AL7 .... 148 B
Withy Cl *LTNW/LEA* LU4 .... 68 A
Withy Pl *LCOL/BKTW* AL2 .... 188 E
Witney Cl *PIN* HA5 .... 231 C
Witter Av *HTCH/STOT* SG5 .... 40 C
Wiveton Cl *LTNE* LU2 .... 69 J
Woburn Av *BSF* CM23 .... 105 F
Woburn Cl *BUSH* WD23 .... 221 H
   STVGE SG2 .... 96 C
Wodecroft Rd *LTNN/LIM* LU3 .... 69 H
Wolsey Av *CHESW* EN7 .... 196 D7
Wolsey Rd *HHNE* HP2 .... 8 A
   RKW/CH/CXG WD3 .... 229 H
Wolston Cl *LTN* LU1 .... 4 A
Wolvescroft *KNEB* SG3 .... 96 B7
Wolves Mere *KNEB* SG3 .... 96 B
Woodacre Dr *WLYN* AL6 .... 123 C
Woodbank Dr *CSTG* HP8 .... 226 A
Woodbine Cl *HLWW/ROY* CM19 ..... 6 E
Woodbine Gv *ENC/FH* EN2 ...... 213 G
Woodbridge Cl *LTNW/LEA* LU4 ... 68 C
Woodbrook Gdns *WAB* EN9 .... 215 K
Woodbury Hi *LTNE* LU2 .... 4 C
Wood Cl *HAT* AL10 .... 171 C
Woodcock Hi *RKW/CH/CXG* WD3 .. 228 C
Woodcockhill *STALE/WH* AL4 ... 145 C
Woodcock Rd *LTN* LU1 .... 89 F
   STVGE SG2 .... 76 E
Wood Common *HAT* AL10 .... 171 C
Woodcote Cl *CHES/WCR* EN8 ... 197 C
Wood Crs *HHS/BOV* HP3 .... 8 A
Woodcroft *HLWS* CM18 .... 6 E
Woodcroft Av *WARE* SG12 ...... 153 _
Wood Dr *STVGE* SG2 .... 3 F
Wood End *LCOL/BKTW* AL2 ..... 188 E
Wood End Cl *HHNE* HP2 .... 9 F
Wood End Hi *HARP* AL5 .... 117 K
Wood End La *STALW/RED* AL3 ... 140 E
Wood End Rd *HARP* AL5 .... 117 K
Wood Farm Rd *HHNE* HP2 .... 8 E
Woodfield Av *NTHWD* HA6 ...... 229 J
Woodfield Cl *STSD* CM24 .... 86 D3
Woodfield Dr *HHS/BOV* HP3 .... 165 _
Woodfield Gdns *HHS/BOV* HP3 .. 165 J8 🔲
Woodfield La *BRKMPK* AL9 ..... 194 A
Woodfield Ri *BUSH* WD23 .... 222 A
Woodfield Rd *RAD* WD7 .... 206 D
   STVG SG1 .... 58 C
   WCCE AL7 .... 148 B
Woodfields *STSD* CM24 .... 86 D
Woodfield Ter *STSD* CM24 .... 86 D3
Woodfield Wy *STALE/WH* AL4 ... 169 F
Woodford Crs *PIN* HA5 .... 230 C
Woodforde Cl *BLDK* SG7 .... 148 B
Woodford Rd *WAT* WD17 .... 12 C
Woodgate *GSTN* WD25 .... 204 C
Woodgate Av *POTB/CUF* EN6 ... 211
Woodgate Crs *NTHWD* HA6 ..... 230 B
Wood Green Cl *LTNE* LU2 .... 70 B
Wood Green Rd *LTNE* LU2 .... 70 C
Woodhall Av *PIN* HA5 .... 231 K
Woodhall Cl *HERT/WAS* SG14 ... 151 F1
Woodhall Ct *WGCE* AL7 147

Woodhall Dr *PIN* HA5 .... 230 E7
Woodhall Ga *PIN* HA5 .... 230 E6
Woodhall Gv *BSF* CM23 .... 105 G3
Woodhall La *HHNE* HP2 .... 8 B4
  OXHEY WD19.
  RAD WD7 .... 207 K4 🔟
  WGCE AL7 .... 147 K5
Woodham Wy *WARE* SG12 .... 153 H5 🔟
Woodhill *HLWS* CM18 .... 180 B4
Woodhouse Eaves *NTHWD* HA6 .. 230 B4 🔟
Wood House La *BROX* EN10 .... 175 J7
Woodhurst *LWTH* SG6.............................. 41 K1
Woodhurst Av *GSTN* WD25 .... 204 E5
Wooding Gv *HLWW/ROY* CM19 .... 6 A4
Woodland Av *HHW* HP1 .... 164 A7
  LTNN/LIM LU3 .... 69 G7
Woodland Dr *STALE/WH* AL4 .... 169 F5
  TRING HP23
  WAT WD17 .... 220 A1
Woodland La *RKW/CH/CXG* WD3 ... 217 G3
Woodland Mt *HERT/BAY* SG13 ...... 151 J3
Woodland Rd *HHW* HP1 .... 164 A7 🔟
Woodland Ri *DUN/WHIP* LU6 .... 113 K2
  WGCW AL8 .... 147 H1
Woodland Rd *HERT/BAY* SG13 ...... 152 B3
  RKW/CH/CXG WD3 .... 227 G4
Woodlands *BRKMPK* AL9 .... 193 H5
  BSF CM23 .... 106 B1
  HARP AL5 .... 118 A6
  LCOL/BKTW AL2 .... 188 E5
  LTN LU1 .... 88 D7
  RAD WD7 .... 206 D4 🔟
  ROY SG8 .... 21 J5 🔟
Woodlands Av *BERK* HP4 .... 162 A6
Woodlands Cl *BORE* WD6................. 224 A4
  HOD EN11 .... 177 F4 🔟
  TRING HP23 .... 134 E7
Woodlands Dr *HOD* EN11 .... 177 F5
Woodlands Meade
  HTCHE/RSTV SG4 .... 59 H1
Woodlands Rd *BUSH* WD23 .... 13 F3
  ENC/FH EN2 .... 213 G8
  HERT/BAY SG13 .... 151 J3
  KGLGY WD4 .... 186 A5
  WARE SG12 .... 127 H3
Woodland Wy *BLDK* SG7 .... 43 F3
  CHESW EN7 .... 195 K6
  STVGE SG2 .... 76 B8
  WLYN AL6 .... 123 F2
Wood La *BSF* CM23 .... 86 D7
  BUNT SG9 .... 50 C3
  HHNE HP2 .... 8 A6
Wood Lane End *HHNE* HP2 .... 9 E4
Woodlea *LCOL/BKTW* AL2 .... 188 C5
Woodlea Gv *NTHWD* HA6 .... 229 H5
Woodley Rd *WARE* SG12 .... 127 K7
Woodman Rd *HHS/BOV* HP3 .... 164 D8
Woodmans Yd *WAT* WD17 .... 13 D5 🔟
Woodmere *LTNN/LIM* LU3 .... 52 A8
Woodmere Av *WATN* WD24 .... 204 E8
Woodpecker Cl *BSF* CM23 .... 105 F3 🔟
  BUSH WD23 .... 221 K8
  HAT AL10 .... 170 E7 🔟
Woodredon Cl
  HLWW/ROY CM19 .... 178 C2 🔟
Woodridge Wy *NTHWD* HA6 .... 229 K5
Woodridings Av *PIN* HA5 .... 231 G7
Woodridings Cl *PIN* HA5 .... 231 G6
Woods Av *HAT* AL10 .... 171 F5
Woodshots Meadow *WATW* WD18.. 219 J3
Woodside *BORE* WD6....................... 223 J4 🔟
  BSF CM23 .... 106 C1
  CHESW EN7 .... 213 K1
  HERT/BAY SG13 .... 152 B6
  WATN WD24 .... 204 A7
Woodside Cl *CFSP/GDCR* SL9 .... 226 B8 🔟
Woodside HI *CFSP/GDCR* SL9 .... 226 B8
Woodside La *BRKMPK* AL9 .... 172 B8
Woodside Rd *GSTN* WD25 .... 204 C1
  LCOL/BKTW AL2 .... 188 B8
  LTN LU1 .... 89 F8

NTHWD HA6 .... 230 A6
WLYN AL6 .... 123 F6
Woods PI *TRING* HP23 .... 135 F6 🔟
The Woods *NTHWD* HA6................... 230 B4
  RAD WD7 .... 206 E4
Woodstock *KNEB* SG3.......................... 96 A6
Woodstock Cl *HERT/BAY* SG13 ... 152 A5 🔟
Woodstock Rd *BROX* EN10 .... 176 D5
  BUSH WD23 .... 222 B7
Woodstock Rd North *STAL* AL1...... 168 E4
Woodstock Rd South *STAL* AL1...... 168 E6
Wood St *BAR* EN5 .... 225 H4
  LTN LU1 .... 5 D5 🔟
Wood V *HAT* AL10 .... 171 C4
Wood Vw *HHW* HP1 .... 164 A4
  POTB/CUF EN6 .... 195 G5
Woodville Court Ms *WAT* WD17 ... 12 B1 🔟
Woodwards *HLWW/ROY* CM19 .... 6 B6
Woodwaye *OXHEY* WD19................... 13 D6
Woodwicks *RKW/CH/CXG* WD3 ..... 227 G4 🔟
Woolgrove Rd *HTCHE/RSTV* SG4.. 40 E8
Wooliam Crs *STALW/RED* AL3 .... 167 K2
Woollard St *WAB* EN9 .... 215 H4
Woolmans Cl *BROX* EN10 .... 176 E8
Woolmer Cl *BORE* WD6 .... 207 K8
Woolmerdine Ct *BUSH* WD23 .... 13 E2
Woolmer Dr *HHNE* HP2........................ 9 F5
Woolmers La *HERT/WAS* SG14...... 149 J7
Woolners Wy *STVG* SG1 .... 2 A2
Woolston Av *LWTH* SG6 .... 42 A5
Wootton Cl *LTNN/LIM* LU3 .... 69 G2
Wootton Dr *HHNE* HP2 .... 164 E1
Worboys Ct *ROY* SG8 .... 15 G4
Worcester Rd *HAT* AL10 .... 170 E3
Worcesters Av *EN* EN1 .... 213 K6
Wordsworth Rd *HARP* AL5 .... 118 C6
Works Rd *LWTH* SG6............................. 42 B2
Worley Rd *STALW/RED* AL3 .... 10 C3
Wormley Lodge Cl *BROX* EN10 .... 197 K1 🔟
Worsdell Wy *HTCHE/RSTV* SG4...... 57 F2 🔟
Worsted La *BUNT* SG9 .... 64 E2
Wortham Rd *ROY* SG8......................... 21 J5
Wortham Wy *STVGE* SG2 .... 3 F5
The Wraglins *BSF* CM23 .... 106 A4
Wratten Cl *HTCH/STOT* SG5 .... 56 C3 🔟
Wratten Rd East *HTCH/STOT* SG5... 56 C3
Wratten Rd West *HTCH/STOT* SG5.. 56 B3
Wrayfields *HTCH/STOT* SG5 .... 26 B2
Wraysbury Cl *LTNW/LEA* LU4......... 68 C5
Wrenbrook Rd *BSF* CM23 .... 105 J4
Wren Cl *HTCHE/RSTV* SG4................. 92 E8
  LTNE LU2 .... 70 D3
  STVGE SG2 .... 3 F2
Wren Crs *BUSH* WD23 .... 221 K8
Wrensfield *HHW* HP1 .... 163 K6
The Wrens *HLWW/ROY* CM19 .... 6 A4 🔟
Wren Wd *WGCE* AL7 .... 148 C2
Wright Cl *STALE/WH* AL4 .... 145 G2
Wright's Green La *RBSF* CM22 ...... 133 G2
Wrights Meadow *STVGE* SG2 .... 77 J1
Wrights Orch *STVGE* SG2 .... 77 F7
Wrotham Rd *BAR* EN5 .... 225 K2
Wroxham Av *HHS/BOV* HP3 .... 164 C8
Wroxham Gdns *ENC/FH* EN2 .... 212 D5
  POTB/CUF EN6 .... 209 J1
Wroxham Wy *HARP* AL5 .... 118 B6
Wulfrath Wy *WARE* SG12 .... 127 G6
Wulwards Cl *LTN* LU1 .... 89 C3
Wyatt Cl *BUSH* WD23 .... 222 B7
  HTCH/STOT SG5 .... 40 B5
Wyatt's Cl *RKW/CH/CXG* WD3 .... 217 K3
Wyatt's Rd *RKW/CH/CXG* WD3 ...... 217 J4
Wychdell *STVGE* SG2 .... 96 D1
Wych Elm *HLW* CM20............................. 6 B5
Wych Elm La *KNEB* SG3 .... 95 K6
Wych Elms *LCOL/BKTW* AL2 .... 188 D6
Wychford Dr *SBW* CM21 .... 132 A8
Wychwood Av *LTNE* LU2 .... 69 K5
Wychwood Wy *NTHWD* HA6 .... 230 A6 🔟
Wycklond Cl *HTCH/STOT* SG5 .... 25 J3 🔟
Wycliffe Cl *LTNN/LIM* LU3 .... 69 H3 🔟
Wycombe Wy *LTNN/LIM* LU3........... 69 H1

STALE/WH AL4 .... 168 E3
Wyddial Gn *WGCE* AL7 .... 148 C3 🔟
Wyddial Rd *BUNT* SG9 .... 63 J1
Wyedale *LCOL/BKTW* AL2............... 190 D5
Wykeham Ri *TRDG/WHET* N20 ...... 225 K8
Wyken Cl *LTNN/LIM* LU3 .... 69 F2
Wyldwood Cl *HLWE* CM17 .... 157 F3
Wyllyotts Pl *POTB/CUF* EN6 .... 210 A2 🔟
Wylo Dr *BAR* EN5................................. 225 F6
Wymondley Cl *HTCHE/RSTV* SG4 .. 56 E3
Wymondley Rd *HTCHE/RSTV* SG4.. 56 E3
Wynches Farm Dr
  STALE/WH AL4 .... 169 G6 🔟
Wynchlands Crs *STALE/WH* AL4 .... 169 G6
Wyndham Rd *LTNW/LEA* LU4 .... 68 B7 🔟
Wyndhams End *BRKMPK* AL9 .... 148 A7 🔟
Wynlie Gdns *PIN* HA5 .... 230 C8
Wynn Cl *BLDK* SG7.................................. 27 G8
Wyrley Dell *LWTH* SG6 .... 42 A6
Wyton *WGCE* AL7................................ 148 E3
Wyvern Cl *LTNW/LEA* LU4 .... 68 D6 🔟

Y

Yardley *LWTH* SG6 .... 42 B5
Yardley Av *LBUZ* LU7 .... 110 C5
Yarmouth Rd *STVG* SG1 .... 75 F2
  WATN WD24....................................... 204 C8
Yately Cl *LTNE* LU2 .... 69 J2
Yearling Cl *WARE* SG12 .... 152 E2
Yeomanry Dr *BLDK* SG7 .... 27 G8
Yeomans Av *HARP* AL5 .... 117 K6 🔟
Yeomans Cl *BSF* CM23 .... 105 G4
Yeomans Dr *STVGE* SG2 .... 77 F7
Yeomans Ride *HHNE* HP2 .... 141 F8
Yeovil Rd *LTNE* LU2 .... 5 F1
Yew Cl *CHESW* EN7 .... 196 C5 🔟
Yew Gv *WGCE* AL7 .... 148 D4
Yewlands *HOD* EN11.......................... 177 F4
  SBW CM21 .... 132 C8 🔟
Yewlands Dr *HOD* EN11 .... 177 F4
Yews Av *EN* EN1 .... 214 A6
Yew Tree Cl *STHM* HP5 .... 182 C8
  LBUZ LU7 .... 110 E5
Yew Tree Ct *BORE* WD6 .... 223 G6 🔟
Yew Tree Dr *HHS/BOV* HP3 .... 185 K6
Yewtree End *LCOL/BKTW* AL2 .... 188 D5
Yew Tree Pl *BSF* CM23 .... 105 J1
Yew Wk *HOD* EN11 .... 177 F4
York Cl *AMP/FLIT/B* MK45 .... 36 C5
  KGLGY WD4 .... 186 A7
York Crs *BORE* WD6 .... 224 C2
Yorke Ga *WAT* WD17 .... 12 B1 🔟
Yorke Rd *RKW/CH/CXG* WD3 .... 219 F6
Yorkes *LCOL/BKTW* CM18 .... 7 E6
York Rd *CHES/WCR* EN8................... 214 D4
  HTCH/STOT SG5 .... 56 C1
  NTHWD HA6 .... 230 B8
  STAL AL1 .... 11 E3
  STVG SG1 .... 59 F8
  WATW WD18 .... 13 D4
York St *LTNE* LU2 .... 5 D3
York Ter *ENC/FH* EN2 .... 213 F8 🔟
York Wy *GSTN* WD25.......................... 204 E6
  HHS/BOV HP3 .... 8 B6
  ROY SG8 .... 21 F1
  WLYN AL6 .... 122 B6
Youngfield Rd *HHW* HP1 .... 163 J5
Youngsbury La *WARE* SG12 .... 127 H1
Youngs Ri *WGCW* AL8 .... 147 G3
Yule Cl *LCOL/BKTW* AL2................... 188 B8

Z

Zambesi Rd *BSF* CM23 .... 105 J4 🔟

Index - featured places

Abbey C of E JMI School
  STALW/RED AL3 .... 10 B5
Abbeygate Business Centre
  LTNE LU2 .... 5 D3
Abbey Mead Industrial Park
  WAB EN9 .... 215 G4
Abbey Road Surgery
  CHES/WCR EN8.................................. 214 D4
Abbot's Hill School
  HHS/BOV HP3 .... 186 B3
Abbots Langley Parish Council
  ABLGY WD5 .... 204 A1

Abbots School
  ABLGY WD5 .... 187 F8
Abbotsweld Primary School
  HLWS CM18 .... 6 C6
Abbotswood Medical Centre
  ABLGY WD5 .... 204 B2
Aboyne Lodge School
  STALW/RED AL3 .... 10 C3
Adeyfield School
  HHNE HP2 .... 9 D5
Akeman Business Park
  TRING HP23 .... 135 F6

Alban Wood Infant School
  GSTN WD25 .... 204 C2
Albanwood School
  GSTN WD25 .... 204 C3
Albany School Grant Maintained
  PEND EN3 .... 214 C8
Albury School
  STDN SG11 .... 83 H3
Aldbury Junior School
  TRING HP23 .... 136 D3
Aldenham Parish Council
  RAD WD7 .... 206 D6

Aldenham School
BORE WD6.................................. 222 C2
Aldwickbury Park Golf Club
HARP AL5.................................. 119 G8
Algrey Trading Estate
HTCHE/RSTV SG4 .... 40 E8
Allied Business Centre
HARP AL5.................................. 118 E6
All Nations Christian College
WARE SG12 .... 153 G1
All Saints C of E Junior Middle & Infant School
BSF CM23 .... 106 A1
Almonds Hill Junior Mixed School
STVG SG1 .... 75 J1
Alpha Business Park
BRKMPK AL9 .... 192 C1
A M F Bowling
HHNE HP2 .... 9 E3
Amwell View School
WARE SG12 .... 153 G5
Andrews Lane Junior & Infant School
CHESW EN7 .... 196 E6
Anglian Business Park
ROY SG8.................................... 21 F2
Anstey School
BUNT SG9 .... 49 G3
Applecroft Junior Middle & Infant School
WGCW AL8................................. 147 G4
Apsley Mills Retail Park
HHS/BOV HP3............................. 185 J2
Archway Surgery
HHS/BOV HP3............................. 183 J5
Ardeley School
STVGE SG2 .... 61 H6
Arndale Shopping Centre
LTN LU1 .... 4 C3
Arnetthill School
RKW/CH/CXG WD3...................... 217 K6
Arnold Middle School
AMP/FLIT/B MK45 .... 36 D7
Arseley Football Club
ARL/CHE SG15............................ 24 E6
The Arthur Findlay College
STSD CM24 .... 87 F4
The Arts Educational School
TRING HP23 .... 135 G6
Ascot Business Centre
LTN LU1 .... 4 B4
Ascot Industrial Estate
LWTH SG6 .... 42 B2
Ashcroft High School
LTNE LU2 .... 70 D7
Ashfield Junior School
BUSH WD23............................... 221 J7
Ash Industrial Estate
HLWW/ROY CM19........................ 179 G2
Ashley Business Centre
HTCH/STOT SG5.......................... 56 D1
Ashlyns School
BERK HP4 .... 161 K7
Ashridge Golf Club
BERK HP4 .... 137 J2
Ashville Trading Estate
BLDK SG7 .... 27 F8
Asquith Court School
HARP AL5.................................. 118 B6
Astley Cooper School
HHNE HP2 .... 165 F1
Aycliffe Drive Primary School
HHNE HP2 .... 8 B1
Aylands School
PEND EN3 .... 214 B6
Baldock Health Centre
BLDK SG7 .... 43 F2
Baldock Industrial Estate
BLDK SG7 .... 43 F2
Bancroft Business Centre
HTCH/STOT SG5.......................... 56 D1
Barbara Castle Health Centre
HLWW/ROY CM19........................ 179 H5
The Barclay School
STVG SG1 .... 75 J1
The Barking Dog Theatre Co
BSF CM23 .... 105 J4
Barkway Park Golf Club
ROY SG8.................................... 32 E7
Barkway Va First School
ROY SG8.................................... 32 C5
Barley Vp School
ROY SG8.................................... 23 G8
Barncroft JMI School
HHNE HP2 .... 164 C1

Barnet General Hospital
BAR EN5 .... 225 J4
Barnet Hospital Chest Clinic
BAR EN5 .... 225 J4
Barnfield College
LTN LU1 .... 89 G4
Barnfield College
LTNE LU2 .... 69 J4
Barnfield College
LTNN/LIM LU3............................ 69 G1
The Barn School
MHAD SG10................................ 103 G7
Barn Theatre
WCCW AL8................................. 147 H3
Barnwell School
STVGE SG2 .... 3 F6
Barracuda Swimming Club
POTB/CUF EN6 .... 210 E3
Barratt Industrial Park
LTNE LU2 .... 90 D3
Barton Industrial Estate
AMP/FLIT/B MK45 .... 36 A5
Barton Rovers Football Club
AMP/FLIT/B MK45 .... 36 C7
Batchwood Golf Club
STALW/RED AL3 .... 10 A1
Batchwood School
STALW/RED AL3 .... 10 C1
Batford JMI School
HARP AL5.................................. 119 F5
Bayfordbury College of Hertfordshire
HERT/BAY SG13 .... 150 E8
Bayford Junior Middle & Infant School
HERT/BAY SG13 .... 174 C4
Beaumont School
STALE/WH AL4 .... 169 G5
Bedmond JMI School
ABLGY WD5................................ 187 F6
Bedwell Junior & Infant School
STVG SG1 .... 3 E2
Bedwell Medical Centre
STVG SG1 .... 3 E3
Beechfield Junior Middle & Infant School
WATN WD24............................... 204 B7
Beech Hill Community School
LTNW/LEA LU4 .... 69 G8
Beech Hyde Junior Middle & Infant School
STALE/WH AL4 .... 145 G2
Beechwood Infant School
LTNW/LEA LU4 .... 68 D6
Beechwood Infants & Junior School
LTNW/LEA LU4 .... 68 D5
Beechwood Park Preparatory School
STALW/RED AL3 .... 114 E8
Belcon Industrial Estate
HOD EN11 .... 177 H3
Bellgate JMI School
HHNE HP2 .... 8 B3
Bells House Gallery
LWTH SG6 .... 41 K3
Belswains Infant School
HHS/BOV HP3............................. 185 K2
Bengeo Junior & Infant School
HERT/WAS SG14 .... 126 A8
Benington Primary School
STVGE SG2 .... 78 A4
Bennetts End Surgery
HHS/BOV HP3............................. 186 A1
Bentfield County Primary School
STSD CM24 .... 86 C1
Berkeley Clinic
RKW/CH/CXG WD3...................... 218 B8
Berkhamsted Football Club
BERK HP4 .... 161 J4
Berkhamsted Golf Club
BERK HP4 .... 162 B2
Berkhamsted Health Centre
BERK HP4 .... 161 H4
Berkhamsted School
BERK HP4 .... 161 K5
Berkhamsted School for Girls
BERK HP4 .... 161 J5
Berkhamsted School House
BERK HP4 .... 161 K5
Berkhamsted Tennis Club
BERK HP4 .... 161 K4
Berkley Gallery
BERK HP4 .... 161 J5

Bernards Heath Infant School
STAL AL1 .... 11 E
Beta Health Clinic
HHW HP1 .... 8 A
Birchwood High School
BSF CM23 .... 106 B
Birchwood Leisure Centre
HAT AL10 .... 171 G
Bishops Hatfield Girls School
HAT AL10 .... 171 F
Bishop's Park Health Centre
BSF CM23 .... 105 J
Bishops Stortford College
BSF CM23 .... 105 H
The Bishops Stortford High School
BSF CM23 .... 105 J
Bishops Stortford Town Council
BSF CM23 .... 105 J
Bishops Wood Hospital
RKW/CH/CXG WD3...................... 229 F
Bishop Wood Junior School
TRING HP23 .... 135 F
Blackthorn Junior School
WGCE AL7 .... 148 B
Blessed Cuthbert Mayne RC School
HHW HP1 .... 164 A
Blue Gold Trading Estate
ARL/CHE SG15............................ 24 E
Bondor Business Centre
BLDK SG7 .... 42 E
Bonneygrove Junior & Infant School
CHESW EN7 .... 196 E
Borehamwood Football Club
BORE WD6................................. 224 A
Borehamwood Industrial Park
BORE WD6................................. 224 C
The Borough Industrial Estate
LTNN/LIM LU3............................ 69 F
Borough of Broxbourne
CHES/WCR EN8........................... 197 F
Botany Bay Cricket Club
ENC/FH EN2 .... 212 A
Bournehall Junior & Infant School
BUSH WD23............................... 221 H
Bovingdon Junior Mixed School
HHS/BOV HP3............................. 183 H
Bovingdon Parish Council
HHS/BOV HP3............................. 183 .
Bovingdon Primary School
HHS/BOV HP3............................. 183 H
Bowmans Trading Estate
STVG SG1 .... 75 C
Boxmoor Golf Club
HHW HP1 .... 184 C
Boxmoor House School
HHW HP1 .... 184 D
Boxwell Road Surgery
BERK HP4 .... 161 C
Bramingham Business Park
LTNN/LIM LU3............................ 69 C
Bramingham Medical Centre
LTNN/LIM LU3............................ 69 C
Bramingham Park Medical Centre
LTNN/LIM LU3............................ 69 C
Bramingham Primary School
LTNN/LIM LU3............................ 69 C
Brandles Close School
BLDK SG7 .... 42 E
Brays Grove Comprehensive School
HLWS CM18................................ 180 E
Breakspeare School
ABLGY WD5................................ 203 H
Brickendon Grange Golf & Country Club
HERT/BAY SG13 .... 174 C
Brickfields Industrial Estate
HHNE HP2 .... 9 C
Bridge Cottage Surgery
WLYN AL6.................................. 122 C
Bridger Packaging Football Club
LWTH SG6 41
Bridgewater School
BERK HP4 .... 161 H
Britannia Business Centre
CHES/WCR EN8........................... 214
British Museum Zoological Museum
TRING HP23 135
Brittania Business Park
CHES/WCR EN8........................... 214

Broadfield Infant School
 HHNE HP2 .... 8 C5
Broadfield Junior School
 HHNE HP2 .... 8 C5
Broadfield School
 HLW CM20 .... 7 D3
Broadmead School
 LTN LU1 .... 4 C6
Brockswood JMI School
 HHNE HP2 .... 141 G8
Bromet School
 OXHEY WD19 .... 13 E6
Brookland Junior
 & Infant School
 CHES/WCR EN8 .... 197 J6
Brookmans Park GM
 Primary School
 BRKMPK AL9 .... 192 E4
Brookmead School
 LBUZ LU7 .... 110 E4
Brookside Business Centre
 RBSF CM22 .... 105 J8
Broom Barns Infant School
 STVG SG1 .... 2 C3
Broxbourne Borough Council
 CHES/WCR EN8 .... 197 H4
Broxbourne Business Centre
 CHES/WCR EN8 .... 197 H4
Broxbourne C of E JMI School
 BROX EN10 .... 176 E7
Broxbourne Sailing Club
 HOD EN11 .... 177 J6
The Broxbourne School
 BROX EN10 .... 176 D8
Broxbourne Sports Club
 BROX EN10 .... 176 E7
Brushwood Middle School
 CSHM HP5 .... 182 A7
Buckinghamshire Chilterns
 University College
 CSTG HP8 .... 226 D1
Burleigh Primary School
 CHES/WCR EN8 .... 197 H8
Burnt Mill Comprehensive School
 HLW CM20 .... 7 D2
Burntmill Industrial Estate
 HLW CM20 .... 6 B1
Burvill House Surgery
 HAT AL10 .... 171 F4
Burydale Junior Mixed School
 STVGE SG2 .... 76 C8
Bus Garage
 LTN LU1 .... 4 C5
Bushey & District Synagogue
 BUSH WD23 .... 221 K7
Bushey Hall School
 BUSH WD23 .... 221 G6
Bushey Hall Swimming Pool
 BUSH WD23 .... 221 C5
Bushey Health Centre
 BUSH WD23 .... 221 G6
Bushey Heath Primary School
 BUSH WD23 .... 222 A8
Bushey Manor School
 BUSH WD23 .... 13 F4
Bushey Meads School
 BUSH WD23 .... 221 K5
Bushey Museum & Art Gallery
 BUSH WD23 .... 221 H6
Bushmead Infant School
 LTNE LU2 .... 69 J4
Business Centre
 RAD WD7 .... 206 E4
The Business Centre
 LTNE LU2 .... 5 E2
Byfleet Industrial Estate
 WATW WD18 .... 219 H8
Caddington Sports Club
 LTN LU1 .... 88 E6
Caddington Surgery
 LTN LU1 .... 88 D5
Calcot Medical Centre
 CFSP/GDCR SL9 .... 226 A7
Camp Junior Middle
 & Infant School
 STAL AL1 .... 168 E7
Canary Club Football Club
 HTCH/STOT SG5 .... 56 C1
Canons Brook Golf Club
 HLW CM20 .... 155 H8
Canterbury Way Surgery
 STVG SG1 .... 59 G7
Capel Manor Primary School
 EN EN1 .... 213 K5

Capital Business Centre
 WATW WD24 .... 204 E6
Cardiff Road Industrial Estate
 WATW WD18 .... 12 C5
Cardinal Newman RC School
 LTNE LU2 .... 52 C8
Castle (Remains)
 BERK HP4 .... 162 A4
Cassio Surgery
 WATW WD18 .... 12 C3
The Castlegate Surgery
 HERT/BAY SG13 .... 151 F4
Castle Montessore School
 BERK HP4 .... 162 A5
Castle Walk Clinic
 STSD CM24 .... 86 E3
The Causeway Business Centre
 BSF CM23 .... 105 J2
The Cavendish School
 HHW HP1 .... 164 A5
Cedars First School
 KTN/HRWW/W HA3 .... 231 K7
Cedars Middle School
 KTN/HRWW/W HA3 .... 231 K7
Central Primary School
 WAT WD17 .... 13 D3
Central Surgery
 SBW CM21 .... 132 C7
Chalfont St Peter C of E
 Middle School
 CFSP/GDCR SL9 .... 226 A7
Chalfont St Peter Football Club
 CFSP/GDCR SL9 .... 226 A6
Chalfonts & Gerrards Cross
 Health Clinic
 CFSP/GDCR SL9 .... 226 A7
Challney High School for Boys
 LTNW/LEA LU4 .... 68 B6
Chambersbury JMI School
 HHS/BOV HP3 .... 186 B1
Chancellors School
 BRKMPK AL9 .... 193 H3
Chase Farm Hospitals NHS Trust
 ENC/FH EN2 .... 212 D8
Chater Infant School
 WATW WD18 .... 12 B3
Chater Junior School
 WATW WD18 .... 12 B3
Chaulden Junior & Infant School
 HHW HP1 .... 163 J7
The Chauncy School
 WARE SG12 .... 127 F8
Cheddington Lower School
 LBUZ LU7 .... 110 A2
Chenies Cricket Club
 RKW/CH/CXG WD3 .... 217 F1
Chenies School
 RKW/CH/CXG WD3 .... 200 D8
Cherry Tree JMI School
 WATN WD24 .... 204 B6
Chesham Preparatory School
 CSHM HP5 .... 182 C5
Cheshunt Community Hospital
 CHES/WCR EN8 .... 214 B4
Cheshunt Football Club
 CHES/WCR EN8 .... 214 B2
Cheshunt School
 CHES/WCR EN8 .... 197 C8
Cheshunt & Waltham
 Cross Council
 CHES/WCR EN8 .... 214 D4
Chesterfield Junior
 & Infant School
 PEND EN3 .... 214 D7
Chiltern Open Air Museum
 CSTG HP8 .... 226 C1
Chinese Medical Centre
 BAR EN5 .... 225 K3
Chinese Medical Centre Watford
 WAT WD17 .... 13 D3
Chipperfield Junior
 & Infant School
 KGLGY WD4 .... 201 K1
Chorleywood Golf Club
 RKW/CH/CXG WD3 .... 217 G4
Chorleywood Health Centre
 RKW/CH/CXG WD3 .... 217 F4
Chorleywood Parish Council
 RKW/CH/CXG WD3 .... 217 H3
Chorleywood Primary
 RKW/CH/CXG WD3 .... 217 F6
Christ Church C of E
 Primary School
 BAR EN5 .... 225 J2

Christ Church Junior Middle
 & Infant School
 WARE SG12 .... 127 J8
Christ Church School
 RKW/CH/CXG WD3 .... 217 J4
Churchgate C of E
 Primary School
 HLWE CM17 .... 157 J6
Church Langley Primary School
 HLWE CM17 .... 181 F1
Church Street Surgery
 WARE SG12 .... 127 H7
Cinema
 LTN LU1 .... 4 C4
Civic Centre & Dacorum
 Borough Council
 HHW HP1 .... 164 B6
Clarklands Industrial Estate
 SBW CM21 .... 132 C4
Club House
 LBUZ LU7 .... 110 B4
The Club House
 HERT/WAS SG14 .... 98 B6
Coach House Surgery
 WATW WD18 .... 12 B3
Coates Way School
 GSTN WD25 .... 205 F3
Cobden Hill Infant School
 RAD WD7 .... 206 E6
Codicote Junior & Infant School
 WLYN AL6 .... 94 D8
Coleman Business Centre
 HTCHE/RSTV SG4 .... 93 F7
Collenswood School
 STVGE SG2 .... 76 D5
The Collett School
 HHW HP1 .... 164 A5
Colnbrook School
 OXHEY WD19 .... 230 D1
Colne Bridge Retail Park
 WAT WD17 .... 13 E4
Colney Heath JMI School
 STALE/WH AL4 .... 170 B8
Colonial Business Park
 WATN WD24 .... 220 D1
Commonside School
 HLWS CM18 .... 180 C5
Commonswood JMI School
 WGCE AL7 .... 148 C6
Community Clinic
 HLWS CM18 .... 180 C4
Community Mental
 Health Centre
 GSTN WD25 .... 204 D4
Community Mental
 Health Centre
 HHNE HP2 .... 8 A4
Corn Exchange
 HERT/WAS SG14 .... 151 G3
Cotswold Business Park
 LTN LU1 .... 88 C7
Council Offices
 OXHEY WD19 .... 230 E2
Countess Anne C of E
 Primary School
 HAT AL10 .... 171 H3
County Hall
 HERT/BAY SG13 .... 151 F5
Cowley Hill First School
 BORE WD6 .... 224 A1
CP House Business Centre
 GSTN WD25 .... 221 G1
Crabtree Junior Mixed School
 HARP AL5 .... 119 F8
Crabtree Lane Infant School
 HARP AL5 .... 118 E8
Cranborne Industrial Estate
 POTB/CUF EN6 .... 192 E8
Cranborne Primary School
 POTB/CUF EN6 .... 209 K1
Cranbourne School
 HOD EN11 .... 153 G8
Crawley Green Primary School
 LTNE LU2 .... 5 F3
Creswick Primary School
 WGCE AL7 .... 147 J6
Crews Hill Golf Club
 ENC/FH EN2 .... 212 C4
Cricket Squash Tennis
 & Hockey Club
 BSF CM23 .... 105 F1
Crown Court
 STAL AL1 .... 11 D4
Crown Prosecution Service
 LTN LU1 .... 4 C4

Crown Prosecution Service
STAL AL1 .... 10 C4
Cuffley School
POTB/CUF EN6 .... 195 H8
Cunningham Hill Junior
Middle & Infant School
STAL AL1 .... 11 F6
Dacorum Athletics Track
HHS/BOV HP3 .... 164 E8
Dacorum District Sports Centre
HHW HP1 .... 164 B8
Dacre Industrial Estate
CHES/WCR EN8 .... 197 J7
Dagnall CP School
BERK HP4 .... 112 E4
Dallow Junior School
LTN LU1 .... 4 A3
Dalroad Industrial Estate
LTN LU1 .... 89 G1
Dame Alice Owens School
POTB/CUF EN6 .... 209 K3
Danesbury Park Golf Club
WLYN AL6 .... 122 C2
Datchworth School
KNEB SG3 .... 96 E6
Deer Leap Swimming Pool
BERK HP4 .... 112 D8
Delrow School
GSTN WD25 .... 221 K1
Denbigh High School
LTNN/LIM LU3 .... 4 A1
Denbigh Infant School
LTNN/LIM LU3 .... 69 G7
The Dentist Surgery
OXHEY WD19 .... 230 C4
Denture Clinic
HARP AL5 .... 117 J5
Dewhurst St Mary Junior Middle
& Infant School
CHESW EN7 .... 197 F7
Diamond Industrial Centre
LWTH SG6 .... 42 C2
Discover Bible School
GSTN WD25 .... 204 D5
Divine Saviour RC JMI School
ABLGY WD5 .... 203 J2
The Downs CP School
HLW CM20 .... 6 C4
Downside Junior & Infant School
LTNW/LEA LU4 .... 68 D8
Dr P J Walkers Surgery
HTCHE/RSTV SG4 .... 93 H2
Duncombe School
HERT/WAS SG14 .... 151 F2
Dundale Infants School
TRING HP23 .... 135 F4
Dundale J M School
TRING HP23 .... 135 F4
Dunstable Road Infant School
LTN LU1 .... 4 A3
The Earl Gallery
POTB/CUF EN6 .... 210 A2
Eastbrook Junior School
HHNE HP2 .... 164 E1
Eastbury Infant School
NTHWD HA6 .... 230 A3
Eastfield Primary
& Infant School
PEND EN3 .... 214 C8
East Herts District Council
BSF CM23 .... 105 J1
East Herts District Council
HERT/BAY SG13 .... 151 F4
East Herts District Council
HERT/WAS SG14 .... 150 C2
East Herts District Council
SBW CM21 .... 132 C7
East Herts Golf Club
BUNT SG9 .... 81 C4
East Herts Golf Clubhouse
WARE SG12 .... 152 B1
Edwinstree Middle School
BUNT SG9 .... 63 H1
Egerton Rothesay School
BERK HP4 .... 161 C5
Eleanor Estate
CHES/WCR EN8 .... 214 E4
Elliswick Lawn Tennis Club
HARP AL5 .... 118 D7
The Elms Health Centre
POTB/CUF EN6 .... 210 D1
The Elms Medical Practice
HARP AL5 .... 118 D7
The Elms Medical Practice
STALW/RED AL3 .... 142 B4

Elstree & Borehamwood
Town Council
BORE WD6 .... 224 A3
Elstree Studios
BORE WD6 .... 223 K3
Elstree Way Clinic
BORE WD6 .... 224 A2
Emmanuel C of E School
NTHWD HA6 .... 230 A6
Enfield Chace Lower School
ENC/FH EN2 .... 213 H8
Epping House School
HERT/BAY SG13 .... 173 K7
Essendon Primary School
BRKMPK AL9 .... 173 G3
Essex County Council
WAB EN9 .... 215 H3
Everest House Surgery
HHNE HP2 .... 9 D5
Everest Sports Club
CHES/WCR EN8 .... 197 F7
Eversley College
SBW CM21 .... 132 B7
Factory
STVG SG1 .... 2 A5
Fairbrook Medical Centre
BORE WD6 .... 224 A2
Fairfield Primary School
RAD WD7 .... 206 B6
Fairfields Junior Middle
& Infant School
CHESW EN7 .... 196 E5
Fairlands Junior Middle
& Infant School
STVG SG1 .... 2 B2
The Fairways
CHES/WCR EN8 .... 197 H4
Falconer School
BUSH WD23 .... 221 C5
Farley Hill Primary School
LTN LU1 .... 4 A6
Farnham School
BSF CM23 .... 85 G3
Fawbert & Barnards
Primary School
HLWE CM17 .... 157 F6
Fearnhill School
LWTH SG6 .... 41 G4
Fearnhill Sports Centre
LWTH SG6 .... 41 G4
Featherstone Wood
Primary School
STVGE SG2 .... 76 D6
Fernville Surgery
HHNE HP2 .... 8 A5
Ferrars Infant School
LTNW/LEA LU4 .... 68 A6
Fiddlebridge Industrial Centre
HAT AL10 .... 171 F3
Field Junior School
WATW WD18 .... 13 D4
Firbank Industrial Estate
LTN LU1 .... 89 F1
The Firs Junior School
BSF CM23 .... 105 H3
Fisher Industrial Estate
WATW WD18 .... 13 D4
Five Oaks School
LTN LU1 .... 88 E6
Five Springs School
LTNN/LIM LU3 .... 68 E2
Flamstead End Junior School
CHESW EN7 .... 196 E5
Flamstead Junior Middle
& Infant School
STALW/RED AL3 .... 116 B8
Fleetville Infant School
STAL AL1 .... 11 F4
Fleetville Jm School
STAL AL1 .... 11 F4
Florance Nightingale
Health Centre
HLWE CM17 .... 181 F1
Flowers Industrial Estate
LTN LU1 .... 4 C5
Football Club
TRING HP23 .... 135 J5
Football & Social Club
WCCE AL7 .... 148 C1
Forres CP School
HOD EN11 .... 153 G8
Forty Hill C of E School
EN EN1 .... 213 K7
Foulds Primary School
BAR EN5 .... 225 J3

The Four Swanns JMI School
CHES/WCR EN8 .... 214 D3
Foxdell Infant School
LTN LU1 .... 89 F1
Foxdell Junior School
LTN LU1 .... 88 D1
Foye Gallery
LTN LU1 .... 4 B5
Francis Bacon School
STAL AL1 .... 189 K1
Francis Combe
Secondary School
GSTN WD25 .... 204 D2
Frithwood Primary School
NTHWD HA6 .... 230 A5
Frogmore Road
Industrial Estate
HHS/BOV HP3 .... 185 H1
Furneux Pelham C of E School
BUNT SG9 .... 66 C5
Furzehill School
BORE WD6 .... 223 K4
Gaddesden Row CP School
HHNE HP2 .... 140 B2
Gade Valley JMI School
HHW HP1 .... 164 A5
The Garden City Practice
WGCW AL8 .... 147 J2
Garden City Surgery
LWTH SG6 .... 41 K3
Garden Court Business Centre
WGCE AL7 .... 148 A3
Garden Fields Junior Middle
& Infant School
STALW/RED AL3 .... 10 C1
Garston Clinic
WATN WD24 .... 204 C6
Garston JMI School
GSTN WD25 .... 204 E5
Garston Manor School
GSTN WD25 .... 204 D2
Garston Medical Centre
GSTN WD25 .... 204 D6
Gascoyne Cecil Primary School
HAT AL10 .... 171 G2
Gazelda Industrial Estate
WAT WD17 .... 13 D4
The Giles Infant & Junior School
STVG SG1 .... 59 F6
Gillmark Gallery
HERT/BAY SG13 .... 151 F4
Goffs Oak JMI School
CHESW EN7 .... 195 K6
Goffs School
CHESW EN7 .... 196 E7
Goldfield Infant School
TRING HP23 .... 134 E6
Golf Club Flat
NTHWD HA6 .... 229 J6
Gooseberry Hill Health Centre
LTNN/LIM LU3 .... 69 G2
Gorhambury
STALW/RED AL3 .... 166 C5
Gothic Mede Lower School
ARL/CHE SG15 .... 24 E4
The Gowan Gallery
SBW CM21 .... 132 C7
Grange Junior Mixed School
LWTH SG6 .... 25 K7
Grange Paddock Swimming Pool
BSF CM23 .... 85 J8
Grange Street Doctors Surgery
STALW/RED AL3 .... 10 C3
Graveley Junior Mixed School
HTCHE/RSTV SG4 .... 58 B5
Great Gaddesden JMI School
HHW HP1 .... 139 G6
Great Hormead C of E School
BUNT SG9 .... 65 F1
Green End Business Centre
RKW/CH/CXG WD3 .... 201 K7
Greenfield Primary School
OXHEY WD19 .... 230 D4
The Greenhouse Health Centre
LTN LU1 .... 4 B3
Green Lane Industrial Estate
LWTH SG6 .... 42 B2
Green Lanes School
HAT AL10 .... 146 E8
Green Side School
STVGE SG2 .... 3 E6
Greenway County First School
BERK HP4 .... 161 H5
Greenwood Park Leisure Centre
LCOL/BKTW AL2 .... 188 D3

The Greneway School
  ROY SG8.......................... 21 J2
Griffin Galleries
  PIN HA5...................... 230 D8
Griffin Golf Club
  LTN LU1........................ 88 C3
Grimsdyke First & Middle School
  PIN HA5...................... 231 G5
Grimsdyke Golf Club
  PIN HA5...................... 231 H4
Grosvenor Gallery
  NTHWD HA6................. 229 K5
Grovehill Medical Centre
  HHNE HP2....................... 8 C1
The Grove Infant School
  HARP AL5..................... 144 A1
The Grove JMI School
  HARP AL5..................... 144 A1
Grovelands Business Centre
  HHNE HP2....................... 9 F3
Grove Road Primary School
  TRING HP23................. 135 G4
Grundy Park Leisure Centre
  CHES/WCR EN8.............. 197 J8
Guardian Industrial Estate
  LTN LU1.......................... 4 A3
Guilden Morden School
  ROY SG8......................... 15 G4
Haberdashers Askes School
  for Girls
  BORE WD6................... 222 E3
Haberdashers Rugby Club
  BORE WD6................... 223 J2
Hadley Wood School
  EBAR EN4..................... 210 D8
Haileybury College
  HERT/BAY SG13............ 152 C7
Hailey Hall School
  HOD EN11..................... 152 E7
The Hammond Junior
  Mixed Infant School
  HHNE HP2....................... 8 C1
Happy Valley Industrial Estate
  KGLGY WD4................... 186 B6
Harefield Cricket Club
  DEN/HRF UB9................ 228 C8
Harefield Health Centre
  DEN/HRF UB9................ 228 B7
Harefield Hospital
  DEN/HRF UB9................ 228 B7
Harefield Infant School
  DEN/HRF UB9................ 228 A7
Harefield Junior School
  DEN/HRF UB9................ 228 B7
Haresfoot Prep School
  BERK HP4..................... 161 J8
Haresfoot Senior School
  BERK HP4..................... 162 D3
Hare Street County Junior
  & Infant School
  HLWW/ROY CM19.............. 6 B4
Harkness Industrial Estate
  BORE WD6................... 223 K4
Harlequin Shopping Centre
  WAT WD17..................... 13 D3
Harlowbury School
  HLWE CM17.................. 157 G5
Harlow Business Park
  HLWW/ROY CM19........... 179 F1
Harlow College
  HLW CM20....................... 6 B4
Harlow College
  HLW CM20....................... 7 D3
Harlow Museum
  HLWS CM18..................... 6 B5
Harlow Rugby Football Club
  HLW CM20....................... 6 A2
Harlow Sports Centre
  HLW CM20....................... 6 B2
Harlow Sports Centre
  HLW CM20....................... 6 C1
Harlow Urban District
  Swimming Pool
  HLW CM20....................... 7 D2
Harpenden Common Golf Club
  HARP AL5..................... 143 J3
Harpenden Golf Club
  HARP AL5..................... 143 G4
Harpenden Health Centre
  HARP AL5..................... 118 C7
Harpenden Hospital
  HARP AL5..................... 118 C5
Harpenden Memorial Hospital
  HARP AL5..................... 118 D7

Harpenden Preparatory School
  HARP AL5..................... 118 B7
Harpenden Rugby Football Club
  HARP AL5..................... 143 F3
Harpenden Sports Centre
  HARP AL5..................... 143 H1
Harpenden Swimming Pool
  HARP AL5..................... 118 C8
Harperbury Hospital
  RAD WD7...................... 207 F1
Hart Hill Junior School
  LTNE LU2......................... 5 D3
Hartsfield Junior Middle
  & Infant School
  BLDK SG7........................ 43 F1
Hartsping Industrial Park
  GSTN WD25................... 221 H2
Hartsping Sports Centre
  BUSH WD23................... 221 H2
Harvey Centre
  HLW CM20....................... 6 B4
Haselmere Industrial Estate
  BSF CM23..................... 105 K5
Haslemere Industrial Estate
  HLWW/ROY CM19........... 179 H2
Haslewood Junior School
  HOD EN11..................... 177 F2
Hatch End High School
  KTN/HRWW/W HA3......... 231 J6
Hatfield House
  BRKMPK AL9.................. 171 J4
Hatfield London Country Club
  BRKMPK AL9.................. 173 G5
Haverfield Surgery
  KGLGY WD4................... 186 A7
Havers Infant School
  BSF CM23..................... 105 H4
Hawridge & Cholesbury
  C of E Primary School
  CSHM HP5..................... 159 J7
Hazel Grove JMI School
  HAT AL10...................... 170 E7
Heathcote School
  STVGE SG2......................... 3 E6
Heathfield Lower School
  LTN LU1........................ 88 D5
Heathlands School
  for Deaf Children
  STALW/RED AL3.............. 11 D1
Heath Mount School
  HERT/WAS SG14............. 98 E7
Heath Sports Club
  ROY SG8......................... 21 G3
Hemel Hempstead Rugby Club
  HHW HP1...................... 163 J8
Hemel Hempstead
  General Hospital
  HHNE HP2....................... 8 A6
Hemel Hempstead
  Rugby League Club
  HHNE HP2....................... 8 C2
Hemel Hempstead School
  HHW HP1...................... 164 B7
Hemel Hempstead
  Town Cricket Club
  HHS/BOV HP3................ 164 B8
Hemel Hempstead
  United Football Club
  HHNE HP2....................... 9 E5
Hengrove School
  TRING HP23................. 158 B5
Heron Trading Estate
  LTNN/LIM LU3................. 68 B2
Hertford County Hospital
  HERT/WAS SG14............ 150 E3
Hertford Police Station
  HERT/BAY SG13............ 151 J2
Hertford Regional College
  WARE SG12................... 152 C1
Hertfordshire Business Centre
  LCOL/BKTW AL2............ 190 B4
Hertfordshire Country Club
  WGCE AL7.................... 147 H6
Hertfordshire County
  Constabulary
  HHW HP1..................... 164 B6
Hertfordshire County Council
  BUSH WD23................... 222 A7
Hertfordshire County Council
  GSTN WD25................... 204 D6
Hertfordshire County Council
  HERT/BAY SG13............ 151 G4
Hertfordshire County Council
  OXHEY WD19................. 230 C2

Hertfordshire County Council
  POTB/CUF EN6.............. 210 D2
Hertfordshire County Council
  RKW/CH/CXG WD3.......... 228 A1
Hertfordshire County Council
  WAT WD17....................... 12 B1
Hertfordshire & Essex
  General Hospital
  BSF CM23..................... 106 B3
Hertfordshire
  & Essex High School
  BSF CM23..................... 106 A2
Hertfordshire Family
  Health Authority Services
  WCCW AL8.................... 147 J2
Hertford Town Football Club
  HERT/WAS SG14............ 150 E4
Hertsmere Borough Council
  BORE WD6.................... 224 B2
Hertsmere Council
  BORE WD6.................... 223 K2
Hertsmere Jewish
  Primary School
  RAD WD7...................... 207 F8
Hertsmere Progressive
  Synagogue
  BORE WD6.................... 223 G6
Hexton Junior Middle
  & Infant School
  HTCH/STOT SG5.............. 37 G8
High Beeches JMI School
  HARP AL5..................... 144 A1
Highbury Infant School
  HTCHE/RSTV SG4............ 56 D3
High Cross Puller Memorial
  Junior & Infant School
  STDN SG11.................... 100 D7
Highfield School
  LWTH SG6....................... 41 H6
Highfield Surgery
  HHNE HP2....................... 8 C3
Highover JMI School
  HTCHE/RSTV SG4............ 41 G8
Hightown Recreation Centre
  LTNE LU2......................... 4 C3
Highview Surgery
  POTB/CUF EN6.............. 210 D3
Highwood Primary School
  BUSH WD23................... 221 F1
Hillborough Junior School
  LTN LU1........................... 4 A5
Hille Business Centre
  WATN WD24.................. 220 C1
Hill Farm Industrial Estate
  GSTN WD25................... 204 A3
Hillgrove Business Park
  WAB EN9...................... 177 H8
Hillingdon Health Authority
  NTHWD HA6.................. 230 B7
Hillmead JMI School
  BSF CM23....................... 86 B8
Hillshott Infant School
  LWTH SG6....................... 42 A3
Hillside Junior & Infant School
  NTHWD HA6.................. 230 B6
Hillside School
  BORE WD6.................... 224 B4
Hitchin Boys School
  HTCH/STOT SG5.............. 56 C1
Hitchin Cricket Club
  HTCH/STOT SG5.............. 56 A2
Hitchin Girls School
  HTCHE/RSTV SG4............ 56 D2
Hitchin Swimming Pool
  HTCH/STOT SG5.............. 56 C1
HM Prison
  CSHM HP5..................... 183 H4
Hobbs Hill Wood Primary School
  HHS/BOV HP3................ 165 G8
Hobletts Manor Junior School
  HHNE HP2....................... 9 D4
Hockerill Anglo European
  GM School
  BSF CM23..................... 106 A2
Hockerill Sports Club
  BSF CM23..................... 106 A4
Hockwell Surgery
  LTNW/LEA LU4................ 68 B4
Hoddesdon Health Centre
  HOD EN11..................... 177 F4
Hoddesdon Industrial Estate
  HOD EN11..................... 177 H2
Hoddesdon Lawn Tennis Club
  HOD EN11..................... 176 E3

Hoddesdon St Pauls
Infant School
HOD EN11 .... 177 G3
Holdbrook Junior Middle
& Infant School
CHES/WCR EN8.................... 214 E4
Holland & Holland
Shooting School
DEN/HRF UB9 .... 229 F8
Hollybush School
HERT/WAS SG14 .... 150 D3
Holly Industrial Park
WATN WD24.......................... 220 D1
Holly Street Trading Estate
LTN LU1 .... 4 C5
Hollywood Bowl
STVG SG1 .... 2 A3
Holmshill School
BORE WD6............................ 224 B2
Holtsmere End Junior
& Infant School
HHNE HP2 .... 165 G1
Holwell Junior & Infant School
WCCE AL7.............................. 148 A4
Holy Cross Boarding
& Day School
CFSP/GDCR SL9.................... 226 A7
Holy Cross RC Primary School
HLWS CM18............................ 7 F6
Holyrood Infant School
WAT WD17............................ 203 J6
Holy Rood Junior School
WAT WD17............................ 203 J6
Holy Trinity C of E
Primary School
CHES/WCR EN8.................... 214 C2
Holy Trinity School
NTHWD HA6 .... 229 H5
Holywell School
WATW WD18 .... 12 A5
Home Farm Industrial Estate
WARE SG12 .... 154 A4
Home Park Industrial Estate
KGLGY WD4 .... 186 B8
Homerswood Junior
& Infant School
WCCW AL8............................ 122 D7
Homewood School
LCOL/BKTW AL2 .... 188 D6
Honilands Junior & Infant School
EN EN14 .... 214 A6
Horseshoe Business Park
LCOL/BKTW AL2 .... 188 D8
Hospital
LTN LU1 .... 4 A4
Hospital Annexe
DEN/HRF UB9 .... 228 B6
Hot Shots Ten Pin Bowling
HHS/BOV HP3 .... 8 C6
Howard Business Park
WAB EN9 .... 215 J4
Howe Dell School
HAT AL10 .... 171 G4
Howe Green House School
RBSF SG22 .... 106 C7
How Wood Junior
& Infant School
LCOL/BKTW AL2 .... 188 E5
Hurst Drive JMI School
CHES/WCR EN8.................... 214 C4
Hyatt Trading Estate
STVG SG1 .... 75 F4
Icknield High School
LTNN/LIM LU3 .... 69 H4
Icknield Infant School
LWTH SG6 .... 41 H3
Icknield Walk First School
ROY SG8................................ 21 J2
Icknield Way Industrial Estate
TRING HP23.......................... 134 D5
Immanuel College
BUSH WD23.......................... 222 B7
Indoor Market
WAT WD17............................. 13 D2
Industrial Estate
DEN/HRF UB9 .... 227 K5
Industrial Park
CHES/WCR EN8.................... 215 F4
International University
BUSH WD23.......................... 221 G4
Ivinghoe Golf Club
LBUZ LU7 .... 111 F3
The Jamie Mosque
STAL AL1 .... 11 F4

Jerounds Junior & Infant School
HLWW/ROY CM19.................. 179 J4
John F Kennedy School
HHW HP1.............................. 163 H5
John Henry Newman RC School
STVG SG1 .... 58 B8
John Penrose School
DEN/HRF UB9 .... 228 C7
The John Warner School
HOD EN11 .... 153 G8
Jubilee Trading Estate
LWTH SG6 .... 42 C2
Junior & Infant School
STVG SG1 .... 2 B1
Jupiter Drive JMI School
HHNE HP2 .... 8 C3
Katherines Primary School
HLWW/ROY CM19.................. 179 H5
Kenilworth Primary School
BORE WD6............................ 224 C3
Kensworth Lower School
DUN/WHIP LU6 .... 114 D1
Kevin Hinds Practice
WARE SG12 .... 127 H8
Killigrew Junior Middle
& Infant School
LCOL/BKTW AL2 .... 188 D3
Kimpton Junior Middle
& Infant School
HTCHE/RSTV SG4 .... 93 F8
King George Surgery
STVG SG1 .... 2 B2
King Harold
Comprehensive School
WAB EN9 .... 215 K3
Kingsbury Watermill Museum
& Waffle House
STALW/RED AL3 .... 10 A4
Kingshott School
HTCHE/RSTV SG4 .... 57 F4
Kings Langley Parish Council
KGLGY WD4 .... 186 A7
Kings Langley Primary School
KGLGY WD4 .... 185 K6
Kingsmoor Junior
& Infant School
HLWW/ROY CM19.................. 179 K5
Kingsmoor Recreation Centre
HLWW/ROY CM19.................. 179 J5
The Kings Oak Private Hospital
ENC/FH EN2 .... 212 D8
Kings Park Industrial Estate
KGLGY WD4 .... 186 B7
Kingsway Industrial Estate
LTN LU1 .... 89 F1
Kingsway Junior School
WATN WD25.......................... 204 B4
Knebworth Golf Club
KNEB SG3.............................. 96 A3
Knebworth Ho
KNEB SG3.............................. 95 H3
Knebworth Physiotherapy Clinic
STVGE SG2 .... 96 D4
Knights Templar School
BLDK SG7.............................. 42 E1
Knowl Piece
HTCHE/RSTV SG4 .... 40 E6
Knutsford Junior & Infant School
WATN WD24.......................... 204 E8
Ladbroke School
POTB/CUF EN6 .... 210 C2
Lady Zia Wernher School
LTNE LU2 .... 70 C6
Laharna Trading Estate
WATN WD24.......................... 204 D8
Laings Sports Ground
BAR EN5 .... 224 D4
Lakeside School
WCCW AL8............................ 147 G5
Lakeside Surgery
HTCH/STOT SG5 .... 25 J3
Langley Terrace Industrial Park
LTN LU1 .... 4 C5
Lannock JMI School
LWTH SG6 .... 42 C5
Larwood School
STVG SG1 .... 3 D1
Laser Clinic
CHESW EN7 .... 197 F8
Latton Bush Business Centre
HLWS CM18.......................... 180 C4
Latton Bush Recreation Centre
HLWS CM18.......................... 180 B4
Laurence Haines School
WATW WD18 .... 12 B5

Lavender Junior & Infant School
ENC/FH EN2 .... 213 H⸱
Layston First School
BUNT SG9 .... 63 K⸱
Lea Farm Junior School
GSTN WD25 .... 204 E⸱
Leagrave Health Centre
LTNW/LEA LU4 .... 68 B⸱
Leagrave Junior & Infant School
LTNW/LEA LU4 .... 68 B⸱
Lea Industrial Estate
HARP AL5............................. 118 E⸱
Lealands High School
LTNN/LIM LU3 .... 68 B⸱
Lea Manor High School
& Community College
LTNN/LIM LU3 .... 68 E⸱
The Leas Junior & Infant School
HARP AL5............................. 118 C⸱
Lea Valley High School
PEND EN3 .... 214 B⸱
Leavesden Green Junior
Middle & Infant School
GSTN WD25 .... 204 B⸱
Leavesden Hospital
ABLGY WD5 .... 204 B⸱
Letchworth Business Centre
LWTH SG6 .... 42 C⸱
Letchworth Garden City
Football Club
LWTH SG6 .... 42 C⸱
Letchworth Golf Club
LWTH SG6 .... 41 K⸱
Letchworth Museum
LWTH SG6 .... 41 K⸱
Letchworth Swimming Pool
LWTH SG6 .... 42 A⸱
The Leventhorpe School
SBW CM21 .... 132 C⸱
Leverstock Green JMI School
HHNE HP2 .... 165 J⸱
Leverstock Green
Lawn Tennis Club
HHS/BOV HP3 .... 165 G⸱
Ley Hill CP School
CSHM HP5 .... 182 D⸱
Ley Park CP School
BROX EN10 .... 176 E⸱
Leys Primary School
STVG SG1 .... 59 G⸱
Lime Walk JMI School
HHS/BOV HP3 .... 164 E⸱
Lincoln Health Surgery
HHNE HP2 .... 8 A⸱
Links Business Centre
BSF CM23 .... 106 B⸱
Lismarrine Industrial Park
BORE WD6............................ 222 E⸱
Lister Hospital
STVG SG1 .... 58 B⸱
Lister House Surgery
HAT AL10 .... 171 F⸱
Lister House Surgery
LTNW/LEA LU4 .... 68 E⸱
Lister Medical Centre
HLWS CM18.......................... 179 K⸱
Little Chalfont CP School
AMS HP6 .... 216 B⸱
Little Furze School
OXHEY WD19........................ 230 C⸱
Little Gaddesden JMI School
BERK HP4 .... 137 K⸱
Little Green CP School
RKW/CH/CXG WD3 .... 219 G⸱
Little Hallingbury C of E
Primary School
RBSF CM22 .... 133 G⸱
Little Heath Junior Mixed School
POTB/CUF EN6 .... 193 J⸱
Little Munden JMI School
WARE SG12 .... 99 H1
Little Reddings Primary School
BUSH WD23.......................... 221 J5
Little St. Helens School
NTHWD HA6 .... 230 A6
Liverpool Road Health Centre
LTN LU1 .... 4 B3
Llewelyn Surgery
WAB EN9 .... 215 H3
Lochinver House School
POTB/CUF EN6 .... 193 H8
Lockers Park School
HHW HP1.............................. 164 A6
Lodge Clinic
LTN LU1 .... 4 C4

North & West Essex Adult
Community College
HLW CM20 6   B2
Northwood College Educational
Foundation
NTHWD HA6 229   J6
Northwood Football Club
NTHWD HA6 230   A8
Northwood & Pinner Community
Hospital
NTHWD HA6 230   B7
Northwood Pinner
Liberal Synagogue
NTHWD HA6 229   K5
Northwood Preparatory School
RKW/CH/CXG WD3 229   H1
Northwood School
NTHWD HA6 230   C7
Northwood Sports Centre
PIN HA5 230   C7
Northwood United Synagogue
NTHWD HA6 229   K6
Norton Road Primary School
LTNN/LIM LU3 68   E5
Norton School
LWTH SG6 42   A1
Nucleus Gallery
CFSP/GDCR SL9 226   A7
Nup End Industrial Estate
WLYN AL6 95   G5
Oaklands College
BORE WD6 224   B2
Oaklands College
HARP AL5 118   D8
Oaklands College
STAL AL1 11   D4
Oaklands College
STALE/WH AL4 169   H5
Oaklands College
WGCW AL8 147   J2
Oaklands JMI School
WLYN AL6 122   E1
The Oakley Surgery
LTNW/LEA LU4 68   C5
Oakmere School
POTB/CUF EN6 210   E2
The Oaks Industrial Estate
HLW CM20 7   E1
Oakwood Estate
HLW CM20 7   F1
Oakwood JMI School
STALE/WH AL4 169   F5
Odeon Cinema
HHS/BOV HP3 8   C6
Odeon Cinema
HLW CM20 6   B3
Odhams Industrial Estate
WATN WD24 204   D7
Odhams Trading Estate
WATN WD24 204   B6
Old Airfield Industrial Estate
LBUZ LU7 109   K4
Old Boys School
STDN SG11 82   A2
Old Fold Manor Golf Club
BAR EN5 225   K1
Old Harlow Health Centre
HLWE CM17 157   F5
Old Merchant Taylors Sports Club
RKW/CH/CXG WD3 219   G4
Old Millhillians Sports Ground
PIN HA5 231   H7
Old Oak Close Industrial Estate
ARL/CHE SG15 24   E1
Old Verulamians
Rugby Football Club
LCOL/BKTW AL2 190   A3
Orchard County Primary School
WATN WD24 204   A6
Oughtonhead Junior
& Infant School
HTCH/STOT SG5 40   A8
Our Ladys Catholic
Primary School
WGCE AL7 147   K5
Oxen Industrial Estate
LTNE LU2 5   D2
Oxhey First School
BUSH WD23 13   F4
Oxheywood Junior
& Infant School
OXHEY WD19 230   D3
Palace Theatre
WAT WD17 12   C2

Panshanger Golf Club
WGCE AL7 148   D1
Panshanger JMI School
WGCE AL7 148   B2
Paramount Industrial Estate
WATN WD24 204   D8
Park Avenue Clinic
WAT WD17 12   B1
Park Avenue Industrial Estate
LTNN/LIM LU3 68   A2
Parkbury House Surgery
STAL AL1 11   D3
Park Farm Industrial Estate
BUNT SG9 47   H8
Park Farm Industrial Estate
BUNT SG9 63   H1
Parkfield Medical Centre
POTB/CUF EN6 210   C2
Parkgate Infant School
WATN WD24 204   D7
Parkgate Junior School
WATN WD24 204   D7
Park Industrial Estate
LCOL/BKTW AL2 189   D3
Park Lane Surgery
BROX EN10 176   E6
Parkside First School
BORE WD6 207   J8
Park Street C of E
Primary School
LCOL/BKTW AL2 189   F5
Parmiters School
GSTN WD25 204   D1
Parndoni Mill Gallery
HLW CM20 6   A1
The Parochial Church
Council of Goffs Oak St James
CHESW EN7 196   B6
Parsonage Farm
Industrial Estate
STSD CM24 86   E6
Passmores
Comprehensive School
HLWS CM18 6   C6
Peerglow Industrial Estate
WATW WD18 219   G7
Peterswood Junior
& Infant School
HLWS CM18 180   A5
The Picture House
HLW CM20 6   B3
Pinehill Hospital
HTCHE/RSTV SG4 57   F2
Pine Wood School
WARE SG12 152   C2
Pin Green JMI School
STVG SG1 3   D2
Pinner Wood School
PIN HA5 230   D7
Pirton Hill Infant School
LTNW/LEA LU4 68   A3
Pirton JMI School
HTCH/STOT SG5 38   E5
Pitstone Surgery
LBUZ LU7 110   D4
Pixies Hill JMI School
HHW HP1 163   J7
Pixmore Junior School
LWTH SG6 42   A4
Ponsbourne St. Marys JMI School
HERT/BAY SG13 195   G2
Pope Paul RC Primary School
POTB/CUF EN6 210   A3
Portland Industrial Estate
ARL/CHE SG15 24   D7
Potten End School
BERK HP4 162   E3
Potterells Medical Centre
BRKMPK AL9 192   D3
Potters Bar Cricket Club
POTB/CUF EN6 210   C2
Potters Bar Golf Club
POTB/CUF EN6 210   B1
Potter Street Primary School
HLWE CM17 180   E3
Prae Wood JMI School
STALW/RED AL3 167   H7
Presdales School
WARE SG12 152   C1
Prince Hotel
STALW/RED AL3 167   H4
Prince of Wales Junior
& Infant School
PEND EN3 214   E8

Princess Alexandra Hospital
HLW CM20 6   A3
The Princess Helena College
HTCHE/RSTV SG4 73   H3
The Print Room/Museum Books
& Prints
BAR EN5 225   K5
Priors Wood JMI School
WARE SG12 128   A6
Priory School
HTCH/STOT SG5 40   C7
Public Swimming Pool
OXHEY WD19 231   F4
Pump House Theatre
WAT WD17 13   D4
The Purcell School
BUSH WD23 221   G2
Purford Green School
HLWS CM18 7   F6
Purwell JMI School
HTCHE/RSTV SG4 57   G4
Putteridge High School
& Community College
LTNE LU2 70   D4
Putteridge Junior
& Infant School
LTNE LU2 70   D4
Queen Elizabeth II Hospital
BRKMPK AL9 148   B7
Queen Elizabeths School
BAR EN5 225   J3
Queen Mother Theatre
HTCH/STOT SG5 56   D2
Queensway Health Centre
HAT AL10 171   G3
Queenswood School
BRKMPK AL9 193   K6
Queen Victoria
Memorial Hospital
WLYN AL6 122   A5
Radburn JMI School
LWTH SG6 42   C4
Radlett & Bushey
Reform Synagogue
RAD WD7 206   D5
Radlett Cricket Club
RAD WD7 206   E2
Radlett Lodge School
RAD WD7 206   E2
Radlett Parochial Church Council
RAD WD7 206   D6
Radlett Preparatory School
RAD WD7 207   F8
R A F Edlesborough
DUN/WHIP LU6 112   B3
Ramridge Infant School
LTNE LU2 5   F1
Ramridge Junior School
LTNE LU2 5   E1
Ramsey Manor Lower School
AMP/FLIT/B MK45 36   D2
Raynham Road Industrial Estate
BSF CM23 106   A1
Real Tennis Club
BRKMPK AL9 171   J6
Recreation Centre
LTNE LU2 70   D4
Recreation Ground
LTN LU1 5   D1
Redbourn Golf Club
STALW/RED AL3 117   H3
Redbourn Industrial Centre
STALW/RED AL3 142   C4
Redbourn Junior & Infant School
STALW/RED AL3 142   B4
Redbourn Recreation Centre
STALW/RED AL3 142   B4
Reddings JMI School
HHS/BOV HP3 164   E4
Red House Surgery
RAD WD7 206   D5
Reed First School
ROY SG8 31   J4
Regal Chambers Surgery
HTCH/STOT SG5 56   C2
Rhodes Museum
& Commonwealth Centre
BSF CM23 105   K3
Richard Whittington JMI School
BSF CM23 105   H1
Richmond Hill School
LTNE LU2 4   C4
Rickmansworth
Public Golf Course
RKW/CH/CXG WD3 228   E4

Rickmansworth School
RKW/CH/CXG WD3 .... 218　E6
Rickmansworth Sports Club
RKW/CH/CXG WD3 .... 218　D6
Riverside Business Park
STSD CM24 .... 86　C3
Riverside Estate
HARP AL5 .... 118　E5
Riverside Industrial Estate
LCOL/BKTW AL2 .... 190　C5
R N I B Sunshine House School
NTHWD HA6 .... 229　J5
Roaring Meg Retail Park
STVG SG1 .... 2　C5
Roaring Meg Retail Park
STVGE SG2 .... 2　C6
Robertswood County
Combined School
CFSP/GDCR SL9 .... 226　C6
Roebuck JMI School
STVGE SG5 .... 3　D6
Roecroft School
HTCH/STOT SG5 .... 26　A3
Roger Bannister Sports Ground
KTN/HRWW/W HA3 .... 231　K5
Roger De Clare School
STDN SG11 .... 81　K6
Roman Theatre
STALW/RED AL3 .... 167　H6
Rosary Priory High School
BUSH WD23 .... 222　B6
Rosedale Clinic
CHESW EN7 .... 196　E5
Roseland Junior Middle
& Infant School
HOD EN11 .... 152　E8
Rossgate JMI School
HHW HP1 .... 163　K4
Round Diamond School
STVG SG1 .... 76　C1
Roundwood Park School
HARP AL5 .... 118　A7
Rowans Junior Mixed
Infant School
WGCE AL7 .... 123　G8
The Royal Masonic School
RKW/CH/CXG WD3 .... 218　C6
Royal Veterinary College
BRKMPK AL9 .... 192　D6
Roydonbury Industrial Estate
HLWW/ROY CM19 .... 179　G1
Roydon CP School
HLWW/ROY CM19 .... 178　C1
Roydon Leisure Park
HLWW/ROY CM19 .... 154　B8
Roysia Middle School
ROY SG8 .... 21　H1
Roysia Surgery
ROY SG8 .... 21　H1
Royston & District Hospital
ROY SG8 .... 21　H5
Royston Golf Club
ROY SG8 .... 21　G3
Royston Health Centre
ROY SG8 .... 21　H3
Royston Museum
ROY SG8 .... 21　G3
Royston Swimming Pool
ROY SG8 .... 21　H3
Royston Town Football Club
ROY SG8 .... 21　H2
Rudolf Steiner School
KGLGY WD4 .... 185　J7
Rugby Club
BSF CM23 .... 85　G8
Russell Clinic
STALW/RED AL3 .... 10　C4
Russell County Primary School
RKW/CH/CXG WD3 .... 216　E4
Ryde College
WATW WD18 .... 219　K6
Ryde Junior Mixed Infant School
BRKMPK AL9 .... 171　H1
Rye House Stadium
HOD EN11 .... 177　J1
Ryelands JMI School
HOD EN11 .... 177　G2
Sacred Heart Junior Middle
& Infant School
OXHEY WD19 .... 221　G6
Sacred Heart RC Junior
& Infant School
LTNE LU2 .... 70　B6
Sacred Heart RC School
WARE SG12 .... 127　H8

Saffron Green First School
BORE WD6 .... 224　C4
St Adrians RC JMI School
STAL AL1 .... 188　E1
St Albans City Football Club
STAL AL1 .... 11　E4
St Albans City Hospital
STALW/RED AL3 .... 10　B2
St Albans Girls School
STALW/RED AL3 .... 168　B2
St Albans High School for Girls
STAL AL1 .... 11　D3
St Albans Lawn Tennis Club
STALE/WH AL4 .... 169　F4
St Albans Museum
STAL AL1 .... 10　C3
St Albans Musical Museum
LCOL/BKTW AL2 .... 188　D6
St Albans Music School
STALW/RED AL3 .... 10　C1
St Albans Organ Museum
STAL AL1 .... 168　E7
St Albans Principal Health Centre
STAL AL1 .... 10　C4
St Albans RC Primary School
HLW CM20 .... 7　E2
St Albans Retail Park
STAL AL1 .... 10　C6
St Albans School
STALW/RED AL3 .... 10　B4
St Albans & Stephen RC JMI School
STAL AL1 .... 11　F4
St Albans Synagogue
STAL AL1 .... 11　D5
St Alban & Stephen Junior
& Middle School
STAL AL1 .... 11　E5
St Albert the Great RC
Primary School
HHS/BOV HP3 .... 165　F8
St Andrews C of E Primary School
HERT/WAS SG14 .... 150　C2
St Andrews JMI School
HTCHE/RSTV SG4 .... 56　E2
St Andrews School
WARE SG12 .... 153　J5
St Anthonys RC Junior School
WATW WD18 .... 219　K5
St Bernadette JMI School
LCOL/BKTW AL2 .... 190　A5
St Catherine of Siena RC School
GSTN WD25 .... 204　E2
St Christopher School
LWTH SG6 .... 41　K6
St Clement Danes School
RKW/CH/CXG WD3 .... 217　G2
St Clements Mixed Junior School
CHES/WCR EN8 .... 197　J5
St Columbas College
Preparatory School
STALW/RED AL3 .... 10　B6
St Cross RC Primary School
HOD EN11 .... 177　F5
St Dominic RC School
HARP AL5 .... 143　J1
St Edmunds College
STDN SG11 .... 81　F8
St Elizabeths School & Home
MHAD SG10 .... 130　D3
St Francis College
LWTH SG6 .... 41　J5
St Giles C of E Primary School
POTB/CUF EN6 .... 209　F2
St Giles C of E Primary School
POTB/CUF EN6 .... 209　G3
St Helens School
NTHWD HA6 .... 229　K5
St Helens School
STALE/WH AL4 .... 145　G1
St Hildas School
HARP AL5 .... 118　B7
St Ignatius College
EN EN1 .... 213　K7
St Ippolyts School
HTCHE/RSTV SG4 .... 57　F6
St James Church School
HLWS CM18 .... 180　A5
St Joan of Arc RC School
RKW/CH/CXG WD3 .... 218　D7
St John Baptist School
WARE SG12 .... 153　F4
St John Fisher RC JMI School
STALE/WH AL4 .... 169　F3

St Johns C of E Junior
& Infant School
ENC/FH EN2 .... 212　E6
St Johns C of E Primary School
WCGW AL8 .... 146　E4
St Johns C of E Primary School
WLYN AL6 .... 123　F7
St Johns Infant School
RAD WD7 .... 206　C5
St Johns RC JMI School
BLDK SG7 .... 43　F2
St Johns RC Junior Middle
& Infant School
RKW/CH/CXG WD3 .... 218　A8
St Johns School
NTHWD HA6 .... 230　C5
St Josephs Junior & Infant School
LTNN/LIM LU3 .... 69　F5
St Josephs RC JMI School
CHES/WCR EN8 .... 214　D3
St Josephs RC Junior Middle
& Infant School
BSF CM23 .... 105　G3
St Josephs RC School
OXHEY WD19 .... 230　C2
St Lukes RC Primary School
HLWW/ROY CM19 .... 6　B6
St Luke's School
STALW/RED AL3 .... 142　B3
St Margaret Clitherow JMI School
STVGE SG2 .... 3　D6
St Margarets of Scotland
Junior School
LTN LU1 .... 89　F4
St Margarets of Scotland RC
Va Infant School
LTN LU1 .... 89　F4
St Margarets School
BUSH WD23 .... 221　H7
St Marks RC
Comprehensive School
HLWS CM18 .... 7　D5
St Martins School
NTHWD HA6 .... 229　J4
St Marys Catholic School
BSF CM23 .... 105　H2
St Marys C of E Primary School
STSD CM24 .... 86　D2
St Marys High School
CHESW EN7 .... 197　F8
St Marys Infant School
WLYN AL6 .... 122　B5
St Marys Junior & Infant School
BLDK SG7 .... 42　E3
St Marys Junior Mixed School
WARE SG12 .... 127　H6
St Marys RC JMI School
ROY SG8 .... 21　H2
St Marys School
STVGE SG2 .... 77　F6
St Marys Voluntary Lower School
HTCH/STOT SG5 .... 26　A3
St Matthews Infant School
LTNE LU2 .... 5　D2
St Meryl Junior Middle
& Infant School
OXHEY WD19 .... 231　F2
St Michaels C of E JMI School
STALW/RED AL3 .... 10　A4
St Michaels Primary School
BSF CM23 .... 105　H2
St Michaels RC School
GSTN WD25 .... 204　E2
St Nichaols Recreation Centre
STVG SG1 .... 59　H6
St Nicholas C of E
Primary School
STVG SG1 .... 3　D4
St Nicholas Health Centre
STVG SG1 .... 59　F7
St Nicholas House School
HHS/BOV HP3 .... 186　B3
St Nicholas Junior
& Infant School
LWTH SG6 .... 26　C8
St Nicholas School
HLWE CM17 .... 157　J6
St Nicholas Voluntary
Primary School
HARP AL5 .... 118　C8
St Pauls Primary School
KGLGY WD4 .... 203　H4
St Pauls Roman Catholic
JMI School
CHESW EN7 .... 197　F5

St Pauls Walden Junior School
HTCHE/RSTV SG4 .... 93 G2
St Peters JMI School
STAL AL1 .... 11 D5
St Peters Junior Middle
& Infant School
RKW/CH/CXG WD3 .... 218 A8
The St Philip Howard
Catholic Primary School
HAT AL10 .... 171 G4
St Roses Infants School
HHW HP1 .... 163 K8
St Teresas RC School
KTN/HRWW/W HA3 .... 231 K7
St Thomas Moore RC JMI School
BERK HP4 .... 161 H5
St Thomas More RC Junior
& Infant School
LWTH SG6 .... 41 H5
St Thomas of Canterbury
Catholic School
STDN SG11 .... 81 H6
Salisbury Hall
LCOL/BKTW AL2 .... 191 F7
Salisbury Infant School
HAT AL10 .... 171 G2
Salisbury Lawn Tennis Club
STAL AL1 .... 168 E5
Sandon Junior & Infant School
BUNT SG9 .... 29 K8
Sandridge Gate Business Centre
STALW/RED AL3 .... 168 C2
Sandridge JMI School
STALE/WH AL4 .... 145 G7
Sandridge Youth Club
& Sports Centre
STALW/RED AL3 .... 144 E8
Sandringham School
STALE/WH AL4 .... 168 E2
Sarbir Industrial Park
HLW CM20 .... 157 F4
Sarratt Junior Middle
& Infant School
RKW/CH/CXG WD3 .... 201 K6
Sawbridge Health Clinic
SBW CM21 .... 132 C7
Schidegger Mis College
LTN LU1 .... 4 B3
Schopwick Surgery
BORE WD6 .... 223 G6
Sebright School
STALW/RED AL3 .... 115 H5
The Sele School
HERT/WAS SG14 .... 150 C3
Service Practice
BERK HP4 .... 161 K5
Shaftesbury Industrial Centre
LWTH SG6 .... 42 B2
Shaftesbury School
KTN/HRWW/W HA3 .... 231 J7
Shakespeare Industrial Estate
WATN WD24 .... 204 B8
Sheepcot Medical Centre
GSTN WD25 .... 204 D4
Sheering C of E Primary School
RBSF CM22 .... 133 H8
Shenley JMI School
RAD WD7 .... 207 J4
Shen Nong Chinese
Medical Centre
STAL AL1 .... 10 C4
Shenval Industrial Estate
HLW CM20 .... 156 D5
Shephall Infant School
STVGE SG2 .... 3 F6
Shephall Way Surgery
STVGE SG2 .... 3 F6
Sheredes School
HOD EN11 .... 176 E4
Sherrardswood School
WLYN AL6 .... 122 D4
Shirley's Temple
LTN LU1 .... 4 B3
Silk Mill House Museum
STALW/RED AL3 .... 142 B5
Simon Balle School
HERT/BAY SG13 .... 151 H4
Sir Frederic Osborn School
WGCE AL7 .... 148 C2
Sir John Lawes School
HARP AL5 .... 118 E6
Sir John Newsom School
WGCE AL7 .... 147 K6
Ski Centre
HHS/BOV HP3 .... 164 D8

Skidmore Clinic
RKW/CH/CXG WD3 .... 218 D8
Skyswood JMI School
STALE/WH AL4 .... 169 F3
Slip End Lower School
LTN LU1 .... 89 G8
Smug Oak Green
Business Centre
LCOL/BKTW AL2 .... 188 D7
Snap Theatre
BSF CM23 .... 105 K2
Someries Castle
LTNE LU2 .... 91 F4
Someries Infant School
LTNE LU2 .... 70 D7
Someries Junior School
LTNE LU2 .... 70 D6
Sopwell House Hotel
& Country Club
STAL AL1 .... 189 H2
South Bedfordshire Golf Club
LTNE LU2 .... 52 D7
South Bedfordshire
Magistrates Court
LTN LU1 .... 4 A4
Southdown Industrial Estate
HARP AL5 .... 143 K1
Southgate Health Centre
STVG SG1 .... 2 B4
South Hill JMI School
HHW HP1 .... 164 B7
South Lodge Queens School
BUSH WD23 .... 221 H3
South Street Surgery
BSF CM23 .... 105 J3
Spellbrook JMI School
BSF CM23 .... 132 D2
Spencer Primary Jm School
STALW/RED AL3 .... 11 D1
Sphere Industrial Estate
STAL AL1 .... 11 F5
The Spinney Junior School
HLW CM20 .... 7 F3
The Spires Shopping Centre
BAR EN5 .... 225 K3
Sports Centre
BORE WD6 .... 224 B1
Sports Centre
HHS/BOV HP3 .... 8 C6
Sports Centre
LCOL/BKTW AL2 .... 205 K1
Sports Ground
BAR EN5 .... 224 D6
Springmead JMI School
WGCE AL7 .... 148 D3
Stadium Industrial Estate
LTNW/LEA LU4 .... 68 A7
Stags School
STALW/RED AL3 .... 168 B2
Stanborough School
GSTN WD25 .... 204 C5
Stanborough School
WCCW AL8 .... 147 G5
Standon Health Centre
STDN SG11 .... 81 K7
Stanmore Road Health Centre
STVG SG1 .... 2 A1
Stansted Clinic
STSD CM24 .... 86 D2
Staple Tye Shopping Centre
HLWS CM18 .... 180 A4
Steeple Morden School
ROY SG8 .... 15 H7
Stevenage Borough Football Club
STVG SG1 .... 2 B3
Stevenage Borough Football Club
STVGE SG2 .... 2 C6
Stevenage Business Park
STVG SG1 .... 59 J7
Stevenage Cricket Club
STVG SG1 .... 2 B2
Stevenage Mosque
STVG SG1 .... 2 B1
Stevenage Museum
STVG SG1 .... 2 C3
Stewards Comprehensive School
HLWS CM18 .... 179 K5
Stirling Industrial Centre
BORE WD6 .... 224 C5
Stocks Hotel Golf
& Country Club
TRING HP23 .... 136 D2
Stockwell Lodge Medical Centre
CHESW EN7 .... 196 E6

Stockwood Park Museum
LTN LU1 .... 89 J5
Stockwood Park Rugby Club
LTN LU1 .... 89 J5
Stonehill JMI School
LWTH SG6 .... 25 J8
Stopsley High School
& Community College
LTNE LU2 .... 70 A5
Stopsley Infant School
LTNE LU2 .... 70 B5
Stormont School
POTB/CUF EN6 .... 210 D1
Stortford Hall Industrial Park
BSF CM23 .... 106 A2
Stort Valley Industrial Estate
BSF CM23 .... 86 A7
Stotfold Health Centre
HTCH/STOT SG5 .... 25 J3
Strathmore Infant School
HTCH/STOT SG5 .... 40 C7
Stream Woods School
HAT AL10 .... 171 G5
Stroud Wood Business Centre
LCOL/BKTW AL2 .... 189 G5
Studham VC Lower School
DUN/WHIP LU6 .... 113 K5
Studlands Rise First School
ROY SG8 .... 21 J4
Summercroft Junior
& Infant School
BSF CM23 .... 106 B1
Summerswood Primary School
BORE WD6 .... 224 A4
Sumners Community
Recreation Centre
HLWW/ROY CM19 .... 179 H5
Sunderland Estate
KGLGY WD4 .... 186 B7
Sundon Business Park
LTNN/LIM LU3 .... 68 A1
Sundon Industrial Estate
LTNN/LIM LU3 .... 68 A1
Sundon Medical Centre
LTNN/LIM LU3 .... 68 B2
Sundon Park Junior School
LTNN/LIM LU3 .... 68 B1
Sunshine Riding School
LTNE LU2 .... 69 J1
Superstore
WAT WD17 .... 13 E4
Surrey Street School
LTN LU1 .... 5 D5
Swimming Pool
HERT/WAS SG14 .... 151 G1
Swimming Pool
STVG SG1 .... 2 B3
The Symonds Green
Health Centre
STVG SG1 .... 75 F2
Tabard Rugby Club
RAD WD7 .... 206 E7
Tanners Wood Junior
& Infant School
ABLGY WD5 .... 203 K2
Tannery Drift School
ROY SG8 .... 21 G3
Tanys Dell Junior School
HLW CM20 .... 7 F1
Telephone Exchange
WATW WD18 .... 12 C3
Telmere Industrial Estate
LTN LU1 .... 4 C5
Templewood School
WGCW AL8 .... 147 H1
Tennyson Road Primary School
LTN LU1 .... 4 C6
Tewin Road Business Centre
WGCE AL7 .... 147 K2
Tewin School
WLYN AL6 .... 124 A7
Tewin Water School
WLYN AL6 .... 123 H7
Therfield First School
ROY SG8 .... 30 D2
Thomas Alleyne School
STVG SG1 .... 75 H1
The Thomas Coram
Middle School
BERK HP4 .... 162 A7
Thomas Rivers Medical Centre
HLW CM20 .... 157 F2
The Thomas Rivers
Medical Centre
SBW CM21 .... 132 A8

Thorley Hill JMI School
  BSF CM23 .... 105 J5
Thorn Grove Primary School
  BSF CM23 .... 106 A3
Three Rivers District Council
  OXHEY WD19 .... 230 D2
Three Rivers District Council
  RKW/CH/CXG WD3 .... 218 D7
Thumbswood Infant School
  WGCE AL7 .... 148 B4
Thundridge JMI School
  WARE SG12 .... 127 H2
Tonwell School
  WARE SG12 .... 126 C2
Town Council
  HAT AL10 .... 171 F3
Town Hall & Council Offices
  LTN LU1 .... 4 B4
Townsend C of E School
  STALW/RED AL3 .... 167 K1
Trestle Theatre Co
  STALE/WH AL4 .... 169 F7
Tricor Business Park
  CHES/WCR EN8 .... 214 D4
Tricor Trading Estate
  CHES/WCR EN8 .... 214 D4
Trident Industrial Estate
  HOD EN11 .... 177 H3
Tring Health Centre
  TRING HP23 .... 135 G5
Tring & New Mill Pre-school
  TRING HP23 .... 135 G2
Tring School
  TRING HP23 .... 135 G5
Tring Sports Centre
  TRING HP23 .... 135 G5
Tring Town Council
  TRING HP23 .... 135 F6
Trotts Hill JMI School
  STVG SG1 .... 59 F8
Tudor School
  HHS/BOV HP3 .... 164 D8
Turnford School
  CHES/WCR EN8 .... 197 J6
Two Waters JMI School
  HHS/BOV HP3 .... 185 H3
Twyford Business Centre
  BSF CM23 .... 105 K4
Underhill Junior & Infant School
  BAR EN5 .... 225 K5
University of Hertfordshire
  GSTN WD25 .... 205 J6
University of Hertfordshire
  HAT AL10 .... 170 C1
University of Hertfordshire
  HAT AL10 .... 170 E5
University of Hertfordshire
  HERT/BAY SG13 .... 151 J5
University of Hertfordshire
  STAL AL1 .... 11 D5
University of London
  ENC/FH EN2 .... 213 K6
University of Luton
  LTN LU1 .... 4 C4
University of Luton
  LTN LU1 .... 4 C5
University of Luton
  LTNE LU2 .... 70 E3
Vale Industrial Estate
  WATW WD18 .... 219 H8
Verulam Golf Club
  STAL AL1 .... 11 E6
Verulam Industrial Estate
  STAL AL1 .... 11 E6
Verulamium Museum
  STALW/RED AL3 .... 10 A4
Verulam School
  STAL AL1 .... 11 F3
Victoria C of E Primary School
  BERK HP4 .... 161 K5
The Village Surgery
  PIN HA5 .... 231 F8
Virgin Cinemas
  HLW CM20 .... 156 C5
Waltham Abbey Swimming Pool
  WAB EN9 .... 215 J5
Waltham Holy Cross Council
  WAB EN9 .... 215 G3
Waltham Holy Cross
  Junior School
  WAB EN9 .... 215 J3

Warden Hill Infant School
  LTNN/LIM LU3 .... 69 H2
Warden Hill Junior School
  LTNN/LIM LU3 .... 69 H2
Warden Lodge Surgery
  CHES/WCR EN8 .... 214 C1
Ward Freman School
  BUNT SG9 .... 63 H1
Wardown Park Museum
  LTNE LU2 .... 69 H1
Wardown Swimming
  & Leisure Centre
  LTNN/LIM LU3 .... 4 B1
Warrendell School
  OXHEY WD19 .... 230 D2
Watchlytes JMI School
  WGCE AL7 .... 148 C3
Waterside Industrial Estate
  HOD EN11 .... 177 J4
Waterside (School)
  BSF CM23 .... 85 H1
Waterways Heritage Museum
  RKW/CH/CXG WD3 .... 218 D8
Watford Arches Retail Park
  WATW WD17 .... 13 D4
Watford Borough Council
  WAT WD17 .... 12 B2
Watford Business Centre
  WATW WD18 .... 12 C2
Watford Central Swimming Bath
  WAT WD17 .... 12 B1
Watford County Court
  WAT WD17 .... 12 C1
Watford Eye Clinic
  WATN WD24 .... 204 C8
Watford Football Club
  WATW WD18 .... 12 C4
Watford General Hospital
  WATW WD18 .... 12 C4
Watford Grammar School
  for Boys
  WATW WD18 .... 12 A3
Watford Grammar School
  for Girls
  WATW WD18 .... 13 D4
Watford Museum
  WAT WD17 .... 13 D4
Watford Sports & Leisure Centre
  GSTN WD25 .... 204 D3
Watford Springs Pool
  WATW WD18 .... 13 D4
Watford United Synagogue
  WAT WD17 .... 220 C1
Watling View School
  STAL AL1 .... 189 F2
Waulds Bank Junior
  & Infant School
  LTNN/LIM LU3 .... 68 D2
Wedgewood Gate
  Industrial Estate
  STVG SG1 .... 59 H7
Welwyn Garden City Cricket Club
  WGCW AL8 .... 122 C7
Welwyn Garden City Golf Club
  WGCW AL8 .... 147 G2
Welwyn Garden Hebrew
  Congregation Synagogue
  WGCW AL8 .... 147 G3
Welwyn Hatfield District Council
  HAT AL10 .... 171 G3
Welwyn Hatfield
  Museum Service
  BRKMPK AL9 .... 171 K1
Welwyn Rugby Football Club
  WGCW AL8 .... 147 G4
Welwyn Tennis Club
  WLYN AL6 .... 122 B5
Wenlock C of E School
  LTNE LU2 .... 5 F3
The Wenta Business Centre
  WATN WD24 .... 204 E7
Westbrook Hay
  Preparatory School
  HHW HP1 .... 184 B1
Western House Hospital
  WARE SG12 .... 127 H7
Westfield JMI School
  HOD EN11 .... 176 E2
Westfield School
  WATW WD18 .... 12 A5

West Hertfordshire College
  WAT WD17 .... 204 B8
West Herts College
  BUSH WD23 .... 13 E2
West Herts College
  HHW HP1 .... 164 B5
Westminster Lodge
  Sports Centre
  STALW/RED AL3 .... 10 B6
Wheatcroft JMI School
  HERT/BAY SG13 .... 151 K2
Wheatfields Junior
  & Infant School
  STALE/WH AL4 .... 168 E2
Whipperley Infant School
  LTN LU1 .... 89 F3
Whipsnade Park Golf Club
  BERK HP4 .... 113 G4
Whitefield Infant School
  LTNN/LIM LU3 .... 68 D1
Whitehall Estate
  HLWW/ROY CM19 .... 179 F2
Whitehill Junior School
  HTCHE/RSTV SG4 .... 56 E4
The Whitewebbs Museum
  of Transport & Industry
  ENC/FH EN2 .... 212 E5
Whittings Hill School
  BAR EN5 .... 225 H5
Whittlesea School
  KTN/HRWW/W HA3 .... 231 K6
Whyllotts Council Offices
  POTB/CUF EN6 .... 210 A2
Widford Junior & Infant School
  WARE SG12 .... 129 K5
Wigginton JMI School
  TRING HP23 .... 135 J8
Wigmore Primary School
  LTNE LU2 .... 71 F7
Wilbury Junior Mixed School
  LWTH SG6 .... 41 J3
William Austin Infant School
  LTNN/LIM LU3 .... 69 H5
William Austin Junior School
  LTNN/LIM LU3 .... 69 H5
William Penn Leisure Centre
  RKW/CH/CXG WD3 .... 217 J8
William Ransom JMI School
  HTCHE/RSTV SG4 .... 57 F2
Willow Field School
  LTN LU1 .... 88 E5
Windermere JMI Primary School
  STAL AL1 .... 168 E8
Windmill Trading Estate
  LTN LU1 .... 5 D4
Wisteria House Clinic
  WLYN AL6 .... 122 B3
Wodson Park Leisure Centre
  WARE SG12 .... 127 G5
Wolsey Business Park
  WATW WD18 .... 219 J7
Wood End JMI School
  HARP AL5 .... 117 K6
Woodfield School
  HHS/BOV HP3 .... 165 H8
Woodhall Farm Surgery
  HHNE HP2 .... 141 G8
Woodlands Infant School
  BORE WD6 .... 223 K1
Woodside Industrial Park
  LWTH SG6 .... 42 B3
Woodside JMI School
  CHESW EN7 .... 196 A7
Woolenwick Junior
  & Infant School
  STVG SG1 .... 75 G3
Woolgrove School
  LWTH SG6 .... 42 D4
Worcesters Infant
  & Primary School
  EN EN1 .... 213 J8
Wormley JMI School
  BROX EN10 .... 197 J1
Wroxham JMI School
  POTB/CUF EN6 .... 209 J1
Wymondley Junior
  & Infant School
  HTCHE/RSTV SG4 .... 57 H5
York House School
  RKW/CH/CXG WD3 .... 218 E2

Page 4

C5
1 Essex Cl
2 James Ct
3 Langley St
4 May St
5 New Town Rd
6 Oxford St
7 Union St
8 Victoria St
9 Windsor St

Page 8

A3
1 Andrews Cl
2 The Bounce
3 Boxhill
4 Broadcroft
5 Mead Temple
6 Sharpcroft
7 Typleden Cl

C5
1 The Queen's Sq
2 Sawyers Wy
3 Sheepcote Rd

Page 9

F6
1 Church Rd
2 Coniston Cl
3 Cumberlow Pl
4 Gravely Ct
5 Hartsbourne Wy
6 Ryecroft Cl

Page 13

D1
1 Anglian Cl
2 Aston Cl
3 Keele Cl
4 Octavia Cl
5 Orphanage Rd
6 St Pauls Wy

D3
1 Cambridge Rd
2 Chapmans Yd
3 Church St
4 The Crescent
5 Derby Rd
6 Granville Rd
7 Kings Cl
8 Lower Derby Rd
9 Market Pl
10 New St
11 Smith St
12 Water La
13 Watford Field Rd
14 Woodmans Yd

E5
1 St Matthews Cl

Page 56

E3
1 Kardwell Cl
2 Kingfisher Ct
3 Lovell Cl
4 Orlando Cl
5 Riddy Hill Cl
6 South Hill Cl
7 Whitegale Cl

Page 69

F2
1 Croxton Cl
2 Cubbington Cl
3 Green Milverton
4 Quickswood

G4
1 Belvedere Rd
2 Fenwick Cl

H7
1 Chaucer Rd
2 Sheridan Rd

K8
1 Arncliffe Crs
2 Kinghamway

Page 70

E8
1 Alderton Cl
2 Barnston Cl
3 Chelsworth Cl
4 Friston Gn
5 Hickling Cl
6 Melford Cl
7 Mutford Cft
8 Pinford Dell

Page 89

J2
1 Alma Link
2 Buxton Rd
3 Gordon St
4 Hastings St
5 King St
6 Mersey St
7 Napier Rd
8 Regent St
9 Rothesay Rd

K2
1 Barbers La
2 Bute Sq
3 Castle St
4 Chapel St
5 Cheapside
6 Cheapside Sq
7 Flowers Wy
8 George St West
9 Library Rd
10 Park St
11 Stuart St

K5
1 Essex Cl
2 James Ct
3 Langley St
4 May St
5 New Town Rd
6 Oxford Rd
7 Union St
8 Victoria St
9 Windsor St

Page 105

K2
1 Fuller Ct
2 The Old Maltings

K3
1 Great Eastern Cl
2 Station Rd

Page 122

C4
1 Church Pl
2 Holly Hall Rd
3 Mimram Rd
4 Orchard Rd
5 Prospect Pl
6 St Marys Cl
7 Welwyn Hall
8 Wendover Ct

Page 147

H3
1 Barleycroft Gn
2 Handside Cl
3 Lanefield Wk
4 Palmerston Cl

H4
1 Fordwich Rd
2 Hobbs Wy
3 Honeycroft
4 Stanborough Cl

K4
1 Athelstan Wk North
2 Edgars Ct
3 Moatwood Gn
4 Oaktree Garth
5 Peartree Ct
6 Regent Ct

K7
1 Drycroft
2 Katescroft

Page 148

A5
1 Home Meadow
2 Swallowfields
3 Verlum Cl

C2
1 Buddcroft
2 Claycroft
3 Kingscroft
4 Nettlecroft
5 Smallcroft
6 Strawfields
7 Waterfield
8 Wheatbarn

C4
1 Amwell Common
2 Batford Cl
3 Bushey Cl
4 Bushey Gn
5 Gravely Dell
6 Thundridge Cl
7 Wareside Cl

D3
1 Andrewsfield
2 Bericot Wy
3 Beverley Rd
4 Douglas Wy
5 Elizabeth Cl
6 Jackdaws
7 Lindbergh
8 Mitchell Cl

D4
1 Aspen Wy
2 Birchall Wd
3 Copperfields
4 Forresters Dr
5 Glenwood
6 High Wickfield
7 Holwell Hyde
8 Pelham Ct
9 Ploughmans End
10 Poppyfields

E3
1 Hunsdon
2 Northwood
3 Oakington
4 Roseacre Gdns
5 Somersham
6 Stapleford
7 Sylvan Wy
8 Tempsford
9 Waterbeach

Page 151

F3
1 Brewhouse La
2 Bridges St
3 Castle St
4 Hertingfordbury Rd
5 Mill Br
6 Old Cross
7 Old Cross B158
8 Port Hl

G3
1 Bell La
2 Bircherley Ct
3 Bluecoats Av
4 Church St
5 Maidenhead St
6 Maidenhead Yd
7 Market Pl
8 Market St
9 Millers Yd
10 Nicholas La
11 Nicholas St
12 Oldhall St
13 Parliament Sq
14 St John's St
15 Salisbury Sq
16 The Wash

J3
1 Beechwood Cl
2 Braziers Fld
3 Caxton Hl
4 Copperwood
5 Extension Rd
6 Mountsorrel
7 Watermark Wy

Page 161

H3
1 Beckets Sq
2 Delifield
3 Dukes Wy
4 Montgomerie Cl
5 Pages Cft

J6
1 Ashlyns Cl
2 Gresham Ct

K5
1 Cavalier Cl
2 Clarence Rd
3 Greene Field Rd
4 Manor Cl
5 Prince Edward St
6 The Wilderness

K6
1 Old Orchard Ms
2 Pheasant Cl
3 Plover Cl

Page 164

A4
1 Cooks Vennel
2 Pierian Spring
3 Timplings Rw
4 Willow Wy

A5
1 Bards Cnr
2 Lockers Park La
3 Minstrel Cl
4 Saffron La

C5
1 The Brackens
2 Chapel Cottages
3 Fensomes Alley
4 Fensom's Ct
5 Garland Cl
6 Normandy Ct
7 Pine Tree Cl
8 Union Ln

D1
1 Helston Gv

D6
1 Chalkdell Hl
2 Quendell Wk

D8
1 Satinwood Cl

E1
1 Clyde Sq
2 Great Palmers
3 Mersey Pl
4 Robin Hood Meadow

E2
1 Cwmbran Ct
2 Kilbride Ct
3 Peterlee Ct
4 Sherwood Pl
5 Welwyn Ct

E3
1 Callisto Ct
2 Ganymede Pl
3 Pentland

E5
1 Coral Gdns
2 Hammer La
3 Rice Cl

E7
1 St Albans Rd
2 Wadley Cl

E8
1 Bennetts End Cl

Page 165

F5
1 Saracens Head
2 Southernwood Cl

H7
1 Church Rd
2 Coniston Cl
3 Cumberlow Pl
4 Gravely Ct
5 Hartsbourne Wy
6 Ryecroft Cl

H8
1 Crossett Gn
2 Manan Cl
3 Stroma Cl
4 Stronsay
5 Westray

Page 168

B7
1 Approach Rd
2 Black Cut
3 Devon Ct
4 Henrys Grant
5 Hopkins Yd
6 Lime Tree Pl
7 Lower Paxton Rd
8 Vernon's Cl

D2
1 The Berries
2 Bolingbrook
3 Lay Brook

E8
1 Cell Barnes Cl

Page 171

G7
1 Downsfield
2 Richmond Ct

H1
1 Highlands
2 Lowlands

Page 185

H2
1 Edward Ct
2 Frogmore Rd
3 Henry St
4 Kents Av
5 Millbank
6 St Andrew's Rd
7 White Lion St
8 William Ct

Page 196

D5
1 Bay Tree Cl
2 Glover Cl
3 Grenadine Cl
4 Lavender Cl
5 Musgrave Cl
6 Northwood Cl
7 Rennison Cl
8 Sycamore Cl

Page 197

H6
1 Campine Cl
2 The Colonnade
3 Drakes Cl
4 Faverolle Gn
5 Hamburgh Ct
6 Southbrook Dr
7 The Spur
8 Symonds Cl

J6
1 Bromleigh Cl
2 Cordell Cl
3 Fraser Rd
4 Goodwin Ct
5 Lensbury Cl

J8
1 Foster Cl
2 Guinevere Gdns
3 Roberts Cl
4 Roswell Cl

K1
1 Fern Cl
2 The Square
3 Virgil Dr
4 Wormley Lodge Cl

K3
1 Farmhouse Cl
2 Felton Cl
3 Juniper Cl

K5
1 Priory Ga

Page 204

B1
1 Lapwing Wy
2 Nightingale La
3 Oriole Cl
4 Redwing Gv

B3
1 Ganders Ash
2 Nottingham Cl

C2
1 Bramley Ct

C8
1 Callowland Pl
2 Halsey Pl
3 Lea Rd
4 St George's Rd

D5
1 Biddenham Turn
2 The Conifers
3 Rochester Dr

Page 214

C4
1 Dumbarton Av

C7
1 Hartmoor Ms

D4
1 Abbey Rd
2 Lodge Crs
3 Station Ap
4 Trust Rd

D7
1 Coldham Gv
2 Cornhill Dr
3 The Generals Wk
4 Johnby Cl
5 Newport Cl

Page 220

C2
1 Albert Rd North
2 Canterbury Rd
3 Franklin Rd
4 Keston Ms
5 Shady La
6 Wellington Rd
7 Westland Rd
8 West St

C7
1 Brookmill Cl
2 Silk Mill Rd
3 The Willows

D2
1 Anglian Cl
2 Aston Cl
3 Keele Cl
4 Octavia Ct
5 Orphanage Rd
6 St Pauls Wy

D3
1 The Broadway
2 Earl St
3 Lord St
4 Ottoman Ter
5 Queen's Pl
6 Queen's Rd
7 Shaftesbury Rd
8 Stanley Rd
9 Trinity Hall Cl

D4
1 Cambridge Rd
2 Chapmans Yd
3 Church St
4 The Crescent
5 Derby Rd
6 Granville Rd
7 Kings Cl
8 Lower Derby Rd
9 Market Pl
10 New St
11 Smith St
12 Water La
13 Watford Field Rd
14 Woodmans Yd

E2
1 Beasant House
2 Bevan House
3 Gandhi Ct
4 Mandela Pl
5 Orwell Ct

Page 221

J6
1 Baird Cl
2 The Close
3 Fidler Pl
4 Herkomer Cl
5 Meadowcroft
6 Mortimer Cl
7 Ryder Cl
8 Wheelright Cl

Page 230

A6
1 Cervantes Ct
2 Church Cl
3 Kemps Dr
4 Wychwood Wy

A7
1 Manor Cottages

D4
1 Bognor Gdns
2 Bromborough Gn
3 Darwin Gdns
4 Doncaster Gn
5 Harborne Cl
6 Huntercrombe Gdns
7 Kenilworth Gdns
8 Morriston Cl
9 Muirfield Cl

E3
1 Crowborough Pth
2 Glencorse Gn
3 Lundin Wk
4 Markeston Gn
5 Mullion Wk
6 Newport Mead
7 Piltdown Rd

E4
1 Ashford Gn
2 Falkirk Gdns
3 Gleneagles Cl
4 Letchworth Cl
5 Leven Cl

E8
1 Chesswood Wy
2 Willow Dean

Notes

Notes

Notes

Notes